Language & Communication in Israel

Studies of Israeli Society *Volume IX*

Language & Communication in Israel

Hanna Herzog
&
Eliezer Ben-Rafael
editors

Publication Series of the Israel Sociological Society
Series Editor Ernest Kraus

Routledge
Taylor & Francis Group
LONDON AND NEW YORK

First published 2001 by Israel Sociological Society

Published 2021 by Routledge
2 Park Square, Milton Park, Abingdon, Oxfordshire OX14 4RN
605 Third Avenue, New York, NY 10017

Routledge is an imprint of the Taylor and Francis Group, an informa business

First issued in hardback 2020

ISSN: 0734-4937
ISBN 13: 978-1-56000-998-6 (pbk)
ISBN 13: 978-1-56000-347-2 (hbk)

Sponsored by the Schnitzer Foundation for Research on the Israeli Economy and Society—Bar-Ilan University.

Contents

Acknowledgements

This volume brings together a representative collection of studies about language and communication in Israel in the last decade or so. This was by no means an easy task seeing the vast dispersion of interests of Israel's scholars in these fields. Yet, our determination to pursue with our scheme stemmed from a strong feeling that such a volume is strongly missing and is something to be done, and soon. Language and communication are, indeed, growing fields in Israeli scholarship which have not yet been given much attention by commentators. Hence, we felt we should bring to the attention of the interested public the quite impressive scope, variety of subjects, diversity of orientations, and—last but not least—fundamental dilemmas of Israel's academic activity in these domains.

We had the privilege to be encouraged in our task, by the sympathy of two prominent figures of these fields who happened to have been themselves deeply involved in the development of Israeli research in their respective domains—Elihu Katz, is the pillar of Communication Studies in Israel for decades, and Josuah Fishman has been the one to give life to the sociology of language here, while he was sojourning in Jerusalem for several years in the early 1970s. We want to thank Elihu Katz and Josuah Fishman for this encouragement. A special thank, moreover, goes to Ernest Krausz, the founding father and chief editor of the series of Israeli Studies, at Transaction, who has been the one who suggested a series volume dedicated to language and communication. An initiator of the project, he has been its most loyal supporter at all steps. Together with him, we also enjoyed the indefectible support of the Israel Society of Sociology and its present president, Yitzhak Samuel. We are thankful to our Faculty of the Social Sciences and Department of Sociology at the Tel-Aviv University for their support.

We want also to thank Nelly Alias and Hagai Boas, our assistants. They took on themselves all daily and so-called "small tasks" that, in actual fact, are the principal activity involved in this kind of compilation. Sylvia, the head of the typing service of the Faculty of Social Sciences at the Tel-Aviv University has been a dedicated typist whose talents in this matter have been the guarantee of the completion of the work.

The large majority of these works are re-published and we want to thank the publishers for their kind permissions. Among journals, we are indebted to *Comparative Politics, European Journal of Communication, International Journal of Group Tensions, International Journal of the Sociology of Language, Israel Social Science Research, Journal of Communication, Language and Society, Media, Culture and Society, Political Communication and Persuasion, Research on Language and Social Interaction, Symbolic Interaction, Text, Theory and Society, Women and Language,* and *Youth and Society*. Among the publishers of books, we are indebted to *Curzon Press, Harwood Academic Publishers, State University of New York Press, Westview Press* and *Tel-Aviv University Press*. We are grateful to all of them of their readiness to cooperate in their way, to this volume.

Last but not least, we also want to thank the "house", that is the people in Transaction who have been in contact with us—Mary E. Curtis and Cristina Kollet, and, of course, Professor Irving Horowitz—for their support as well as the work that they have been ready to invest in the publication of this volume.

HANNA HERZOG AND ELIEZER BEN-RAFAEL

Sources

1. Katriel, Tamar, 1992, " 'Lefargen': A Study in Israeli Semantics of Social Relations", *Research on Language and Social Interaction*, 26/1:33-55.

2. Hazan, Haim, 1993, "That's How We Were: Individual, Group and the Collective in the Tel Aviv of 'Late Summer Blues'" in D. Nahmias and G. Menachem (eds.) *Tel-Aviv Jaffa Studies*, Tel Aviv University, pp. 261-280.

3. Blum-Kulka, Shoshana, 1993, " 'You Gotta Know How to Tell a Story': Telling, Tales and Tellers in America and Israeli Narrative at Dinner", *Language and Society*, 22:361-402.

4. Zilberg, Narspy, 1995, "In-Group Humor of Immigrants from the Former Soviet Union to Israel", *Israel Social Science Research* 10/1:1-22.

5. Raz, E. Aviad and Shapira, Rina, 1994, "A Symbolic Interactionist Guide to the Answering Machine: 22 Reflections on Vocal Encounters in an Emerging Social World", *Symbolic Interaction*, 17/4:411-429.

6. Ben-Rafael, Eliezer, 1994, "A Sociological Paradigm of Bilingualism: English, French, Yiddish and Arabic in Israel", *Israel Social Science Research*, 9:181-206.

7. Fisherman, Haya, 1990, "Attitudes Toward Foreign Words in Contemporary Hebrew" *International Journal of Sociology of Language*, 86:5-40.

8. Bentolila, Yaakov, 1994, "Bilingualism in a Moroccan Settlement in the South of Israel", *Israel Social Science Research*, 9:89-108.

9. Cromer, Gerald, 1995, " 'Secularism Is the Root of All Evil': The Haredi Response to Crime and Delinquency" *International Journal of Group Tensions*, 109-120.

10. Amara, Muhammad and Spolsky, Bernard, "The Construction of Identity in a Divided Palestinian Village: Sociolinguistic Evidence", in Yasir Suleiman (ed.) *Language and Identity in the Middle East and North Africa*, Great Britain: Curzon Press, pp. 81-100.

11. Ben-Rafael, Eliezer and Brosh, Hezi, 1995, "Jews and Arabs in Israel: The Cultural Convergence of Divergent Identities", in Ron Vekler (ed.) *Medieval and Modern Perspectives on Muslims Jewish Relations*, London: Harwood Academic Publishers, pp. 17-34.

12. Katz, Elihu and Haas, Hadassah, 1994, "Twenty Years of Television in Israel: Are there Long Run Effects on Values and Cultural Practices?" in *Journal of Communication*, 47:2 Spring pp. 3-20

13. Schneller, Rafael, 1988, "Video Watching and its Societal Functions for Small-Town Adolescents in Israel", *Youth and Society*, 19/4: 441-459.

14. Shinar, Dov, 1993, "VCR Narrow Casting in the Kibbutz", *Israel Social Science Research*, 8/1: 175-196.

15. Wolfsfeld, Gadi, 1995, "Voters as Consumers: Audience Perspectives on the Election Broadcasts" in A. Arian and M. Shamir (eds.) *The Election in Israel—1992*, Albany, SUNY, pp. 235-253.

16. Herzog, Hanna, 1990, "Was It on tha Agenda? The Hidden Agenda of the 1988 Campaign" in A Arian and M. Shamir (eds.) *The Elections in Israel-1988*, Westview Press. pp. 37-62.

17. Lemish, Dafna and Tidhar, E. Chava, 1991, "The Silenced Majority: Women in Israel's 1988 Television Election Campaign", *Women and Language*, 14/1: 13-22.

18. Liebes, Tamar, 1992, "Decoding Television News: The Political Discourse of Israeli Hawks and Doves" *Theory and Society*, 21/3: 357-381.

19. Loshitzky, Yosefa, 1991, "The Intifada as a Meta-Televisual Dialogue", *Media, Culture and Society*, 13: 557-571.

20. Roeh, Itzhak and Cohen, A. Akiba, "One of the Bloodiest Days: A Comparative Analysis of Open and Closed Television News", *Journal of Communication*, 42/2: 42-55.

21. Weimann, Gabriel, " 'Redefinition of Image': The Impact of Mass Mediated Terrorism", *International Journal of Public Opinion Research*, vol. 2: No. 1 pp. 16-29

22. Lehman-Wilzig, Sam, 1989, "Protest, Television, Newspapers and the Public: Who influences Whom?" *Political Communication and Persuasion*, 6:21-32.

23. Etzioni-Halevy, Eva, 1988, "Inherent Contradictions of Democracy: Illustrations from National Broadcasting Corporations", Comparative Politics, April: 325-340.

24. Caspi and Limor, 1999. *The In/Outsiders: The Media in Israel*, Cresskill, NJ: Hampton Press

25. Roeh, Itzhak and Nir, Raphael, 1990, "Speech Presentation in the Israeli News: Ideological Constraints and Rhetorical Strategies", Text, 10/3: 225-244.

26. Peri, Yoram, 1997, The Rabin Myth and the Press-Reconstruction of the Israeli Collective Identity" European Journal of Communication, 12/4: 435-458.

Part 1

Introduction

1

The Study of Language and Communication in Israeli Social Sciences

Hanna Herzog and Eliezer Ben-Rafael

Theories and Practice

From the inception of the series, each volume of *Studies of Israeli Society* has been devoted to one major topic in the sociology of Israeli society in recent years. The current volume deviates from the tradition only by widening this practice and combining two fields of knowledge and research: the sociology of language and the sociology of communication. The rationale underlying this choice is that while the two fields have experienced their own separate development, they tend to converge and focus on the same subject matter, where language is the support of communication and communication constitutes the ground of language activity.

Already in 1690, John Locke analyzed the nature and the importance of communication in human life by describing the relationship between words and exploring internal meaning and the role of language as the basis of both mind and society (Locke 1975). These bonds between language and communication are strikingly expressed in the first books and readers in the sociology of language and communication, which intimately interwove the two fields (e.g. Bryson 1948; Hertzler 1965; Miller 1950). As areas of study, communication and language historically share not only the same interests but very often the same research questions as well. Harold Lasswell, a leading figure in communication studies, articulated the key sentence that for years stood as the motto of the field: "Who says what, in which channel, to whom, with what effect?" (Lasswell 1948). A similar agenda of sociological language studies was formulated by Joshua Fishman, encapsulated in the phrase: "Who speaks what language to whom and when?" (Fishman 1965:67). Of course, this is not to gainsay that each field has evolved separately by elaborating and expanding its own range of inquiry, raising new questions, and seeking independent modes of institutionalization. Among other tangible signs, one finds the emergence of distinct journals and book series as well as professional associations both local and international, research budgets, and colloquia and conferences on subjects which brook no confusion. Last but not least, language and communication have distinct programs of study, up to independent departments in universities.

The sociology of language focuses on the study of linguistic data with the intention of learning about society as a whole. This approach is conceptually different from sociolinguistics, which, to the contrary, proceeds from the social context toward an understanding of linguistic variation. In practice, though, the boundary lines between these differentiations tend to blur, allowing the use of both terms indiscriminately. Certainly, this field is one of the most dynamic areas in the social sciences. It is grounded in the ethnomethodological assumption that individuals construct their world by asserting their identities through words and language: "Speech is the most important device by which humans create and distribute meanings" (Hill 1989: 14). Goffman (1987: 61) points out that it hardly seems possible to name a social variable that does not relate to speech behavior. J. A. Fishman elaborates further: "The sociology of language examines the interaction between [two] aspects of human behavior: the use of language and the social organization of behavior" (Fishman 1987:45). The importance of this kind of study, according to Ardener, (1989: 159) is that it enables "society [to] be analyzed [like] a text," including the generation and circulation of identities and their symbols.

Social scientists, as we know, are divided by their espousal of divergent theoretical perspectives; some emphasize social cohesion, others the subjective construction of the social order or the coercive role of power. However, all share attentiveness to the role of language. As early as 1704, Vico asserted that objects of culture do not exist independently from what we think they are (Vico 1948). Wittgenstein contends that as representation, language is both social and accessible to introspection—in other words, it is both normative and subjective—and that the primarily social nature of language consists of conventions between people and not people's traits (Wittgenstein 1958). Language is basically an intentional object of mutual belief, the most characteristic medium of social exchange, which simultaneously reflects and influences all facets of social existence. The appeal of studying language in its social context lies in the possibility that this might offer a key to an understanding of society itself (Newmeyer 1986: 5). While linguistic facts are not just social–they also constitute a reality of their own–the "linguistic turn in the social sciences," as Giddens puts it (Giddens 1987: 199), involves both the extension of ideas taken from the autonomous study of language to other aspects of human activity, and the exploration of the intersection between language and social practices.

Communication takes the lion's share among these practices. As shown by Carey (1989: 14-23), the term communication encapsulates two basic meanings, both of which refer to the social structure and to the actors' perceptions. One views communication as a process of transmission, the second as a ritual. The transmission view models communication as a process in which ideas, knowledge, and information are spread, transmitted, and disseminated in order to control people and space. The ritual view of communication emerges from the common root of the terms "community" and "communication." It is linked to such notions as "sharing," "participation," "association," "fellowship," and the "possession of common faith." While the transmission view is directed toward the extension of messages in space, the ritual view is oriented toward the maintenance of society in time, the representation of shared beliefs, and the preservation of a meaningful cultural world. The transmission view leads researchers to ask about the effect of transmitted information on audiences; it emphasizes the role of technology, raising questions about the persuasive power of the mass media and its contribution to individuals' changes of attitude.

The ritual view focuses on the ways the world is portrayed, represented, confirmed, and changed. As delineated by Clifford Geertz (1973), rituals are an active symbolic arena and have the potential for both representing models *of* society and creating models *for* society. Such a notion of communication entails examining actual social processes wherein significant symbolic forms are created, apprehended, and used; this is a process of generating and exchanging meanings (cf. Herzog 1987b). The core of this phase lies not in the social process, as in the transmission model, but in the text and its impact on the production and absorption of culture. These two views of communication are not mutually exclusive, and Carey suggests defining communication as "a symbolic process whereby reality is produced, maintained, repaired, and transformed" (Carey 1989: 23). This definition is comprehensive and includes all forms, conventions, and practices of speech and writing (Williams 1962), thus broadening the term communication to embrace culture as a whole and re-associate it with language studies. Such a conception re-establishes the original link between the sociology of language and communication. It elicits questions about communities of meanings and speech communities in which the media is another locus of the production of the symbolic order.

The study of language and communication in Israel is embedded in the contemporary academic development of these fields. At the same time, it has also its roots in both the old Jewish scholarly tradition and Israel's particular—and quite exceptional—experience in the realm of language. The importance is known of the role played by Old Hebrew as the charismatic code of the Bible, and this kind of interest is not alien to Jews' longstanding preoccupation with matters of language–up to and including the political militancy inspired by Yiddish among both anti-Zionists (e.g., the socialist-revolutionary Bund and among the ultra-Orthodox) and Zionists (Ber Borochov, a founder of socialist Zionism, was a prominent Yiddish linguist). Furthermore, prominent Jews in the development of linguistics as an academic discipline have also contributed significantly to the scientific study of Jewish languages. Max Weinreich, a leading linguist, was also a dedicated Yiddishist, and W. Chomsky was one of the first modern Hebrew linguists. Nevertheless, the contemporary social study of language and of communication in Israel relates, in one way or another, to the extraordinary revival of Hebrew as a spoken language, which was set in motion at the turn of the century and has ever since acted as the melting pot of the Israeli society. Its singularity resides in the fact that, for the first time in history, individuals who already had a language in common (nearly all the early participants in the revival were Eastern Europeans who shared Yiddish) made the switch to another language, Hebrew, which they did not know as a vernacular but which belonged to their "collective consciousness" as the Jews' sacred and literary tongue.

A Canaanite variant spoken in Judea (Sarfatti 1990), Hebrew was in use until the end of the First Commonwealth in 587 BCE. It was influenced by Aramaic during the Babylonian exile and by Greek later, until the Scribes reshaped it and created a new literary language. This Hebrew was spoken until the end of the second century CE, when it lost its function as a vernacular. Yet, even then, scholars continued to write books in Hebrew, and the language remained a subject of sacred study. As a result, Hebrew continued to absorb innovations originating from a wide range of languages—especially Arabic. Moreover, for many Jews of the Diaspora, Hebrew remained "on the tip of their tongue" (Fellman 1974:352) because it was used on many occasions, such as festivals, or lectures of rabbis visiting from remote communities (Rabin 1969). Hebrew was also the language of publicly chanted prayer and was of course heard when the Bible was read during synagogue services. Furthermore, Hebrew words and expressions are legion in Yiddish, Jewish Arabic, and Ladino, indicating a supplementary role of Hebrew in speech.

Hebrew became a language of secular writing again in the nineteenth century, with the advent of the *Haskalah* (Enlightenment) movement in Eastern Europe. The great turn came with Zionism. A modernized Hebrew, serving both as the language of culture and rite, and as a daily common vernacular, became the emblem of Jewish nationalism. Induced by anticipation of the ingathering of Jews from all corners of the globe in the Land of Israel and the necessity of a unifying language for all, this linguistic revival actually triumphed half a century before the ingathering itself occurred. By 1898, Palestine already had six all-Hebrew schools and fourteen part-Hebrew elementary schools, attended by a total of about 2,500 pupils. The first didactic book for teaching modern Hebrew was published in 1900. In 1906, a first Hebrew-speaking high school was founded, in Jaffa, and in 1914 a second one was established in Haifa, together with the first Hebrew-speaking institution of higher learning, the Technion. Citing these grounds, Zionist lobbying in 1921 succeeded in making Hebrew an official language of the British Mandate regime in Palestine. Thus, when the State of Israel was proclaimed, in 1948, Hebrew was already established as a legitimate language by major educational and other institutions. Although the revival had been launched by a small coterie of intellectuals (Fellman 1978) led by Eliezer Ben-Yehuda (compiler of the first modern Hebrew dictionary) and a number of teachers (often writers and poets themselves) (see Silbergschlag 1981), the language was later on vigorously transmitted to the massive immigration of the early 1950s (Bachi 1956; Rosenbaum 1983). Fellman (1974; 1975; 1978) has given a comprehensive account of this revival, and Rabin (1969), echoed by Cooper (1989), has shown how the revival extended its functions to include low-culture uses through inventiveness in semantics and lexicon, opening the language to the influence of Jewish vernaculars, Western languages and Arabic (Blanc 1968; Chomsky 1957). Since the 1950s, the transmission of Hebrew to immigrants has been channeled through intensive courses given within the framework of the *ulpan*, which is part of the state-run "absorption" process, and the revival of Hebrew itself was reproduced for the edification of every student (Katz 1982).

This genuine cultural revolution has had enormous ramifications for the social study in Israel of all related fields. To begin with, it has impeded efforts to investigate Jewish languages other than Hebrew. Hence the relative paucity of works focusing on social, historical, or cultural aspects of the development of Jewish languages such as Yiddish (Wexler 1987), Judezmo (Marcus 1965), or Judeo-Arabic (Schwartzwald 1981). As for the study of Hebrew itself, what mattered most to many sociolinguists was how well Israeli Jews learned the language and switched to it for their regular linguistic activity. Sociolinguistic studies (Bachi 1956; Bachi 1974; Carmon and Manheim 1976; Hofman and Fisherman 1972) have thus shown that factors including long stay in the country, lower age on arrival, higher level of education, greater urban experience, higher social status, or ethnic heterogeneity of spouses correlate positively with a rapid assimilation of Hebrew (for a review, see Rosenbaum 1983). Other works have looked into the influence of specific social categories on the development of Hebrew. More particularly, professional groups were shown to play a determinant role in lexical innovations related to their special requirements (Hofman 1974a; Hofman 1974b; Nahir 1978) and in the context of their orientation toward their international professional community (Fisherman 1990). Nadel and Fishman (1977) found that newspapers are also important agents of diffusion of new terms which spring from Hebrew roots but are of foreign-mainly English-origin (see also Ronen et al. 1977). While discourse and conversational analyses (Weil 1983), similar to comparable works elsewhere, indicate a differentiation according to class and gender regarding various aspects of speech, we are also informed that among the educated, women are generally more normative than men in their use of Hebrew. Other researchers have investigated the Hebrew language usage of specific ethnic categories which brought to Israel their own habits of speech. A leading example is Morag (1963), who has delved into the Yemenites' Hebrew (see also Hofman and Fisherman 1972). In a similar vein, a number of works have investigated the speech of the growing category of native-Israeli Jews. To take one example, a study of requesting language (Blum-Kulka and Olshtain 1984) reveals that being born in the country definitely matters and is bound up with rougher linguistic behavior. In another investigation, this one of complaining behavior (Olshtain and Weinbach n.d.), both Israeli-born and non-Israeli-born appeared to prefer, in identical frustrating situations, strategies expressing "disapproval, complaints, and accusation" to softened, polite expressions "below the level of reproach." However, the native-born are clearly more inclined to employ rougher expressions.

Such works have prompted researchers to ask new questions and delve into more problematic issues; they signal a shift among sociolinguists from a discussion of the success of Hebrew to reflection on social problems in language. A pioneering example is the work by Katriel (1986) which investigates the *dugri* (frank, in Arabic) speech model associated with the Israeli-born. It is described by Katriel as a style of speech embodying sincerity and frankness, naturalness, and a spirit of community. *Dugri* speech, moreover, is an anti-style, reacting to the supposed wordiness, exaggerated politeness, and manipulative speech behavior of Diaspora Jews as perceived by the Israeli-born. This anti-style developed its own rituals which, like all rituals, involved a departure from spontaneity and sincerity. The perceived image of Diaspora Jews as being weak and dependent on non-Jews translates into the feeling of superiority toward both the Diaspora and toward recent immigrants that can be found among native Israelis. In a similar vein, Almog (1997) goes so far as to assert that the Israeli-born exhibit a cult of nativeness, Orientalism, and elitism, which are conveyed by "Army Hebrew." The reference is to numberless new words and expressions created by youngsters during their military service, which maintain direct, intense relations with the slang which dominates Tel Aviv pubs, university cafeterias, or offices of young professionals. The aura of the *sabra* generation, however, is gradually fading with the constant increase in their number and, concomitantly, the structural and cultural transformation of Israeli society.

Urbanization, higher education, professionalization, and changing power relations in society pressurize the legitimate language in new directions. At some points, the slang component of *sabra* Hebrew seems to be giving way to more standard forms, which play a more acute role in the expression of social distinction. At the same time, English is gaining increasing importance in Israeli society as a second language.

This development has effectively brought the revolution of Hebrew to a curious point: just when the language has effectively become the mother-tongue of a whole population, it is losing its role as the language in which everything can be said, produced, and enjoyed. Related to such concerns, the study by Spolsky and Cooper (1991) in Jerusalem is another illustration of the new directions in Israeli sociolinguistics. The work maps the linguistic landscape of Jerusalem (Jews and non-Jews included) and charts the reality of power relations in society by analyzing the languages used throughout the city in formal and informal discourse.

Still another perspective is exemplified by Ben-Rafael (1994), who investigates Israeli society from the viewpoint of the bilingualisms attached to social cleavages. This methodology has disclosed new sociological perspectives. The diffusion of parochial vernaculars, on the one hand, and of English, the first foreign language in Israel, on the other, reveal that while ethnic and localist values are dominant in the lower classes, non-ethnic, national, and cosmopolitan orientations prevail in the middle and upper classes. Furthermore, the study of the penetration of Hebrew and the retention of Yiddish among the ultra-Orthodox unveils the community's inclination not only to adjust to its environment but also to be impactful. Last but not least, the patterns of bilingualism among Israel's Arabs underline their far-reaching cultural Israelization, notwithstanding the tensions existing between them and the Jewish majority and their potent desire to retain their Palestinian identity.

The institutionalization of the sociological study of language in Israeli academia received a major boost from Joshua Fishman during his stay at the Hebrew University in the first part of the 1970s. His direct collaborators, Bernard Spolsky (in the Department of English at Bar-Ilan University) and Robert Cooper (Department of Sociology, Hebrew University), later settled in Israel. They were not isolated, however, as sociolinguistic studies in Israel had acquired a presence in linguistics or language departments since the 1970s, and afterward in schools of education, as an aspect of the study of the diffusion of languages. Still later, one finds sociolinguists in communications and sociology departments. In the early 1990s, an inter-university Center for the Study of Language Policy was created (at Bar-Ilan), and the Israeli Association of Sociolinguistics was founded in the mid-1990s.

In the meantime, the field of communication studies was also well on its way, in the context of the development of mass media. The

Hebrew press was one of the harbingers of the revival of Hebrew (Kressel 1964; Yardeni 1969) (Halevy 1976), and an important locus for the crystallization of the national society (Kena'an 1979), even though, as in any country of high immigration, the foreign-language press also flourished (Ben-Rafael and Weitman 1984: 247-252; Frenkel 1994). In addition, there has always been an Arabic press which never tried to attract immigrant Jews from Arab countries but addressed itself almost exclusively to the country's Arab citizens. This chapter in the historical sociology of the press still awaits research.

In 1936, the written word was augmented by the establishment of the Voice of Jerusalem, the official radio station of the Mandate government, joined at the beginning of the 1940s by underground broadcasts sponsored by the leadership of the Yishuv (pre-Israel Jewish community in Palestine). After the creation of the state, radio was utilized by the government to implant norms, transmit concepts, and inculcate Hebrew (Caspi and Limor 1992), as a means to achieve control and oversight (Galnoor 1979). Programs aimed at the new immigrants were broadcast in a variety of languages. Arabic radio, like the Arabic press, was geared mainly to Israel's non-Jewish citizens and to listeners in neighboring countries. Until 1960, the Voice of Israel broadcast on one station in Hebrew to the local audience and on two other stations abroad: the Voice of Zion to the Diaspora and the Israeli Broadcasting Service to the Arab states (Caspi and Limor 1992: 98). Army Radio was introduced alongside the state network already in 1950 (ibid.: 106-110). This evolution of radio in Israel was marked by constant decentralization, a steady increase in the number of stations, and by commercialization. A similar process is discernible in Israeli television. It started with one state channel in 1968, to which a second channel was added in 1986, soon followed by an array of local and foreign channels made available through cable television (Caspi and Limor 1992: 115-133). Computer communication is introducing a new dimension, which makes Israelis residents of the global village. Indeed, Israel is a leading country in terms of per capita number of personal computers and in the number of Internet users. How much power, however, do the Israeli media wield? What role do they play? These questions have become central in the study of the communications media in Israel.

Parallel to the growth and consolidation of the social study of language, communication research in Israel has developed to meet all the criteria of scientific activity, further manifesting its institutionalization. The subject is taught and studied in the universities within the framework of existing departments—the Hebrew University of Jerusalem was the pioneer in the establishment of a separate Department of Communications, and today similar departments and/or study programs exist in all Israeli universities. Recently the journal *Patuah—Journal of Politics, Communication and Society* has appeared under the auspices of Bar-Ilan University, and a new association of communication was formed which also supports a journal, *Dvarim Achadim—Israel Journal of Communication, Culture and Society*. The Open University plays a special role in developing written courses and in publishing readers (e.g., Caspi and Limor 1998). From the outset, communication study developed as an interdisciplinary field of research which was nourished by and in turn nourished the social sciences (mainly sociology, anthropology, political science, and psychology) and the humanities (mainly linguistics, cinema, rhetoric studies, and education). Sociology has contributed significantly to the development and shaping of communication research by laying the foundation for the investigation of the interface of culture and society—the underpinnings of communication study. The pioneer scholars of the field in Israel were sociologists, preeminently, of course, Elihu Katz, a leading scholar in communication studies worldwide. Dina Goren was the first to introduce to Hebrew readers the basic conceptual frames and theories in studies of mass communication (Goren 1975; Goren 1986).

The transmission model that dominated the research agenda in American scholarship of communication studies until the mid-1970s (Katz 1987) influenced Israeli studies as well. Consequently, the main concerns were with the process of communication (Fiske 1990). Most of the early studies dealt with media effects (e.g., Adoni 1979; Cohen 1976), the media's agenda-setting function (Caspi 1981), media consumption (Adoni 1985; Dotan J. 1976), and uses and gratification (Cohen et al. 1988; Weimann 1982).

Israeli research was especially attentive to the subject of leisure-time culture and to the question of how much of that time was devoted to the consumption of the mass media (Katz and Gurevitch, 1976). The major themes were: who consumed what, and when (Ben-Ami 1988); and how did the advent of the new media affect communication consumption from the introduction of television (Katz and Hass in this volume), the proliferation of communication channels (Lachman-Messer 1997; Weimann 1995), the expansion to cable television (Weimann

1996), and, more recently, the rise of the Internet (Bar Ilan et al. 1997; Danet et al. 1997; Karniel 1997; Wolman 1997).

Interestingly enough, Israeli communication studies have been dominated by political communication studies. The leading question has been, and still is nowadays: How do the means of communication interact with the democratic process? Are the mass media the watch dogs or servants of the politicians (e.g., Caspi 1997)? Does information enhance democracy or it is just another fiction of the age of enlightenment (Ezrahi 1997)? Political communication during elections has intrigued Israeli scholars, especially since the advent of television. They have investigated intensively the role of the media in political campaigns (Elizur 1986; Elizur and Katz 1979; Eyal 1985; Peri 1975), testing theories of media effects, agenda setting, and uses and gratification (Caspi 1984; Cohen 1985). Considerable research has been devoted to pre-election polls (Shamir 1987; Weimann 1983; Weimann 1990), the social distribution of political attitudes among the population, and the messages and strategies that characterize the basic patterns of Israeli political culture (Gerts 1984; Greilsammer 1984; Herzog 1987a; Nir 1988).

Surprisingly, although the media in Israel have been centralized and controlled by politicians and the state, the issue of who controls the media, and how, has not been given prominence on the Israeli scholarly agenda. Among the very few studies, one notes the works on government-news media relations of Dina Goren (1979), Itzhak Galnoor (1982), Dan Caspi (1983) and Eva Etzioni-Halevy (1987). On the other hand, the juridical relations between the press and the State are more often discussed (e.g., Lahav 1993; Segal 1990). It was shown that several control mechanisms have limited freedom of speech and assured the media's support for government policies. To take one example of many, Military Censorship (Elyada 1990) and the Editors' Committee arrived at an arrangement in which the senior editors in both the written and the electronic media would meet with representatives of the Army and the government to decide together on publication policy concerning major national events (Lavi 1987). The press's self-censorship, especially during wartime, was another significant factor in this regard. While in many cases the press's self-restriction was intentional (Goren 1976), in many others it was the outcome of taken-for-granted social and political frames of reference (Koren 1994; Levi 1994) and the rhetoric of conformity (Raphael and Roeh 1992).

The ongoing decentralization and privatization of the media that have already produced a multi-channel media system call for new studies on the relationship between politicians and the media and on the impact of economic control on the structure and culture of Israeli media. First steps in that direction have been taken by Caspi (1986b) in his study of local newspapers, and by Caspi and Limor in their work on the changes within the Israeli media between 1948 and 1990 (Caspi and Limor 1992). The researchers' conclusion is that despite the multiplicity of channels and programs, the seemingly pluralistic structure of public-state broadcasting in Israel is illusory. The communications establishment, which is in large measure controlled by the political establishment, exercises a virtual monopoly on information (Caspi and Limor 1992). Katz (1996) supports this conclusion by shedding light on the monopoly of small, private owners of Israeli cable TV and their dependency on the political system.

The growth of local communication channels permits an examination of the media's place and role in shaping communal patterns as well as of the community's impact on the character of the media. We find an incipient treatment of these issues in a study of the new press in the ultra-Orthodox community (Michalson 1990; Zrachia 1989) and in the use of audiotapes as a communication channel within that community (Caplan 1997). Other studies examined the communications media in the kibbutz movement (Shur 1985), in the periphery (Avraham 1993), and among the elderly (Shinar 1984). However, this area of study needs additional research: Are genuine "communication communities" springing up? What are their distinguishing features? Are they developing their own language and distinctive contents? How does the use of local communication intersect with local politics and social life? Communication channels create alternative, imagined communities of viewers and readers. An experiment to study an imagined community in the media has been undertaken by Ehud Graf (1991) who focuses on the Tel Aviv weekly *Ha'ir*. Another attempt to cope with this question is made by Dafna Lemish (1997) in a study of the emergence of a community of "wrestlers" in schools among viewers of wrestling shows on television. Among other questions awaiting researchers: What can be said about the character of the youngsters who watch children's programs, are enthralled by video clips, and chat on the Internet?

Under the inspiration of critical cultural analysis, several researchers have adopted the models prevailing in European academia (Carey 1989:19-20; Fiske 1990; Gitlin 1978). The so-called "ritual view" has opened the field to a growing number of critical studies of group representations (e.g., Herzog 1998; Shohat 1979; Tidhar 1988; Tidhar and Lemish 1993). It has encouraged scholars to focus on the construction of social meanings and to delve into communities of shared meanings (Herzog and Shamir 1994; Liebes 1988; Liebes and Katz 1990) and frames of social interpretation used by media and audiences (Herzog et al. 1992; Liebes 1984). Concomitantly, the research venue has shifted to private homes (Liebes and Rivka 1991), media events (Dayan and Katz 1993), and talk shows as new public spheres (Liebes 1997). Moreover, instead of seeing in the audience a passive object of communication or an actor that at most chooses among options, current research and theories view audiences as active actors who interpret meaning and resist or use the media in "subversive" ways (Liebes 1992; Liebes 1993).

A Road Map of the Book

This volume presents a collection of articles originally published in the mid-1980s and in the 1990s. Reflecting the current state of research, it seeks to present the broadest possible range of the approaches and themes that characterize Israeli sociology in the fields of language and communication. Taken as a whole, the volume does not necessarily reflect the relative weight of the various paradigms and interests of the researchers. However, it includes articles that are representative of as many conceptual thrusts–and universities–as possible, within the constraint of the space limitations. In brief, it is primarily intended to give expression to the breadth of Israeli research in these fields, during the 1980s and 1990s.

Hence, and according to our inter-field approach, the book is divided into sections which cover, successively, *language and communication in daily life* (2), *in a pluralistic society* (3 and 4), *during elections* (5), and *in the shadow of the Israeli-Arab conflict* (6). We continue with works focusing on the relations of *society, state, and mass media* (7), before we turn, under the title of *thinking about the future* (8), to Josuah A. Fishman's and Elihu Katz's special and enlightening contributions which map future agendas for the sociological study of language and communication in Israeli society.

The first chapter of Part 2 is Tamar Katriel's. She traces the semantic journey of the term lefargen, which originates from Yiddish and means, roughly, "to be supportive and not to begrudge" and is employed in everyday speech by Israelis. Comparing the term with "supportive talk" in other languages, she explores the cultural logic of speech communities in which such metacommunicative terms are embedded. Katriel situates the emergence of *firgun* in the partial and uneasy shift from a communal to an individualistic orientation in Israeli society. Following Katriel's chapter, Haim Hazan deals with these two orientations through an anthropological analysis of a cinematic text, the Israeli film "Late Summer Blues." Viewing it as an event taking place at the critical crossroads between cultural life cycle and personal life cycle, Hazan re-reads the film's symbolic meaning and interprets its strategies as simultaneously controlling, subverting and altering cultural forms. In an examination of daily speech acts, Blum-Kulka analyzes dinner-table conversations. Comparing middle-class Jewish-American and Israeli families, she shows how cultural styles come to the fore in private domestic communication. While Blum-Kulka emphasizes the way cultural patterns are reflected in the act of storytelling, Zilberg explores how humor, as an act of speech, provides a forum for new immigrants to reconsider values and cultural and social norms. Humorous journalism as a mass media vehicle, Zilberg suggests, is a crucial element in the resocialization of immigrants from the former Soviet Union. Raz and Shapira then offer a sociological analysis of the technological aspects of communication, focusing on the answering machine. This device, which expands our communication reach, also restricts face-to-face relationships, masking and distorting "reality". The nature of verbal interaction is changed while technology becomes personified and actual. This kind of investigation, to be sure, will become increasingly timely in our Internet-dominated era, as "virtual reality" plays a growing role.

Part 3 addresses the issue of pluralingualism in Israeli society. This issue is of particular interest here, not only because pluralingualism is a major aspect of many multicultural modern societies, but also, and above all, because of Israel's experience of the revival of Hebrew as a spoken language and, indeed, as the very epitome of the new Israeli culture. The chapters in this section show, however, that the adoption of Hebrew as a legitimate language on behalf of Jewish nationalism has by no means reduced this society to monolingualism. Ben-Rafael shows that a variety of codes, such as French, English, Yiddish, and Arabic, coexist with Hebrew and experience different types and kinds of diffusion, according to both their social values and the status of their original carriers. Similarly, Fisherman indicates that people's attitudes regarding the use of foreign words within Hebrew language is influenced by age, education and occupation, and social-linguistic background. Bentolila focuses, more specifically, on profiles of bilingualism in a Moroccan community. The use of Hebrew and Judeo-Arabic appears to depend on both practical (e.g., linguistic skills) and emotional factors. The respective uses of Hebrew and Arabic depend, it appears, not only on the age of individuals but also on their education and status. Focusing on another aspect of verbal activity in a different type of community, Cromer analyzes the rhetoric of the *haredi* (ultra-Orthodox) leadership on crime and delinquency, showing how *haredi* politicians and rabbis portray these problems as the logical and natural outcome of the forsaking of religion—in short, the result of secularism. This rhetoric reveals the *haredis*' view of their own world as much as it does their perception of the secular society. It is yet another Israeli setting that Amara and Spolsky consider in their article: the Arab minority. More specifically, and focusing on a peculiar case, they study the language and symbols of collective identity of Arabs in Israel by comparing the two parts of a village that until 1948 was split down the middle between Israel and Jordan, but since the 1967 war has been wholly under Israeli administration. Their sociolinguistic investigation finds that the section that was part of Israel since 1948 shows a clear thrust toward Hebrew and Israeli culture, whereas the formerly Jordanian part shows an evolution toward Palestinian culture and identity. In a similar vein, Ben-Rafael and Brosh consider the mutual attitudes of Jews and Arabs in Israel toward each other's language. The main finding is that Jews and Arabs differ less in terms of how they perceive each other than of how they evaluate each other's language. Both Jews and Arabs feel remote from each other socially and culturally. Yet, on the other hand, while Jews see Arabic more or less in the same terms as they see Arabs, Arabs see Hebrew in much more positive terms than they see Jews. The findings support the hypothesis that from the viewpoint of language—hence also of culture—Arabs tend to converge toward Jews, though this by no means signifies that they are not deeply convinced of their distinct identity.

Following a section which dealt with social aspects of language activity, Part 4 brings together several works dealing with communication in Israeli society. As reflected in our selection, the mass media constitute the major interest. Most communication studies in Israel are indeed focused on radio broadcasting, the written press, and television. Elihu Katz, who headed the team in charge of introducing television to

Israel (in the late 1960s), was deeply involved at the time in the debates about that medium's possible negative educational and cultural effects on society. In his chapter with Hass these issues are reconsidered, though now with more than twenty-five years of experience to draw on. The researchers remind us that the medium's opponents thought that renascent Hebrew culture would be undermined by the introduction of foreign values, that the People of the Book would turn into the people of television, that ascetic and pioneering values would be uprooted by consumerism, and that ideological politics would be displaced by personality politics. The findings and the authors' careful interpretations suggest that television served as a bulwark against individualistic and hedonistic trends, offering an agenda to society. More specifically but no less instructive regarding the role of the media in society, other scholars delve into the social impact on community life. Schneller addresses the question of video watching and its societal functions for small-town adolescents, and Shinar discusses the role of the VCR in the community life of the kibbutz.

Part 5 offers three electioneering studies, a well-established field in Israeli communication studies. Most of the Israeli scholars in this field have been involved at least once during their careers in the study of election campaigning, especially via television party ads. These studies cover issues such as the media role in the formation of public opinion (Adoni 1979), in voting decisions (Caspi 1984), in influencing the agenda of politicians (Eyal 1985), and in gratification of campaigns (Cohen 1985). Also investigated were the language of politics and the rhetoric of political debates (e.g., Caspi 1986a; Gerts 1984; Greilsammer 1984; Nir 1988). Professionalization in election campaigns (Caspi and Eyal 1983; Elizur and Katz 1979) has also awakened a growing interest in pre-election polls (Shamir 1986; Shamir 1987; Weimann 1983; Weimann 1990; Weinamann 1983). In brief, electioneering has become a genuine industry in its own right in Israel. Millions of shekels are poured into political advertising, and the section's three chapters approach, from different perspectives, the question of whether this investment has paid off and in what ways. Wolsfeld looks at elections as "occasions for civic education" and asks whether the election broadcasts in Israel meet this criterion. His findings confirm that election ads reinforce existing attitudes far more than they change them. The study discovered that the vast majority of Israelis watched fewer election ads in the 1990s than they did in the past. They are far from satisfied with what they see, and in general do not take these ads seriously. Herzog shows that although election campaigns do not change voters' attitudes, they nevertheless play a role in the long-term process of shaping political cognition. Election ads frame and interpret information and thus construct reality. While the symbolic contest over issues on the open agenda emphasizes the differences between the parties (e.g., over where the country's borders should run), this very competition also enforces a hidden agenda of taken-for-granted assumptions. Such assumptions are, for instance, the definition of the collective "that counts" as the Jews, and the right of the Jewish people to the Land of Israel. It is in this vein that Herzog finds that election ads help reproduce a nationalistic society. Similarly, Lamish and Tidhar explore the role of TV commercials in reproducing a gendered social structure. The ads, they suggest, marginalize women and represent them through traditional stereotypes.

Part 6 focuses on the social and cultural impact–as expressed in language and communication-of the fact that Israelis live under the shadow of a protracted conflict with neighbors. This centrality of the conflict in daily life is deeply related to the intense consumption of news throughout the day. The chapters of this section discuss the role of the media and language in reporting about current events linked to Israeli-Palestinian tensions, portraying enemies, and commenting on rival political perspectives regarding the conflict. These chapters are but a small sample of the work carried out in this sphere, which is extremely popular among Israeli researchers of language and communication (e.g., Cohen and Wolfsfeld 1992). Liebes explores the role of television news in the process of political socialization. Her study is based on observations of interactions within Israeli families watching and discussing television coverage of the Intifada (the Palestinian uprising). Loshitzky's analysis refers to the way foreign television stations covered the Intifada. More specifically, she analyzes an encounter of Israelis and Palestinians organized by ABC, which was viewed simultaneously by a live audience and panelists in Jerusalem and the United States. This analysis tends to see news within the terms of ideological construction. In line with such preoccupations, Itzhak Roeh and Akiba Cohen address the classical question of objectivity in television news reports on the basis of the reports by five channels in different countries about the same incident in a West Bank village during the Intifada. The analysis of verbal and visual texts reveals substantial ("open" versus "closed") differences in the presentations of the incident. The last chapter in this section turns to another role of the media in conflict—their becoming a major aspect of the conflict setting itself (Wolfsfeld 1997). Weinman's chapter on terrorism-as-theater peels away the layers of the multifaceted relations between the terrorist, his target, the bombing or ambush, and the public. Putting the Israeli case in comparative perspective, he asks the question of what, if any, are the effects on public opinion of mass-mediated terrorism.

Part 7 addresses the question of the relationship between society, the state, and the media. Because Israel is a highly politicized society–due, in large part, to the permanent conflictual situation–this question is of particular interest here. Israelis, according to Lehman-Wilzig's findings, believe in television's power to promote political causes–at least as far as protesters are concerned. Although newspapers were found to be independently better reporters of news, television is considered the most efficacious channel through which citizens can affect state policies. The study by Etzioni-Halevy probes the structure of broadcasting and its interaction with the political elite. The tensions and struggles between the two, she explains, are inherent in the democratic game. While Caspi and Limor survey external patterns of political control imposed on the media, Roeh and Nir deal with the media's self-regulating mechanisms operating in the area of news presentation. Their claim is that ideology does not fully determine the rules of presentation, but does delineate the limits of linguistic variations. Yoram Peri's contribution addresses the overwhelming role played by the media in the ultra-dramatic event of Yitzhak Rabin's assassination, an event that shattered Israeli democracy and threw the entire country into a state of anomie. Peri's analysis of the coverage of the event and its aftermath shows how far the media were a factor in overcoming the following spiritual and social crisis, by reconstructing Rabin's biography as the nation's collective experience.

These six sections encompass, to the best of the editors' ability–with all the limitations that space constraints impose–the state of the art, so to speak, in the social study of language and communication in Israel, in recent years. The bibliography that closes the book aims to fill the lacunae caused by the space factor. However, as a way of concluding the volume, Part 8 offers some thoughts about the necessary agenda for these fields, the sociology of language and of communication, that form the subjects of this volume. We have here the privilege of special contributions by two international renowned figures in these fields. Their contributions should influence the future research efforts of Israeli scholars in this area. As already noted, Fishman, who founded the study of the sociology of language, was at the Hebrew University of Jerusalem for several years in the early 1970s. The sociology of language, he says, has never been a major field of research here in either sociology or linguistics. This, despite the fact that as a country of immigrants and as the place where the revival of Hebrew as a spoken language took place, Israel could well have served as an ideal laboratory for such research. In Israel especially, he maintains, sociolinguistics could have become a highly productive area of study that might have shed much light on the dynamics of society. Fishman deplores that for many researchers, sociolinguistics has remained a "sometime thing." On the one hand, sociologists have often failed to grasp the importance of this area, while on the other, linguists have remained focused on Hebrew's triumph in becoming a dominant language. Fishman points, then, to sociolinguistic issues of major importance in present-day Israel, such as the spread of English, the patterns of sociolinguistic integration of the Jews from the former Soviet Union, the changing role of Yiddish among the ultra-Orthodox, and the evolution of the Arabic spoken by Israeli Arabs. He urges social scientists to address these crucial issues, and it is his hope that the dedication of the present volume to this topic will strengthen this stream of sociology in Israel and also attract the commitment of linguists.

Elihu Katz, the founder of Israeli communication studies, reminds us that a communication miracle–the Holy Book and the language it perpetuated, Hebrew–is what has kept the Jews a living people. Like Fishman regarding language, Katz urges sociologists to see in communication a major area of investigation–though many sociologists in fact deal with communication unknowingly. Communication is as central to democracies as it is to non-democracies. A current agenda for communication studies should include both interests which turn to the past–such as reexamining how the Bible has safeguarded the Jewish people, and with it Hebrew–and current, ongoing reality, such as Israel's institutional structure of communication, the division of labor among media and types of media, the relations between the media and politics, and external influences: media roles in Israel's internal and external conflicts. Last but not least, this agenda should also focus on what lies ahead in terms of the media's part in the making of Israel's culture and future society.

The importance of these views derives from the simple truth that communication, through language, comprises the human experience anytime and everywhere, even when we are not conscious of it. "The one thing of which the fish is unaware is water, the very medium that forms its ambiance and supports its existence" (Marshall McLuhan, cited in Carey 1989:24).

References

Adoni, H. 1979. 'The Functions of Mass Media in the Political Socialization of Adolescents'. *Communication Research* 6: 84-106.

Adoni, H. 1985. 'Media Interchangeability and Co-Existence: Trends and Changes in the Television Era'. *Libri* 3: 202-217.

Almog, O. 1997. *The Tsabar - A Portrait*. Tel Aviv: Am Oved (Hebrew).

Ardener, E. 1989. *The Voice of Prophecy*. Oxford: Basil Blackwell.

Avraham, E. 1993. *The Media in Israel: Center and Periphery*. Tel Aviv: Breirot Publishers (Hebrew).

Bachi, R. 1956. 'A Statistical Analysis of the Revival of Hebrew in Israel'. *Scripta Hierosolymitana* 3: 179-247.

Bachi, R. 1974. *ThePopulation of Israel*. Jerusalem: The Hebrew University of Jerusalem.

Bar Ilan, J., Lazinger, S.S. and Peritz, B.C. 1997. 'Internet Use by Faculty Members at the Hebrew University of Jerusalem'. *Dvarim Ahadim - Israel Journal of Communication, Culture and Society* 2: 153-164.

Ben-Ami, I. 1988. '«Who is Reading What?» Reading Newspapers in Israel as a Mode of Cultural Consumption' *Department of Sociology*. Tel Aviv: Tel Aviv

Ben-Rafael, E. 1994. *Language, Identity and Social Division: The Case of Israel*. Oxford: Oxford University Press.

Ben-Rafael, E. and Weitman, S. 1984. 'The Reconstitution of the Family in the Kibbutz'. *European Journal of Sociology* 25: 1-27.

Blanc, H. 1968. 'The Israeli Koine as an Emergent National Standard' in Fishman, J. A., Fergurson, C. A. and Das Gupta, J. (eds.) *Language Problems of Developing Nations*. New York: Wiley.

Blum-Kulka, S. and Olshtain, E. 1984. 'Requests and Apologies: A Cross-Cultural Study of Speech Act Realization Patterns'. *Applied Linguistics* 5: 196-213.

Bryson, L. 1948. 'The Communication of Ideas'. New York: Harper & Brothers.

Caplan, K. 1997. 'God's Voice: Audiotaped Sermons in Israeli Haredi Society'. *Modern Judaism* 17: 253-279.

Carey, J.W. 1989. *Communication as Culture*. Boston: Unwin Hyman.

Carmon, N. and Manheim, B. 1976. *Achieving Goals through Housing Polices*. Haifa: Technion (Hebrew).

Caspi, D. 1981. 'The Agenda-Setting function of the Israeli Press'. *Knowledge* 3: 181-193.

Caspi, D. 1983. 'On the Control of Media by Politicians: A New Perspective'. *Political Communication and Persuasion* 2: 263-277.

Caspi, D. 1984. 'Following the Race: Propaganda and Electoral Decision' in Gutman, E., Caspi, D. and Diskin, A. (eds.) *The Roots of Begin's Success: 1981 Israeli Elections*. London: Croom Helm.

Caspi, D. 1986a. 'Electoral Rhetoric and Political Polarization: The Begin - Peres Debates'. *European Journal of Communication* 1: 447-462.

Caspi, D. 1986b. *Media Decentralization - The Case of Israel's Local Newspapers*. New Brunswick and London: Transaction Publishers.

Caspi, D. 1997. 'Communication and Democracy in Israel'. Tel Aviv: Van Leer Jerusalem/Hakibbutz hamemeuchad Publishing House.

Caspi, D. and Eyal, C.H. 1983. 'Professionalization Trends in Israeli Election Propaganda: 1973-1981' in Arian, A. (ed.) *The Elections in Israel - 1981*. Tel Aviv: Ramot Publishing Co.

Caspi, D. and Limor, Y. 1992. *The Mediators: The Mass Media in Israel 1948-1990*. Tel Aviv: Am Oved Publishers.

Caspi, D. and Limor, Y. 1998. 'Mass Media in Israel'. Tel Aviv: The Open University of Israel.

Chomsky, W. 1957. *Hebrew: The Eternal Language*. Philadelphia: Jewish Publication Society of America.

Cohen, A. A. 1976. 'Radio versus Television: The Effects of the Medium'. *Journal of Communication* 26: 29-35.

Cohen, A. A. 1985. 'Attention to the Mass Media among Straight and Split Ticket Voters'. *Human Communication Research* 2: 75-78.

Cohen, A. A., Levy, M. R. and Golden, K. 1988. 'Children's Uses and Gratifications of Home VCRs: Evolution or Revolution'. *Communication Research* 6: 772-780.

Cohen, A. A. and Wolfsfeld, G. 1992. 'Framing the Intifada: People and Media'. Norwood, New Jersey: Ablex Publishing Corporation.

Cooper, R.L. 1989. *Language Planning and Social Change*. Cambridge: Cambridge University Press.

Danet, B., Rudenberg-Wright, L. and Rosenbaum-Tamari, Y. 1997. 'Virtual Virtuosos: «Where's All that Smoke Coming From?» Writing, Play and Performance on IRC'. *Dvarim Ahadim - Israel Journal of Communication, Culture and Society* 1: 143-164.

Dayan, D. and Katz, E. 1993. *Media Events*. Cambridge, Mass.: Harvard University Press.

Dotan J., C.A.A. 1976. 'The Uses of Mass Media in War and Peace: Israel 1973-74'. *Communication Research* 3: 393-402.

Elizur, J. 1986. 'The Media in the Israeli Elections of 1981' in Penniman, H. H. and Elazar, D. J. (eds.) *Israel at the Polls: The Knesset Elections of 1981*: American Enterprise and Indiana University.

Elizur, J. and Katz, E. 1979. 'The Media in Israeli Elections of 1977' in Penniman, H.R. (ed.) *Israel at the Polls: The Knesset Elections of 1977*. Washington D.C.: American Enterprise Institute.

Elyada, U. 1990. 'Journalism and Censorship in 1948' *From the Yishuv to the State/ 1947-1948: Continuity and Change*. Haifa: Hertzel Institute, Haifa University.

Etzioni-Halevy, E. 1987. *National Broadcasting under Siege - A Comparative Study of Australia, Britain, Israel and West Germany*. New York: St. Martin's.

Eyal, C. 1985. 'Newspaper Political Advertising and News in the 1984 Israeli Elections'. *Journalism Quarterly*: 601-608.

Ezrahi, Y. 1997. 'Myths of Information and Democracy'. *Dvarim ahadim* 1: 19-25 (Hebrew).

Fellman, J. 1974. 'The Hebrew Revival: A Myth?'. *Orbis* 23: 350-354.

Fellman, J. 1975. 'The Hebrew Language on the Eve of Revival'. *Orbis* 24: 349-353.

Fellman, J. 1978. 'A Note on the Hebrew and the Irish Revival'. *Orbis* 27: 315-316.

Fisherman, H. 1990. 'Attitudes toward Foreign Words in Contemporary Hebrew'. *International Journal of the Sociology of Language* 86: 5-40.

Fishman, J. 1965. 'Who Speaks What Language to Whom and When?'. *La Linguistique* 2: 67-88.

Fishman, J.A. 1987. 'The Sociology of Language' in Giglioli, P. P. (ed.) *Language and Social Context*. Harmondsworth: Penguin Books.

Fiske, J. 1990. *Introduction to Communication Studies*. London and New York: Routledge.

Frenkel, E. 1994. *The Press and Politics in Israel: The Jerusalem Post from 1932 to the Present*. Connecticut, West Port: Greenwood Press.

Galnoor, I. 1982. *Steering the Polity: Communication and Politics in Israel*. Beverly Hills: Sage Publication.

Galnoor, I. 1979. 'The Politics of Public Information'. *Transaction/Society* May/June: 20-30.

Geertz, C. 1973. *The Interpretation of Culture*. New York: Basic Books.

Gerts, N. 1984. 'Propaganda Style of Election Ads from 1977 to 1984' in Arian, A. (ed.) *The Elections in Israel - 1984*. Tel Aviv: Ramot Publishing Co.

Giddens, A. 1987. 'Structuralism, Post-Structuralism and the Production of Culture' in Giddens, A. and Turner, J. (eds.) *Social Theory Today*. Oxford: Basil Blackwell, Polity Press.

Gitlin, T. 1978. 'Media Sociology: The Dominant Paradigm'. *Theory and Society* 6.

Goffman, E. 1987. 'The Neglected Situation' in Giglioli, P. P. (ed.) *Language and Social Context*. Harmondsworth: Penguin Books.

Goren, D. 1975. *Mass Communication*. Tel Aviv: Am Oved-Tarbut Vechinuch (in Hebrew).

Goren, D. 1976. *Secrecy, Security and the Freedom of Press*. Jerusalem: Magnas (Hebrew).

Goren, D. 1979. *Secrecy and The Right to Know*. Ramat Gan: Turtledove.

Goren, D. 1986. *Communication and Reality - Basic Concepts in Mass-Communication*. Jerusalem: Keter Publishing House (in Hebrew).

Graf, E. 1991. 'From «White City» to a «Metropolitan»: The Universalistic City in «The City»' *Department of Sociology and Anthropology*. Tel Aviv: Tel Aviv University.

Greilsammer, I. 1984. 'Campaign Strategies of the Israeli Religious Parties 1981-1984' in Arian, A. (ed.) *The Elections In Israel - 1984*. Tel Aviv: Ramot Publishing.

Halevy, S. 1976. 'The Beginning of the Hebrew Press in the Land of Israel' *Chapters in the History of Jewish Community in Jerusalem*. Jerusalem: Yad Ben Zvi (Hebrew).

Hertzler, J. O. 1965. *A Sociology of Language*. New York: Random House.

Herzog, H. 1987a. *Contest of Symbols - The Sociology of Election Campaigns through Israeli Ephemera*. Cambridge, Massachusetts: Harvard University Library.

Herzog, H. 1987b. 'The Elections Campaign as a Liminal Stage: Negotiation over Meanings'. *The Sociological Review* 35: 559-574.

Herzog, H. 1998. 'More Than a Looking Glass: Women in Israeli Local Politics and the Media'. *The Harvard International Journal of Press/Politics* 3.

Herzog, H., Camp, A. and Drori, G. 1992. 'What the U.S. is Doing Here? Public Discourse on the U.S Involvement in the Middle East Conflict'. *Patuach* 1: 31-48 (Hebrew).

Herzog, H. and Shamir, R. 1994. 'Negotiated Society? Media Discourse on Israeli Jewish/Arab Relations'. *Israel Social Science Research* 9: 55-88.

Hill, J. H. 1989. 'Language, Culture and Worldview' in F.J., N. (ed.) *Linguistics: The Cambridge Survey: The Socio-Cultural Context*. Cambridge: Cambridge University Press.

Hofman, J.E. 1974a. 'Predicting the Use of Hebrew Terms among Israeli Psychologists'. *International Journal of the Sociology of Language* 3: 53-65.

Hofman, J.E. 1974b. 'The Prediction of Success in Language Planning: The Case of the Chemists in Israel'. *International Journal of the Sociology of Language* 1: 39-65.

Hofman, J.E. and Fisherman, H. 1972. 'Language Shift and Language Maintenance in Israel' in Fishman, J. (ed.) *Advances in the Sociology of Language*. The Hague: Mouton.

Karniel, Y. 1997. 'Freedom of Speech on the Internet'. *Dvarim Ahadim - Israel Journal of Communication, Culture and Society* 2: 165-185.
Katriel, T. 1986. *Talking Straight in Dugri Speech in Israeli Sabra Culture*. Cambridge: Cambridge University Press.
Katz, E. and Gurevitch, M. (eds.). 1976. *The Secularization of Leisure*, London: Faber and Faber.
Katz, E. 1987. 'Communications Research Since Lazarsfeld'. *Public Opinion Quarterly* 51: 25-45.
Katz, P. 1982. 'Ethnicity Transformed: Acculturation in Language Classes in Israel'. *Anthropological Quarterly* 55: 99-111.
Katz, Y. 1996. 'The Development of Cable Television in Israel and its Connection to the Socio-Political System'. *Patuach* 3: 65-94.
Kena'an, H. 1979. *The Newspapers Struggle - The Struggle of the Hebrew Press in the Land of Israel against the British Mandate*. Jerusalem: The Zionist Library (Hebrew).
Koren, A. 1994. 'Coverage of the «Land Day» (1976) in the Israeli Press'. *Patuach* 1: 3-16 (Hebrew).
Kressel, G. 1964. *History of the Hebrew Press in Israel*. Jerusalem: The Zionist Library (Hebrew).
Lachman-Messer, D. 1997. 'The Map of Israeli Media'. *Dvarim Ahadim - Israel Journal of Communication, Culture and Society* 1: 66-87.
Lahav, P. 1993. 'The Press and National Security' in Yaniv, A. (ed.) *National Security and Democracy in Israel*. Boulder and London: Lynne Rienner Publishers.
Lasswell, H. D. 1948. 'The Structure and Function of Communication' in Bryson, L. (ed.) *The Communication of Ideas*. New York: Harper & Brothers.
Lavi, Z. 1987. 'The Editors Committee - The Myth and the Reality'. *Kesher* 1: 11-35 (Hebrew).
Lemish, D. 1997. 'School as a Wrestling Ring: The Role of a Televised Wrestling Series in the Lives of Elementary School Children'. *Dvarim Ahadim* 1: 116-132 (Hebrew).
Levi, D. 1994. 'The Ideological role of News in TV'. *Patuach* 1: 9-30.
Liebes, T. 1984. 'Ethnocriticism: Israeli of Moroccan Ethnicity Negotiate the Meaning of 'Dallas''. *Studies in Visual Communication* 10: 46-71.
Liebes, T. 1988. 'Cultural Differences in the Retelling of Television Fiction'. *Critical Studies in Mass Communication* 5: 277-292.
Liebes, T. 1992. 'Decoding Television News'. *Theory and Society* 21.
Liebes, T. 1993. 'Television News and the Politicization of Women in Israel'. *Zmanim-A Historical Quarterly* 12: 188-199 (Hebrew).
Liebes, T. 1997. 'Talk Shows: The New Public Sphere?' in Caspi, D. (ed.) *Communication and Democracy in Israel*. Tel Aviv: Van Leer Jerusalem Institute/ Hakibbutz Hammeuchad Publishing House.
Liebes, T. and Katz, E. 1990. *The Export of Meaning - Cross Cultural Reading of Dallas*. N.Y.: Oxford University Press.
Liebes, T. and Rivka, R. 1991. 'A Mother's Battle against TV News: A Case of Political Socialization'. *Discourse and Society* 2: 203-222.
Locke, J. 1975. in Nidditch, P. (ed.) *An Essay Concerning Human Understanding*. Oxford: Clarendon Press.
Marcus, S. 1965. *The Judeo-Spanish Language*. Jerusalem: Kiryat Sefer.
Michalson, M. 1990. 'Haredic Press in Israel'. *Kesher* 8: 11-22 (Hebrew).
Miller, G. A. 1950. *Language and Communication*. New York: McGraw-Hill Publishing Co.
Morag, S.H. 1963. *The Hebrew Language Tradition of the Yemenite Jews*. Jerusalem: The Academy of the Hebrew Language (Hebrew).

Nadel, E. and Fishman, J. 1977. 'English in Israel: A Sociolinguistic Study' in Fishman, J., Cooper, R. Conard, W. (ed.) *The Spread of English - The Sociology of English as an Additional Language*. Newbury: Rowley.

Nahir, M. 1978. 'Normativism and Educated Speech in Modern Hebrew'. *International Journal of the Sociology of Language* 18: 49-67.

Newmeyer, F.J. 1986. *The Politics of Linguistics*. Chicago: Chicago University Press.

Nir, R. 1988. 'Electoral Rhetoric in Israel - The Televised Debate'. *Language Learning* 38: 187-208.

Olshtain, E. and Weinbach, L. n.d. 'Interlanguage Features of the Speech Act of Complaining'. Tel Aviv: Tel Aviv University, School of Education.

Peri, Y. 1975. 'Television in the 1973 Election Campaign' in Arian, A. (ed.) *The Elections in Israel - 1973*. Jerusalem: Jerusalem Academic Press.

Rabin, C. 1969. 'The Revival of the Hebrew Language'. *Ariel* 25.

Raphael, N. and Roeh, I. 1992. 'Intifada Coverage in the Israeli Press: Popular and Quality Papers Assume a Rhetoric of Conformity'. *Discourse and Society* 3: 47-60.

Ronen, M., Seckbach, F. and Cooper, R.L. 1977. 'Foreign Loan Words in Hebrew Newspapers' in Fishman, J., Cooper, R.L. and Conard, A.W. (eds.) *The Spread of English - The Sociology of English as an Additional Language*. Newbury: Rowley.

Rosenbaum, Y. 1983. 'Hebrew Adoption among New Immigrants to Israel: The First Three Years'. *International Journal of the Sociology of Language* 41: 115-130.

Sarfatti, G. 1990. ' 'L'Hebreu: De la langue de la Bible la langue d'aujourd'hui' Louvain-la-Neuve: Conference on 100 Years to the Revival of Hebrew (lecture delivered in French) Universite Catholique de Louvain-la-Neuve'.

Schwartzwald, O. 1981. *The Language of Oriental Groups*. Jerusalem: The Hebrew University of Jerusalem, Department of Linguistics (Hebrew).

Segal, Z. 1990. .

Shamir, J. 1986. 'Pre-Election Polls in Israel - Structural Constrains and Accuracy'. *Public Opinion Quarterly* 4: 62-75.

Shamir, J. 1987. 'Horse Race Journalism and Pollsters' Performance in Israel'. *Political Communication and Persuasion* 4: 371-383.

Shinar, D. 1984. *Communication at Old Age - To come with the Mountain to Muhammad*. Jerusalem: Academon.

Shohat, E. 1979. *Israeli Cinema East/West and the Politics of Representation*. Austin, Texas: University of Texas Press.

Shur, S. 1985. 'Editorial Board of Kibbutz Journal as Communication Institute'. Haifa: Haifa University, The Institute for the Study of Kibbutz and the Cooperative Idea (Hebrew).

Silbergschlag, E. 1981. 'Eliezer Ben-Yehuda: A Symposium at Oxford'. Oxford: Oxford Centre of Postgraduate Studies.

Spolsky, B. and Cooper, R. 1991. *The Languages of Jerusalem*. Oxford: Calderon Press.

Tidhar, C. E. 1988. 'Women in Israel's broadcasting Media and on Israeli Television' in Kawakami, Y. (ed.) *Women and Communication in an age of Science and Technology*. Tokyo: Atom Press.

Tidhar, C. E. and Lemish, D. 1993. 'Women in the Intifada: A Television News Perspective' in Cohen, A. A. and Wolfsfeld, G. (eds.) *Framing the Intifada: People and Media*. Norwood, New Jersey: Ablex Publishing Corporation.

Vico, G. 1948. *The New Science*. Ithaca, NY: Cornell University Press.

Weil, S. 1983. 'Women and Language in Israel'. *International Journal of the Sociology of Language* 41: 77-91.

Weimann, G. 1982. 'The Prophecy that Never Fails: On the Uses and Gratifications of Horoscope Reading'. *Sociological Inquiry* 52: 274-290.

Weimann, G. 1983. 'Pre-Election Polls in the Israeli Press'. *Journalism Quarterly* 60: 283-300.
Weimann, G. 1990. 'The Obsession to Forecast: Pre-Election Polls in the Israeli Press'. *Public Opinion Quarterly* 54: 396-408.
Weimann, G. 1995. 'Zapping in the Holy Land: Coping with Multi-Channel TV in Israel'. *Journal of Communication* 45: 97-103.
Weimann, G. 1996. 'Cable Comes to the Holy Land: The Impact of Cable TV on Israeli Viewers'. *Journal of Broadcasting and Electronic Media* Forthcoming.
Weimann, G. 1983. 'Every Day is Election Day' in Gutman, E., Caspi, D. and Diskin, A. (eds.) *The Roots of Begin's Success: The 1981 Israeli Elections*. London: Croom Helm.
Wexler, P. 1987. 'Interdialectical Translation as a Reflection of Lexical Obsolescence and Dialect Distance: The West Yiddish Bible Translation of 1679 in the Biblia Pentapla'. *Journal of the Sociology of Language* 67: 7-26.
Williams, R. 1962. *Communication*. Harmondsworth: Penguin.
Wittgenstein, L. 1958. *Philosophical Investigations*. Oxford: Oxford University Press.
Wolfsfeld, G. 1997. *Media and political conflict*. Cambridge: Cambridge University Press.
Wolman, Y. 1997. 'The Internet in the Interpersonal Scientific Community'. *Dvarim Ahadim - Israel Journal of Communication, Culture and Society* 1: 165-169.
Yardeni, G. 1969. *The Hebrew Press in the Years 1863-1904*. Tel Aviv: (Hebrew).
Zrachia, Z. 1989. 'The Haredic Press' *Department of Communication*. Jerusalem: The Hebrew University.

Part 2

Language and Communication in Daily Life

2

Lefargen: A Study in Israeli Semantics of Social Relations

Tamar Katriel

1. Introduction

The term *lefargen* and its derivatives—roughly translatable as "to support, not to envy or begrudge another's success"—is routinely employed in everyday discourse among Israelis. As Netser (1988) pointed out, and as many adult speakers of colloquial Hebrew confirm in sociolinguistic interviews, this has not always been the case. Although the spread of the term cannot be determined precisely, the sense of lexical novelty attending its use can still be glimpsed now and then as when people readily respond to questions of linguistic usage by recalling "the first time I have heard the word." Or, more pointedly, when a person who has been away from the country for a number of years explicitly wonders about the semantics of *lefargen,* as did a repatriated colleague of mine who, upon hearing about my interest in this term, said: "I was really wondering about this word. I just learned it coming back now, and am not quite sure how to use it." Indeed, I, too, found myself tenuously trying to pin down the semantics of *lefargen,* which I clearly remember to have first encountered upon my return from an extended stay in the United States in early 1988 in the often-heard expression "*etslenu lo mefargenim*" "Here, by us, people don't support each other, are envious of each other's well-being." Notably, however, younger informants, students in their early 20s, consider *lefargen* and its derivatives as part of their taken-for-granted everyday vocabularies. In fact, they are somewhat surprised to learn that the term has not been part of the active, standard repertoire of speakers of colloquial Hebrew until relatively recently.

Thus, whereas the lexemes morphologically derived from the root stem *f-r-g-n* have found their place in dictionaries of Hebrew slang for quite a number of years now (Sappan, 1965; Ben-Amotz and Ben-Yehuda, 1972), they seem to have been incorporated into colloquial Hebrew speech in a gradual manner over the past decade or so. These items have also gained increasing sociolinguistic legitimacy as their usage proliferated. For example, they can be heard in relatively formal speech events such as lectures or formal TV interviews with high-profile artists or politicians, and they no longer tend to appear in the press in single quotation marks, which are typographical devices used to mark the nonstandard status of linguistic items. As one person put it, smilingly: "When I heard Shimon Peres [former prime minister and leader of the Labor bloc who is considered an intellectual] use the word *lefargen,* I knew it was OK to use it."

Like other metacommunicative terms that verbally chart culturally focal "ways of speaking" (Hymes, 1974), *lefargen* is considered both routine and symbolically potent. In Ortner's terms (1973), it is a verbal "key symbol," affirmed as much in positive injunctions about the value of supportive conduct falling under the heading of *firgun* and in ongoing complaints about a prevailing attitude of nonsupportiveness, or lack of *firgun.* Thus, the culturally focal status I claim for the verbal symbol *lefargen* is predicated not only on its proliferation in everyday speech, a matter of frequencies, but more importantly on the emotional and moral overtones attending its discussion among cultural members. As I show, the wider circulation and broader legitimacy related to the use of the family of terms morphologically associated with *lefargen* (verb) and *firgun* (noun) have been accompanied by a broadening of its semantic scope. For example, *lefargen* and its derivatives have assumed a central "summarizing" role in descriptions of a social milieu as a whole (Ortner, 1973), as exemplified in the generalized expression *avira mefargenet,* "a supportive atmosphere."

The extent to which the term *firgun* has become "naturalized" in Israeli speech can be gleaned from a somewhat facetious newspaper article by Amnon Rubinstein (1990), professor of law, member of parliament, and student of Israeli society (Rubinstein, 1977). This article explicitly supports my selection of *lefargen* as a culturally focal key (verbal) symbol in contemporary Israeli society. The article is entitled "*Fargen Li l-firgun Katan,*" roughly, "Don't begrudge me a bit of begrudging," and carries a subtitle (given in parentheses), that reads: "If you understand this title it is a sign that you are an Israeli." Further commenting on the title, Rubinstein wrote: "Every true Israeli will understand it with a little effort. If I don't begrudge you, [do] begrudge my failure to begrudge you. But who will understand this title except for us? And how the hell do you translate this title into English or French—or into any other language" (p. 8)? He continued by writing that the word has spread so much that "it is difficult to imagine a newspaper article without it being employed in both expected and unexpected places" (p. 8).

Whereas parsing out the semantic features of *lefargen* would in itself be an interesting analytic task (which was partially accomplished by Netser, 1988), my main interest lies in reflecting upon the larger contextual issues associated with the adoption (through lexical burrowing) and spread of the term as part of Israeli social semantics. I submit that in commending a person as someone who "knows how to express support" (*ehad shejodea lefargen*), in presenting oneself as "someone who likes to express support" (*ohev lefargen*), or in complaining of "lack of support" (*hoser firgun*), speakers give voice to an ethnosociological model in which social relations and interpersonal patterns of a particular kind are verbally reified and valorized.

As I demonstrate, the particular conception and scope of the notion of "interpersonal support" embedded within this model, and the behavioral expectations associated with it, are indeed a matter of empirical exploration.[1] To what extent this verbally encoded cognitive model in fact shapes actual behaviors is another question. The constant complaints about people's failure to stand up to expected standards of *firgun* suggest that social expectations are, in fact, often thwarted by the actual realities of everyday interpersonal conduct. These expectations, however, whether followed or not, are central components in Israeli "behavioral ideology." Behavioral ideology, according to Volosinov (1973, p. 91), is "that atmosphere of unsystematized and unfixed inner and outer speech which endows our every instance of behavior and action and our every "conscious" state with meaning."

The particular flavor of *lefargen* as an interpersonal support term can be gleaned from the explications found in slang dictionaries. Thus, Ben-Amotz and Ben-Yehuda (1972) noted that *lefargen* is a borrowing from Yiddish, and they exemplified its use with the negative *Hu lo mefargen leaf ehad shum davar,* which is explicated as "He cannot stand it when someone has an advantage over him.... He is envious." Sappan (1965) similarly explicated *lefargen* as "relating to another without envy." This explication goes back to the German-derived Yiddish term *ferginen,* which denotes an interpersonal attitude anchored in the ability and willingness to overcome one's envy in another's good fortune, and not to begrudge his or her success.[2] This account indeed captures a core component in the semantics of this family of terms but does not cover the whole array of meanings and uses currently associated with it.

Interviewees' renderings of *lefargen* similarly mark it as a social support term, pointing to various dimensions of its meanings. Thus, a 39-year-old male informant explained: "*Lefargen* is to give advance credit, to want somebody else's advantage. To give them a chance, to want them to succeed, and to be pleased with their success. For example, when someone succeeds in business, I show him I am pleased for him (*ani mefargen lo*)." A 37-year-old woman said that "*lefargen* is to give someone a chance to do things, not to judge them harshly." And a 22-year-old woman said that "*lefargen* is generally speaking a positive expression, a positive form of expression that is externally expressed in words, bodily behavior, or smiles. The classical example: a teacher-student encounter. When the student gives a correct answer, the teacher supports him (*mefargen lo*) by repeating the student's words and making use of what he said." And, finally, a 40-year-old man said: "*Lefargen* is supporting someone you like, i.e., if your colleague received a promotion and you didn't, then *lefargen* is when you are as happy for him as if it was you who received the promotion. It is not just giving compliments, it's when you identify with, encourage, and feel proud of the other person."

As is further discussed in the next section, the notion of support is not invoked here in its more usual sense of extending goodwill in times of stress, but rather in the sense of partaking in another's success or good fortune, for example, by being willing and able to express delight in another's accomplishment with no trace of envy. Notably, this kind of "facework" (Goffman, 1967) involves expressive behavior that in Brown and Levinson's (1987) extension of Goffman's facework model would fall under the category of "positive politeness." But it actually refers to conduct that goes beyond matters of politeness as culturally interpreted in Israeli ethnosemantics. Thus, one can be quite polite (*menumas*) and yet not act in the mode of *firgun*, whereas acting in the mode of *firgun* actually precludes the interpretation of conduct as involving politeness (in the native rendition as *nimus*).

That *nimus* and *firgun* semantically exclude each other was brought home to me one day when, standing at a bus stop on campus, I overheard two young students who were discussing a third person. One of them said: "*Ani davka ohevet ota, ki hi mefargenet kazot*" "I actually like her because she is a supportive type." The other replied: "*Hi lo kol kah joda'at lefargen, hi stam kazot nimusit*" "She doesn't really know how to show support, she's just sort of polite." From an emic standpoint, politeness is associated with the social conventions governing "dutiful" behavior rather than with individually motivated, voluntary, spontaneous conduct expressive of sincere feeling (see Katriel, 1986). So that although conduct culturally perceived as "polite," together with conduct that would earn the label of *firgun* in cultural members' talk, similarly fall into Brown and Levinson's (1987) category of "positive politeness" as far as their universal model of politeness strategies goes, the interpersonal scenarios these two metacommunicative terms invoke are clearly differentiated within the ethnosemantics of colloquial Hebrew.

We are now in a better position to delineate the semantics of *lefargen* more closely. It denotes 'support," like the more standard expression for support (*tmiha*), but is semantically differentiated from *tmiha* in its scope of application within the ethnosemantics of social support in Israeli everyday speech (referring to supportiveness and appreciation in good rather than in bad moments). *Lefargen* also denotes attentiveness to one's interlocutor's "positive face wants," but in such a way as to assure him or her that one's expressive conduct is not a matter of "mere politeness."

My interest in tracing the semantic journey of *lefargen* and its derivatives was triggered on one level by the aforementioned experiential sense of lexical novelty and widespread linguistic presence, and on another level by an ongoing attention to the lexical coding of social relations in colloquial Hebrew and their communicative manifestations as ways of speaking and acting. Given the proliferation of *lefargen*, and the considerable animation attending its discussion in preliminary explorations, I decided to trace its "language game" (Wittgenstein, 1968) in a way similar to earlier studies of Israeli metacommunicative terms, hoping it would similarly offer new inroads into the study of central aspects of the semantics of social relations in Israel (Greifat and Katriel, 1989; Katriel, 1986, 1991).

Identifying my enterprise as a study in the "semantics of social relations" implies a particular research focus on the *language of social relations* as culturally coded in the form of the lexicalization of metacommunicative dimensions of speech conduct. In line with one of the standard foci of ethnography of communication research (see, e.g., Hymes, 1974; Stross, 1974), I am interested in studying the discursive uses of lexically codified "talk about talk" as a way of exploring the "behavioral ideology" (Volosinov, 1973) of a speech community. On given occasions, cultural members may hold divergent opinions as to whether a particular communicative act counts as *firgun*, yet they share a cultural logic in terms of which their interpretations of particular acts are constructed and, at times, debated. It is this underlying cultural logic that I seek to uncover—not so much through attention to instances of interactional behavior that I or my informants might interpret as involving *firgun*, but rather through a focus on the metacommunicative acts that invoke the cultural construct of *firgun* as actional attributions.

Based on many examples of the uses of the family of terms related to the root stem *f-r-g-n* recorded over the past 5 years (1988 to 1992) during casual conversations and from media sources, as well as in sociolinguistic interviews with 58 native speakers of colloquial Hebrew, I attempt to delineate the type of conduct that would be encompassed within this metacommunicative category by cultural members as well as the attitudes it invokes. However, there is always some measure of slipperiness to such behavioral attributions both in actual everyday usage and in retrospective analysis. When, for example, is an act of recognition of a friend's success considered a well-meaning, spontaneous act of *firgun*, and when is it considered a self-serving act of calculated flattery? Attributions of this kind are clearly contingent on assessments of intentions and degrees of sincerity. Notably, these kinds of judgments are always external to the act—one can name as *firgun* the act of another or one's own past acts, for example, but one cannot preface one's utterance with a prefix explicitly identifying and framing it as an act of *firgun* in the way that *dugri* utterances can be prefaced with "I'll tell you *dugri*..." (Katriel, 1986, chapter 3).

In fact, the characterization of an act as constituting *firgun* is not only a matter of intentions but also of uptake. An utterance cannot be considered as having involved *firgun* if its supportive function is not acknowledged by the party to whom the *firgun* was directed. One cannot say: "*Firganti lo aval hu hitragez alai bitguva*" "I acted toward him with *firgun* but he was angry with me in response." One would say: "Nisiti *lefargen* lo..." "I tried to act toward him in the mode of *firgun* but...."

My data, therefore, consist of reports of linguistic usage (involving *lefargen/firgun* and their derivatives) encountered either in natural settings of casual interaction when conversational partners used them spontaneously, in press reports of verbal conduct identified as involving *firgun*, or in the more formal setting of interviews in which informants were asked to discuss the semantics and scope of the terms and give examples. Such examples involved reports of relevant past interpersonal conduct or speculations about possible usage.

In the next section, I draw cumulatively on the data I have collected in further exploring the social semantics of the family of terms derived from the root stem *f-r-g-n* as linguistic articulations of a culturally focal idiom. I also inquire into the sociocultural implications of the prevalence and salience of this and related lexemes in spoken Hebrew in recent years. In so doing, I consider the language game of *firgun* in relation to the aforementioned studies of Israeli *dugri*, "straight" talk, and the *gibush*, "crystallization," metaphor that, I believe, denote ways of speaking and feeling that point to different cultural models of social relations than the one encapsulated in the notion of *firgun* in the Israeli context.

2. *FIRGUN* as a Cultural Idiom

The most common derivations of *f-r-g-n* are the verb *lefargen*, as in the often-heard, self-critical comment, "*Etslenu lo yod'im lefargen*," roughly, "Here people don't know how to display support," or in an inflected form, such as past tense, third person singular, male "*hu firgen li mikol halev*," roughly "He supported me with all his heart." The noun *firgun* is also routinely employed, as in "*Hajta avira tova, harbe firgunim hadadi'im*," roughly "There was a good atmosphere, lots of displays of mutual support." A commonly used nominal expression relates to the state of a lack of support, natively referred to as *hoser firgun*, which is quasi-ritually lamented in many casual discussions of social life. Finally, the root stem is used adjectivally, as in an example that appeared in Rubinstein (1990), "*Nai'm li lihtov katava mefargenet*," roughly, "It is pleasant for me to write a supportive, complimentary article." Netser (1988, p. 50) did not include this adjectival form in his list, but he included the form *mefurgan*, which denotes the recipient of positive, supportive feelings, rather than their giver, citing the one example he found: "*Ha'ish hahi mefurgan bakongress...,*" roughly, "The person who received the most compliments, recognition in the congress..." I have not encountered this inflection elsewhere, whereas the adjectival form *mefargen* (appropriately inflected for number and gender) is quite common.

The rather impressive morphological productiveness of the root stem *f-r-g-n,* including such creative, immediately intelligible, nonstandard forms as *mefurgan* and its widely varying contexts of occurrence, points to the semantic richness of the term. As Netser (1988, p. 50) pointed out, and as the definition of the term found in the Ben-Amotz and Ben-Yehuda (1972) slang dictionary suggests, *lefargen* is often defined negatively in terms of its implied emotional content—as involving *lack* of envy, as *not* begrudging another's good fortune. Informants' folk interpretations, however, even though they did not contradict these definitions, referred more specifically to the communicative displays associated with acts of *firgun,* delineating a sense of the term that captures its behavioral dimensions as well. Acts of *firgun* are thus said to involve gestures of goodwill, expressions of positive feelings and sympathy, compliments, verbal encouragement, and displays of appreciation. These may be either generalized as part of an overall supportive attitude (*jahas mefargen*) designed to affirm and reinforce the positive self-image of the recipient of the *firgun,* or, as is more often the case, they may indicate a more localized response of appreciation ("positive feedback," in some informants' words) for specific accomplishments by individual actors for which they should "get credit."

As noted, although a few informants rendered *lefargen* as involving social support in the sense of providing encouragement and comfort, the interpretation of the term pointed overwhelmingly to support and encouragement extended to a person who finds himself or herself in a position of advantage, cultivating a sense of achievement and self-worth. The ability to respond to another's success in the mode of *firgun* both presupposes and implies a sense of connectedness, a selfless identification with another's accomplishment. Many informants commented that one does not speak of *firgun* between strangers, that it assumes some measure of solidarity. When someone is accused of lack of *firgun* *vis-à-vis* the accomplishments of another, it does not imply that the accomplishment goes unacknowledged, but that it is denied *public* recognition. Mostly, such recognition is accorded verbally, so that *firgun* tends to be heard as a discursive act. In a few rare cases, I have heard it used to refer to nonverbal acts, as when a teenager described a gossip session in which a friend of hers was maligned. She said that she kept silent, later describing (and accounting for) her reticence as a matter of *firgun* toward her friend. Some informants referred to attentive listening on the part of an addressee as displays of *firgun* as well.

The overwhelmingly discursive contexts of *firgun* point to an important semantic dimension of the term: *Lefargen* involves acts that are both interpersonally oriented, in the sense that they are predicated on the positive feelings of one individual toward another, *and* they are publicly oriented in the sense of being performed as much for a wider audience as for the individual in question. As a supportive act, in other words, use of the term is designed not only to help cultivate another's self-image in a direct way but also to do so indirectly through the social repercussions attending public announcement. Acts of *firgun* serve to enhance the favorable reputation of the person whose performance or character is the object of the expressed positive evaluations referred to as *firgun*. Given their public resonance, acts of *firgun* can be performed in the absence of the person they are "about," the expectation being that news will travel and he or she will eventually learn of them.

The enhancement of reputation associated with acts of *firgun* applies no less to the person who "knows *lefargen*" than to the person whose praises are sung. A person who acts with *firgun* not only exudes goodwill but is also seen as secure enough in his or her personal standing to publicly express recognition and delight in another's accomplishments. This becomes particularly meaningful in contexts of actual or potential competition, professional or otherwise, when another's recognized success may have direct consequences for one's own position. Thus, frequent examples given to me of *firgun*-related conduct involve superordinate-subordinate relations (e.g., commander in the army and his or her soldiers, supervisor at the workplace and his or her staff, schoolteacher and his or her students) or collegial relations among equals who are willing to give each other credit for their contributions to a cooperative project or to acknowledge each other's professional merits. Thus, many examples I have collected involve assessments of the degree to which a person can be described as *mefargen/et* or not *vis-à-vis* a rival. The ability to give public recognition to the merits of one's competitor(s) is sometimes even described as nobility (*atsilut*) and has been an often-discussed feature of the lore surrounding local celebrities (e.g., pop stars, actors, and politicians) as it appears in gossip columns in the popular press.

In the context of hierarchical relations, it is the person higher in the hierarchy who can be said to display appreciation toward his or her subordinates in the mode of *firgun.* The reverse situation, when appreciation is displayed by the person lower in the hierarchy to the person higher in it, may be spoken of in an idiom of respect (*ha'araha*) but not of *firgun.* This structural constraint on participation in supportive exchanges falling under the rubric of *firgunim* throws further light on the semantics of the term. Displaying appreciation toward one's superior is mandated by a code of respect. Failure to do so indicates either that one does not know one's proper social place, or that one refuses to acknowledge it, and may imply direct or indirect sanctions. Displaying appreciation toward one's social equals or inferiors, on the other hand, is recommended by a code of sincerity and generosity. Failure to do so may reflect on one's attitude or character but is not a directly sanctionable act.

Lack of *firgun* is therefore an index of lack of positive identification, not of ill will. It is to be distinguished from the opposite of *firgun,* which is said to involve verbal acts designed to discourage rather than encourage, to hurt rather than to enhance reputations, to act in the aggressive interactional mode of *kasah* (Katriel, 1986, pp. 52-54). Someone who is said to be "*ehad kaze shelo ohev lefargen,*" "a person who does not like to support others in the way of *firgun,*" is thought of as a kind of "social miser," who inwardly acknowledges another's success or merit but refuses to express this knowledge through a public display of appreciation. Thus, for example, critical comments about the competitiveness of career women are routinely phrased as a semiformulaic complaint that "*nashim lo mefargenot ahat lashni'ja,*" "women do not support each other."

That acts of *firgun* are considered as tokens of both forthrightness and generosity was succinctly expressed in a student paper I received, which dealt with autograph books and which contained the following statement: "The youth of today are much more direct, *mefargen,* do not hesitate to express feelings and write praises."

The association of *firgun* with directness is interesting, particularly in view of the fact that some informants contrasted *firgun*-related conduct with the "thorniness" of the Sabra, which is associated with the straightforwardness of the *dugri* idiom (Katriel, 1986). Both *firgun* and *dugri* imply an openly and sincerely expressed evaluative stance. The former involves a positive and the latter a negative evaluation of another's situation or conduct, which is, however, articulated as a corrective act, with the addressee's interest in mind. In both cases, it is the speaker's personal, active choice that propels the act. Opting to invoke the *dugri* code, a speaker implies or explicitly signals that he or she has chosen to suspend the politeness requirements standardly holding in everyday interaction. A person's choice to act in such a way as to convey *firgun* is similarly predicated on the self-regulated enactment of individual intentions rather than on conforming to a closely prescribed set of social rules. Both *dugri* speech and acts of *firgun* can thus be said to articulate and mediate basic cultural codes of forthrightness and goodwill with individuals' needs for personal support in the one case and for social information in the other. Both these cultural communication codes, however, have their limits. One's straightforwardness can exceed the parameters encapsulated in the *dugri* code, sliding into bluntness (*gasut ru'ah*); and one's appreciative displays can exceed the parameters set out in the code of *firgun*, sliding into flattery (*hanfanut*).

The problem of flattery and lack of sincerity arises with particular force in contexts of *firgun* between status equals, when the issue of manipulativeness may become salient, as relationships are not as closely regulated in terms of structural arrangements. A specialized context of this kind involves courtship relations in which *firgun* is both highly functional and most vulnerable to accusations of insincerity and manipulativeness. Hence, there is a frequency of such expressions as *lefargen mikol halev*, which underscores the sincerity of an act of *firgun*, indicating the speaker's perception that it might be put into question. It may be the double burden of providing support and communicating the sincerity of one's intentions that has given rise to the sense that *firgun* is not only a matter of willingness to display appreciation, but also a matter of doing so in such a way as to inspire credibility, so that, as mentioned earlier, one can speak of "knowing how to *lefargen*."

As discussed so far, *firgun* marks a specific response to a specific occasion in which it is felt to be deserved. A more diffuse usage, however, refers to *avira mefargenet*, a social climate in which *firgun* is said to take place routinely. The cultivation of a climate of *firgun* is associated with the de-emphasis of competition and conflict and the overall enhancement of good feeling. It is interesting to compare the generalized notion of *avira mefargenet*, "supportive climate," to another, older, Israeli cultural idiom of social relations centered on group solidarity, which is natively referred to as *gibush*, "crystallization" (see Katriel, 1991, chapter 2). Whereas both *gibush* and *firgun* (as applied to groups) refer to a diffuse notion of social climate, they denote subtly different social emphases. The ethnosociological notion of *gibush* "crystallization" subsumes individuals within a group formation, metaphorically envisioning them as the equalized, equidistant "atoms" that have come to form a crystal (Katriel, 1991), whereas the idiom of *firgun* can be said to encapsulate a group-centered yet *interpersonally grounded* social pattern.

As both *gibush* and *firgun* are similarly used in describing the social feeling prevailing in such contexts as the work teams of status equals, the introduction of the idiom of *firgun* in such discursive contexts is indicative of a newly emerging cultural emphasis on the quality of interpersonal relations as reflected in and cultivated by acts of *firgun*, rather than processes of group formation under the heading of *gibush*. In particular, a "supportive atmosphere," labeled *avira mefargenet*, is considered to serve the function of diffusing tensions associated with a (potentially) competitive situation between status equals. Tension is diffused by turning the success of individual members of the group into an affiliative resource through the cumulative effect of spontaneously engendered interpersonal acts of *firgun*. In this way, the social support idiom of *firgun*, although grounded in interpersonal gesture, has, in turn, become semantically extended in such a way as to recapture the communal focus that is such a salient feature of Israeli cultural ethos (see Katriel, 1991). The semantics of *firgun* thus suggest the contours of a newly emergent Israeli pattern of social relations: an interpersonally grounded communal ethos in which individual experience and accomplishment are both acknowledged and transported, becoming a source of shared social feeling.

We are now in a position to address the question that gave the first impetus to this study. Given, as Netser (1988) argued, that the frequency of use and range of uses of *firgun* and its derivatives have proliferated in recent years, serving to fill a semantic void in colloquial Hebrew, the sociocultural question still arises of how we can account for the emergence of this "void" in the first place, which has triggered the lexical borrowing of the term and its subsequent elaborations. Assuming that the naming of social relations and sentiments through a process of lexicalization is a significant if subtle step in the cultural coding of both experienced and danced social attitudes, one wonders what this particular change can teach us about the dynamics of the cultural construction of social relations in contemporary Israel.

Considering the newly emergent cultural focus on *firgun* as an expression of the softening of the *dugri* mode (Katriel, 1986, pp. 48-52), it is notable that these two interactional styles both partake in a common idiom of forthrightness and goodwill, although this underlying idiom is differently articulated and interpreted in each. In both cases, also, the enactment of the style is a matter of individual intention and expressive choice that have become a measure of relationships and even of the whole social climate of the group. The essential difference between them is, I believe, that the employment of *dugri* speech is predicated on the invocation of a cultural code that allows for the transcendence (or suspension) of interpersonal relations in the name of some higher, impersonal cultural values shared by participants whose membership in the Sabra speech community is both assumed and *ascribed.* Acts of *firgun,* on the other hand, capitalize on the need to attend to the contours of interpersonal relations, harmonizing and leveling situational differences in *achieved* status by acknowledging them in a mutually supportive and participatory vein, rather than by diffusing them within a more broadly shared cultural frame.

The *firgun* matrix has become central in a sociocultural context in which competition and achieved status are acknowledged rather than systematically repressed as they were in the heyday of the nation-building effort. Yet, given the strong traces of an egalitarian ideology in Israel, competition and personal achievement are still often felt to be socially too problematic to be openly celebrated so that, as many informants pointed out, one hears at least as much about lack of *firgun* in Israeli society as about its deployment. That is, although there is a keen sense of the need and value of supportive conduct that will give full social legitimacy to personal success and worth, the very preoccupation with this issue suggests that it has a problematic standing, and the constant complaints concerning lack of *firgun* reinforce this sense.

I believe the poignancy of the term *firgun* and its associated problematics derive from a sociocultural situation that is transitional between the strongly group-oriented, communal orientation of the ethos of *gibush* (Katriel, 1991), which is associated with ascribed positions of group affiliation, and a more individualistic orientation in which personal aspirations and achieved status are both legitimate and valued in their own right. The extension of the notion of *firgun* from an interpersonal act to a social climate pulls it back in the direction of group phenomena and an affiliative orientation. In a work team, family, or friendship network where there is a climate of *firgun,* specific gestures of support are subsumed under a general expectation for interpersonally supportive conduct, diffusing the import of such acts as specifically and uniquely addressed.

In sum, the emergence of *firgun* as a culturally focal term in Israeli discourse in recent years attests to a much more far-reaching cultural tale: the uneasy and partial shift from a communal to an individualistic orientation in Israeli society. Although the contours of this shift can be gleaned in a variety of cultural contexts and forms, it is perhaps their evasive yet persistent traces in the fleeting practices of everyday speech that carry the most persuasive testimony of this shift.

The cultural embeddedness of such terms is evidenced not only in the meaning shifts traced historically within the ethnosemantics of one particular culture, but also in the subtly differentiated social semantics of terms for supportive conduct that can be gleaned from a comparative consideration of in some sense comparable terms in a number of speech communities. I therefore conclude with a brief comparative account of the ethnolinguistics of social support by drawing on a number of studies. I begin with a relatively detailed discussion based on unpublished findings regarding the Arabic metacommunicative notion of doing *mujamala* that my students and I have collected in recent years (the term is mentioned in passing in Greifat and Katriel, 1989). Then I offer brief discussions of Duranti and Ochs's (1988) study of the cultural construct of the *taapua'i* "supporter" in a Samoan speech community, and of the American category of *communication* as studied by Katriel and Philipsen (1981) with an eye to cross-cultural comparison.

3. Social Support Terms: A Comparative Look

Given the centrality of interpersonal support in the social construction of human relations, it is not surprising that social support terms can be found in the social lexicon of many speech communities. I believe the cultural semantics of such terms and their fluctuations offer important clues for understanding the ethnosociologies of particular speech communities as enacted within localized patterns of interactional practices. The following comparative look is hoped to demonstrate the fruitfulness of such an approach.

Arabic Mujamala as a Cultural Idiom

Arab informants who become familiarized with the notion of *firgun* tend to translate it as *mujamala*. A closer semantic exploration, however, reveals that the language games of these two terms bring out subtle differences in the ethnosociologies presupposed by them. The term *mujamala*, which, like *musayara* (Greifat and Katriel, 1989), belongs to the semantic field of politeness terms in Arabic, is derived from the word *jamil* "beautiful." Its etymology thus points to the aesthetisizing gesture inherent in this interactional code, as well as to the fact that the word has long-standing roots in the cultural lexicon rather than being a newly adopted lexical borrowing, as is the case with *firgun*. "Doing *mujamala*" refers to the performance of communicative acts designed to enhance good feelings and social harmony, to "beautify" social relations and thereby maintain a pleasant atmosphere and, by implication, the stability of the social order.

Adherence to the idiom of *mujamala* is a generalized cultural expectation but is claimed to be followed more closely by older than by younger people, by villagers more than by city folk. The injunction to do *mujamala* is experienced as mandatory. It is not internally motivated, spontaneous conduct but acts whose origin is in the social sphere, in the stylized patterning of social relations. Typical examples of doing *mujamala* involve "foregrounding the positive aspect of everything," in the words of one informant. This includes showing deference both verbally and nonverbally by giving compliments and displaying appreciation, by participating in others' life-cycle rituals such as wedding celebrations or funerals, and by following the code of hospitality. One of the informants, a 22-year-old woman, exemplified the notion of *mujamala* as follows: "During the lesson the teacher asked a difficult question and there was only one student who was able to answer it. After class I told that student that I liked his response, I gave him respect, noticed him, that was *mujamala*."

As many informants pointed out, it is not always clear whether a particular social enactment should be viewed as an instance of *mujamala* or as an instance of the concessive idiom of *musayara*, which involves "going along" with the other in such a way as to "give up" something of oneself (Greifat and Katriel, 1989). There seems to be an area of semantic overlap between the terms, and their "operationalizations" are not always clear-cut.

Therefore, rather than attempting a conclusive definition of what counts as *musayara* or *mujamala* in the culture's social semantics, I propose to reverse the definitional question that seemed to beleaguer many of the informants and turn it into an attributional issue, asking instead, "What is communicated to cultural members about a social act when it is said to be an instance of either *mujamala* or *musayara,* respectively?" The sense of personal sacrifice associated with doing *musayara* makes it a more weighty affair than the more casual performance of acts of *mujamala* as social lubricants. Thus, extending an insincere compliment to another, framing it as an act of *mujamala,* makes it part of the obligatory dance of social politeness, whereas framing it as an act of *musayara* foregrounds the sense of personal compromise involved in the performance of a humoring act. The need to do *musayara* is grounded in either structural or situational differentials in power relations, so that the idiom of *musayara* both responds to and re-creates deeply rooted hierarchical social arrangements.

Acts of *mujamala,* on the other hand, are taken to be essentially egalitarian and reciprocal—one does *mujamala* with the expectation that a similar courtesy will be extended in return. Many informants thus interpreted *mujamala* as manifested in the self-initiated, though highly expected, ongoing exchange of pleasantries in the everyday run of events. It is used to refer to positively oriented social conduct designed to overcome embarrassing moments, as well as to the showering of compliments in the more specialized contexts of courting among modernized youngsters. Notably, many informants pointed out that doing *mujamala* is restricted to familiars who are nonintimates, as one expects close family relations not to require such gestures.

Another salient context for the articulation of *mujamala* that was mentioned by many informants involves participation as guests in significant life-cycle celebrations such as weddings or funerals. On such occasions, participants enhance social relations and reaffirm the communal order through a sheer "rhetoric of presence" and the attendant expectation that it will be reciprocated in the future. When attending someone's wedding is referred to as an act of *musayara,* there is an implication that one's presence is more than a taken-for-granted gesture of politeness or respect, that one has needed to overcome some inner resistance (a grudge, perhaps) or outer circumstances (e.g., a competing engagement) that might have prevented one from partaking in the festivities.

A person who routinely orients to others in the mode of *mujamala* is approved of socially as being *mujamel,* and one who does not reciprocate such an act is interpreted as unwilling to uphold social norms of pleasant interaction, signaling social withdrawal and an uncaring attitude (e.g., youngsters who have moved away from village life). Refraining from doing *mujamala* may be subject to explicit social sanctioning, most obviously the reciprocation of social indifference. The opposite of doing *mujamala,* however, involves more than that—it involves directly insulting another to his or her face. In the same way that one can act inappropriately by not being *mujamel* enough, one can also err by overdoing *mujamala* displays so that they are perceived as flattery and self-interested manipulation rather than well-intentioned social courtesy, a desire to exploit social relations rather than to beautify them. In other words, the problem of sincerity becomes an issue in a way similar to the case of *firgun* as discussed earlier.

Finally, juxtaposing *mujamala* and *firgun* as semantically comparable lexical possibilities in the cultural repertoires of their respective speech communities, we are now in a position to further refine our understanding of the cultural logics underlying their use. Both terms refer to social orientations grounded in a desire to maintain and harmonize social relations in contexts in which conflict or threat to face are *not* an issue, that is, when redressive action is *not* called for although some of the verbal actions that can be referred to as displays of either *mujamala* or *firgun* may—in another context—be interpreted as constituting redressive action concerned with either positive or negative face. According to Brown and Levinson (1987), because acts of politeness essentially involve *redressive* gestures, both acting in the mode of *firgun* and doing *mujamala* would not be considered within the domain of politeness theory as ethically conceived within their framework. From an emic standpoint, which is grounded in speakers' own cultural constructions, speakers of Arabic do view *mujamala* as falling within the domain of politeness, whereas speakers of colloquial Hebrew do not conceive of *firgun* as part of the politeness domain.

Furthermore, although it makes sense to speak, in English, of these terms as relating to the display of social support, this labeling covers only some cases for Arabic usage—when *mujamala* involves paying condolences in a formal visit to mourners' home, for example. In other cases, as discussed earlier, *mujamala* involves culturally coded, stylized displays of goodwill and reciprocity in informal and casual encounters, whereas *firgun* denotes the display of appreciation for someone's accomplishment when there is a potential for envy and competition rather than in times of stress.

In sum, whereas *mujamala* denotes a generalized code of reciprocity and mutuality, articulated in what are often expansive interpersonal acts designed to beautify social relations among communal members, *firgun* is much more restricted in scope, articulating a localized sense of potential social tension and competition in a particular class of interpersonal contexts, as well as a culturally preferred way of dealing with it. In doing *mujamala,* one enacts a code of stylized, easy-going sociability and taken-for-granted mutuality, with some consequences in terms of one's presentation of self. In acting with *firgun,* on the other hand—even in the case of the reciprocally extended appreciation and support alluded to in the phrase *firgun hadadi* 'reciprocal *firgun'*—reference is made to spontaneously performed personalized acts of appreciation and goodwill, which signal sincerity and generosity of character.

Clearly, these two cultural idioms of social support represent different degrees of sociolinguistic institutionalization of interpersonal relations in the two speech communities, as they are embedded within significantly different vocabularies of motives. In these vocabularies, social acts are variously constructed as springing from individual motivation (in the case of *firgun*) or from socially coded expectations (in the case of *mujamala*).

Samoan Maaloo Exchange as Verbal Ritual

The *maaloo* exchange is associated with the important concept of the *taapua'i* "supporter" or "sympathizer" in Samoan culture. It exemplifies an even greater degree of sociolinguistic institutionalization of the social support function, as the analysis offered by Duranti and Ochs (1988) brought out.

According to Duranti and Ochs (1988, p. 199), a Samoan rarely does something "without someone next to him to provide recognition of his actions, attempts or accomplishments.... The relationship between the actor and the supporter is truly reciprocal rather than unidirectional. When an actor's work or accomplishment is valued and recognized by a supporter, the supporter's work at recognizing the accomplishment is also recognized by the actor. This relationship is symbolically and routinely instantiated by the use of what we call "*a maaloo* exchange." The following example exemplifies this kind of routinized exchange:

(Driver does something that shows skill, presence of mind.)

Passenger(s): *Maaloo le fa'auli!*

Well done the steering!

Driver: *Maaloo le taapua'i!*

Well done the support!

In the Samoan world view, an accomplishment is seen as a joint product of actor and supporter. Accomplishment is a collective and cooperative enterprise, "in which the individual's competence is defined by his audience appreciation, and his merit is framed within the merit of the group" (Duranti and Ochs, 1988, p. 200). This sociocentric cultural view of task accomplishment finds its discursive expression in the organizational structure of the *maaloo* exchange, which is characterized by two features that differentiate it from exchanges identified as involving *firgun* and *mujamala* alike: (a) A *maaloo* exchange is lexically signaled by the use of the *maaloo* term itself; (b) It takes the form of what conversation analysts refer to as an "adjacency pair" (Sacks, Schegloff, and Jefferson, 1974). As in the case of greetings, given this interactional structure, once a support statement for an act is articulated, there is a strong expectation that it be met with a statement of "support for the support, as indicated in the aforementioned example of accomplished driving."

These structural features enable speakers (and analysts) to identify *maaloo* exchanges unambiguously, whereas the identification of social acts as involving *firgun* and *mujamala* remains potentially a matter of ambiguous attribution. For example, there are no surface structural features that attach to an utterance considered as *firgun* rather than as flattery or mere politeness, or as *mujamala* rather than *musayara.*

Thus, whereas *firgun* is conceptualized as an individually motivated act reflecting personal character, and *mujamala* is grounded in a loosely defined pattern of reciprocal expectations regulating the stylized performance of individually anchored social acts, the *maaloo* exchange reflects a sociocentric view. Ochs (1988) demonstrated this view to be typical of Samoan culture, in which individual action is considered but part of a reciprocal exchange so that "to be skillful (*poto*) at something does not mean to stand out with respect to everyone else as much as to be able to create the conditions for a successful collective endeavor" (p. 200). Each of these terms is central to the semantics of social support in the verbal repertoire of the speech community in which it is employed. Their shared human resonance must not obliterate, but rather bring forth, the distinctive tonalities they carry as culturally embedded focal terms.

American Communication as a Cultural Idiom

Katriel and Philipsen (1981) discussed the metacommunicative term *communication* as it is employed in American discourse as denoting a culturally coded form of flexible, supportive speech. It is associated with the domain of intimate interpersonal relation and finds its quintessential place in the context of what the authors have dubbed "communication rituals"—communicative occasions constructed around relational discourse in which cultural members "sit down and talk" in a way that affirms both "self" and "relationship." The topics elaborated on those ritualized occasions have to do with problems in the life of the person who has initiated the verbal ritual, and the interlocutor is by and large expected to lend an attentive and sympathetic ear, thereby affirming the main speaker's sense of problematicity and self-worth, as well as the viability of the relationship between them.

Communication refers to social support in the sense of Hebrew *tmiha,* that is, support extended to a person in need or in distress rather than the appreciation and encouragement associated with *firgun,* as a form of conduct that signals one's ability to overcome envy in a context of potential competition. However, as a form of supportive speech, *communication* shares with *lefargen* a focus on the individual experience of the person whose problem (in the one case) and success (in the other case) are foregrounded—a focus not shared by the aforementioned, collectively oriented construct of *gibush* 'crystallization." The social scope of the terms differs in that *communication* is relationally restricted to persons considered close, whereas one can *lefargen* to a broad range of people, even, at times, to someone one does not know, such as throwing a passing compliment (e.g., about appearance) in a fleeting encounter. A further difference relates to the fact that the support offered by *firgun* is a gesture one does *for* someone, the originator of the act being the person who offers support. In fact, such an act can be accomplished even in the absence of the focal person (usually with the expectation that the behind-the-back compliment will be reported to him or her), whereas the support offered in the context of the American communication ritual is something one does *with* someone, the originator of the act being the person who receives the support. It is, moreover, essentially a face-to-face dyadic affair in which attentive co-presence is an important precondition.

Both American *communication* and *firgun* differ from both *mujamala* and the *maaloo* exchange in their degree of linguistic institutionalization. Both involve spontaneously generated interpersonal acts as these are perceived by cultural members rather than highly stylized, even formulaic ones that are experienced as a matter of etiquette. However, *communication* remains an interpersonally oriented category, whereas *firgun* can become a more diffuse matter of group climate, transcending the interpersonal sphere in which it is originally grounded.

4. Conclusion

This comparative sketch brings out the many dimensions of meaning and value associated with cultural vocabularies of what we can dub "supportive talk." Cultural variability in this domain is a matter of deeply rooted yet historically situated assumptions about persons, relationships, and social groupings. A consideration of these various culturally focal vocabularies can, therefore, offer insights into that which is specific to the interpersonal ideologies of various speech communities, as well as help to chart points of divergence that are significant in terms of our understanding of the larger cultural configurations in which these metacommunicative terms are embedded. As I have demonstrated in this article (once again), a focus on the meaning dynamics of such terms can be highly rewarding in studying the language/culture interface.

Notes

1. For studies concerned with "social support" as a scientific construct in communication-oriented research, see Albrecht and Adelman (1987). The American category of "communication" as studied by Katriel and Philipsen (1981) is an "emic" American concept for "supportive speech" that seems to inform some of the analytic discussions of social support that appear in the research literature.
2. I am grateful to David Gold for a discussion of the Yiddish and German etymology of the term.

References

Albrecht, T., and Adelman, M. (1987). *Communicating social support.* London: Sage.

Ben-Amotz, D., and Ben-Yehuda, N. (1972). *The world dictionary of Hebrew slang.* Tel-Aviv: Levin-Epstein (in Hebrew).

Brown, P., and Levinson, S. (1987). *Politeness.* Cambridge, England: Cambridge University Press.

Duranti, A., and Ochs, E. (1988). Literacy instruction in a Samoan village. In E. Ochs (Ed.), *Culture and language development* (pp. 189-209). Cambridge, England: Cambridge University Press.

Goffman, E. (1967). *Interaction ritual: Essays on face-to-face behavior.* New York: Doubleday.

Greifat, Y., and Katriel, T. (1989). Life demands *musayara:* Communication and culture in contemporary Israel. *International and Intercultural Communication Annual,* 13, 121-138.

Hymes, D. (1974). *Foundations in sociolinguistics.* Philadelphia: University of Pennsylvania Press.

Katriel, T. (1986). *Talking straight: "Dugri" speech in Israeli Sabra culture.* Cambridge, England: Cambridge University Press.

Katriel, T. (1991). *Communal webs: Communication and culture in contemporary Israel.* Albany: SUNY Press.

Katriel, T., and Philipsen, G. (1981). What we need is communication: "Communication" as a cultural category in some American speech. *Communication Monographs,* 48, 301-317.

Netser, N. (1988). F-r-g-n: A linguistic void filled from Yiddish. *Hebrew Computational Linguistics,* 26, 49-57 (in Hebrew).

Ochs, E. (1988). *Culture and language development.* Cambridge, England: Cambridge University Press.

Ortner, S. (1973). On key symbols. *American Anthropologist,* 75: 1338-1345.

Rubinstein, A. (1977). *To be a free people.* Tel Aviv: Schocken (in Hebrew).

Rubinstein, A. (1990, October 10). Fargen li i-firgun Katan [Don't begrudge me a bit of begrudging]. *Yedioth Aharonot,* p. 8.

Sacks, H., Schegloff, E., and Jefferson, G. (1974). A simplest systematics for the organization of turn-taking in conversation. *Language,* 50, 696-735.

Sappan. R. (1965). *The Israeli slang dictionary.* Jerusalem: Kiryat Sefer (in Hebrew).

Stross, B. (1974). Speaking of speaking: Tenejapa Tzeltal metalinguistics. In R. Bauman and J. Sherzer (Eds.), *Explorations in the ethnography of speaking* (pp. 213-239). Cambridge, England: Cambridge University Press.

Volosinov, V.N. (1973). *Marxism and the philosophy of language.* Cambridge, MA: Harvard University Press.

Wittgenstein, L. (1968). *Philosophical investigations.* New York: Macmillan.

3

That's How We Were: Individual, Group, and Collective in the Tel Aviv of "Late Summer Blues"

Haim Hazan

This chapter offers an anthropological analysis of a cinematic text, the film "Late Summer Blues," which takes place almost entirely in the North Tel Aviv of the early seventies. The heroes of the film are young boys and girls facing army enlistment; the main arena is a high school in the city of Tel Aviv; the plot pivots on the preparation of the graduation party; and in the background is the War of Attrition. One can already see at first glance that these dramatic materials present a mixture of local and universal elements. On the one hand, we have a typically Israeli frame of reference: "pre-enlistment." On the other hand, the film's heroes represent an age-group whose youth culture is based on American cultural models. The graduation party, too, while its contents are distinctly local, is an example of what anthropologists call generically, "rites of passage." I will return later to these pairs of contrasts, and others, in order to show what I consider to be the film's deep infrastructure. Before this, however, it is worth saying a few words about the article's nature and purpose.

"Late Summer Blues" will not be examined here within the cinematic discipline and genre, but from an external vantagepoint from which it may be seen as a cultural document. The premise for this approach is that cinema—like literature, poetry, painting, and other types of art—reflects to a certain extent the socio-cultural context in which it is created. The representation is not manifestly obvious; indeed, it is often vague and indirect. Various methods of analysis are able to trace the outlines of the social and cultural processes reflected in a work, although no method claims to have reached the most correct understanding of the "work's spirit," or, alternatively, the most faithful interpretation of the "author's intentions." Here, however, lies the root of the problem: these methods would claim that the "spirit of the work" or the "author's intentions" are not relevant at all to the purposes of study, since both are a product of the reader's interpretation.[1]

The frames of reference used in this chapter belong to two complementary theoretical agendas. The first deals with models of the study of language, culture, and myth, among whose outstanding representatives are C. Levi-Strauss and R. Barthes. Levi-Strauss (1981) dealt with the understanding of myths in "simple" societies while Barthes (1972) focused on everyday myths in current cultures. The combination of their works may provide us with an efficient key for the rereading of "Blues." The other frame of reference is based on the wealth of anthropological research concerning rites of passage, those symbolic apparatuses which perform the miracle of passage from one identity to another in a short period of time and with the greatest effectiveness. These rites are scattered throughout a person's life-cycle at critical points of alteration and change of status. While turning to the characteristics of rites of passage as the theoretical code, a complementary touch from other Israeli "group films" will be added to the specific analysis of "Blues," in order to establish the premise that some of the characteristics constituting the infrastructure of "Blues" are none other than reflections of ground rules that appear repeatedly in cultural productions (such as other "group films") whose super-language is common.

The examination of "Blues" as a cultural document will focus on those processes that play a central role in the film's plot: processes of identity loss and gain; preserving individuality versus the acceptance of the collective dictate; the struggle between the cosmopolitan alternative hidden in Tel Aviv and the local patriotism it represents. The fact that "Blues" is a very "Tel Avivian" film, and at the same time, a very "Israeli" film, is therefore an important point for our discussion. I call "Blues" a "Tel Avivian film" for reasons which need to be clarified. Many films have been shot in Tel Aviv locations but they cannot be termed "Tel Avivian films." I mean by this term a film where Tel Aviv is not only its geographical arena, but also its symbolic territory; a film which realizes in Tel Aviv those things which the city is conceived as symbolizing, renewing, repressing or distorting. In this respect, "Blues" is a Tel Avivian film just as "Big Eyes" is a Tel Avivian film and *Memorandum* is a Tel Avivian novel. These are works which perceive the city of Tel Aviv through a symbolic, even mythical, prism through which it is seen as an arena for struggles between opposites: hedonism versus responsibility; emotional life versus big ideas; the movement's verdict versus the individual's wishes; the glory and promise of the past versus the disintegration and failures of the present; avant-guard versus conformism; creation and renewal versus treading water and loss of selfhood; and so on.

Of course, none of these is limited to the city of Tel Aviv, since all reflect depth structures in the whole of Israeli society as well; but Tel Aviv, as heroine in the literary or cinematic plot, raises them to the surface, liberates them from their hiding place, provides them with the conditions for their expression, one beside the other, and thus causes their inevitable collision. Just as the Tel Avivian film is a reflection of the contrasts of Tel Avivian culture, so Tel Aviv itself is a reflection of the Israeli culture in which it is situated. The city of Tel Aviv and Israel are not just physical territories; they are symbolic entities, distinguished by their cultural qualities, and complementary to each other, with each one separately forming the identity of the individual living in them. While a country is a "big place"—that is a life level of values, ideas, ambitions and images—a city is a "small place."[2] This means a physical, earthly everyday dwelling place. This does not negate the possibility of the connection between the two, and they may certainly nourish each other, but separation and distancing between them are also possible. Trips with the Nature Preservation Society, for example, represent—in their rhetoric and in practice—a declaration of the contradiction between city life and "nature," as a desirable world of values and ideas. Tourism abroad can also constitute a statement exposing the discomfort of everyday life and the yearning to be released from it into a different reality. "Blues" also touches the heart of the question of deciding between the two places; place of identification and memory or friendship and of a world view which are not necessarily compatible.

The Plot

The film's main thematic units are four life stories.

The first story is that of Yossi Zwillich, who is about to enlist. After the school is informed of the death of one of its graduates, the class does the Zionism exam, during which the principal announces the postponement of the graduation ceremony, due to the tragedy. Zwillich protests, claiming he will miss the ceremony due to his recruitment, to which the principal replies: "You should have been born in Australia." On the eve of his enlistment, the group holds a farewell party for Zwillich, during which he asks one of the girls to become his girlfriend. She conditions it on "parachutist's wings," which he promises to bring her. Zwillich writes a diary describing the parting. On the following day his parting from the group and from his parents, at the entry to the recruitment center, will be documented by Margo's camera. The group goes out to celebrate on the beach and is caught smoking grass, but the members are released from custody, so that their arrest will not place a stain on them in view of their approaching enlistment.

The second story is that of Ahraleh, the rebel among the group, who writes graffiti against the war and against the establishment. During the rehearsal for the graduation ceremony, Ahraleh and his graduation sneak into the principal's office, smoke grass there, put a joint to a photograph of Golda Meir and search for the location of Honduras on the globe. The principal receives a telephone message concerning Zwillich's death in a training accident. Nevertheless, she continues the rehearsal and gives a speech including educational questions, such as: "Are we making correct, fair use of them (the pupils)? Are we preparing them for real life?" Ahraleh protests vigorously that she does not mention Zwillich's death, and walks out to the sound of the principal's response, that "there are some things you don't yet understand." Zwillich's burial is also documented by Margo's camera, and after it the group decides to stage a protest show for the end of the year, a show which will include singing satirical pieces such as "It is good to die for our country": and "We don't want wars, violence, cemeteries." Ahraleh continues to spray protest slogans, is almost caught by the police, and in making his escape reaches the house of Naomi, whom he desires. He finds her in the company of Mussi, reading Zwillich's diary. Kobi and Shoshi, two members of the group, get married. On the beach on their wedding night, which they spend with their friends, an argument erupts between Kobi and Ahraleh, during which the latter is accused of cowardice under the guise of idealism. Ahraleh totters on the pier, shouting: "I am a coward!"

The third story is that of Mussi, a talented musician, who is wondering whether to join a military band or to serve in a combat unit, like his older brother. The commanders of the band wish to persuade him to lower his high military profile. He tries, but fails. The commanders do not give up. They visit the graduation ceremony, and this results in Mussi being accepted to the military band. However after Ahraleh and his girlfriend Naomi accuse him of betraying the group by exploiting the ceremony for his own needs, Mussi changes his mind and joins the parachutists. His enlistment is also recorded by Margo. Meanwhile, the school's secretary discovers the group's protest plans and reports them to the principal, who watches the show and is shocked by an imaginary conversation with Zwillich's ghost who is asked whether it was worth dying and answers in the negative. She forbids the performance of the show and threatens to cancel the ceremony. The group apart from Ahraleh, decide to change the show, to give up the overt protest and to settle for just one song: "Yossi, my successful child." The show and the award of certificates take place with Zwillich's parents present.

The fourth story is that of Margo, the photographer and director of the documentary films, and the narrator of the film itself. Margo is exempt from military service due to his diabetes. He is willing to do anything in order to be fit for enlistment, but since there is no chance of that, he decides to go to Paris to study cinema. He cannot bear the thought of his friends returning from the army and telling their stories, and the feeling that following their enlistment: "Tel Aviv suddenly looks like a deserted city." In Paris he hears about the death of Mussi ("my beloved") in the Yom Kippur War. Being requested by Mussi's parents to find for them the documentaries about their son, he returns to Israel. The film ends with the opening pictures: the group is filmed on the beach, with the poem by Hannah Senesh, "God, God, let it never end," playing in the background.

The Analytic Perspective: Pairs of Competing Contrast

A quick glance at the cinematic text reveals a wealth of existential subjects appearing between the lines of the script and the film: life and death, growing up, family, time, relationships between the sexes and between generations—all these are dialectical binary structures which organize the world of human experience according to common issues applicable to any society and to any culture. The coalescence of these binary structures to form a system of relationships clothed in dramatic storylike form is achieved by means of myth. When I claim that in "Blues" there are mythical elements, I mean that there is a framework story (narrative) based on relationships of opposites; moreover, these opposite are brought, by means of the dramatic development, into a struggle during which they may reverse and change. This struggle is "mythical" in that it is connected to the hub of the cultural forces which dictate the lives of the individual and of society.

A systematic analysis of the elements of myth hidden in "Late Summer Blues," as in its cinematic equivalents—"Such a Group," "Voyeurs," "Eskimo Lemon," "One of Us," and others—may reveal a common cultural code, which has developed out of the same social context. To perform the formal analysis of this code—the exposure of the "mythemes," the basic units (pairs of contrast) of the mythical structure, as Levi-Strauss termed them—we require just two mechanisms. The first mechanism is the one that separates the mythemes and divides them into a series of pairs of contrasts, each pair a thing and its opposite. This mechanism determines borders, defines categories, and creates a pre-determined order The second mechanism, on the other hand, is capable of switching round the two mythemes comprising the pair of opposites. This is a transformative mechanism, turning sacred into secular, individual into subject, youth into man. This mechanism, then, realizes the dynamism of social life and the fluidity and instability of concepts and borders.

The first mechanism—the separating mechanism—is based, among other things on practices of separation and removal, which create cultural conventions concerning the separateness and uniqueness of events and phenomena. Thus, for instance, the definition of a certain occurrence as a "ceremony" actually programs the participants to act within it and to treat it as one of the "rules of ritual," which constitute a certain language, interpretation and performance intended to be suited to the ceremonial situation, but not to "ordinary" reality. Many linguistic expressions which belittle or glorify certain symbol-rich occurrence ("It's only a ritual" or "A dignified ceremony") are everyday testimonies to this distinction. Another separation practice is to ignore the opposite member. Thus, for example, it is possible to live while totally ignoring the possibility of death, to develop a masculine culture with no reference to women, etc. The unilateral and one-dimensional construction of such a world view is characteristic of pure conversational patterns which lack the dialectical element, unless it serves the "absolute truth" to which they claim. This sort of separation can also develop to the level of claim to pure authenticity; this means a statement canceling the distinction between the signifier and the signified and claiming to be "the thing in itself." This does not negate the authenticity of other "things" or "truths," but it removes the connection between those things, so that each one of them becomes a frame of reference independent of the existence or non-existence of other units

Distinct from this mechanism and parallel to it operates the second mechanism. This one dissolves the rigidity of borders and forces the contrasts to confront each other. The capacity of one frame of reference to be reflected in another, to serve as a reverse or distorted reflection of it, creates an active and bilateral communication channel between the two. Not only does one receive and adapt the other's image, but each also nourishes and supports the other. Art, by its very nature, offers ways of representation and imitation, not only between itself and its surroundings, but also and perhaps mainly, within itself. For this reason, art constitutes an outstanding practice participating in this mechanism. Related practices are the joke, the prank, and especially acting, which allows the breaking of the authenticity principle that separates the various units. It appeals to methods of decoding which are based on surmounting the fixedness of "the thing itself" since acting is never the same "thing."

The cinematic syntax in front of us, then, is composed of a series of opposites which connect with each other to form the complete pattern of a world-view surrounding the overt occurrence: the deliberations of young girls and boys before enlistment, during the War of Attrition, to go to their death or survive in safety but bear a social stigma. The basic scheme for the organization of the script's components can be presented by a system of contrasting dilemmas, each of which leads to the next:

1. The personal versus the social.
2. The individual versus the collective.
3. The family collective versus the national collective.
4. Belonging to a sexual category, women versus men.
5. Identification with the present, young people versus the adult past generation.
6. Belonging to a national collective versus humanity in general.
7. Belonging to a special place versus the cosmos.
8. Deciding between historical time and mythical time.
9. Choosing between death perceived symbolically as eternal life and death perceived as impotence.
10. Existential decision versus the renunciation of meaning.

This mythical odyssey colors the script in universal shades and gives it the feel of a story whose development is isolated from the overt plot. The cultural arena of the film is double; on the one hand the city of Tel Aviv in the summer of 1970, with its beach and its northern neighborhoods, and on the other hand the military-national Israel of the same period. These are two places with different laws. The first is earthly, real, personal, familiar and controllable. The second is abstract, general, collective and fatalist. The first is limited in the everyday and in chronological time; the second in myth and the cyclical time of the "eternal repetition."

In order to re-read the story of "Blues," we have only to examine how the cinematic drama is spread out along the two axes described: the axis in which cultural limits are defined and emphasized, and the axis in which the binary oppositions on both sides of the divide win, lose or change.

Analysis of the Text

The four life stories comprising the film's composition are apparently personal stories and even their titles testify to this: "Yossi," "Ahraleh," "Mussi" and "Margo"; however, the content of the stories deals with the systematic location of the lives of these youths within a social framework without which they have no existence as a story. Each one of the youths is, presumably, a person with a background, wishes and connections which distinguish him from the group, but these disappear and are absorbed by his assimilation in the group. The group is, therefore, the justification for the existence of the individual, who confronts (and in fact is forced to confront by the script) a constant choice between his ambitions for self expression and his assimilation in the group. This conflict is presented to us beginning with Yossi Zwillich, who wants to sleep with a girl and to get a driving license; through the rebellious Ahraleh, who wishes to protest against the existing order and change it; to the creative Mussi, whose artistic identity is suborned to the group's directive; and to Margo, who, against his will and to his disadvantage, is rejected from the group due to a physical defect.

This first dilemma, in which there are only two choices—the personal versus the social—is the one that dictates the dynamics of the whole story. The decision the youth must reach does not have limitless scope for the manipulation of possibilities and cannot be resolved while vacillating between both options. The group does allow doubts, soul searching and looking for the right way, but only for a limited period.

The intended and indisputable deadline for this period of doubt is the approaching enlistment to the army, from whose ranks one can only be released by death—or in Margo's case, diabetes. All our heroes—even the black sheep among them, Ahraleh—enlist, and adopt the ethos against which they had wished to rebel. This enlistment is a dramatic and symbolic act of separation from the group, as preparation for the even more extreme cancellation and negation of the private self. The group in this respect is just a preparation for the larger group, the army, and above it the state; the State of Israel as a hierarchy of friends and groups.

A. The Group

The transition from the individual's living space to his annexation by the collective is conducted through the mediating link of the group. This is a social form which, although not local, has gained a special hold in Israeli culture. Groups of various types, from the labor corps and other communes, through the kibbutz, the youth movement and the cooperative, constitute a melting pot for the fusion of the private identity into the collective identity. The group's action can be understood in terms of a myth, since it is organized as a series of contrasts which may be reversed, thus allowing the impossible—the metamorphosis of the personal self into the collective self, with a commitment to totally negate the personal, social and physical.

Group films have become a popular genre in Israel, which undoubtedly reflects Israeli society's frequent (but not necessarily reflexive) concern with the collective ethos, whose sources will be presented briefly in the next section. In the film "Such a Group" (directed by Zeev Havatzelet), an attempt was made to describe a group whose members are flesh and blood. The result, however, is closer to the national collective myth. Burstein (1990, 85) describes how, in one of the film's comic scenes:

> "The kibbutz's newcomer (Gideon Singer) is annoyed when the Palmach members hide ammunition crates under the plants of his beloved garden and ruin the seedlings he has planted. The film 'speaks' about love for the land, but 'shows' the opposite: here Singer is playing the role of a contemptible outsider. He is not 'in'. His love of nature is dwarfed in comparison with the heroic task of liberating the motherland. The newcomer's disaster—the destruction of the garden he has been cultivating with diligence and effort—is not tragic but comic. It is intended to emphasize the tragedy reserved for those who are 'in'; those who die for the motherland and the officers who send them to die. At the same time, it allows the

> representation of these heroes as supposedly 'naughty', which the film's creators interpret as a human quality which makes the characters flesh and blood. But this three dimensionality is applied to the whole group and not to its individual members. The naughtiness of the characters is collective. The three loafers (always three—never one), who escape from field training, practice individual infiltration to Tel Aviv (their natural place) in order to eat ice cream there at the Whitman Café. They decide on this together, and later, when they are prevented from participating in a military action, they regret it together. The sin, like the repentance for the sin, does not stem from the individual's will, but from the group's decision."

The fact that the three loafers escape to Tel Aviv of all places ("their natural place," Burstein adds), is significant for us. The Tel Aviv of "Such a Group" is therefore a sanctuary town, a hiding place from the collective's authority, an open place whose entertainment and leisure sites ("The Whitman Café") provide, with their anonymity and cosmopolitanism an alternative for the steaming melting pot of Israeli society. This, of course, is also the alternative offered by the Tel Aviv of "Blues". But the whole of "Blues" take place in Tel Aviv, and in this respect "there is nowhere to escape to." On the other hand, in the group in "Blues" there is an attempt to give the various heroes distinguishing characteristics and to round out their characters in a way that represents some progress since the days of "Such a Group." But the group's authority is not doubted even here. Burstein (1990), whose book is dedicated to the cinematic history of the Israeli portrait, describes how the surrender to the collective ethos gives rise to a collective photographic ode: "Therefor it is no wonder," he writes (1990:86), "that close-up faces in the film 'Such a Group' are rare and coincidental. Its heroes have to be seen together, and therefore there is usually no choice but for them to be filmed from a distance." This is true also of "Blues", and especially of the opening and closing scenes where the group is filmed on the beach. These scenes, which open and close the film, thereby delimiting it and marking its dramatic boundaries, emphasize the group's being a main part of these confined boundaries.

B. Individualism versus Collectivism

So, the group films made in Israel are in themselves a genre which deserves its own study (on this matter, see Graz, 1987; Klieg and Klieg, 1981; Neeman and Zimmerman, 1987). These films deal with the question of identification with the collective versus the preservation of the individual's uniqueness. "The group" is therefore a social practice which reproduces the collective ethos and with great success.

In "Such a Group," which has just been discussed, all the youths enlisted for training are called "Yosef," and their personal possessions are exposed for all to see as part of the process of their debasement in the face of the collective. Their personal diaries are also turned over to the group, and thus the possibility of personal and private documentation is eliminated. There is no question here of justifying the war or the commitment to the group; this is a reality which is taken for granted, in the face of which all other commitments, and especially the commitment to the family, are negated.

Loyalty to the collective as represented in the group films, expresses inter-generational continuity, between parent and children and between older and younger siblings. This continuity is expressed in the military service, preferably combat service, and it binds the erupting rebellion with bonds of family loyalty, which feeds on national tribalism. The reasons for enlisting are no longer important and of course are never discussed. Even if militaristic ideology has ceased to be accepted, and even if reason is perceived as mistaken and lost, the patterns of identification with the collective action still stand. The women, although they wish to raise families and stick to everyday life ("You can't get married in this country without the news in the middle"), are also part of the group, and they encourage the men in it to show loyalty to the higher collective expressed by the army. Enlistment in an "élite unit" is considered a criterion of the "masculinity" of a woman's potential partner, and the withdrawal towards personal-artistic fulfillment is done stealthily and deceitfully and is perceived as betrayal.

The emphasis on the spirit of collectivism in Israeli society is a subject that has been studied from a sociological point of view, although insufficiently since Israeli sociology also sees itself as part of the collective which it studies and whose own borders it constructs within the framework of academic discourse.[3] There is a sociological consensus that Israeli society is undergoing a continuous process of transition from collectivism to individualism (see Eisenstadt, 1967; Lisak and Horowitz 1989), and the year of transformation usually suggested is 1973, when the Yom Kippur War caused a loss of faith in both the army and the government, the change of government and the rise of an election economy and a new consumer culture. The assumption is that the collectivist ethos grew up in the formative years before the State was founded as part of the communal utopia of socialistic Zionism (Liebman and Don Yehia, 1983; Even Zohar, 1981; Shapira, 1989) and the Jewish Shtetl tradition (Katz and Gurevitch, 1976), which became fixated during the following years by central processes, such as the enforced integrated ideology of the "melting pot" (Etzioni-Halevi and Shapira 1977) and the siege mentality aroused by the routine of war (Schwartz, Zerubavel, and Barnett, 1986). The military conflict in particular, which became a routine of existence and which demanded both the formation of a large and expensive "people's army" and long reserve duty service, established, according to Kimmerling (1974, 1992), the borders of the Israeli-Jewish collective, and turned the army into a social system which replaced and expanded the blood relations system, with army service determining to a large extent the inclusion of the Israeli citizen in the system of social supervision and esteem (Horowitz and Kimmerling, 1974; Gal, 1986; Ben Ari, 1989). This dominant history of Israeli militarism is what gave rise to unique cultural phenomena, such as "critical obedience" (Ben Eliezer, 1991), who states that during a war, the IDF must not be criticized. Since Israel is in a permanent state of war, this "prohibition" has received a permanent status, and its action can be seen even in the most extreme protest wave that Israeli society has known—during the Lebanon war. "Few were those who challenged the very call to enlist for the war, despite the massive protest, which gathered pace from the first weeks of the war. This protest was unprecedented in Israel in wartime. It broke the rule of "Be quiet, we are shooting!", a rule which symbolizes the pushing aside of internal arguments so long as the battle continues. However, the protest did not digress from the pattern of critical obedience—a pattern which allows criticism, but in the end does not translate it into alternative actions or practices" (Helman, 1993: 273).

There are a handful of sociological case studies attempting to demonstrate in specific fields the change from the collectivist ethos to a more individualistic lifestyle. Thus, for example, Roniger and Feige (1992) describe how the "pioneer" turned into the "freier," while Rubinstein (1977) describes in a similar manner the rise and fall of the mythological Sabra; Shapira and Herzog (1983) analyze the pattern changes in memoirs, Har Even (1989) the change in the attitude to the group of emigrants as a social problem, and Burstein (1990), as mentioned, the changing face of Israeli cinema. This collection of studies is certainly too eclectic to be generalized into any conclusion, but makes clear the fact that collectivism is still to a large extent the dominant frame of reference for Israeli culture.

This conclusion is also supported from the specific view point of the film "Late Summer Blues," which consists entirely of a description of the suppression of individualism by the dominant collective's system of reference: the group, the army, the state, the school, the family. "Blues" represents the adult generation—parents and educators—as an authority which cannot be questioned. This generation is composed of Zwillich's parents, who accompany their children to the recruitment center on their way to the reception and sorting base; of people who live their diaspora past; of policemen who are willing not to enforce the law on those facing enlistment; and of a principal and secretary who serve as cultural commissars. Each of these could have been presented as a category opposed to the younger generation, but "Blues," true in its own way to the collectivist ethos, reproduces and eternalizes their cultural dominance and presents them as guardians of the normative order and the cultural capital of Israeli society.

The combination of a value system that is considered legitimate and is supported by inter-generational links stemming from a feeling of common destiny turns the group into an inescapable cultural trap. Universalist statements, such as "there are no just wars," perhaps reflect Western youth culture, but have no real echo in the local culture described in the film. This yearning for the extra-Israeli-national world does not represent a constructive alternative, but merely escapism, like that of Margo who goes to Paris to escape the Friday nights when the group will gather for military conversations in which he will have no patrol.

The ability—limited from the outset—of the heroes of "Blues" to perform soul searching before they are incorporated into the collective results from their being in a liminal position. They are already out of the school framework and not yet in the army; no longer boys and not yet men. The maturation of the group's youths occurs at the meeting place of two opposing cultural frameworks. The streets of Tel Aviv, the school corridors and the beach are earthly environments; the wish to stick to them so that "it will never end," arises, among other things, from the mythical power of the other, alternative, existence worlds which await the Israeli adolescent. The national myths, which give the youth their cultural lives, remove their personal freedom to choose between earthly life and death. These are swallowed up within the justification of existence beyond time and space, which surrounds the generations of fathers and sons and cancels the barriers between periods, places, origins and behavior patterns. The rhetoric of "people," "nation," "the glory of Israel," "it is good to die for our country" and other such phrases is ultimately worn out, but its present realization (for example, by enlistment to the army) still exists and is taken for granted.

C. Liminality, Acting Documentation, and Simulation: Self Reflection

"Blues" is a graduation film told from an autobiographical point of view. As such, it is based on reflections: the youths represent their lives to themselves, to their parents and to their teachers; Yossi Zwillich writes a diary; Ahraleh conducts a graffiti diary on the walls of Tel Aviv "In order to annoy all those who don't care." But the characters are mainly reflected through the lens of Margo's camera. Margo, the outcast from the collective, who is at first considered a nuisance due to his wish to document, becomes the commemorator of the group and its members. The commemorative power of his camera gives Margo a perspective whose exterior is nostalgic but whose essence presents an illusion of "the thing itself." "Were we like that, so stupid, so beautiful, so pure?", asks Margo in his exile, and the process of his alienation from the group is at its strongest at a time when it is he who holds the key to commemoration.

"That's how we were:" Margo, watching his youth with the backdrop of Tel Aviv's foundation stones is reminiscent of Yaakov Shabtai, who looks at his youth in Tel Aviv through the stories of *Uncle Peretz Takes Off* (and especially in "Spotted Leopard"); and who later in *Memorandum* even asks exactly the same question. Shabtai's early Tel Aviv is the Tel Aviv of the Fourth Aliya, a city of plots of sand, vineyards, muddy fields and a wild beach. For Margo also the most pure and nostalgic authenticity is in the sights of the Tel Aviv beach. For Shabtai, early Tel Aviv "is a very homely, familial city, a city of apartments and yards, where the collective life of family members, acquaintances and neighbors happens—everyone goes in and out of each other's life; it is a city of workers' restaurants, narrow streets where the busy traffic is not of vehicles but of people; a city of one story houses and huts, with dovecotes alongside them, like in the Nordia neighborhood (...). Tel Aviv being built in exhausting labor and Zionist and worker awareness"—as Edna Shabtai describes it (1991:58). So collectivity is Yaakov Shabtai's frame of reference for the "small Tel Aviv" and the loss of both—of collectivity and of small Tel Aviv—involve and connects each with the other.

Compared with the small Tel Aviv in the *Uncle Peretz Takes Off* stories, the Tel Aviv of *Memorandum* is a sweaty and crowded city where countless anonymous people wander around aimlessly in the maddening summer heat, and which creates alternately oppression and gloom, and attacks of hedonism; a city of immigrants who came to build their home there, but which does not allow them to settle down. "Yaakov Shabtai" writes Nissim Calderon (1980: 26), "examines in *Memorandum* the class which more than any other class determined behavior patterns and values in Israeli society, since it was the central force in it, until it was broken in the fracture exposed on May 17th, 1977 the people of 'working Israel', Zionists and socialists (...) The family here is the same tight and sticky dough that determines norms and stuffing them into your mouth with a spoon which is much larger than the mouth. The family passes from generation to generation, being the strongest power and also the most transparent lie and also the bitterest failure."

The two faces of Tel Aviv—the beach and the graffiti covered streets, the collectivist nostalgia and the collective fracture, the power versus the lie and the failure—are welded in "Blues" just as they are divided between *Uncle Peretz Takes Off* and *Memorandum*. But "Blues" subscribes neither to Yaakov Shabtai's bleak individualistic awareness, nor to his political and social criticism. In this respect, one must say it is not in Shabtai's league: to surrender these two reference levels is to surrender with them poetic complexity in favor of a more conventional plot—one could almost say a more Hollywood-style plot. But here lies the secret of the appeal and popular acceptance of a film, which among other things was chosen to represent Israel in the Oscar awards competition for the best foreign movie.

The self-reflection methods adopted by the people of "Blues," just like their brief flights of individualism, are limited in advance by the collective frame of reference. Trapped between Israeli society's "rules of ceremony" on the one hand, and its "hero culture" on the other, the youths of the group find release for their criticism in a different mode of representation of relations: parody. The parodic model serves both as a distorted mirror of social ceremonial and as a means of rebutting the myths of the "hero culture." As part of the protest play which was not staged, the group's youths present a parody of Yossi Zwillich's taken-for-granted enlistment ("Get up and join the Jewish Battalion"), and even a parody on the character of Trumpeldor ("It is good to die for our country"), who represents the collective hero.

The satire on Zwillich's death, during which the Holy of Holies of Israeli national existence—the myth of the fallen soldier—is smashed, is presented only as a "rehearsal," and is not staged in front of the adults. It remains as an exercise, as a possibility of rebellion that is not realized. In fact, quite the opposite happens. The provocative act of presenting questions concerning the fatalism in Israeli national existence ends with a sort of acceptance of answers which have never been given and whose source is not in accepted reason or logic. This acceptance leads to participation in the inevitable Israeli social practice of memorializing the fallen. The parents, the friends, the school, and the whole of society require the continued presence of the dead among them, so that the social life of the deceased will not end with their physical demise.[4] The memorialization which follows this acceptance is "Yossi, my successful child"—a song that constitutes, in the context of the graduation ceremony and the presence of Zwillich's parents there, a softened ironic protest about the child, who is partly a disappointment to his parents since he does not fulfill their expectations and is partly an original child going his own way.

The possibility for self reflection and the ability (although limited) to reject, if only for a moment, the "rules of ritual" by means of parody and satire, are rooted in the unique situation of the heroes of "Blues," a state which anthropology terms a "liminal situation." "Late Summer Blues" is located at a critical crossroads between two life cycles: a person's cultural life cycle versus his personal life cycle. In most human societies known to anthropologists there are mechanisms for adapting between these two cycles, and the meeting between them is performed in planned social situations, called rites of passage.[5] These rites are intended by society to cause changes in the initiate's symbolic and functional identity. During them, the initiate is separated from his immediate surroundings and taken "outside the camp"—to somewhere not recognized a social place. The separation is expressed by removing signs of personal identity—removing clothes, wearing uniform, forbidding the use of language and blurring the differences between people of different status. The previous social structure is turned into an "anti-structure," in which the familiar social order ceases to exit and its place is taken by a different human experience. This receives strong experiential expression in the second stage of the rite (the liminal stage), when, alongside difficult humiliations and physical torture, the mutilation of organs and the survival of life-threatening challenges, the initiate is confronted with his society's central myths. These become part of the experience of the rite and the initiate is not a passive observer of them, but participates in their occurrence as part of an alternative, mythical reality, devoid of chronological time. At the center of this stage is a phenomenon that is apparently completely opposite to the purpose of the whole process. This phenomenon involves the desecration of the most holy object of worship in the society—a totem, an image of a certain animal or place. This objet is slaughtered, sacrificed, smashed or desecrated. Only after such a desecration has taken place properly can the initiate return to his society, with a new status and identity. The accepted anthropological explanation of this contradiction of holiness and its desecration stems from the assumption that the main power of the rite of passage results from its being a total subjugation of the person's existence to the authority of society and the collective. This subjugation becomes effective through the demonstration of society's power. The peak of this show of power occurs when society proves it ability to smash its own idols. It is not the initiate who desecrates the sanctity, but society, which uses initiates as pawns fulfilling its will.

The graduation play of the heroes of "Blues" is a rite of passage which becomes a parody due to the lack of connection between the myth and the reality in the lives of those youths. The national myth, the hero culture, Zionism and militarism—all these do not constitute for them the contents of an ordered and clear world view. They are more like norms and dictates of "see and do." Zwillich dies in the name of the myth, even though his death was not a hero's death, but during a training accident; and Ahraleh enlists despite his doubts concerning the validity of the myths in whose name he might die. Mussi, unlike them, makes a decision based on commitment to the myth as embodied in his brother and family. Margo, forced to watch all of them, is prepared to exchange his diabetes for a recruitment paper.

Living between an exhausted myth and a reality based on other principles does not allow the group to accept Zwillich's death as an integral part of the taken-for-granted mosaic of "Israeli culture." Their feeling is that he died in vain, that he had a death not only biological, but also and mainly social. They cannot hold a memorializing ritual for Zwillich, and on the other hand, they cannot rebel against the chains of the collective which bind them. The lack of ability is the key to understanding the group's existential dilemma. Unlike other groups, e.g., in "Such a Group" on the one hand and "Eskimo Lemon" on the other, that have clear commitments to a certain context—the former to the context controlled by the myth, the latter to the context stemming from everyday life—the life cycle of the Tel Avivian high school students is in a culturally unclear context. Israeli society is not undergoing a process of connecting and fusing the opposites within it in order to create reality. On the contrary, this is a society where various processes inside it, whose nature and origins cannot be discussed here, amplify the polarization and widen chasms between myths and improvisations, between beliefs and the desire and needs to "settle down" and survive. As a result, a culture is created built on two dimensions with no connection between them, and which therefore cannot make the connection. The first dimension finds expression in fanatical loyalty to fundamentalist religious or nationalistic value systems, while the second is revealed in "projects," "operations," and other short term improvisations.

The lack of connection between myth and daily life leads to the fatalism of the first not being softened and controlled by the pragmatism of the second, but becoming borderless, due to its distance from the earthly pull of the second. In other words, considerations of communications, benefit and circumstances do not nourish and form the uncompromising loyalty to the myth. The separation between the two allows the maximum self-fulfillment of each. Various events may be explained on the basis of this analysis—from the phenomenon of "critical obedience" mentioned above, to the culture of driving, and the attitude to emigration from Israel, to the popular rhetoric of "that's what there is,"—as a justification for the impotence to preserve and control any context. "Late Summer Blues" is an additional artistic testimony to this cultural system and its implications on the maturation process of young boys and girls in a space where place, time and meaning exist in a chaotic state and cannot serve as a basis for the formation of the self as a social subject with a consistent identity. The wandering between belonging to the cosmic entities of nation and land on the one hand, and life in the realistic city on the other hand, causes the "large place"—the country—to stand in contrast to the "small place"—the city. The declaration of one of the participants in the school's graduation play, "I have no place to die," is a desperate statement of someone whose maturation places his personal life cycle on the threshold of his society's death cycle.

The "city" and the "country," Tel Aviv and Israel, are two forms of place and of time, in both of which none of the heroes of "Blues" can find a resting-place for himself. Without a place to die, there is also no place to live, and the youths of the group are inevitably absorbed into the collective "self," which is subject to the total authority of the mythical fate, which negates the individual's freedom of choice. The solution offered by the film to this state of affairs is outside myth and outside everyday life. This is a solution dealing with representation and reflection by means of diaries, graffiti and documentary films. This reflexivity, in which irony and nostalgia are mixed in equal doses, testifies above all to the inability of the observer to change his pre-programmed behavior according to the Israeli-tribal code.

Zwillich, Ahraleh and Mussi pass through the group on their way to personal annulment, which confuses them to the point of loss of any critical sense and judgment. The group's confusion is reflected in the fact that all its statements and commitments are overturned and are all phrased on the level of reflection, joke and game. The attempt to separate the life outside—society, state, army—from the life in school and within the group itself, by means of creating ritual frameworks, does not succeed, since the ceremonial mold is open to penetration by all the other forms of symbolization, which compete with it and shatter it. The ritual mold is especially destabilized by self reflection concerning its contents and rules, by reflexive patterns of irony, acting, satire and parody. These are the patterns that the group's heroes wish to insert into the ritual mold, which has lost the justification for its existence from their point of view. The principal's battle against this "subversive" attempt is successful only because against both the ritual and the acting, she places an absolute truth, which is, in the reality of the groups' life, the mother of all values—the image of Yossi Zwillich's parents' suffering. This is the cultural axiom which is beyond dispute and argument. It is the root of the contrasts and the factor uniting the political disputants. On the other hand, she is the one demonstrating the no-escape situation into which the participants have been drawn. In a situation where the deceased are no longer heroes, their memorialization loses its value as a mythical-symbolic basis for the "hero culture." The irony, the nostalgia, the simulation of the idea of collective sharing, while the authentic feeling of this is disappearing, can only be interpreted as intermediate stages in the rejection of collectivism, whose whole effect and meaning can only be appreciated correctly when the time comes.

Instead of Conclusions: the "Tel Aviv Syndrome"

One of the phenomena attributed to the spiritual influence of Jerusalem to some of its visitors is known as the "Jerusalem Syndrome." This is an agitated mental state, in which the atmosphere of Jerusalem drives the tourist insane and causes him to do things and to see hallucinations which he would not have done or hallucinated elsewhere. There is no parallel phenomenon connected with Tel Aviv, and this raises questions. Here is the key to some of the conclusions and the questions raised by the analysis in this article.

Jerusalem is a combination of a "small place" and a "large place;" it has myth and eschatology combined with a reality of residence and everyday life. In other words, the heavenly Jerusalem and the earthly Jerusalem are mixed up, and create, for the visitor, a distorted temporal world, in which the boundaries between mythological time and earthly existential time collapse. The lack of coordinates stems from Jerusalem's unique cultural place in the awareness of the historical religions in particular, and in the Western world in general. Tel Aviv is a place of one time—earthly, local, existential and immediate—a time of mortals, managing their lives along a social life cycle. The other time, the mythical, immortal time, invades this temporal existence in special circumstances, such as an enlistment ceremony. The need to decide between the times arises when the question of the meaning of life and death is raised in the framework of the collective self, and not as part of the private self. The behavioral handling of this question is performed in the group by a reflective game of contrasts, which avoids, by its being a game, a commitment to one time or the other.

The contrasts composing the lives of the youths are not really bridged but serve as dramatic elements in this game of suspense for a reality which is itself one dimensional and uni-temporal: completely mythical. This ultimate reality is unnegotiable, irreconcilable and cannot be softened; it demands a decision between the two methods of selfhood and of existence in time. In this respect, Tel Aviv serves as a small place in which there is no room for a large place. These are two mutually excluding alternatives, and the impossible confrontation between them occurs only in game time, where everything is possible: the well-known proximity of play to madness raises a comparison between the "Jerusalem Syndrome" and the acting of the group members. The loss of sanity happens to a stranger arriving in a place with an ambivalence of time, whose regular inhabitants have learnt to distinguish between its dimensions and to deal with the non-local, mythical time. He stumbles upon a state of foreignness, and as a stranger to his own world he loses the ground of his everyday existence and exchanges it for a game of theoretical choice which stands in for the lack of real choice. The personal self is actually memorialized even in the small place Tel Aviv.

Notes

* The film "Late Summer Blues" was produced in 1987 by Ilan De-Vries, Ranan Shor and Doron Nesher. Director: Ranan Shor.

** I would like to thank Ranan Shor for encouraging me to write this article, and Aviad Raz for his assistance in writing.

1. The assumptions described here somewhat simplistically, are those of the Post-Structuralist approach. Various "methods" are included in this approach, such as "The Archaeology of Knowledge" (Foucault, 1976), "Germatology" and Deconstruction (Derrida, 1976), and the Semiology of Literature (Barthes, 1967, 1975), Symbolic Exchanges (Baudrillard, 1983) and also Mytho-Poetic, Psychoanalytic approaches and so on. "The Death of the Author" has already become a sort of axiom of Structuralist research (see Foucault, 1979), focusing on the reader's position and on the analysis of the text-as-it-is-read in different social situations and historical periods, and, therefore, in different meanings. This "reconstruction" of the text's meaning requires, therefore, a poetics of acceptance (see Iser, 1978; Holub, 1984; Fish, 1980). The general rationale guiding this research is that there are literary phenomena which cannot be explained fully out of the text itself, "from the inside," but should be interpreted as symptoms whose roots are on a different level, the social and cultural level.
2. The big place and the small place are a pair of terms proposed by Aran and Gurevich (1991), which the present article uses as part of a specific cultural paradigm of big place/small place—country/city = Israel/Tel Aviv = collective/individual.
3. The dominant approaches in the sociology of Israeli society have been, and still are, characterized by a perception of the "Israeli-Jewish collective" as an ontological object *a priori*, and taken for granted. Thus, for instance, the structural-functionalist approach, whose outstanding representatives in Israeli sociology are Eisenstadt (1967), and also his students Horowitz and Lisak (1977), saw the collective as an objective entity at the navel of the nation-state; a delimited society with a clear identity and consensus, various functional sub-systems, etc. (see also Herzog 1992 for a similar critique). The verdict passed on Israeli sociology so far is quite damning: thus, for example, Kimmerling (1992) claims that Israeli sociology has harnessed itelf to the building of the nation and thus lost the little neutrality which could have been attributed to it as a scientific discipline; while Ram (1989) presents the various approaches existing in Israeli sociology (modernization, elite, class, pluralism, ethnicity and colonialism) as various alternatives whose common source is ideological and the justification of whose existence is the "collective" that they define.
4. The external life provided to the deceased by means of memorializing ceremonies are in fact the basis of what I have called the "hero culture." This term was developed by Becker (1973) and expanded by Lifton (1986). In the specific Israeli context of "hero culture," see the important work of Meron (1992).
5. These characteristics are borrowed from the important theoretical work of Van Gennep (1969) on rites of passage, a work which Victor Turner (1969) later used and expanded.

Sources

Aran, G. and Gurevitch, Z. (1991). "On Place: Israeli Anthropology." *Alpayim*, 9-44 [Hebrew].

Barthes, R. (1967). *Writing Degree Zero*. London, Jonathan Cape.
Barthes, R. (1972). *Mythologies*. New York: Hill and Wang.
Barthes, R. (1975). *S/Z, the Pleasures of the Text*. London, Jonathan Cape.
Barthes, R. (1979). "From Work to Text" In: J.V. Harari (ed.), *Textual Strategies: Perspectives in Post-Structuralist Criticism*, Ithaca: Cornell University Press, 73-81.
Baudrillard, J. (1983). [1975]. *Simulation*. New York: Semitext.
Becker, E. (1973). *The Denial of Death*. New York: The Free Press.
Ben Ari, E. (1989). "Masks and Soldiering: The Israeli Army and The Palestinian Uprising." *Cultural Anthropology* 44, 372-389.
Ben Eliezer, U. (1991). *The Meaning of Political Participation in a Non-Liberal Democracy: The Example of Israel*. (Mimeo) Washington, Seattle, Jackson School of International Studies.
Burstein, Y. (1990). *The Face as a Battlefield: The Cinematic History of the Israeli Face*. Tel Aviv, Hakibbutz Hameuchad. [Hebrew].
Calderon, (1980) N. *In a Political Context: Four Articles on Authors*. Siman Kriya Books: Hakibbutz Hameuchad Press.
Derrida, J. (1976). *Of Grammatology*. Baltimore: Johns Hopkins University Press.
Eisenstadt, S.N (1967). *Israeli Society - Background, Development and Problems*. Jerusalem: Magnes [Hebrew].
Eisenstadt, S.N. (1985). *The Transformations of Israeli Society: An Essay in Interpretation*. London: Weidenfeld and Nicholson.
Etzioni-Halevi, H. and Shapira, R. (1977). *Political Culture in Israel: Cleavage and Integration among Israeli Jews*. New York: Praeger.
Even-Zohar, I. (1981). "The Emergence of a Native-Hebrew Culture in Palestine: 1882-1948." *Studies in Zionism*, 4, 167-184.
Fish, S. (1980). *Is There a Text in This Class? - The Authority of Interpretive Communities*. Harvard: Harvard University Press.
Foucault, M. (1976). *The Archaeology of Knowledge*. New York: Harper and Row.
Foucault, M. (1979). "What is an Author?" Trans. Karl Hanet, *Screen*, XX (1), 13-33.
Gal, R. (1986). *A Portrait of the Israeli Soldier*. New York: Greenwood Press.
Graz, N. (1987). "The Company Was Walking." *Seratim*. Issue no. 3, April [Hebrew].
Har Even, Y. (1989). *Emigration as a Social Problem*. Master's Thesis, Department of Sociology and Anthropology, Tel Aviv University [Hebrew].
Helman, W. (1993). *Refusal to Serve in the Army as an Attempt to Redefine Citizenship*. Doctoral Thesis, The Hebrew University, Jerusalem [Hebrew].
Herzog, H. (1992). "Review of the book: Distress in Utopia." *Megamot*, 34(3), 479-84 [Hebrew].
Holub, R. (1984). *Reception Theory: A Critical Introduction*. London: Methuen.
Horowitz, D. and Kimmerling, B. (1974). Some Social Implications of Military Service and the Reserve System in Israel." *Archives Européenes de Sociologie*, 15, 2652-2676.
Horowitz, D. and Lisak, M. (1977). *From Settlement to State*. Tel Aviv, Am Oved [Hebrew].
Horowitz, D. and Lisak, M. (1989). *Distress in Utopia*. Am Oved: University Library [Hebrew].
Iser, W. (1978). *The Act of Reading: A Theory of Aesthetic Response*. Baltimore, MD: The Johns Hopkins University Press.
Katriel, T. (1991). "Gibush: The Crystallization Metaphor in Israeli Cultural Semantics." Chapter 2 in her *Communal Webs: Culture and Communication in Israel*. Albany: SUNY Press.

Katz, E. and Gurevitch, M. (1976). *The Secularization of Leisure: Culture and Communication in Israel.* Faber and Faber: London.

Kimmerling, B. (1974). "Anomie and Integration in Israeli Society and the Salience of the Israeli-Arab Conflict." *Studies in Comparative International Development*, 9(3), 64-89.

Kimmerling, B. (1992). "Sociology, Ideology and Nation Building: The Palestinians and Their Meaning in Israeli Sociology. *American Sociological Review* (August).

Klieg, Ira and Uric (1981). "We Were Simply in the Army Together." Kolnoa, *Summer Issue* [Hebrew].

Levi-Strauss, C. (1981). *The Naked Man: Introduction to the Science of Mythology.* London: Jonathan Cape.

Liebman, C. and Don Yehia, E. (1983). *Civil Religion in Israel: Traditional Judaism and Politics, Culture and Society*, 3(2), 255-272.

Lifton, R. (1986). *The Broken Connection.* New York; Basic Books.

Meron, D. (1992). *Opposite the Silent Heart: Studies in Poetry of the War of Independence.* The Open University: Keter [Hebrew].

Neeman, Y. and Zimmerman, M. (eds.). (1987). *Introduction to Israeli Cinema - Textbook.* The Department of Cinema and Television, Tel Aviv University [Hebrew].

Ram, U. (1989). "Civic Discourse in Israeli Sociological Thought." *International Journal of Politics, Culture and Society*, 3(2), 255-27.

Roniger, L. and Feige, M. (1992). "From Pioneer to Freier: the Changing Models of Generalized Exchange in Israel." *Arch. Europ. Sociol.* XXXIII, 280-307.

Rubinstein, A. (1977). *You Chose Us for Freedom*, Tel Aviv, Schoken. [Hebrew].

Schwartz, B., Zerubavel, E. and Barnett, B.M. (1986). "The Recovery of Masada: A Study in Collective Memory." *The Sociological Quarterly*, 27, 147-164.

Shabtai, E. (1991). "Tel Aviv in the Prose of Yaakov Shabtai." *Achshav*, 56, 54-78 [Hebrew].

Shapira, A. (1989). *Visions in Conflict.* Tel Aviv: Am Oved [Hebrew].

Shapira, R. and Herzog H. (1983). "Top Secret Memoirs as a Reflection of Age and of Period." *Megamot*, 24, 513-30.

Turner, V. (1969). *The Ritual Process - Structure and Anti-Structure.* Chicago, Aldine.

Van Gennep, A. (1969) (1980). *The Rites of Passage.* Translated by M.B. Visedom and G.L. Caffee, Chicago, University of Chicago Press, Phoenix Books.

4

"You Gotta Know How to Tell a Story": Telling Tales, and Tellers in American and Israeli Narrative Events at Dinner

Shoshana Blum-Kulka

This chapter explores the degree of cultural diversity in the dinner-table conversation narrative events of eight middle-class Jewish-American and eight Israeli families, matched on family constellation. Conceptualized in terms of a threefold framework of telling, tales, and tellers, the analysis reveals both shared and unshared narrative event properties. Narrative events unfold in both groups in similar patterns with respect to multiple participation in the telling, the prevalence of personal experience tales, and the respect for children's story-telling rights. Yet, cultural styles come to the fore in regard to each realm as well as their interrelations. American families locate tales outside the home but close in time, ritualizing recounts of "today"; Israeli families favor tales more distant in time but closer to home. While most narratives foreground individual selves, Israeli families are more likely to recount shared events that center around the family "us" as protagonist. In modes of telling, American families claim access to story ownership through familiarity with the tale, celebrating monologic performances; but in Israeli families, ownership is achievable through polyphonic participation in the telling. (Ethnography of communication, language and culture, conversation analysis, folklore, narrative).*

Story-telling in ordinary talk between inmates is one of the most common enactments of narrative discourse. We tell stories to each other as a means of packaging experience in cognitively and effectively coherent ways (Labov and Fanshel 1977, Sacks 1974), or in the terms of J. Bruner (1990), as a way to test the borderlines between the exceptional and ordinary. Fisher (1987) considers the narrativization of experience a basic human need; the essential nature of human beings is captured by the metaphor of man as *homo narrans.* Extending Kenneth Burke's definition of man as a symbol-making and symbol-using animal, Fisher proposes an all-encompassing definition for the role of narratives (Fisher 1987:63):

> The idea of human beings as storytellers posits the generic form of all symbol composition. It holds that symbols are created and communicated ultimately as stories meant to give order to human experience and to induce others to dwell in them in order to establish ways of living in common, intellectual and spiritual communities in which there is confirmation for the story that constitutes one's life.[1]

Although the narrative use of language, as insisted by Hymes (1981), is a universal function, such use can be expected to vary culturally as do other ways of speaking. Indeed, oral narrative styles vary by culture for both adults and children, as shown both by work adopting a cross-cultural perspective (e.g. Scollon and Scollon 1981, Tannen 1980) and by comparative studies in the context of language socialization (e.g. Heath 1983, Schieffelin and Ochs 1986). My goal here is to apply a culturally sensitive analysis to narratives told in the course of dinner-table conversations in middle- to upper-class Jewish-American and Israeli families. To apply such an analysis, we need first to understand the nature of the narrative event in question.

Conversational story-telling can be looked at from a social-interactionist position, as interaction, with a focus on how the narrative emerges in its context, and/or as discourse, with a focus on the textual end product abstractable from the context. The first approach is represented by work on conversational story-telling from the perspectives of both ethnomethodology (e.g. Jefferson 1978, Sacks 1974) and discourse analysis (Polanyi 1989, Schiffrin 1984, Tannen 1984); such work shows the manner in which the structure of oral narratives is conversationally accomplished. Particularly relevant here are studies focusing on narratives during family dinner-table conversations (Erickson 1982, 1988; Ochs et al. 1989; Ochs et al. 1992). A complementary, rich source of information on this dimension is provided by studies in folklore that highlight the poetic and social interactional aspects of performance (Bauman 1986, Briggs 1988, Hymes 1981, Kirshenblatt-Gimblett 1975, Shuman 1986). By contrast, the discourse approach is best illustrated by Labov's influential work (Labov and Fanshel 1977, Labov and Waletzky 1967), which unveils the structural coherence of seemingly chaotic conversational renderings of personal experience.

Figure 1
Dimensions of narrativity.

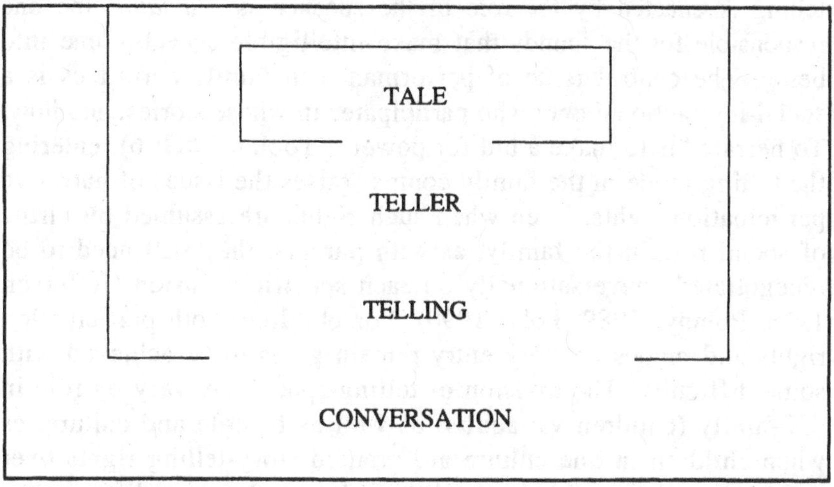

The narrative events examined here, performed by both adults and children, function as crucial socializing contexts for family interaction in general, as claimed by Bernstein 1971. Hence a further perspective that needs to be added is cross-cultural and cross-ethnic studies of language socialization (Blum-Kulka and Snow 1992, Heath 1983, Miller et al. 1990, Schieffelin and Ochs 1986).

Yet, none of these approaches on its own captures the unique nature of family narratives. We need an approach that accounts simultaneously for family story-telling as an event, a social action unfolding in real time, as well as (at the discourse level) a text about other events. The links and transitions between these two realms are provided by performer/tellers. Dinner-table narrative events are unique: they represent a three-way intersection of the act of narration, the textual content and form of the narrative, and the persons responsible. Taking all three dimensions together, narratives become *narrative events.*[2] Like other speech events, narrative events have their specific norms governing the scene, participation rights, message content, message form, and rules of interpretation (Hymes 1974: 55-8). In narrative events, these features can be seen as subsumed under three dimensions of narrativity: telling (narration), tales (narratives), and tellers (narrators). In oral storytelling, the realm of telling is embedded (in an open-ended fashion) in the realm of conversation, and the realm of tales within that of telling, as depicted in Figure 1.[3]

Telling is the act of narrating in real time, the actual performance of a story before an audience. In the terms of Goffman (1981: 144-5), telling is enacted by the role of the speaker as *Animator,* the one responsible for the sounds that make intelligible speech come into being. The central issue of performance in family narratives is a social-interactional one: who participates in whose stories, and how. To narrate "is to make a bid for power" (Toolan 1988: 6); entering the telling mode in the family context raises the issues of narrative participation rights. Even when such rights are assumed by virtue of social role in the family, as with parents, they still need to be renegotiated conversationally on each specific occasion (Jefferson 1978, Polanyi 1989, Polss 1990). For children, both participation rights and modes of story entry remain goals to be achieved with some difficulty. The division of telling-space may vary by role in the family (children vs. adults) as well as by role and culture, as when children in one culture are granted story-telling rights over and beyond their rights in another. Cultures also may differ in the framing of transitions from the realm of conversation to the realm of telling, as well as in the importance of the telling with relation to the tales.

Tale is the stuff from which narratives are made. The term refers to the two dimensions of narrative captured in the poetics of narrative fiction by the distinction of *fabula vs. sjuzet* (in the Russian formalists' terms) or *story vs. narrative* (Rimmon-Keenan 1983). The *fabula* or the *story* of narratives "designates the narrated events, abstracted from their disposition in the text and reconstructed in their chronological order, together with the participants in these events" (Rimmon-Keenan: 3). In other words, in experience-based narratives, the *fabula* consists of the real-world building blocks used for the construction of the story. The *sjuzet,* on the other hand, relates to the way in which the story is shaped in the making: the "spoken or written discourse that undertakes the telling." In the actual discourse, events do not necessarily appear in chronological order, and content is filtered through some perspective, sometimes called a "focalizer" (Rimmon-Keenan: 74). It is the responsibility of the *author* (Goffman 1981: 144-5) to select the words in which the *fabula* is encoded in a way that is still retrievable for the audience. Cross-cultural variation in *fabula* choice may be expressed in spatio-temporal orientation of narrative plots (e.g. recent vs. not-recent past) or in the type of protagonists that are foregrounded (self vs. others). However, cultural attitudes to the preferred style of *sjuzet* may be expressed through critical comments to children about the way they are telling a story. As one father told his son, who failed to give a convincing performance of a joke learned from the father, "You gotta know how to tell a story."

Tellers (performers) may or may not be the persons accountable for the story. This is the role called the *Principal* by Goffman (1981: 144-5): the one committed to what the words say. In personal narratives, all three speaker roles (principal, author, and animator) can merge into one. In a personal narrative, it is the Principal who has actually experienced the events recounted and claims authorship for the narrative, acting also as Animator. But more generally, and especially when children are involved, the three speaker roles may be realized by different speakers. A mother who repeats to the father a story of personal experience, recounted to her earlier by her child, may act only as Animator (if she quotes verbatim); or she may take authorship rights, if she edits the child's version. In either case, the child remains the principal for the story. From a cross-cultural perspective, the relation of tellers to telling and tale raises issues of authorship vs. performance: How is authorship emically defined? Who, in each culture, is entitled to tell whose stories?

Background and Method

The database for the study consists of 264 narrative events that occurred during two dinner-table conversations with eight middle-class Jewish-American and eight Israeli families.[4] All Jewish-American families were residents of the Boston area; all Israeli families lived at the time in Jerusalem. The narrative events were examined as part of a larger project investigating the pragmatic socialization of children in the presence of a member of the research team who came from the same cultural background as the family. Following initial contacts by phone, the observer visited the home and got acquainted with the family prior to recordings. The same observer stayed with the family throughout the research period. The families were told that we were interested in comparing Israeli to American family dinners, and they were provided with details when interested. The observers were invited to join the families for dinner as a matter of course. Hence, the situation in which we are comparing the groups is that of families interacting with a semi-official guest.

As will be discussed later, interaction with the observer proceeded differently in the two groups, revealing a cultural difference in this mode of family self-presentation. All families participating in the project came originally from a European background (mainly from Russia and Poland) and hence share a Jewish Eastern-European heritage. The parent generations are native-born American or native-born Israeli. The American and Israeli families were matched for number and ages of children.

Segmentation and Coding

Narrative events were defined broadly as conversations that recapitulate past events. Since the perception of what constitutes a narrative may well differ from children to adults, or across cultures, we deliberately avoided imposing further structural criteria on tales (e.g. number of events mentioned).[5] The segments extracted from full transcripts of the dinner conversations vary in length from brief exchanges, of a few seconds, to long elaborated happenings, of up to 10 minutes. Boundaries of the segments were decided textually, in agreement among three analysts, on the basis of transition markers signaling entrances and exits from the telling realm. Analysis of the texts proceeded by a set of quantifiable coding categories, designed to capture variation in each dimension of narrativity. The categories used and the findings from the coding are integrated into the discussion.

In the following, I address the degree of cultural diversity between Jewish-Americans and Israelis in their attitudes toward telling, tales, and tellers in family narrative events. I argue that, considered from this threefold framework, family narrative events of the two groups share certain features attributable to the speech event in which they are embedded. Yet the groups differ culturally in the structuring of each dimension of narrativity, and in the relative importance granted to each: Jewish-American narrative events foreground tellers and the act of telling, while Israeli narrative events prefer to focus on tales and tellers. The argument is developed as follows: the degree of cultural diversity is discussed, first, in terms of the division of narrative space between members of the family and styles of story initiation; second, in terms of the spatio-temporal orientation of tales, and the degree of conventionalization in the transformation of tales into telling; and third, in terms of the relationships between ownership of the tale and participation in the telling.

Figure 2
Number of participants in narrative events

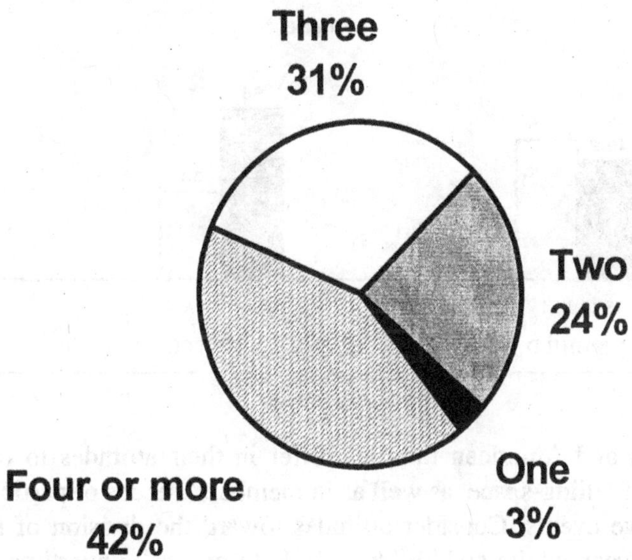

Issues of Telling

Gaining Access to Narrative-Space: Children and Adults

Family dinner-table narratives tend to be jointly constructed affairs (Erickson 1988, Ochs et al. 1989). In our case, collaboration takes several forms: stories are co-narrated, constructed through question/answer sequences, or told with sporadic but meaningful contributions from an active audience. In all these, telling is shared by several members of the family, sometimes including the observer. Collaborative process is at work in both Israeli and American narrative events: in almost half of the narratives, more than four members participate. By contrast, less than 5% are performed by just one participant; see Figure 2. What these numbers mask, though, are cultural styles of participation; as will be shown, Israeli and Jewish-American families differ greatly in the way they draw lines of demarcation between *teller(s)* and *audience*.

Figure 3
Maintellers: Division of telling space

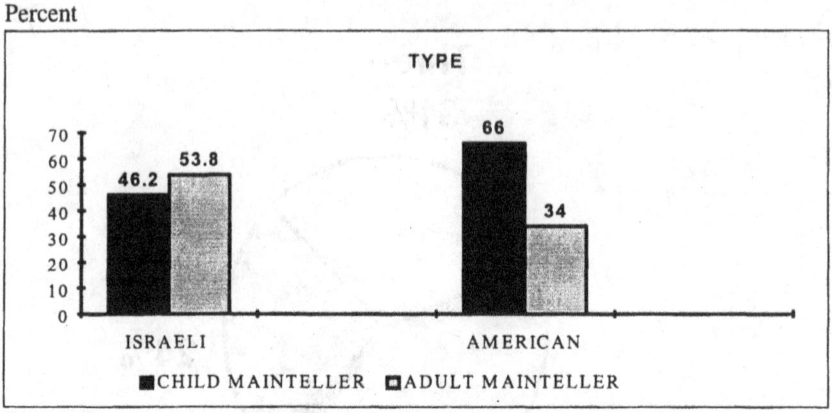

Israeli and American families differ in their attitudes toward the division of telling-space, as well as in members' modes of participation in narrative events. Consider attitudes toward the division of telling-space between adults and children. In both groups, dinnertime is perceived as a prime occasion for spotlighting children as narrators. To reveal attitudes toward children, we first divided narrative events in terms of identity of the predominant *mainteller(s),* as either *child* (or children) or *adult(s);* see Figure 3. In a further analysis, we identified the initiator of the narrative event by role in the family as *child, father, mother,* or *observer;* see Figure 4.

Figure 4
Narrative initiation

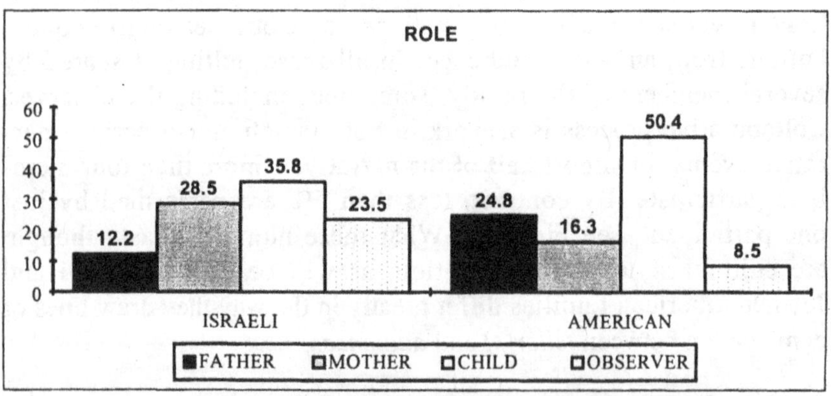

The degree to which children are considered conversational partners in adult company is noteworthy across the two cultures. In discussing determinants of cultural variability in conversation, Schieffelin and Eisenberg (1984: 382) note:

> Cultures vary along a continuum ranging from societies in which children are not allowed or expected to talk to adults or strangers and/or are not thought of as co-conversationalists to those in which children are actively encouraged to talk to adults, who in turn support this interaction and try to understand it. In some societies adults think it is important to elicit speech from children, socializing them in terms of production and interaction skills (e.g., Kaluli in Papua New Guinea, white middle-class American); but in other cultures children are encouraged to be quiet and speak only when spoken to (e.g., rural Louisiana Blacks, Luo in Kenya).

We found that, across the two groups, children take up 42% of all narrative space (see Fig. 3). The case of the middle-class families studied here well exemplifies a cultural pattern which treats children as rightful co-conversationalists; in both the Jewish-American and Israeli families, children around the dinner table share, in the terms of Goffman (1981: 131-2), an official status as *ratified* participants.[6] The pattern is most salient in the American families (see Fig. 3). American children act as maintellers in 66% of all narrative events, leaving the adults as maintellers of 34%. But, the adults in the Israeli families take up a much higher proportion of narrative space, playing the dominant role in 54% of narrative events. In line with the overall attitude toward the division of narrative space between adults and children, American children are also more active story-initiators (by 15%) than Israeli children.

This difference points to a cultural distinction in modes of narrative socialization at dinner. Notions of tellability and cultural styles of telling are acquired by children both by engaging in the telling and by being exposed to stories told by others. The American families tend to emphasize socialization by allowing for the display of narrative practice; but in the Israeli families, children are given a higher chance to act as active (or non-active) story recipients.

This does not necessarily mean that Israeli children engage generally in less display of narrative than do American children; stories may be told by children at other points during the day, to siblings or one parent. But it does mean that dinner-table conversations, where both adults and children jointly participate, are perceived by the American families as an occasion to focus on the children as narrators; in the Israeli families, narrative space is divided between adults and children. From the children's point of view, different gains are involved in each practice. Being encouraged to tell stories may be important in developing confidence in performing rights and the skills of narration (Blum-Kulka and Snow 1992); however, acting as primary or even secondary audience to adult stories allows access to the experience of significant others, thereby expanding the bases for identification (Miller et al. 1990) and shaping cultural notions of tellability or *reportability* (cf. Hymes 1981).[7]

Narrative Initiation: Insiders and Outsiders, Women and Men

Adult roles are also differently distributed across the two groups, most notably in regard to the observer. Observers in the Israeli families initiate 15% more narrative events than do the observers in the American families (see Fig. 4). In other words, the observers in the Israeli families seem much more confident in their story-telling rights than their American counterparts. Or, as suggested by Deborah Tannen (personal communication), the Americans may have different ideas about their *obligations*, rather than their rights: with their scientific tradition of "objectivity" in social science, perhaps they feel it incumbent upon them not to participate any more than necessary. This result ties in with other observations on the relations between observers and families in the two groups.

In both groups, observers (with one exception) were invited to join the dinner table as a matter of course; but the nature of their interaction with the family differed in key, and consequently in rules of interaction. In terms of the continuum of formality proposed by Irvine (1979), the generally prevailing key of family discourse (because of intimacy among participants) is that of informality. Yet there are differences of degree between the two groups: Israelis seem to celebrate the outermost informal end of the continuum. Consequently, observers are drawn into the circle of conversation from the onset, and interact with all family members, not only in the role of familiar guests, but rather as actual or potential friends. This is in line with the ethos of solidarity in Israeli culture, which tends to symbolically minimize social distance (Blum-Kulka et al. 1985, Katriel 1986). One of the privileges granted to friends is that of both self-directed and other-directed narrative initiation. Observers in the Israeli families accordingly share initiation almost equally with other members present.

Being a familiar guest at the American family's somewhat more formal dinner table does not bestow on the observer the privileges granted to friends; though partaking in the interaction, the observer does so cautiously, under the rules of interaction governing communication between nonintimates. Not being overtly active in narrative initiation is one way in which such caution is exercised. Hence it is not surprising to find that observers in the American families are engaged in less than 10% of story initiations.

Another difference between Israelis and Americans is in the relative parts played by mothers vs. fathers in narrative initiation. In the Israeli families, mothers have twice as many initiations; in the American families, fathers play a slightly more active role. This finding is in line with general patterns of participation rates in dinner-table talk. Following the categories proposed by Bublitz (1988) for topical action, we have analyzed the proportional role of fathers vs. mothers as topic initiators throughout the entire conversation: out of 47 parent-introduced topics, Israeli mothers introduced 76.5%; but out of 67 parent-introduced topics in the American families, fathers introduced 66%.

One reason for these findings may be the American perception of the occasion as having formal overtones because of the presence of the observer. Though the serving of food is accomplished mostly by the mothers, the fathers in these families take it upon themselves to *entertain the guest,* e.g. to introduce topics and to use narratives to keep the conversation going. By contrast, in the Israeli families, the mothers seem to take charge of the event, both in instrumental terms (here too it is mostly the women who serve the food) and by keeping the conversation going.[8]

Styles of Narrative Initiation

The solidarity ethos of Israeli society, as manifested in attitudes toward the observer, finds further expression in styles of narrative-event initiation. Consider story entry. In an independent study of the same corpora, Polss (1990) has analyzed in detail the types of devices used by initiators and story recipients in the course of story-entry talk. Germane to the discussion of attitudes toward telling is her analysis of the types of devices used in responsive utterances. Following Tannen's distinction (1984, 1985, 1989) between *high-involvement* and *high-considerateness* conversational styles, Polss distinguishes between high-involvement and low-involvement narrative response strategies.

High involvement responses focus on the tale and the teller; in Tannen's terms, they show active "participatory listenership" (1984:

30). These include devices such as requests for information, confirmation of information, and listener contribution to the narrative. Low-involvement responses focus on the telling; they signal message reception, thereby confirming the teller's success in aligning story-recipients. These include different types of *uptakers* (Edmondson and House 1981: 62-3), e.g. neutral back-channeling responses (*mhmm, uhhuh, yeah, right, okay*, etc.) and emotively colored ones (*really? good, for heaven's sake*).

Polss found interactive, high-involvement style more characteristic of story entry in Israel than in America: the proportion of high to low involvement styles is 82% to 18% in the Israeli narratives, compared to 69% to 31% in the American stories. Thus, Israeli story-opening exhibits a higher emphasis on co-participation and demonstration of personal involvement. Israeli co-participants frequently interpret story-initiator information, showing their concern with tale and teller.

(1) Israeli family 7: The conversation takes place as the family is getting ready to sit down at the table. Present also are the daughter (16) and the two sons (12 and 10).[9]

1	Observer:	*etmol hayinu* [//] *hayiti ecel pnina ve +...*	Yesterday we were [//] I was at the home of Pnina and +...
2	Mother:	*ve-cvika?*	And Cvika?
	Observer:	*ve-cvika ken.*	And Cvika, yes.
	Mother:	*nu # ve-ex halax?*	So how did it go?
	Observer:	*haya meod nexmad.*	It was very nice.
		[Story]	

The fast rate of speech, lack of interturn pauses, and dialogic unfolding of this story entry places it high on the involvement continuum. The story recipient's high engagement can further be seen by her use of what Tannen (1984: 118) calls "cooperative promptings" at every turn (e.g., "So how did it go?"). Americans, by contrast, exhibit less relative focus on interpersonal involvement, devoting their efforts to floor-management tasks aimed at securing the telling.

(2) American family 2: The children are Martin (8m), Daniel (6m), and Tamara (4f). The conversation takes place in the middle of dinner.

Martin:	My best friend got about + ...	
		You see me and my best friend were studying *rockets*-?
Observer:	Uhhuh.	
		[Story]

The shared features noted here are high degrees of collaboration and of inclusion of children in narrative events. Cultural diversity is revealed in attitudes toward tellers—the question of who participates—and in styles of story entry. This trend for cultural diversity of a gradient nature, against a background of shared orientations, is also noticeable in attitudes toward tales.

Transforming Tales to Telling

Cultural Variation in Spatio-Temporal Orientation of Tales

Where do tellers find the tales for constructing narratives at dinnertime? Certainly not in fiction; the vast majority of narratives in both groups (90%) are derived from real-life experience. In predominantly adult narratives, fictional topics do not exceed 4%.

In child-involved narratives, fiction does play a role (14%). Israeli children mention fictional characters from story books (Aladdin is one) and tell the contents of movies and books. American children talk about fictional characters from television: Sesame Street, Bugs Bunny, etc.

We have analyzed spatio-temporal framing by coding the two dimensions independently. First, since our definition of narratives included only stories of the past (see Ochs et al. 1989 for a different notion of temporal framing in family narratives), we distinguished narratives by temporal reference, including *today* ("I finished my assignment today in um and ..."), *recent past* ("I met an interesting man on the beach last week"; "Last night Debbie..."), or *distant past* ("that happened abut five years ago"). Cases which were either timeless (such as jokes and fiction), or lacking in cues for reliable assignment to a "recent" or "distant" time frame, were excluded from this analysis, leaving a corpus of 195 clearly time-framed marked narrative events (out of 264). Second, we defined narrative spatial orientation as geared either toward the *home,* the *world of school* and/or *work,* or any other location in the *world.* For example, a narrative about how the substitute teacher behaved that day is considered a "today/school" narrative, a visit to the museum last week is a "recent-past/world" story, and a teenager's early childhood memory about a family pet is a "distant-past/home" story.

In terms of their spatio-temporal framing, family dinner narratives defy the expectations of literary critics. Toolan (1988:1-2) defines narratives as "a recounting of things spatio-temporally distant." This might be true for fictional narratives; but most family narratives are definitely not temporally, and only partially spatially, remote from tellers and audience. Considered together for both groups, the majority of temporally marked narratives (63%) concern events of the very recent past—today, yesterday, or last week—leaving 42% to focus on events from the distant past (*n* = 195); see "Past 1" and "Past 2" in Figure 5. In terms of location, half the narratives analyzed fall into the third group, being located in the world. A third concern school or work, with the rest (12%) being located in the homes; see Figure 6.

Figure 5
Temporal tale frames.

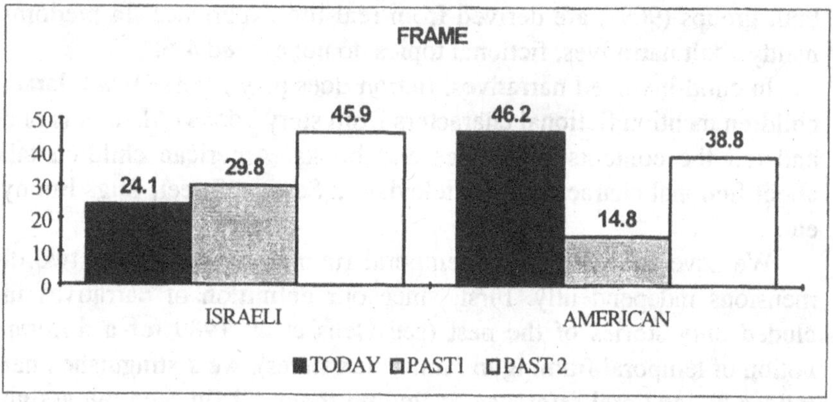

Within this general framework, however, we find cross-cultural preferences. The distribution by story time in Israeli and American narratives shows that story time is very different in the two groups (Fig. 5). The most striking difference is revealed in regard to the "today" frame: in the American families, almost half the time-marked narratives focus on *today* (46%). Telling about the happenings of the day thus stands out as the most important single timeframe for American narratives. By contrast, in Israeli narratives, "today" stories take up only one-quarter of narrative space (24%). For Israelis, the recent and non-recent past are the preferred timeframes, taking up over three-quarters of narrative space (76%). The difference lies in general preference for timeframes, not in choice of topics within the frames chosen. For example, for both Americans and Israelis, stories of the distant past cover a rich variety of topics. These include a series of humorous anecdotes about house painters that the family employed over the years, the story of an exceptional shopping expedition, several camping and travel stories, and anecdotes from the children's earlier years.

Cultural preferences for the tale's spatial frame are revealed in the choices of home orientation vs. school or work orientation (see Fig. 6). For both groups, about half the narratives are world-oriented, concerning spatial frames such as museums, camping grounds, or shopping malls. But Israeli narratives are markedly more home-oriented than American. In a considerable proportion of Israeli narratives (20%), the locus of the tale is at the home; by contrast, home stories are quite rare (6%) in the American corpus. The Israeli home stories include stories about birthday celebrations, family pets, grandparents visiting, or specific incidents that link the world and the home, such as the story of a mother's anxiety on coming home and not finding her two (early teen) sons there when she expected them.

Figure 6
Spatial tale frames

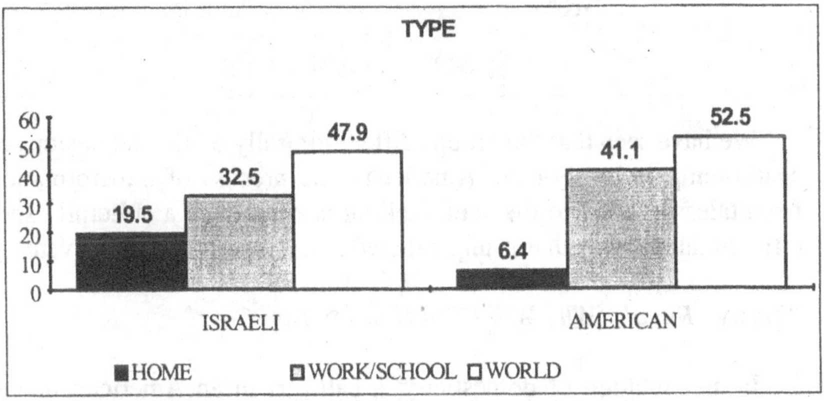

An interesting corollary to Israeli home orientation is provided by analysis of the types of protagonists foregrounded in family narratives (Figure 7). We have divided protagonists as *self, other,* or *us.* For both Israelis and Americans, attention is divided almost equally between stories that involve the self as protagonist and those concerning others. The prominence of the self as protagonist is not surprising, given that family dinners provide a unique opportunity for each member to use the narrative mode for raising issues of personal concern before a presumably supportive audience. Stories about others often involve the self too, e.g. the self as critical observer, as when the narrative concerns a teenager recounting an incident between the teacher and another student. The third category, "us stories," are quite rare in both groups; but they are more likely to appear in the Israeli narratives than the American. Furthermore, the nine Israeli "us narrative" events are rather long and elaborated happenings, lasting up to seven to eight minutes each, while the two American "us narrative" events are much shorter (3-4 minutes) and less elaborated.

Figure 7
Tale protagonists

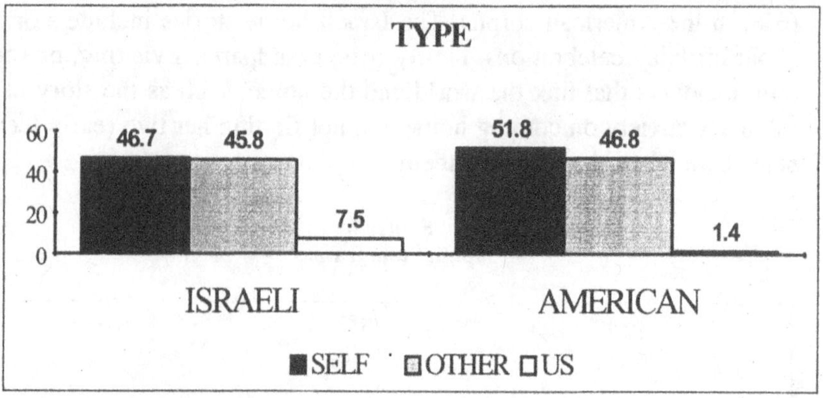

We have seen that the groups differ culturally on the dimensions of spatio-temporality. For the Americans, the process of transformation from tales of today to the actual telling is enacted in a culturally specific, ritualistic way that is unparalleled in the Israeli narrative events.

"Today" Rituals: Who Will I Tell How My Day Goes?

In an imitation of domesticity, a call girl in an American movie from 1990 (*Pretty Woman*) greets her customer with "How was your day, dear?" But judging by our dinner-table conversations, this conventional query functions socially in much richer ways than merely a sign of wifely concern. Narratives about the day's happening figure in both Israeli and American dinner-table talk, but it is only in the American families that such narrative events take on the features of a proper interaction ritual (Goffman 1976). "Today" narratives seem to combine three ritualistic features: the recurrent nature of the activity type, and the role expectations that it entails; the formulaic, repetitive language of the opening phase; and the ritual constraints governing the type of conversational contribution expected.

As an activity type, "today" narratives resemble early childhood *formats of interaction,* which are "standardized...interaction patterns between adult and infant that contain demarcated roles and eventually become reversible" (J. Bruner 1983: 120). Within the family context, the roles of demarcation cut across *insiders* and *outsiders:* thus the observer at the family dinner table has in this case no participation rights, never asks (and is not being asked) about other's or his/her own day. This is not surprising, given that "today" rituals, like early childhood interaction formats, are based on a very high level of shared assumptions of both a cognitive and an affective nature. Members of the family have basic cognitive scripts about each other's activities during the day, and they act on the assumption that deviations from such scripts (the stuff narratives are made of) are a matter of mutual interest and concern.

Theoretically, within the family circle, all members have reciprocal rights and duties to participate; but in practice, reciprocity is limited to spouses, since children either self-initiate participation or are invited by parents to do so, but as a rule fail to show the same initiative toward their parents.

Whereas childhood interaction formats act as a language acquisition support system (J. Bruner 1983), "today" narratives act as a critical socializing context for the acquisition of narrative skills. As the analysis of the texts will show, the ritual can be performed with varying degrees of success. The processes involved in causes of success or failure provide contexts of socialization in regard both to the choice of acceptable topics and to appropriate ways of telling.

The opening phase of "today" rituals is marked by clear discourse boundaries at the point of initiation. The stylistic features of the opening gambit are of a formulaic and repetitive nature, allowing for only a limited degree of lexical and syntactic variation.

Consider modes of initiation. Transition from any other topic to the "today" narrative is enacted either by an other-initiated formulaic question (some variation on *How was your day?*), or by a self-initiated *today + action verb* phrase ("I had lunch at the Parka today").

(3) American family 6: The children are Andrew (10m), Jessica (8f), and Joshua (3m). This "today" story is the first, to be followed by several others at the same meal.

1 Father: Jessie, how was your day?

2 Joshua: Ooooh aaah

3 Mother: What was the best part of your day, Jessie?

4 Jessica: After lunch.

5 Joshua: I get xxx

6 Jessica: xxx

7 Father: You were out playing in the rain.

8 Jessica: Uh-huh. [=! affirmative]

9 Mother: Do you have your templates, Jessie?

10 Jessica: XXX

11 Father: [=! talking to Andrew] Really? What happened after lunch? You left for the beach yesterday?

The transition from the previous topic is often minimally marked by the use of a discourse marker (cf. Schiffrin 1987), e.g. *so.*

(4) American family 2: Present are also the children: Daniel (6m), Marvin (8m), and Tamara (3f).

1 Father: So, Tamara, what did you do today?

2 Mother: <xx help yourself> [>]

3 Father: What'd you do today, Tamara?> [<]

End@

(5) American family 7: The children are Aaron (9.5m) and Abigail (7f).

1 Mother: So what did you accomplish today?

2 Father: xxx

3 Aaron: Uh, uh.

4 Father: Yes

5 Mother: Yes [=laughing]

6 Father: Well #

[Story]

The salience of the ritual becomes particularly evident through self-nomination. The right for telling your day is implicitly felt to be equally shared, as voiced by 4-year-old Sandra. With no preliminaries, Sandra at some point in the middle of the dinner turns to her mother and asks a question.

(6) American family 4: The children are Jordan (7.5m) and Sandra (4f). Sandra's initiation takes place half an hour into the dinner.

1 Sandra: Mommy to who will I tell how my day goes?

2 Mother: OK let's hear your day

3 Sandra: Well # I xxx played puzzles xxx I made xxx [continued]

Sandra's question shows that she is already aware of her rights for displaying her day, and moreover that she offers her day as a gift to be received. It is the duty of her family to appoint a receiver for the gift; and indeed, her mother acknowledges the gift, accepting it on behalf of all present (*Okay, let's hear your day*), thereby giving the signal for the ritual to begin. In other words, the ritual requirement in the case of self-nomination is for recipients to display positive acceptance—not only yielding the floor for the teller, as is the case in all narratives, but also paying homage to the specific offering made.

In other-initiated narratives, the opening gambit creates a slot that the recipient is expected to fill with a narrative of the *doings* and *accomplishments* of the day. In this way the ritual constraint that operates determines the type of contribution expected from both initiators and respondents. In ex. 4, the child is *probed to conform* to this *conversational demand* (cf. Dascal 1983: 109), while in ex. 5 the adult provides the expected narrative. What distinguishes the family "today" ritual from similar rhetorical routines in other types of interaction (e.g., *How was your weekend?* at the office) is apparently the notion of accountability. In the family, a question like *How was your day?*, especially when addressed to children, implicitly invites a narrative no less than does an explicit query about the day's happenings. In other contexts, of course, a narrative may be neither invited nor much wanted. It is through the notion of accountability that we can understand how somebody's day can be topicalized, objectified, distanced, and contemplated with care.

(7) American family 8: The children are Jared (11m) and Robin (9f). The mother's move follows a request from Robin to change the subject discussed previously.

1 Mother: I want to talk to Jared about his day, because he said it was so horrible.

2 Jared: It was not horrible, it was just boring.

3 Mother: Why was it boring Jared?

4	Jared:	It was really [//] actually that's not quite true. This person who studies lungs came in for science +\
5	Mother:	Lungs?
6	Jared:	Yeah, and she said [//] she showed us some slides and brought in a plastic dog's lung

[continued]

As these examples show, both children and spouses are invited to participate in the ritual. But as noted, nomination rights are not quite equally distributed. We encountered only one instance where a child tries to nominate a parent, rather than vice versa.

(8) American family 7: The children are Aaron (9.5m) and Abigail (7f).

1	Aaron:	What happened at work today Mother?
2	Mother:	Well I bet you, one power trouble at work today.
3	Aaron:	Oh really. [=! laughs]
4	Mother:	[=! laughs] Oh God
5	Abigail:	You should drop your jobbie.
6	Mother:	I know.
7	? :	Drop your jobbie.

END@

This example shows one way in which the ritual may fail: neither party (certainly not the mother) seems to consider the question as a serious attempt to initiate a "today" ritual. When no narrative comes forth, another child offers a personal comment (T5), which serves to change the topic. In the case of successful "today" narratives, the same slot often is filled by prompts to continue, worded in no less formulaic ways than initiations.

(9) American family 4: Sandra is 4; also present is Jordan (7.5m).

1	Father:	So what else did you do today Sandra?
2	Sandra:	Um xx beads, puzzles and I played clock

[continued]

(10) American family 4.

1 Mother: What else did you do today, dear?

2 Father: That's all.

Such constraints on initiation and participation rights, as well as on modes of telling, turn "today" narrative events into clearly delimited speech events that impose specific rights and duties on all participants. For the gift of a *today story* to be well received, it must be a substantial gift. The first operating constraint is one of selection. Not all the day's happenings are worthy of telling: adults explicitly call upon nominated tellers to exercise criteria of interest in regard to the tale before launching into the telling; thus 8-year-old Jessica (T3 in ex. 3) is asked to tell *the best part of her day*. A long account of a soccer game by an 8-year-old boy is interrupted as follows.

(11) American family 4: Jordan is 7.5.

Father: Jordan, would you like to tell us something? Other than soccer, what happened today?

Child tellers are required to order the day's happenings by relevance (*Tell us the worst/best part of your day; What were the highlights of your day?*) prior to foregrounding one particular chain of events as a narrative topic. Children are also explicitly socialized in modes of telling. They are required, in the terms of Genette 1980, to turn *stories* into true *narratives*. An extreme example of this process is illustrated by the narrative event I refer to as "Everybody's Day."

(12) Everybody's day: American family 5. The family has three children: Dorothy (13f), Beatrice (10f) (also called Harriet), and Matthew (4m).

1 Father: So how was your day Harriet? <You're supposed + \> [>]

2 Bea: <Daddy [=! offended]> [<].

3 Father: What?

4 Bea: Cut that out. [%com: Bea does not like to be called Harriet]

5 Father: You're supposed to say "Oh it was wonderful xxx"

6 Bea: Daddy [=! annoyed] no lozzie [unclear ?] [/] <lozzie> [?][>]

[=! laughs].

7 Father: <=! laughs> [<]

8 Mother: xx Why don't you tell us about your day now?

9 Matthew: My [//] your day.

10 Bea: Mine?

11 Matthew: xxx.

12. Father: Your first?

13 Matthew: And your tenth.

14 Father: Oh [=! laughs].

15 Matthew: Bea tell your day.

16 Bea: I woke up and I got dressed and xxx [=! speaks very softly].

17 Matthew: What?

18 Father: Speak up.

19 Bea: # um # I woke up and got dressed and went to xx xx

20 Father: You didn't bother to eat any of breakfast or lunch?

21 Bea: Nope.

22 Father: And I made you such nice French toast too.

23 Matthew: No then <my day!> [>].

24 Father: <Oh is it your turn now?> [<]¬

25 Matthew: After Bea comes me [=! laughter]# my day # washed and woke up # then go do nothing # then googo then dodo [=! laughs].

26 Father: Matthew!

27 Matthew: Oh [=! laughs]

28 Father: You can do any of that # whatever it was.

29 Dorothy: Matthew now # can I go?

30 Matthew: No. First I wake up # then go to bed # then wake up<then go to bed # then I wake up # then go to bed> [>] [=! laughing].

31 Father: Oh [=! laughs] <you just lost your turn> [<]

32 Matthew: First I wake up # then + \

33 Bea: Matthew!

34 Father: No, stop.

35 Matthew: xxx.

36 Bea: Matthew you had a very <boring day> [>].

37 Matthew: <Here go Mommy> [<]

38 Father: First I wake up # then I go to nursery school

%com: [=! imitates the way Matthew speaks]

39 Mother: Listen to this family.

40 Mother: First I woke up and then had breakfast.

41 Matthew: Then you had nothing [=! laughs].

42 Mother: Then I had my shower.

43 Matthew: Then you had nothing [=! laughs].

44 Mother: Then I did the wash. I made the lasagne+…

45 Dorothy: Now it's my turn Matthew.

46 Father: First I ate breakfast # then I got up.

47 Bea: Daddy [=! annoyed tone].

48 Mother: Oh [=! laughs].

49 Father: Then I didn't take a shower. Then I brushed my teeth # then I went outside # then I got dressed +\

50 Bea: Daddy [=! shouting]!

51 Mother: Oh [=! laughs].

52 Father: Then I took my shoes off and put my pajamas back on # went to the basement # did some work # caught a pigeon # <made the pigeon for lunch> [>]

53 Matthew: <Oh [=! laughs]> [<].

54 Father: <Then I drove you all to> [<] [/] then I [/] then I went to # Woolworth's bought something that I had to return later in the day as usual because I always have to return everything I buy.

55 Bea: You can't buy things.

56 Father: um # then we went to the library.

57 Bea: And found nothing.

58 Father: And I went with a girl who found nothing. Then we went out <of the library +\> [>]

59 Bea: <Okay> [=! shouted]!

[Turns into a discussion about whose books are on whose library card]

"Everybody's day" displays the typical features of the "today" ritual in its insistence on equality in rights of participation (on turn-taking, see particularly T24, T25, T29, T45), on the repetition of the formulaic questions (T1, T8, T15), and on the type of sequential coherence built up from "your day" questions responded to by action verb series. But it is a ritual gone sour, negative rather than positive in affective outcomes.

Several indicators in the discourse combine to show us what is going wrong, and thereby also reveal underlying norms for how it should have gone. First, there is a double message in the father's initiation: he uses the formulaic *How was your day?* but prefixes it with an unusual term of address (which his daughter does not like), and follows it with a metacommunicative statement (*you're supposed to say...*). He thus sets a playful tone for the interaction, implying that it is not to be taken seriously. But the mother shifts the key back to a serious tone (T8), and the children spend a considerable amount of metacommunicative energy—in line with the general tendency of American family dinner talk to topicalize turn-taking (Blum-Kulka and Sheffer 1993)—arguing for their share in the family's "today" narrative space.

By shifting the argument constantly from the realm of telling, in which the issue at hand is a share in the "today" ritual, to the realm of conversation, in which the issue is floor management, the speakers indicate most clearly a dissatisfaction with the unfolding of the event. Thus, in T23, Matthew claims his share in the ritual of telling one's day; his utterance is an attempt to enter this specific telling realm. His father's response, *Oh, is it your turn now?*, switches back to the realm of conversation, thereby implicitly inviting talk for talk's sake rather than compliance with the demanding task (in terms of content) of telling one's day. In T24, the framing of the event shifts from the frame of telling one's days, in which it is meaningful to exchange and evaluate personally owned days, to the loosely defined frame "talk about the day," in which the focus is on having a share in the talk, rather than on telling one's own day. Subsequently, the realm of the tale is affected as well, yielding extremely poor "today" stories in terms of information.

The first child to speak on the topic, Beatrice (T16-22), fails to provide an interesting narrative; she is interrupted by her younger brother, Matthew (T23), who is dismissed (T33-34) as having defied expectation for making a substantial contribution of any kind. While Beatrice still conforms to the rules, though not very successfully, Matthew steps out of the rules completely. Deliberately or not, his account actually parodies both the requirement for informative substance (T25, T31) and relevance. His father dismisses him by moving from the realm of telling to the realm of conversation, negating a conversational turn that fails the "today" requirement (*You just lost your turn*); but Beatrice's evaluation of the tale (*Matthew you had a very boring day*) implies a critique of the teller as principal (T36). The mother's metacomment in T39 (*Listen to this family*) suggests an awareness that things have gone wrong; yet her own attempt at a change of *footing* (Goffman 1974: 124-60) goes back to the earnest, but not good enough, report mode earlier initiated by her daughter (compare T16 to T40 and T44).

The event culminates with the father giving an echoed, free indirect speech, mocking imitation of Matthew's account (T38), only to go on (T46ff.) to offer a parodized version of a "today" report of his own. Framing the report as a parody of the real thing is indicated by an unlikely reversal of chronology (*First I ate breakfast then I got up*), followed by the negation of an event (*then I didn't take a shower*). Audience response (T47, 48, 50, 53) wavers between clear annoyance, which in the case of the daughter may mean taking offense (see T47), and laughter, which seems to indicate in this case that both mother and son align with the father's choice of telling-frame.

The overall message of this failed narrative event relates to tales, telling, and tellers. In regard to the tale, it evokes the requirements of "today" tellability: to provide a significant contribution to the ritual, you have to select, order, and dramatize the events of the day. A failure to do so shifts the focus of the narrative event from the realm of telling back to the realm of conversation, and changes its key; these transformations result in the disintegration of the "today" ritual. Tellers, encompassing in this event both the role of animator and an accountable principle (Goffman 1981), are highly vulnerable to such transformations, finding themselves being challenged both on account of their roles (e.g. *boring day*) and their participation in the telling.

What is the overall function of the "today" rituals in the American families? In terms of discourse goals, they occupy a curious place between transactional and interactional speech (Brown and Yule 1983: 1-2). The role of the ritualistic question *How was your X* can set off different types of speech events. In case it is completed in a two-move exchange, as might be the case among co-workers in an office situation, we have before us an interaction ritual (in Goffman's sense) that will tend to serve mainly phatic interactional goals, aimed predominantly at the maintenance of social relations, rather than the transmission of information. But in the family the same question sets off very different kinds of expectations. Here the transmission of (narratively filtered) information is not only tolerated, but actually required, and the interactional goal achievable is not just social harmony but rather "affective convergence" (Aston 1988: 255). The ritualistic mode seems to satisfy this variety of expectations; it provides conventionalized ways for the show of reciprocal interest and affect in the family, while simultaneously serving as a socializing context for transmitting cultural notions of appropriate ways to transform tales into telling.

In contrast, the Israeli time-framed narratives exhibit only few of the features of the "today" ritual. We do find that the activity type is enacted, especially by parents asking their children about the activities of the day. As in the American families, such questions expect a response in the form of a narrative, rather than phatically. Failure to provide a narrative is responded to by further probing (see T4, 5, 8 in ex. 13).

(13) Israeli family 4: The family has two daughters, Ruti (12f) and Naomi (8f), and one son, Yaron (4m).

1 Mother: Yaron # tesaper lanu <ma asita ha-yom ba-gan> [>]
Yaron, tell us what you <did in school today> [>]

2 Ruti: <ma [//] ex haya ba-gan> [<] <What [//] how was school> [<]

3 Yaron: naim Pleasant.

4 Mother: naim? ma haya naim? tesaper lanu ex haya naim? Pleasant? What was pleasant?

Tell us how it was pleasant.

5 Yaron: sixaknu We played.

6 Mother: be-ma sixaktem? What did you play with?

7 Yaron:	be-misxakim.	With games.
8 Mother:	eze? ba-xuc? ba-xacer?	
	[continued]	Which? outside? in the yard?

But initiation of such narrative events varies with child and family. Transition to a narrative concerned with the day's happenings is initiated either by a variant of *What did you do in school (today)?*, as in ex. 13, or more typically, by a topically specific question, as in ex. 14.

(14) Israeli family 6, with twin girls aged 6: Lilax and Iris.

Father:	lean halaxtem hayom be-shiur teva?	Where did you go today during your "nature" lesson?
Lilax:	la-giva hazoti she-pa'am she-avra halaxnu	
[continued]	To this hill that we went to last time.	

The time marker *today* tends to appear in stories about children, rather than by children in response to "today" elicitations. An example is a story told mainly by a mother, with some participation from a child, about the adventure her 4-year-old daughter had at school when a rooster jumped on her; or a story, again told by a mother, about how 6-year-old Rami missed the bus to school. The need to mark narratives temporally tends to be reserved by Israelis for stories from the past. One device is the use of *pa'am;* literally *pa'am* means 'once'; and as in English, it figures in conventional story beginnings. Examples from the family narratives vary in topic, as seen in ex. 15-17.

(15) Israeli family 2: The children are Shlomit (12f), Riki (10f), and Mika (5f).

Father:	hayiti pa'am be-shuk aravi ve-ani halaxti liknot kishuim vehayu sham
[continued]	I visited once an Arab market and I went to buy some zucchini and there were

(16) Israeli family 2:

Mika:	any roca lesaper bedixa. pa'am axat halax ish	I want to tell a joke. Once a man went...

(17) Israeli family 1: Yoash is a guest, a friend of the family.

Yoash: shamati pa'am et ex korim la, hagveret Milo

[continued] I once heard, what's her name, Mrs. Milo

Other time-marking devices used include concrete specifications of time (*last week/yesterday/last year/about a month ago*), as well as sequential ordering of events relative to self (*the first time I went to the University*).

Talk about the day's activities lacks the ritual constraints on participation structure: we found no indication in the Israeli discourse of an expectation for all to participate, as in the American families. What seem to be missing are both the accountability requirement, in regard to the most recent time frame, and the expectation for a display of reciprocal interest in each other's day.

The difference between the two groups in regard to "today" narratives reflects to some extent a wider cultural difference in the way verbal elements of social interaction are conventionalized. Relative to Israeli society, American social interaction seems much more governed by situationally conventionalized scripts (see Blum-Kulka 1992 for elaboration), which in turn pale by comparison with the degree of linguistic conventionalization observed for Japanese social behavior (Ide 1987). From this perspective, *How was your day,* apart from its broader cultural and familial functions, is yet one more instance of the rich repertoire of routinized interaction rituals in the United States.

Cultural Styles of Collaboration

Issues of Co-Ownership vs. Co-Performance

The degree of participation in the telling raises the issue of how access to the information contained in the tale, i.e. the *tale-ownership,* is related to the *entitlement* to tell the story (Shuman 1986: 137-41). In other words, whose stories in the family are told by whom and to whom? In discussing narratives that call for audience response, Sacks (1978: 261) notes that it is the "involvement in it [the story] that provides for the story's telling." Personal experience grants ownership, and shared experience grants joint ownership: "Parties who have experienced an event together are jointly in a position to describe it to someone else" (Goodwin 1981: 159). As noted by Miller et al. (1990:

298), "The conditions giving rise to joint ownership are more likely to occur in intimate relations than in non-intimate ones." Members of the family, being part of an intimate network, come to the dinner table with knowledge of both shared and unshared events. Although the conditions for claiming joint ownership may be met, the fact that several people are in a position to tell a story does not result necessarily in joint performance: Mothers regularly tell stories *about* children in the presence of the children (Miller et al. 1990), claiming sole performance rights on jointly *owned* stories. The reverse may be true as well: at least during the dinner-table conversations studied here, highly involved audience response to a story of personal experience (or knowledge) may turn the telling into a joint performance, implying a process-motivated claim to joint ownership. Hence ownership rights through access to the tale have no one-to-one correspondence to performance rights through access to the telling.

As the first step in exploring the interrelations between these two dimensions, I consider each independently, and then explore the culturally preferred intersections observed in the family narratives.

One way to approach story ownership is by considering access to the knowledge of the events recounted: is the narrated event (the fabula) known to the teller only, or is it shared by any other participants? Abstracting the nature of the narrated events from the verbal narratives by considering textual indicators, we follow Labov and Fanshel (1977: 62-4) in distinguishing individually known *A-events* (known to teller only) from two-party shared *A-B events* (known to teller and one other participant) and generally known *O-events*. Specific to the family scene is a fourth type of fabula, *F-events,* which are shared by all members of the family.[10] A breakdown of the data using these categories, as presented in Figure 8, suggests that Americans and Israelis only partially share attitudes regarding the degree of novelty expected from narratives around the dinner table.

In both groups, A-events dominate (66% and 69%). This is not surprising, given that dinner time provides a unique opportunity for all to share personal experiences with intimates. Family dinners with young children do not seem to occasion stories concerned with the state of the world; O-event narratives are almost absent from this speech event. For Americans, the next most frequent category following A-events is A-B events (30%). For the most part, these recount events experienced jointly by a child and one of the parents. For the American families, there is a marginal 3.5% of F-event stories. On the other hand, for the

Israelis, F-event narratives prove a viable category, representing 9% of all stories told. It is interesting to note that, for Israelis, the percentage of F-event narratives in child-involved narratives rises to 15%, while in the equivalent set of American stories it drops to 2%.

Figure 8
Tale event-types

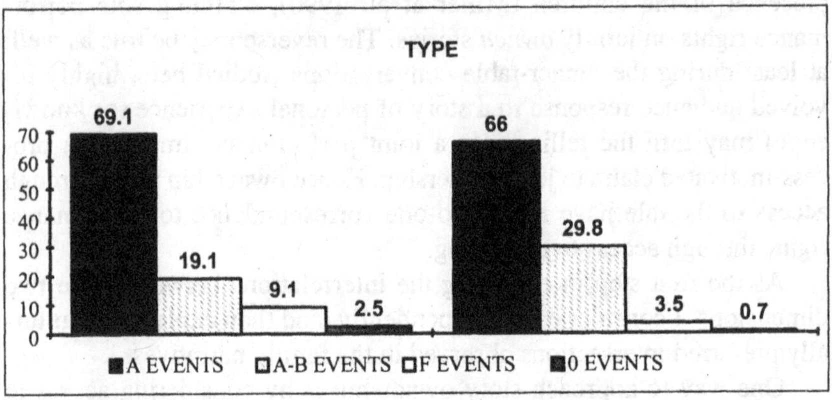

Consider now modes of performance. We can distinguish three major modes of telling: *monologic, dialogic,* and *polyphonic.* Even though family narrative events are jointly constructed affairs, styles of collaborations vary from low to high participation by participants other than the primary narrator(s). At the dominantly single-voice end of the continuum, we find monologic narratives, in which one primary narrator remains in control of the floor throughout the event. The audience at such events responds indirectly, sustaining the telling but not involved in the tale. At the multi-voiced, polyphonic end, we find narratives that defy the distinction of primary vs. secondary narrator(s), being constructed in close collaboration between several participants. Between these two ends, we find dialogic narrations, constructed typically through a question/answer format.

A multiplicity of voices at the level of telling (in the polyphonic mode) can also transform relations between tellers. In the terms of Goffman (1974: 127), the audience at such events is transformed into "fellow performers" who become "inhabitants of the same realm." For Tannen (1989: 12), it is an issue of involvement: "an internal, even emotional connection individuals feel which binds them together to other people as well as to places, things, activities, ideas, memories and words. However,...[it is] not a given but an achievement in conversational interaction." In Tannen's analysis of a dinner conversation between friends (1984) she found this achievement of high involvement through conversation style to characterize the three Eastern-European Jewish speakers present.

Monologic narratives tend to be self-initiated, though they may follow a question from another participant. For example, in the Robbery Story analyzed by Polanyi (1989: 66), the topic is put forward by a participant other than the storyteller, appealing to the appointed participant's expertise on the events to be narrated. Turning to the two women who got robbed, their friend asks: "I heard secondhand or whatever that you got robbed.—Yeah.—What happened?" Nor do tellers of monologic narratives necessarily have to claim experiential warrants for the tale—although, around the dinner table, tales do tend to be stories of personal experience. The distinctive feature of monologic narratives is the recognizability of a single narrator's voice.

In the dialogic mode, narration proceeds through a question/answer format, whether the story is self- or other-initiated. This is the mode that children use to tell stories from the very early stages of language acquisition (Ninio 1988, Sachs 1979). A well-documented subset of such stories is the joint evocation of shared events, in which the caretaker and the child jointly recount the story (Heath 1982, Snow 1991). But whether or not the events to be recounted are known to both adult and child, elicited narratives with young children tend to remain collaborative, with story contributions distributed between adult and child (Snow and Goldfield 1982).

Polyphonic narration is enacted in principle through both co-performance and co-ownership. Co-performance requires access to the tale, or at least shared access to its social context. This access takes into account an individual teller's *information state* (cf. Goffman 1974: 133) as to "why events have happened as they have," as well as participant's familiarity with the underlying sociocultural scripts that make narratives "ring true with the stories they know to be true in their lives" (Fisher 1987: 63). Co-ownership may be culturally interpreted as entitling all co-owners with story-telling rights (but not necessarily so; see Miller et al. 1990, Shuman 1986).[11] The outcome will be a jointly constructed narrative, where division lines between primary and secondary narrators are blurred. The issue of telling rights in such cases may vary culturally in regard to all participants, or only in regard to children. If children are included in the circle of right-holders, a child may feel licensed to contribute on topics felt relevant, whether the story is initiated by an adult or another child.

Israelis and Americans seem to differ in preferences for these three modes of performance. Quantitative analysis of a subsample of the narratives included here (Blum-Kulka and Snow 1992) shows that Americans prefer the monologic, display mode in 60% of the cases, with a preference for the dialogic mode in 29%. Israelis, by contrast, make use of all three styles, preferring both the dialogic (49%) and the polyphonic (30%) to the monologic (24%).[12]

Table 1
Styles of participation

	Mode	
Event-type	Polyphonic	Monologic
Shared	Israeli/American	American
Unshared	Israeli	Israeli\American

But the cultural difference in regard to both ownership and performance rights is revealed mainly in the diverse ways the groups interpret the relationship between these two dimensions. Excluding dialogic, typically adult/child narration from this analysis, we can detect four types of interaction between access to the tale and participation in the telling. In the following I argue that the two groups differ in their preferences for these, as shown in Table 1.

Among the four possible configurations between event type and mode of telling, Israeli and American narratives seem to share two: telling shared experiences collaboratively in the polyphonic mode, and allowing predominantly solo performances of personally known stories. However, the American families support monologic performances even when tales are known to more than one participant; and Israeli narration may unfold in a highly collaborative way, even in unshared tales.

The distribution among these four modes shows these preferences as representing a gradient phenomenon; see Figure 9. In both groups, shared experiences told collaboratively and single experiences told monologically constitute the bulk of narrative events (77% for Israelis, 84% for Americans). For Israelis, the third choice is to tell unshared events in a polyphonic mode (18%); for Americans, it is to tell shared events in the monologic mode (12%). In the following, I illustrate the way cultural styles are manifested within each of the two major modes of telling.

Figure 9
Ownership vs. performance in telling tales

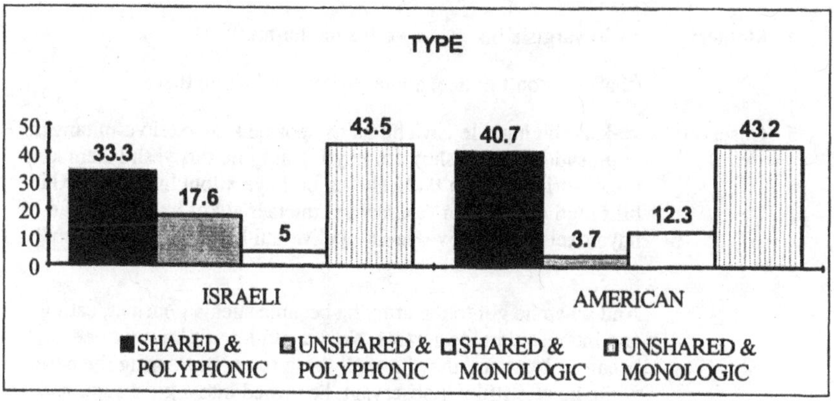

The Monologic Mode: Telling Shared and Unshared Events

A culturally shared and highly prevalent mode of telling (43% for both groups) is the dominantly monologic performance granted occasionally to sole tellers who recount (mostly but not exclusively) personal experience. In one such case, an Israeli woman describes in great detail the nightmarish dream she had about getting lost on one of the campuses of the Hebrew University in Jerusalem. In another instance, an American teenage girl recounts a confrontation she had with a teacher in school. In the following example, the story offered by the observer terminates a series of stories concerning memories of food from childhood, all embedded in members' attitudes towards the religious practices of the parent and grandparent generations.

(18) Israeli family 1: The children are Nadav (11m) and Jonathan (10m). The segment follows several exchanges concerning food and eating habits.

1 Observer: aval ha-ax sheli Avner haya noda be-bareranuto be-oxel. hu mamash hayu shlosha dvarim she-hu axal ve-zehu.

But my brother Avner was well-known for his pickiness in food. There were actually three things he ate and that's it.

2 Mother: ma? What?

3 Observer: chips ve-stek ze haya ha-xx, ve-ani zoxeret she-od basar bishvil she-hu yoxal basar notnim lo. Sonya hayta notenet lo avatiax be-onat ha-avatixim xotexet lo she-yaani kaxa + \

Chips and steak it was xx # And I remember that more meat so he'll eat meat they would give him. Sonya [%com: Sonya is the teller's stepmother] would serve him watermelon in season # would cut it so + \

4 Mother: ++ lo yargish. bis-me-ze ve-bis me-ha-hu.

(that) he won't notice; a bite ¬ here and a bite there.

5 Observer: ve-kshe-hu higia le-cava hu na'asa gorme kaze oxel ve-mitanyen be-misadot. hayom shuv ani lo yoda'at ki hu dos yesh lahem kol mine isurim, aval ba-tkufa she-hu od haya xiloni hu na'asa axlan bilti ragil ve-hu amar "axshav ani mictaer al kol ha-shanim she-haya oxel kol kax tov <ve-ani. [>] ve-ani lo neheneti me-klum."

And when he got to the army he became such a gourmet, eating and interested in restaurants. Now again I don't know, since he became observant, they have all these rules. But during the period while he was still nonobservant, he turned into a great eater and said, "Now I'm sorry for all these years when there was such good food and I, and I didn't enjoy it at all."

6 Mother: <ken?> [<] <Yes?>

7 Nadav: ani af pa'am lo ectaer. I shall never regret it. ¬

8 Observer: lo # kol ze ba lomar lax she-ata lo yaxol lada'at ma yihye be-od + |
@End

All this means that you can never know what will happen in an other + \

The story of Avner, the non-eating child transformed into a gourmet adult—only to lose access (from the teller's point of view) to gourmet food, through newly acquired religious practices—is exceptionally rich in cultural themes, negotiating transitions between life cycles in the Israeli context (child/soldier/adult) and Jewish life styles (non-observant/observant); see Polanyi (1989) for analysis of cultural themes in American stories. For the purposes of the present analysis, the mode of telling is of interest. The example illustrates that, even in the monologic mode, when recounting unshared events, Israeli audience response goes beyond brief *uptakers* (Edmondson and House, 1981). In T4, the evaluative detail added by the mother is her own logical inference, never mentioned by the main teller. The child's comment in T7 indicates how carefully he had been listening to the story; in the Israeli families, children typically act as active audience to all stories told, regardless of tellers (adults or children) and topic. In the American families, child participation in the role of active audience seems more restricted to child-related topics (Blum-Kulka and Snow 1992).

In the American families, monologic telling is not restricted to unshared events. In 12% of the American (non-dialogic) narrative events, a sole performer is granted telling rights for a tale; this happens in only 5% of the parallel cases in the Israeli families. Consider the following personal experience narratives told with the explicit purpose of entertaining.

(19) The bug: American family 3. The children are Samuel (10m), Joshua (6m). Talk on hikes precedes this segment.

1 Mother: Daniel loves that.

%com: [Daniel is her husband]

2 Samuel: Really?

3 Mother: I on the other hand [//] He loves to commune with nature. Me, I can take nature through a glass window.

4 Samuel: xxx

5 Mother: A glass window # with the bugs out # and anything that's more ¬ than four feet removing themselves from my presence I can't deal with them [=! laughs]. We had a bug once in the shower # and Samuel called me in on a Friday afternoon # wouldn't you know it # and he screams "Ma!" and there is this thing # if it wasn't two inches big # I thought it was the most disgusting and somehow as disgusting as they are small # they get worse when they get larger # and there I was # it wasn't even afraid # it wasn't running # it was taking its time # it was sort of taking a little walk across the shower. I would at least appreciate it if they were afraid + /

6 Observer: But no. ¬

7 Mother: +^But no, it sat there, very territorially, so I said "Get rid of it,:" he said "I'm not getting rid of it, you get rid of it," and of course Daniel was nowhere around.

8 Observer: Of course, right. ¬

9 Mother: So we had to shpritz it to death.

10 Observer: Of course. ¬

11 Mother: Oh, it was horrible, and the darn thing was so resilient it wouldn't die, you know I find that absolutely appalling +\

12 Observer: It wasn't xxx

13 Mother: That's right, well by the time we finish with them, they would be + … Cockroaches are going to inherit this earth one of these days.

14 Father: Well, you weren't using insecticide though.

15 Mother: I was using mildew spray xxx and that bug had the nerve to walk around in it yet # but finally it gave up # the ghost # and then we had to dispose of it. So I said "Go ahead # Samuel # dispose of it." He says "I'm not touching it # you touch it." So I took it out with thirty layers of tissue # so that I wouldn't even feel its shape and I picked it up and I threw it into the bathroom toilet.

16 Observer: She hasn't gotten over it.

17 Mother: I'm still thinking about it. I can see that bug # and I have visions of it rising up yet like a phoenix to haunt me.

END@

The Bug Story is initiated by the mother, who remains the primary narrator for its duration. Though both father and older son (Samuel) are familiar with the events, audience response is limited to sustaining the act of telling through appropriate backchanneling and clarification comments (T6, T8, T10, T12, T16). The teller's comment on her relations with nature (*I can take nature through a glass window*, T3) serves as bridging talk to introduce her dramatic encounter with a spider in her bathroom on a Friday afternoon. She then manages to entertain her listeners by using several evaluative devices to highlight the turning points of her narratives (e.g. direct quotes, a shift to the use of the present tense; see T5, T7). Her efforts are fully appreciated—as can be seen by audience reactions in T6, T8, and T16. Finally, she concludes by providing a Labovin coda (Labov and Waletsky 1967: 39); visions of the bug rising like a phoenix clearly link the past to the present.

The Bug Story shows that co-ownership of the tale does not necessarily entail equal rights for the telling. Narrative events can distinguish tellers from experiencers. In the Bug Story, the teller is the chief but not sole experiencer in the events narrated; yet she is granted full telling rights, foregrounding her story-telling skills as individual performer.

The Polyphonic Mode: Telling Shared and Unshared Events

As listeners, we tend to expect collaboration in the telling when access to the tale is shared by several of the participants. Thus stories about a couple's trip abroad may be told to friends jointly, or in a monologic style, but with frequent interceptions from the other "knowing" participant. Shared ownership of the tale in the family may cut across generations, or create ownership affiliations between any group of members, either by true experience or by claimed familiarity with the events. Events that happen to parents jointly, prior to their children's birth, are one source for generationally defined ownership. In one case, the story of the parents' courtship is told in collaboration by both parents in response to a 10-year-old's question: *ex at ve-aba higatem le-ahava me-aruxat-erev pshuta?* "How did you and Dad come to be in love from a simple dinner?"

The story of the parents' courtship is an example of the type of narrative which may be told again and again, because of its relevance to the history of the family. Memories from a shared past carry the potential to become part of the familial narrative repertoire, their telling triggered by the presence of a new audience. Our presence at the dinner table might have occasioned the retelling or construction of several such *family fables.* Consider the potential of the following recollection of a family reunion as a candidate for being or becoming a family fable.

(20) American family 7: Children are Aaron (9.5m) and Abigail (7f).

1 Father: Yeah # anyway we had a big family reunion.

2 Abigail: What's a family reunion? [= softly]

3 Mother: That was all the members of the family [//] all relations.

4 Father: Well # you can't be more specific.

5 Mother: Not all.

6 Abigail: All the members of his side of the family. ¬

7 Father: Yes # it was all of my father's [//] my father and both of his sisters and all their children # and all the grandchildren.

8 Aaron: We were one of the grandchildren # right? ¬

9 Father: Right.

10 Mother: Um hm.

11 Father: So all these people were at this big reunion. And there wasn't enough room to sleep inside the house. So a lot of people bought # had or rented.

12 Mother: Rented. Nobody had # everybody rented.

13 Father: Yeah? Everybody rented RVs, which are these motor homes which you sleep in. And are not real comfortable.

14 Mother: And they're not real private.

15 Father: xx didn't seem to mind.

16 Mother:	Well you just [//] you were so shy Abigail # you wouldn't talk ¬ to anybody. And you just stayed inside the RV and you never wanted to come out # see everybody. You just wanted to stay inside and read books and play with your toys.
17 Aaron:	She could read then?
18 Mother:	Well she had some books that she looked at the pictures # you know.
19 Aaron:	Yeah.
20 Abigail:	Picture book? Picture book?
21 Aaron:	Pretended to read # pretended she was grown up.
22 Mother:	Uh huh. And when anybody tried to talk to you # you'd run away and hide in the RV.
23 Father:	Except for Pearson.
24 Abigail:	Yeah in the RV I would go. ¬
25 Father:	You visited xxx P. He picked you up. xxx feet and sat you on his back xxx started asking you about the pictures.
26 Abigail:	Huh
27 Father:	You succumbed to his charms. xxx have [=! laughter]
	END@

The polyphonic mode of telling is particularly suitable for stories that have the family "us" as protagonist, and which are relevant in terms of contribution to the building of familial and individual identities. The Family Reunion story is not about self or other, but rather reflexively about "us," the family, and the way we were then. Its relevance stems from stressing family continuity: it seems to be saying, "Here is something we did together, even if you children do not remember it all." Revealing several sides of Abigail's younger personality, the story is particularly relevant for the child protagonist: it provides her with a sense of the continuity of the self, combined with the opportunity to reflect on her younger self as compared with her current self. The suggested key for reflection is a humorous one; the child is invited to join the others in laughing at her own shyness then, and the attraction that broke it. The text contains indicators that the story has been told previously. Abigail's first contribution to the narrative (*all the members of his side of the family*, T6) suggests familiarity with the tale, or at least parts of it. A later remark (*yeah in the RV I would go,*

T24) can be taken either as her recollection of the events, or as her acceptance of her parents' version. The story is thus on its way to becoming a family fable.

Telling is carried by both parents, with a shift in appointed audiences. The father seems to be talking first to the Observer; but the mother deliberately shifts perspective, appointing Abigail, the heroine of the story, as primary audience (*you were so shy Abigail,* T16). Aaron, the older brother, takes the role of the challenger, doubting his mother's version (*She could read then?* T17)—and once reassured, insisting on his sister's limitations ([*She*] *pretended to read,* T21). The mother aligns with her son by picking up the 3rd person reference to Abigail (*Well she had some books,* T18); then, treating the exchange with Aaron as a "side-sequence" (Jefferson 1972), she shifts back to addressing Abigail directly. Thus, although in different narrative roles, eventually all family members collaborate in constructing a narrative that may well become part of the family's fable repertoire.

In the Israeli narratives, by contrast, sharing the tale is no prerequisite for participation in the telling. Even when the specific events are strictly of the A-event, "only teller knows" type, in the family they are told against the background of shared sociocultural scripts which in turn provide occasions for nonexperiencer participation. Israeli dinner-table participants seem to take full advantage of their familiarity with such scripts. In 18% of the (non-dialogic) Israeli narrative events, singular tales get a polyphonic telling. In the American families, we detected only three such examples (4%). In the following narrative, the fact that the story concerns an A-event does not prevent other members from taking an active part in the construction of the story.

(21) *Saving a watermelon:* Israeli family 4. The family has two daughters (Ruti, 11, and Naomi, 8) and one son (Yaron, 4). The story follows an account of a car accident the mother was involved in the same day.

1 Father: ani etmol [/] ani etmol hicalti avatiax.
I yesterday [/] I saved a watermelon yesterday.

2 Observer: Oh [=! laughs]

3 Naomi: ex [/] ex? How? How?

4 Ruti: ex hu hicil? How did he save it?

5 Father: atem lo ta'aminu. ani nasati li # hayiti ba-boker # ze haya etmol # ken # hayiti hare etmol ba-boker ba-bank <lifnei hacaharayim.>[>]

You won't believe it. I was driving, in the morning, it happened yesterday, yes, I was at the bank yesterday before noon.

6 Mother: <avatiax al ha-sakin.> [<]

Watermelon by the knife. [an expression used by watermelon vendors]

7 Father: lo ze lo al ha-sakin. mazal. No, it's not by the knife. Lucky.

8 Observer: ani mekava she-lo <sikanta et acmexa> [>]

[=! laughs] I hope you didn't endanger yourself [=! laughs]

9 Father: <ve-ani nosea li> [<] me-ha-super be-giva hacarfatit # ma at mekava?

And I'm driving from the supermarket on French Hill # what do you expect?

10 Observer: she-lo sikanta et xayexa + \ That you didn't risk your life

11 Father: kimat. almost.

12 Mother: oy va-avoy li. [=! exclamation]

13 Father: be-super lemata le-kivun ha-ramzor ve-pitom ani roe holexet shamisha im ezo yalda ve-pitom ve-eze sakit mitxila lehitgalgel bamorad # ve-he-yalda roca laruc <le-sham ve-coraxat> [>] ve-ha-ima maxzika ota.

Near the Super in the direction of the traffic lights, and suddenly I see a woman walking with a child (female) and suddenly a bag starts rolling down the slope, and the child wants to run there and is yelling and her mother is holding her.

14 Observer: <ha-yalda xx [<] The child.

15 Father: az ba-hatxala lo raiti ma ze aval ze hitgalgel be-merec.

So at the beginning I didn't see what it was but it rolled with great vigor; everybody is laughing.

16 Ruti: avatiax dafuk Shitty watermelon.

17 Father: raiti [/] raiti she-lo keday la'acor et ze im ha-oto, maher acarti et ha-oto ve-racti ve-hiclaxti litfos et ha-avatiax she-hitgalgel be-tox sakit # ve-lo kara lo shum davar # bari ve-shalem hexzarti oto le-zro'ot ha-yalda.

I saw that it's not worth stopping it with the car, so I stopped the car quickly and ran, and managed to catch the watermelon that was rolling in the bag, and it came to no harm, I returned it safe and sound into the arms of the little girl.

18 Ruti: +> <ha-yalda ha-mityapaxat>.

[>] The sobbing child.

19 Mother: <acarta et ha-mexonit>> [<] [/] acarta et ha-me + \
You stopped the car, you stopped the + \

20 Father: avarti oto. acarti et ha-mexonit + \
I passed it. I stopped the car.

21 Mother: acarta ve-yaradta me-ha-mexonit ve-hicalta et ha-avatiax?
You braked, got out of the car and saved the watermelon?

22 Father: natati la avatiax ve-hicalti et xaye ha-mishpaxa sham.
I gave her a watermelon and saved the life of the family there.

23 Mother: ve-ma amru lexa ha-mishpaxa ha-zot?
And what did they say to you, this family?

24 Observer: Oh [=! laughs]

25 Father: "toda raba be'emet toda ve-shuv toda."
"Thank you very much really and thanks again."

26 Mother: be-amerika ish lo haya ose et ze.
In the States nobody would have done it.

27 Father: be-amerika avatixim ze masoret lehacil.
In the States there is a tradition to save watermelons.

28 Mother: ze rak ba-arec <mishehu yored me-ha-mexonit.> [>]
It's only here that somebody would get out of the car.

29 Father: <ma at medaberet xx> [<>] dvarim kaele + …
What are you saying, things like this…

30 Ruti: <be-amerika yesh xx xx xx> [<].
You have in the States.

31 Father: hem meod adivim ba-dvarim ha-ele.
They are very polite in these things.

32 Observer: aval avatiax, im ha-yalda hayta raca la-avatiax az haya yaxol lihyot nora mesukan.
But a watermelon, if the child would have chased the watermelon things might have become very dangerous.

33 Father: lo. hayta sham beaya, zot omeret ha-ba'aya shel ha-isha hayta o ha-avatiax o ha-yalda.

No. There was a problem. I mean the woman's problem was either the watermelon or the child.

34 Mother: ve-hi hexlita ha-yalda <be-shlav dey mukdam [>].

And she decided for the child quite early on.

35 Father: <hi hexlita ha-yalda> [<] # aval ha-yalda hexlita avatiax.

She decided (for) the child, but the child decided (for) the water melon.

END@

This story is offered as a humorous counterpoint to the preceding narrative by the mother, recounting her near escape from a car accident. The father embeds the upcoming story in the ongoing conversation by repeating the verb *save* (in the previous story, *saved from the incident*) in the new and unexpected context of *saving a watermelon.* Unlike the Bug Story, the watermelon incident is based on events known to the teller only. Yet, in the Israeli family, participants take an active part in the performance from the onset. The high level of involvement (Tannen 1984, 1989) can be glimpsed by just scanning the names of the participants making comments during the event (wife, Observer, both older children) and by noticing the high proportion of overlapped talk.

The nature of the audience participation changes with different phases of the narrative event. The event is composed of three phases: the opening (T1-13), which provides the abstract and the general setting (time and place); the main body of narrative (T14-18); and the discussion of its point (T19-35); cf. Polanyi (1989). In the opening phase (T1-13), audience response takes the form of what Tannen (1984: 118) calls "cooperative prompting": both children display interest (T3-T4), the wife debates jokingly the kind of watermelon in question (T6), and the observer expresses empathy for the teller experiencer (T8).

The teller presents the main events of the story—including setting, complication, and resolution in Labovian terms—in turns T13, T15, T17. Audience response at this stage is diminished, recipients confining themselves mainly to backchanneling.

But once the happy ending becomes evident, the audience takes on a highly active part both in embellishing the story and in debating its point. In T18, Ruti uses a phrase borrowed from the language of written Hebrew fairy tales ('the sobbing child'), which serves to dramatize the scene of the story's denouement. The child's sobbing is implied in an earlier statement by the teller ('she is yelling', T13), but is never mentioned again. This evaluation of the tale is offered because it coheres with the rest, not because the speaker has first-hand or vicarious proof for it being "true."

The point of the narrative emerges in collaboration among several participants. In response to his wife's clarification question (T21), the teller reformulates the point of the story as concerning 'the saving of a family' rather than 'saving a watermelon' (T22). In the side-sequence that follows, wife and husband disagree about the plausibility of the event taking place anywhere but in Israel. The mother's attempt to explain the narrative's coda, in terms of cross-cultural variability as regards norms of politeness (T26, T28), is rejected by both father and daughter (T29, T30, T31). Note that the girl shows her alignment with her father's position by cooperatively overlapping talk (Tannen 1984: 118) that actually completes the father's utterance (T30).

In T32-T35, the three adults return to the issue of the point of the story. By rephrasing the "true" nature of the complication as a case of real danger (T32), the Observer reinforces the transformation of the narrative's point, from being an entertaining anecdote about "saving a watermelon" to being a serious story about saving lives. The discussion foregrounds the status of the narrative as a moral construct (cf. Fisher 1987), giving it meaning through negotiating the nature of the moral dilemma at hand. Husband and wife collaborate in underscoring this new angle, by shifting perspectives (T34-35) to the viewpoint of the woman with the child, for whom the problem was one of protecting her child rather than the watermelon.

This example shows that Israeli participants do not feel restrained by non-access to actual experience to claim authorship for the story. Though the fabula of the watermelon is derived from the personal experience of the teller, the other participants in the event take a highly active part in the story's construction, especially in negotiating its macrolevel point. The process culminates in a joint agreement as to the point of the story; this agreement, as well as the high degree of participation throughout, reveal a preference for a multivoiced mode of performance in this group. But collaboration goes beyond performance: through the process of becoming *fellow performers* in the telling, participants claim joint ownership of the tale. In other words, in monologic unshared event narratives, ownership rights are reconfirmed through the telling; but in the process of a joint performance of an (initially) unshared event, ownership rights may be generated performatively through the very act of participation in the telling.

These examples show that the two groups differ in attitudes toward the relationship between ownership and performance. Israeli families reveal a flexibility in regard to both dimensions; they strive toward joint ownership for all narratives. This trend is manifested by the high degree of participation in the telling of both personal narratives and shared family events. By partaking in the construction of the story, members of the Israeli family use narrative authorship (Shuman 1986: 174-8), to make claims for joint narrative ownership.

In the Jewish-American families, however, participation in the telling seems preconditioned by joint access to the tale. Thus, the recollection of shared family memories (the Family Reunion story) is accomplished with the help of several family members. But, in contrast with the Israelis, story authorship is highly valued. Hence we note a trend to allow for the display of individual story-telling skills even in cases where the tale is known to more than one participant (the Bug Story). For these families, authorship through performance is used to assert and/or achieve individual ownership.

Conclusions

I have grounded my analysis of family narrative events in the threefold framework of telling, tales, and tellers. The distinction between the first two dimensions is certainly not my discovery. Under different guises, it concerns students of both narratology (e.g. Genette 1980, Rimmon-Keenan 1983) and folklore (e.g. Bauman 1986, Briggs 1988, Young 1987). My inclusion of tellers within the same paradigm is meant to emphasize the social constitutive nature of oral story-telling--and within it, the role of individual selves (e.g. in the presentation of self as protagonist and/or performer) in relation to the other two realms.

This model permits us to isolate the shared and unshared properties of Jewish-American and Israeli family narrative events. We have found similar patterns with respect to multiple participation, the prevalence of personal experience stories, and a respect for children's story-telling rights. These patterns probably derive as much from a common Eastern-European oral story-telling tradition as from narrative practices prevalent in middle-class families in the Western world. As documented by Kirshenblatt-Gimblett (1974: 283), oral story-telling has been a cultural focus in Jewish society from time immemorial; it was frequent and important in traditional Eastern-European communities, it was egalitarian (everybody could tell), and was not limited to specific speech events. By contrast, features like the dialogic nature of many oral narratives (Polanyi 1989) or the deliberate involvement of children in story-telling (McCabe and Peterson 1991) characterize White North American mainstream practices.

However, the two groups also differ in many respects. The differences show up both in the ways of construing each of the three narrativity dimensions independently, and in the interplay between them. Access to telling is less available to Israeli than American children, but is more available to Israeli than American observers. Spatio-temporal framing of tales in the American families locates stories outside the home, but close in time; Israeli families favor stories more distant in time, but located in the home. While most narratives in both groups recount individually known events with self as protagonist, Israeli families are more likely than Americans to recount family-shared events that center around the family ("us") as protagonist.

In transitions between the realm of conversation and the realm of telling, American families search for clear demarcation lines, occasionally ritualized, as in the "today" stories. The high-involvement style of Israeli story entry tends to blur the boundaries between the two realms. Israeli narrative events often begin and end in a highly polyphonic mode; while the opening phase establishes shared access to the tale, the closing phase focuses on negotiating a shared interpretation of the story's meaning, seamlessly moving back to the realm of conversation.

The relations of the tellers to the tales and/or telling is also perceived in culturally distinct ways. Americans support tellers by attending to individual telling rights, but Israelis tend to support tellers by attending to the tale. Access to story ownership in the American families is asserted through familiarity with the tale, but in the Israeli families it is also achievable through participation in the telling. As a result, monologic modes of telling in the American families extend to shared events, while telling of unshared events is celebrated by Israelis in the polyphonic mode. The proposition unique to the Americans seems to be "Let me tell our story"; for Israelis, it is "Let us (all) tell your (singular) story."

Yet, all these families share an Eastern-European background. As such, all could be expected to manifest in narratives the high-involvement conversational style found by Tannen 1984 to typify Jewish New Yorkers from the same background. Spolsky and Walters (1985: 64) argue that this high-involvement style has an analogy in Eastern-European learning styles of the Yeshiva, where participatory listenership and rapid turn-shifting "mark the discussion of equals." Another analogy is provided by styles of worship in the synagogue: the Eastern-European temple is seemingly chaotic, compared to the Asian or Western European, yet this "chaos" is governed by underlying ideological principles, which allow for a higher involvement on the part of the individual worshiper.

Ideology is also a strong motivating factor in understanding Israeli conversational style. As elaborated by Katriel 1986, the Israeli style emerged against the background of a strong ideological opposition to all things associated with Eastern-European diaspora traditions, including ways of speaking. On many dimensions of language use, the Israeli style has indeed been shown to break away from traditional modes (e.g. Blum-Kulka 1992, Katriel 1986). But simultaneously it seems to show strong traces of cultural continuity. We first noted this trend in the prolific use of affective nicknames and endearments, which echo in their suffixes Yiddish and Slavic sound patterns (Blum-Kulka and Katriel 1991). The study of family narrative events provides a second example. Compared to the Jewish-Americans, the Israelis are more involved in all aspects of narrative discourse, sharing both tellings and tales.

From this comparative perspective, the impact of Eastern-European traditions is less noticeable in the narrative discourse of Jewish-American families. In their case, it is American culture which seems to have played the formative role. Thus the emphasis on individual rights and self-accomplishment, seen in attitudes toward the telling, could be expected from sociological accounts of American society (e.g. Bellah et al. 1985). The ways that Jewish-American narratives differ from Israeli narratives echo American ways of speaking, although they may well differ in style from narratives in other American speech communities.

Notes

* An earlier version of this article was presented at the Boston University Child Language Conference, October 1989. The research reported was funded by Grant no. 87-00167/1 from the Israel American Binational Science Foundation (BSF).

I am indebted to Leslie Polss, Naomi Mazoz, Talya Miron-Shatz, and Sigal Ravina, who participated in coding and analyzing the data. Special thanks are due to the participants at the 1990 summer Dubrovnik Inter-University Graduate Seminar on Cross-Cultural Pragmatics—especially Guy Aston, Juliane House, Gabi Kasper,

Tamar Katriel, Susan Paulston, Catherine Snow, and Elda Weizman—for many insightful comments on the family narratives. I also thank Deborah Tannen, who graciously identified herself as the reviewer for the manuscript. Her comments were extremely helpful.

1. Other approaches to narrative stress the *socioculturally* constitutive role of narrative practices (Bauman 1986, J. Bruner 1986, E. Bruner and Gorfain 1984). As formulated by Bauman (p. 113), "narrative...is not merely a reflection of culture, or the external character of social institutions, or the cognitive arena for sorting out the logic of cultural codes, but is constitutive of social life."
2. I borrow the term from Bauman (1986), who follows Roman Jakobson in distinguishing the narrative context of the situation, namely the narrative event, from the story-world evoked through the telling, namely the events narrated.
3. See Young 1987, especially chapters 1-2, for a philosophically attuned discussion of the phenomenological framework for the analysis of the different narrative realms involved (in her terms *storyworlds* and *talewords*).
4. The families were selected by the snowball technique: all adults had to be college-educated, professionally employed, and native-born Israelis or Americans. The full sample includes three groups: native-born Israelis, native-born Jewish-Americans, and native-born Jewish-American immigrants to Israel. Three dinner conversations were recorded (twice by audio and once by video) for each family, within a period of two to three months; all families (including children) participated in an ethnographic interview following the recordings. For further details on the project see Blum-Kulka 1990, Blum-Kulka and Katriel 1991, Blum-Kulka and Sheffer 1993, Blum-Kulka and Snow 1992, Olshtain and Blum-Kulka 1989.
5. The common practice in studies of children's narrative development is to insist on two consequent and causally or temporally related events (Labov and Waletzky 1967) as a minimal requirement for a segment of text to be considered a narrative. On one occasion, we used this definition to allow for comparability across data sets collected under different conditions (Blum-Kulka and Snow 1992). But we found the definition inadequate for capturing the richness of conversational narratives at dinner. From a young child's perspective, recounting a single past event during one short speaking-turn (not an "extended turn," as in conversation-analytical accounts of story-telling) may very well count as "telling a story." Operational definitions of what constitutes a narrative need to accommodate the type of discourse in which the narrative is embedded, as well as variation in participants' emic perspectives.
6. Goffman (1981: 131-2) distinguishes official, ratified participants vs. unofficial (unintentional) *eavesdroppers* and (intentional) *overhearers*.
7. I use "reportability" here in the sense of Hymes (1981: 82): the knowledge that competent members of a culture or community have as to what behavior is reportable in that community.
8. An interesting issue, beyond the scope of this article, is the gender differences between the parents, noted at the family dinner table, as related to possible gender differences in speech in the two respective societies at large.
9. Transcription follows the CHILDES system (MacWhinney 1991: 122-5) as follows: < > overlap; [>] overlap follows; [<] overlap precedes; # short pause; [/] retracing without correction; [//] retracing with correction; + \ interrupted utterance; +... trailing off; +^ quick uptake; +, self-completion; ++ other-completion; [=! text] paralinguistic material; [%com] contextual information. Punctuation marks are used to mark utterance terminators. Some deviations from CHILDES were introduced: the use of capitals and quotation marks for reported speech, to ease

reading; and the segmentation of the text by turns (the relevant units here), rather than utterances. Participants are identified by role (for adults) and by name (for children). Age and sex of child are given in parentheses, in that order: Andrew (8m) = Andrew, aged 8 years, male. Conversational features (e.g. interruptions and overlaps) are marked approximately on English translations from Hebrew. Leftward arrows to the right of the transcript point to the passages being discussed.

10. Examples of textual indicators for event type would be: *A funny thing happened to me today* (A-event); *Remember the time I walked you to school?* (A-B event); *Remember our last camping?* (F-event); *I was surprised by the results of the election* (O-event).
11. As Shuman (1986: 31) notes: "One must have information in order to talk about something. However, people with the information are not necessarily entitled to tell what they know."
12. Included in this analysis were all narrative events from one meal of 10 American (five middle-class and five working-class) families and five Israeli middle-class families (n = 73).

References

Aston, Guy (1988). *Learning comity: An approach to description and pedagogy of interactional speech.* Bologna: Cooperativa Libraria Universitaria Editrice Bologna.

Bauman, Richard (1986). *Story, performance and event.* Cambridge and New York: Cambridge University Press.

Bellah, Robert N., Madsen, Richard, Sullivan, William M., Swidler, Ann, and Tipton, Steven (1985). *Habits of the heart.* New York: Harper and Row.

Bernstein, Basil (1971). A socio-linguistic approach to socialization, with some reference to educability. In Dell Hymes and John Gumperz (eds.), *Directions in sociolinguistics.* New York: Holt, Reinhart and Winston. 465-98.

Blum-Kulka, Shoshana (1990). You don't touch lettuce with your fingers: Parental politeness in family discourse. *Journal of Pragmatics* 14: 259-88.

——— (1992). The metapragmatics of politeness in Israeli society. In R.J. Watts et al. (eds.), *Politeness in language: Studies in its history, theory, and practice.* Berlin: Mouton de Gruyter. 255-81.

———; Danet, Brenda; and Gerson, Rimona (1985). The language of requesting in Israeli society. In Joseph Forgas (ed.), *Language and social situations.* New York: Springer. 113-41.

———, and Katriel, Tamar (1991). Nicknaming practices in families: A cross-cultural perspective. In Stella Ting-Toomey and Felipe Korzenny (eds.), *Cross-cultural interpersonal communication.* Newbury Park, CA: Sage. 58-78.

———, and Snow, Catherine (1992). Developing autonomy for tellers, tale and telling in family narrative-events. *Narrative and Life History* 2: 187-217.

———, and Sheffer, Hadas (1993). The metapragmatic discourse of American-Israeli families at dinner. In Gabriele Kasper and Shoshana Blum-Kulka (eds.), *Interlanguage pragmatics.* Oxford and New York: Oxford University Press. 196-223.

Briggs, Charles (1988). *Competence in performance: The creativity of tradition in Mexicano verbal art.* Philadelphia: University of Pennsylvania Press.

Brown, Gillian, and Yule, George (1983). *Discourse analysis.* Cambridge and New York: Cambridge University Press.

Bruner, Edward, and Gorfain, Phyllis (1984). Dialogic narration and the paradoxes of Masada. In E. Bruner (ed.), *Text, play and story: The construction and reconstruction of self and society.* Washington, DC: American Ethnological Society. 56-80.

Bruner, Jerome (1983). *Child's talk: Learning to use language.* New York: Norton.
——— (1986). *Actual minds, possible words.* Cambridge, MA: Harvard University Press.
——— (1990). *Acts of meaning.* Cambridge, MA: Harvard University Press.
Bublitz, Wolfram (1988). *Supportive fellow-speakers and cooperative conversations.* Amsterdam: Benjamins.
Dascal, Marcelo (1983). *Pragmatics and the philosophy of mind. 1.* Amsterdam: Benjamins.
Edmondson, Willis, and House, Juliane (1981). *Let's talk and talk about it: A pedagogic interactional grammar of English.* Munich: Urban and Schwarzenberg.
Erickson, Frederick (1982). Money tree, lasagna bush, salt and pepper: Social construction of topical cohesion in a conversation among Italian-Americans. In Deborah Tannen (ed.), *Analyzing discourse: Text and talk.* Washington, DC: Georgetown University Press. 43-71.
——— (1988). Discourse coherence, participation structure, and personal display in family dinner table conversation. *Working Papers in Educational Linguistics* 4: 1-26.
Fisher, Walter (1987). *Human communication as narration.* Columbia: University of South Carolina.
Genette, Gérard (1980). *Narrative discourse.* Ithaca, NY: Cornell University Press. (French original published 1972).
Goffman, Erving (1974). *Frame analysis.* Harmondsworth, England: Penguin.
——— (1976). *Interaction ritual: Essays on face to face behavior.* Garden City, NY: Anchor.
——— (1981). *Forms of talk.* Philadelphia: University of Pennsylvania Press.
Goodwin, Charles (1981). *Conversational organization: Interaction between speakers and hearers.* New York: Academic.
Heath, Shirley Brice (1982). What no bedtime story means: Narrative skills at home and at school. *Language in Society* 11: 49-76.
——— (1983). *Ways with words: Language, life and work in communities and classrooms.* Cambridge and New York: Cambridge University Press.
Hymes, Dell (1974). *Foundations in sociolinguistics: An ethnographic approach.* Philadelphia: University of Pennsylvania Press.
——— (1981). "In vain I tried to tell you": Essays in Native American ethnopoetics. Philadelphia: University of Pennsylvania Press.
Ide, Sachiko (1987). Strategies of "discernment" and "volition" for linguistic politeness. Paper delivered at the International Pragmatics Conference, Antwerp, August.
Irvine, Judith (1979). Formality and informality in communicative events. *American Anthropologist* 81: 773-91.
Jefferson, Gail (1972). Side sequences. In David Sudnow (ed.), *Studies in social interaction.* New York: Free Press. 294-338.
——— (1978). Sequential aspects of storytelling in conversation. In Jim Schenkein (ed.), *Studies in the organization of conversational interaction.* New York: Academic. 219-48.
Katriel, Tamar (1986). *Talking straight: Dugri speech in Israeli Sabra culture.* Cambridge and New York: Cambridge University Press.
Kirshenblatt-Gimblett, Barbara (1974). The concept and varieties of narrative performance in East-European Jewish culture. In Richard Bauman and Joel Sherzer (eds.), *Explorations in the ethnography of speaking.* Cambridge and New York: Cambridge University Press. 263-83.
——— (1975). A parable in context: A social-interactional analysis of story-telling performance. In Dan Ben-Amos and Kenneth S. Goldstein (eds.), *Folklore: Performance and communication.* The Hague: Mouton. 106-30.

Labov, William, and Fanshel, David (1977). *Therapeutic discourse: Psychotherapy in conversation.* New York: Academic.

———, and Waletsky, Joshua (1967). Narrative analysis. In June Helm (ed.), *Essays on the verbal and visual arts: Proceedings of the 1966 Meeting of the American Ethnological Society.* Seattle: American Ethnological Society. 12-44.

MacWhinney, Brian (1991). *The CHILDES Project: Tools for analyzing talk.* Hillsdale, NJ: Erlbaum.

McCabe, Allyssa, and Peterson, Carole (1991). Getting the story: A longitudinal study of parental styles of eliciting narratives and developing narrative skills. In A. McCabe and C. Peterson (eds.), *Developing narrative structure.* Hillsdale, NJ: Erlbaum. 217-53.

Miller, Peggy; Potts, R.; Fung, H.; Hoogstra, L.; Mintz, J. (1990). Narrative practices and the social construction of self in childhood. *American Ethnologist* 17: 292-309.

Ninio, Anat (1988). The roots of narrative: Discussing recent events with very young children. *Language Science* 10: 35-52.

Ochs, Elinor; Smith, Ruth; and Taylor, Carolyn (1989). Detective stories at dinnertime: Problem solving through co-narration. *Cultural Dynamics* 2: 238-57.

Ochs, Elinor; Taylor, Carolyn; Rudolph, Dina; and Smith, Ruth (1992). Storytelling as a theory-building activity. *Discourse Processes* 15: 37-72.

Olshtain, Elite, and Blum-Kulka, Shoshana (1989). Happy Hebrish: Mixing and switching in American-Israeli family interactions. In Susan Gass et al. (eds.), *Variation in second language acquisition: Discourse and pragmatics.* 59-83. Clevedon, England: Multilingual Matters.

Polanyi, Livia (1989). *Telling the American story.* Cambridge, MA: MIT Press.

Polss, Leslie (1990). Starting the story: A cross-cultural analysis of conversational story entrance talk. M.A. thesis, Hebrew University, Jerusalem.

Rimmon-Keenan, Shlomit (1983). *Narrative fiction: Contemporary poetics.* London: Methuen.

Sachs, Jackie (1979). Topic selection in parent-child discourse. *Discourse Processes* 2: 145-53.

Sacks, Harvey (1974). An analysis of course of a joke's telling in conversation. In Richard Bauman and Joel Sherzer (eds.), *Exploration in the ethnography of speaking.* Cambridge and New York: Cambridge University Press. 337-53.

——— (1978). Some technical considerations of a dirty joke. In Jim Schenkein (ed.), *Studies in the organization of conversational interaction.* New York: Academic. 249-70.

Schieffelin, Bambi, and Eisenberg, Ann R. (1984). Cultural variation in children's conversation. In Richard Schiefelbusch and Joanne Pickar (eds.), *The acquisition of communicative competence.* Baltimore: University Park Press. 378-420.

Schieffelin, Bambi, and Ochs, Elinor, eds. (1986). *Language socialization across cultures.* Cambridge and New York: Cambridge University Press.

Schiffrin, Deborah (1984). How a story says what it means and does. *Text* 4: 313-46.

——— (1987). *Discourse markers.* Cambridge and New York: Cambridge University Press.

Scollon, Ron, and Scollon, Susan (1981). *Narrative, literacy and face in interethnic communication.* Norwood, NJ: Ablex.

Shuman, Amy (1986). *Storytelling rights: The uses of oral and written texts by urban adolescents.* Cambridge and New York: Cambridge University Press.

Snow, Catherine E. (1991). Building memories: The ontogeny of autobiography. In Dante Cicchetti and Marjorie Beeghly (eds.), *The self in transition: Infancy to childhood.* Chicago: University of Chicago Press. 213-42.

———, and Goldfield, B. (1982). Building stories: The emergence of information structures from conversation and narrative. In Deborah Tannen (ed.), *Analyzing discourse: Text and talk.* Washington, DC: Georgetown University Press. 127-41.

Spolsky, Bernard, and Walters, Joel (1985). Jewish styles of worship: A conversational analysis. *International journal of the Sociology of Language* 56: 51-65.

Tannen, Deborah (1980). A comparative analysis of oral narrative strategies. In Wallace Chafe (ed.), *The pear stories.* Norwood, NJ: Ablex, 51-87.

——— (1984). *Conversational style: Analyzing talk among friends.* Norwood, NJ: Albex.

——— (1985). Relative focus on involvement in oral and written discourse. In David R. Olson et al. (eds.), *Literacy, language, and learning.* Cambridge and New York: Cambridge University Press. 125-47.

——— (1989). *Talking voices: Repetition, dialogue and imagery in conversational discourse.* Cambridge and New York: Cambridge University Press.

Toolan, Michael J. (1988). *Narrative: A critical linguistic introduction.* London: Routledge.

Young, Katharina (1987). *Taleworlds and storyrealms: The phenomenology of narrative.* Dodrecht: Nijhoff.

5

In-Group Humor of Immigrants from the Former Soviet Union to Israel

Narspy Zilberg

The content and function of in-group, ethnic humor of Russian Jewish immigrants to Israel is explored. The argument is made that satire and humorous journalism is a crucial element in the study of the resocialization of this immigrant group. The study concludes that ethnic humor has defensive and social control functions (as a vehicle to vent aggression). It provides a forum for reconsideration of values and cultural and social norms. The compensational functions of nostalgia for the old culture, lost status and traditional ways of life are also important. In-group humor helps immigrants to uphold high self-esteem and cultural levels, reducing the stigma of marginality.

Introduction

During the period from 1989 to 1992, more than half a million Russian Jews emigrated from the former Soviet Union to Israel. For these new immigrants, prior stressful social changes in their country of origin combined with immigration and post-immigration hardships have brought about the breakdown of habitual assumptions, a reconsideration of values, and an active search for new orientation markers for social and ethnic identification. As early as 1991, humorous journalism emerged as one important response to the challenges faced by the Russian *aliyah* [immigration wave; lit. to go up] to Israel. One of the publications is *Beseder?* [OK?], a four-page weekly newspaper (circulation 12-15,000) devoted to political satire, commentary on important events in the immigrant community, cartoons and parodies of both Russian- and Hebrew-language mass media. Humorous journalism in the Russian-language press has evolved into a sophisticated and flexible social barometer, highly sensitive to the emotional changes, conflicts and frustrated aspirations of the new immigrants. This article focuses on the content and functions of this ethnic—or, more precisely, sub-ethnic, in-group—humor, and argues that the satire and humorous journalism of Russian Jews in Israel is a crucial element in the study of their resocialization process. Using Ehrlich's definition that, "A joke told by a Jew about Jews to an audience of Jews is an instance of ethnic humor" (Ehrlich, 1979: 383), the magazine as a whole may be considered a paradigmatic example of in-group sub-ethnic humor of Russian Jews in Israel.

The Social Functions of Humor

Humor has long been recognized as a molding force in society, performing a variety of important social functions. In his classic study of jokes and the unconscious, Freud identified humor as "the highest defensive process." Humorous displacement, according to Freud, functions by "finding a means of withdrawing the energy from the release of displeasure that is already in preparation and of transforming it, by discharge, into pleasure" (Freud, 1966[1905]:233). Freud analyzed the structure and functions of jokes in detail, identifying four major types: hostile jokes (serving the purpose of aggressiveness, satire or defense); obscene jokes (serving the purpose of exposure); cynical or critical jokes; and skeptical jokes which attack neither persons nor institutions, but the certainty of our knowledge itself (Freud, 1966:90-116). Jokes are allied with dreams, he explained, not only in their structure (both depend heavily on condensation, displacement, representation through absurdity, and oppositions), but also in their shared ability to produce a sense of wish fulfillment. Significantly, many of the jokes Freud quotes as paradigmatic examples are jokes told by Jews to other Jews. The tendency toward self-mockery in the jokes told by Diaspora Jews prompted Freud to claim this self-criticism as the most distinguishing feature of Jewish humor.

Both Vladimir Propp (1976) and Mikhail Bakhtin (1984) also elaborate on the "culture of laughter" using the methods of formalistic analysis and placing humor in the context of people's social and cultural lives. According to Bakhtin, a particular "humorous world outlook"—a folk carnival culture, in his terms—overturns social hierarchy and creates a change in social roles. He concludes that humor plays an equalizing role and establishes a "golden age" of common equality. "Seriousness burdens us with hopeless situations," he writes, "but laughter lifts us above them and delivers us from them. Laughter does not encumber man, it liberates him. The social, choral nature of laughter strives to pervade all people and the entire world" (Bakhtin, 1986:132-158). Bakhtin's ideas on heteroglossia can explain the linguistic syncretism of Russian and Hebrew that occurs among immigrants, which is one of the sources of their in-group humor.

More recent research on humor as a social process in hospital and laboratory settings indicates that, in addition to serving more general defensive purposes, humor provides a means of entertainment, reassurance, communication and mutual reinterpretation of collective experience. It also may result in clarification of group objectives and individual roles (Stephenson, 1951; Coser, 1959; Goodchild and Smith, 1964; Ziv, 1984), and in re-establishing positive group distinctiveness (Gadfield, Giles, Boughis and Tajfel, 1979). But, as Levine concludes in his overview, we still know little that is fundamental about national and ethnic differences in humor behavior (Levine, 1968).

The Tradition of Jewish Humor among Russian Jews in the former Soviet Union and in Israel

According to Coven, author of *Jewish* Wry (1987), Yiddish humor of the late nineteenth century was a principal element in the self-identification of the Jews of Eastern Europe.

> It is an instructive paradox (writes Alter [1987:25]), that one of the grimmest stretches in Jewish history—the recent centuries of Yiddish- speaking culture in Eastern Europe—should also prove to be the period in Jewish history that produced the most richly distinctive humor...In such circumstances, it has been suggested, a shrewdly ironic humor became a source of necessary inner strength, a mode of survival.

This tradition of Jewish folk humor found numerous outlets in the Yiddish literature of Russian Jews. In the more recent past, the Jews of the former Soviet Union continued to develop this culture of humor.

Characteristically, they became the leading humorists on Soviet variety shows and theater stages, as well as in the literature of the Soviet period. In addition, outside the official framework of culture there existed an underground folk culture, which, owing to its unofficial status, had an extremely radical and free character. Within this culture, the "Odessite anecdote"—a kind of modern urban folklore of Russian Jews with a clear anti-Soviet direction—was especially popular. In addition to employing such traditional features of Jewish humor as self-deprecation and irony, the Odessite anecdote had a particularly sharp political and anti-totalitarian emphasis (Shturman, 1987).

This traditional use of humor among Russian Jews was developed further in Israel under post-immigration conditions. Humorous journalism evolved in the Russian-language press, first in the form of special sections devoted to humor in all the leading newspapers, and soon after by the publication of several specialized humor magazines. *Balagan*, whose title [which means "chaotic mess"] is a common word both in its original Russian and in Hebrew, was first published in 1991; *Beseder?*, the ubiquitous Hebrew word for "OK" or alright [literally, "in order"], in 1991; and *Balagasha*, a humor magazine for children, in 1992.

Due to its wide readership, *Beseder?*, which first appeared as a Friday supplement to *Nasha Strana* (the oldest Russian-language newspaper in Israel) merits a special place among Russian-language publications in Israel. It was launched at the beginning of 1991, when immigration from the former USSR reached its peak. In addition to the weekly, a separate edition of *Beseder?*, bound with color covers, has also been published each year since its editorial board formed a publishing *amuta* [cooperative enterprise] in 1991.

Beseder? can be distinguished from its sister humorous publications by its commitment not only to entertain, but also to provide commentary on more substantive issues, as well as its commitment to publish recent work by new immigrants, rather than merely reprinting CIS (Confederation of Independent States) authored works and translations from Hebrew and foreign humor (as does *Balagan*), or focusing on the "disintegration products" of Soviet ideology (as does *Absats* [Paragraph]).

For *Beseder?*, the main goal is the attempt to comprehend the situation of post-Soviet Jews in Israel and to comment upon immigrants' experiences during the most difficult period of initial adaptation. Thanks to its original materials and orientation toward the interests of its readers, the Russian-language Jews living in Israel, the magazine can be rightly called the quintessential new immigrant publication. Its inclusion of many common associations and allusions contributes to the pleasure of the jokes and renders the humor a particularly funny form of in-group ethnic humor (Ehrlich, 1979).

While the literature on humor is extensive, the humor of the most recent wave of *aliyah* from the Soviet Union to Israel has yet to be discussed. This *aliyah*, which began in 1989, has created the largest sub-ethnic group in the country after native-born Israelis, and can be distinguished from previous waves of immigration in several important respects. Perhaps most significant for the Russian-language community in Israel was the convergence of their emigration with the effects of perestroika and glasnost. The break-up of the former Soviet Union, the challenge to communist ideology, rising nationalism among the peoples of the former Soviet Union, and the economic and social crises in their country of origin left the nature of "home" in almost as much flux for these immigrants as the nature of the new country to which they arrived. Even as newly-arrived Russians struggled to make sense of their new situation, they also found themselves needing to make sense of their past in light of the enormous changes taking place in the CIS.

A central concern among Russian-language speakers in Israel, therefore, is not only the traditional immigrant concern with assimilation into mainstream society, but also the requirement that they forge some common identity out of their very disparate pasts and negotiate relationships with those immigrants who arrived in the 1970s and 1980s—the *vatikim* [lit., the veterans]. The *vatikim*, like other immigrant groups of the same ethnic identity whose arrival has preceded that of a later wave of immigration (Shokeid, 1993), greeted the newcomers' arrival with some ambivalence and resented the challenges their arrival posed to the *vatikim's* newly achieved assimilated status.

The scope of the most recent *aliyah* also brought with it a set of unique problems, most notably, unemployment and underemployment for large numbers of professionals.

Given these factors, what role, we asked, does ethnic, in-group humor play in this immigrant community? In what ways does this humor function to name and then to address the concerns of the group? Is it even appropriate to call the recently arrived Russian-language speakers in Israel a community? If so, how has in-group humor functioned to forge a sense of communal identity?

Research Methods

This study of humor in the Russian-language press in Israel relied on interviews with staff and a content analysis of the publications. Using the notion of layers of context (Roswell, 1992), examples of humor in the Russian language press were placed in the immediate context provided by the readers and writers of these newspapers, and then more generally in the context of the Russian-language community living in Israel. Data sources included all issues of the magazine *Beseder?* published from 1991-1994 (200 issues comprising 800 pages in the standard-size magazine format generally used by Israeli weeklies), supplemented by additional examples of humor in the Russian-language press from *Balagan* and *Absats* (appearing in the daily newspaper *Vesty*). In addition to analyzing the contents of these newspapers, following the procedures for qualitative research (Glaser and Strauss, 1967), I conducted extensive interviews with the editors of *Beseder?*, during which I elicited the editors' explanations of their work, sought to verify my emerging interpretations of the data, and developed new categories with which to analyze the data. These interviews were further embedded in extensive fieldwork within the Russian-language community in Jerusalem. As a recent immigrant to Israel myself, I had many advantages of the "insider/outsider," or participant observer, critical to insightful fieldwork, and my familiarity with the community greatly simplified such issues as negotiating entry and identifying key informants. Data analysis continued this pattern of triangulation, and I engaged in a range of analyses, including techniques derived from narratology (Bakhtin, 1986; Labov, 1972) and content analysis.

The Editorial Staff: Some Sociological Remarks

Beseder? is a specifically immigrant magazine, established and written by journalists who are themselves new immigrants, published in Russian, and oriented almost exclusively toward the immigrant audience. As one of the founders of the magazine, Deputy Editor Anatolii Livshitz, noted in an interview with the author of this paper, from the moment *Beseder?* appeared, all who read it and those who wrote it were placed in a flood of events, in a completely new reality. The authors perceived and discovered Israel in exactly the same way as the readers perceived and discovered it. The only difference was that the former could better formulate and generalize what was happening.

Beseder? is best described as a small business, with a staff of only three full-time employees and a small number of free-lance contributors (living both in the CIS and in Israel). Most members of the editorial board are non-professional humorists. Most are under forty and, like a large percentage of the new immigrants, have earned advanced degrees. Some of them, who viewed work on *Beseder?* as a temporary job or an intermediate step to higher positions in journalism, have already left the magazine. The best known of these is cartoonist Oleg Shwartzburg, who after failing to get work as a physician, started working for *Beseder?*, and in a short period of time became one of the leading cartoonists for the international edition of *The Jerusalem Post.* Shwartzburg represents the only case of integration of a Russian-language journalist into the national Israeli press, perhaps because the cartoonist relies on a special visual humor which works primarily through symbols and is not dependent on specific knowledge of Russian, Hebrew, or English.

Over the years, *Beseder?* has cultivated an involved readership and maintained close ties with humor amateurs and connoisseurs, guaranteeing that as soon as new anecdotes, funny expressions and stories are born in the community, they are published in the magazine.

The Structure and Content of *Beseder*?

The structure of *Beseder?* repeats a structure familiar to its readers from Soviet newspapers. The content repeats the exaggerated ideological emphasis. In fact, the first element of parody operates on the level of content itself, as the Soviet and Israeli Russian-language presses, with their often skewed priorities, peculiar ways of interpreting information, and penchant for prescribing readers' conduct, are themselves satirized in this four-page weekly magazine.

The front page of *Beseder?* contains slogans and appeals; it is an "editorial page" patterned after and parodying the Soviet "general line" [official response] to major events, arranged in the table of contents under such headings as "Official Chronicle" and "Associated Stress News Agency." These columns vary considerably from week to week, providing the flexibility to respond to developing events. During the 1992 election campaign, for example, one column was headed "Meet The Elections With Shock Labor." Frequently, the comic effect is produced by the names of the columns' authors. The editorial column is signed by Pogranzon (formed from the Russian word *granitsa* [state border], plus the typical Jewish surname ending "zon"), alluding to the notorious Soviet border-guard vigilance and ideological control. The weekly commentary on the *Torah* reading (a genre familiar from both the Hebrew- and Russian-language press in Israel), is signed by "Sergeant Petrov." Another comic clash of the Soviet past and Israeli present: "News" is reported by a certain "Sopha Hadashot" (*Sof ha-Hadashot* is a well-known Hebrew radio program phrase meaning the end of the news broadcast.)

The second page includes commentaries and interviews located in sections or columns with such headings as "Actual Interview," "Sniffing of Events," and "Editor's Corner." Commentary and advice columns by such experts as lawyers, doctors and insurance agents are also parodied here, as are commentaries on the weekly *Torah* chapter.

The third page contains literary texts and comments, including satirical book reviews, a "Nostalghetto" section (which reprints humor classics), as well as "Lenin's Readings," "Useful Heritage," and so on. As a rule, "official" Soviet classics and serious literature, movies, and TV, children's reading and literature taught in school courses—in fact everything that has shaped CIS immigrant cultural assumptions and norms—serve as material for the newspaper's parodies. A characteristic device transfers familiar personages and plots into Israeli reality, and the appreciation of the joke therefore requires the reader to master a wide range of symbolic and allegorical allusions. As Freud explains in his attempt to account for the power of this kind of humor, "In discovery of the familiar, recognition is experienced as pleasure" (Freud, 1938:714).

A special section, "The Russian Press Digest," pokes fun at the most obvious shortcomings of the Russian mass media. The "Political Map of the World" (subtitled "On Israel Russian Periodicals Materials") parodies the fact that the Israeli Russian-language press places little emphasis on world events, giving disproportionate attention to the CIS, US, Israel, and the press—its cliches, its low credibility and its sensationalism. At the same time, parodying major Israeli Russian press announcements, *Beseder?* addresses such substantial issues as emigration from Israel, new immigrant businesses, and prostitution and youth problems among recent immigrants. Self-irony and jokes are used here as a means of regulating deviant behavior.

The fourth page of the magazine is named "Your Leisure Time." It features parodied or genuinely funny advertisements, horoscopes, crosswords with satirical names (like "The Triumph of Zionism," "From Everyone According to His Abilities," etc.), and a "Children's Page." Throughout the paper, but especially on this final page, much space is devoted to cartoons, sketches, one-liners and comics.

The fact that *Beseder?* is designed as a newspaper allows it to provide immediate responses to actual events in the life of Israel and its Russian-language community. At the same time, the newspaper format encourages a critical attitude toward the press as a whole. Anatolii Livshitz sums up this component of the magazine's editorial philosophy when he explains that,

> it is not rare that a Russian immigrant comes to think that he is already finished here, and loses the ability to read between the lines. I consider it relevant to return self-esteem to the man, so that he realizes that he came from an ideological country to a place no less ideological, and in this situation has no right to relax. He has to analyze the information and put to himself the same question: "To whom does the profit go?"

New Methods of Being Funny

Reconsideration of the Soviet past on the one hand, and the search for a place in Israel on the other, have determined the focus of the magazine. As Livshitz remarks, "We draw from the two cultures, the two realities, and then check by our old measuring instruments all that we experience here. The funniest things are born from the incongruities of the two cultures."

Beseder? draws widely, for example, on the Russian-language mass media outlets which reflect the life and spirit of the immigrant community. These publications include numerous, sometimes low quality daily newspapers as well as daily 12-hour radio broadcasts in the Russian language. Everything is subject to parody here—commercial advertisements, readers' letters, TV-program announcements, weekly commentaries on passages from the *Torah*, the heavily Hebraized Russian language of new immigrants (Markowitz, 1993).

Perhaps even more important as a source of Russian immigrant humor has been classic Russian literature transferred into a different reality—everything from Pushkin to Tolstoi to Lenin. The centrality of these references can be explained in part through one of the stereotypes of assimilated Soviet Jews who have adopted Russian language and culture as their own and who regularly assert the superiority of Russian culture over the "aboriginal" culture. This sense of cultural superiority has exacerbated the dilemmas of assimilation experienced by other ethnic groups that have immigrated, and has made the costs of assimilation particularly poignant.

The fourth specific source of *Beseder?* humor is parody of the Soviet mass media—the system which over many decades had been strictly controlled to express only the perspectives of the Communist Party and the goal of the Soviet regime. As Livshitz explained, in many cases, the comic effect is achieved by linking or associating well-known Soviet ideology clichés and slogans with Israeli reality. Well-known quotations of Marx, Lenin or Stalin, as well as other Soviet and revolutionary texts and slogans that were routinely generated by the Soviet propaganda machine, are often parodied, as in such examples as: "We all descended from Egypt..." (*cf.* the popular revolutionary song, "We all descended from the people..."); or, "Our armed forces are the most armed of all forces in the world!"

In addition, a comic effect is often based on puns and wordplay involving rhyme, double-entendre or transliteration of Hebrew words into Cyrillic letters—a whole range of jokes which are, unfortunately, lost in the process of translation.

Key Problems Explored in Russian Immigrant Humor

It is a major argument of this paper that the pages of *Beseder?* provide a unique window into the problems experienced by the newly arrived Russian-language community in Israel and that the humor of *Beseder?* is not only reflective of, but also constitutive of, the community's attempts to forge a new collective identity for itself in order to respond effectively to these challenges. We now turn, therefore, to a more detailed consideration of how the problems of Russian immigrant life in Israel are represented in *Beseder?*. The following themes emerge as most central:

1. Problems of absorption (finding jobs, attaining financial security, etc.) and status anxiety caused by a decline in social and professional status.
2. Challenges of defining and creating relationships with members of the mainstream or "target" society (Israelis), as well as with the country's many sub-ethnic and social groups.
3. Iconoclastics of ideology.
4. Problems of self-identification for the assimilated and usually secularized Russian Jews and the challenges of developing new attitudes toward religion.

Problems of Absorption

An indisputable priority is given to new immigrant absorption problems. The magazine demonstrates a sharply satirical perspective toward the government's stated concern for new immigrants, showing the conflict between the bureaucrat and the newcomer over jobs, housing and other emotionally laden issues.

The marginal state in which new immigrants found themselves in Israeli society, and the socio-economic and cultural crises they experienced, have created ground for detachment and satirical perception of the new realities surrounding them. At the same time, humor has provided an outlet for aggression ("Thus to Berlyne and Kant, sudden relief from tension is the key to all humor" [Levine, 1968:1]). Humor controls aggression as much as it violates social taboos.

One of the most difficult problems of the Russian *Aliyah*-90 lies in the fact that the high educational and professional level which the majority of Soviet Jews had attained in the USSR cannot be sustained in Israeli society.

The situation of this group of immigrants, who, percentage-wise, have had higher status and prestige in Russia (most being of the upper middle class), is supposed to be the most severe of any group in previous *aliyot* with regard to the problem of professional fulfillment and absorption into Israeli society. The Russian-language press molded a collective image of the *Aliyah*-90: "Professor with a broom," the pictorial depiction of the new immigrant with unrealized potential. When the Association of Scientists from the former Soviet Union was founded in January 1994, the broom crossing the model of an atom became its symbol.

The humorous effect in the treatment of this problem is based, as a rule, on the incongruity of the "high" style of the characters' speech or their literary prototypes and associations (Pasternak, Descartes, Goethe, Lermontov) with the low social status of immigrant street-sweeper.

A motto: I sweep, hence I exist.

A resume: A Prof. Descartesman, Ph.D., ex-Marxist-Leninist, now street-sweeper -philosopher, 2 years in the country

A tourist's observation: A remarkable change has occurred among Israeli street-sweepers: two years ago, they spoke only Arabic. But in the last two years, they have all learned Russian and completed advanced degrees.

Relationships with Israelis and Other Ethnic and Sub-Ethnic Groups in Israel

In contrast to the problems of absorption, problems of other sub-ethnic groups and native Israelis [*sabras*], as well as other new immigrants' attitudes toward them, are represented poorly and one-sidedly, which may be caused by the rather marginal place of "Russian" newcomers of the 1990s in Israeli society. A small section, "For you, Sabras," is based on everyday observations both of Israeli television and of behavior in the street, on buses and in shops. Appearing in this column, for example, has been tongue-in-cheek advice on how to use the multiplication table to teach *sabras* arithmetic, and detailed instructions on how to use a trash can.

It is interesting to note that many stereotypes presented here function as a kind of mirror image of a whole series of materials in the Israeli press and on television about "uncivilized ways" of the new immigrants (Leshem, 1993). The tone of critical alienation regarding Israeli culture and Israelis was especially characteristic for the first year of the magazine's existence. Subsequently, the emphasis was transferred to criticism of government policies regarding new immigrants.

The general tone is critically detached. The feelings of resentment and loss of a considerable part of the new immigrant population concerning their social and professional status is reflected in the way Israeli popular and professional cultures are portrayed, since the Russian community (because of the absorption conditions) contacts predominantly the lower strata of Israeli society. A story, "If I Were Not Myself," is revealing in this respect. I reproduce it in full here, because it is a particularly clear example of the most common stereotypes.

> If I were a *sabra*, I'd be a *kablan* [building subcontractor], a member of the Knesset [Israeli Parliament], and a hereditary *balabayit* [landlord]. I'd buy watermelons in the supermarket and perfumes in Paris. I'd drive a Subaru, speculate on the stock-exchange, dodge taxes, rent out two apartments, and say "*Kak dila*" [How are you?] in Russian.

> If I were a *vatik* [veteran Russian immigrant], I'd have a good job, pay taxes, drive a Renault, curse Russian newspapers in Hebrew ones, vote for the Likud, speak with my children in Hebrew, buy at the *shuk* [market] in the morning [when the food is freshest and the prices are highest], and wouldn't be indebted to the Bank Idud [immigrant bank]. I'd rent out a flat, ask the *olim* [new immigrants] "Where were you earlier?", explain to them where they will be later, and tell them about the swamps and Zionism.

If I were a new immigrant, I'd wish I were a *sabra*, or at least a *vatik*, rent an apartment, go to the *shuk* in the evening, work at staircase cleaning and receive a dole. I'd have arrived as a single mother two flights before my husband, and my pensioner parents would have providently divorced beforehand [to get more benefits]. I'd [write horrifying letters, swear at my wife who had "lured me here," buy a Daihatsu-Applause, dream about going to America, and not pay the TV tax as a revenge that here is bureaucracy and Socialism.

However, I'm a tourist, and I like being here among *sabras, vatiks*, and *olim*. And asked why have I come on a guest visa, I answer: "We're all only guests in this world."

I. Winterman

In this story, the typical behavior of different social groups is compared by way of the juxtaposition of two quite different genres. On one hand, the author presents himself as a tourist (outsider), assuming the stance of disinterested "objectivity" and employing the familiar genre of taxonomy or classification. The use of taxonomy is itself a particularly significant choice, not only because it calls attention to the strict, if unspoken, status divisions separating the different groups living in Israel, which is largely based on the length of time they have lived in the country, but also because it very precisely "draws the map" of the new social situation in which the immigrants find themselves. The use of the pseudo-scientific language of classification delineating the habits, possessions and common expression of each group makes manifest the "rules of the game" and renders those rules part of the shared knowledge of the in-group. Almost as satisfying as, and crucial to, ultimately attaining the status of the *sabra* or the *vatik* as mastering the code of symbols that broadcasts that status within the society.

At the same time, the joke also resonates with the self-deprecation familiar from the Jewish humor of such masters as Shalom Aleichem, who frequently employed the theme of a hypothetical situation and the refrain of "If I were..." In another version of this joke that appeared in *Beseder?* in the same year, the skepticism is even more obvious. An unemployed new immigrant is sitting on the seashore and dreaming of being in the situation of the veteran immigrant. The veteran, who has overcome the problems of the new immigrant, is dreaming of attaining the status of the *sabra*. And the *sabra*, who has succeeded in fulfilling the immigrant's and veteran's dreams, only wishes that he could sit on the seashore and do nothing. In this case, the humor serves as a kind of wish-fulfillment, helps to control inter-group tensions and aggressive feelings, and also provides opportunities for immigrants to rehearse—and also to reject—the different roles available in Israeli society.

The magazine also comments on the stress in the relationship between two generations of USSR immigrants. A special column called "Nasha Strana"..."Years Ago" features selections from the Israeli-Russian press of the 1970s. These fragments emphasize the smoother absorption conditions of the previous *aliyah* from Russia. An obvious *vatik* tendency to stress the advantages of their status and their detached attitude to newcomers are hyperbolized to great comic effect, as in a sketch called "Vatik's Pride." Employing the technique Freud called "representation through absurdity" (1966:125-127), a *vatik* boasts to an *oleh*, "Do you see these forests? It was I who planted them. Here is Jerusalem. It was I who built it. There, look, is the Dead Sea. It was I who murdered it."

Speaking about the relationship of new immigrants and native Israelis, the short story "A Man to a Man is a Jew" (a reference to the well-known Soviet saying, "A Man to a Man is a Friend, Comrade and Brother," or, alternatively, *homo homini lupus est.)* explores the oppositions between the stated ideals of Zionism and the realities immigrants often confront. Here is how Livshitz, author of the story, comments on his idea:

> It was an attempt to realize the process of the *aliyah* absorption. Undoubtedly, a man is to another man a Jew and a brother here. At the same time, a brother would take $400 a month as his brother's apartment rent, and add $100 for moral sufferings for this high price, and pay his brother five shekels an hour instead of ten for working for him. Because there are things which are stronger than this brotherhood [which] lays at the level of normal human interest. Interest will always take an upper hand over principle. Much has been written about the end of Zionism. We laugh at that, as well as at any other "-isms," since this is an idea, which, when put in a foundation, cannot carry the construction. We had an epigram about Sharon [then Minister of Housing] and his idea of caravan sites for new immigrants:
>
> "The houses' walls are made from shit when ideology is the base of it."

Iconoclastics of Ideology

An inoclastic view toward any ideology is a typical feature of the new immigration wave of the 1990s, since its world outlook formation years date back to the 1970s–1990s, when the growing crisis of the Socialist system together with social de-ideologization were advancing at full speed.

In this respect, new immigrant conduct during the Israeli elections in 1992 was highly typical, using ideological jargon, drawing on supposedly unquestionable principles, and moralistic in tone. This was especially the case when the majority of *olim* voted for the Labor Party. The situation prompted the following "Confession" by the Chief Editor of *Beseder?*, Mark Galesnik:

A Fault Confessed...

I, *Beseder?* Chief Editor Mark Galesnik, immigrated in 1990 to Israel harboring a malicious and corrupt plan to harm the veteran Israeli population by bringing the Labor Party into power. Being politically unripe and socially irresponsible, I gave my vote to the above-mentioned. My behavior, however, was partially caused by my bad habit of totalitarianism and red flags, acquired in my childhood. I also sucked my left thumb and had an oral/anal Communist complex. I completely realize my terrible crime and herewith apply to be accepted as a member of Likud or Mossad. Or both.

Obviously, the humor in this "confession" operates at many levels and gains its effectiveness by parodying the much publicized "confessions" of the Soviet period by likening the ideological certainty of Likud supporters to that of Communist hard-liners, and by exaggerating to absurdity the "psychological" explanations for behavior included in these forced confessions. In the final line, Galesnik reveals the insincerity pervading such forced confessions with the blind willingness to apply to Likud, Mossad or both.

During the 1992 election campaign, the magazine established its own political party called *Beseder?-Achshav!* or BA, which may be translated as "Order-Now." To a considerable degree, it is a parody of the new immigrant party DA (*Democracy ad Aliyah*, the abbreviation of which means "yes" in Russian), and at the same time a reference to the Israeli Peace Party, *Shalom Achshav* [Peace Now]. Its "ethnic candidate," imaginary Jewish astronaut Pupyrchatyi, sends a note from his spaceship, *Shtele* [village; *cf.* "Shuttle], protesting the votes of non-confidence for his "heroic efforts to zionize the Earth adjacent to space and spacenize the Earth adjacent to space and spacenize the Earth adjacent to Zionism." In this declaration, not only is the attempt to found a "Russian" party satirized, but also the ideological excesses of Zionism and Israel's pretensions toward first world status by launching a spaceship. The technique of humorous paradox and playful judgment, studied in detail by Freud (1966:10-14), is used there.

The Problems of Self-Identification

The skepticism of the last joke is also extended to the religious pronouncements and beliefs the new immigrants encounter. In their history as almost totally secularized Jews, this new immigrant population introduced a completely new dimension to the definitions and categories of Jewish identity that were prevalent in Israel before their arrival. On one hand, they openly repudiate the Jewish tradition. For example, *Beseder?* regularly ridicules the rules of *kashrut* [a body of religious laws governing the preparation and consumption of food] and the often arcane legalistic reasoning supporting such rules, posing such seemingly *halachically* [Jewish religious law] grounded questions as, "Is it permitted to eat meat with milk teeth?" The daily life of the orthodox community, as well as religious party machinations (e.g., the arrest of Interior Minister Arie Deri for, among other things, alleged misallocation of funds to religious institutions), are also mocked in cartoons. *Beseder?'s* editorial policy states unequivocally that the editor "respects religious people's feelings, but reserves the right to laugh at whatever seems funny" to him. The weekly *Torah* commentary is, above all, a parody of such commentaries appearing in the Russian press, where the political and partisan attitudes are not controlled enough.

Self-image and identity in Israel is one of the categories of ethnic humor peculiar to new immigrants The background for the jokes essentially lies in the controversial understanding of Jewishness in the USSR and in Israel.

The level of cultural assimilation or auto-emancipation of Jews in the former Soviet Union was high. They adopted the Russian language and culture, and Soviet norms and regulations of behavior. Nonetheless, the feeling of national identity and its consciousness was strong. Loyalty of Soviet Jews and their attempts to be part of "a new Soviet nation" were reactions to denationalization of this group and of state-instigated anti-Semitism.

In Israel, post-Soviet Jews find their Jewishness without Judaism and their traditions challenged. Many of them feel uncomfortable with and resentful of their identification as "Russians" by Israelis. The humor created to respond to these dilemmas is made more biting by the many controversies concerning falsified identities and illegal immigration as in the following jokes:

Announcement:

Soviet Jews! Immigrate to Israel! Only here your long-cherished dream to become Russians will come true!

A Parodox:

—Look, what a paradox: In Russia I was a Jew, and here I'm a "Russian!"

—So you're an idiot.

—And you, you're smart, aren't you?—Sure I am; there I was a Russian, and here I'm a Jew!

Although the humor of *Beseder?* can be divided into commentary on social status, inter-group relationships, skepticism toward ideology, and a search for a new identity, many of the funniest pieces address these interlocking concerns together. In a lengthy column, "All the best to Sabras," which we excerpt here, we see, for example, many of the tensions experienced by the immigrant community addressed simultaneously:

Be Spock

Sabras—they are like children.

Many people ask: How should we behave with *sabras*? Read Doctor Spock! But in the meantime, here are some important ideas.

The perception of *sabras* differs from the perceptions of those who are more mature. The *sabra* is joyful, happy-go-lucky, and often disobedient He doesn't know about our adult problems—about apartments, work, banks, immigrant loans...Like all other children, a *sabra* may wake during the night and cry and ask you to take him into bed. In these cases, you must kindly but firmly speak to him and explain that tomorrow you must go to work, and if you will not go, there will be nothing for him to eat...

Many *sabras* cannot manage to button up their shirts or zip their zippers. You must patiently show them how to do it. But it is not worthwhile to do this for them, because they will get used to your help and it will create problems in the future.

Sabras are very sensitive. They take your faults and difficulties in absorption close to their hearts. They pick up your mood immediately, and may become nervous. In this state they may even rebuke you with questions, asking: "Why have you come here? Why have you made us and you so unhappy?" In moments like these, they can use nasty words they may have heard from friends. Do not take this too seriously. They themselves do not know what they are saying.

Sabras are very curious. Every five minutes they ask you a question and patiently wait for your answer. "*Kama zman atah po?*" "*M'ayn atah?*" "*Lama Batah?*" [How long have you been in the country? Where are you from? Why did you come?] Don't try to give abstract or evasive answers like, "I was brought by the stork," or "That's the way it is." They will get the information anyway that they find interesting, perhaps in the streets and from hooligans...You must sit with the *sabra* comfortably and explain the physiological details—that Jews in the country appear because of their grandfather Herzl. *Sabras* are generally afraid of him and respect him....

D. Zillber

At the risk of spoiling some of the fun of this piece, it seems worth analyzing this particular column in some detail. Unlike much of the humor analyzed in the literature (Freud, 1966; Cohen, 1987), this column is not a single joke that culminates in a definitive punch line. Instead, like much of the Russian immigrant humor, it is an extended parody that relies on a complex web of allusion for its full effect. At the same time, it is this reliance on allusion and shared references that contributes to the nature of "Be Spock" as the quintessential example of how in-group humor develops and operates in the immigrant Russian community in Israel.

Numerous elements of in-group humor operate simultaneously here. The premise of the entire piece—that *sabras* are like children and that the advice of an expert like Dr. Spock can enable new immigrants to deal effectively with these sometimes troublesome youngsters—at once exaggerates and reverses the role of immigrants as consumers of paternalistic advice, reverses the assumed status relationships between immigrants and long-time residents, and also, of course, satirizes the familiar genre of self-help literature for weary parents, and particularly the style of Dr. Spock himself.

In its basic structure, the parody also employs displacement (Freud, 1966:232-233) appropriation, and carnival (Bakhtin, 1984), and the mixture of self-criticism and criticism of others considered to be so essential to ethnic Jewish humor.

Like the "If I were" stories, the joke makes manifest the much greater knowledge that the immigrant group has of the dominant group than vice versa by highlighting such typical elements of Israeli culture as the unbuttoned shirt (even in the most formal of circumstances), the freedom Israelis feel to ask personal questions about age, status and income (considered inappropriate in many other cultures), and the famed Israeli informality. In representing the *sabras* as illiterate children, immigrants see themselves as members of a more elite, educated, mannered and mature community. The parody also enacts the Russian immigrants' feelings of cultural superiority and, through the use of shared reference, reiterates the importance of shared texts and helps to constitute the in-group by way of its canonical texts. Like the title of the magazine *Beseder?*, "Be Spock" also enacts the process of appropriation of taking the words of another and making them one's own (Bakhtin, 1986) in its use of common Hebrew phrases transliterated into Russian. When recounting the common questions asked by *sabras*, "Be Spock" demonstrates the ability of the immigrant to speak the language of "the other"—and their exercise of power in deciding which of the other's language and culture they wish to make their own.

In short, this joke operates as much more than a simple release of aggression. Instead, it serves to define the in-group to newly arrived Russian immigrants through the parodied description of the *sabras*. To fully appreciate the humor of the piece, one must know Russian, must know some Hebrew, must have read Dr. Spock, have been subjected to lots of press analyses of the "problems of absorption" that subtly liken new immigrants to children (now reversed), be familiar with canonical Russian texts, and be familiar with the details of contemporary Russian society—in short, part of the pleasure of the joke is the confirmation that one is, in fact, a member of a particular community constituted by these shared concerns, knowledge, language—that one is a member of the in-group.

Conclusion

The immigrant humor of the Russian-language press in Israel serves, we believe, as a means of accommodation through a self-ironic attitude on one hand, and a vehicle to vent aggression on the other.

The major *Beseder?* concern is the socio-economic and professional status of Russian Jews in Israel. Through its satiric commentaries, *Beseder?* constitutes a kind of a club, with its own cultural tradition, rules, professional argot and language. While in its first stages, its audience consisted mainly of intelligentsia whose situation was supposed to be most gruesome. Nevertheless, it should be noted that, if at the beginning of their absorption all immigrants were in the same transitional, status-less state, over the past three years the situation has begun to change. The *aliyah* has become stratified, as some of the newcomers have been able to restore their pre-emigration status, while others have become lumpenized. Some indications of a Russian-language community formation with its inner hierarchy have appeared. These new dynamics promise to change the emphasis of the Russian immigrant humor, as it strives to address, not only in-group, but also inter-group and intra-group concerns.

As the in-group humor of the Russian immigrant community, this humor has social control functions (approval or disapproval of old and new social norms and attitudes of the new immigrants). Another aspect of the social function of humor is related to in-group interaction. Humor helps the community to reinterpret its experience, to gain political strength and to improve the position of immigrants in the society (using social criticism in the form of satire). Immigrant humor provides a forum in which cultures can mix and overlap and become laminated. Mutual reconsideration or rejection of the negative and positive elements in the past and the adoption or appropriation of elements from the new Israeli experience can reinforce group cohesiveness and common identity. Humor also has defensive functions (to defend through satire the interests of the whole immigrant community and its most problematic groups). The compensational function of immigrant humor for nostalgia for the old culture, lost status and traditional ways of life, and for a marginal position in Israel, must also be important. Humor helps to uphold self-estimation and cultural levels, providing enjoyment from the intellectual games, reducing the stigma of marginality.

At the same time, it should be noted that many examples of the humor of the Russian Jewish immigrant community in Israel are unique; it remains rather obscure to the Jews of the CIS and of other Jewish Russian Diaspora, owing to its Israeli specificity as well as the language pertaining to Hebraisms. But the patterns used in the technique of immigrant humor in the Russian-language community in Israel are often common to other emigrant groups of Jews from the former Soviet Union. Some materials from *Beseder?* were used in the immigrant humor magazine *Okay!!*, a monthly, published since 1994 in the United States. The humorous combination of American reality and Soviet past by post-Soviet Jews demonstrates the same methods of being funny which were used in *Beseder?*. The experience of the international humor competitions of CVN (The Club of Joyous and Inquisitive Ones) in 1992-1994, with *Beseder?* represented by its editorial board members, is another example of the common basis for ethnic humor of the post-Soviet Jews in Israel and in the Diaspora. These shows were successfully performed in Israel, the United States, and the ex-USSR, and broadcast by the cable TV.

The substrate of Russian literature and communist phraseology evokes either no associations or wrong ones in veteran Israelis and non-Russian Jews. However, such elements as the structure of humor, its self-criticism and skepticism, its contents highlighting the problems of assimilation, identification, attitude to religion, and the search for status, are traditional for the Jewish humor of the post-emancipation period.

Acknowledgments

I am grateful to Dr. Barbara Roswell and to Professor Paul Hare and Gideon Kressel for their invaluable comments and assistance in preparing this paper for publication.

References

Alter R. (1987) "Jewish humor and the domestication of myth." Pp 25-37 in S.B. Cohen (ed.), *Jewish Wry*. Bloomington, IN: Indiana University Publications.

Bakhtin, M. (1984) *Rabelais and His World.* Bloomington, IN: Indiana University Publications.

———(1986) *Speech Genres and Other Late Essays*. Slavic Series No. 8. Austin, TX: University of Texas Press.

Cohen, S.B. (1987) "Introduction: The varieties of Jewish humor." Pp. 1-16 in S.B. Cohen (ed.), *Jewish Wry*. Bloomington and Indianapolis, IN: Indiana University Press.

Coser, R. (1959) "Some social functions of laughter: A study of humor in a hospital setting." *Human Relations*:12.171-132.

Ehrlich, H.J. (1979) "Observations on ethnic and intergroup humor." *Ethnicity* 6:383-398.

Freud, S. (1938) *The Basic Writings of Sigmund Freud*. Modern Library, NY

——— (1966) *Jokes and Their Relation to the Unconscious*. London: Routledge & Kegan Paul. [Originally published in 1905].

Gadfield N., H. Giles, R. Boughis and H. Tajfel (1979) "Dynamics of humor in ethnic relations." *Ethnicity* 6:373-382.

Glaser, B.B. and A.L. Strauss (1967) *The Discovery of Grounded Theory: Strategies for Qualitative Research*. Chicago, IL: Aldine.

Goodchild, J.D. and E.E. Smith (1964) "The wit and his group." *Human Relations* 17:23-31.

Labov, W. (1972) *Sociolinguistic Patterns*. Philadelphia, PA: University of Pennsylvania Press.

Leshem, E. (1993) "The Attitude of Israeli Population to Olim of the 90s." *Social Security* 40(8):54-72. [Hebrew].

Levine, J. (1968) "Humor" *International Encyclopedia of Social Science. Vol. 7.* New York: Macmillan & Co., and The Free Press.

Markowitz, F. (1993) "Israelis with a Russian accent." *The Jewish Journal of Sociology* 35(2):97-111.

Propp, V. (1976) *Problems of Humor and Laughter.* Moscow: Iskousstvo. (Russian).

Roswell, B. (1992) "The tutor's audience is always a fiction." Doctoral Dissertation. Philadelphia, PA: The University of Pennsylvania.

Shokeid, M. (1993) "One-night stand ethnicity: The malaise of Israeli-Americans." *Israel Social Science Research* 8(2)23-50.

Shturman, D. (1987) *The Soviet Union in the Mirror of the Political Anecdote, 2nd Ed.* Jerusalem: Express. (Russian).

Stephenson, R (1951) "Conflict and control functions of humor" *American Journal or Sociology* 56:569-576.

Ziv, Z. (1984) *Personality and Sense of Humor.* New York: Springer-Verlag.

6

A Symbolic Interactionist User's Guide to the Answering Machine: 22 Reflections on Vocal Encounters in an Emerging Social World

Aviad E. Raz and Rina Shapira

Having entered the market more than 20 years ago, the answering machine is now a popular commodity, one that is actively changing our daily life. The following essay offers some sociological reflections on this new communication technology. Research on the issue is scarce and only little more is available with regard to the answering machine's older and more influential kin—the telephone (see, e.g., De Sole 1977; Fischer 1987; Umble 1992). Most approaches in the sociology of technology and communication address such questions as the commodity's reception, socio-economic aspects of its marketing, or its technological implications by assuming that technology affects society in a direct and linear manner. In contrast, our aim will be to understand how new technologies interact with and are shaped by pre-existing cultural categories and social relationships. In addition, this study is based on the analysis of texts—excerpts selected from literature, television, cinema, and answering machines' tapes. It does not, perhaps cannot, aim to cover the full spectrum of such an analysis but offers a first sociological look at a timely subject, evoking an interpretive collage of illustrations and queries, a list of recorded messages that still wait to be answered.

The chapter is divided into four sections. In the introduction, we present a semiotic model of "machine talk" and discuss its linguistic, as well as social, implications. The following two sections are concerned, respectively, with the construction of the answering machine as both a cultural idiom and a social agent. The former describes its construction as a meaningful object in cultural discourse; the latter deals with its social use and the practical logic by which it operates. This distinction is largely analytic. The ensuing conclusion inter-connects these two complementary aspects, and suggests a broader, postmodernist perspective that encompasses them both.

Introduction: The Two Faces of the Answering Machine

Unlike the telephone, the answering machine is essentially a selective mechanism of communication. Its purpose is to record all incoming calls, so that at some future time, one can select whom to call back. The selectivity of the answering machine is, in fact, a product of its two complementary aspects: restricting and expanding communication. The dual aspects of both expanding the availability of the recipient and restricting his or her actual response are combined in the functional selectivity of the machine. The machine can thus be transformed into a "barrier", a screen, a buffer regulating the callee's communicative involvements (see this observation in the first discussion of the "telephone answering service" by Roth and Lepionka [1973]). The answering machine is a time capsule of suspended talk, of messages in an electronic bottle. It replaces (literally re-places) former face-to-face conversation with a simulation of talk where neither the semiotic maxims of proximity and synchronization—nor their derived interactional concepts of intimacy, visibility, and presence—any longer hold. However, this simulation of talk is also predesigned to reproduce an almost exact reflection of "the original", namely, face-to-face conversation (see item 12). Later on, the concept of the answering machine as a simulation will be discussed through the social world perspective, with allusions to Baudrillard's view of the postmodern (tele)technologies of representation. But first, the following list sets out to further articulate our point of departure, which is the dual, selective character of the answering machine:

(1) On the one hand, the answering machine restricts communication, as you talk to a machine and not with its human owner. On the other hand, the machine provides the caller with access to the callee any time. It offers a technological solution to the problem of availability, which is so characteristic of telephone interaction (Schegloff 1972).

(2) The machine can be regarded as contributing to its owner's privacy, as it enables us to receive messages without interacting directly with the caller. On the other hand, the answering machine may become an "irresistible intruder" (McLuhan 1965:271), the representative of public life even in one's absence (see, for example, items 10 and 17).

(3) For many people, the first encounter with an answering machine is a disorienting experience. They encounter a recorded message instead of a human voice willing to talk back to them, and are expected to leave their own message, short and concise. Knowing that one's message will be recorded gives some people the feeling that they have to plan carefully what they want to say, which leads in many cases to hanging up (see also Dingwall 1992:97). Talking to the machine is perceived as a kind of test to be successfully mastered, as if the machine tests you, dubs you as guilty (of unfluency, redundancy, nagging) until proven otherwise. In contrast, new strategies for identity management and dialogicity can also be invented. For example, callers may bestow on their message (which is recorded in life-time) the character of the immediacy of the voice (Alvarez-Caccamo and Knoblauch 1992:475). More significantly perhaps, leaving a message on an answering machine usually follows a common scheme which is perhaps used more often and followed more strictly by those whose experience with the machine is the most disorienting.

(4) In principle, messages could consist of anything. In fact, there is a limited range of things callers do when leaving a message. For one thing, the limited time available exerts strong restrictions on what is said. Furthermore, messages are, to a large extent, standardized (see Wojcik 1987; Gold 1991; Sayad 1985), consisting of the following scheme (Alvarez-Caccamo and Knoblauch 1992:493):

-opening/greeting

    -excuse/justification/request

        -offer/request/proposal

        -request for agreement/okay

    -thank you

-closing/goodbye

(5) The one-sidedness of leaving a message may be connected to the flattening of face-to-face, personal interactions in modern society, and perhaps even to the increasing solitude of urban life. Even if one

can devise innovative ways of using the machine to symbolize his/her identity, one is not directly aware of how that identity is being read by others. Answering machine self-presentation (see items 12-15) hence becomes a monologist practice, lacking all the subtle clues (e.g., facial expressions, bodily gestures, the physical distance/proximity between interlocutors) that we generally look for when we are involved in face-to-face interaction. "Real" conversation is a tango, a carefully coordinated, synchronized dance in space, whereas the answering machine provides a one-sided experience, both to the caller and the callee, who are separated by both space and time. In contrast, the machine can also contribute to personal relationships. Instead of representing a disjunction in the verbal interactional history of caller and callee, many private messages analyzed by Alvarez-Caccamo and Knoblauch (1992; see also item 11) show anaphoric and cataphoric references which allude to prior or future actions by the caller and callee. The answering machine is hence capable of linking together past, present and future—a significant feature that we shall later come back to in our discussion of ellipsis (see item 8).

(6) Compared to other forms of spatially-remote discourse—both oral and written—the answering machine seems to "behave" more like letters than like telephone calls (Dingwall 1992:96). Mail (electronic as well as hand written) and machine talk are potentially permanent and allow little interaction between the producer and the receiver but potentially more time for the producer to plan what he/she wants to say; both are fairly independent of the immediate context and the response to the "summons" is delayed. However, the comparison with letters is obviously limited and a more suitable metaphor for machine talk will be sought for and suggested later on.

By virtue of its selective screening, the answering machine becomes a gatekeeper (see also item 10), and the home that one uses is turned into a communicative territory. The notion of "communicative territory" may explain the interesting observation that the machine is often placed in the hall. The hall is evidently not the only possibility: there are alternative places, such as a phone extension in the study or the bedroom. [1] But placing the machine in the hall—that is, as the gatekeeper of the house entrance—symbolically defines it as a "communicative territory". Single persons living in rented apartments often place the machine near their bedroom extensions. This hints at the more practical reasons underlying the machine's placement. As with many other objects of home consumption, when many of the family members use the object, it means that it has to be placed in a "public" spot. This is probably why the answering machine is situated in the hall in the case of both families and roommates, while single persons may place it as they choose. [2]

Enabling one to select one's calls means that, once a principal of selection is formed, it can be viewed as defining one's pattern of involvement and participation in various concentric social circles, whose core consists not of the person but of the answering machine. Thus, many answering machine users may recall an extreme situation of selective (or perhaps suspended) communication, in which one activates the machine while at home, so as to answer the phone only when certain people call. This situation has become so widely practiced that one can find oneself, on hearing the machine instead of its human owner, uttering into it: "Come on, Jack, I know you're at home, I'm waiting for you to pick up the phone."

Selective communication demands a delay in time between the incoming and the returned call. When the phone rings and we hurry to pick it up, we have no option of selection (except for the binary choice "to answer or not to answer") since the identity of the caller is unknown. Both the telephone and the answering machine are technologies of telecommunication; that is, they enable two (or more) remote persons to communicate. While telephone communication is synchronous (the two communicators, though spatially remote, can speak and hear each other in the same time), the answering machine represents a form of communication which "takes place" in different times. This, precisely, is the reason why the telephone is regarded as a mediator of "conversation", while the answering machine is not. The form of communication we call "conversation" entails a specific spatio-temporal organization. Vocal and auditory communication in humans has certainly evolved under specific conditions (proximity; synchronization), but modern technology changes that. It is only as a result of telecommunication that we can begin to think of earlier forms of communication as bounded by space and/or time.

A simple semiotic typology of forms of talk according to parameters of space/time should illustrate our claim. Thus, while a face-to-face conversation (presently still considered as "the real thing") occurs in the same place and in the same time, it is a telephone conversation which exists in the same time but not in the same place; whereas communicating through an answering machine (what we term here, for the sake of simplicity, as "machine talk") is carried out neither in the same place nor at the same time (as one may listen to the message well after this had been uttered).

The fourth possible combination, that of same space but different times, poses a rather intriguing problem, for how can a human conversation, the human condition being inherently temporal as it is, be conducted on the same spot but over quantal periods of time? It seems that the speakers should somehow possess the ability to switch themselves on and off while their discourse is continually kept alive. If human speakers, temporally bounded as they are even when technologically is released from spatial boundaries, cannot perform such feats, then perhaps their "voices" can—as is the case with the telephone and the answering machine. The Jewish example of a Gemmara page, [3] within which different ("polyphonic") voices from different times take part in a continuous discourse on exegesis, is a case in point. A more secular and modern instance of the same-space-different-time category is the graffiti wall, that is, an urban wall on which various graffiti which refer to each other have been inscribed over time; or its bourgeois counterpart, namely, the notes left throughout the day by members of the family, usually on the door of the refrigerator, concerning various issues on the family agenda. Another case in point here is the "names book", in which "memories" are inscribed in different times by different children (Shapira and Herzog 1984).

There exists, we suggest, a paradigmatic relation of the following form: cohesive temporality/spatiality = personal/territorial connexity. [4] The "paradigm" of such a relation is, indeed, the conversation. Still, modern technology provides us with all the other combinations, as table 1 exemplifies. Interestingly, the four squares of the table reflect not only a certain technology of communication, but also a respective social form of human interaction. Notably, whereas the fragmentation of the first pair (temporality/spatiality) has been connected with machine talk, the dissolution of the latter couple (personal/territorial) characterizes social worlds.

Table 1
A Spatio-temporal Model for a Typology of Forms of Talk

	Same Time	Different Times
Same Space	"Real" Conversation	Gemmara/Graffiti Page/Wall
Different Spaces	Telephone Conversation	"Machine Talk"

We use here the term "social world" as a concept focusing on the unique role of a certain communication network from which emerges a distinct mode of social interaction. Consider, for a recent example, the system of electronic mail (e-mail). There are relatively formal procedures that allow participants to enter or leave this abstract network of communication, which can operate independently of personal knowledge and face-to-face interactions. Geographical-territorial boundaries, formerly a must in community studies, are here given secondary importance, if at all. The concept was suggested by Shibutani (1955), who considered social worlds as configurations of shared communication in industrial societies, and further elucidated by Strauss (1978; 1982). The approach has since been employed as a core idea in a number of studies concerning the world of art (Becker 1982), computers (Kling and Gerson 1978), alcoholism (Denzin 1977, 1978), the elderly (Unruh 1983), and photography (Rosenblum 1978). The symbolic core of many social worlds is not human relationships per se, but human relationships as revolving around a certain object, such as the computer, the painting, the liquor bottle, or "the community," "the club," and "the factory." In our context, this object is the answering machine; take the answering machine out, and the social world revolving around it falls apart.

To study the answering machine, we needed a symbolic-interactionist perspective that interconnects social interaction and communicative networks, while emphasizing the role of objects, and not human participants, in sustaining relationships. Hence, the social world perspective was suggested as relevant. Moreover, the discourse of social worlds arises exactly when social relationships can no longer rely on face-to-face interaction, when territorial boundaries collapse and time is fragmented by the involvement of participants in multiple and often contrasting life-worlds. Hence, the atemporal rhetorics of "community" can serve as the new symbolic core of the social world in an artificially-designed urban renewal setting (Hazan 1990), the ex-territoriality and impersonality of the social world of a coffeehouse can act as a substitute form of sociability and privacy in urban life (Shapira and Navon 1991), and the atemporality of folktales as well as the impersonality of symbolic types can replace conventional forms of discourse and social negotiation in the social world of a members club for the elderly (Raz 1992/3).

The core object of the social world should hence embody, through its symbols and discursive practices, the ability to bridge over dissolved boundaries of geographical territories, the absence of synchronous face-to-face interaction, and the fragmented time of participation. These postmodernist predicaments are, indeed, the symptoms of "the homeless mind," as suggested by Berger, Berger, and Kellner (1973). Indeed, "machine talk" seems like a natural extension of the postmodernist "nomadic" identity (Giddens 1991). Whether the social world perspective as described here produces "real" interaction, or only simulations of such, will be later discussed. In our case, this is somewhat tantamount to the question of whether machine talk is indeed a "real talk" or not. At this stage, our answer will be that it is a new mode of communication, which should be analyzed on its own grounds and through a novel set of analytic constructs. The social world perspective is one such construct. While face-to-face interaction is related to same-place/same-time personal relationships, these are irrelevant to machine talk; the concept of the social world was hence chosen as a new context, a new paradigm of nomadic interaction. Just as the machine both extends one's communication network and fragments one's relationships, so the social world both extends one's social involvements while allowing one to remain largely anonymous.

Both machine talk and social worlds are substitutes that have now taken on lives of their own. Both should be subject to careful examination. Our argument here is that machine talk and machine use can be regarded as belonging to a specific brand of social worlds, perhaps, better called "social worlds of telecommunication;" other members of that category are e-mail, tele-conferencing, BBS, home shopping and banking, teletexts, etc.—all currently exerting their global impact (Singleton 1989). The semiotic properties of the answering machine produce the sort of disembodied, formal, impersonal, spatially and temporally disjointed discursive practices that characterize social worlds. Arguing that the machine now stands at the core of a social world also implies that the machine has become a cultural idiom and a social agent. Whether such a social world indeed emerges in the context of the answering machine is the subject of the following reflections:

The Answering Machine as a Cultural Idiom: An Array of Textual Representations

The first example of what we call the "idiomatic use" of the term "answering machine" is taken from Israel. However, this example is not culturally unique. As answering machines began to flood the Israeli market about ten years ago, the original term "answering machine" was replaced, among native Hebrew speakers, by the locution "electronic secretary," which denotes the same object. This connotative expression has recently been at the center of a public debate carried in the name of feminism over the pages of several Israeli daily newspapers. The quarrel began when a journalist, well known for his feminist column, attacked the idiom "electronic secretary" as reproducing the male conception of the stigma of the female-secretary (note that "secretary" in Hebrew is a feminine noun). The article triggered various responses from both sides and resulted in a quest for more "gender-free" terms. This search was concluded with the alternative title "answerer" ("me'shivon"—a masculine noun in Hebrew), though others (notably women) have propounded the use of "listener"—since the Hebrew word they suggested, "shimon," was in fact a pan made out of both a semantic derivative of the form "to listen," while at the same time denoting a Hebrew male name. Neither name caught on and the term "electronic secretary" remained.

Evidently, there is no ontological connection between the answering machine and the image of the female secretary. That whole debate, however, could be taken as an example of the cultural discourse of new technological objects of communication, which are perhaps familiarized and inserted into public awareness by personifying them, that is, relating to them as "having" a gender, a name, a "character." The popular reference to the television as our "big brother," a term whose ongoing usage has endowed it with a certain familiarity quite opposite to its original alienating connotation, is another example.

Even more interesting is the evolving role of the answering machine in literature and the cinema. For example, in one of the memorable scenes from the American version of "Breathless" (1982), starring Richard Gere, a girl, on entering her apartment while accompanied by a male friend, immediately replays her answering machine (which is found, by the way, in the living room). When a friendly message uttered in a male's voice is heard, the man suddenly disconnects the machine and smashes it on the floor in an act of (sublimative?) aggression. Other films, such as "Broadcasting News" (featuring William Hurt) or "Jumping Jack Flash" (starring Whoopi Goldberg) make dramatic use of recurrent scenes in which the characters, having returned home, replay their machines—which contain messages involving significant clues for the rest of the plot. Harrison Ford, in Polansky's "Frantic", discovers the whereabouts of his wife's abductor through a message left on an answering machine.

These instances represent the growing use of the machine as a compositional short-cut, a dramatic vehicle enabling condensed flow of past information relevant to the present, thus mediating a leap to the future and advancing the plot. Whereas the old private eye of the "Film Noir" genre had to collect information by shaking it out of people, the modern, hi-tech, timesaving answering machine has it all instantly.

Douglas Adams, who earned international fame through his series of the "Hitch Hiker's Guide to the Galaxy" novels, makes some innovative uses of the answering machine as the navigator of plot in his novel, *Dirk Gently's Holistic Detective Agency*. The characters, who are extremely fond of leaving messages for their often-not-at-home plot partners, follow each other by listening to messages left on their answering machines. At the height of the story, the characters are gathered to listen to the final words, which are recorded on an answering machine, of a man who died in what appears to be a case of murder. This final message is supposed to contain the clue to the mystery; however, it only deepens it, as few minutes after the noise of shooting, the ghostly voice of the deceased is suddenly heard from the same machine.

In the above mentioned examples taken from various texts of the modern Western culture industry, the answering machine is charged with what discourse analysis terms as "ellipsis function": "a structural relation between parts of a text, which forces the reader, when he encounters it, back into the text while providing him with new information" (Brown and Yule 1983:193). Consider the following grammatical example of elided form: "Jules has a birthday next month. Elspeth has, too." Thus, in accordance with Halliday and Hasan's (1976:229) recognition that "it is the underlying semantic relation, which the reader is forced to look for... that actually has the cohesive power," we contend that within the poetical (rather than grammatical) level of the plot, the texts produced by the answering machine exert, by virtue of their elliptic nature, a cohesive textual effect and, by doing so, also serve to promote the unfolding of the plot. More importantly, the answering machine can, indeed, serve this function as a result of its special spatio-temporal attributes, articulated in the beginning of this article.

A form of communication existing in different times and spaces, the texts of the answering machine become, like other supra-linear ("spatial," in the literary jargon) forms (such as rhyme, analogies, character-pairing or counterpoint), compositional components which must be set out, abstracted the temporal flux of the story, and re-integrated by the reader. These texts are then used to dynamize the plot along what Sternberg (1984) has ingeniously phrased as "the crooked corridor of discourse." The dramatic use of the elided function of the machine was illustrated in item 7, especially in the examples of "Frantic" and *Dirk Gently*; for a "real" message exemplifying this function in everyday machine talk, see item 11. Ellipsis, it should be noted, is precisely the textual by-product of a medium of communication capable of linking past and present as well as here and there.

At the risk of sounding pseudo-poetical, we might suggest that it is this elided function that the answering machine serves when it is replaying its vocal contents into that polyphonic plot which is our life. Making the answering machine work as a means of ellipsis, as a compositional shortcut, is part of its emerging role as a "character" in its own right. The answering machine as character can thus either "conceal" its messages from other human characters or "reveal" them at the right time; it can provide clues, trigger flashbacks, foretell the future, pretend as if we are not at home, and introduce us to strangers.

The abstract notion of ellipsis alone does not capture the social dimension related to machine talk, which has become connected, for instance, to life in the big city. Many films and novels portray the men and women of the modern megalopolis as being quite prepared to intimately address the "other" through his/her machine—while often not sure whether it will be the addressee who will actually hear the message, and whether he\she will then be on their own. This can be exemplified by a scene from the popular American TV series, "thirtysomething," in which we witness, for some long minutes, how one of the characters, Ellen, utters a romantic monologue straight into her boyfriend's machine.

The one-sidedness of this monologue and the solitude embedded in it later become a metaphor for that relationship. This example adds another dimension to our discussion of the machine as a cultural idiom, which goes beyond its function in the plot and connects it to the modern predicament of loneliness and isolation as often experienced in urban life.

It is the American idiom of "phone tag" which fully captures the duality of the machine as being both a gatekeeper and an "irresistible intruder". The machine may permit us the privilege of not answering the phone, but it also commits us to reply to its messages. It answers in our place, but it will not answer for us. The "phone tag" also adds to this practical predicament a negative sense which relates to technologies substitution of human interaction. "Tag" is a kids' play in which one player has to catch the others; "telephone tag" respectively denotes a state in which two persons find themselves constantly leaving messages on the other's machine and never seem to catch the other person at home. It is in the constant absence of the other person that talking to the machine becomes frustrating; it is here that the gate-keeper becomes a nuisance, the Golem(5) turns into a Frankenstein's monster.

_______ 1. Hi. Much more preferred to have an interactive conversation

_______ 2.with you Milka = but. This s- seems to be: the- uh pattern

_______ 3 of our co(h)mmunication (of) weeks.

_______ 4. hh I will once again leave a message on the machine?

_______ 5. for you. Uhmm. Uh [click]

_______ 6. Sorry I missed you today when you called; I was at work

_______ 7. (.) I've got back to work (...)

(...)

_______ 10. I'm going out tonight, and I probably won't be in

_______ 11. till late; but you can call me tommarow morning if you want.

(...)

_______ 15. I hope everything is OKAY, (hh) uh I love ya too,

_______ 16. a::nd I'll talk to you later. Bye bye [whisper]

In Alvarez-Caccamo and Knoblauch (1992:488)

The Answering Machine as a Social Agent: Tele-Communicative Strategies of Embodiment

The technological design of the answering machine reflects longstanding conventions of communication. It is designed to store verbal locutions of two categories. These are contained in the machine's two cassettes—the cassette holding the pre-recorded announcement of the machine's owner and the cassette receiving the incoming messages.

In attempting to analyze the linguistic procedure involved in this dyad, an evident structural analogy may be drawn to face-to-face conversation. The latter is known to involve fairly complex forms of politeness called "phatic" functions by semiologists (see Jakobson 1960). When we say, "Hello, how are you?" we signify our availability for substantive communication. We close the communication line with another set of rituals, such as "it's time I get going, see you around." The fact that this set of communicative rituals is culturally required is hilariously illustrated by small children's inability to decide who will "hang up" first (see Bjelic 1987).

However, in the context of machine talk, these phatic functions of establishing face-to-face communication are replaced by an opening performative speech act (Austin 1962) such as "John is speaking" or "this is John," and usually closed in a meta-communicative utterance, e.g., "call me." All these locutions might be analyzed linguistically, as presenting common denominators of "machine talk." Moreover, intriguing questions such as age-related differences, social and sexual markers in speech, "hyper-correction" (Labov 1973) in machine talk, and, in contrast, the use of some local vernacular form of speech such as "straight talk" (see Katriel 1986) in it, can also be posed. As a sufficient linguistic database of announcements as well as messages is presently not at hand, these are posed here not to be answered but in order to draw the attention of sociologists to a yet uncharted territory.

A basic feature of all communication, and one that takes a special form in the case of machine talk, is the management of identity. By this term, we refer here to the techniques individuals employ to control their self-presentation, techniques which differ from one medium to another. New electronic media enabling impersonally transacted yet personally interpreted communication are currently proliferating. Yet, sociologists have largely neglected their potential long-term effect on the structure of social interaction. One exception is Feenberg's (1989) study on the pragmatics of computer-mediated communication, which states that "users of electronic bulletin boards, dialogue systems and computer conferences...though appearing to each other only through explicit written language...possess the "literary" capability to project their personalities in written texts" (p. 261). This, of course, applies just as well to the spoken texts of the answering machine. In both cases, then, the loss of the interlocutor's bodily presence does not necessarily signify impersonality.

The chronic absence from home of young, working people is one of the major reasons stated by them for purchasing a machine—"be out and stay in." This situation, combined with the modern predicament of individual loneliness together with collective socializing, places the answering machine in a unique position. Its recorded voice becomes not just an announcement, but also a metonymy of its utterer's self. This recorded message is often much more than a voice, involving long pieces of music and sound effects. Preparing such imaginative messages takes time, thought and technical knowledge—a considerable investment that clearly attests to its significance. For example, we were told of a recorded message which had Elvis singing "White Christmas" for at least a minute (imagine getting this kind of recorded message while on a long-distance call). [6]

These kinds of recorded messages are, perhaps, responsible for the growing number of persons who find themselves getting nervous prior to making a call, thinking what they will have to say if they run into an answering machine. Thus, while on the one hand enabling the presentation of its owner's self, the machine also serves as a self-processor, in which the hearer to engender some sort of coherent impression processes vocal fragments of the speaker.

In a species whose evolution has emphasized the visual senses as the major form of communication—compared to other animals, we have a very limited spectrum of auditory, not to mention olfactory, sensations (see Sebeok 1968)—it is interesting to inquire as to the sort of relations that are created between the self and its disconnected vocal embodiments. Carpenter (1972) describes the intriguing example of a New Guinea chief who, having been disobeyed by his subjects, tape-records his ordering voice in the local urban governmental office; to which, once replayed to them through the tape recorder, the former "rebels" immediately consent.

The "formal authority" attributed to the bodiless voice, indeed, also characterizes our modern society, reflecting its bureaucratic character, whereas in the case of simple societies its authority stems from a mystical propensity. However, both attributes, from the most formal to the most intimate, can be found in the vocal messages of the machine. A-propos of bodiless voices and mystical propensities, the best metaphor found to describe the act of listening to messages appears in Adams's *Dirk Gently's Holistic Detective Agency* (1989), in which it is compared to a séance. After all, both are one-sided and have to do with hearing bodiless voices that begin and end in an uncontrollable manner, though we have the power to summon them.

Indeed, the fact that ghosts—real ghosts—are able, as it happens, to record their messages on the answering machine, as Adams has it, is a logical extension of this metaphor. While the vivid conception of the "ghost in the machine" is to be regarded as adding a metaphorical touch to the sociological consideration, it also implies that the machine is not only a self-processor, but also a medium.

The surrogate self of the machine, combining the opposite parameters of formality and intimacy, finds various expressions within the modern processes of alienation and solitude. Thus, one of Adams's characters continuously leaves messages on machines, since he is:

> "one of these people that cannot think unless they speak; when new ideas cross his mind, he has to convey them to those who would listen. If no one would, and this happens ever too often, their answering machines will. He has a secretary whose sole job is to recollect these recordings. When asked why he does not use an 'executive's' tape-recorder, he replies that he doesn't like talking to himself." (p.64)

This theme reappears, in a more interesting way, in Beckett's (1959) play, "Krapp's Last Tape and Embers," in which the protagonist, Krapp, rediscovers tapes on which he has previously recorded a daily diary. The theme of recorded diary thus becomes a life review, with the answering machine turned into a modern confession booth, its vocal announcement the counterpart of the confessional parson. This refiguration of the voice into a person is hilariously exemplified by one of Mashi'ach's (1989:9) interviews, in which a man explains why he placed the machine in his study room by saying that his girlfriend was "...opposed to the existence of another woman in the home." [7]

A popular Israeli television series, "Bein Hakis'ot" (literally, "between the chairs", meaning "mixed bag") recently dedicated one of its programs to the issue of dating and featured the following story. A young man, the male member of a couple sitting in front of the interviewer, told the camera how he dialed a number by mistake, found himself listening to an answering machine with an agreeable announcement, and left a message with his telephone number. The owner of the machine heard his message, and—so she said—dialed it out of curiosity. She was answered by a machine, and, finding the announcement to be quite pleasant, left her own number. At the end of the day, concluded the interviewer, they both found themselves married.

This example illustrates the potential imbued in the answering machine to open up communication in new and innovative ways, whereas former examples (e.g., Ellen's monologue) portrayed the one-sidedness of the caller and the passivity of the recipient—almost as if to imply that the machine, only by its presence, restricted personal relationships. The active use of the machine is, in itself, as this section argues, worthy of close consideration, for it has to overcome the lack of visibility (the hallmark of face-to-face conversation) as well as synchronization (which the telephone still maintains) by finding new ways of vocal embodiment.

Conclusion: Space-Time Distancing, Spectrality and Simulation

Unlike the popular issue of passive exposure to the media, research on the social meaning of the active use of telecommunication is scarce. One such piece of research is that of Guillaume (1982), who introduced the concept of "spectrality" to describe the subject of these new forms of telecommunications between individuals who are reduced to anonymity by the society in which we live and yet succeed in turning that anonymity to their own profit, using it to shelter and assert their identity.

"Teletechnologies, considered as a cultural sphere, respond to a massive and unconfessed desire to escape partially and momentarily both from the symbolic constraints which persist in modern society and from totalitarian functionality. This escape does not take the still ritualized form of those brief periods of celebration or disorder permitted by traditional societies, but is initiated at the convenience of the subject, who pays for this freedom by a loss. He becomes a spectre... in the triple sense of the term: he fades away in order to wander freely like a phantom in a symbolic order which has become transparent to him" (1982:23).

The spectrality of which Guillaume speaks is a combined outcome of both the anonymous mass society of modern times and the time-space distancing involved in telecommunications. By "time-space distancing," we mean the dissolution of spatial and temporal boundaries implied by the use of telecommunication, which, however, does not lead to the merging of social boundaries, but rather to the deepening fragmentation of human interaction. The telephone and the answering machine both expand our communication lines and change the character of our social interactions, in that they have the potential to make physical contact obsolete. Face-to-face interactions are connected with a whole symbolic array of traditional forms of sociability, in which proximity implies intimacy and synchronization means involvement and attachment.

As face-to-face interactions are increasingly substituted by telecommunication, this symbolic array undergoes an immense change.

Consider, for a lively illustration of that proposition as well as the audience's compelling interest in it, the success of a recent novel titled *Vox* (by Nicholson Baker). Vox consists entirely of the increasingly warm phone conversation between Jim and Abby—professional middle class singles who have met through an "adult party line" and shunted themselves of to a "one-on-one" connection to share private sexual fantasies.

Most critics considered Vox as a post-AIDS tragedy of non connection, a techno-safe-sex love story which is "the very opposite of Erica Jong's zipless sex" (e.g., Gates 1992; Stengel 1992; Garrison 1992). That interpretation, however, fails to locate Vox within the larger matrix of telecommunication forms of talk/interaction. Vox makes use of the telephone's capacity to mediate talk of the same-time/different-place kind. While synchronization is kept, physical proximity is obliterated. Moreover, now it is synchronization which takes over proximity as the source of intimacy, yet it is a unique kind of an "anonymous intimacy" (Jim and Abby probably will never meet, and need not meet). It is perhaps no surprise that in Vox, synchronization replaces proximity as the source of intimacy: are we not persuasively and persistently told by legions of sexologists that it is the harmony between partners (ultimately exemplified in the synchronization of orgasm), rather than physical proximity, that makes the difference?

Incidentally, moving from Vox and its telephone conversation to the answering machine, which also obliterates synchronization, is a small step. It is easy to imagine a state of affairs (not too far in the future) when the other voice on the hot line will come from a prerecorded, sophisticated answering machine that can be activated through the caller touch-tone telephone technology. And cyberspace simulations of talk/interaction/eroticism are of course merely a small step further. Welcome to telecommunications, the realm of simulations.

The connection between time-space distancing, telecommunication and alternative social forms (in the Simmelian sense) leads us to the work of Jean Baudrillard (1983; 1988), who has written extensively on the substitution of meaning by its signs and of "truth" by its simulations. In his most recent study, Baudrillard (1992) argues that the Gulf War did not, literally, "take place" ("n'a pas eu lieu"); it existed, for its audience as well as its American generals, on TV screens and through CNN reports. The Gulf War brought to an extreme the substitution of reality by media-projected simulacra. This all-embracing substitution constitutes what Baudrillard terms as "hyper-reality." We propose that "machine talk" should be regarded as a type of simulation—a simulation of "real" conversation. This is because machine talk, like the Gulf War, does not take place. It exists only by virtue of an electronic recording device, which stores reality and then replays it.

The Baudrillardian view of the precession of simulacra has another important parallel with our treatment of the four types of talk/interaction (see Table 1) as structured by the two semiotic vectors of time and space. Baudrillard (1983, p.11) defines a list of four successive phases of the simulation: (1) the reflection of a basic reality; (2) simulation which masks and perverts a basic reality; (3) simulation which masks the absence of a basic reality; and (4) simulation which bears no relation to any reality whatever: it is its own pure simulacrum. Our types of talk/interaction can be located within these phases. As time/space distancing advances, the participants respectively ascend in Baudrillard's phases of the simulation. Face-to-face conversation, presumably a "reflection of reality", fits the first phase; telephone talk, with its invisibility effect (the "mask") fits the second; machine talk, in which "talk" is conducted with absent interlocutors, belongs to the third order of simulacra (here is also found the gemmara page/graffiti wall); and cyberspace, the imaginary world of computer communication (see Fontana and Tillet 1993; Balsamo 1989) in its various possibilities of "virtual reality", is an expression of the fourth phase: its own pure simulacrum.

All our telecommunication technologies carry with them a two-pronged prospect. We use them in order to expand our reach, to maximize productivity, to eliminate geographical boundaries. But then again telecommunication also restrict face-to-face relationships, mask and distort "reality", and emphasize the distance among people. Most important, as this article has attempted to demonstrate, tele-technologies, by substituting face-to-face interaction, provide the terms for novel forms of talk/interaction. They often change the very nature of the nexus between these two basic counterparts. There is also the possibility that the substitutes will take over. If this happens—perhaps, it already did—then the simulation becomes reality; persons are turned into specters while technology becomes personified and actual.

This evidently spells a new phase in the deepening ambiguity inherent in the human-machine relation. "While the machine is a sign of human inventiveness, it also conjures up the spectre of control, thus ranging from ally of humans to feared enemy" (Fontana and Tillett 1993, p. 38). The answering machine is perhaps not as likely to be cast as a feared enemy, but it does condition us, its users, in subtle ways. As technological (not social) progress seems unavoidable—as does time-space distancing—we should not worry about whether or not to "accept" the simulacra (they are already here), but rather what to make of them. To answer this question, another inquiry, parallel to this one, should be conducted 20 years from now. Perhaps, by then, vocal messages will have completely substituted human conversation; and, face-to-face interactions will have become obliterated by various combinations of human-to-machine, machine-to-human, and machine-to-machine communication.

You are invited to leave your message after this beep.

Beep.

Notes

The authors wish to thank Prof. Haim Hazan, who read a former version and provided helpful comments, and whose specter dwells in this paper.

1. This observation, along with various others, is based on interviews carried out by Ms. S. Mashi'ach (1989), who has kindly permitted us access to them, for which we are very grateful.
2. The issue of the geographical location of the answering machine within the home connects us with the literature concerning the territorial aspects of the home. Thus, Shamgar-Handelman and Belkin (1984), as well as Sebba and Churchman (1986), who studied the territorial behavior of Israeli families within the home, have suggested that space allocation is an index of the power structure in a given family, and that it is the parents, rather than the children, who generally have control over space. It would seem logical, therefore, to consider the selection of place for the machine as part of a the family issue of "control over space." This pattern seems to be pertinent, indeed, not only to Israeli families.
3. Basically, a "Gemmara page" is part of a voluminous text of exegesis called "the Talmud" and written by Jewish scholars in Babylon and Jerusalem approximately between the 2nd century and the 5th century (A.D.). Each page in the Talmud contains many sources referring to the same question, and this polyphony of voices, which belong to various scholars working in different times, are all "debating," so to speak, on the exact interpretation of another, earlier text of exegesis called the "Mishna." Together, these form the codex of Jewish life.
4. The "Golem" in Jewish folklore is a bulk of clay which is brought to life, by the power of certain formulae of Hebrew letters, in order to serve its creators. It is a kind of robot with no free will which must obey its creator's commands—unlike the rebellious monster in *Frankenstein*, which turned against its creator.
5. This example was conveyed to us by reviewer #3; we were taken by its vividness and the striking similarity to this kind of recorded messages one can hear in Israel.
6. It should be kept in mind here that the Hebrew popular idiom for "answering machine" is, in fact, "electronic secretary."

References

Adams, Douglas 1989. *Dirk Gently's Holistic Detective Agency*. New York: Simon and Schuster.

Alvarez-Caccamo, C., and H. Knoblauch. 1992. "'I Was Calling You': Communicative Patterns in Leaving a Message on an Answering Machine." Text 12(4):473-505.

Austin, J. L., 1962. *How To Do Things With Words*. London: Oxford.

Balsamo, A. 1989, "Imagining Cyborgs: Post-Modernism and Symbolic Interactionism," pp. 369-379 in Studies in Symbolic Interaction, Vol. 10b, (N. K. Denzin, ed.), Greenwich City, GAI Press

Baudrillard, J. 1983. *Simulations*. NY: Semiotext(e).

———————, 1988. *The Ecstasy of Communication*. NY: Semiotext.

———————, 1992. *La Guerre du Golf n'a pas eu Lieu*. Paris: Galilee

Becker, H. 1982. *Art Worlds*. Berkeley, CA: University of California Press.

Beckett, S. 1959. *Krapp's Last Tape and Embers*. London: Faber and Faber.

Berger, P., B. Berger and H. Kellner. 1973. *The Homeless Mind*. Random House: Vintage.

Bjelic, D. 1987. "On Hanging Up in Telephone Conversation." Semiotica 67-3/4, 195-210.

Brown, G., and G. Yule. 1983. *Discourse Analysis*. Cambridge Textbooks in Linguistics. New York: Cambridge University Press.

Carpenter, E. 1972. *Oh, What a Blow that Phantom Gave Me!* St. Albans, UK: Paladin Books.

De Sole, P.I. (ed.) 1977. *The Social Impact of the Telephone*. Cambridge, MA: MIT Press.

Denzin, N.K. 1977. "Notes on the Cuminogenic Hypothesis: A Case Study of the American Liquor Industry." American Soc. Rev. 42:905-920

——————1978. "Crime and American Liquor Industry." pp. 87-118 in Studies in symbolic Interaction, Vol. I, Greenwich: JAI Press.

——————, 1992. The Conversation. Symbolic Interaction 15(2):135-149.

Dingwall, S. 1992. "Leaving Telephone Answering Machine Messages: Who's Afraid of Speaking to Machines?" Text 12(1):81-101

Feenberg, A. 1989. "A User's Guide to the Pragmatics of Computer Mediated Communication." Semiotica 75-3/4, 257-278.

Fischer, C.S. 1987. "Women and Telephone in North America 1890-1940: Technologies of Sociablity." Am. Jou. of Soc.

Fontana, A. and S. Tillet, 1993, "Deconstructing the Self: New Metaphores for a Post-Modern Self," pp. 35-43, *Studies in Symbolic Interaction*, Vol. 14 (N. K. Denzin, ed.), Greenwich City, GAI Press

Garrison, D. 1992, "Phoning It In." *New Yorker*, March 9, pp. 93-95

Gates, D. 1992, "Sex that Goes Over the Line." *Newsweek*, Jan. 27

Giddens, A. 1991. *Modernity and Self Identity: Self and Society in the Late Modern Age* Cambridge, UK: Polity Press

Gold, R. 1991. "Answering Machine Talk." *Discourse Processes* 4:243-60

Guillaume, M. 1982. "Telespectres." Traverse 26.

Halliday, M.A.K., and R. Hasan. 1976. *Cohesion in English*. London: Longman.

Handelman, D. 1992. *Symbolic Types, the Body, and Circus*. Semiotica 85-3/4:205-27

Hazan, H. 1990. *A Paradoxical Community*. Greenwich: JAI Press.

Jakobson, Roman, 1960. "Linguistics and Poetics." in T. Sebeok (ed.) *Style in Language*. Bloomington: Indiana University Press, pp. 350-77.

Jameson, F. 1991. *POSTMODERNISM, or, The Cultural Logic of Late Capitalism*. Durham: Duke University Press.

Katriel, T. 1986. *Talking Straight: 'Dugri' Speech in Israeli Sabra Culture*. Cambridge: Cambridge University Press.

Kimmerling, B., 1985. "Between the Primordial and the Civil Definitions of the Collective Identity: Eretz Israel or the State of Israel." in E. Cohen, M. Lissak, U. Almagor (eds.), *Comparative Social Dynamics*, Westview Press, pp. 262-283.

Kling, R. and E.M. Gerson, 1978. "Patterns of Segmentation and Interaction in the Computing World." Symbolic Interaction 1:24-43

Labov, W. 1973. *Language in the Inner City*. Philadelphia: University of Penn. Press.

Mashi'ach, S. 1989. "Different Aspects of the Usage of Answering Machines for Private Purposes: Interviews and Data." Unpublished paper, Tel-Aviv University.

McLuhan, M. 1965. *Understanding Media: The Extensions of Man*. NY: McGraw-Hill.

Raz, A. 1992/3. "The Reinherited Self: A Case Study in The Dynamics of a Social World." Forthcoming in N.K. Denzin (ed.), *Studies in Symbolic Interaction*.

Rosenblum, B. 1978. *Phat Work*. NY: Holmes and Meier.

Roth, J.A., and M.E.R. Lepionka. 1973. "The Telephone Answering Service as a Communication Barrier: A Research Note." Urban Life and Culture 2(1):105-112.

Sayad, A. 1985. "Du Meassage Oral au Message Sur Cassette, la Communication Avec l'Absent." Actes de la Recherche en Sciences Sociales 59:61-72.

Schegloff, E. 1972. "Sequencing in Conversational Openings." In *Directions in Socio-Linguistics: The Ethnography of Communication*, J. Gumperz and D. Hymes 9eds.), 346-80. NY: Holt, Rinehart and Winston.

Sebba, R. and A. Churchman 1986. "The Uniqueness of the Home." Architecture and Behavior 3 (1): 7-24.

Sebeok, T.A., (ed.) 1968. *Animal Communication*. Bloomington, Indiana: University Press.

Singleton, L. 1989. *Global Impact: The New Telecommunication Technologies*. NY: Harper and Row.

Shamgar-Handelman, L. and R. Belkin 1984. "They Won't Stay Home Forever: Pattern of Home Space Allocation." *Urban Anthropology* 13 (1): 117-144.

Shapira and Herzog. 1984. "The Autograph Book as a Mirror of Age and Period: The Israeli Case, " *Megamot*, Vol. 28(4) pp. 513-531 (in Hebrew).

Shapira, R. and D. Navon. 1991. "Alone Together: Public and Private Dimensions of a Tel-Aviv Cafe." *Qualitative Sociology*, Vol. 14, No. 2, 107-125.

Shibutani, T., 1955. "Reference Groups as Perspectives," *American Journal of Sociology* 60: 562-568.

Stengel R., 1992, "1-900-AURALSEX." *Time*, Feb. 3, pp. 59

Sternberg, M. 1984. "Spatiotemporal Art and the Other Henry James." in: *Poetics Today*, 5.

Strauss, A. 1978. "A Social World Perspective," in: N.K. Denzin (ed.), *Studies in Symbolic Interaction*, Vol. 1. Greenwich C.T.: JAI Press, pp. 119-128.

———, 1982. "Social Worlds and Legitimation Processes," in N.K. Denzin (ed.), *Studies in Symbolic Interaction*, Vol. 4. Greenwich, C: JAI Press, pp. 171-190.

Wojcik, D. 1987. "'At the Sound of the Beep': An Analysis of the Structure and Traditional Speech Forms of Answering Machines." *Folklore and Mythology Studies* 11:81-103.

Umble, D. 1992. "The Amish and the Telephone: Resistence and Reconstruction," in R. Silverstone and E. Hirsch (eds), *Consuming Technologies*, New York: Routledge.

Unruh, D.R., 1983. *Invisible Lives: Social Worlds of the Aged*. Beverly Hills, CA: Sage.

Part 3

Language in a Pluralistic Society

7

A Sociological Paradigm of Bilingualism: English, French, Yiddish, and Arabic in Israel[1]

Eliezer Ben-Rafael

Bilingualisms: Cultural and Status Aspects

Bilingualism means that the individual's allegiance to language is divided between two (or more) codes. Spolsky (1989: 100) says that "Scholars in the field treat bilingualism as a relative rather than an absolute phenomenon, and consider anyone able to produce (or even understand) sentences in more than one language as the proper object of their study." For a society, bilingualism means that various languages are diffused at diverse degrees (see Lieberson, 1981). Models and typologies widely vary (Hamers and Blanc, 1989). Fishman (1980; 1989) emphasizes that codes may differ according to the domains of their use; considering the notion of *diglossia*, Romaine (1989) emphasizes the complexity of contemporary situations and speaks of *triglossia* or *polyglossia*. Mackey (1968) points to functions like counting, praying, cursing, dreaming, diary-writing, or note-taking (see also Grosjean, 1982 for a list). A distinction is also made between *subtractive* and *additive* bilingualisms and Dorian elaborates on the notion of *semi-speaker* ((1981; 1982; see also Dressler, 1989). All of these are relevant mainly for *second languages* known besides the legitimate and dominant language, which, in contrast to the former, is usually protected by specialized institutions, and is transmitted by official socialization.

One may focus on such *not-indispensable* languages through different perspectives. One perspective relates to the notion of *cultural pluralism*, and another to the notion of *linguistic capital*. To the notion of cultural pluralism are linked these approaches which elaborate on the role of languages as markers of collective identities (Fishman, Cooper et al., 1971; Bell,1983: 132)), and the practice of bilingualism, as their negotiation (Scotton, 1980; 1983). Fishman's concept of *di-ethnia* (1980) applies when more than one ethnocultural norm exists in society in relation to different languages. Second languages warrant a cultural accumulation, which may uphold the social cohesion of restricted communities (Sapir, 1974; Stevens, Swicegood, 1987) and protect their sociocultural personality (Labov, 1976: 116-142)). The social importance of languages then fluctuates with the social location, wealth, power, and prestige of their carriers. Models of bilingualism anchored in social divisions and inequality (see also Scotton, Ury, 1977; Grosjean, 1982: 117-161) call for a distinction between *elitist* bilingualism, which involves the privileged, and *folk* bilingualism, which refers to popular strata (see Harding, Riley 1986: 24)). Gumperz (1976) explains further on that "...the majority language, the *they-code* is associated with more formal, stiffer and less personal out-group relations, whereas the minority language, the *we-code*, becomes associated with in-group and informal activities." Hence, the relation of linguistic variety and cultural pluralism comes out to the role of carriers and their status. Giles and his colleagues (Beebe, Giles, 1984; Street, Giles, 1982) elaborate on the benefits of locutors to adjust to the language of the addressee.

On the other hand, says Grosjean (1982: 121), language contacts create differences of status among the languages themselves. Lambert (1975; 1977) has elaborated on their differential prestige and power. Determined by a variety of factors including, but by no means exclusively, the status of their original carriers, this differentiation influences the general attitudes toward those languages. Corollarily, languages may be forgotten or acquired, independently, or at least distinctively, from what happens to their original carriers in society. Romaine (1989) has shown that bilingualism can be a phase of decline for *old* languages confronting the penetration of *new* ones; Gal (1979), that borrowing and interferences from an expanding language along with social relations with its speakers cause the decline of mother tongues.

As a specific category of symbolic resources, second languages circumscribe their own social market and get rated relative to each other. This accounts for their power of attraction as objects of eventual acquisition. Hence, one may speak of the status *per se* of languages. Bourdieu elaborates on *linguistic resources* as *symbolic capital* (Bourdieu, Passeron, 1970: 50; Bourdieu, 1987: 147-166); Bourdieu, 1982). This attribute is not only a function of their association with the privileged and situations which concern them particularly (Bernstein, Henderson, 1972), but also of their conditioning access to wanted services, signaling recognized social values and warranting symbolic manipulation (see Marcellesi, Gardin, 1974: 35-38;). They establish social distances between social categories and reproduce them (Chilland, 1971; Baudelot, Establet, 1971).

When widening this perspective to include bilingualisms—Bourdieu himself focuses only on variants of the legitimate language—the accumulation of different languages may too be seen as symbolic power. The modern structures of international communication account, particularly, for the universal use, power, and prestige of worldwide codes that represent—as any prized resource—targets of investment for, nay, even of monopolization by, the privileged.

In sum, linguistic symbols are bound to cultural pluralism when they distinguish between collective identities; they act as a symbolic capital when they create a difference of social distinction between strata. These two analytically distinct aspects cannot be seen as absolutely independent, and it is at this point that our own contention is that *the status of cultural carriers of a language and the symbolic-capital status of the language itself interact, and together widely determine the dynamics of linguistic resources in society.* Elaborating—on the basis of a twofold dichotomization—on these aspects, Table 1 draws out the possibilities implied by the paradigm, which they delineate. This paradigm raises theoretical questions.

(1) Related to original carriers of high-status symbolic resources, who themselves belong to the privileged, it may be asked if being gratified by the social order encourages or discourages the retention of symbols which set this group in contrast with the rest of society (case 1).

(2) Where linguistic markers are socially prized—and wanted by the privileged—but the carriers—for independent reasons—exhibit as for them, social weakness, one may question the capability of such elements to resist a hold over of their resources by the stronger (case 2).

(3) A strong group, conveying a language that is of rather low status, may not have anything to lose socially by sticking to its linguis-

tic legacy; on the other hand, one may question what its interest is to do so as an entity privileged by the social order (case 3).

(4) A weak group might get rid of low-prestige linguistic resources that damage its status. Though, the less prestigious a language, the weaker, also, the competition for its mastery on the side of others, which should allow it to retain its linguistic identity more easily (case 4).

Table 1
A paradigm of languages—markers of groups versus linguistic capital values[a]

Status of carriers	Cultural capital value +	Cultural capital value -
+	1:+/+	3:+/-
—	2:-/+	4:-/-

a '+' signifies that the given language or variant is of high linguistic-capital value or constitutes a marker of a high-status group; '-' signifies the contrary.

A privileged group does not necessarily carry a prestigious marker, and an underprivileged group a low-status code. This statement guides the following analysis of the social dynamics of second languages in Israel as it is generated by the very revival and diffusion of a new national language. Each of the four types outlined in Table 1 applies here to different codes and we will focus on the four principal ones—English, French, Yiddish, and Arabic.

The Revival of a Language: The Generation of Bilingualisms

Influenced by European nationalism (Katz, 1960; Laqueur, 1972; Avineri, 1981: 3-13), Zionism was primarily embedded in Jewish cultural notions (Buber, 1973: XVII) and, as says Avineri (1981: 13), "substituted a secular self-identity of the Jews as a nation for the traditional and Orthodox self-identity in religious terms." It is in this vein that the Zionist enterprise started with a linguistic revolution, revived Hebrew, the language of the Bible, and imposed it as the new nation's legitimate language. The following uncompromising struggles against the Gola languages recall the imposition of the language of the *Ile de France* over all Frenchmen in the Great Revolution (Grillo, 1989).

However, modern Hebrew was first to be invented (see Chomsky, 1957). Hebrew (Rabin, 1973: 69; Cooper, 1989: 12-14), the Language of the Scriptures, was to be transformed into a vernacular. Nahir (1978) defines the revival of Hebrew cautiously as *speech revival* rather than *language revival*"(for a discussion see Schur, in preparation) and Blanc (1968) speaks of a *koine* to mean that modern Hebrew combines a variety of earlier forms with elements of different contemporary languages. Anyway, during the 1950s, the mass immigration was channeled to the *Ulpan*, a period of temporary residence in a center of absorption where immigrants are taught the language intensively; this course focuses especially on speech competence. Up to now, the *ulpan* is not just a form of diffusion of the language; it reproduces the revival itself for every immigrant and consists of a deconstruction and reconstruction of identities (see Selwyn, 1990; Katz, 1982). Because Hebrew was the sacred language of all Jewish legacies, and therefore *a priori* a symbol of identity and identification, this process has never raised protest among newcomers. In particular, the popular underprivileged Middle-Eastern and North African communities who mostly immigrated during the 1940s and 1950s accepted willingly the shift to Hebrew because of their traditionalist Zionism.

Some groups, to be sure,—such as the Yemenites, have found it easier to grasp Hebrew than others,—such as the Germans, (Hofman, Fisherman, 1972). Length of stay in the country, lower age on arrival, level of education, urban experience, social status, or ethnic heterogeneity of families correlate positively with a rapid assimilation of Hebrew (Bachi, 1956; 1974; Hofman, Fisherman, 1972; Carmon, Manheim, 1976; see for a review, Rosenbaum, 1983).

While the dominant aspiration was the building of one unified nation grounded in a Hebrew culture, later cultural and structural changes in Israeli society have, however, witnessed new developments. The growing importance of reference to the Western world—in technology, economic development, and social organization—exposed Hebraization to the diffusion of English and to a re-appraisal of foreign languages. Moreover, Hebrew has actually been acquired much more quickly than the mother-tongues have been forgotten. From both viewpoints, and while public debates moved by ideological concerns rarely discuss this aspect, the shift to Hebrew has also meant the generation of *bilingualisms*. The dynamics of this bilingual reality reveals forms and models that the interaction between social and linguistic resources may take on.

The following overviews selected findings of a set of studies which we led during 1988-1990 about the roles of English, French, Yiddish, and Arabic. Because of the diversity of the *parcours*, these works used different research tools and a variety of methodologies. When considered as a whole, however, these works yield models that respond to the questions of our paradigm. Because our concern focuses on the part of the Israeli population which has experienced the revival of Hebrew, it excludes references to groups like the Arab minority, which retains Arabic as a first language, or the ultra-Orthodox community, which widely retains Yiddish as its vernacular.

English: The Prestigious Language of the Privileged

English was one of the three official languages of the British Mandate (1922-1948), together with Hebrew and Arabic. Ever since the creation of the state, it is the second language in the Hebrew-speaking school—though its formal status was terminated by Parliament. This language is compulsory in elementary and high school. A requirement for graduation and for admission to the university, a given competence in English conditions the continuation of academic studies (see also Isaacs, 1967). A study of middle class students in 11th and 12th grades (Cooper, Fishman, 1977) reveals a general fair level of proficiency. Youngsters exploit opportunities to use the language outside the classroom. English is seen as "beautiful, rich, musical" and the good students of English are also good in any matter, which often correlates with a privileged social status of the family. Many middle- and higher-rank jobs require a fluent knowledge of English and this tendency increases over time (Ronen, Seckbach, Cooper, 1977). The language is perceived as of a growing importance in numerous domains—foreign trade, tourism, and technological development. Besides Hebrew, English is the most popular language in the country—(Rosenbaum, Nadel et al, 1977).

Over the years, the number of books, journals and magazines published in Israel in the English language increases considerably. About 10% of all newspaper and periodicals printed in the country are published in English, many in specialized areas. A survey of 307 libraries showed 37% of books in English. In specialized libraries—museums, universities, or institutes—this figure is more than 50%. A survey of names of stores shows that the use of English is frequent and loaded with notions of modernity, fashion, and, good business. In 1990, Israel's Broadcasting Authority instituted a fifteen-minute daily TV news program in English. Last but not least, a study (Alony-Fainberg, 1977) shows that the dictionary of the Israeli Academy for the Hebrew Language lately borrows more and more from English. A recent study (Ben-Rafael, 1974) found that English is the first language parents want their children to learn. This language, as shown in Table 2, is far ahead in this respect among the four major languages known in Israel besides Hebrew.

Table 2
The relative importance of languages
(What language do you want your children to learn?)

	Grades[a]	*Standard deviation*
English	2.714	.022
French	1.413	.026
Arabic	.944	.028
Yiddish	.077	.011

[a] The grades were obtained by granting 3 points to the first choice, 2 to the second and 1 to the third.

The same research has found that the knowledge of English is dispersed throughout society but is higher among the privileged strata. It is in middle- and upperclass milieus, that the language is acquired by personal investments and is of real presence—with relatives from abroad, tourists, and colleagues—serving as well for selected cultural, leisure, and professional needs. The language that is most praised by individuals of *all* classes best differentiates the privileged from the underprivileged.

This development has a special impact on the attitude toward English of those who immigrated here and whose language of origin is English. These immigrants are a small cohort—less than 2% of the population, but they heavily concentrate in middle- and upper-middle professional strata, and represent the communities of the English-speaking countries which amount to more than 50% of all Jews in the world. An evolution has taken place over the years in their attitudes toward English. In the mid-1960s, Isaacs (1967) found that parents hardly spoke with their children in their language of origin. Because of their Zionist ideology, they preferred Hebrew. Ten years later, another study (Seckbach, Cooper, 1977) reported that English speaking mothers of recent immigration and professional background, did not refrain from speaking in English with their children, on public sites among themselves as well as with people who are not native English speakers.

These developments were delved into by our own research in the late 1980s. A first step took us to Kohav Yair where we questioned 23 informants in in-depth interviews—teachers, town hall officials, and managers of community centers (11 informants), and members of the active families of the English-speaking group (12 informants). Kohav Yair is a new town created in 1986 in Samaria, 10 km from Israel's veteran town of Kfar Saba. The settlement numbers 750 families with 4,000 souls 15% of "Anglo-Saxon origin," mostly South African. The town's population is overwhelmingly middleclass—three-quarters of the employed are professionals—and middle-aged—the average age of the adults is 40, and the children are 62% of the population. Many families consider themselves as moderately religious. These families are now, three years after immigration, very active in the community and of undeniable weight in the public and political arena. On the other hand, South Africans are also active within frameworks that they created for themselves. Hence, there is the weekly rugby game of men and there also is the charity Ezra organization of women. Everything here is in English as is almost any social interaction involving Anglo-Saxons—on public sites as well as in the family and with children. In the homes, one would hardly find books, videotapes, magazines or newspapers in another language than English. The children use Hebrew with their mates but Hebrew and English with their parents.

English is recognized by the local authorities as a nearly official language: local cable-TV broadcasts in both Hebrew and English. This does raise the reservations of not a few non-Anglo-Saxon residents. One female member of the local council warns that: "One is to confess that the way things go, the new immigrants will never learn Hebrew; they are spoiled by everyone far beyond the normal. They continue to use English as their first language. When one get to their homes, one may forget that Hebrew is the language of this country."

The South Africans contribute to the community. The very presence of an English-speaking group of immigrants is considered a symbol of status for the settlement. To integrate English-speaking families is seen as important for its public image. Of middleclass background themselves, many inhabitants of non-Anglo-Saxon origin know English and like speaking this language with South Africans. For the mayor: "We are all educated people, and we all know English. This is not a foreign language to us. We feel pleased with the use of English ...After all, we all were abroad, in the States or elsewhere; we all learned English at school."

The Anglo-Saxons make up a powerful group able to raise demands and obtain satisfaction. They imposed several members of their group as English teachers in school despite the fact that they lack formal qualification. Such achievements endow them with a feeling of status. They are convinced that the use of English grants them prestige, rather than criticism. The stigmatization, which might be bound to the retention of linguistic particularism, does not find in them a vulnerable target.

Raanana (North of Tel-Aviv) is another example. South Africans started settling here in the early 1960s. Their neighborhood became a pole of attraction for English-speaking immigrants who expanded in other quarters and became the major concentration of English-speaking families in the country—five thousand families in a town of. 25,000 souls. We interviewed 15 South African families who immigrated in the 1960s or 1970s and we conducted systematic observations in public sites and institutions—a kindergarten, a primary school, the absorption center of the town, a supermarket, and of course, the main street.

All our informants pointed out that South African immigrants here belong overwhelmingly to the professional class. Both husbands and wives usually work outside the home. South African families in Raanana generally use Hebrew when addressing non-English speakers in public, but speak only English among themselves—including parents with children. Even when only one of the spouses is South African, the family still uses English together with Hebrew. Children know both languages and use them indiscriminately when they address their parents. Among themselves children use Hebrew.

The opinion of all informants is that English is so important in Israel that any English-speaking individual feels that using the language is gratified by the environment. Yet, as a rule, South Africans in Raanana know Hebrew, which they had often already learned in their country of origin in Jewish schools. Hence, TV and radio broadcasts watched or listened to are by no means exclusively in English. Hebrew newspapers are read, even though a majority do not give up the pleasure of reading an additional English paper—at least a weekly. While reading books in Hebrew may seem too difficult—, among parents, Hebrew is still of wide use. The network of friends is mostly heterogeneous from the linguistic viewpoint and but a minority remains confined to a milieu that is uniformly English-speaking. In interactions with people who are not native English-speakers, Hebrew is the principal language.

Raanana's South African families are not religious in general, but often consider themselves traditionalist. The majority attend synagogue services on Rosh Hashanah (the Jewish New Year) and Yom Kippur (the Day of Atonement). By habit, on the eve of Shabbat, many attend synagogues that are known as *Anglo-Saxon* and are of Conservative—as opposed to Orthodox—rite; the prayer may be in Ashkenazi Hebrew, as usual in South Africa. This could be seen as a sign of ethnicization. There also are the numerous activities held in English, which are sponsored by the *ESRA* (English Speakers Residence Association)—tours, parties, or social services—or by the *Federation of South African Immigrants*—counseling for immigrants, information about jobs, or aid for lodgings.

Among the children, Hebrew is, of course, the first language; however, English is fluent and of large use—at home and outside home. At school, children of South African origin do not speak with each other in English. On the other hand, though, South African parents finance special classes for English advanced studies for their children, instead of the regular English lessons, which their children do not need. This creates, within the school, a partial framework particular to these children of native English-speaking families. These children also participate in a variety of activities offered by the South African organizations—which may require rituals and uniforms—and mostly revolving around typical South African sport.

We found, however, another face of South African immigration in Orot, a cooperative village—moshav—about 40 kms southeast from Raanana. Today, 40% of the members are South African; 20% English, American, or Australian; and 40% Israeli-born. Most members have jobs outside the *moshav* in addition to their work on their land, which they labor with the help of salaried workers. The Zionist ideology of the *Return to the Land* of the *moshav* movement and its consequent cult of Hebrew are still vivid components of the culture of the village.

The South African families are here, too, mostly of wealthy origin and of higher education; they immigrated and joined the *moshav* for ideological motives. Unlike the residents of Raanana or Kochav Yair, the *moshavniks*, however, are not traditional though the atmosphere is here characterized by more simplicity and ascetism. People rarely journey abroad. The Committee for Cultural Activities organizes events including lectures, movies, celebrations, or circles of studies. The principal activity consists in the celebration of feasts. For some years, there was in the *moshav* a dramatic circle which performed in English. Yet, the South Africans of Orot have no strong commitment to their language of origin. As a member of Orot told us, "To be a *moshavnick* is incongruent with remaining a non-Hebrew speaker. To be a Hebrew-speaker means to stop to be a South African." The *moshavniks* have adopted Hebrew as their daily language, and they speak it not only with the Israeli-born members of the *moshav* but among themselves as well. Hebrew is spoken between spouses, as well as with children. They are interested, of course, in having their children learn English at school as well as possible, yet they evoke in this respect merely instrumental reasons.

Hence, because of the strong Hebraist ideology and Zionist culture of the *moshav*, the use of English in Orot as a daily vernacular is but feebly gratified, and the motivation to retain collective features on the basis of the use of English is weak. Hence, the tendency of the South Africans in Raanana and in Kochav Yair to emphasize their linguistic identity cannot be seen as simply dictated by a primordial commitment to English, but rather as a function of the prestige English grants in those urban communities.

French: The Prestigious Language of the Underprivileged

French is, up to now, used by about 250,000 Israeli Jews (6%) (see ICBS, 1983). The sources of this *francophonie* are varied. For many Bulgarian, Greek, or Turkish Jews, French has been learned in the school of the *Alliance Israelite Universelle* as the carrier of modernization. In the Eastern European bourgeoisie, French was a marker of social status. Three quarters of Israel's French speakers consist, however, of North Africans for whom French has been a cultural identity. Here, the North African communities are widely lower-class and make up the most underprivileged Jewish category. As a result, the North African origin itself has been associated with the lowest step in the hierarchy of ethnic status (Kraus, 1982; Ben-Rafael, Sharot, 1991).

At the same time, however, and as previous work shows (Ben-Rafael, 1994) French, as a worldwide code, is seen by Israelis in general, as a major Western European language and is granted a prestige which is well above Arabic's and Yiddish's (see Table 2). It is as such that it is diffused by the Israeli school as a second foreign language. The language is chosen by approximately 7% of the general school enrolment of the 12to18 age bracket (1986), i.e., 34,000 students. The investigation (see Ben-Rafael, Gani et al., 1989) of a random sample of this population—747 students of 34 schools or about 20% of all schools where French is taught in the country—reveals its social characteristics.

This research shows that a speaker of French- origin—i.e., those who have at least one parent who, according to the respondent's own testimony, masters a fluent French—is here over represented—28% which is almost as twice the 15% figure among Israeli Jews in general (ICBS,1983). *Francophonie* is primarily associated with a North African origin—less with Balkan and still much less European origins. Though, the French-speakers are still a restricted minority—on the basis of our findings, we estimate that less than 10% of the North African students of appropriate age, study French at school (see Ben-Rafael, Herzlich et al, 1990). French is here by no means an ethnic niche.

On the other hand, homogeneity reigns among our respondents as for their parents' social status and their own status at school. The fathers of more than two thirds of the students (70%) have a white-collar occupation and nearly half belong to the professional. Three-quarters (73%) of the families enjoy a comfortable material situation (one person at most per room of residence). According to an index of socioeconomic status (SES) (see Ayalon, Ben-Rafael et al, 1987), 57% of the students belong to the upper-middle class, 16% only to the inferior stratum, and 27% to the intermediary stratum. In parallel, a two-thirds (67%) majority of students are "good" or "very good" students in the principal matters of study. Their teachers confirm that they constitute a gifted cohort.

As for their motivation, less than one-tenth of the sample explains that it took on French studies because of the constraints of the school's programs, although learning this language is not considered either as useful for the acquisition of technological knowledge or scientific information. Moreover, only a minority is interested in French literature and culture—the notion of French culture being generally associated with stereotypes carried by the media like gastronomy (53%), fashion (17%), tourist interests (8%), or romantic values (6%). Nearly none is motivated by ethnocultural incentives, while less than 10% aspire to strengthen their relations with members of their family, thanks to French. In fact, the most important motives of learning French are associated with the notion of cultural capital. Half of our respondents emphasize the pleasure of speaking French; more (two-thirds) consider this knowledge to be a mark of social distinction and education ("to be cultivated"), and almost all are convinced that French is a privileged means of international communication. The knowledge of French is thus firstly a symbol of status and a valued resource. This type of allegiance to French by no means implies a rejection of other languages—90% wish that their future children know French as well, 98% English.

Similarly, for more than half of our respondents (53%), a family norm has been a determinant factor, of the individual's choice. This presence of the family turns the attention to what differentiates parents who have children in classes of French and those who do not. Hence, a sample of parents completed this study (Ben-Rafael, Gani, et al., 1989). This investigation was led with parents of students of high schools where French is offered and it numbered both parents whose children do and do not study French at school (n=573, 201 of whom or 35% had children who studied French).

French, in fact, is principally offered in academic frameworks, and rarely in vocational schools. A sample like ours thus counts a relatively larger share of the stronger strata of society—the main clients of this kind of education—than in the population as a whole. Hence, only 35% respondents were of North African or Middle Eastern origins; a wide majority had at least a complete secondary education (85%); on the basis of the husbands' occupations, 28% of the respondents belonged to higher SES strata, 50% to the middle stratum and 22% to the lower salaried blue-collar stratum. While the principal language of this sample is Hebrew (91%), many know English (78% as a second or third language), and a few know Arabic (28%) or French (24%).

The general attitudes toward French are favorable: 66% are very positive and consider this language as worth studying; 27% are indifferent; only 7% are hostile. The French language is seen as cultural (85%), respectable (73%), and international (61%). The utility of French is understood as being related to a *good education* (69%); its knowledge is (for 45%) a source of pleasure and it helps to occasion interesting social contacts (32%). On the other hand, French is practically useful for less than half of the respondents (46%), and only a small minority considers it important for the acquisition of scientific or technological knowledge (10%). French culture or literature is not of much interest either (13%).

Only one-third of those in our sample have children who are learning the language, but nearly two-thirds (63%) would like their children to do so. Most interestingly, the parents of students who learn French are of significantly higher SES than the non-learning category: among the former, 45% are from the higher SES stratum, 53% of the middle stratum, and but 2% of the lower stratum. The distribution among the families whose children do not learn French is 19%, 48% and 33% respectively. Moreover, the same tendency is revealed within all groups of geocultural origin. The difference in average SES ratings (summing up to .29, while .16 among others) is particularly salient among the North Africans. Higher status North Africans are much more likely to have children studying French at school than lower status North Africans. Seeing that their ethnic status is associated with social inferiority and is incongruent with their class position, the attraction of the former to French may be interpreted as an ambition to assert an allegiance to a prestigious marker and valuable resource by exploiting the familiarity with the language acquired originally as an ethnic marker.

The non-mobile North Africans, however, are the representatives of the very bulk of the Israeli *francophonie*, i.e., the North African—mostly lower-class—communities. An investigation into the extent that French is still alive in its original environment was thus led in the Moroccan working-class neighborhood of Bat-Yam—a city of 130,000 inhabitants in the direct southern vicinity of Tel-Aviv—with the help of 25 informants—teachers, merchants, social workers, or townhall officials—and by means of observation—seventy hours of observation in cafes, synagogues, and other public sites. We found that French is here still a living language and very much spoken by the elderly and between them and the middle-aged generation. This French, usually a form of popular North African parlance, shares its popularity with the Moroccan Judeo-Arabic. Both French and Arabic songs can be heard at weddings or other festive opportunities. These vernaculars are often switched from one to the other in the speech of the elderly. Since the family is usually large—six to eight children—and stable in this setting, the elderly retain a strong presence, which is significant for the transmission of the languages of origin to the young.

Many residents of this neighborhood have relatives in France, Morocco, or Quebec. Visiting these relatives means *seeing the world* at a not inconsiderable expense and hosting relatives from abroad in Bat Yam is a source of legitimate pride. Reciprocal visits constitute an incentive for the retention of some French. On the other hand, there are also the visits from and to Casablanca which favor a retention of some Arabic. This reality is remote from the evolving of French in the educational institution where it is dispensed in an elitist perspective and where French, as second language taught after Hebrew and English, appears as a luxury difficult to afford for a socially deprived category.

In fact, the models of diffusing French in the school encourage the language to migrate from underprivileged groups where it constitutes an integral part of the culture, to stronger and more prestigious groups where it represents additional assets and a symbol of distinction. The same applies to the middle- and upper-classe North Africans who exhibit a special allegiance to French. The North African community as a whole hardly retains this rare, valued resources, which is gradually losing its principal setting of daily utilization. This deterioration of the intrinsic value of the language takes place, however, at the same time that it undergoes social valorization. The main problem with this process resides in the fact that it illustrates a phenomenon of cultural polarization between underprivileged and privileged strata.

Yiddish: A Non-Prestigious Language of a Privileged Category

The best known Jewish diasporic vernacular is Yiddish, the language of origin of more than 80% of the Jews in the world, and of 50% of the Israeli Jews. Yiddish (see Katz, 1986) emerged, following the settling of Jews in Germany, as a language which allied Semitic and German components. By 1350, Yiddish was the language of the Jews who lived on German-speaking territory; it was developing independently from German and expanding eastward (Susskind, 1987; Wexler, 1987). Yiddish became a world language during the 19th century with the emigration of Eastern European Jews to the West. A new and secular Yiddish literature, theatre, and journalism developed during the last decade of the 19th Century and the first decades of the 20th (Susskind, 1987; Fishman, 1980). At the 1908 Conference of Tshernovits, Yiddish was declared the language of the Jews; it was boosted, against the partisans of Hebrew, by the Socialist Bund Party. Though, among the Zionists too, many sustained Yiddish, starting with Ber Borochow, one of the founders of Socialist Zionism and a Yiddish linguist.

Nowadays, Jews have mostly integrated into non-Jewish environments and speak local languages. Moreover, Hebrew has been the language of a Jewish state since 1948. Here and there, Yiddish is still transmitted by Jewish schools, but with limited success. About 100 Yiddish books are published annually in the world for about 250,000 or 300,000 Yiddish-speakers. Throughout the world, some three million

Jews share a semi-competence in this language. Called a *jargon* by its own speakers, the only contemporary adepts of Yiddish, those who, paradoxically enough, have succeeded the old socialist Bund in this capacity, are the non-Zionist ultra-Orthodox. These sects confine Biblical Hebrew to holy learning and have long blamed the profane use of this language as the "greatest danger of heresy for the innocent". To be sure, the role of Yiddish in ultra-Orthodox communities in Israel makes it, in the eyes of the non-ultra-Orthodox, a marker of an alien and elapsed way of life.

The struggle of Zionism against Yiddish had been harsh, indeed. Nearly all ideological and political forces had been united in the boycott of anything Yiddish—cultural manifestations or publishing literary pieces—and conversations in Yiddish overheard in the street could attract the protests of youngsters. Today, Yiddish still belongs to the less esteemed languages in Israel (see Table 2) far after English, French, and even Arabic. On the other hand, the Ashkenazi Jews, the original carriers of Yiddish, belong, in the overwhelming majority (by about 80%), to the middle and upper-middle classes where they constitute the predominant component (Ben-Rafael, Sharot, 1991). In fact, they are the ones who, as the bulk of the Zionist movement, have pushed this language to the bottom of the prestige ladder of languages.

However, a genuine change has taken place in recent years. Yiddish is now given more respect. It has been instituted as an optional—secondary—subject of study in high school, and about 800 pupils study this language for matriculation. This is revealing. On the media, Yiddish expressions, jokes, and songs are now frequent and Yiddish culture is a frequent object of reference in public speech. All these are short from meaning a revival of Yiddish as a public language. Yet, one definitely witnesses ever since the early 1980s public efforts aimed at reviving Yiddish culture.

The most outright manifestation of these efforts is the new Tel-Aviv Yiddish Theater. After years without success, a repertoire Yiddish-speaking theater in Israel was finally created in 1987 and, a few months were enough for it to achieve an undeniable cultural impact. For years, Yiddish-speaking actors had met an unbreakable wall and had to make do with small audiences in remote halls. The slogan *Speak Hebrew* was an unbridgeable obstacle to the diffusion of Yiddish culture. Dzigan and Schumacher, two illustrious Yiddish comedy players, succeeded for a time, in the 1950s, but they never were a part of the country's mainstream artistic milieu. Several Yiddish theaters in the

1960s tried vainly to overcome the official disdain for the culture they represented. A national Yiddish theater in Tel-Aviv inaugurated in 1974 carried on for only one year. A last attempt of Dzigan to set up a new scene in 1978 was without success.

The 1987 attempt, in contrast, enrolled a group of actors and a director who came from the Habima National Hebrew Theater itself. Its declared goal was to preserve the Yiddish culture as due to a major mould of Jewish history. Rejecting any intention to set up a museum, it aspired to rejuvenate Yiddish artistic production. The target audience was not only the Yiddish-speaking elderly but also those younger who were still somehow familiar with the language. The theater also set up evenings of poetry readings, circles of study of the Yiddish literature, and seminars of initiation to Yiddish culture.

An investigation of the theater's actors and audience found that the demand for Yiddish plays in Israel is by no means negligible. Performances are given daily and the hall never fills less than four-fifths of its 500 seats. The majority of the audience consists of veteran, post-Holocaust immigrants. Their age is generally over 60, many are over 70, but about a quarter of the spectators are Israeli-born younger people—in their 30s and 40s—who are familiar with Yiddish as the language of their parents or grandparents. The conversations during the recess or before the show overheard in the cafeteria or in the hall reveal that attending the Yiddish theater is in no way an expression of counterculture directed against Hebrew: Hebrew is here too the dominant language. We found rather that the performance is looked at as valuable on its own right, as bringing memories back, or as still relevant nowadays to one's cultural world.

Interviews of the director and several actors and actresses (9) added to this picture. The initiative of the theater has been collective; it emerged from the conviction of a group of intellectuals who belong to the main stream of Israeli culture, that the Yiddish culture is not to be abandoned to oblivion. They felt that they must do something on behalf of the maintenance of this culture, to bring the younger generations closer to the language of their ancestors, and to enlighten that Yiddish is at the root of contemporary Jewish culture. This is, above all, an obligation to the victims of the Holocaust. "This Yiddish theater has been created long after the battle of Hebrew with Yiddish...since everybody turned to Hebrew, there is no need anymore to maintain a hostile attitude toward Yiddish...If for the first performances we had only aged Yiddish speakers; recent checkings show that the audience becomes younger. This is not the time, anymore, when...the police could come in the middle of the show and complain for the noise." The theater is supported by the mayor of Tel-Aviv who is quoted as saying that "Tel-Aviv without Yiddish is not Tel-Aviv anymore".

The repertoire is made of both classic plays and contemporary works, and the theater numbers about 14 permanent actors strengthened by additional performers according to the needs of particular plays. Several actors have a rich artistic biography, which mainly includes performances in Yiddish theaters in Russia, Romania, or Poland. Several artists were tenured Hebrew actors of the Habima—though not from among its first ranks. Others played independently in both Hebrew and Yiddish. All actors are young or middle-aged. First-rate Israeli actors have not been convinced to turn to Yiddish acting—though it now may happen that the Habima itself may set up its own Yiddish play. Ambitious artists have been encouraged to join the theater. The critique, however, is not unanimous. Some praise the theater's performances; others do not see in the new institution a workable enterprise since, as one prominent critique told us, "There is no Yiddish school of acting anymore nor any genuine repertoire". If the Yiddish theater remains in the periphery of the cultural life, it has gained in vigor in comparison with the past.

It is among the elderly that one may still find Yiddish as living language in secular Israel; we found this practice in a Tel-Aviv home for the elderly. This 13-floor home hosts 400 residents. The ground floor is occupied by administrative, health and social services and it includes the club, the dining room, and the cafeteria. The residents like sitting in the lobby and playing cards or chess, conversing, or reading. It is there that they receive their visitors. We observed them, spoke at length with 40 of them, collected anything written referring to life in the home, and interviewed 12 members of the staff. In total, our research spanned a 15-week period, with on average two four-hour visits per week. The youngest resident was 72; the average age was 83; two-thirds were women. Only 5% were Israeli-born; about 70% of the residents originated from Poland, Russia, Rumania, Hungary, Czechoslovakia, or Germany. 25% were from Bulgaria, Turkey, Greece, Egypt, or Yemen. Nearly all non-Israeli born immigrated to the country between 1914 and 1939—85% of them in their twenties. This was thus the generation of the Hebrew renewal.

Hebrew is the dominant language of the home and nearly all organized activities. The only exceptions are reading evenings of Yiddish poetry, two or three times a year. Though, competence in Hebrew among these founding fathers of a Hebrew-speaking society is uneven. A wide majority, (two-thirds), have seemingly never entirely assimilated the language they revived. They appear to have accepted being linguistically handicapped for the sake of the new language. On the other hand, when asked what is the dominant language in the home, quite a few—of 7 out of 40—understood the question as asking about the language more widely spoken among the residents, and answered "Here, one speaks Yiddish". For eleven respondents, there are two dominant languages in the home, Hebrew and Yiddish; for five, Hebrew is the dominant language but Yiddish is also widely used. 17 out of 40 replied: "Everyone has here his own language".

The residents use Yiddish as the major language after Hebrew. 70% of our respondents use Yiddish to some extent. Some read a daily or a weekly in this language and regularly listen to Yiddish broadcasting. All happen to use the language with other residents. A few (3) speak only Yiddish—even with the staff. About half of the conversations in the dining room, the club or the lobby involving Yiddish-speaking residents take place in this language. When a non-Yiddish speaker joins a table of Yiddish-speakers, the language switches to Hebrew, only to return to Yiddish when the non-Yiddish speaker leaves. A minority of Yiddish-speaking residents would never initiate a conversation in Yiddish but they would follow when addressed in this language. In the lobby, one always finds two or three groups of five to eight persons speaking in Yiddish. There are always the jokes about the residents' origins and the staff. Stories about the past also abound, and they bring the past back. The family and the relatives are another subject of talk and so is the matter of health. Last but not least, there is the gossiping about residents and the staff. When it comes to the sting of gossip, the language is *necessarily* Yiddish.

The staff always use Hebrew both with themselves and in addressing residents. Yet, they learn some Yiddish over time and use several ready-made expressions. The cook of Moroccan origin, here for nine years, was able to answer the residents' queries in Yiddish. The residents, who mostly address the staff in Hebrew, do not always resist using Yiddish sentences. When it comes to relatives on visit, the share of Hebrew increases but Yiddish is still widely spoken. Hebrew and Yiddish utterances of residents addressing adult sons, daughters, and grandchildren may be of equal importance. On the other hand, grandchildren invariably answer in Hebrew. Very often, one may hear "What have you said, Grandma?" or "Say it in Hebrew, please."

When asked why they, who have spoken Hebrew for decades, may now show such a renewed eagerness for Yiddish, as a rule they point out that speaking Yiddish is easier for them than speaking Hebrew. Apparently, the longstanding pro-Hebrew ideological constraints, which dictated their behavior for years, have weakened with the growth of age and life in the home. Deep-rooted inclinations seem to have been released, inhibitions lifted, and new norms generated. In particular, Yiddish seems indispensable when it comes to health: "Only a doctor who understands Yiddish will understand me."

This interest for Yiddish does not delegitimize Hebrew and for all respondents but five, Hebrew is more important than Yiddish as a language. However, they are no longer willing at this stage to ignore the easier speech which Yiddish offers them. The non-Ashkenazim have to accept this role of Yiddish and the difficulty it represents for them as residents. The practice of Yiddish by children and grandchildren at every visit paid to their parent or grandparents contributes, on the other hand, to instill in them a familiarity with the language. In this sense, those elderly persons constitute now a real factor of diffusion of the Yiddish language.

In Israel, our language survey (Ben-Rafael, 1994) shows that Yiddish is principally used for inter-generational communication. The Israeli-born are rarely more than semi-competent in the language, and ready-made expressions are actively retained but as markers of an Ashkenazi origin—more in lower social strata than in the middle-class. That Ashkenazim overwhelmingly belong to the privileged might have accounted for a capacity to retain particular symbols. Furthermore, there is the rise to power since the late 1970s of a regime depending on the votes of the Middle Easterners which has increased their symbolic and cultural presence on the public scene. This development has sharpened the Ashkenazim's consciousness of the threads that bind their culture to legacies of their own. Such feelings seem to stand behind the success of the Tel-Aviv Yiddish theater and other recent expressions of assertion to *Yiddishkeit*—Yiddish culture. Though, one is to remember that the ideology of nation building and its concomitant revival of Hebrew has been carried out, in their time, by these Ashkenazim who form nowadays Israel's upper strata. *Noblesse oblige* postulates an attachment to models which they themselves, or their fathers, imposed not only on themselves but also on others.

Arabic: The Non-Prestigious Language of the Underprivileged

Arabic is the language of the neighboring states, the Occupied Territories, and a national Arab minority. It is also the language of origin of 50% of Israel's Jewish population; these experienced Hebraization and belong, therefore, to the present discussion. Arabic is an official language even though Hebrew enjoys a preferential status in some dispositions (Landau, 1987). It is present in the media (Kraemer and Olshtain, 1989) with 31% of Israeli TV broadcasting; one full-time radio station; three dailies, and several periodicals. Arabic is also diffused by the Hebrew school. Spoken Arabic is compulsory in the fourth-to-sixth grades of elementary school, and literary Arabic is optional, alternately to French, in high schools. Here, the study of a second language in addition to English is intended for Humanistic studies, but in recent years, the Ministry of Education encourages the learning of Arabic in all tracks. Arabic, however, is still given in Israel by the public a prestige far behind English and French (Table 2).

On the other hand, the groups characterized here by an allegiance to Arabic are also of lower social status: it has been shown (Semyonov, Lewin-Epstein, 1987) that the Palestinians are the most unprivileged in the labor market, after the Israeli Arabs (themselves preceded by the Middle-Eastern and North African Jews). As for the latter, Algerian Jews had been adopted by France in 1860 and they widely assimilated to French culture ever since (Cohen, 1981). The rural communities remained closer to Judeo-Arabic until their exodus in the 1960s. Moroccans and Tunisians remained speakers of Jewish Maghrebian—influenced by Hebrew, Aramean, and French—even when they acquired French as a first language. Judeo-Arabic vernaculars were also much in favor in the Yemenite, Iraqi, or Syrian communities. A study led in Hebrew-speaking schools (see Brosh, 1988; Ben-Rafael, Brosh, 1991) wanted to throw light on both the educational policy and the attitudes of students and parents toward the teaching of Arabic in the Israeli schools.

Official documents sustain the acquisition of Arabic by Jews only as the *language of the Arab*. Knowing Arabic is seen as forwarding understanding between Arabs and Jews, promoting peaceful relations in the Middle East, improving the Jews' acquaintance with the Arabs and encouraging face-to-face contacts (Yaffe,1977). The President of the State, Herzog, declared in 1984 (*Hamanit*, 1984:4) that "We live in an area where we are but a small minority, while the vast majority speaks Arabic. We must get to know the Arab people, to respect its tradition, literature, and culture." Similarily, the Minister of Education stated in 1986 in Parliament (*Haaretz*, 29.8.1986) that "By no means can we accept that citizens of Israel, in this area will not be acquainted with Arab culture and Arab language." Textbooks such as *Mil'arai'a* (Ministry, 1985), *The Essentials of the Arabic Language* (Landau, Y., 1973) or *Arabic in Second Year* (Dana, 1969) always focus on Islamic values and symbols—the ritual pilgrimage to Mecca (Hadj), the Ramadan, the figure of the Prophet, the Koran, or the Khalifes. As for non-religious topics, these books invariably describe the Arab peasant and its village. Learning Arabic is never presented in reference to the fact that this is also one of the major diaspora languages, that a large part of Jewish civilization has been written in Arabic and that hundreds of thousands of Israelis share a familiarity with Arabic as a language of origin. Recognizing Arabic as a Jewish language could mean encouraging parochial cultures and a pluralization of the society. This, it seems, is understood as opposed to the Zionist ideology of national integration and Hebraization. Hence, while special school programs are aimed at upgrading the contribution of non-Ashkenazi Judaisms, in no case are they related to the Arabic language.

The survey itself investigated Jewish students of Arabic—890, in the Tel-Aviv area, a random sample of 27 classes in 10 high schools randomly chosen. The questionnaire—40 statements—focused on the perception of the teacher, the learning situation, educational contents and the sociocultural context. The data (see Brosh, 1988; Ben-Rafael, Brosh, 1990) show that students of Arabic in general share negative feelings toward this matter. This is true—for Middle-Easterners and North Africans and Ashkenazim alike—of motivational aspects as well as social images. Negative feelings are especially sharp vis-a-vis teachers (62%), the practical utility of the language (88%), its value *per se* (59%), and the image of Arab society (84%) (see Brosh, 1988). Respondents are not interested in visiting Arab countries, nor are they willing to work with Arabs. They do not see either any point in relations with Arab individuals. As one of them said it: "I will not go to an Arab doctor or an Arab tailor, and I won't buy anything in an Arab shop. Why thus should I learn Arabic?"

Arabic-speakers are often described as "hostile toward Jews" and opposed to the Western label they use in reference to Israeli society as a whole. The language is for many "backward and useless". Hence, the subjects also contended that Arabic is not an asset for social mobility.

As a clear indication of this lack of prestige, students who excel in this matter are reluctant to see in their achievements a source of pride. The students feel that society, as a whole, disregards Arabic. Their conviction is that the prestige of this language does not hold in comparison with English or French. Respondents were quite unwilling to invest in Arabic any effort beyond the formal requirements. Many opposed the idea of encounters with Arab youth or watching Arabic TV broadcasts. Students conceded that Arabic is important for roles related to national security: however, they saw these considerations as the Army's and not theirs.

Parents are reported by their children as sharing similar appreciations of the language, even though they may emphasize more its practical advantages. Teachers reported that at school gatherings of parents , only a few inquire about their offspring's achievements in Arabic. When the children have difficulties in Arabic, many a parent sees the solution in obtaining an exemption. They rarely think of private lessons to improve the achievements of their children—as it is often the case of other subjects. In many schools, the alternative to Arabic, French is limited to students of above-average level. This leaves Arabic compulsory for pupils of lower school-status, downgrading further its prestige. These data confirm works like a Haifa study (Adir, 1985) where elementary school pupils appeared to share strong negative stereotypes associating Arabic with hostile and dangerous feelings toward Jews. In this context, teaching Arabic encounters the greatest motivational problems on the side of students (Piamenta, 1984). It seems that this discipline has not yet become an integral part of the curriculum (Atzmon, 1985). The low linguistic capital value of the language makes its learning definitely unattractive to learners—and primarily to stronger and privileged social elements.

To be sure, the Middle-Eastern and North African students are by no means greater supporters of Arabic than the Ashkenazim: on a five-step attitude ladder, on nearly no count do the means of neither Middle-Easterners and North Africans, nor of Ashkenazim reach the median value of 2.5; on none, the minimally positive score of 3.0. At some particular respects, however, the Middle-Easterners and the North Africans' attitudes differ from the Ashkenazim's. Less negative attitudes concern the perception of the learning situation, the image of the teacher, the evaluation of the contents of study, and the encouragement of parents. Regarding three other aspects—the communicative importance of Arabic, the desirability of its mastering, and the desire to learn it—

point to a systematic—though not significant—tendency in the same direction. Arabic thus obtains here some—though weak—ethnic support of Middle-Easterners and North Africans. At the same time, one finds that the Middle-Easterners and the North Africans are more negative than others when it comes to the appreciation of Arab society. If among Ashkenazim, a lesser negative image of Arabic is bound to a lesser negative image of Arab society, among Middle-Easterners and North Africans, there is no such correlation.

Hence, the Middle-Easterners' and North Africans'less negative attitudes toward Arabic is not accounted for by greater empathy for Arabs. Their linguistic attitudes actually appear to stem from another source than their image of Arab society—in contrast with the Ashkenazim. "Arab" some said, "is one thing, Arabic is another" or "When I learn Arabic, I don't think of Arabs, as it was not their language". This kind of statement could not have been gathered from Ashkenazim. It remains that Arabic itself is but feebly supported by its natural constituency within the educational setting. This questions the role of Arabic in Israel's Middle-Eastern and North African communities.

Community studies show, in fact, that Arabic has not yet been lost here a rapid Hebraization. One example among many, the *Yemenites* of Rosh Ha'ayin. About 12,000 Yemenites, 15% of all Yemenites in Israel, live here, in the Northern area of metropolitan Tel-Aviv. The majority of the population belongs to the working class and to the lower-middle class. Investigations of 37 informants has shown us that this population is generally very traditional—some are even ultra-Orthodox—and possesses numerous parochial synagogues, with a local museum dedicated to Yemenite Judaism. The influence of Israeli education and life experience is undeniable and a stratum of young adults, some of them back from academic studies, dominate the local government. But "*up to now*" we were told by the mayor "*our children read the Bible and learn with the Mori* (the traditional teacher) *who teaches 'Yemeniteness' after regular school hours*." I. L. who is in charge of a local project of neighborhood rehabilitation informs us that: "*...the Yemenite speaks differently from other Jews*." Because of their religious fervor, the Yemenite Jew honors Hebrew which has always been the liturgic language and definitely dominates the public life of Rosh Ha'ayin. Yet, the language is spoken with a characteristic accent and imprinted with numerous borrowings from the original Jewish Arabic variant (*Jewish Yemenite*) still used here by many as a principal vernacular—the poor, uneducated, and elderly. Middle-aged males and females mostly know Yemenite Hebrew which they speak with their parents.

As a rule, youngsters adopt the Israeli common Hebrew, mitigate their accent, and use much less than their parents the Yemenite vernacular. They do not, however, abandon every Yemenite characteristic. A major factor of transmission, "*There are about 120 synagogues here, or 1 for every 20 or 30 men aged 13 or more...and each member of a synagogue has a chance to read the Bible in public every other Shabbat*", we are told by the director of the local museum."...*up to now we sing the Bible, sacred poems and traditional songs. The songs are mostly in Arabic...in about one fourth of the homes of Rosh Ha'yin, the principal language is Judeo-Arabic.*" Young adults confirm both that Yemenite linguistic particularism is waning among the new generations, and that the synagogue, the guardian of the linguistic legacy, is still central to the community.

On the basis of additional works reported elsewhere (Ben-Rafael, 1994) we led among Iraqis in Ramat-Gan, Tripolitanians in Holon or Moroccans in Dimona, we may generalize about the continued use of Arabic in Middle-Eastern and North African communities. The use of this vernacular is declining but gradually over the generations while still retaining a role in some rituals and folkculture. At least symbolically, the bulk of the Middle-Eastern and North African communities, its original carriers, retain some allegiance to Judeo-Arabic. At the same time, our data about the school setting, show that the low linguistic-capital value of Arabic correlate with a feeble power of attraction on the privileged milieus—which are mostly Ashkenazim. In fact, this weakness of the appeal of Arabic among the privileged may well be a factor of the slowness of the decline of the language in low-class Arabic-speaking communities.

It is true, however, that it is difficult to distinguish any Middle-Eastern and North African allegiance to Arabic in the attitudes of pupils at school. Their less negative feelings vis-a-vis the language at some respects is far from consisting a real support. This is partly due, it may be suggested, to these Middle-Eastern and North African students who are of socially mobile families and who are seemingly particularly influenced by middle-class Ashkenazim. Such an explanation draws from studies that show the assimilatory tendencies of mobile non-Ashkenazim to Ashkenazim (see Ben-Rafael, Sharot, 1991). As for Middle-Eastern and North African students of weaker background, the low linguistic-capital value of Arabic in society and at school—as seen in the above—should be an obstacle to an open expression of their familiarity with the language. This familiarity cannot but be stigmatizing in a framework that these weaker cohorts share with—and which is dominated by—stronger elements who assert and impose that derogatory attitude toward Arabic. Furthermore, the Middle-Easterners and the North Africans—and mainly those of lower classes who are a majority in their categories—experience in Israeli society the difficult social location which consists in making up the weaker stratum of a dominant category. To emphasize an allegiance to Arabic which, in the educational ideology, is presented as the language of the Arabs, could evidence their cultural closeness to a subordinate entity and endanger their status. This may account for negative attitudes here, toward a language which is still their grandparents', if not their parents' or their own. It is indeed easier for them to openly express their link to Arabic within their communities.

The Language Market: The Different Syndromes

The previous has considered four major codes under the twofold angle of their own value or status on the market of languages and the status of their original carriers in society (Table 3).

Table 3
Syndromes of linguistic resources

Status of language	Status of carriers	Examples	Syndromes of social outcomes in Israel.
High	High	English	Marker of higher strata Singularization of nat.speak.
	Low	French	Expansion in higherstrata Decline in original community
Low	High	Yiddish	More retention in low.strata Decline in original community
	Low	Arabic	Some retention in low.cl.comm. Feeble societal interest

In brief, the strong value of *English* accounts for its control—at a high level—by privileged strata. This value is such that while middle- and upper-class individuals and groups tend in Israel to loosen their ethnic commitments, English-speaking immigrants are encouraged to draw from, retain and transmit their original language as an identity. Their own belonging to privileged classes grants them the strength to stand stigmatization of self-seclusion on the side of the unifying national ideology.

Still alive in the North African popular communities, *French* is mainly spoken by the elderly and to some extent, the middle-age generation. Youth, however, shows no enthusiasm. On the other hand, the general attitude valorizes the language independently and privileged milieus encourage their offspring to acquire it as a cultural capital. Institutional encouragement is given to the migration of French from the underprivileged groups where it plays an identical part, toward stronger groups where it but represents an additional asset and a symbol of distinction. Because of their social weakness, the native speakers are unable to resist linguistic pauperization. A more vigorous allegiance to French is principally found among mobile North Africans. This might express the pressure exerted by the incongruence of their lower ethnic status and their class position to convert their French acquired as an ethnic symbol, into a symbolic-capital resource relevant for mobility and social acceptance.

Yiddish is a low status language which, however, pertains to a privileged social category. The ideology of national integration especially commanding in upper strata spells out why the Ashkenazims who implemented and imposed the revival of Hebrew fought against their own vernacular. Yiddish tokens and expressions used in conversation, thus mainly serve as group markers and not for communication. Yiddish is the object of more loyalty among those who, because of their own social marginality, feel less committed to the central cultural values. Yet, the strong status of the original carriers explains that Yiddish may still come back as a cultural reference.

Arabic is encouraged by Israel's educational policy. This policy, however, defines the language as the Arab's exclusively, associating it with a hostile environment and a low-class national minority. On the other hand, Arabic continues, at some degree and under the form of Jewish vernaculars, to characterize lower-class Middle-Eastern and North African communities. A low market value of Arabic in the absence of competition, makes some retention of the language possible among the weaker groups. Yet, that the language is diffused by the school as the *Arabs'*, belittles the motivation of Middle-Eastern and North African offspring to exploit the programs to assert an allegiance to the legacies of their families.

These syndromes contribute elements of answer to the questions we raised at the start of these pages, as far as major linguistic resources characteristic of Israeli reality are concerned. *Where languages are of high status*, as we have seen with English and French, (1) their carriers are rather encouraged to stick to them when they themselves are socially strong and able to stand the social price implied; (2) they are less able to do this when they belong to the underprivileged. *Where languages are of low status*, (3) carriers of strong status are feebly motivated to keep to these languages; (4) they more motivated—though not always with the greatest determination—when they are a weaker element less committed by national ideologies nor pressurized by interested parties.

Our approach has assumed that two perspectives on the social role of second languages in bilingual situations—the notions of *cultural particularism* and *linguistic capital*—respond to different aspects. The perspective bound to cultural pluralism emphasizes the concepts of marker and identity, and comes to focus on the power of carriers. The perspective bound to the notion of linguistic capital insists on the social value, and thereby the power of attraction, of languages in society. These aspects shape together the social dynamics of languages. Bourdieu's perspective recalls the cultural pluralist that languages are resources that as such are a factor of the social dynamics; Fishman reminds the theory of linguistic capital that languages represent commitments. Under this twofold angle, a picture comes out which responds to a variety of models. The paradigm we elaborated was applied to the Israeli case where the revival of Hebrew has created a multiplicity of bilingualisms.

Notes

1. First published as E. Ben-Rafael "A Sociological Paradigm of Bilingualism: English, French, Yiddish and Arabic in Israel" *Israel Social Science Research*, vol. 9/1 and 2, 1994: 181-206.

Bibliography

Alony-Fainberg, Y. (1977) "The influence of English on formal terminology in Hebrew" in J. A. Fishman, R. L. Cooper, A.,W. Conrad (ed) *The Spread of English—The Sociology of English as an Additional Language*, Rowley (Mass.): Newbury, 1977: 137-167

Atzmon, N. (1985) *Teaching Arabic in Israelli Jewish Schools—A Program Proposal*, Jerusalem: Ministry of Education

Ayalon, H., Ben-Rafael, E., and Sharot, S. (1987) "Class and Class Consciousness in Israel", *International Journal of Comparative Sociology*, 28/3-4: 158-172

Avineri, S. (1981) *The Making of Zionism: The Intellectual Origins of the Jewish State,* New York: Basic Books

Bachi, R. (1956) "A Statistical analysis of the revival of Hebrew in Israel" in *Scripta Hierosolymitana* 3: 179-247

Bachi, R. (1974) *The Population of Israel,* Jerusalem: The Hebrew University of Jerusalem

Baudelot, C., Establet, R. (1971) *L'ecole capitaliste en France,* Paris: Maspero

Beebe, L.M., Giles, H. (1984) "Speech-accommodation theories: a discussion in terms of second-language acquisition" *International Journal of the Sociology of Language* 46: 5-32

Blanc, H. (1968) "The Israeli koine as an emergent national standard" Fishman, J.A., Ferguson, C.A., Das Gupta, J. (eds) *Language Problems of Devoloping Nations,* New York: Wiley, 237-251

Bell, R.T. (1983) *Sociolinguistics—Goals, Approaches and Problems* London: B.T. Batsford

Ben-Rafael, E. (1994) *Language, Identity, and Social Divisions: The Case of Israel,* Oxford: Oxford University Press/Clarendon

Ben-Rafael, E. and Brosh, H. (1991) "A sociological study of second language diffusion: The obstacles to Arabic teaching in the Israeli school" *Language Problems and Language Planning* 15/1: 1-24

Ben-Rafael, E., Gani, L., and Herzlich, R. (1989) *Enquete aupres des parents d'eleves, des professeurs de francais et de directeurs d'ecole en Israel,* Paris: Recherche Conjointe Franco-Israelienne

Ben-Rafael, E., Herzlich, R., and Freund, M. 1990) "Symbole d'identite ou capital symbolique: Le parcours social du francais en Israel" *Revue Francaise de Sociologie,* 31-2: 315-329

Ben-Rafael, E. and Sharot, S. (1991) *Ethnicity, Religion and Class in Israeli Society,* Cambridge: Cambridge University Press

Bernstein, B., Henderson, D. (1972) "Social class differences in the relevance of language to socialization" in Fishman, J. A. (ed) *Advances in the Sociology of language II,* The Hague: Mouton

Bourdieu, P. (1987) *Choses Dites,* Paris: Les Editions de Minuit

Bourdieu, P. (1982) *Ce que parler veut dire,* Paris: Fayard

Bourdieu, P. Passeron, J.-C. (1970) *La Reproduction—Elements d'une Theorie du Systeme d'Enseignement,* Paris: Les Editions de Minuit

Brosh, H. (1988) *The Effect of Learning on Arabic in Elementary and School on Achievement in Literary Arabic in the Seventh Grade* Tel-Aviv: Ph.D. Thesis: The School of Education, The Tel-Aviv University

Buber, M. (1973) *On Zion,* Bath (UK): East and West Library

Carmon, N., Manheim, B. (1976) *Achieving Goals through Housing Policies,* Haifa: Technion (Heb)

Chilland, C. (1971) *L'enfant de 6 ans et son avenir,* Paris: PUF

Chomsky, W. (1957) *Hebrew: The Eternal Language* Philadelphia: Jewish Publication Society of America

Cohen, D. (1981) "Remarques historiques et sociolinguistiques sur les parlers arabes des Juifs maghrebins" *International Journal of the Sociology of Language,* 30: 91-105

Cooper, R.L. (1989) *Language Planning and Social Change,* Cambridge: Cambridge University Press

Cooper, R.L. and Fishman, J. A. (1977) 'A study of language attitudes' in Fishman, J.A., Cooper, R.L., Conrad, A.W. (eds) *The Spread of English—The Sociology of English as an Additional Language,* Rowley (Mass): Newbury, 239-276

Dana, M. (1969) *Arabic in the Second Year,* Tel-Aviv: Yavneh (Hebr. and Arabic)

Dorian, N. (1981) *Language and Death: The Life Cycle of a Scottish Gaelic Dialect,* Philadelphia: University of Pennsylvania Press

Dorian, N. (1982) "Language loss and maintenance in language contact situations" Lambert, R.D., Freed, B.F. (eds) *The Loss of Language Skills,* New York: Rowley

Dressler, W.U. (1989) "Language death" in Newmeyer (ed) *op.cit.* 184-192

Fishman, J. (1989) *Language and Ethnicity in Minority Sociolinguistic Perspective* Clevedon, Philadelphia: Multilingual Matters

Fishman, J. A. (1980) 'Bilingualism and biculturalism as individual and as societal phenomena' *Journal of Multilingual and Multicultural Development* 1/1: 3-1

Fishman, J., Cooper, R. and Ma, R. (1971) *Bilingualism in the Barrio,* Bloomington: Indiana University Press

Gal, S. (1979) *Language Shift—Social Determinants of Linguistic Change in Bilingual Austria,* New York: Academic Press

Grillo, R. D. (1989), *Dominant Languages: Language and Hierarchy in Britain and in France,* Cambridge, U.K.: Cambridge University Press

Grosjean, F. (1982) *Life with Two Languages—An Introduction to Bilingualism,* Cambridge (Mass): Harvard University Press

Gumperz, J.J. (1976) "The sociolinguistic significance of conversational code-switching" in Cook-Gumperz, J., Gumperz, J. J.(eds) *Papers on Language and Context,* Berkeley: University of California, Berkeley

Hammers, J. and Blanc, M. (1983) *Bilinguality and Bilingualism,* Cambridge: Cambridge University Press

Harding, E., Riley, P. (1986) *The Bilingual Family,* Cambridge: Cambridge University Press

Hofman, J.E. and Fisherman, H. (1972) 'Language shift and language maintenance in Israel', in J. A. Fishman (ed) *Advances in the Sociology of Language* 2, The Hague: Mouton, 1972: 342-364

Isaacs, H., (1967) *American Jews in Israel,* New York: J Day

ICBS (1983) *Data Bank,* Tel-Aviv: Institute of Social Research, Tel-Aviv University

Katz, D.(1986) "On Yiddish, in Yiddish and for Yiddish—Five hundred years of Yiddish scholarship" Gelber, M.H.(ed) *Identity and Ethos,* New York, Bern: Peter Lang: 23-36

Katz, J. (1960) *Between Jews and Gentiles,* Jerusalem: Bialik Institute (Heb)

Katz, P. (1982) "Ethnicity Transformed: Acculturation in Language Classes in Israel" *Anthropological Quarterly* 55: 99-111

Kraemer, Rand and Olshtain, E. (1989) "Perceived Ethnolinguistic Vitality and Language Attitudes: The Israeli Setting" *Journal of Multilingual and Multicultural Development* 10/3: 197-212

Labov, W. (1976) *Sociolinguistique* Paris: Editions de Minuit

Lambert, W.E. (1975) "Culture and Language as Factors in Learning and Education," in Wolfgang, A. (Ed) *Education of Immigrant Students,* Toronto: Ontario Institute for Studies in Education

Lambert, W.E., (1977) "Culture and language as factors in learning and education" in Eckman, F. (ed) *Current Themes in Linguistics: Bilingualism, Experimental Linguistics and Language Typologies,* Washington, D.C.: Hemisphere Publishing

Landau, Y. (1973) *The Essentials of the Arabic Language,* Jerusalem: Achiemeier (Heb)

Laqueur, W. (1972) *A History of Zionism,* London: Wiedenfeld and Nicolson

Laudau, J. M. V. (1987) "Hebrew and Arabic in the State of Israel: Political Aspects of the Language Issue" *International Journal of the Sociology of Language,* Vol. 67

Lieberson, S. (1981) *Language Diversity and Language Contact,* Stanford: Stanford University Press

Mackey, W.F. (1968) "The description of bilingualism" in Fishman, J. (ed) *Readings in the Sociology of Language,* The Hague: Mouton, 554-584

Marcellesi, J.B. and Gardin, B. (1974) *Introduction a la Sociolinguistique—La Linguistique sociale,* Paris: Larousse

Ministry of Education (1985) *Arabic for the Hebrew School—Bil'arabyyaa,* Jerusalem (Heb)

Nahir, M. (1978) 'Normativism and educated speech in modern Hebrew' IJSL 18/1978: 49-67

Piementa, M. (1984) "Arabic as a tool and as a national value" *Hed Hakhinuch* 9/58.

Rabin, C. (1973) *A Short History of the Hebrew Language* Jerusalem: the Jewish Agency

Romaine, S. (1989) *Bilingualism,* Oxford: Basil Blackwell

Ronen, M., Seckbach, F. and Cooper, R.L. (1977) 'Foreign loanwords in Hebrew newspapers' in Fishman, Cooper, Conrad (ed) *The Spread of English—The Sociology of English as an Additional Language,* Rowley (Mass): Newbury, 239-276

Rosenbaum, Y. 'Hebrew adoption among new immigrants to Israel: the first three years' *International Journal of the Sociology of Language* 41/1983: 115-130

Rosenbaum, Y. Nadel, E., Cooper, R.L. and Fishman, J. A. (1977) 'English in Keren Kayemet street' in Fishman, Cooper, Conrad (ed) *op.cit.* 179-194

Sapir, E. (1974) "Language" in Blount, B.G. (ed) *Language, Culture and Society,* Cambridge (Mass): Winthrop: 46-66

Scotton, C.M. (1980) "Explaining linguistic choices as identity negotiations" in Giles, H., Robinson, P., Smith, P. (eds) *Language: Social Psychological Perspectives,* Oxford: Pergamon

Scotton, C.M. (1983) "The negotiation of identities in conversation: a theory of markedness and code choice" *International Journal of the Sociology of Language* 44: 116-136

Scotton, C. and Ury, W. (1977) "Bilingual strategies: the social functions of code-switching" *Linguistics*, 193: 5-20

Seckbach, F. and Cooper, R.L. (1977) 'The maintenance of English in Ramat Eshkol' in Fishman, Cooper and Conrad, *op.cit.* 168-178

Selwyn, T. (1990) "Teaching nationalism to language learners: The case of the Israeli Ulpan" *The SOAS Language Revival Conference*, London, 7, 8 June

Semyonov, M., Lewin-Epstein, N. (1987) *Hewers of Wood and Drawers of Water* Ithaca (NY): Cornell Institute of Labor Studies

Spolsky, B. (1989) "Bilingualism" in Newmeyer, F.J. (ed) *op.cit.*, 100-118

Stevens,G. and Swicegood, G. (1987) "The linguistic context of ethnic endogamy" *American Sociological Review* 52: 73-82

Street, R. J., Jr. and Giles, H. (1982) "Speech accommodation theory: a social and cognitive approach to language and speech behavior" in Roloff, M., Berger, C. (eds.) *Social Cognition and Communication,* Beverly Hills: Sage

Susskind, N.(1987) "A partisan history of Yiddish" Katz, D.(ed.) *op.cit.*, 127-134

Wexler, P.(1987) "Interdialectal translation as a reflection of lexical obsolescence and dialect distance: the West Yiddish Bible Translation of 1679 in the Biblia Pentapla (1711)" *International Journal of the Sociology of Language*, 67: 7-26

Yaffe, A. (1977) *Characteristics of the Teaching of Arabic in Hebrew Schools* (the Piamenta Committee Report), Jerusalem: Ministry of Education (Heb)Yaffe, 1977

8

Attitudes toward Foreign Words in Contemporary Hebrew

Haya Fisherman

Introduction

Foreign words are commonly used in all countries and languages. This is a sociohistorical phenomenon rather than a linguistic one. Interlanguage contact is regarded by anthropologists as an aspect of cultural contiguity, and linguistic interference as a form of acculturization. No language is ever immutable, and words are added to denote new objects and ideas as well as fresh attitudes to familiar concepts. These are parallel to social innovations and newly-acquired values and serve as a mirror to society.

The use of foreign words is influenced not only by in-language factors but by others, such as the prestige of the lending language.

The bewildering dimensions reached by word borrowing today are due to two main reasons: the accelerated changes in the sciences and a growing tendency to follow fashions in language which, in turn, makes it into a creation of fashion. The influence of American English, so conspicuous in Europe, has also reached Hebrew. American English and the Americanization process in particular proliferate in a situation reminiscent of the growing domination of Latin in the Middle Ages or of the influence of Greek in the days of the Second Temple.

Foreign words (those of European origin that have infiltrated Hebrew since its revival from 1880) are not integrated into Hebrew. They tend to avoid formations such as verb inflections, the construct state, and possessive pronominal suffixes. Etymologically and morphologically, they remain extraneous to the language.

The importance of describing the phenomenon as it exists among speakers of Hebrew in Israel lies in the extensive use of foreign-language words in Hebrew today, an important and natural element in the development of Hebrew and its revival process.

The Struggle Against Foreign Words

"Purism" is the name given to a protective attitude by the language which strives to avoid use of foreign words. This is one of the major principles of today's normative grammarians. Linguistic purism in Europe was part of nineteenth-century national reawakening. Few languages were as open to foreign words as English, for example, whose welcoming attitude to these was a direct result of contact with numerous countries. This attitude helped the language achieve a cosmopolitan status. Various European countries and also America reacted to foreign-word borrowing with opposition and a demand to purify their language of foreign elements, made mostly by writers, linguists, politicians and scientists.

In Italy, every linguistic reform was accompanied by a program to uproot the Gallicisms from the language. In Germany, the language societies upholding linguistic purism were imbued with patriotic fervor and, during the First World War, chauvinism and linguistic purism were rampant. The rise of Nazism initiated a campaign against foreign elements in the language, particularly those from France. In Turkey, one of the primary targets of linguistic reform which increased in the time of the New Turks' movement and Ataturk was to abolish thousands of Arabic and Persian words from Turkish. In Norway, in the 1950s, there were arguments about using foreign words, and the government demanded that Norwegian be reinforced to withstand their invasion. In France, there are those who mock "*franglais*," so prevalent with the public and in the language of the media. Nevertheless, the opposition to borrowing from foreign languages has diminished over the last few years in many countries, to be replaced by a more tolerant attitude which, in turn, has weakened the purist approach to language.

In Israel, since the revival of the language, the subject of foreign words has raised normative problems. Should the practice be encouraged, accepted, or rejected?

In 1914, the Language Committee convened to discuss possible sources for filling the voids in the Hebrew language, and Eliezer ben Yehuda declared that the Committee would do everything in its power to stick to the principle of avoiding non-Semitic foreign words. His opposition was ideological, based on the viewpoint of a linguistic element there, regarding as he did foreign words as strangers in the temple of our language, hard to adapt to Hebrew and its grammar. They could ultimately destroy the Semitic character of the language. Better to create a new root in the spirit of the language than admit strangers into the temple.

Yellin, Lifschitz, and other participants in the discussion regarded foreign words as a lesser evil than the danger of fresh creations not in the spirit of the language, of temporary usage, soon to be replaced by Hebrew words. According to Lifschitz, the danger lay in using them more than necessary, as embellishments to speech taken from a foreign culture more prestigious than our own. Echoes of that discussion still ring in public attitudes expressed today.

During the last few years, there has been an outcry in Israel against foreign words which seems to indicate a negligent attitude toward Hebrew, cultural licentiousness and a tendency to ape. Not only is the language studded with foreign words, but there is an enormous infiltration of foreign culture in syntax and style, in whole sentences lifted from other languages, in cultural imitation, especially that of American, in the field of commerce and advertising. These protests are voiced in interviews with public figures, in public meetings, in letters to the press and in newspaper articles and periodicals. There is even a society called KELA [Hebrew Language Fund], which in 1979 started a campaign for the reinforcement of the Hebrew language, whose membership includes "professors, writers, members of the Knesset, actors and public figures." The society held a national congress at the home of the President in Jerusalem on January 21, 1981. The Chairman of the Committee for Education and Culture in the Knesset proposed a "Law of the Hebrew Language," a tenet of which was an unmitigated fight against excessive prettification of the language with foreign words. The arguments voiced during the discussion in the Knesset reflected attitudes rooted in linguistic, social, cultural and national considerations.

Those demanding the use of foreign words for linguistic reasons stressed that without them no translation would be exact. Those who rejected them, also for linguistic reasons, stressed the difficulty in understanding them. Those holding social attitudes, who were resigned to the phenomenon, regarded it as sociolinguistic, fashion-oriented in nature, while the rejectors objected to having the language permeated with American words in writing, signboards and advertisements, all motivated by snobbery and a desire to impress.

Those opposed to the use of foreign words on national grounds were deeply concerned for the status of the native language as a spiritual value, a symbol of national identity. Excess in the use of foreign words spelled, in their view, danger to the national feelings.

There are, conversely, more moderate attitudes protesting against linguistic extremism They regard the phenomenon as natural, one that characterized our language in the past, in the Bible, in the times of the Sages, and in the Middle Ages. It is accepted by all nations and is a part of today's reality.

In the course of the public controversy on the subject, both in the early days of language renaissance and today, the purists object to the use of foreign words while others accept them, regarding them as a necessary stage in the present development of the language.

Basic Assumptions

Linguistic attitudes are not created in a vacuum but grow out of experience influenced by basic background data such as age, education and occupation, and social-linguistic background. The background data may be regarded as go-betweens or independent variables while the attitude is the dependent variable—the attitude toward the use of foreign words, that is, tolerance or opposition brought to bear by the background data.

Social psychologists distinguish between three components of every attitude: the conscious, the behavioral, and the emotional. Attitude should be seen in the context of familiarity with foreign words and their uses and should not be isolated from those factors.

The examination of attitudes toward foreign words was based mainly on the following assumptions:

a: *The influence of personal data on the attitude—age group, educational and occupational level, land of origin*

1. The "teenage" group vs. an older age group: the younger the age group, the greater the tendency to regard the danger of using foreign words as a threat to the language. The emotional factor and the lack of

experience characteristic of the youngsters, who tend to see things in black and white, prevent them from discerning intermediate stages.

2. The educational and occupational level: higher levels familiarize the speaker with foreign words. Those with a formal education learn them during their studies at a higher rate than those lacking such an education. An occupation which provides such a confrontation will influence familiarity with the phenomenon and sharpen the awareness of the problem more than any other occupation. A specific specialization within the Hebrew language will foster a greater loyalty to it coupled with an intolerance toward the use of foreign words.

3. The land of origin of the interviewee and his parents: these have a bearing on his exposure to the phenomenon and the resulting attitude.

Speakers of European origin who grew up speaking a European language are better acquainted with foreign words and the way they sound, so that they are liable to show more tolerance of the phenomenon. Conversely, speakers from Arabic-speaking countries may regard them as obstacles to be avoided. (The education of the interviewee interferes here, of course. He may have studied foreign languages at school, thereby encountering foreign European languages, even if his origin would naturally prevent such exposure).

b: *The knowledge and use of foreign words*

Different social groups vary from each other in the word inventory they use and the relative popularity of the various words it contains, this being a result of the differences between the background data such as age group, education and occupation, etc. Knowledge of foreign words can be manifested by passive acquaintance or by active use. Presumably, there is not necessarily a correlation between passive acquaintance and active use. Linguistic behavior is not an inevitable result of the conscious element or of the emotional one, so that there need not be a correlation between actual linguistic behavior and attitude. A speaker may express a positive stand regarding the use of foreign words but might actually use them sparingly or, conversely, he may express opposition to such use but indulge in it liberally.

Findings

The collection of empirical material is based on questionnaires filled out by a student population, nurses and high-school pupils. These consisted of 100 students of the Hebrew Language Faculty at the University of Haifa, 85 nurses specializing in sociology at the Section of External Studies of the University of Haifa, and 110 pupils age 16-17 of the Ironi Gimmel High School in Haifa. In choosing the participants of the sample, it was assumed that they all had a certain degree of literacy, enabling them to answer the questionnaire. The sample was not presumed to be representative, but we think that even if the participating groups had been larger, it is doubtful whether the results would have been different.

In the course of a regular lesson, the interviewees were given a questionnaire containing 23 questions whose purpose was to check their use of foreign words, their familiarity with them and their Hebrew equivalents, and their attitudes to foreign words as such.

Question 23 ascertains the interviewees' backgrounds, making it possible to examin the correlation between their replies and their personal data, age group languages spoken at home, and social background.

In addition to the questionnaire, some open-ended questions were set on the subject, eliciting their opinions on it freely.

The Influence of the Personal Data of the Interviewee on His Attitudes

Age group. The group of pupils is less aware of the subject, as it lies outside their fields of interest and their meager experience (see Appendix 1, Table 1).

Interviewees of this group are neutral as regards users of foreign words or their Hebrew parallels (see Appendix 1, Tables 8-9). They evince neither sympathy nor lack of it toward users of foreign words. Due to little experience in the subject, a high percentage of the group (30%) answered "I don't know" regarding the future of Hebrew parallels, for an estimation not based on knowledge and experience is not dependable (see Appendix 1, Table 5). Seeing things in black and white is typical of youngsters, and this is reflected in their anxiety about the future of the language which might be destroyed and forgotten as a result of foreign words (see Appendix 1, Table 4).

Education and occupation. In contrast with the other two groups, that of the students specializing in the Hebrew language is more sympathetic to the users of Hebrew parallels (see Appendix 1, Table 9). On the other hand, they have certain reservations and are more opposed to the use of foreign words and to their users (see Appendix 1, Table 3 and 8). This group, therefore, approves of combating this phenomenon (see Appendix 1, Table 7). The position of this group is influenced not just by the norm and by what is expected of students of the Hebrew Faculty, but also by their general observations of the language and their comprehension of its inner processes. They therefore consider, more than the other two groups, that the contribution of foreign words is large to medium (see Appendix 1, Table 2). For this group, the subject is no problem (see Appendix 1, Table 1) nor does it consider it a danger to the future of the language (Appendix 1, Table 4). Compared to that of the students, the nurses' group is more tolerant of the phenomenon and reflects the attitude of the average speaker, who regards the use of foreign words as an inseparable part of modern speech. As a nonpartisan group in this context, it approves less of the use of Hebrew parallels and more of the use of foreign words (see Appendix 1, Table 8-9).

The tolerance regarding the use of foreign words. This is higher among children of academics and officials than among those of technicians, self-employed laborers and farmers (see Appendix 1, Tables 10-11).

For children of academics and officials, there are opportunities for encounters with foreign words because of their parents' education and occupation as a result of which they develop a more tolerant attitude toward these words than others. This tolerance is expressed not only by an absolute agreement to their use but by an appreciation of their contribution to the language. Children of academics, more than others, answered that the use of foreign words was a medium contribution. Conversely, the nurses' group, which had a high percentage of interviewees whose fathers were laborers, answered that there was no contribution.

Country of origin. In all the groups, the higher percentage of those supporting the campaign against foreign words was among those of Asian and African origin (see Appendix 1, Table 12). For them, the use of foreign words in Hebrew was a source of difficulty and a hindrance. A comparison of the groups shows the highest percentage opposing the campaign to be among those of European-American origins in the nurses' group. They had grown up using a European language and saw no need for a campaign against foreign words.

Languages Spoken at Home

Among the group of pupils who speak Hebrew and a European language, a higher percentage saw little danger in the phenomenon or none at all as compared with those speaking only Hebrew (see Appendix 1, Table 13). A high percentage of those speaking only Hebrew, in both the pupils' and students' groups, had reservations about using foreign words and even opposed it. Those speaking and a European language are more tolerant of the phenomenon, as they are familiar with more European words than those who speak Hebrew alone. Familiarity with the phenomenon makes for tolerance.

A high percentage of speakers of a European language among the nurses (100%) accepted the phenomenon absolutely. In the students' group, a higher percentage regarding the phenomenon as a great and medium danger was among the speakers of Arabic only, as contrasted with those who spoke both Hebrew and a European language or just Hebrew. The group of Arab speakers is faced with the problem more than the others in the course of its studies, and therefore regards it as a danger to the language.

Familiarity with Foreign Words

Among the pupils' group, there is a lower percentage of those who always or frequently come up against foreign words as compared with other groups (see Appendix 1, Table 14). Their youth has prevented such a confrontation, unlike the more mature age groups. On the other hand, there is a higher percentage among the student interviewees who are constantly or often confronted by them in comparison with the two other groups, so that the students are more highly exposed to foreign words than the two other groups. In the word lists, graded according to their frequency, we can distinguish differences among the groups—the world of the interviewees is revealed beyond the words. A word like "terminology" is more frequent in the field of academics and is therefore closer to the student group. Conversely, a word like "socialization" is often used in the social sciences at school and even more so in the lectures for the introduction to sociology in which the nurses participating in the sample took part. Words like "symptom" and "sterile" have a higher rating among the nurses' group as compared with the two other groups, being connected to their occupation. Words like "association" and "motive" have a lower grading among the nurses than among the pupils and students, who encounter them more often. Words like "aggressive," "administration," "alternative," "analogy," "mentality," "simultaneous," "sector," "provocation," "combination," "regression" and "relevant" have a low rating among the pupils' group as compared to that of the students because these words are used in the adult world and have little to do with that of pupils. On the other hand, the following words had a high rating among them: "maximum," "minimum," "drastic," "normal," "panic," "antenna" and "model." They have often heard their teachers say, "Don't get into a panic," or "There has been a drastic decline in discipline!"

The high grading of the word "normal" among the pupils' group as compared to the other two groups is worth noting. This is probably due to the frequent use of "normal" and "not normal" in slang. In this group, the word "model," too, received a high grading, as it is widespread in the context of motor cars and their year of production.

Frequency of Use of Foreign Words

The average number of those who use foreign words constantly or frequently is 50 percent, a percentage higher among the pupils' groups and lower among the students (see Appendix 1, Table 16). In the field of speech, the extensive use of foreign words among the pupils is interesting. This finding is probably rooted in the words' presence in the slang used by the younger age group. But in writing, the percentage of constant or frequent users is lower when compared to their speech, due to greater control and less spontaneity. In writing, it is among the nurses that we find a higher percentage of constant or frequent users, more than in the other two groups. Among the students, this percentage is lower than in the other two groups.

The students' group which, from the viewpoint of encountering foreign words is first and foremost (see Appendix 1, Table 15), comes last as regards using them, whether in speech or in writing. The pupils' group, encountering the least number of foreign words, heads the list in using them in speech. Is there any correlation between familiarity of foreign words and their use? According to the findings, this is not necessarily so (see Appendix 1 Table 17). Among the nurses' group, such a correlation is apparent, so that those who used foreign words were more familiar with them than those who didn't.

It is possible that the interviewees declared that they used foreign words in speech and even in writing, while their available variety was meager. When asked to refer to a specific list of words, it appeared that only a small percentage of them had constantly or frequently encountered them. Certain words may not belong to the user's repertoire, nor does he encounter them, but he cannot be considered a user of foreign words. Moreover, his knowledge of them does not make his use obligatory. Such words as "socialization," "sterile," "simultaneous," "symptom," "selection," "spontaneous," "project," "communication," and "relevant" were, according to a high percentage of the pupils, words they had encountered constantly or often, though they used them rarely compared with others. Knowledge of the words is passive; using them is active.

One encounters foreign words at various opportunities and, when used in society, they become public property, although their use is limited to the individual's needs and his personal data.

The Difference Between the Use of Foreign Words and Their Hebrew Equivalents

Regarding the synonymity of foreign words and their Hebrew equivalents, the interviewees seemed to feel it was not perfect (see Appendix 1, Tables 18-19). Even when the Hebrew parallel was intended as a perfect replacement for the foreign word, there was a sense of difference, caused in most cases by habitual use which tended to favor the foreign word.

Besides the difference caused by habitual use, there is another—that of creating an impression. Linguistic imitation and word borrowing from other languages because of their prestige are common phenomena in the cultures of various nations. The infiltration of foreign words from a prestigious language is impressive even if there are perfectly good Hebrew parallels to replace them. The interviewees felt that words like "prestige," "regression," and "hobby" create an impression not to be achieved by the Hebrew parallel.

The Absorption of Hebrew Parallels in the Language

Regarding the absorption of Hebrew equivalents into the language, the interviewees' attitudes toward the social factors that influence the differences of this absorption appear to tend to the social rather than to linguistic factors (see Appendix 1, Table 20-21).

Fashion and the appearance of the Hebrew equivalent at the right moment are more heavily emphasized in the interviewees' replies than are linguistic factors such as the word root, its grammatical form and its length.

The moment circumstances combine to absorb the word in the social sense, be it a new fashion or exigent reality, it is not the root or the grammatical form that will determine its chances of absorption. There are words that, in this sense, are transparent, yet the use of foreign words will continue while their Hebrew parallels will not be absorbed. Some words have been absorbed into the language not because of their transparency to the public as regards their root and grammatical form but because they have become fashionable.

In comparing foreign words with their Hebrew equivalents from the point of view of use and the absorption differences of the Hebrew replacements, the social factor is stressed. The interviewees pointed out the habit of using foreign words and the fashion of using the Hebrew equivalents. The latter, being so highly publicized socially, are all the more easily absorbed into the language and are used beside the foreign words until the latter finally disappear.

The Connection Between the Use of Foreign Words while Knowing the Hebrew Equivalents and the Attitude toward Using Foreign Words

This connection may be assessed by means of the interviewees' answers reflecting the coordination between the Hebrew parallels and the foreign words (see Appendix 2, Figures 6-10), for example, the word "interest."

In a pupil group of 46 which agreed absolutely with the use of foreign words, 43 knew the Hebrew equivalent of the word "interest," 9.3 percent of them use foreign words, 69.8 percent do so frequently, and 20.9 percent seldom do. Out of 52 who agree to using foreign words, 51 knew the Hebrew equivalents, 43.1 percent use them frequently, 54.8 percent rarely, and 2 percent never. Among ten who had reservations about using foreign words, ten knew the Hebrew equivalents. Of those, 70 percent use foreign words frequently and 30 percent seldom. Two who opposed using foreign words knew the Hebrew equivalents. They use foreign words often or rarely. Those who use foreign words are always found in groups agreeing absolutely to the practice, but not in those belonging to a different level of agreement.

The percentage of foreign-word users is often higher among those who agree absolutely as contrasted with the percentage of those who agree. Conversely, the percentage of users is higher among the group agreeing than among those agreeing absolutely. In most of the examples, the percentage of foreign-word users rarely expands according to their level of disagreement.

As to the knowledge of Hebrew equivalents, there is no correlation between it and the measure of agreement to continue using foreign words. There is also a marked knowledge of foreign words among those having reservations regarding their use and those who oppose it.

Summary of Attitudes toward the Use of Foreign Words Manifested According to Interviewees' Sample

Two kinds of linguistic attitudes are discernible: those regarding the language as a value, a symbol of national identification, and those for whom language is a communication instrument serving their personal needs.

The interviewees' attitudes indicate that they regard the phenomenon both from the ethnical, national viewpoint and as an instrument of communication.

a. Ethically speaking, the phenomenon is regarded with tolerance. Eighty-eight percent of interviewees expressed approval of the use of foreign words, claiming that this was a natural process of a living, growing language and was of a universal nature. It is hard to avoid external influences where everybody imitates everybody in fashion, technique, and language. One should regard language as a whole so that the use of foreign words does not create an anomaly in the natural development of the word. Nevertheless, 60 percent in each group see a great and medium danger to the language in such practice. They adduce national reasons, those of national prestige and preservation of identity. According to them, we must insist on purity of language if we wish to have one of our own. Just as every people should be characterized and made unique by its culture and customs, it should also do so by means of its language. The uniqueness of a people lies in its linguistic culture, and when the language is impure, the uniqueness is lost.

There is an element of self-abasement in the use of foreign words when compared to more respected languages. It is an injury to the Israeli identity. Yet, in spite of the threat inherent in the phenomenon, it is not regarded as endangering the language in the future.

According to the interviewees in the students' group, foreign words were used in both Biblical times and those of our Sages, yet this did not harm the image of the language. Those whose business is language do not foresee its destruction as the result of such use—such things have happened before. Conversely, among the pupils' group the apprehension is greater. According to them, the use of foreign words injures the language and, with the passage of time, many more of them are assimilated, so that in several decades more the Hebrew words will be entirely forgotten. As to the chances of the Hebrew equivalents being absorbed, there is little optimism among them

b. Among those who regard the language as a communicative instrument there is a tolerance of the use of foreign words. About 60 percent of every group of interviewees regards it as a contribution to the language, a bridge toward communicative quality. Many foreign words cannot be translated exactly, and their use provides a more impressive emotional charge. As to the struggle against such words, opinions are divided.

In the nurses' group, the percentage of those approving a struggle is lower as compared to the other two groups. According to them, a foreign word may be more precise and hard to replace as regards content and meaning. Those who approved of a struggle in the students' group claimed that the use of foreign words makes understanding of the contents difficult. The foreign words are not clear in formation. In all the groups, however, very few are ready to put up a fight, which perhaps indicates adaptation to the phenomenon.

c. As to the emotional attitude to the subject, there is a marked tolerance of foreign words. In all the groups, when asked, "How do you regard those who use foreign words?" a high percentage answered, "It's their private affair." The interviewees show no fanaticism in their attitude toward the phenomenon, rather a kind of neutrality.

Summary

Attitudes are highly significant in the study of sociolinguistic behavior in macro and micro. They are used to predict phenomena and influence linguistic behavior and are influenced by it.

Many subjects in sociolinguistics are supported by the study of linguistic attitudes such as language planning (Haugen 1966; Hofman 1974a, 1974b, 1977, 1980, 1985; Fishman 1968; Ferguson et al. 1968); language maintenance and language shift (Herman 1961; Fishman 1965, 1968); and acquisition of a second language (Lambert et al. 1968).

The question of whether to use foreign words or to replace them with elements of the language itself is dealt with in language planning. This is related to the choice of a norm, be it a new one or an improvement on an old one. A change in norm depends on social attitudes—the language planner must be aware of the affinity existing between linguistic and social processes, every linguistic usage being subservient to social norms. Attitudes toward the use of foreign words are influenced by the nature of the times in which the language is used. They are a result of processes occurring at a certain time and in certain circumstances. A discussion of the problems of language in which it is conceived as a symbol and a value and not particularly as an instrument of communication also reflects a social norm. Factors characterizing social norms such as habitual use and fashion are more highly stressed in a confrontation between foreign words and their Hebrew equivalents.

Today, however, there is a further dimension to the problem which reflects the spirit of the time. There is concern not only for the language and its prestige, but also for social image. If, during the renascence, the argument centered on "foreign words," today it centers on "foreignness" and everything that this term implies. The present attitude toward the phenomenon is directed toward everyday language and not, as in the early days, toward the more theoretical problem of the nature of language or its actual use and experience. Today, discussions are more sociolinguistic in nature than purely linguistic.

References

Ater, Moshe (1980). Foreign words in contrast with and in Hebrew (in Hebrew). *Parakim B.* Petach Tikva.

Ben Yehuda, Eliezer (1971). *The Dream and its Solution* (in Hebrew). Mosad Bialik, Jerusalem.

Ferguson, CA., Fishman, J.A., and Das Gupta, P. (1968). *Language Problems of Developing Nations.* New York.

Fishbein, M. (1967). Attitude and Prediction of Behavior. In *Attitude Theory and Measurement.* M. Fishbein (3ed.), 477-492.

Fishman, J.A. (1965). Language maintenance and language shift—the case of Yiddish in the U.S.A. *Europa Ethnica* 22, 146-158.

——— (1968). *Readings in the Sociology of Language.* The Hague: Mouton.

Glixon, Moshe (1923). On the usage of foreign words (in Hebrew). *Sefatenu B*, 17-23.

Haugen, Einar (1966). *Language Conflict and Language Planning—The case of Modern Norwegian.* Cambridge, MA: Harvard University Press.

Heath, S.B. (1976). A national language academy? Debate in the new nation, *International Journal of Sociology of Language.* 11:26-31.

Hed, Uriel (1954). *Language Reform in Turkey.* Jerusalem: Israel Oriental Society.

Herman, S.N. (1961). Explorations in the social psychology of language choice. *Human Relations* 14, 149-164.

Hofman, J.E. (1974a). The prediction of success in language planning—the case of chemists in Israel. *International Journal of the Sociology of Language* 1, 39-65.

——— (1974b). Predicting the use of Hebrew terms among Israeli psychologists. *International Journal of the Sociology of Language* 3, 53-65.

——— (1977). Language attitudes in Rhodesia. In *Spread of English*, J.A. Fishman, R.L. Cooper, and A.W Conrad (eds.), 277-301, Rowley, MA: Newbury House.

——— (1980). The use of Hebrew terms as a function of personal background and attitudes towards language. *Educational Studies* 26, 27-32.

——— (1985). The commitment to modern Hebrew value or instrument. In *Readings in the Sociology of Jewish Languages*. J.A. Fishman (ed.). Leiden: Brill.

Hope, T.E. (1971). *Lexical Borrowing in the Romance Languages*, vols. 1-2, Oxford.

Lambert, W. et al. (1968). A study of the roles of attitudes and motivation in second language learning. In *Readings in the Sociology of Language*, J.A. Fishman (ed.). The Hague: Mouton. 473-491.

Lifschitz A.M. (1923) Foreign words (in Hebrew). Isefatenu A, *26-31*.

Memories of the Hebrew Committee *(1914). Sources to fill in the lack in our language (in Hebrew).* Mahberet *4, 3-66.*

——— (1960). What was said by the participants in the discussion on the foreign words problem (in Hebrew). *Session* 36, (7-8) 136-146.

Mencken, H.Z. (1937). *The American Language*. New York: Knopf.

Migliorini, V. (1943). La questione della lingua purismo e neopurismo. In *Lingua Contemporara. Biblioteca di lingua nostra,* 49-67.

Moreshen M. (1967). Our attitudes towards foreign words in our language (in Hebrew). *Katif* 4-5, 264-271.

Nir, Rafael (1984). *Language Medium and Transmission* (in Hebrew). Jerusalem: Pozner.

Perez, Y. (1963). Purism in Nation and in Israel (in Hebrew). *Molad* 21, 563-566.

Rabi, Ya-akov (1973). Foreign words in Israeli press: positive and negative (in Hebrew). *Sefer Hashana shel Haitonaim* (Tel Aviv), 304-312.

Rabin, Chaim (1968). Our Hebrew: How shall we speak in 2000 (in Hebrew). *Sefer Hashana Shel Haitonaim*, 125-127.

Serjeantson M.S. (1935). *A History of Foreign Words in English*. London: Routledge and Kegan Paul.

Sivan, Reuven (1976). Foreign words today—their way and their behavior (in Hebrew). *Al Ovnei Leshon Yamenu* (Jerusalem) 79-93.

——— (1980). Changes in the language nowadays (in Hebrew). *Leshoneu La'am*. Mahzor 31, 203-301.

Viereck, W. (1979). Englisches in der Österreichischen Pressesprache. In *Fremdwort Diskussion*, Peter Braun (ed.)., 314-320.

Von Polenz, P. (1979). Fremdwort und Lehnwort. In *Fremdwort Diskussion* Peter Braun (ed.), 9-32.

Waterman, J.T. (1966). *A History of the German Language*. Seattle: University of Washington Press.

Weinrich, U. (1963). *Languages in Contact—Findings and Problems*. The Hague: Mouton.

Wexler, P.J. (1964). Frein—the naming of the vehicle brake. *Cahiers de Lexicologie* 5, 69-83.

Wicker, A.W. (1969). Attitudes vs. actions—the relationship of verbal and overt behavioral responses to attitude objects. *Journal of Social Issues* 25, 41-73.

Zoref, E. (1962). Don't leave the language in the hands of the mockers (in Hebrew). *Hachinuch*, 36, 500-501.

Appendix 1. Tables

Table 1
Question 11: have you ever considered the problem of the presence of foreign words in Hebrew?

Preoccupation with the problem	Interviewee group: Pupils		Nurses		Students	
	no.	%	no.	%	no.	%
Constantly/often	49	43.5	74	87	59	59
Seldom	46	42	8	9.5	33	33
Never	15	14.5	2	3.5	8	8
Total	110	100	85	100	100	100

Table 2
Question 13: Do foreign words, in your opinion, contribute to the Hebrew language?

Contribution to the language	Interviewee group: Pupils		Nurses		Students	
	no.	%	no.	%	no.	%
High	29	26.4	17	20	25	25
Medium	38	34.5	33	38.8	42	42
Small	22	20	21	24.7	20	20
Not at all	21	19.1	14	16.5	13	13
Total	110	100	85	100	100	100

Table 3
Question 20: Do foreign words, in your opinion, constitute a danger to Hebrew?

Danger to the language	Interviewee group: Pupils		Nurses		Students	
	no.	%	no.	%	no.	%
High	26	23.6	15	17.6	28	28
Medium	42	38.2	36	42.4	31	31
Small	29	26.4	26	30.6	32	32
Not at all	13	11.8	8	9.4	9	9
Total	110	100	85	100	100	100

Table 4
Question 21: Do you think the use of foreign words can endanger the existence of Hebrew in the foreseeable future?

Danger to the language in the future	Interviewee group: Pupils no.	%	Nurses no.	%	Students no.	%
Probably/Certainly	36	32	19	23	30	30
Probably not	50	46	40	47	60	60
Don't know	24	22	26	30	10	10
Total	110	100	85	100	100	100

Table 5
Question 22: Do you think the Hebrew equivalents will replace the foreign words in the foreseeable future?

Hebrew equivalent replacing foreign words	Interviewee group: Pupils no.	%	Nurses no.	%	Students no.	%
Probably/Certainly	21	19	28	33	34	34
Probably not	49	45	34	40	45	45
Don't know	40	36	23	27	21	21
Total	110	100	85	100	100	100

Table 6
Question 12: Do you agree to the use of foreign words in Hebrew?

Agreeable to the use	Interviewee group: Pupils no.	%	Nurses no.	%	Students no.	%	Total no.	%
Agree absolutely	46	42	28	33	42	42	116	40
Agree	52	47.2	47	55.3	45	45	114	48
Agree but prefer	10	9	10	11.7	12	12	32	11
Against Hebrew equivalents	2	1.8	—	—	1	1	3	1
Total	110	100	100	100	85	100	295	100

Table 7
Question 13: Do you think a campaign is desirable against foreign words?

Campaign	Interviewee group: Pupils no.	%	Nurses no.	%	Students no.	%
Desirable	55	50	35	41	52	52
Undesirable	55	50	50	59	48	48
Total	110	100	85	100	100	100

Table 8
Question 14: What is your attitude towards the Hebrew speaker who uses foreign words?

Attitude	Interviewee group: Pupils no.	%	Nurses no.	%	Students no.	%
Positive	20	18	16	19	12	12
It's his own affair	71	65	48	56	56	56
Though I disagree with him, I understand him	10	9	16	19	24	24
Negative	9	8	5	6	8	8
Total	110	100	85	100	100	100

Table 9
Question 19: What is your attitude towards the user of a Hebrew equivalent instead of a common foreign word?

Attitude	Interviewee group: Pupils no.	%	Nurses no.	%	Students no.	%
Positive	49	45	38	45	53	53
It's his own affair	55	50	34	40	42	42
Though I disagree with him, I understand him	4	3.5	8	9	4	4
Negative	2	1.5	5	6	1	1
Total	110	100	85	100	100	100

Table 10
Question 12: Do you agree to the use of foreign words in Hebrew? (interviewees listed by origin, education and employment of father)

Father's land of origin	Total in %		Father's education and occupation: Academic	Clerk	Technician	Self-employed laborer	Professional		
A. Pupils' group[a]									
Israel	30.4	100	64.3	14.3	7.1	14.3	—		
Asia-Africa	13	100	16.7	33.2	16.7	16.7	16.7		
Europe-America	56.6	100	61.3	19.3	7.7	7.7	3.8		
Total	100								
B. Nurses' group[b]									
Israel	25	100	42.9	28.6	14.2	14.3	0	0	0
Asia-Africa	17.9	100	0	40	40	0	20	0	0
Europe-America	57.1	100	12.5	31.3	25	6.4	18.5	0	6.3
Total	100								
C. Students' group[c]									
Israel	21.4	100	44.4	11.1	0	22.2	11.2	0	11.1
Asia-Africa	26.2	100	18.2	45.5	18.1	9.1	9.1	0	0
Europe-America	52.4	100	27.3	22.7	9.1	22.7	9.1	9.1	0
Total	100								

[a] 46 out of 100 (46%) answered absolutely in the affirmative (agree absolutely).
[b] 28 out of 85 (33%) answered absolutely in the affirmative (agree absolutely).
[c] 42 out of 100 (42%) answered absolutely in the affirmative (agree absolutely).

Table 11
Question 13: Does the use of foreign words contribute to the language? (answer in %)

Contribution to Language	Father's education and occupation: Academic	Clerk	Technician	Self-employed laborer	Professional			
A. Pupils' group								
large	21.3	36	10	46.2	40			
medium	40.4	32	35	23.1	20			
small	21.3	20	20	15.4	2			
none at all	17	12	35	15.3	20			
Total	100	100	100	100	100			
B. Nurses' group								
large	0	35.7	17.4	18.6	11.1	—	0	—
medium	60	35.7	34.8	28.6	22.2	—	66.7	—
small	26.7	17.9	34.8	28.6	22.3	—	0	—
none at all	13.3	10.7	13	14.2	44.4	—	33.3	—
Total	100	100	100	100	100	100	100	100
C. Students' group								
large	25	28.6	20	11.1	45.5	0	50	0
medium	41.7	42.9	50	50	27.3	0	25	66.7
small	25	14.3	30	16.7	18.2	50	0	33.3
none at all	8.3	14.2	0	22.2	9	50	25	0
Total	100	100	100	100	100	100	100	100

Table 12
Question 13: Is a campaign against foreign words desirable? (based on country of origin) (answers in %)

Father's country of origin	Campaign against foreign words?						
	Total.	Pupils		Nurses		Students	
		yes	no	yes	No	yes	no
Israel	100	45.2	54.8	44	56	53.3	46.7
Asia-Africa	100	54.8	45.2	44.4	55.6	58.3	41.7
Europe-America	100	48.4	51.6	35.7	46.3	55.7	44.3
Total		50	50	41	59	52	48

Table 13
Question 20: Is there a danger in using foreign words in the language? (based on language spoken at home) (answers in %)

Language at home	Danger to language:					
	Totally	Great	Medium	Small	None at all	Total
A. Pupils' group						
Hebrew	78	24.4	39.7	26.9	9	100
Hebrew/European	28	21.4	35.7	21.4	21.5	100
Hebrew/Arabic	2	50	0	50	0	100
Arabic	—	—	—	—	—	—
European	2	0	50	50	0	100
Total	110					100
B. Nurses' group						
Hebrew	48	22.9	39.6	31.3	6.2	100
Hebrew/European	19	5.2	57.9	31.6	5.3	100
Hebrew/Arabic	5	0	40	0	60	100
Arabic	10	10	40	40	10	100
European	3	66.7	0	33.3	0	100
Total	85					100
C. Students' group						
Hebrew	64	29.7	25	34.4	10.9	100
Hebrew/European	16	31.3	37.5	25	6.2	100
Hebrew/Arabic	6	16.7	33.3	50	0	100
Arabic	7	28.6	42.9	14.3	14.2	100
European	7	14.3	57.1	28.6	0	100
Total	100					100

Table 14
Frequency of encountering foreign words (for the 40 words in the list) (answers in %)

Words		Foreign word encountered always/frequently		
		Pupils	Nurses	Students
1.	aggressive	70.9	83.5	84
2.	administration	56.3	60	89
3.	improvisation	37.3	35.3	39
4.	instinct	89.1	87	89
5.	information	95.4	91.8	96
6.	alternative	82.7	91.8	93
7.	antenna	97.2	98.8	98
8.	analogy	39.1	61.2	71
9.	association	92.7	84.8	96
10.	aspect	74.6	90.6	94
11.	ecstasy	79.1	61.1	75
12.	drastic	96.3	90.6	95
13.	terminology	20.9	30.6	52
14.	transformer	72.7	75.3	80
15.	model	95.5	95.3	91
16.	motive	90	75.3	91
17.	minimal	94.5	96.5	99
18.	mentality	81.1	85.9	98
19.	maximum	98.1	95.3	98
20.	normality	97.3	88.2	94
21.	socialization	50.9	67	45
22.	structural	2.2	23.5	28
23.	starter	70.9	65.9	79
24.	sterile	90.9	92.9	85
25.	simultaneous	60.9	60	68
26.	symptom	71.8	89.4	84
27.	selection	86.3	84.7	89
28.	spontaneous	90.9	97.6	95
29.	specialization	30	45.9	53
30.	sector	71.8	85.9	91
31.	panic	97.3	82.3	06
32.	function	90.9	92.9	93
33.	player	86.4	71.8	73
34.	provocation	62.7	51.8	75
35.	project	95.5	92.9	95
36.	communication	80.9	75.3	84
37.	critical	94.5	88.2	98
38.	regression	17.2	50.6	50
39.	relevant	89.1	94.1	99
40.	prescription	84.7	88.2	84
Average total		74.7	77	82.5

Table 15
Distribution of frequency of encountering foreign words among interviewee groups for the 40 words in the list

Percent encountering words always or seldom[a]	Number of familiar words:					
	Pupils		Nurses		Students	
	no.	%	no.	%	no.	%
91-100	14	35	13	32	19	48
81-90	9	22	11	28	8	20
71-80	7	18	4	10	5	12
51-70	4	10	8	20	4	10
41-50	—	—	1	2.5	2	5
21-40	4	22	11	28	8	20
1-20	2	5	—	—	—	—

Table 16
Frequency of use of foreign words

Interviewee group	Uses words always/often		sometimes/never		Total	
	no.	%	no.	%	no.	%
General use						
Pupils	66	60	44	40	110	100
Nurses	43	51	42	49	85	100
Students	42	42	58	58	100	100
Total	151	51	144	49	295	100
Use in speaking						
Pupils	68	62	42	38	110	100
Nurses	37	44	48	56	85	100
Students	40	40	60	60	100	100
Total	145	49	150	51	295	100
Use in writing						
Pupils	31	28	79	72	110	100
Nurses	28	-33	57	64	85	100
Students	16	16	84	84	100	100
Total	75	25.5	220	74.5	295	100

Table 17
Correlation between familiarity and use of foreign words (answers in %)

Words	Pupils		Nurses		Students	
	knows and uses	knows and doesn't use	knows and uses	knows and doesn't use	knows and uses	knows and doesn't use
1. aggressive	66.7	77.3	93	73.8	85.7	82.8
2. administration	50	65.9	79.5	59.6	90.5	88
3. improvisation	31.8	45.5	37.2	33.3	38.1	39.7
4. instinct	81.8	100	93	81	90.5	87.9
5. information	96.5	95.5	95.4	88.1	97.6	94.9
6. alternative	81.8	84.1	97.6	85.7	92.8	93.1
7. antenna	96.9	97.7	100	97.6	100	96.5
8. analogy	33.3	47.7	69.7	52.4	76.2	67.2
9. association	93.9	90.9	93	76.2	100	93.1
10. aspect	72.8	77.3	97.7	83.4	95.2	93.1
11. ecstasy	74.2	86.3	67.5	54.8	85.7	67.2
12. drastic	97	95.5	95.4	85.7	95.3	94.8
13. terminology	21.2	20.2	30.2	30.9	61.9	44.9
14. transformer	68.2	79.5	81.4	69.1	78.6	81
15. model	95.4	95.4	97.7	92.9	97.7	92.9
16. motive	89.4	90.9	83.7	66.7	88.1	93.1
17. minimal	93.9	95.4	97.6	95.2	100	98.2
18. mentality	80.3	84.1	88.4	83.3	97.6	98.3
19. maximum	100	95.4	100	90.5	97.6	98.3
20. normal	98.5	95.5	100	100	100	100
21. socialization	48.5	64.6	72.1	61.9	57.1	36.2
22. structural	7.6	9.1	23.2	23.8	38.1	20.7
23. starter	75.7	63.6	67.5	64.3	76.2	81
24. sterile	89.4	93.1	97.7	88.1	83.3	86.2
25. simultaneous	45.5	84.1	67.5	52.4	73.8	63.8
26. symptom	62.1	83.4	93	85.7	83.3	84.5
27. selection	81.8	93.1	86	83.3	85.7	91.4
28. spontaneous	89.4	93.2	100	95.2	97.6	93.1
29. specialization	33.3	25	53.5	38.1	61.9	46.6
30. panic	96.9	97.7	88.4	76.2	95.3	96.6
31. function	90.9	90.9	97.7	88.1	90.4	94.8
32. player	84.8	88.6	74.4	69	64.3	72.3
33. provocation	62.1	63.7	69.8	33.3	76.2	74.2
34. project	93.9	97.7	97.7	88.1	95.2	94.8
35. communication	77.2	86.4	79.1	71.4	90.5	79.3
36. critical	97	90.9	97.7	78.6	100	96.6
37. regression	18.1	15.9	58.1	42.8	61.9	41.4
38. relevant	84.9	95.5	93	95.3	100	98.2
39. prescription	86.3	90.9	90.7	78.6	85.7	82.8
40. sector	71.2	72.8	93	78.6	92.8	89.7
Average total	62.8	66.4	70.1	61.8	72.1	66.2

Table 18
Question 7: Do you feel a difference between the use of foreign words and the use of their Hebrew equivalents?

Difference in use	Interviewee group: Pupils		Nurses		Students	
	no.	%	no.	%	no.	%
Yes	99	90	62	73	85	85
No	11	10	23	27	15	15
Total	110	100	85	100	100	100

Table 19
Types of difference indicated by those answering question 3 in the affirmative, with reference to 20 word pairs (answers in %)

Interview group	Type of difference: Emotional	Creating an impression	Content	Habitual use	Other	No difference	Total
Pupils	3.6	24	8.7	45.4	5.5	12.8	100
Nurses	5.1	32.4	10.2	47.1	3.5	1.7	100
Students	10.9	22	9.8	42.7	4.2	10.4	100

Table 20
Question 9: Is there a difference among various Hebrew equivalents as to their rate of absorption into the language?

Difference in rate of absorption into the language	Interviewee group: Pupils no.	%	Nurses no.	%	Students no.	%
Yes	81	74	33	39	85	85
No	29	26	52	61	15	15
Total	110	100	85	100	100	100

Causes for Differences among various Hebrew equivalents as regards their absorption into the language

Referring to question 10, "What causes the difference in the rate of absorption of Hebrew equivalents into the language?" the interviewee was given seven linguistic and social possibilities influencing the chances of the Hebrew equivalent to be absorbed into the language.

1. The length of the Hebrew equivalent
2. The degree of fashion of the Hebrew equivalent
3. The sound of the Hebrew equivalent
4. The 'luck' of the Hebrew equivalent (the word reveals the inability to show clearly and precisely what it is that causes the word's absorption or rejection)
5. Grammatical form of the Hebrew equivalent
6. A known form of the Hebrew equivalent
7. The appearance of the Hebrew equivalent at the right moment.

The length of the word, its sound, grammatical form, and root—all these are linguistic elements influencing the absorption or non-absorption of the Hebrew equivalent. The fashionable use of the word, its appearance at a suitable time—when an event reaches the headlines that calls for its use—all these are social factors, influencing the absorption or non-absorption of the Hebrew equivalent.

Table 21
Interviewees' attitudes to ten foreign words and their equivalents (causes for differences from the list above)

Interviewee group	Causes for differences in the absorption of the word into the language (%) 1	2	3	4	5	6	7	No answer	Total
prestige									
Pupils	7.3	32.7	19.1	3.6	6.4	1.8	4.6	24.5	100
Nurses	2.4	18.8	3.5	2.4	2.4	3.5	8.2	58.8	100
Students	9	49	12	4	2	8	3	13	100
hobby									
Pupils	0.9	32.7	23.6	8.3	3.6	1.8	4.6	24.5	100
Nurses	2.4	15.3	2.3	4.7	4.7	2.4	9.4	58.8	100
Students	3	44	15	9	3	10	2	14	100
normal									
Pupils	4.5	30	18.2	10.9	4.6	2.7	4.6	24.5	100
Nurses	1.2	15.3	4.7	1.2	2.3	4.7	11.8	58.8	100
Students	5	34	18	15	3	9	2	14	100
segment									
Pupils	3.6	29.2	18.2	12.7	5.5	1.8	4.5	24.5	100
Nurses	1.2	16.5	2.4	5.9	2.3	2.3	10.6	58.8	100
Students	4	34	14	15	11	5	3	14	100
bureaucracy									
Pupils	1.8	30.9	19.2	9.1	9.1	0.9	4.5	24.5	100
Nurses	2.4	16.5	2.4	3.5	2.3	2.3	11.8	58.8	100
Students	6	38	10	11	10	9	2	14	100
parasite									
Pupils	4.5	26.4	20	10.9	7.3	1.9	4.5	24.5	100
Nurses	2.4	14.1	4.7	2.4	2.3	3.5	11.8	58.8	100
Students	5	40	13	10	5	11	2	14	100
politician									
Pupils	3.6	26.5	20.9	12.7	7.3	0	4.5	24.5	100
Nurses	1.2	17.6	5.9	2.4	2.4	1.1	10.6	58.8	100
Students	7	36	9	15	4	13	2	14	100
regression									
Pupils	4.5	30.9	16.4	10	6.4	2.7	4.6	24.5	100
Nurses	1.2	15.3	2.4	4.7	4.7	2.3	10.6	58.8	100
Students	2	38	18	10	3	11	4	14	100
transformer									
Pupils	5.5	31.8	16.4	9.1	5.5	2.7	4.5	24.5	100
Nurses	1.2	16.5	3.5	3.5	4.7	2.4	9.4	58.8	100
Students	5	33	17	18	4	7	2	14	100
generator									
Pupils	6.4	28.2	21.8	9.1	4.6	0.9	4.5	24.5	100
Nurses	1.2	14.1	2.4	4.7	4.7	3.5	10.6	58.8	100
Students	4	35	16	17	4	8	2	14	100

APPENDIX 2. FIGURES

Figure 1
Do you agree to the use of foreign words in Hebrew (Hebrew mother-tongue respondents).

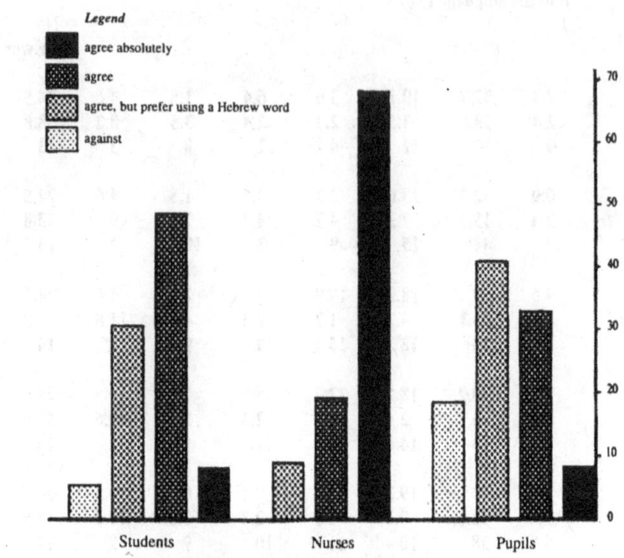

Figure 2
Do you agree to the use of foreign words in Hebrew (respondents who use a European mother tongue at home).

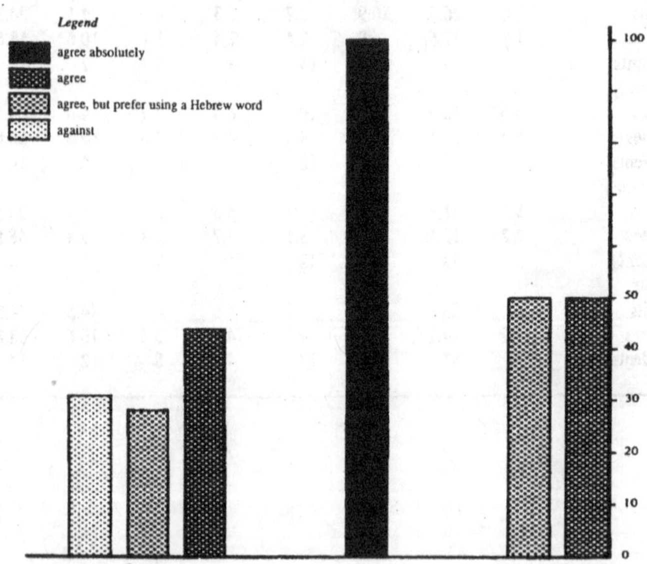

Figure 3
Do you agree to the use of foreign words in Hebrew (respondents who use both Hebrew and a European mother tongue at home.

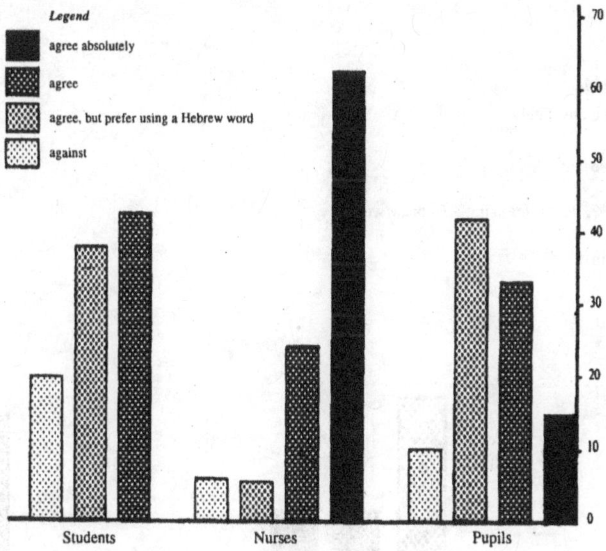

Figure 4
Do you agree to the use of foreign words in Hebrew (respondents who use both Hebrew and Arabic at home.

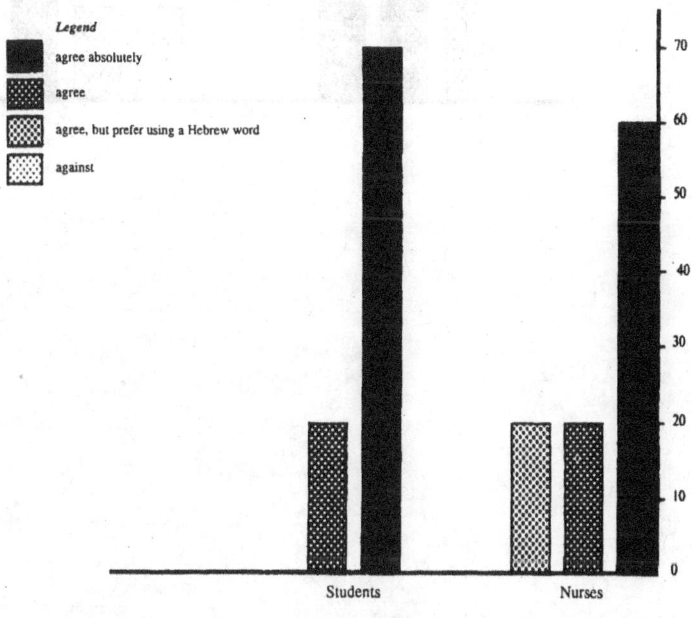

Figure 5
Do you agree to the use of foreign words in Hebrew (respondents who use Arabic at home).

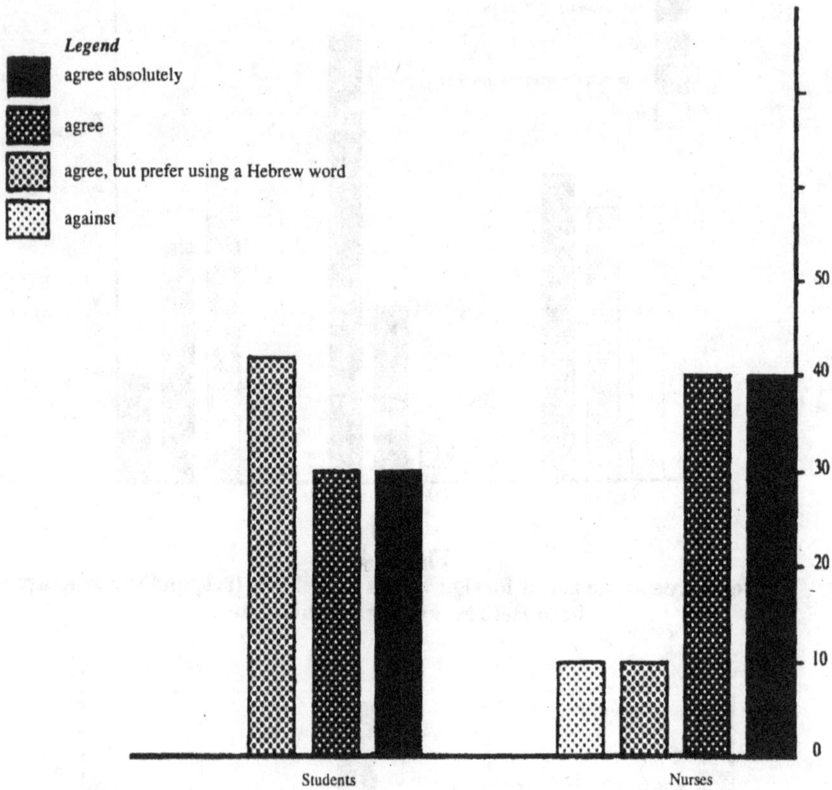

Figure 6
Relation between use of foreign words, knowledge of Hebrew equivalents, and attitudes towards use of foreign words: interest.

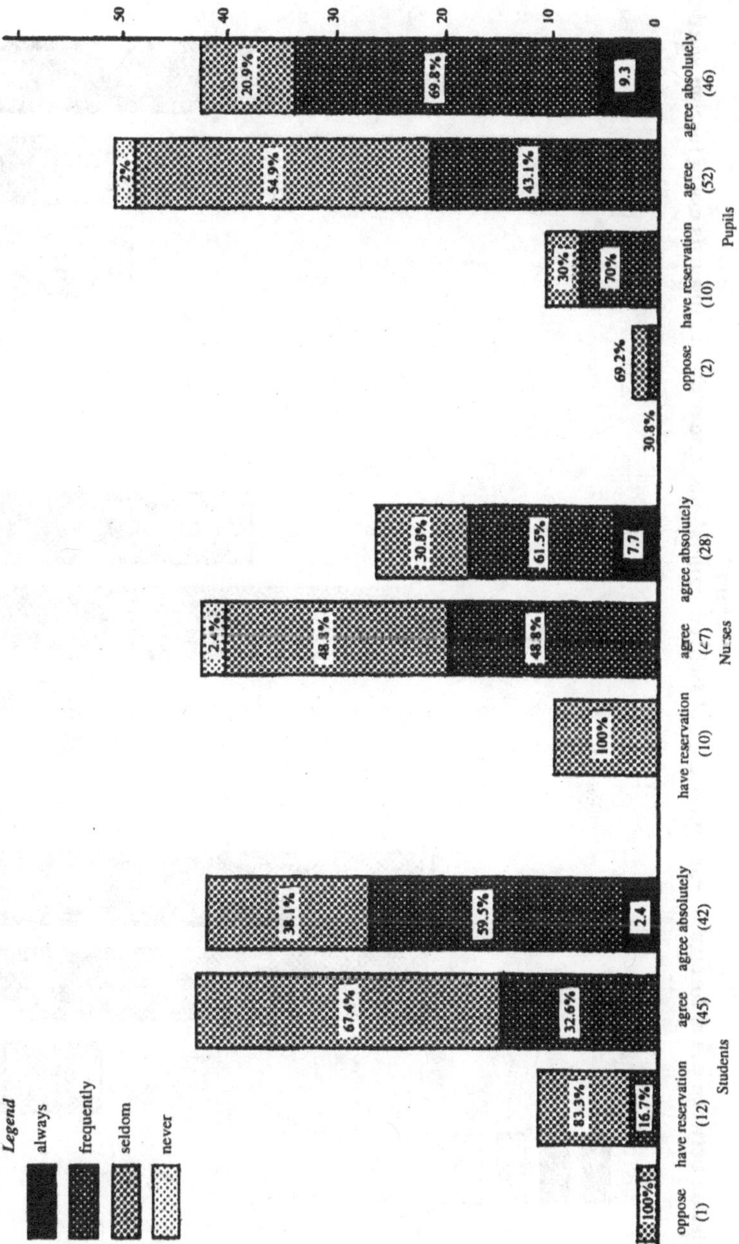

Figure 7

Relation between use of foreign words, knowledge of Hebrew equivalents, and attitudes towards use of foreign words: index

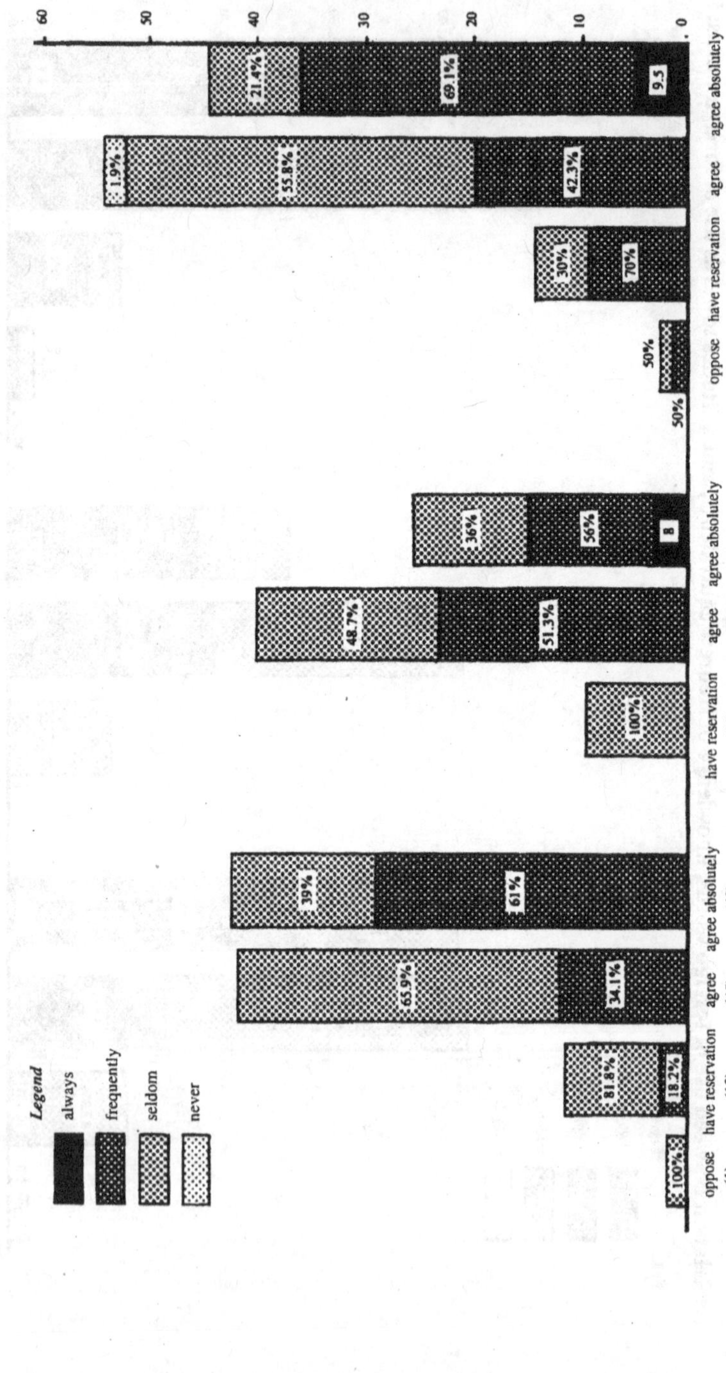

Figure 8
Relation between use of foreign words, knowledge of Hebrew equivalents, and attitudes towards use of foreign words: information

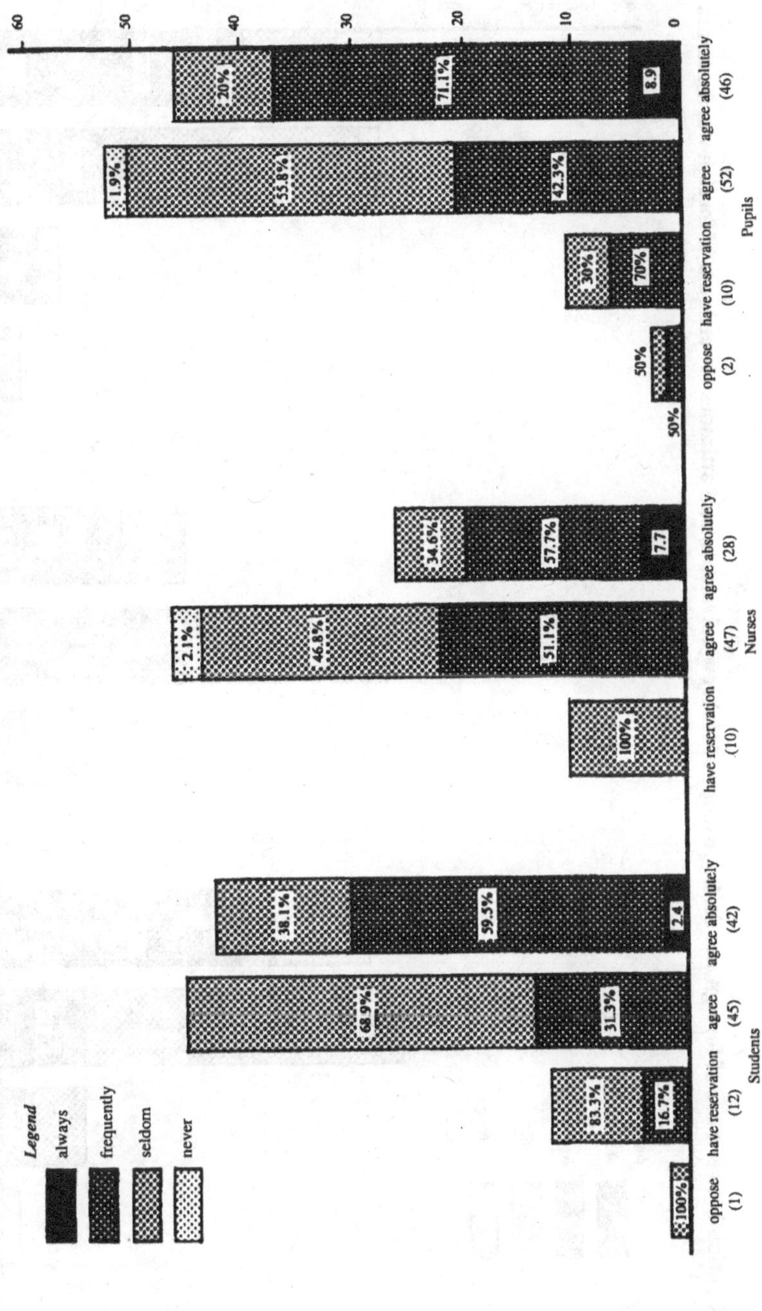

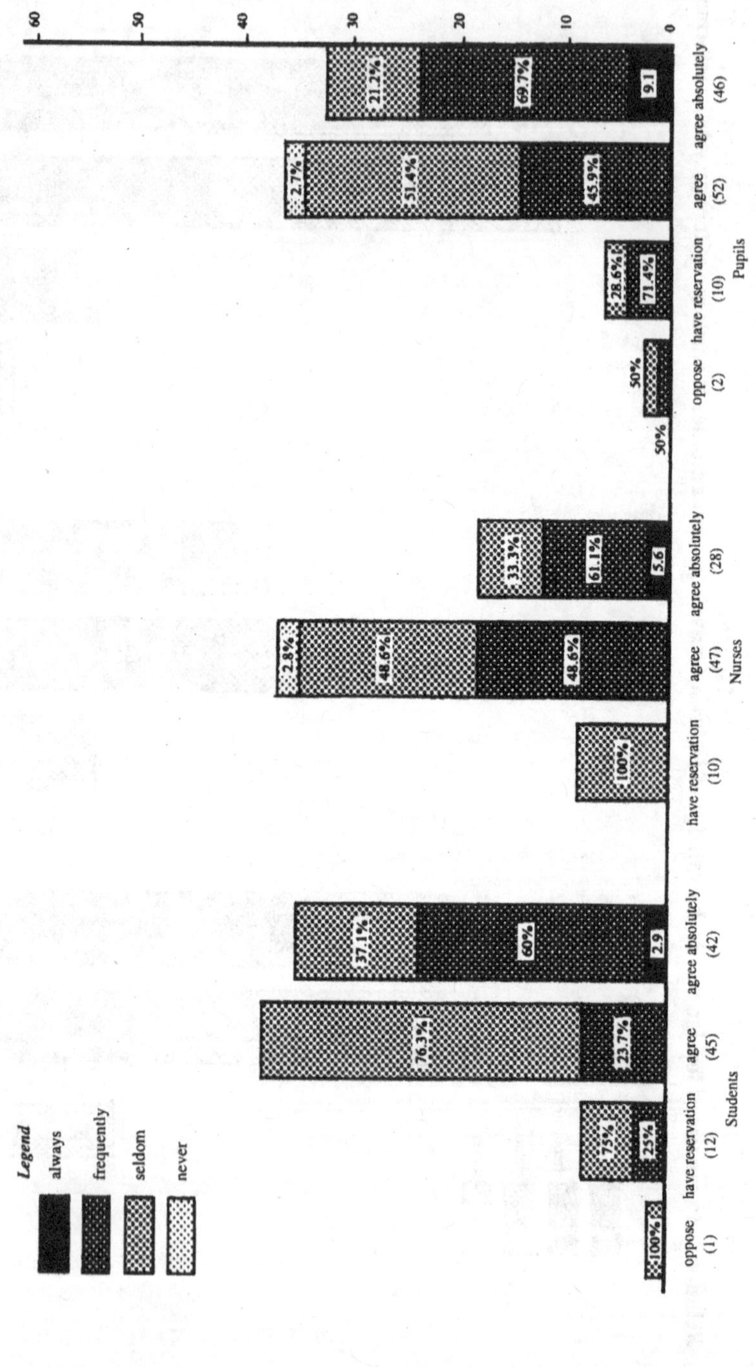

Figure 9
Relation between use of foreign words, knowledge of Hebrew euivalents, and attitudes towards use of foreign words: terminology

Figure 10

Relation between use of foreign words, knowledge of Hebrew equivalents, and attitudes towards use of foreign words: switch

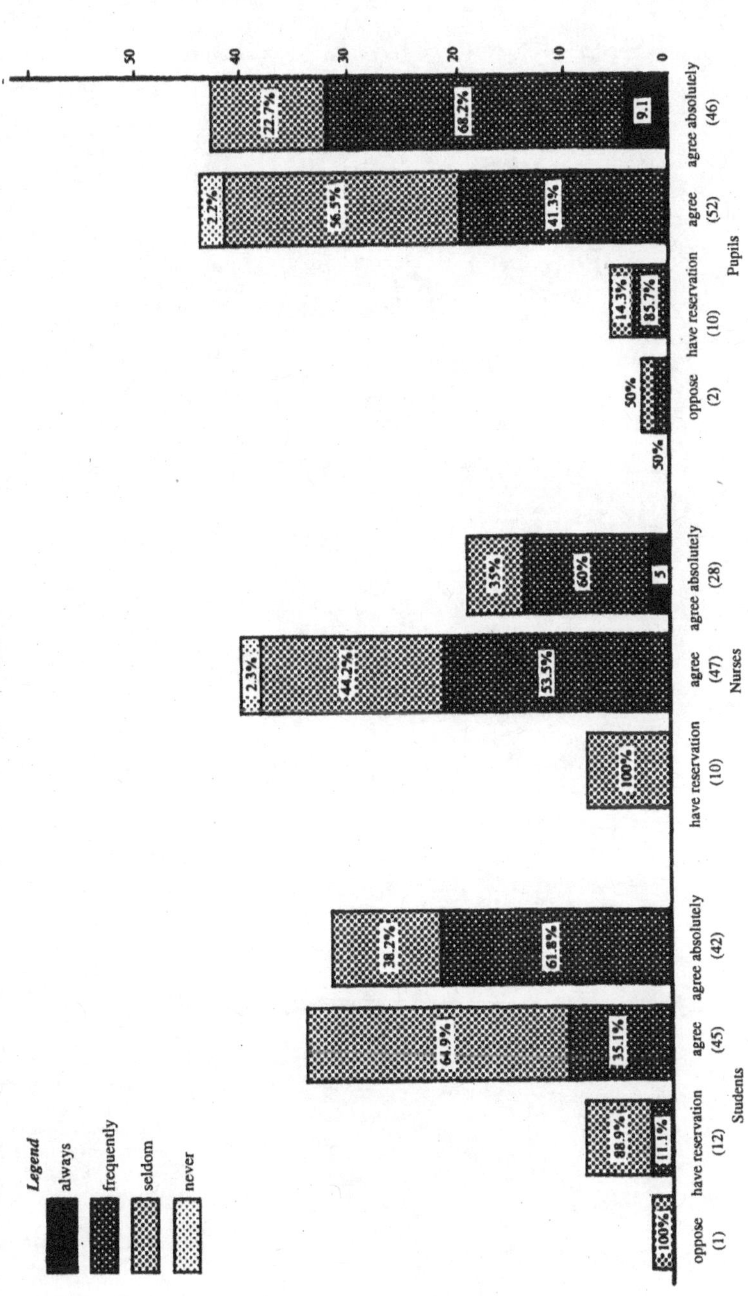

9

Bilingualism in a Moroccan Settlement in the South of Israel[1]

Yaakov Bentolila

Bilingualism in Israel

Among the various topics in Israeli sociolinguistics that have attracted scholarly attention,[2] few have been concerned with issues of bilingualism. The most prevalent manifestation of bilingualism in Israel concerns the retention by new immigrants of their languages of origin. It is a transitional bilingualism,[3] since Israeli-born children (or sabras), with a few notable exceptions, are immersed in Hebrew, which is, used everywhere (in the kindergarten, at school, in the army, etc.). They either do not learn their parents' tongue at all, or do so to such a limited extent that it can no longer be considered a primary language, let alone a mother tongue. It is therefore evident that we should clearly distinguish between the generations: that of the immigrants—whatever proficiency they may have reached in Hebrew—and that of their children—the second generation. Since Hebrew is the official language of the country and necessary at all times, we can assign to it the status of L1, i.e., the majority language in a bilingual situation. Similarly, the immigrants' original languages may be considered as L2, i.e., minority or secondary languages (regardless of whether we are dealing with a "remote" Jewish dialect, like Moroccan Judeo-Arabic, or with a major international language of high cultural level, such as English or Russian). Generally speaking, we assume that the second generation will be located more closely to the abandonment end of the continuum, which mirrors the degree of maintenance of L2.[4]

Affinity with the language of origin exists in differing degrees and for different reasons in the various communities.[5] Immigrants who are English or French speakers, for example, may well be inclined to continue using their "prestigious" languages of origin, which are associated with universally-recognized cultural values and which offer undeniable benefits.[6] For immigrant families from western countries, it seems most uncommon to refrain from teaching their children their European language of origin.[7] I have often noticed that sabras in families from the United States, France, or the Netherlands, retain their parents' language as their mother tongue, or at least they know it equally well. The parents, aware that they are providing their children with good opportunities for advancement, continue speaking with them in their language of origin and manage to teach them, by means of private lessons or the like, even how to read and write in that language.[8] They have no reason to worry about Hebrew, which will undoubtedly be learned outside the family network.

A different case occurs when very strong feelings of solidarity are the cause of retaining the language of origin. This happened as regards the Romanian community, which was the object of a research study in Israeli bilingualism by Fisherman.[9] In a sample of youth (N=95), Fisherman found 80 (representing 84%) who spoke Romanian quite well. Nevertheless, the case of young Romanians differs from that of English- or French- speakers. It is true that the percentage of young Romanians totally ignorant of their parents' language proved to be null; however, not all can read and write in Romanian. In youth gatherings, they generally use Hebrew, notwithstanding the fact that "if someone in the younger crowd insists on Hebrew as a matter of principle he is derided as a snob" (Hofman andand Fisherman, 1971: 225).

It seems therefore that the nature of Israeli bilingualism should be studied separately for each community. Such diverse factors as the prestige of the language of origin, its cultural background, the social stereotypes it conjures, its role in the feelings of communal solidarity, its educational advantages[10]—all these factors must be considered when it comes to tracing the profile of bilingualism for the second generation in Israel. In the present article, we have tried to describe a specific case of bilingualism within a rural population of Moroccan origin in Israel.

Romema

Romema is the pseudonym given[11] to a *moshav*[12] established in 1956 in the Northern Negev by Moroccan immigrants. The founders all came from a single *mellah*[13] called Amran,[14] situated on one of the northern slopes of the High Atlas. The settlers numbered, upon arrival, 33 families, mostly related, due to interval marriage over several generations. Six years later, a new group of Moroccan immigrants joined the Romemites. They, too, originated in rural areas of Morocco, but not the Atlas. Shokeid's studies trace the phases of their acculturation and adaptation to the norms of organized cooperative agriculture in Israel. This was often a painful process, whereby ancient values, especially those concerning the social hierarchy between the diverse groups, were called into question. Twenty years after their settling,[15] however, most of the Romema farmers, a population of about 300 persons, have become financially independent. They have achieved a certain degree of economic security, becoming assimilated to the modern way of life and accustomed to a relatively prosperous standard of living. They have acquired modern furniture, electrical appliances, radio and TV. Some own cars, tractors and trucks. The children go to the communal school, where they mix with pupils and teachers of European origin. To a certain extent, older children go to high schools, either academic or vocational, locally or in other parts of the country. Some, born in Morocco but having lived in Israel since early childhood, have even attended university. On the other hand, a large number have only completed primary school; others have not even achieved that much. Boys go to the army at age 18; most girls are exempt from military service for religious reasons.

Bilingualism Among the Romemites

Romemite bilingualism did not begin in Romema. In Morocco, these people all spoke Moroccan Judeo-Arabic,[16] while using Hebrew as the language of religious study and worship.[17] The Jewish vernaculars have always been in a state of stable bilingualism with Hebrew, or rather, by definition, in a state of diglossia.[18]. In our particular case, it is actually a triglossia, because the district where the mellah Amran (see above) was situated was Berber-speaking. Thus, the Amranites used three languages: (1) Judeo-Arabic, as their communal everyday language, (2) Berber, with their non-Jewish neighbors, and (3) Hebrew, for religious purposes. One can say that the first generation of Romema has always been trilingual. In Morocco, they used Judeo-Arabic, Berber, and Hebrew; in Israel, the order has simply been changed to Judeo-Arabic, Hebrew and, to a certain extent, Berber.[19]

The Roots of Hebrew in Romema

Therefore, Hebrew functioned in Morocco both as a language of religious studies and prayers and as a supplier of lexical elements into Judeo-Arabic. The elders of Romema, like so many other Moroccan immigrants, easily recognized familiar words and phrases in Israeli Hebrew, and this undoubtedly facilitated the acquisition of their new required language. To this day, the elders of Romema still utilize quaint, archaic Hebrew expressions in their daily speech. This is by no means a sententious style, but rather a natural retention of what had been learned at school and recited in the synagogue.

The Attitude of the Elders of Romema towards Hebrew and towards Judeo-Arabic

In 1961, the Central Bureau of Statistics performed a nation-wide census, inquiring among other issues, about the use of Hebrew and other languages in Israel. The analysis of the results was published in an important article, which constituted a balance sheet of the progress of Hebrew thirteen years after the proclamation of the State of Israel (Shmeltz and Bachi, 1973). Professor Shmeltz kindly sent us the detailed data concerning the usage of Hebrew in Romema, as gathered in this census. This information is presented in the following table (Table 1).

Table 1
Hebrew as everyday language at Romema, according to the 1961 census.

	Total	Male	Female
The entire population	190	105	85
Percentages	100	100	100
Hebrew only language (%)	—	—	—
Hebrew first language (%)	74	81	65
Hebrew second language (%)	5	—	12
Non Hebrew-speaking (%)	21	19	23

It is difficult to accept these findings without reservations. Apparently, only those men who spoke no Hebrew at all were considered as not possessing it as their primary language (?); this means that even the slightest knowledge of Hebrew was enough for it to be considered a first language! Only among the women were there some who admitted speaking Hebrew as a second language: the women's responses thus seem more credible. The Romema elders surely looked upon Hebrew with the highest esteem. If they did not make more proficient use of this language, it was only because they did not know it well enough to utilize as their daily tongue. In Morocco, to be sure, the men had studied "the Holy Language" in the framework of their traditional schooling, but not in sufficient measure for fluent use as the modern everyday idiom. Indeed, only after a certain period of acclimatization to Israel, do they succeed in expressing themselves to a reasonable extent in Hebrew.

The Attitude of the Romema Youth towards Hebrew and towards Judeo-Arabic

With the Romema youth, things are more complex. They explain their use of Judeo-Arabic as a necessity, especially in their communication with elderly family members who do not know Hebrew. A young Romemite described the bilingualism of the moshav in these terms: the young adults, who as children spoke Judeo-Arabic with their parents (that is, who had previously used Judeo-Arabic as their mother tongue), have gradually begun to speak Hebrew with their younger brothers or with their own children. Thus, there are children in Romema who had not acquired Judeo-Arabic in infancy, but who learned this language later, through interaction with the entire Romemite society. These children then learned Hebrew first and Judeo-Arabic later. In many families, elderly parents address their children in Hebrew, doubtlessly influenced by the norms adopted by their elder children (especially the girls), thus transferring Hebrew from a "fraternal language" into a true "maternal language."

However, not all the youth have identical attitudes towards Hebrew. Two young instructors[20] have observed the following facts: between the ages of 13 and 21, boys (as opposed to girls), and especially those who have discontinued their studies after primary school, use Judeo-Arabic most regularly. Before and after these ages, they use more Hebrew. Judeo-Arabic, then, is quite widespread especially among young boys with a limited or interrupted education. This behavior may be understood as resulting from a need affiliation (Atkinson 1964), i.e.

the necessity to maintain positive relations with the surrounding people, a need that was related to social privation, just like hunger relates to a lack of food.[21] Findling (1971) found a positive correlation among Puerto Ricans in New York between utilization of English and the need affiliation, especially outside the family context. In other words, when a Puerto Rican wants to further his social status in the society at large, he uses English rather than Spanish.

I believe that the aforementioned explanation is also valid, in certain cases, for a preferred secondary language in a bilingual situation. We may attribute this preference too to what Labov calls *linguistic insecurity.*[22] As noted by Labov, a stigmatized linguistic variant may reassume a certain prestige, originating in an opposing system of subjacent norms.[23] Thus, certain speakers will regularly use a vernacular variant, notwithstanding the fact that they are perfectly conscious of its low status. This seems to explain the situation of the disadvantaged males among the Romema youth. As a matter of fact, the majority of Romemite youth display behavior patterns characteristic of a psychological state of *linguistic insecurity*[24], but with the less prosperous, this trait seems to be strong enough to turn them away from Hebrew. Striving for social status, they turn to a restricted group of "buddies," after having given up hope of attaining social prestige within a larger body. This consequently contributes to a more prestigious status of Judeo-Arabic, which appears here as an affiliating factor, among other manifestations of intra-group comradeship, that creates solidarity and an identity.

In an article drawing a comparison between Jewish and Arab high school students in Israel and their respective ethnolinguistic vitality and language attitudes, Kraemer and Olshtain (1989: 210) found that "Arab students who saw their group prestige and political power as lower had a higher evaluation of their language." Interpreting this fact according to social identity theory, they cite the following principle as formulated by Tajfel (1978:210):

> perception of low status and lack of political power foster the need to seek an adequate social identity based on positively valued distinctiveness from the dominant group. One strategy used by subordinate groups to achieve this end is the evaluation of some existing characteristic as positively differentiating between themselves and the dominant group...Language is often an appropriate object for such differentiation.

Although the cases under study by Kraemer and Olshtain differ from ours in very important details, nevertheless, it seems that they obey similar attitudinal principles.

The Use of Two Languages in Romema

Concerning the use of Hebrew and Judeo-Arabic in Romema, we questioned only the youth, since the older men are subject to objective constraints (Cf. ~ 2.3). According to the responses obtained, it seems that all but one of the principal factors associated with the use of each language, were the result of various subjective constraints, as follows:

1) *The linguistic competence of the person addressed.* Judeo-Arabic is used when addressing people who do not know Hebrew very well. The fact that usage of a language in a bilingual community correlates directly with the linguistic competence of the addressees is well-known from other studies. Cooper has found that people are addressed in a certain language to the extent that their fluency in that language is known (Cooper 197 1:282).
2) *Replies correspond in language to the utterance.* The Romemite youth partially explain their usage of Judeo-Arabic by the fact that they are addressed in this language.
3) *The linguistic competence of the speaker.* In general, the youth think that they speak more Hebrew because they are more fluent in it than in Judeo-Arabic.
4) *Judeo-Arabic is used for swearing and other manifestations of anger.* Expression of strong emotions, especially of disdain, may bring forth the most vulgar linguistic variants. Moreover, since swearing requires the usage of ready-made locutions, the new bilingual may continue using the old expressions for a long time. It is therefore in Judeo-Arabic that the adults of Romema insult each other,[25] and these are probably the only conveyances of displeasure that the children of this community have heard since their earliest childhood.
5) *The only clear-cut function of Judeo-Arabic not attributable to any subjective constraint is its use as a secret language.* For example, take this dialogue, which we have recorded with S. B. (16 years old):

We: "Who, for example, speaks Judeo-Arabic with you?"

S. B.: "The lads, and also..."

We: "Of your age?"

S. B.: "Yes. When we don't want...that—when we don't want anybody to understand us, then we speak Judeo-Arabic..., and also my mother. . . "

We: "That who won't understand?"

S. B.: "Uhm...somebody...an Ashkenazi or...from another community..."

We: "But among yourselves what do you speak?"

S. B.: "Mostly Hebrew."

This distribution of language use is not entirely evident to the young Romemites. Their testimony was probably influenced by their attitudes, as regards Hebrew or Judeo-Arabic, yet the principal tendencies are quite manifest.[26]

Inquiry Into the Usage of Languages at Romema

Fishman et al., in their large-scale study of bilingualism among Puerto Pecans in New York (Fishman, Cooper, and Ma 1971), have discussed psychological, sociological, and linguistic aspects of the subject. A study of such dimensions exceeds the limits that we have taken upon ourselves here. Nevertheless, we have attempted a methodical observation of the question, be it only on an experimental level. We were assisted by two young civil servants in daily contact with the population of Romema, including home visits, invitations to family meals, etc.[27] At our request, they recorded their observations on the use of languages in a seven-family sample of the Romema population[28]. Our assistants were asked to note the language chosen by the participants (parents; adults living in the house; other adults; youth, i.e., young people over the age of 18; children: boys and girls from 5 to18 years old; children not belonging to the family; infants under the age of 5). This survey was conducted during conversations on various *topics*[29] (we defined five: the family; work; the moshav; miscellaneous; religion, education and culture) which took place in diverse *settings*[30] (the home; the club,[31] other). Furthermore, they were required to define the speech act as either "conversation" (i.e., flowing dialogue) or as "summons"[32] (in which case both the summoner and the summoned were to be identified).

Conversations

In the category "conversations" (N =: 210 records) we found that the younger generation, that is, the youth and the children (those of the household and others, but excluding the infants), only use Judeo-Arabic when speaking with adults; among themselves they only use Hebrew. On the other hand, the adults converse most often in Judeo-Arabic, but with the young—in inverse proportion to their age—they speak more Hebrew than Judeo-Arabic (cf. Tables 2 and 3).

Table 2
Number of "conversations" recorded, classified according to the speakers and the languages

	Addressers			Addressees			
	Adults	Youth	Children	Adults	Youth	Children	Total
JA	76	4	4	74	6	4	168
Hebrew	35	24	67	50	4	72	252
Totals:	111	28	71	124	10	76	420

Total X2: 140.019 p =: .0001

Table 3
Number of "conversations" recorded, classified according to interacting speakers (Ad[ults], You[th] and Ch[ildren]) and the languages

	Ad/Ad	Ad/You	Ad/Ch	You/Ad	You/Ch	Ch/Ad	Ch/Ch	Totals
JA	66	6	4	4	0	4	0	84
Hebrew	18	3	14	9	15	23	44	126
Totals:	84	9	18	13	15	27	44	210

Total x2: 104.039 p= .0001

Our assistants could not jot down notes during the meetings and had to reconstruct their findings later from memory; in addition, one assistant did not understand Judeo-Arabic, a fact which naturally impeded her ability to precisely evaluate the subject of the conversation. It should also be remembered that the very presence of the assistants could have influenced the course of the conversation to a certain extent. Moreover, we have considered each record as a single observation, whereas it may have often been the case that a note like "the parents used Judeo-Arabic at home when discussing moshav affairs," for example, refers to several such conversations. All these factors may naturally diminish the validity of the results. Our intention is to discover the general tendency, even if definitive conclusions can not be reached at the present time.

Summonses

Records defined as "summonses" probably reflect reality in a more reliable manner since these are short events which often constitute an entire act of speech on their own. This impression is due not only to the fact that the results seem "less logical" and more in keeping with the young Romemites' testimony; it also has to do with the fact that these findings seem to be singularly precise, kept intact in the memory of our assistants. In considering the distribution of the usage of the two languages in the category "summonses," two factors stand out as decisive in the choice of the linguistic variant:

a) *The age of the summoned (or "the authority factor").* With respect to adult speakers, a young age of the summoned correlates precisely with a tendency of the summoner to use Judeo-Arabic. Adults summon children in Judeo-Arabic (and in Hebrew as well, especially regarding children from outside the household); on the other hand, they summon other adults exclusively in Hebrew (Table 4).

b) *Intimacy*—A relation of intimacy brings about a more frequent use of Judeo-Arabic; the youth summon adults of the household in both Judeo-Arabic and in Hebrew, but they address other adults of the moshav in Hebrew alone (Table 5).

Effect of the Topic and of the Setting of the Event

From all said so far, by virtue of data elicited from informants as well as from the records of "conversations" and "summonses," it has become clear that the functions of the two linguistic variants in Romema, while depending on the linguistic competence of the speakers, are also linked to role relationships. Now, however, it may be worth investigating if the topic of the conversation or the setting in which it takes place (Cf. ~3.0) have a bearing on the language choice.

Table 4
Number of "summonses" recorded, classified according to interacting speakers (Ad[ults] and Youn[g]) and the languages

	Ad/Ad	Ad/Youn	Totals
J. A.	0	21	21
Hebrew	8	9	17
Totals	8	30	38

Total X2: 12.518 p = .0004
X2 with continuity correction: 9.846 p = .0017

Table 5
"Summonses" by the young, i.e., youth and children, classified according to the summoned and the languages

	To home-residents	To other members of the *moshav*	Totals
JA	24	0	24
Hebrew	18	17	35
Totals	42	17	59

Totalx2: 16.376 p =.0001
X2 with continuity correction: 14.093 p = .0002

Effect of the Topic

In the data elicited from the category "conversations" over the entire sample, it appears that the topic of conversation had no significant effect on the choice of the language (Table 6). This result remains unchanged, even if we exclude the youth (since we have seen that they nearly always speak Hebrew among themselves).

Table 6
Effect of the topic on the choice of the language in the category "conversations" over the entire sample

	Family	Work	Moshav	Varia	Culture	Totals
JA	21	19	16	14	14	84
Hebrew	25	25	32	18	26	126
Totals	46	44	48	32	40	210

Total X2: 2.291 p = .6824

Effect of the Setting

Tables 7 and 8 show—in the category "conversations"—the distribution of language choice according to the *setting*, in the whole sample and in the adult group, respectively. It seems clear that the *setting* is important for the question at hand: the adults show a greater tendency to use Hebrew outside the home.

Table 7
Effect of the setting on the choice of language in the category "conversations" in the whole sample

	Home	Club	Elsewhere	Totals
JA	67	0	17	84
Hebrew	48	27	51	126
Totals	115	27	68	210

Totalx2: 40.353 p = .0001

Table 8
Effect of the setting on the choice of language in the category "conversations"—adults sample

	Home	Elsewhere	Totals
JA	55	11	66
Hebrew	5	13	18
Totals	60	24	84

Total X2: 21.389 p = .0001
X2 with continual correction: 18.753 p = .0001

Conclusion

Romema is a relatively homogeneous society, somewhat intimate and also fairly isolated. The fact that the discussed *topic* had no significant effect on the choice of language proves that there is no tendency in this community to assign specific functions to each of the two linguistic variants. The elderly are more naturally inclined to use Judeo-Arabic, especially in contexts of intimate speech or contexts of parental authority. With the young, on the other hand, feelings of inferiority or of social frustration, translated to *linguistic insecurity*, push them to resort to that language.

In most other bilingual societies, where social barriers between rulers and subordinates are the norm, different degrees of stable bilingualism have been established. Diglossia, in Ferguson's sense (1959), is theoretically assumed to be the most stable of all bilingual situations. In immigrant societies, however, the language of the majority (L1) has an overwhelming impact outside, while the mother tongue of the immigrants (L2) tends to be retained longer at home. Scholars familiar with indigenous societies prefer to define all bilingual situations as mutually conflicting. Factors of resistance may delay a linguistic shift for very long periods of time, but such transitions are eventually inevitable.[33] In Romema, however, the "language of the rulers," Hebrew, is considered by the "subordinates," as we will call them for our purposes,[34] most legitimately as theirs, and somehow they come to know that their subordinate status is but temporary. Factors of resistance to Hebrew, then, only exist at a most individual level. A process of Judeo-Arabic shift toward Hebrew is, therefore, accepted as quite normal by the speakers themselves. Hebrew's imminent total victory in Romema cannot be doubted.

Notes

1. This paper represents a completely revised version and translation of Chap. 3 of Bentolila 1984. Here I would like to thank Dr. Roni Henkin, who helped me with the translation, and Prof. Chaim Cohen, who proofread the translation. I am indebted also to Prof. Pierrette Thibault, for her important comments on an early draft of this paper.
2. Cf Cooper and Danet 1980.
3. For the distinction between stable and transitional bilingualism, cf. Fishman 1967.
4. For the representation of transitional bilingualism as a continuum, going from a total maintenance to a total loss of the minority language, see Giles, Leets, and Coupland 1990.
5. For a study of the psychological aspects of this attachment, cf. Herman 1968.

6. On the prestige of English and French in Israel, and the public usage of these languages by immigrants from countries where these languages are spoken, cf. Herman 1968: 498-499.
7. When that happens, it implies an attitude dictated by strong ideological motives. It may be the case in the *Kibbutz*, where the situation surely differs from that described here for an urban population.
8. Naturally, English speakers find it very convenient that their language is taught at school. In general, English speakers enjoy certain advantages in the Israeli setting, like the existence of a very highly prized newspaper, the *Jerusalem Post*, or the fact that a great number of foreign TV programs or cinema films are spoken in their original English versions.
9. Cf.: Hofman and Fisherman 1971: 222-226; Fisherman 1971.
10. English (and to a lesser degree French) is part of the high school curriculum, and is obligatory at the university.
11. By Professor Moshe Shokeid, who conducted long anthropological studies in the area in question; cf. Shokeid 1971, Deshen and Shokeid 1974.
12. A cooperative village in Israel.
13. mellah is an Arabic term designating a Jewish community in Morocco, be it a Jewish quarter in a city or a Jewish village in a typically rural district.
14. 13 By Shokeid; cf. n. 10.
15. The data for our research were gathered between the years 1976- 1979.
16. Moroccan Judeo-Arabic is mutually comprehensible with Moroccan Arabic, as spoken by the Muslim population of that country. As a Jewish language, Moroccan Judeo-Arabic is distinguished especially by its lexicon, where Hebrew or Aramaic words and phrases, drawn from the traditional Jewish sources, are more or less integrated (notably as regards the designating of objects and concepts associated with culture and religion). Some aspects of Moroccan Judeo-Arabic have been described in Brunot and Malca 1939, 1940, Leslau 1945, Bar-Asher 1978, 1991, Heath and Bar-Asher 1982, Ch?trit 1980, 1986.
17. In the context of its cultural-religious use in the Diaspora, the term Hebrew includes also Aramaic, since Jewish sources often utilize both languages together within the same documents.
18. For the distinction between diglossia and bilingualism, cf. Ferguson 1959. In Fishman 1967, we find more developed distinctions. An analysis of the state of the Jewish languages in terms of diglossia is given by Rabin 1981.
19. Berber in Romema is heard only among the elder population. Its role is limited to a sort of secret language (in presence of children, outsiders, etc.). It may also be used occasionally in relaxed contexts (humor, jokes, etc.).
20. Miss M. Ben-Ezra and Miss H. Bernstein who, at the time of our research, fulfilled socio-educative functions in the moshav. They have also assisted us in gathering data for our research on the usage of competing languages in Romema (Cf. 5 3.0).
21. Cf. Findling 1971: 338.
22. Labov 1972: 132-133.
23. Labov 1972: 249.
24. Cf. Bentolila 1984, chap. 5 and 6.
25. One of the poorest domains supplied by the traditional written sources is the vocabulary of swear-words. Israeli Hebrew has borrowed all sorts of expressions—especially from Arabic, Russian, and English—for these emotional needs.
26. Although many isolated phenomena remain unexplained. For example, we may suppose that the high-school pupils of Romema should speak only Hebrew among themselves. This was confirmed in a conversation, which we recorded, between

Rivka (16) and Rachel (15). They did, indeed, speak Hebrew, but one phrase was pronounced in Judeo-Arabic:

Rivka: "Has your brother brought the tickets?"

Rachel: "What tickets?"

Rivka: "Haven't you heard? You are supposed to buy tickets!"

Rachel: "What tickets?"

Rivka: "Wait...I'm going to David's today and...There's a group, from <Tel Aviv>..."

Rachel: "Ah!"

Rivka: "They're the best...and they're...true Yemenites..."

Rachel: "But where are they (= going to perform?)"

Rivka: "Pardon?"

Rachel: "Where? In Tequma (= name of a neighboring moshav) or where?"

Rivka: "In Tequma."

Rachel: "Always in Tequma..."

Rivka: (says a non-intelligible phrase)

Rachel: "Is it new?"

Rivka: "Yes."

Rachel: "No...I didn't notice...I am dressed.../**wai li wai li wai li ma 'andi daba ma nelbab = adda**/ (in Judeo-Arabic: *"Oh, Lord! Oh, Lord! Oh, Lord! I have nothing to wear tomorrow..."*), I have nothing to wear tomorrow...eh...more...I have not...no...I won't wear it anymore."

What is the reason for the sudden change to Judeo-Arabic? And why was this phrase first uttered in Judeo-Arabic, then repeated in Hebrew translation?

27. Cf. n. 19.
28. We are grateful to Professor Robert Cooper for his advice as to the method of notation for these observations.
29. The topic is a sub-type of the domain, both concepts conceived by Fishman (1965), for analyzing the functions of languages in a bilingual community (Cf. Fishman, Cooper, and Ma 1971, pp. 585-586). In the model elaborated by Cooper (1969) only domain appears. The domain represents either the basic context in which the act of speech takes place, or else the limits of social activity, which constitute the subject of a conversation. Five domains were defined: family, friendship, religion, education and occupation (Greenfield 1968). As for the topic, it refers to the immediate subject at hand. For example: two businessmen talking about "currency rates" (the topic) are speech-interacting in the domain "occupation." According to Fishman, topic and domain are parallel notions, the first concerning a "Micro-context," the second a "Macro-context."
30. In the Fishman-Cooper model (Cf. Cooper 1969), the serving regards the situational context (site, participants, etc.), in which the speech act takes place.
31. The club, or mo'adon, is a local meeting place, used for diverse social, cultural, and administrative activities, such as the general assembly of moshav members. This category also includes the synagogue, which similarly constitutes a communal meeting place.
32. The term "summons" is used here in the sense of "attention-getting device," i.e., a term of address, a courtesy phrase, etc., following Schegloff 1972 (Cf. especially pp. 357-358).
33. Those are the conclusions of Mexican scholars investigating bilingual rural societies in Mexico (Cf.Hamel and Sierra 1983; Hamel 1990).
34. As long as they still maintain true new immigrant status.

Bibliography

Atkinson, J. W.
1964 *An Introduction to Motivation*, Nostrand, Princeton.
Bar-Asher, M.
1978 "The Hebrew Elements in the Spoken Arabic of Moroccans Jews" (in Hebrew), *Leshonenu* 42: 163-189.
1991 "Hebrew Elements in North African Judeo-Arabic: Alterations in Meaning and Form", in Kaye, Alan S. (ed.), *Semitic Studies in Honor of Wolf Leslau*, vol 1. Wiesbaden: Otto Harrassowitz.
Bentolila, Y.
1984 *The Sociophonology of Hebrew as Spoken in a Rural Settlement of Moroccan Jews in the Negev*, PhD thesis (in Hebrew), The Hebrew University, Jerusalem.
Brunot, L. and E. Malka
1939 *Textes Judeo-Arabics de Fès; textes, transcription, traduction annotee*, Rabat.
1940 *Glossaire Judeo-Arabic of Fès*, Rabat.
Chitrit, J.
1980 "Niveaux, registres de langue et sociolectes dans les langues judéo-arabes du Maroc," in J.-L. Miège (ed.), *Les Relations entre Juifs et Musulmans en Afrique du Nord*, Paris.
1986 "Stratégies discursives dans la langue des femmes judéo-arabophones du Maroc," *Massorot* 2: 41-66.
Cooper, R.
1969 "How can we measure the roles which a bilingual's languages play in his everyday behavior," in Kelly, L. G. (ed.), *Description and Measurement of Bilingualism: An International Seminar, University of Moncton (June6- 14, 1967)*, University of Toronto Press, Toronto.
1971 "Degree of Bilingualism," in Fishman, Cooper and Ma 1971: 273-309.
Cooper, R.L. and B. Danet
1980 "Language in the melting pot: the sociolinguistic context for language planning in Israel," *Language Problems and Language Planning* 4: 1-28.
Deshen S. and M. Shokeid
1974 *The Predicament of Homecoming; Cultural and Social Life of North African Immigrants in Israel*, Cornell University Press, Ithaca.
Ferguson, C. A.
1959 "Diglossia," *Word* 15: 325-340.
Findling, J.
1971 "Bilingual need affiliation and future orientation in extra-group and intra-group domains," in Fishman, Cooper, and Ma 1971: 337-344.
Fisherman, H.
1971 "The status of the Hebrew language in the Roumanian Community" (in Hebrew), in Sh. Kodesh (ed.), *Kamrat Memorial Volume, Essays on the Teaching of Hebrew as a Second Language* (in Hebrew), Council of the Teaching of Hebrew, Jerusalem.
Fishman, J. A.
1965 "Who speaks what language to whom and when," *La linguistique*, vol. 2: 67-88; also in Fishman, Cooper and Ma 1971: 583-604, under the title: "The relationship between micro- and macro-sociolinguistics in the study of who speaks what language to whom and when."
1967 "Bilingualism with and without diglossia; Diglossia with and without bilingualism," *Journal of Social Issues* 23, No. 2: 29-38.

Fishman, J. A., R. Cooper, and R. Ma
1971 *Bilingualism in the Barrio*, (Language Science Monographs, Vol. 7), Indiana University Publications, Bloomington.
Giles, H. Leets, L. and Coupland N.
1990 "Minority language group status: A theoretical conspectus," *Journal of Multilingual and Multicultural Development*, 11: 37-55.
Greenfield, L.
1968 "Situational measures of normative language views of person, place and topic among Puerto Rican bilinguals," in *Bilingualism in the Barrio*, Final Report, Yeshiva University, New York.
Hamel, R.E.
1990 "Lengua nacional y lengua indigena en el proceso historico de cambio," in *Anuario de Antropología*, Universidad Autónoma Metropolitana, Iztapalapa (Mexico)
Hansel, R.E. and M.T. Sierra
1983 "Diglosia y conflicto intercultural: La lucha por un concepto o la danza de los significantes," in *Antropología Americana* 8, Instituto panamericano de geografía e historia.
Heath, J. and M. Bar-Asher
1982 "A Judeo-Arabic dialect of Tafilalt," in *Zeitschrift für arabischeLinguistik*, OttoHarrassowitz, Wiesbaden.
Herman, S. R.
1968 "Explorations in the social psychology of language choice", in Fishman, J.A. (ed.), *Readings in the Sociology of Language*, Mouton, The Hague.
Hofman, J. E. and H. Fisherman
1971 "Language shift and maintenance in Israel," *International Migration Review* 5: 204-226.
Kraemer, R. and E. Olshtain
1989 "Perceived ethnolinguistic vitality and language attitudes: The Israeli setting," *Journal of Multilingual and Multicultural Development* 10:197-212.
Labov, W.
1972 *Sociolinguistic Patterns*, University of Pennsylvania Press, Philadelphia.
Leslau, W.
1945 "Hebrew elements in the Judeo-Arabic dialect of Fez," *Jewish Quarterly Review* 36: 61-78.
Rabin, H.
1981 "What constitutes a Jewish language?" *International Journal of the Sociology of Language* 30: 19-28.
Schegloff, E. A.
1972 "Sequencing in conversational openings," in Gumperz, John J. and Dell Hymes (eds.), *Directions in Sociolinguistics—the Ethnography of Communication*, Holt, Rinehart and Winston, Inc., New York.
Shmeltz, A. and R. Bachi
1973 "Hebrew as an everyday language of Jews in Israel" (in Hebrew), *Leshonenu* 37: 50-68, 187-201.
Shokeid, M.
1971 *The Dual Heritage: Immigrants from the Atlas Mountains in an Israeli Village*, Manchester University Press, Manchester.
Tajfel, H.
1978 "The achievement of group differentiation," in H. Tajfel (ed.), *Differentiation between Social Groups*. London: Academic Press.

10

"Secularism Is the Root of All Evil": The Haredi Response to Crime and Delinquency

Gerald Cromer

An analysis of haredi rhetoric on crime and delinquency indicates that political and rabbinical leaders alike portray these problems as the logical and natural conclusion of secularism and as completely absent from their own community. This invidious comparison provides the basis for a further argument—that the acceptance of the yoke of the Torah is the only way to ameliorate the situation. Together, these claims are used both to keep the faithful within the fold and to attract others to it. They are cited as proof, not only of the efficacy of haredi Judaism, but also of its veracity.

Introduction

Research studies of the ultra-Orthodox or haredi[1] community in Israel have generally emphasized the extent to which its adherents segregate themselves from non-observant Jews in order to avoid being contaminated by them.[2] This defensive response, it has been argued, arises out of a fear that any form of contact is more likely to endanger the traditional community's existence than to attract the surrounding society to its way of life. Recently, however, a number of observers have drawn attention to a new mood amongst haredi Jews. They argue that the trauma of erosion has given way to a feeling of superiority or triump. Rabbinical and political leaders alike are no longer satisfied with simply defending those within the fold against the process of secularization; they are now intent on taking the offensive against the surrounding society.[3] Haredim now employ strategies of withdrawal and conquest at one and the same time (Liebman 1983:77).

Withdrawal from Israeli society and the conquest of it focus on the haredi community and its secular neighbors, respectively. Both approaches though are designed to achieve the same end—the furtherance of ultra-orthodox Judaism. This is the major concern of haredi leaders. As far as they are concerned, the value of Israeli society is measured "only by the extent to which it brings the people of the Lord closer to the Torah, the commandments and the faith." (Ravitsky 1989:95) Everything pales into insignificance in comparison with this lofty cause.

Haredi spokesmen use a wide variety of arguments in support of their twin policies of withdrawal and conquest. Recent studies, however, (Elor, 1991; Levi 1990) indicate the overriding importance of one particular kind of rhetoric—the claim that secularism is the root of all evil. They draw attention to the incessant haredi warnings about the perils of modernity and the evil machinations of those who purvey it. The article that follows provides a detailed analysis of this kind of argumentation with regard to the problem of crime and delinquency. After describing the various rhetorical strategies used in the haredi attack on modernity, the paper suggests that this particular claim—that secularism is the root of all evil—is especially popular because it appeals to both rationality and rectitude (Best 1987:116- 117) at one and the same time.

Etiology Story

Haredi claimants use the same kind of data as their secular counterparts do in order to show the extent of the crime problem. They cite incidence and growth estimates to show its present level and how it has increased over a given period of time respectively (Best, 1987:106-108). Comparisons between Israel and other Western countries, especially the United States, suggest that the situation will likely worsen in the future. The fact that they have higher crime rates is never thought of as a consolation; it is always regarded as a portent of what is to come.

This overall portrayal of the crime problem is often accompanied by horror stories (Johnson, 1989) that provide a detailed description of specific criminals or particular instances of crime. These tales not only attract more attention than crime statistics, however alarming the latter may be; but they also enable readers to better grasp the enormity of the problem and the need to take appropriate action to ameliorate it.

It must be pointed out though that these claims go hand in hand with a further argument—that crime and delinquency are not, in fact, the real problem. Haredi leaders, political and rabbinical alike, constantly take pains to point out that they are rather symptoms or effects of a much more basic malaise—the lack of religious observance and religious belief in Israeli society. That, haredi claimants insist, is the crux of the problem.

In this haredi etiology story (Pfuhl, 1980:142), crime and delinquency are dematerialized. The favored affinity of poverty (Matza, 1969: 94-100) is rejected in favor of secularism. These and, for that matter, other social problems, are attributed to spiritual rather than material deprivation. Thus, haredi claimants explain the high rates of crime and delinquency amongst Israelis of African and Asian origin in terms of their decline in religious observance rather than their low socio-economic status. They drive this message home by pointing to the complete absence of these problems in the diaspora. Oriental Jews, haredi leaders argue, never engaged in crime and delinquency even though they were much poorer in their countries of origin than they are in Israel. Their adherence to Jewish law ensured their compliance with the law of the land.

Haredi spokesmen pay particular attention to those youngsters who are not "classical child criminals." Political and rabbinical leaders alike are invariably at the forefront of the moral panics about "delinquents from well-to-do families." Because these offenders violate the widely accepted type-scripts concerning those kinds of behavior that the middle and upper-classes are seen as unlikely or unable to commit (Harris, 1977:11-15), they lead to a questioning of the conventional wisdom about the causes of crime. In contrast, haredi leaders contend that middle-class delinquency confirms their etiology story.[4] Thus, in response to the killing of a taxi driver by two high school students, *Hamodia* (13 January 1994), the official organ of Agudat Yisrael,[5] argued that

> There is no difference between children of well-to-do families and those from the poorest ones...In both cases, the education system did nothing at all to curb the spirit of the country's youth. They never learn the values of Judaism that have always prevented trouble in the past...As a result, everyone does whatever is right in his own eyes.

In this and similar cases, haredi claimants draw attention to the surprise and shock of secular Israelis. Although they express the hope that these cause célèbres will prompt the country's leaders to search their souls and, in turn, take the necessary action to rectify the situation, they are not very optimistic in this regard. In fact, haredi spokesmen invariably make prophecies of doom. They predict that crime and delinquency are likely to become both more widespread and more serious. In short, that the worst is yet to come.

In contrast, haredi leaders claim that there is one aspect of the situation that remains constant. Their community, they insist, is and always will be crime-free. Their argument is simple. Secular Israelis engage in crime and delinquency because they have transgressed God's commandments. It follows, therefore, that haredim, who are religiously observant, will not break the law. Obedience to God's commandments always leads to compliance with the rules of man.

A Slippery Slope

Haredi claimants do not simply posit a causal connection between secularism and crime; they insist that it is "the logical and natural conclusion of a life devoid of Jewish law and morality." Thus, political and rabbinical leaders alike use the slippery slope argument (Lamb, 1988:1-9) or what Edwin Schur (1980: 144-145) has somewhat cryptically referred to as the doctrine of horrible consequences, in order to explain the inexorable nature of this process. Their etiology stories include a wide variety of metaphors, but they are all designed to achieve the same aim—to show that crime is bound to occur in, or is endemic to, secular society.

The slippery slope is often envisaged as the workings of divine justice. Crime and delinquency, haredi claimants argue, are punishment from God for the initial rejection of traditional Judaism by the founding fathers of the Jewish state. According to this view of things, man only has to make the first retrograde step; the rest is in the hands of the Lord.

This belief in divine retribution does not prevent haredi leaders from using images borrowed from the natural sciences. Thus, they frequently resort to the illness metaphor (Sontag 1979), arguing that secularism inevitably leads to "the cancer of crime," and that orthodox Judaism provides immunity against this and other social ills. Of particular interest to this study, however, are those metaphors that are popular amongst haredi claimants and are only rarely used by their secular counterparts. Political and rabbinical leaders alike use the image of growth to describe both the source of the problem and its deleterious consequences. Thus, they accuse Israeli secular leaders of having "prepared the ground" or having "provided a hothouse" for crime and delinquency. On other occasions, haredi spokesmen denounce secular Zionism as the root of the problem or the seed of the trouble. And, continuing the analogy, they also refer to the offenders in botanical terms—as rotten fruit, a wild growth, or foreign vines in the vineyard of Israel.

The vacuum image is, perhaps, the most frequently used one. Orthodox youngsters are portrayed as being full of spiritual content. They therefore have no need or, to continue the spatial metaphor, no room for crime and delinquency. Secular youth, in contrast, are characterized by spiritual emptiness. This void, haredi spokesmen insist, leaves them open to "foreign and dangerous influences" which, in turn, cause them to break the law. Drawing on well-known rabbinical interpretations of Joseph in the pit, *Shearim* (24 December 1972), the official organ of Poalei Agudat Yisrael,[6] explained this point in the following way.

When the pit is empty, serpents and scorpions are always to be found in it. When a person is empty of substance, of "water," negative influences will always be found to fill the vacuum. This is the case with regard to both individuals and society as a whole. "With no vision, the nation will be in travail."

The metaphor of decline is based on the premise that only orthodox Judaism can prevent the flouting of all moral standards. Throwing off the yoke of the kingdom of heaven, haredi leaders argue, not only leads to a decrease in religious observance, but also results in the abandonment of every human value. "Without orthodoxy, there are no limits, anything goes." To quote *Shearim* (24 December 1972) once again, "When a person raises a hand against the sacred tenets of Israel, against the values of Judaism, he cannot stop halfway. There is nothing or nobody who can stop him." Everything is permitted.

This, and, for that matter, other images used to portray the inexorable decline from secularism to crime and delinquency, suggest that the offenders themselves are not to blame. Causal and political responsibility (Gusfield, 1981: 13-16), haredi claimants insist, lie elsewhere.

Corrupting Agents

Political and rabbinical leaders sometimes portray the secularization process as a kind of cultural diffusion. According to this view of things, Israelis have simply adopted behavioral patterns from abroad. More frequently, however, haredi spokesmen attribute the present situation to purposive action on the part of the country's leaders. Secularization did not just happen; they did their utmost to bring it about. According to *Hamodia* (22 December 1972), "these people thought that the first thing to be done in the new state was to uproot religion and not to leave a single branch."

In order to emphasize the severity of these changes, haredi claimants compare the leaders of the Jewish state to the external enemies of the Jewish people. Thus, *Hamodia* (22 December 1972) went on to say that,

> they became a kind of kidnapper, like the notorious kidnappers during the reign of Alexander of Russia. They kidnapped children from religious parents and transferred them to kibbutzim and similar places in the state. They rejoiced at the fall of every additional child. They were happy when a boy cut off his earlocks. They were particularly pleased when he ate non-kosher food or violated the Sabbath for the first time in his life.

Maayan Hashavua, a weekly pamphlet of the Sephardi Shas Party,[7] took this argument a step further. It compared Israel's political leaders to Amalek—the apogee of evil in the Jewish tradition. Drawing on a number of rabbinical commentaries on the biblical text, *Maayan Hashavua* (No.94) made the following analogy between the Labor government in the 1950's and the first enemy of the Jewish people.

> Amalek took advantage of an hour of fatigue and weariness on the way to the Land of Israel in order to inculcate its poison, the poison of doubt and heresy, in the hearts of the weak. Unfortunately, a similar process occurred just a generation ago. The Jews came out of exile to the Holy Land, full of hope and in high spirits. However, there were people who took advantage of their exhaustion and weakness on arrival. Those who did not fear God did their utmost to make them irreligious.

With the passage of time, haredi claimants turned their attention from the Labor Party and the different kibbutz movements to other "corrupting agents." They now tend to single out the mass media for special attention. Occasionally, the national press is accused of being "public enemy number one." Usually, however, this invidious honor is reserved for Israeli television. Thus, the "Committee for the Purity and Holiness of our Camp" described it as "the new way which the devil has devised to undermine the essentials of the Jewish home. Its only purpose," the flier continued, "is to be an instrument of pollution, and to cause idolatry, incest and bloodshed."

Of course, haredi spokesmen do not claim that the leaders of the Jewish state intended for these phenomenon to occur. They were simply unaware of the fact that by destroying the roots of belief and tradition in the soul of Israeli youth they would deprive them of "the only education for self-restraint and the only awareness that there are limits to human desire—the limits of the Torah." Israeli leaders, haredi claimants insist, did not understand the wisdom of the sages. In such a situation, they asked, "How could a boy help sinning?" (Babylonian Talmud Berakhot 32a).

The most frequently used image in this regard is the talmudic one of "children who are taken capture among Gentiles." Haredi leaders portray offenders in general, and juvenile delinquents in particular, as having been enticed into a secular lifestyle and, thereby, into a life of crime. Invariably, they are depicted as being victims of circumstance and, therefore, not to blame for their misdeeds. Israeli secular leaders, haredi claimants insist, should be "on the suspect's bench." They, rather than their followers, are "on trial."

Miraculous Stories

Rabbinical and political leaders alike have little or no faith in the ways usually suggested for dealing with the increase in crime and delinquency. They are convinced that neither stiffer penalties nor new rehabilitation programs will solve these problems. What is needed, haredi claimants insist, is a "complete revolution" in the education system. There has to be "a return to the primal values of Judaism—to a belief in God and to the observance of His commandments." Only this works; everything else is of no avail. Haredi spokesmen have made this claim ever since, and even before, the establishment of the state. In recent years, however, both rabbinical and political leaders have backed it up with a description of haredi accomplishments in this field. They cite the large number of delinquents who have accepted the yoke of the Torah and thereby abandoned their criminal lifestyle. Invariably, these estimates are accompanied by stories about individual delinquents that are designed to show how the Torah has helped to rehabilitate even the most hardened criminals, those who everyone felt were "lost and beyond hope."

In an attempt to back up this claim, haredi leaders quote laudatory statements by academics who study the problem of crime and delinquency and control agents who try to deal with it. They also attest to the "extraordinary success" of religious rehabilitation programs both within the prison system and in the community at large.[8] Not surprisingly, however, the most compelling spokesmen in this regard are the delinquents themselves or, to be more precise, those who have managed to escape the world of crime. Thus, one repentant delinquent made the following rather arresting analogy:

> It's the only solution for the Jewish people. You can take somebody who is on drugs to a thousand psychologists; you can take him to all the psychologists in the world, but it won't help. He'll carry on using them. But you can see from this yeshiva (talmudic academy) that if he returns to the Torah, he'll give up drugs. Not all at once, but slowly and surely. When somebody repents, he has limits, because G-d is checking up on him all the time. It's like having your own policeman 24 hours a day. That's the difference between secular and religious rehabilitation (interview with author, June 1987).

This argument is often couched in more personal terms. Repentant delinquents recount their life histories in order to show how they have benefited from accepting the yoke of the Torah. Gabriel Hacham, for instance, described how he got into bad company at the age of 15 and began smoking hashish. Within a short period of time, he moved on to hard drugs. Needing money to support his habit, Gabriel began to commit burglaries and engage in the selling of drugs. After serving time in Beersheva prison, he made contact with an Arab drug dealer in Ramallah, but then events took an unexpected turn.

> A day before the deal was supposed to go through, an old friend of mine who had become religious six years before begged me to come to his yeshiva. That night was a turning point in my life. I heard about the suffering of our fathers in exile and how they held on to Judaism. I heard about western culture and how it destroyed us. My eyes were opened, and I decided to stay in the yeshiva for a few days...The rabbi told me that everything would be alright. I found it difficult to believe. To my surprise, though, I received drugs in the yeshiva, albeit of a very different kind. The real revolution took place when I spent a Sabbath in the yeshiva. That showed me that drugs are worthless. They are like a drop in the ocean compared to the true enjoyment of the Holy Sabbath. The Sabbath meals and songs did not leave any room in my heart for doubts. I was free of drugs. Those who say that we do not have the means to fight the war against drugs are wrong. During the course of two years in yeshiva, I have become a new man. I am like a newborn infant (*The Light of the Torah* Av 5743).

Other repentant delinquents tell a similar story to that of Gabriel Hacham. They also talk about a steady decline, followed by a dramatic metamorphosis and subsequent rehabilitation. In many instances, the storyteller posits a causal connection between the two periods. Only because they had sunk so low, the delinquents argue, did they decide to expose themselves to, and eventually accept the teachings of the Torah. Despite or, to be more precise, because of their dismal past, everything worked out fine in the end.[9]

These miraculous stories constitute a microcosm of the haredi argument concerning the etiology of crime and delinquency. Thus, they always point an accusing finger at secular Zionism. In certain cases though, the delinquents also accept a certain amount of blame for their misdeeds. With the benefit of hindsight, they understand that their involvement in crime and drugs arose out of a desire to "be a man" or even "to be king." Now having accepted the yoke of the Torah, the repentant delinquents realized the error of their ways. Quoting the Ethics of the Fathers (4:1), they now define manhood in terms of strength of character. "Who is the mighty? He who subdues his passions." The real battle is against the evil inclination.

The Evil Inclination

The haredi critique of Israeli society focuses on its secular orientation. This line of attack implies that the situation was better before the advent of the Zionist movement. However, haredi interpretations of biblical and rabbinical sources suggest that this was not, in fact, the case. On the contrary, the contemporary situation is by no means *sui generis*. Crime is a phenomenon that characterizes humankind rather than secular man.

Haredi darshanim (expositors of the sources) go back to the beginnings of the Jewish people (e.g., the waters of Massah and Meribah and the sin of the golden calf) and even to the dawn of history (e.g., Sodom and Gemorrah and the Noachide flood) in order to prove their point. They even make explicit analogies between the situation then and now.

> The flood is a terrible deluge that sweeps the sinner into the spiritual depths. But, do we not live in the generation of a flood? A flood of heresy, a flood of corruption, a flood of insane pursuit of vanity, in which the vexation and pressure will eventually drown us all (*Maayan Hashavua* No. 72).

In certain instances, the darshanim draw attention to the fact that history repeats itself, and that it is necessary to learn the lessons of the past. More frequently, however, they couch their argument in psychological terms. The darshanim point out that man has always had a yetzer hara (evil inclination) that tries incessantly to lead him astray.

> The evil inclination always makes tremendous efforts to prevent us from obeying the commandments...There is no realm which is exempt from its influence. It is, therefore, imperative to warn against being in contact with any forbidden thing even if it does not appear attractive...This lesson can be learned from the very first sin, the sin of Adam and Eve. Precisely that tree which was forbidden turned out to be "good for food and a delight to the eyes." The evil inclination works in every realm, even in those which appear to be totally irrational (*Hamodia* 28 August 1992).

According to Jewish tradition, God created the Torah as an antidote to the evil inclination. Haredi darshanim therefore stress the need for punctillious observance of the commandments. Only those who live within the four cubits of halacha (Jewish law), they insist, "can say no to their desires and be master of them." Everybody else is always at risk; their yetzer hara will sooner or later get the better of them.

This dichotomy is, in fact, not such a clear-cut one. Haredi darshanim often take pains to point out that even the most observant Jews can be tempted by their evil inclination. Like the snake in the Garden of Eden, their yetzer hara uses all its guile in order to entice them into sinning. In particular, it always knows exactly how to adapt itself to the situation at hand. Thus, in the case of haredi Jews, the evil inclination begins by trying to persuade them not to observe a seemingly unimportant custom. However, it knows full well that this initial misdeed is just the beginning of the slippery slope. From then on everything is downhill. To quote *Yeted Neeman* (8 May 1992), the official organ of Degel Hatorah,[10]

> This is the way of the evil inclination. One day it says do this, and the next day it says do that. Consequently, we must not belittle even the most minor custom of Israel. It constitutes a fence that guards the Torah. The evil inclination is always to be found amongst these fences. However, that is only the beginning. By tearing down the fences, the evil inclination can eventually destroy the most basic tenets of our Torah.

According to this view of things, the absence of crime and delinquency in the haredi communities by no means a given; the situation can always take a turn for the worse. In fact, there is only one way to prevent this from happening. Haredi Jews have to continue fighting "the big battle against the evil inclination." That is the key to winning the war against crime.

Conclusions

Repentant delinquents recount how they managed to overcome their evil inclination. Haredi darshanim enjoin their readers of the need to do so. They also point out that this "holy war" is by no means a new one; it has engaged humankind ever since the beginning of time. Clearly, however, these psychological and historical perspectives must not be allowed to hide the major thrust of the haredi response to crime and delinquency. Political and rabbinical leaders alike focus their attention on the deleterious effect of contemporary Israeli society. "Secularism," they insist, time and time again, "is the root of all evil."

In actual fact, the haredi argument takes the form of an invidious comparison. Claimants always take pains to point out the contrasting fortunes of secular and haredi Jews. In certain instances, they simply argue that there are lower rates of crime and delinquency amongst the latter. Invariably, however, haredi spokesmen make much more far-reaching claims. They argue that these problems are endemic to secular society and that they simply cannot happen within the haredi community. "Those who tremble at His word" are immune to these and other social ills. The conclusion is therefore clear. Secular control agents cannot eradicate crime and delinquency; repentance and acceptance of the yoke of the Torah is the only way to deal with the problem.

Haredi spokesmen obviously draw attention to the practical implications of this state of affairs. They suggest that the costs of secular society and the benefits of living in accordance with the Torah are sufficient reason to stay within or to join the fold. However, this is by no means the only rationale for living within the four cubits of halacha. The cost-benefit analysis also provides the basis for a much more far-reaching argument concerning the relative value of the competing lifestyles.

The contrasting fortunes of the haredi and secular world-views are frequently cited as proof of their truth and falsity, respectively. Thus, in answer to the question of "whether the utility of belief constitutes a proof of its veracity," *Hamodia* (26 May 1957) argued as follows:

> The healthy intuition of millions is not likely to lead one astray. In the eyes of Judaism, the consequences of a particular world-view have always been a criterion of its veracity. The people of Israel said, "We will keep the commandments and then we will understand them." After we perform the commandments and see their beneficial effects, then we will understand the true intention of the Torah. Adherence to the truth is bound to have positive consequences, and positive consequences testify to the fact that the source from which they draw inspiration is the real truth.

According to this way of thinking, the efficacy of the Torah and its veracity are not separate entities; they are intertwined. Warnings of the horrible consequences of secularism are also a way to relegate it to an inferior ontological status. The haredi etiology story about crime and delinquency is not just a cautionary tale about the dangers of going beyond "the four cubits of Jewish law;" it is also a way of telling people what is true and what is false.

Despite, or maybe because, they are physically and culturally separated, haredi Jews see themselves as the mirror image of the surrounding society. They construct their identity in opposition to the secular other. There are, of course, several ways of doing this. However, the telling of etiology stories seems to be a particularly popular one. Comparing the costs of contemporary secular culture with the benefits of traditional religious life enables haredi spokesmen to talk in physical terms and draw spiritual implications at one and the same time. Claims of success in this world furnish the basis for promises of future rewards in the world to come.

This research was carried out with the help of grants from the Lucius N. Littauer Foundation and the Bar Ilan University Research Authority.

Notes

1. This designation is taken from Isiah 66:5—Hear the word of the Lord, you that tremble (haredim) at His word.
2. See, for instance, Shilhav and Friedman (1985).
3. See, for instance, Heilman (1994).
4. Haredi spokesmen make a similar point whenever secular kibbutz members are suspected of engaging in illegal behavior of one kind or another.
5. Union or Association of Israel. A political party founded in 1948 to promote the observance of Jewish law in public life.
6. The Workers of the Union of Israel. A haredi party that has sometimes run together and sometimes separately from Agudat Israel.
7. Shas is an acronym for Sephardi Torah Guardians, an oriental haredi party established in 1983 following a split in Agudat Yisrael.
8. Haredi spokesmen frequently contend that secular Israelis portray the process as a form of brainwashing, in order to explain or, to be more precise, to explain away its achievements with even the most hardened criminals and delinquents
9. These miraculous stories also play an important role in the actual rehabilitation process. This was first pointed out in Cromer (1978; 1981) and later analyzed in much greater detail by Timor (1988).
10. Flag of the Torah. A new haredi party established in 1988 following a split in Agudat Yisrael.

References

Best, J. (1987) Rhetoric in Claims Making: Constructing the Missing Children Problem *Social Problems* 34(2): 101-121.

Cromer, G. (1978) Linguistic Aspects of Transformative Labeling: The Case of Repentant Delinquents *Mental Health and Society* 5(3) 186-193.

Cromer, G. (1981) Repentant Delinquents: A Religious Approach to Rehabilitation *Jewish Journal of Sociology* 23(2) 113-122.

Elor, T. (1991) The Perception of Secular Jews in the Ultra- Orthodox Community in Israel *Megamot* 34(1) 104-121 (in Hebrew).

Gusfield, J. R. (1981) *The Culture of Public Problems: Drinking-Driving and the Symbolic Order.* Chicago: University of Chicago Press.

Harris, A. R. (1977) Sex and Theories of Deviance: Towards a Functional Theory of Deviant Life-Scripts *American Sociological Review* 42(1) 3-16.

Heilman S. C. (1994) Quiescent and Active Fundamentalisms: The Jewish Cases. pp.173-196 in M. E. Marty & R. S. Appleby *Accounting for Fundamentalisms: The Dynamic Character of Movements* Chicago: University of Chicago Press.

Johnson, J. M. (1989) Horror Stories & the Construction of Child Abuse. pp. 5-19 in J. Best_*Images of Issues: Typifying Contemporary Social Problems* New York: Aldine De Gruyter.

Lamb, D. (1988) *Down the Slippery Slope: Arguing in Applied Ethics* London: Croom Helm.

Levi, A. (1990) The Haredi Press and Secular Society. pp. 21-44 in C. S. Liebman *Religious & Secular: Conflict and Accommodation Between Jews in Israel* Keter: Jerusalem.

Liebman, C. S. (1983) Extremism as a Religious Norm. *Journal for the Scientific Study of Religion* 22(1) 75-86.

Matza, D. (1969) *Becoming Deviant* Englewood Cliffs, N.J: Prentice Hall.

Pfuhl, E. M. (1980) *The Deviance Process* New York: D. Van Nostrand Co.

Ravitsky, A. (1989) Exile in the Holy Land: The Dilemma of Haredi Jewry_*Studies in Contemporary Jewry* 5: 89-125.

Schur, E. (1980) *The Politics of Deviance: Stigma Contests and the Uses of Power* Englewood Cliffs, N.J.: Prentice Hall.

Shilhav, J. & M. Friedman (1985) *Growth and Segregation: The Ultra-Orthodox Community of Jerusalem*: Jerusalem Institute for Israel Studies (in Hebrew).

Sontag, S. (1979) *Illness as Metaphor* New York: Vintage Books.

Timor, U. (1988) *Commitment to the Jewish Religion as a Way of Rehabilitating Delinquents: A Phenomenological Study Among Ex- Prisoners* Ph.D. diss., Hebrew University of Jerusalem, Israel (in Hebrew).

11

The Construction of Identity in a Divided Palestinian Village: Sociolinguistic Evidence

*Muhammad Amara** *and Bernard Spolsky*

Palestinization or Israelization?

The identity of Israeli Arabs is a matter of current academic dispute. One group of scholars (including Ganem and Ostazki-Lazar, 1990; Ginat, 1989; Lehman-Wiltzig, 1991; Smooha, 1989, 1992; and to a lesser extent, Al-Haj, 1989 and Rouhana, 1989, 1990) claims that the Arab minority is undergoing a process of Israelization. Israeli Arabs, they argue, are moving towards integration into Israeli society and perceive themselves as citizens of Israel. Their struggle is for a state of normal coexistence with civil rights and full equality. The fact that Israeli Arabs limited themselves to moral and financial support of the Intifada is considered to support this view. The opposing group (such as Landau, 1984, 1989; Lustick, 1980; Regev, 1989; Cohen, 1989; Rekhes, 1989; Soffer, 1986, 1989) argue that Israeli Arabs identify with Palestinians in the territories not only in politics, but also in culture. In this view, the reunification of the Palestinians in the West Bank and Gaza Strip with Palestinians in Israel since 1967 has accelerated the Palestinization process and the alienation of Israeli Arabs.

Amara *et al.* (1994) suggests that the dichotomous choice is too simplistic. Paradoxically, the Intifada has strengthened both the Israeli and the Palestinian identities. Israeli Arab society is in transition from a traditional to a modern society. For Israeli Arabs, the principal source of modernization and urbanization is Israeli society. At the same time, Palestinization represents their desire to preserve their identity. While rapprochement with Israeli society has given them the chance to achieve their ambitions as citizens with equal rights, acculturation to their fellow Palestinians satisfies their aspirations for national identity and cultural uniqueness. The sociolinguistic study of a divided Palestinian village[1] has given us a chance to look at empirical evidence of this growing double identity.

The Village of Barta'a

In this chapter, we look at some aspects of the linguistic, social, and cultural dislocation that followed from the political and economic dislocation and subsequent reintegration of one of several Palestinian Arab-speaking villages that were divided between Israel and Jordan in 1948 and reunited after 1967.

Barta'a is a Palestinian[2] village in the Ara valley, in the hills of Samaria, halfway between the Jordan river and the Mediterranean. It is about fifteen kilometers north of the Israeli town of Hadera and twenty-five kilometers south of the Israeli town Afula and the West Bank town Jenin. The Rhodes Armistice Agreement, signed in 1949 between the newly independent State of Israel and the newly named Hashemite Kingdom of Jordan, arbitrarily drew a border in the middle of the village. For the next twenty years, the village came under two separate jurisdictions, with Eastern Barta'a under Jordanian rule and Western Barta'a under Israeli.

Studying the village now, twenty-five years after the formal boundary line was removed, we have found in the speech of its inhabitants, including those who were not born while the border was in place, unmistakable evidence of the continuing social division between the two halves of the village. In sociolinguistic interviews, we identified several hundred lexical items that were used by the inhabitants of one half of the village rather than the other, and we found significant differences between the two sectors in usage of some of the key phonological and morphological features that have come to typify modernization and urbanization in Palestinian Arabic speech. While the village can be considered a single speech community, this is only by virtue of its being a community that recognizes the existence of the marked differences in the speech of people living in each of its sectors.

The first explanation that we offer for this continued linguistic frontier is the continuing and parallel social, political, economic and cultural differences between West Barta'a, essentially an Israeli Arab Palestinian village, and East Barta'a, a West Bank Palestinian village. In the study of the geopolitical and economic history of the village, we found how these distinctions have been maintained by the differential treatment received by the two sectors and their inhabitants under Israeli government policy. Exacerbated by the Intifada, the relations of the two sectors to each other and to the rest of the world have produced noticeable differences in economic, educational and cultural development. The sociolinguistic facts are thus directly correlated with political and demographic differences.

But correlation is not causation. There is a third set of factors, a mediating cluster of attitudinal factors, that makes even clearer the nature of the differences between the two sectors and provides a possible explanatory factor for differential change. These attitudinal factors, forming what can be thought of as identities, are both the result and transmitting force of the demographic and economic facts, and the putative cause and effect of the linguistic differences. In our studies, we have found evidence of clusters of factors on what we call the macrolevel (the social, political, and economic levels) that are linked through mediating attitudinal clusters with the microlevel of specific sociolinguistic phonological, lexical and grammatical variables.

Methodology

The sociolinguistic survey of the village took two years. Initial ethnographic studies lasted six months, from November 1992 until May 1993. We observed uses of linguistic variants in various settings and domains such as homes, neighborhoods, mosques, schools, and wedding parties, and recorded and later transcribed over forty hours of conversations about topics such as the political situation, schooling, transport, the Intifada, the peace process, construction, and the economic situation. Based on analysis of these data, a protocol for a structured interview was designed.[3] It started with open-ended questions about work or school, leisure time, the importance of electricity, and the village. This part of the interview, with a tape-recorder running, gave evidence of the careful style of speech used in such circumstances. To see what happened when the speakers were even more careful, we asked them to name the objects shown in sixty pictures selected to check variations in both pronunciation and lexicon. Each interview lasted from one hour to one hour and a half.

A total of 81 villagers were interviewed by three different interviewers.[4] Forty were from Eastern Barta'a and forty-one from Western Barta'a, half men and half women. Nineteen had been born before 1948, 30 between 1948 and 1967, and 32 after 1967. The villagers from each sector were more or less matched for educational level, with about ten in each of the levels of elementary, junior high, high, and tertiary education. Occupations, too, were matched. There was a range of religious observance in both samples, and there were differences in amount of contact with Jews.

The Linguistic Repertoire and Sociolinguistic Differentiation

The language of both sectors of Barta'a is categorizable as a variety of the Palestinian Arabic dialect. With growing exposure to Arab media (mainly TV and radio) and the rapid increase in the educational level, the knowledge and usage of features of Standard Arabic have increased. Some words from Standard Arabic have replaced local vernacular words (see Amara 1986; Kaplowitz 1992). Modern Standard Arabic has influenced even people with minimal education. Features from other dialects of Palestinian Arabic, especially those of the more prestigious towns and cities, and features from dialects of other Arabic countries (spread mainly through television) have also invaded the general speech.

In addition to the changes in the village variety that have come from other varieties of Arabic, there has been important influence from English and Hebrew. English is the third language learned in Western Barta'a (after Hebrew), and the second school language in Eastern Barta'a. It is important because of its role as the international language of science, technology, and commerce and the popularity of American culture.

Hebrew knowledge and usage is different in the two sectors of the village. In Western Barta'a, Hebrew is learned formally and informally. Since Hebrew is one of the official languages of Israel, Israeli Arabs learn Hebrew as the language of the country and not as a foreign language (see Winter, 1981). Hebrew is taught in Israeli Arab schools from the third grade, but the influence of informal learning from outside contact is even more important (see Reves, 1983). All age groups, regardless of gender, have informal contact with Hebrew speakers—though in varying degrees.[5]

Hebrew knowledge and usage in Eastern Barta'a follow the same pattern as in the rest of the West Bank. Hebrew is learned informally, mainly at work.[6] Young and mature men speak Hebrew best, since they work in Israel. Hebrew is not a compulsory subject in West Bank schools. However, thousands of Palestinian prisoners learned Hebrew in Israeli prisons.

In analyzing the sociolinguistic data, we tried to answer the question of whether Barta'a is to be considered two villages or one. To the casual outside observer, the residents of Barta'a all appear linguistically similar. Their dialect of Arabic contains the same sounds, their vocabulary is more or less the same, they know the same other languages. In our study, however, we found clear evidence of differences. First, the respondents themselves believed that they could recognize differences in the speech of the two sectors of the village. In an attitudinal study, all reported that their variety was different from that of the other half of the village, although there were fascinating differences in the features that they said were different. Second, when we analyzed the speech in the interviews, we found noticeable differences in lexicon and in the percentage use of certain important grammatical and phonological variants. In addition, there were clear differences in the level of mastery of Hebrew.

Basically, we found that demographic factors such as residence in West or East Barta'a, age, gender, education, occupation, place of work, and religious orientation could account for a large amount of the variation. Although direct correlations between residence in East or West Barta'a on the one hand and the specific linguistic variables were significant in only two cases, when we looked more closely at specific age, educational, gender, religious or occupational groups, the place of residence regularly emerged as a significant factor.

We found a number of features of particular interest. One is the realization of the phoneme /k/; the standard variant is [k] and the vernacular [tò]. Another is the phoneme /q/, [q] in the standard and [k] in the vernacular. A third is the voicing (standard) or voicelessness (vernacular) of the phoneme /d?/. Vowel deletion in certain environments is standard. The morphemes /fi/ and /'ala/ are standard, with the vernacular variants /bi/ and /'al/. Also of importance was the percentage of use of words from Standard Arabic and from Hebrew.

Age correlated significantly with most of the linguistic features. We divided our subjects' ages by political milestones. Those born before 1948 were the oldest group, those born between 1948 and 1967 the adult group, and those born since 1967 the youngest. The youngest respondent was 18. The picture that emerges is one of language change in progress, with a general tendency for younger subjects to be moving away from the village vernacular and in the direction of more general or Standard Arabic.

Age, however, is not a causal factor. We are not dealing with an age-graded social structure in which there is an old people's variety. Rather, it is the different social experiences (especially the increase in education and outside contacts) which are themselves correlated with age that are the putative causes of the change. The educational revolution, a feature of the newly defined Palestinian people in which parents who did not themselves complete elementary school commonly have children studying at university, emerged in fact as one of the strongest factors accounting for the choice of the more standard linguistic variables.

In a diglossic situation, the main linguistic goal of the school system is to "correct" the vernacular by teaching the normative Standard forms. Consequently, the more education a speaker has, the more he or she has been encouraged and enabled to learn the Standard Literary Language and the more she (or, to a lesser extent, he) is likely to modify her or his vernacular speech in the direction of the Standard, phonologically, grammatically and lexically.

At first glance, it appeared that men use the standard features more than women. Closer analysis revealed that these statistics disguise the effect of differential education. The existence of a larger group of less educated women among the older groups and in Eastern Barta'a leads to the mistaken impression that males lead in adopting the new and prestigious variants. In fact, Barta'a supports the basic generalization that women who have access to education are more likely than men to use the standard forms.

Barta'a as a whole is participating in a language change whereby, as a result of education and changed communication patterns, standard normative features are entering educated speech. As a general rule, the more educated the respondent, the higher the percentage of the normative /k/ variant. In all these groups, too, the respondent is more likely to use the normative variant when being careful (as in the picture naming task) than when speaking in the interview. An important exception is the adult men of Western Barta'a, whose probability of use of some normative features is lower than expected, and who use more of the local village vernacular variant in the picture naming task than they do in the freer interview. This we label vernacular loyalty. In Eastern Barta'a, a similar phenomenon seems to be the explanation for the fact that highly educated youth (mainly) use village vernacular vocabulary more than other groups. It is these cases of vernacular loyalty that encouraged us to continue our pursuit of the study of identity.

Collective Social Identities

As Ferguson (1991:183) reminded us, "Tying together findings from macro- and micro-level research has been recognized as a major problem since the earliest days of explicitly sociolinguistic research." The macrolevel studies, whether studies of language maintenance in the sociology of language tradition (such as Fishman, 1966) or of language attitudes in the social psychology mode (such as Bentahila, 1983) have tended to remain unconnected to the microlevel sociolinguistics (or, in its own terms, secular linguistics) research following Labov (1966). To this has been added the recent challenge presented in Fishman (1991) to strengthen the ties between sociolinguistic study and the discipline of sociological methodologies and theoretical concepts. We attempt here to go beyond the social psychological studies of attitude to a model that relates the sociological to the sociolinguistic via the social psychological. It is here that we looked at identities.

In the preliminary ethnographic study, we distinguished the following relevant labels for identities in the two sectors: Arab, Muslim, Palestinian, Israeli, Villager, and Kabaha (Hamula). Our first aim was to find whether there is any principled basis in the choice of these identities by villagers and whether there are differences in the choices made in the two sections of Barta'a. We hoped also to be able to use the resulting construct as a possible explanation for sociolinguistic differences. It should be noted that these labels for identities come from different domains: *Israeli, Palestinian,* and *Arab* are national, *Muslim* is religious, *Kabaha* is kinship, and *Villager* is local.

First, we looked at the definition and significance of the various identities in the two sectors. The respondents were asked, "How do you define yourself?" or "Who are you?" They offered thirteen different sets of labels. The most common identity chosen in Eastern Barta'a was *Palestinian* (selected by 19); in Western Barta'a, the two most popular choices were *Arab* and *Palestinian* (8 each). Other choices (*Muslim, Israeli, Kabaha, and Villager*) were made by few respondents.

The number of compound answers was good evidence of the complexity of identity in the village. Thirty-two of the respondents did not satisfy themselves with a single term. To simplify our analysis, however, we forced their choice by looking at their primary identity (taken to be the second term in a compound like "*Muslim* ***Palestinian***"). Looked at this way, *Kabaha, villager, Israeli*, and *Muslim* appear even less important. The resulting distribution of *Palestinian* and *Arab* in the two sectors is even clearer. Whereas *Palestinian* is the most important in Eastern Barta'a (21), followed by *Arab* (15), in Western Barta'a, equal weight is given to both *Arab* and *Palestinian* (19 each). We may tentatively conclude that in Eastern Barta'a, *Palestinian* is the primary identity, followed by *Arab*. In the West, two primary identities emerge; *Arab* and *Palestinian*.

One problem with these results is that they depend on a respondent's choice of a label for identity, provided as answers to the question, who or what are you? We therefore asked another question about the importance of the various identities to the respondents. *Muslim* was ranked as most important (5.44), followed by *Palestinian* (4.6), and *Arab* (4.4), then the local identities *Kabaha* (2.25) and *villager* (1.75), and in the last place *Israeli* (0.76). There are differences between the sectors. In Eastern Barta'a, *Muslim* is the most important, followed by *Palestinian*, then *Arab. Kabaha* and *villager* identities were in the last place and *Israeli* not a possible choice. In Western Barta'a, *Muslim* was most important, followed by *Arab* and *Palestinian*. *Kabaha* was in fourth place, and *Israeli* and *villager* received the same ranking.

We found, as might have been predicted, that *Palestinian* is the most important among younger people and the least among older adults in Eastern Barta'a. Younger people in Eastern Barta'a considered the *Palestinian* identity as the most important, and other groups choose *Muslim*. In Western Barta'a, *Muslim* was the most important, *Arab* was second and *Palestinian* was third. Interestingly enough, the younger the respondent, the less important was *Israeli*. The *local* identities were considered the least important among all the age groups.

There are interesting differences according to gender by sector. In Eastern Barta'a, the most important identity among females was *Muslim*, followed by *Palestinian* and *Arab*. However, among Eastern men and Western women, *Muslim* was the most important, and *Arab* and *Palestinian* were equal. Among Western men, *Muslim* was the most important, with *Arab* second and *Palestinian* third. The local identities were last. *Israeli* is more important for men than women in Western Barta'a.

All educational groups in both sections ranked *Muslim* identity as the most important. Second in the east for all educational levels was *Palestinian*, strongest among elementary and junior high school groups. *Arab* identity emerged as the third most important identity among the easterners, though a little bit higher in the university group. *Hamula* (Kabaha) was strongest among elementary and high school groups. The higher the education of the respondent, the weaker *villager* identity was.

In contrast, in Western Barta'a, *Arab* identity was the second most important identity after *Muslim*. The higher the education, the stronger was *Arab* identity. For *Palestinian* which ranked third, the higher the education the stronger the identity. *Villager* and *Israeli* identities received similar rankings. *Israeli* identity was strongest among the illiterate and university groups.

The third question asked, which identity label best describes the respondent, permits us to look at these preferences again. On both sides, *Muslim* remains the term mentioned as describing respondents best, though more strongly in the western sector. In second place was *Palestinian*, stronger in Eastern Barta'a. The local identity was chosen as the best trait by only two people in Western Barta'a. Nobody chose *Israeli* or *Villager* as describing them best. Young people in Eastern Barta'a chose *Palestinian* rather than *Muslim*. The higher the level of education (especially in Eastern Barta'a), the more respondents reported *Palestinian* as the best trait.

All respondents then stressed their Islamic identity as most important. This is understandable in the case of Western Barta'a, where claiming *Muslim* identity is much more convenient and not accompanied by specific requirements. The other identities involve cognitive dissonance, since respondents know that they do not perform their obligations as *Palestinians* and as *Arabs* fully. That is to say, the symbols and practices attached to these identities are not as evident in their daily life as among Palestinians in the occupied territories. Thus, while the people of Western Barta'a are proud to be part of the Palestinian people and proud of their achievements especially during the Intifada, they did not take an active role in it. In Eastern Barta'a, the respondents also stressed the importance of Islamic identity, seeing this as a wide circle and the strongest identity through which it is possible to achieve national goals.

As Jean-François Legrain (1994) suggests, the opposition to the secular leadership of the PLO in opposing or dealing with the Israeli occupation of the West Bank and Gaza Strip was essential and crucial to the formation of the Islamic movement. He explains that patriotism and fighting the occupation through the Intifada was a condition for expansion. For Palestinians, the *Muslim* identity is an alternative to their national identity, following their disappointment with Arab countries.

The Eastern ranking for *Palestinian* is 4.8, in contrast to 4.4 in the west. The rank for *Arab* is 4.2 in the east, and 4.65 in the west. The rank of 4.4 given to the *Palestinian* identity in Western Barta'a is quite high, showing a process of Palestinization which has been accelerated during the Intifada. *Arab* is more important in the western sector than in the eastern. This may be attributed to the fact that the westerners were not directly affected by the Arab countries, whereas the easterners were directly affected and experienced the corruption of their regimes, which during the Intifada did not offer any help.

Hamula (or Kabaha) is in fourth place among the two sides. This identity is an expression of traditional values that still have some influence on the two sides. It is a little higher among the easterners (2.4) in contrast to (2.1) in the west. The *Hamula* identity is held as an expression of the numerical power of the members and it is potentially a factor unifying the two sides. In contrast, the village identity expresses the separation and the differences between the two sides. However, we have to be careful regarding the *Hamula* identity, since it is a strong expression of the power and paradoxes of the Intifada. The Intifada enhanced the feelings of solidarity and unity among the Palestinian people. However, at the same time, it also enhanced local (village) and *Hamula* identities. *Hamula* membership became a sign of solidarity and brotherhood. Some youth worked together on a *Hamula* basis during the Intifada for reasons of secrecy and trust. *Hamula* identity is not extremely important in Western Barta'a, where it is not vital or practical in daily life.

The *village* identity is weak on both sides, since it stresses the difference and not the unification between the two sections. Traditional values are a little stronger in the eastern than in the western sector. We may explain the weakening of the *Hamula* and *village* identities as a result of the modernization and urbanization taking place among Israeli Arabs; in Eastern Barta'a this change may be attributed to accelerated political socialization as a result of the Intifada.

Language and Identity

We now examine the relationship between identities and sociolinguistic variables, looking for a mediating level between politics and language. This will help us explain some of the features of sociolinguistic variation that were left unexplained by the demographic factors earlier.

In this section, we look at important correlations between selected identity, demographic and sociolinguistic variables to propose an underlying causal model for our observations. We assume a model with three clusters of relevant factors. The socio-demographic factors (like age, gender, education, occupation, village sector) are assumed to be primary, in that they account for the differential experience of the subjects over the past years. From these emerge the collective social identities (Palestinian, Arab, Villager, Israeli) which the villagers have constructed in various complex combinations. These, in turn, are expressed by or reflected in the sociolinguistic choices (standard or local phonology or morphology or lexicon, or Hebrew borrowing) in the third cluster. The simple causal interpretation is, of course, wrong, for the sociolinguistic choices are part of the construction of identity and related to social roles.

Applying this model and looking at only cases where correlations are highly significant (at the .01 level),[7] the following preliminary picture has emerged from our analysis to date:

> Palestinian identity is positively correlated with Arab identity (0.43), and negatively correlated with Religious identity (-0.5). It is equally spread among all demographic groups, with the exception implied in the negative correlation with Religious identity, namely, that it is also weakly correlated with occupational status. Sociolinguistically, its major reflex (with a surprisingly high 0.82 correlation) is with phonological changes from village to standard forms. From earlier discussion, we also know that there is a tendency for adult West Barta'a men to resist consciously some of these changes.

Arabic identity is positively correlated with Palestinian identity, but distinguished from it by also being positively correlated with being male (0.32). It is significantly correlated with two sociolinguistic factors: standard phonology (0.32) and standard morphology (0.37).

Israeli identity is, as one would expect, strongly related to Western Barta'a (0.55), to males (0.4), and to higher occupational status (0.36). Linguistically, it is most strongly expressed by the use in spoken Arabic of words borrowed from Hebrew (0.32), and, as we noted before, in a resistance to some phonological standardization (vernacular loyalty).

Religious identity (fundamentalism) is positively correlated to age (0.32) and negatively to occupation (0.34). Sociolinguistically, it is marked by a low use of Hebrew borrowings (0.34).

Village identity is a strongly marked category. First, it is negatively correlated with Israeli identity. It is also marked for gender, being negatively correlated with male and, by logical extension, with occupational status. Sociolinguistically, it is shown by low values for standardization of phonology, morphology and lexicon. We have here further evidence on the controversy over the sociolinguistic tendencies of women in the Arab world, showing that uneducated women tend to conservatism rather than innovation.

Hamula or Kabaha identity is also marked for gender as female. It is strongly correlated negatively with education, and expressed sociolinguistically by low percentage of use of standard phonology, morphology and lexicon and Hebrew borrowings.

What do these results mean? The significant negative correlation between local identity and the linguistic variables indicates that being identified as such does not entail the use of standard features or Hebrew features. Those who tend to identify themselves as Kabahas or villagers use the local vernacular features, showing their loyalty to their local vernacular, a behavioral pattern fitting the local identification. Regarding Israeli identity, the significant positive correlation is with Hebrew items and was restricted to residents of Western Barta'a.

Though the religious identity was the most important among both sides, this has not emerged as an important construct when correlated with linguistic variables. This means that identifying as a Muslim does not require one to use aspects of the standard in order to be identified as such. Probably it is enough to carry out the duties of Islam in order to express this identification and its associated behavioral patterns.[8]

What seems of particular interest is the Palestinian and Arab identity. Highly positive significant correlation is found between Palestinian identity and the phonological variables. The primary identity on the eastern side is Palestinian. This suggests that being identified as Palestinian entails the use of some standard aspects. We suppose that the high correlation with phonological variables rather than with morphological or standard Arabic items is because they are more salient in speech. We may tentatively conclude that Palestinization is related to use of standard Arabic features. If the Intifada is the political concrete aspect of the increasing Palestinization, then at the linguistic level also the use of standard features reflects this trend. The tendency among adult male Western Barta'ans to vernacular loyalty makes clear the limitations they impose on their acceptance of Palestinian identity.

Arab identity, on the other hand, is positively expressed in standard phonological (though less than the Palestinian) and morphological variants. The Arab identity is the primary identity in the western sector. These results strengthen the "two village" view. The sociolinguistic differences between the two sectors have resulted from the political division of the village in 1949, accompanied by massive changes in their economies, education and politics. The identities are the result and the transmitting force of the demographic and economic facts, and the putative cause and effect of the linguistic differences. The two halves differ in their perception of Israeli identity, which in the western section constitutes a part of their multi-identity, and thus another linguistic resource and prestige (as shown in Amara 1986, 1995) available to them in daily life. The Eastern Barta'ans react negatively to this Israeli identity. While both sides claim they are Palestinians, this is functional in the eastern section and symbolic in the western.

This was shown in the highly positive significant correlation between Palestinian identity and critical linguistic variables. In Eastern Barta'a, Palestinian identity as a transmitting force is a strong mediator between linguistic variants and the macro sociological level. In the western section, being identified as Palestinian does not lead to either linguistic (e.g., towards standard Arabic) or political action (e.g., in taking an active role in the Intifada).

Though both easterners and westerners identify as Arabs, in the western section, this identification is much stronger. Arab identity in the West is the explanation of standard features. The eastern side is disappointed with the Arab world, mainly its regimes, because they did not offer any help during the Intifada.

With the changes taking part on both sides of the village, it is the marginalized groups (the uneducated and older men and women) who maintain the local identities (villager or Kabaha), which is shown also by the maintenance of vernacular features, but without the special loyalty shown to these features by Western males. It is their lack of education that accounts for their speech as it accounts for their traditional identity.

Conclusion

In Western Barta'a, the two major identities which serve as transmitting forces are Israeli and Arab. The construction of Israeli identity is mainly through use of borrowed features. The Arab-Palestinian identity encourages standard Arabic features, setting up a tension and modifying the degree of use. In Eastern Barta'a, the most influential identity is Palestinian, explaining the rapid linguistic change in progress towards standard Arabic and the great sensitivity to its use.

These results show that the study of language in relation to identity reveals interesting explanations for sociolinguistic variation. Most sociolinguistics studies have been satisfied with correlations between language behavior and socio-demographic facts, and causation is seldom analyzed. In this study, we have started building a unified model, bringing sociology (and politics and economics) into sociolinguistics through social psychology.

Notes

* Bar-Ilan University and Beit Berl College.

1. This paper was written for the Edinburgh Symposium on Language and Identity in the Middle East and North Africa, July 3-5, 1995.The study on which it is based was made possible by a grant from the Israel Foundations Trustees to Bar-Ilan University.
2. As sociolinguists, we recognize the political loading that terms like "Palestinian," "Samaria" and "West Bank" have taken on, but, short of creating a new set of neutral terms, are constrained by these realities. Thus, while *Palestinian* was used in the 1940s in English to refer mainly to Jews living in the British Mandatory territory, it is now generally used to refer to Arabs who live or who once lived in the same area. Similarly, the term "West Bank" refers to the territory on the west bank of the Jordan River that was occupied by Jordan and is now under Israeli control. Many Israelis prefer to refer to the same area by its Biblical names (Judea and Samaria), and many Palestinians prefer to call it Occupied Territory. New names will presumably develop as Palestinian autonomy becomes a reality.
3. The structured interview was based on Amara's interviews (1991). Some questions regarding identity were adapted from Schimmel (1990). The interviews were piloted with eight subjects from the two sections of the village and modified.
4. Some effects of this difference are discussed in Spolsky and Amara (1995).
5. See Amara & Spolsky (1986) and Amara (1995) for details of Hebrew knowledge in nearby Zalafa village.
6. See Spolsky & Cooper (1991).
7. These results are based on simple inspection of correlations. In preliminary analysis using more powerful statistical tools, we are finding support for the three part model, with demographic features as the cause of the attitudinal, and the attitudinal as the cause of the sociolinguistic.
8. To some degree the non-significant correlation of Islamic identities with linguistic variables is surprising, since Islam is associated with Classical Arabic. Part of the explanation lies in the fact that the recent increase in religious fundamentalism is among less educated and older villagers.

References

Al-Haj, Majid. (1989). Elections in the Arab street under the Intifada. In Landau, J. (ed.), *The Arab Vote in the Knesset Elections, 1988*. Jerusalem Institute, Jerusalem. 35-49. (In Hebrew)

Amara, Muhammad. (1986). The Integration of Hebrew and English Lexical Items into the Arabic Spoken in an Arab Village in Israel. MA Thesis, Bar-Ilan University, Ramat-Gan.

Amara, Muhammad. (1991). Sociolinguistic Aspects of Variation and Change: A Study of the Languages Spoken in an Arab Village in Israel. Ph.D. Dissertation, Bar-Ilan University, Ramat-Gan.

Amara, Muhammad. (1995). Hebrew and English lexical reflections of socio-political changes in Palestinian Arabic. *Journal of Multilingual and Multicultural Development.* 16, 3:165-172

Amara, Muhammad, Sufian Kabaha and Riyad Kabaha. (1994). *The Struggle of Eight Villages in Wadi 'Ara Against an Imposed "Rural Council."* The Institute for Peace Studies, Giv'at Haviva. (In Hebrew)

Amara, Muhammad and Bernard Spolsky. (1986). The diffusion and integration of Hebrew and English lexical items in spoken Arabic in an Israeli village. *Anthropological Linguistics* 28, 1:43-58.

Bentahila, Abdul. (1983). *Language attitudes among Arabic French bilinguals in Morocco.* Clevedon, Avon: Multilingual Matters Ltd.

Cohen, Ranan. (1989). *The Complexity of Loyalty: Society and Politics in the Arab Sector.* Am Oved, Tel Aviv. (In Hebrew)

Ferguson, Charles A. (1991) Individual and social in language change: diachronic changes in politeness agreement in forms of address. In Robert L. Cooper and Bernard Spolsky (Eds.), *The influence of language on culture and thought: essays in honor of Joshua A. Fishman's sixty-fifth birthday* (pp. 183-197). Berlin: Mouton de Gruyter.

Fishman, Joshua A. (1991) Putting the "socio" back into the sociolinguistic enterprise. *International Journal of the Sociology of Language 92:* 127-138..

Fishman, Joshua A and others. (1966). *Language loyalty in the United States: the maintenance and perpetuation of non-English mother tongues by American ethnic and religious groups.* The Hague: Mouton.

Ganem, Asad and Sara Ostazki-Lazar. (1990). *Green Line, Red Lines: Israeli Arabs in the face of the Intifada.* The Institute for Arabic Studies, Giv'at Haviva. (In Hebrew)

Ginat, Joseph. (1989). Voting patterns and political behavior in the Arab sector. In Landau, J. (ed.), *The Arab Vote in the Knesset Elections, 1988.* Jerusalem Institute, Jerusalem. 3-21. (in Hebrew)

Kaplowitz, I. (1992). Arabic in Israel: the sociolinguistic situation of Israel's Arab minority. *International Journal of the Sociology of Language* 98: 29-66.

Labov, William (1966). *The stratification of English in New York City. Washington,* DC: Center for Applied Linguistics.

Landau, Jacob. (1984). The Arab vote. In Caspi, D., Diskin, A., and Gutmann, E. (eds.), *The Roots of Begin's Success.* Croom Helm, London: 169-189.

Landau, Jacob. (ed) (1989). *The Arab Vote in the Knesset Elections of 1988.* Jerusalem Institute. (in Hebrew)

Lehman-Wiltzig, Sam. (1991). *Stiff-Necked People, Bottle-Necked System: The Evolution and Roots of Israeli Protest, 1949-1986.* Bloomington: Indiana University Press.

Legrain, Jean-François. (1994). Palestinian Islamism: Patriotism as a condition of their expansion. In M. Marty and F. Appleby (eds) *Accounting for Fundamentalism: the dynamic character of movements.* Chicago: University of Chicago Press, 413-27.

Lustick, Ian. (1980). *Arabs in the Jewish State: Israel's Control over a National Minority.* Austin: University of Texas

Regev, A. (1989). *Israeli Arabs: Political Issues.* Jerusalem Institute, Jerusalem. (In Hebrew)

Rekhes, Eli. (1989). Israeli Arabs and the Arabs of the territories: political ties and national identity (1967-1988). *Hamizrah Hehadash*, 22: 165-191. (In Hebrew)

Reves, Thea (1983). What makes a good language learner? Personal characteristics contributing to successful language acquisition. Unpublished Ph.D. Dissertation, The Hebrew University of Jerusalem.

Rouhana, Nadim. (1989). The political transformation of the Palestinians in Israel: from acquiescence to challenge. *Journal of Palestine Studies*, 18: 38-59.

———— 1990. The Intifada and the Palestinians of Israel: Resurrecting the Green Line. *Journal of Palestine Studies*, 19: 58-75.

Schimmel, Malka. (1991). How Israeli Palestinians Construe their Identities. Ph.D. Dissertation, University of Chicago.

Smooha, Sam. (1989). The Arab minority in Israel: Radicalization or politicization? *Studies in Contemporary Jewry*, 5: 1-21

———— (1992). *Arabs and Jews in Israel: Change and Continuity in Mutual Tolerance* (Vol. 2). Westview, Boulder.

Soffer, Arnon. (1986). The territorial struggle between Jews and Arabs in Israel. *Horizons in Geography*, 17-18: -23. (In Hebrew)

———— (1989). Israeli Arabs—from village to the metropolis, what's next? *Hamizrah Hehadash*, 32: 125-138. (In Hebrew)

Spolsky, Bernard. and Robert L. Cooper. (1991). *The Languages of Jerusalem*. Oxford: Clarendon Press.

Spolsky, Bernard and Muhammad Amara. (1995). *Sociolinguistic reflexes of political division: a study of a divided village* (Final scientific report, Israel Foundations Trustees, No.59/92). Language Policy Research Center, Bar-Ilan University.

Winter, Michael. (1981). Basic problems in the Arab education system. In Lish Aharon (ed.) *Arabs in Israel: Continuity and Change*. Magnes Press, 168-79. (In Hebrew)

12

Jews and Arabs in Israel: The Cultural Convergence of Divergent Identities*

Eliezer Ben-Rafael and Hezi Brosh

The Purpose of the Study and Its Background

The relations between Arabs and Jews in Israel have been generally discussed as a conflict between an underprivileged national minority and a better-off majority (see among many others, Smooha, 1976; Rosenfeld, 1978; Lustick, 1980). The social, political and cultural disparities, which separate Jews from Arabs are, indeed, manifest. The Israeli Arabs make up 18% (ICBS, 1989) of Israel's population; about 80% of them reside in their own villages and towns. Those who live in the mixed neighborhoods of Tel-Aviv-Jaffa, Haifa or Acre make up less than 20% of the total Arab population. These Arabs are widely characterized by social deprivation (Horowitz and Lissak, 1989). While nearly 90% of Arab manpower—including those Arabs who live in homogeneous villages or towns—is employed in the all-Israeli economy, 80% of these individuals hold lower-class or working-class jobs—in contrast to 45% of the Jewish population (see Semyonov, Lewin-Epstein, 1987). Moreover, the definition of the State of Israel as a Jewish state reduces these Arabs to the status of national minority. However, the status of a national minority also signifies that the dominant culture endorses a pluralistic approach vis-a-vis Arabs (see Gorny, 1986; Landau, 1987). The Arabs' own notions of identity, moreover, define them as a part of the Arab nation—which excludes the Jew. Furthermore, the state of belligerency between Israel and the Arab countries creates quite a hardship for the Jewish-Arab relationship.

The linguistic reality of Israel is a major dimension of these complex relations. The Zionist enterprise, it must be remembered, started with the renewal of Hebrew as the nation's legitimate language (see Chomsky, 1957; Cooper, 1989). Even so, Arabic has remained an official language of the State. It is much less employed in official documents and dealings than Hebrew, and many an official ignores it (Brosh, 1988), but the presence of Arabic in Israel is nevertheless real. In all universities, one finds departments of Arabic and of Middle-Eastern Studies, and language courses in Arabic. Arabic is supported by daily TV and radio broadcasting, daily newspapers and periodicals. Above all, Arabic is the teaching language of the Arabic educational system where more than 90% of Arab children study—from kindergarten to teachers' colleges. Moreover, in the Hebrew-speaking school system, Arabic is an optional third language. About two-thirds of the students in the non-vocational and non-scientific tracks where Arabic is offered choose to study it, in addition to English, which is compulsory. On the other hand, Hebrew is obligatory from the third grade on in Arabic-speaking schools. The high competence which Arab students generally achieve in Hebrew—the wide majority of Arabs under forty know Hebrew well (Rubinstein, 1980)—contrasts with the feeble dedication of many Israeli Jews to the learning of Arabic in the Hebrew educational system (Ben-Rafael, Brosh, 1991; Kraemer, 1990; Brosh, 1988).

As for English, it is one of the principal—and obligatory—subjects in Hebrew-speaking and Arabic-speaking schools alike. It is the second language to be taught in the former, after Hebrew, and the third in the latter, after Arabic and Hebrew. English is actually a requirement for admission to the university (Isaacs, 1967), as well as for many middle- and high-rank jobs (Ronen, Seckbach, Cooper, 1977). The knowledge of English is, in fact, widely characteristic of Israel's privileged strata (Cooper, Fishman, 1977; Seckbach, Cooper, 1977; Rosenbaum, Nadel et al., 1977; Ben-Rafael, 1994).

Hence, the same three languages—Hebrew, Arabic, and English—are diffused by school and other social agencies throughout both the majority and minority groups. This offers wide room for studying Jewish-Arab relations not only as a conflict, i.e., as a case of *divergence in collective identities*, but also, through the diffusion, uses and attitudes toward those languages, as a case of *cultural convergence*. Rarely considered as such by researchers, this aspect questions the very evolution and transformation of Jews and Arabs—and, thereby, of Israeli society itself, through the very unfolding of their uneasy relationship. It is this aspect of the Jewish-Arab relationship that is investigated and analyzed in the following pages. This question of the cultural convergence of a majority and a minority conveys theoretical significance at several levels of discussion.

Investigating Cultural Convergence through Language

By cultural convergence, we mean (Gumperz, 1982, 1987; Giglioli, 1987) the integration into one's own culture of symbols which originate from another group's culture. This convergence is best illustrated by language activity (Fasold, 1987; Edwards, 1988), the very core of culture (Habermas, 1988; Giddens, 1987). More specifically, patterns of bilingualism may be of the greatest relevance in this respect: bilingualism signifies that the individual's allegiance to language is divided into two or more codes (Spolsky, 1989), which, in contemporary society, generally involves local or community languages known and used in addition to the national language and, possibly, to international codes.

One may find in the sociological literature, including the sociology-of-language literature, three major references to cultural convergence, i.e., related to majority-minority *inter-group relations*—i.e., when each side is influenced by the other by the very fact of their coexistence in the same setting; *inter-individual relations* of members of the majority and the minority; exposure of the setting as a whole to external influences—i.e., *inter-setting relations.*

Inter-Group Relations

Cultural influences stemming from majority-minority inter-group relations are primarily determined by the distribution of power. Researchers (see Grillo, 1989) refer, in this respect, to different models of bilingualism: a majority which has become bilingual, and thereby converges toward the minority, isolates the latter culturally. A majority which imposes its code on the minority downgrades the social value of the latter's language but compensates it by widening the range of social opportunities made consequently available to it. In both cases, a common language is used which, in itself, is a factor of cultural convergence. Grillo posits here, however, that a majority is not necessarily attached to the destruction of any form of socio-cultural and linguistic pluralism and that there are majority groups which aspire to retain their distinction from minority groups, not out of their respect for the minority cultures, but rather out of their disregard for them.

Hechter (1978; 1975), who formulates a theory of internal colonialism and proposes a contrary hypothesis, claims that the language of the majority is necessarily the only one to remain relevant to social life in any majority-minority setting. This approach finds support in numerous well-known cases of attrition and death of a minority language (see Dorian, 1982; ed., 1989). It signifies that the minority is driven by a depreciation of its code and symbols concomitantly with an identification with those of the majority.

Grillo and Hechter both agree, however, that the majority is, in any event, the factor which determines the patterns of cultural convergence prevailing in a given setting. Others do not take this assumption for granted. Ben-Rafael (1994) contends that within the framework determined by the majority's perspective, be it pluralistic or unifying, there is room for the minority to express its own aspirations: i.e., to choose whether to retain its identity or to assimilate. The minority, it follows, does influence—to a lesser extent than the majority, but still undeniably—the pace of its cultural convergence toward the majority.

This perspective makes it possible to conceive additional patterns of bilingualism expressing and implement in particular models of majority-minority relations. To the extent, for instance, that the minority aspires to retain some particularism while the majority itself is pluralistic, one may suppose that bilingualism should be less unbalanced than in the two models mentioned above. The minority may appreciate and acquire the majority's language without being prevented from retaining its own language as a community code. Actually, the culture and language of the minority might even be recognized by segments of the majority for its cultural or communicative importance.

Inter-Individual Relations

Face-to-face personal interactions are another factor of cultural convergence. Gordon (1964) and Horowitz (1975) speak of the assimilationist influence on members of the minority, of their interactions with members of the majority (McKay and Lewine 1978; Lal, 1983). This hypothesis suggests that individuals of the minority who have more contact with members of the majority converge toward it more resolutely. More categorical, contact-hypothesis theory contends that face-to-face relations between members of the majority and the minority forward cultural convergence by destroying mutual misconceptions generated by conflict (Brewer and Kramer, 1985; Brewer and Miller, 1984; Hewstone and Brown, 1986). This approach thus assumes that both elements of the minority and the majority who have more face-to-face contacts in their respective categories with members of the other group personify stronger cultural convergence toward the other group.

These approaches gainsay Myrdal's (1962) "poor white" theory, which contends that increased contacts between the minority and the majority involved the latter's lower strata. People who belong to these strata perceive the social advancement of the minority as threatening their own status. Such feelings, says Myrdal, nourish velleities to retain segregative practices against the minority and impede cultural convergence. It may be pursued that those members of the minority who have more contact with the majority encounter its more hostile elements which, in turn, drives them to become more hostile toward the majority. In this perspective, more personal interaction between members of the majority and the minority lead to stronger social and cultural divergence.

Inter-Setting Relations

Another facet of cultural convergence concerns the cultural impact of inter-setting relations. Fishman (1987) has formulated an approach which sees in the expansion throughout the world of what he calls *worldwide communication languages* (WCLs) the basis for the formation of a world culture. Fishman, however, acknowledges that this diffusion of WCLs takes place through a strengthening of elites who have, more than others, access to these linguistic resources. In the framework of Bourdieu's approach (1987: 59-95; 1982; Bourdieu, Passeron, 1970), WCLs are endowed cultural-capital value which can be measured by the profits of distinction warranted by their control of their carriers (Wardhaugh, 19878; Fishman, 1989). Hence, WCLs make the world more unified, and thereby more egalitarian and, at the same time, constitute an aspect of social stratification. Prestigious resources which penetrate societies under the control of the privileged (Woolard, 1989) draw social categories closer to each other by their internalization of a common appreciation of outside resources, but also draw them apart by their uneven distribution in society.

At this point, exchange-theory (Homans, 1974; Blau, 1964) would object that an unequal distribution of linguistic resources should unavoidably entail a differentiation of the evaluation of such resources among groups. Those who possess these resources should obviously tend to upgrade their value; those who do not possess them should downgrade their value in view of limiting the social price, which they pay for their lack of control of those resources.

In sum, regarding all three levels of cultural interaction, the literature of the field proposes different and often opposing perspectives. These levels structure the notions of cultural convergence and divergence of a majority and minority. Majority-minority interaction is the level among the three that involves the more central aspect of social order. Inter-personal interaction refers to variance within both the majority and the minority, which makes its impact secondary to majority-minority interaction. Inter-setting interaction refers to influences which are not endemic to the social condition itself.

The Research and Its Methods

The data were collected (1990) by means of a Lickert-type questionnaire of semantic-differential items. The first section asked about attitudes toward, and images of, the other group. The second section asked about images of the other group's language (Arabic for Jews, and Hebrew for Arabs), and a third section about both groups' attitudes toward English. These second and third sections concerned images of, and attitudes toward, teachers, the learning situation, value-contents conveyed by language programs, motivational aspects, parental support and uses of the languages acquired.

We surveyed Jewish and Arab ninth grade students who learned all three languages in Hebrew- and Arabic-speaking schools, respectively; each sample was itself made up of two sub-samples of students living in a heterogeneous Jewish-Arab or in a homogeneous, either Jewish or Arab, neighborhood. We assumed that this criterion would efficiently differentiate between individuals who have daily contact with members of the other group, and individuals who have much less contact of this sort outside the work setting. The total sample consisted of 544 male and female students randomly selected: 72 Arabs and 98 Jews who live in a Jaffa heterogeneous neighborhood in the southern part of Tel-Aviv, 84 Arabs who reside in Kfar Kassem (35 km from Tel-Aviv), a homogeneous Arab town; and

290 Jews who live in a Northern Tel-Aviv homogeneous Jewish neighborhood.

Findings and Discussion

Inter-Group Relations

The divergence of identity between Jews and Arabs is unambiguous. The Jews are the most extreme in this respect (see Table 1). The data clearly show that they lack any enthusiasm for social intermingling with Arabs, confirming thereby what we know from former works (see Levy, Guttman, 1976; Peres, 1976). The Arabs' attitudes toward Jews are more favorable from all aspects taken into account, which shows that they define their own social boundaries in terms which are less exclusionist.

However, while Jews perceive in the Arabs fewer positive attributes than Arabs notice in Jews, Jews also see in Arabs fewer negative attributes than Arabs do in Jews. This makes it appear that Arabs refer to Jews more intensely than Jews do to Arabs, and that this more

Table 1
Reciprocal perceptions of Jews and Arabs

Perceptions	*Arabs*			*Jews*			
	N	*Mean*	STD	N	*Mean*	STD	*F-test*
Other's social attributes[1]	145	0.60	0.81	272	-0.30	0.93	98.16*
Other's unsocial attributes[2]	150	0.22	1.03	271	-0.08	0.95	9.02*
Other's social closure[3]	150	3.28	1.82	275	3.36	1.54	0.21
Aspirations to group intercourse[4]	143	0.49	0.78	286	-0.28	1.01	64.20*

* $p < 0.01$

[1] Integrated variable of perceptions of the other group as polite, cooperative, educated, good-hearted

[2] Integrated variable of perceptions of the other group as miserly and outspoken

[3] Perception of the other group as self-segregated

[4] Integrated variable of readiness to have a relationship with members of the other group, as guests in each other's home and as neighbors

intense reference is innately contradictory. It is plausible that the Arab is driven vis-a-vis the Jew by opposing forces stemming from his minority status which emphasizes the identitional divergence from the majority, as well as pushing them to view the majority as a reference. The Arabs, who are a minority, seemingly leave the members of the Jewish majority more indifferent. In either case, however, identity divergence is clear.

Our questionnaire then shows that, according to self-ratings, Arabs know the majority language, Hebrew, better than the Jews know the minority language, Arabic (Table 2). We can already speak here of a cultural convergence since Hebrew and Arabic appear to be conveyed to both Jews and Arabs, albeit at unequal levels of acquisition.

Table 2
The knowledge of the other's language

Knowledge *of Languages*	*Arabs*			*Jews*			
	N	*Mean*	STD	N	*Mean*	STD	*F-test*
Self-ratings of knowledge of other's language	155	4.49	0.77	289	3.17	1.37	123.59*

*p < 0.01

Yet, as shown by Table 3, the members of the majority generally, though not unanimously, evince a low motivation to learn Arabic; they tend to underrate the general importance of Arabic, its value in the school curriculum, its instrumental importance, communicative role and social utility. In contrast, the Arab respondents appreciate Hebrew on all counts and assert an undeniable motivation to learn it. Jews and Arabs thus illustrate inverse tendencies regarding the code, which is the maker of the other's identity.

When we set the findings of Table 3 in relation to the findings of Table 1, a lack of symmetry appears between Jews and Arabs. The Jews' attitudes toward Arabs and Arabic are quite similar: they appear as distant from the Arabs as a group as from Arabic as a language. Among Arabs, the attitude toward Hebrew tends to be more positive and concomitant with divided and contradictory attitudes toward Jews.

Thus, these findings firstly show that (1) the majority shares an orientation of self-distinction from the minority, and (2) the minority

Table 3
Perceptions of the other's language

Perceptions	*Arabs vis-a-vis Hebrew*			*Jews vis-a-vis Arabic*			
	N	*Mean*	STD	N	*Mean*	STD	*F-test*
General importance[1]	142	1.16	0.51	282	-0.50	0.65	709.34*
Score among other topics[2]	155	-1.16	0.55	288	0.55	0.62	836.25*
School status3	138	0.33	0.75	287	-0.39	0.86	219.48*
Instrumental importance4	149	0.91	0.72	288	-0.39`	0.82	264.90*
Communication role[5]	152	4.40	0.92	286	2.67	1.29	213.11*

*$p < 0.01$

[1] Perception of the other's language related to its uses for the respondent: further education, job prospects, reading papers and books, social relations, TV watching and movies, tourism.

[2] Score of the other's language as an expression of a lack of priority related to other matters of study.

[3] Status at school of the language as a function of the attitude toward the teacher, the atmosphere of the class, the interest level of school books.

[4] Instrumental aspect as relating to the association of the language as a condition for social mobility and encouragement of parents to learn the language for reasons of future mobility.

[5] Expresses the willingness to learn the language for the purpose of speaking with people and drawing pleasure from it.

itself views the majority as a reference only in specific respects, and not in those in which it strongly asserts its distinctiveness from the majority. Accordingly, the data describe majority-minority relations where (3) the minority acquires and appreciates the importance of the majority's language, but at the same time (4) retains the use of its own language in the community.

On the other hand, (5) the general attitude of the majority is one of disrespect for both the language and the group, (6) which, however, does not prevent given segments of the majority from recognizing the value of the minority's language.

In brief, Hechter, who emphasizes the diffusion of the dominant culture and the erasing of that of the minority is not supported by our data. We are closer to Grillo's approach which spotlights the possibility that a dominant culture, i.e., the orientation of the majority, is not necessarily unifying but may also encourage pluralism. We, however, also consider the minority's velleities as having an impact, albeit less than that of the dominant culture, which was confirmed in the kind of *bilingualism* which we found in the case investigated.

Inter-Individual Relations

It is on the basis of the models of bilingualism exhibited by Jews and Arabs in Israel that we now consider the impact of inter-individual relations and the extent to which they account for intra-group variation in attitudes toward languages and groups.

The subcategories within both the majority and the minority, which have more frequent relations with individuals of the other group are, in fact, principally from mixed Jewish-Arab neighborhoods. The Jewish population of these neighborhoods is, in general, made up of Middle-Easterners and North Africans (83% of the Jewish Jaffa respondents, by country of origin of grandfathers, but only 33% of the Jewish respondents of Tel-Aviv). These Jews belong to the Jewish lower class and were, in many cases, native speakers of Arabic who shifted to Hebrew after immigrating to Israel. On the part of the minority, it is, instead, most often spoken by people who have limited prospects for social mobility: settled blue-collar, petty-bourgeoisie or lower-strata of clerks. Table 4 shows that this holds as well for our own sample.

Table 4
The distribution of the sample according to settings of residence and social status of fathers

Group of population	N	SES *Mean Scores*[1]	STD
Arabs in Kfar Kassem	84	-0.85	0.40
Arabs in Jaffa	71	-0.61	0.62
Jews in Jaffa	98	-0.58	0.70
Jews in Tel-Aviv	191	0.55	0.83

[1] SES scores were computed on the basis of three factors: occupational prestige of the fathers' occupations, his number of years of formal education and the number of individuals per room in the family apartment.

Table 4 shows that the socioeconomic status of the Jews in the homogeneous neighborhood (Tel-Aviv) is higher than the status of the Jews in the heterogeneous neighborhood (Jaffa). Among the Arabs, however, those who live in the heterogeneous neighborhood (Jaffa) are of a relatively (though modestly) higher status than those who live in the homogeneous village (Kfar Kassem). As a result, Jews and Arabs of the mixed neighborhood tend to be close to each other in terms of socioeconomic status (SES). As in any case where stratification differentiates a majority from a minority, here, too, the mobile elements of the minority tend to have more contact with the lower levels of the majority group. In the context of these ethnic and socioeconomic differences among neighborhood groups, the questions which now arise are:

To what extent is the frequency of inter-personal contacts associated with the reciprocal attitudes of members of the majority and of the minority? To what extent do these contacts influence their perceptions of the other's language? With Tables 5 and 6, we first focus on the latter

Table 5
Jews: Attitudes toward language and group

Perceptions of the other's language						
Percept. other Group	Knowl. score	General import.	Topic score	School status	Instrum. import.	Commun. role
1. *Homogeneous community*						
Social attrib.	-0.0237 173 p = 0.379	0.1324 172 p = 0.042	0.0573 175 p = 0.226	0.0264 175 p = 0.364	0.2028 175 p = 0.004	0.2833 174 p = 0.000
Unsocial attrib.	-0.0085 172 p = 0.456	-0.0258 169 p = 0.370	0.0264 174 p = 0.340	-0.0311 174 p = 0.465	-0.0868 174 p = 0.495	-0.1056 172 p = 0.084
Social closure	0.0218 176 p = 0.387	0.0459 174 p = 0.274	0.0311 178 p = 0.340	0.0066 178 p = 0.465	-0.0090 178 p = 0.495	0.0383 177 p = 0.306
Aspir. to intercrse	-0.0406 186 p = 0.291	0.1898 185 p = 0.005	-0.0093 189 p = 0.450	-0.0070 188 p = 0.462	0.1118 189 p = 0.063	0.3414 188 p = 0.000
2. *Mixed community*						
Social attrib.	0.2653 98 p = 0.004	0.3915 98 p = 0.000	-0.0181 98 p = 0.430	0.3868 98 p = 0.000	0.3286 98 p = 0.000	0.3533 98 p = 0.000
Unsocial attrib.	-0.1892 98 p = 0.031	-0.1216 98 p = 0.116	-0.2473 98 p = 0.007	-0.02871 98 p = 0.002	-0.1907 98 p = 0.030	-0.1938 98 p = 0.028
Social closure	0.0954 98 p = 0.175	-0.0225 98 p = 0.413	0.0641 98 p = 0.265	0.0716 98 p = 0.242	0.1464 98 p = 0.075	0.0348 98 p = 0.367
Aspir. to intercrse	0.2352 98 p = 0.010	0.4119 98 p = 0.000	0.0964 98 p = 0.172	0.3827 98 p = 0.000	0.3524 98 p = 0.000	0.5196 98 p = 0.000

issue. Tables 5 and 6 show that in both groups, and with little difference among categories, two aspects are bound, more than others, to positive attitudes toward the other group's language. These aspects are aspirations to intercourse with individuals of the other group, and, to a lesser extent, positive social images of the other group. This is first true of the Jews of the homogeneous community, and then of the Arabs of both categories, but it is also clear for the Jews of the mixed community.

Table 6
Arabs: Attitudes toward language and group

Perceptions of the other's language

Percept. other Group	Knowl. score	General import.	Topic score	School status	Instrum. import.	Commun. role
1. *Homogeneous community*						
Social attrib.	0.2975 81 p = 0.003	0.3088 70 p = 0.005	-0.1089 81 p = 0.167	0.5353 73 p = 0.000	0.2005 78 p = 0.039	0.3395 79 p = 0.001
Unsocial attrib.	-0.0458 80 p = 0.342	-0.0821 71 p = 0.248	0.1027 81 p = 0.181	-0.1127 73 p = 0.171	-0.1504 79 p = 0.093	-0.2246 79 p = 0.023
Social closure	-0.0022 80 p = 0.492	0.1096 70 p = 0.183	-0.0717 80 p = 0.088	-0.1611 72 p = 0.088	0.1403 79 p = 0.109	-0.0713 78 p = 0.268
Aspir. to intercrse	0.2475 74 p = 0.017	0.3991 65 p = 0.000	0.0454 74 p = 0.350	0.5615 69 p = 0.000	0.4307 74 p = 0.000	0.3560 74 p = 0.001
2. *Mixed community*						
Social attrib.	0.0390 68 p = 0.004	0.1739 63 p = 0.086	0.1710 64 p = 0.088	0.3359 59 p = 0.005	0.1718 63 p = 0.000	0.3045 64 p = 0.007
Unsocial attrib.	0.0001 68 p = 0.500	0.1111 64 p = 0.185	0.0099 69 p = 0.468	-0.0232 61 p = 0.430	-0.0205 66 p = 0.435	-0.1396 68 p = 0.128
Social closure	-0.1349 68 p = 0.135	-0.0385 68 p = 0.378	-0.0023 70 p = 0.492	0.0477 62 p = 0.356	-0.0782 67 p = 0.265	0.0430 69 p = 0.363
Aspir. to intercrse	0.3594 68 p = 0.001	0.2658 67 p = 0.015	0.0765 69 p = 0.266	0.5017 63 p = 0.000	0.4426 67 p = 0.000	0.600 69 p = 0.000

Beyond these correlations, however, in order to investigate the genuine differences among categories in these very respects, we compared the attitudes of the subcategories, in both groups, regarding the various aspects of their images of the other group and of its language.

It has already been reported in former works that inter-group contacts develop on an egalitarian basis, in situations of relative isolation such as in total institutions (Kraemer, 1978, 1990; Mar'i, 1989). Our own data, however, gainsay the contact hypothesis as for an open setting: on most counts, the Jews' and Arabs' attitudes toward the other group and its language do not differ according to the kind of neighborhood where they live (Tables 7 and 8).

As for the Jews, and in drastic contradiction with contact-hypothesis theory, there is little difference between the two subcategories in both their attitudes toward Arabic and toward Arabs. Regarding the two aspects where there were significant differences (the sociability image of Arabs and the general importance of Arabic), it appears that, in comparison to the residents of the mixed neighborhood, the respondents of the Jewish homogeneous neighborhood are less negative in their appreciation of Arabs and more negative in their appreciation of Arabic. The first finding seems to relate to the lower-class condition of the Jewish inhabitants of the mixed neighborhood and to sustain Myrdal's "poor white" theory (1962; see also Ben-Rafael, Sharot, 1991). These elements are seemingly more threatened than are individuals of higher socioeconomic status by the confusion of the social distinction between the majority and the minority. Moreover, it is likely that in this case their negative attitude toward Arabs is further sharpened by the fact that the low-class strata by and large belong to a particular ethnic category, the Middle-Eastern and North African communities. These communities, which share some cultural and linguistic resemblance to the minority group, may see in this resemblance a risk of downgrading their status within the majority, in the eyes of other Jewish groups.

For this very same reason, however, one may explain that the Middle-Eastern and North African respondents are also more appreciative of Arabic, which they are familiar with as their own language of origin. Regarding all these circumstances, however, it seems that we obtained relatively few findings differentiating the two subcategories of Jews. This tends to evince that the general negative attitude of the majority vis-a-vis the minority is here a predominant factor.

Table 7
Jews' perceptions of Arabs and Arabic

	Social Settings						
	Homogeneous			*Heterogeneous*			
Perceptions of	N	*Mean*	STD	N	*Mean*	STD	*F-test*
1. Arabs							
Other's social attributes[1]	175	-0.12	0.85	97	-0.64	0.98	20.68*
Other's unsocial attributes[2]	174	-0.15	0.92	97	0.05	1.00	2.92
Other's social closure[3]	178	3.47	1.45	97	3.14	1.70	2.85
Aspirations to group intercourse[4]	189	-0.24	0.98	97	-0.36	1.06	0.85
2. Arabic							
General importance[5]	185	-0.58	0.61	97	-0.36	0.70	7.10*
Score among other topics[6]	191	0.58	0.55	97	0.47	0.72	2.17
School status[7]	190	-0.39	0.89	97	-0.39	0.80	0.00
Instrumental importance[8]	191	-0.35	0.85	97	-0.45	0.76	0.93
Communication role[9]	189	2.70	1.27	97	2.62	1.36	0.28

*$p < 0.01$

[1] Integrated variable of perceptions of the other group as polite, cooperative, educated, good-hearted

[2] Integrated variable of perceptions of the other group as miserly and outspoken

[3] Perception of the other group as self-segregated

[4] Integrated variable of readiness to have a relationship with members of the other group, as guests in each other's home and as neighbors

[5] Perception of the other's language related to its uses for the respondent: further education, job prospects, reading papers and books, social relations, TV watching and movies, tourism

[6] Score of the other's language as expressing the priority of learning it, related to other matters of study

[7] Status at school of the language as a function of the attitude toward the teacher, the atmosphere of the class, the interest level of school books

[8] Instrumental aspect as relating to the association of the language as a condition for social mobility and encouragement of parents to learn the language for reasons of future mobility

[9] Expresses the willingness to learn the language for the purpose of speaking with people and drawing pleasure from it.

Table 8
Arabs' perceptions of Jews and Hebrew[1]

	Homogeneous Setting			*Heterogeneous Setting*			
Perceptions of	N	*Mean*	STD	N	*Mean*	STD	*F-test*
1. Jews							
Perceptions 1	81	0.62	0.78	64	0.58	0.85	0.07
Perceptions 2	81	0.33	1.01	69	0.08	1.04	2.23
Perception 3	80	3.13	1.71	70	3.46	1.93	1.25
Aspirations to group relations	74	0.35	0.79	69	0.63	0.74	4.76*
2. *Hebrew*							
General importance	73	1.11	0.52	69	1.22	0.50	1.82
Score among other topics	84	-1.15	0.50	71	-1.18	0.61	0.13
School status	75	0.88	0.76	63	0.88	0.75	0.00
Instrumental importance	81	1.04	0.64	68	0.75	0.79	6.05*
Communication role	82	4.63	0.66	70	4.13	1.10	12.18***

*p < 0.05; **p < 0.01; [1] Same variables as in Table 6.

As for the Arab respondents, in either type of neighborhood, Jews are both admired for their "intellectual force" and "sociability," and blamed for their "outspokenness" and "miserliness." The data uphold the assumption that the Arabs of both categories share mixed feelings about the Jews. Here, too, it seems that more inter-personal contact has little effect on Arabs' perceptions of Jews as a group. One may suggest that practical benefits for Arabs from their relations with Jews may counterbalance the outcome of probably frustrating contact with the majority. That this contact is frustrating we can see in the fact that the only significant difference we found between the Arab subcategories refers to aspirations to more contact with Jews: the Arabs who live in a homogeneous setting and have thus less contact with Jews appear to be more willing than those who live in the mixed neighborhood to increase their inter-personal contact with Jews. This finding definitely rules out the contact-hypothesis theory. On the other hand, we also find that those Arabs who live in a homogeneous neighborhood and, consequently, have less interaction with Jews, seem more appreciative of Hebrew.

These data weaken the Contact Hypothesis theory, and corroborate Myrdal's long-standing approach: the members of the majority have more contact with the minority and who exhibit a rejectionist attitude vis-a-vis Arabs do not constitute a factor facilitating the Arab's integration into society at large. To this we add that such negative attitudes also impact these same Arabs' response to the Jewish society. Yet, we add here two remarks. First, we have shown that a predominantly negative attitude on the part of the majority vis-a-vis the minority and its language may leave but little variation which can be accounted for by the frequency of inter-personal contact. Second, for the minority elements who are in greater contact with members of the majority, fringe benefits may attenuate the acrimony resulting from frustrating personal contacts, and thereby lessen the differences in attitudes of minority members who have more or less contacts with the majority.

Furthermore, it is interesting to note that, quite independent of the actual frequency of intercourse between members of the majority and the minority, aspirations to intercourse and positive images of the other group do correlate with more positive images of the significance of learning the other group's language. This leaves the door open for influences and education in both subcategories of the two groups.

Inter-Setting Influences

The third facet of cultural convergence envisaged here consists of external influences stemming from the setting's relations with the outside. We discuss this aspect with respect to the attitudes of Israeli Jews and Arabs toward English.

English is valued in Israel by both Jews and Arabs, which in itself is, undeniably, a factor of cultural convergence. As expected according to Bourdieu's cultural-market theory, however, this common emphasis on English by both groups does not preclude a differentiation between majority and minority with respect to the extent that they obtain control over this resource. Table 9 shows the significant difference in this respect between the samples. The Arab students feel weaker in the mastery of English than the Jewish students, and these self-ratings are easily explained by the fact that for the Arabs, English is a third language of study at school, after Arabic and Hebrew, while for the Jews, it is the second language, right after Hebrew. Jews thus learn more English than do Arabs. Corollarily, the Jews give greater importance than Arabs, to English in general and as a school matter. The Arab respondents also tend to view English much less favorably than the Jews as for its social and communicative utility and general importance in society.

Table 9
Attitudes of Arabs and Jews toward English

	Arabs			*Jews*			
Perceptions of English	N	*Mean*	STD	N	*Mean*	STD	*F-test*
Self-ratings of mastery[1]	155	3.68	1.15	289	4.19	0.88	26.39**
Status at school[2]	131	0.16	1.11	287	-0.06	0.97	4.26*
Instrument. value[3]	141	-0.37	1.22	287	0.21	0.78	35.47**
Uses[4]	140	-0.52	1.06	284	0.22	0.88	57.72**
Motivation[5]	155	-0.08	1.48	289	0.07	0.66	2.21

*p < 0.05; **p < 0.01

[1] Students were asked to rate themselves with respect to their mastery of English

[2] Attitudes of students vis-a-vis English as a matter of school study; this integrated variable includes the image of the teacher, the appreciation of school books, liking the class atmosphere, etc.

[3] The instrumental perception of English includes: the extent that learning English is associated with improving career expectations; pressures of parents in this direction.

[4] Relating the study of English to job opportunities, high education, reading newspapers and books, forming social relationships, TV and movies, tourism.

[5] The priority that the English language is given over other matters of study at school.

The difference of mastery of an attribute which they appreciate but which is better controlled by the Jews seemingly implies for the Arabs a problem of self-esteem and dignity. The smaller practical role which English represents for them is obviously bound to their restricted access to the usually privileged positions which require English. A third language may also seem a luxury for a minority which first faces the challenge of mastering the majority's language in addition to its own.

Hence, it is in accordance with Bourdieu's theory that we obtained a consensus between the majority and the minority about the importance of English as linguistic capital. By the same token, we see that outside influences do imprint themselves on a cultural convergence of the majority and the minority. Within the social reality, however, this status of English means that aside from and through the very consensus which it represents, it also contributes to social inequality. English, indeed, appears now as linguistic capital, i.e., as a kind of cultural capital which distinguishes, in terms of prestige, between a majority better armed to gain control of the language, and a minority less able to. On the other hand, it is along the expectations of exchange theory that the majority's quasi-monopolization of English is concomitant with the minority's underrating of the significance of its own weaker control of the language. This minority is not ready to concede the price, in terms of self-depreciation, for its feeble hold of a prestigious cultural resource, as expected by the majority, which controls this resource and thus tends to overvalue it.

Conclusion

This paper analyzed the cultural convergence of Israel's Jews and Arabs in the area of bilingualism. Israel is a setting where Jews and Arabs represent conflicting identities but where Hebrew, the dominant language, Arabic, the minority's official language, and English, the first foreign language, are all diffused—though unevenly—in the majority as well as the minority. We asked to what extent this diffusion conveys a cultural convergence of Arabs and Jews. This cultural convergence is elaborated on by considering the different sources which it stems from.

The determinant factor of inter-group interaction is the dominant culture, which legitimizes a linguistic and cultural pluralistic model of majority-minority relations. Within this context, Arabic is by no means held in high respect by the majority, which tends to downgrade its value and to associate its status with the condition of its speakers. Among other factors, the underprivileged status of Arabs in Israel, Israel's conflictual relations with the Arab environment, and the fact that Arabic is of little use as a means of communication in Israel since Israeli Arabs know Hebrew, all account for the restricted interest on the part of Jews for Arabic. These factors explain why Arabic is most often left out of the Jews' cultural repertoire—even though it is diffused by school.

On the other hand, the minority, which is dependent on the language majority, is determined to acquire it, though it does not concede its linguistic particularism. Differentiating between Hebrew and Jews, the minority enriches itself—paradoxically enough—linguistically, by becoming bilingual. The price it pays for this enrichment is the downgrading of the social value of its own language.

This case disavows the Hechterian "internal colonialism" unifying model which expects the vanishing of minority cultures and the assimilation of minorities into the dominant culture. Rather, the data support Grillo's acknowledgment of the possibility that a dominant culture itself encourages the retention of particularism by groups from which the majority wants to distinguish itself. Moreover, our findings also support Ben-Rafael's contention (1994) that the minority's own velleities do play a role in this respect. Hence, that the Arab minority is definitely attached to its own identity which basically diverges from that of the Jews, is by no means a neglectable factor in their determination to acquire Hebrew without deserting Arabic as a community language, in spite of its downgrading.

We also found that more personal relations have no positive effect on Arabs' perceptions of Jews as a group. In fact, Arabs who live in a homogeneous setting and have thus less contact with Jews are the ones who are more willing to increase such contact with Jews and are also more appreciative of Hebrew. This finding gainsays the contact-hypothesis theory on the side of the Arabs.

Our data also disavow this theory on the part of Jews. Corroborating Myrdal's approach, the members of the majority who have more contact with the minority—a relatively underprivileged subcategory—appear as a factor which does not facilitate the integration of Arabs. However, the predominantly negative attitude of the majority in general vis-a-vis the minority and its language, in any case, leaves little room for a variation which could be accounted for by the frequency of inter-personal contact. The rather feeble aspirations to intercourse or positive images of the other group—which correlates which more positive images of the other group's language and its learning—do not especially concern those who have, in practice, more interaction with Arabs.

Israeli culture, moreover, comprises a cosmopolite aspect which is the outcome of the inter-setting interaction and is best illustrated by the importance of English. The cultural importance of English is agreed upon by both Jews and Arabs, but the control of the language is much stronger among the majority. In accordance with cultural-market theory, the minority's convergence toward the majority in this respect represents, at the same time, a process of cultural convergence and a recognition and enforcement of the distinction of the majority vis-a-vis the minority. However, and in an exchange-theory vein, the minority also appears to protect its dignity by remaining somehow behind the majority's appreciation of English. The minority appears to minimize the social significance of its weakness, reflecting, by the same token, its immediate and much greater interest in the acquisition of the dominant language, i.e., Hebrew. The paradoxical outcome is that the weaker group appreciates the majority language, Hebrew, more than the neutral foreign language, English, which is not necessarily the case with anyone who belongs to the majority itself. In sum,

(1) as for the more central aspect of majority-minority relations,
- some members of the majority may be sensitive to Arabic culture
- the minority clearly converges toward the majority
- without concession of its own community identity
- despite the social downgrading of Arabic

(2) as for the impact of personal relations,
- inner differentiations of either group are minimal

(3)as for outside influences,
- English creates a convergence of value criteria
- this convergence of English is not symmetrical
- its very diffusion deepens the inequality between the groups

Thus, data in the realm of language activity teach us about aspects of the cultural convergence of Jews and Arabs that could hardly be evinced by other strategies. We learned about the development of a form of bilingualism in the minority which stands in contradiction to the subordinate status of the group. This bilingualism constitutes a pattern of acculturation which does not imply assimilation or positive inter-personal interaction with members of the majority. Arabs do become "Israelis" as far as it is indicated by their Hebraization and their attitudes toward Hebrew and English. Paradoxically, this *Israelization of Arabs* is concomitant with a tendency among Jews to exhibit a stronger outlook toward the outside.

Notes

* In R. Nettler (ed.) *Medieval and Modern Perspectives on Muslim-Jewish Relations,* Reading (UK): Harwood Academic Publishers, 1995.

Bibliography

Ben-Rafael, E. (1994) *Language, Identity and Social Division: The Case of Israel,* Oxford: Oxford University Press.

Ben-Rafael, E., Brosh, H. (1991) "A sociological study of second language diffusion: The obstacles to Arabic teaching in the Israeli school" *Language Problems and Language Planning,* 15/1: 1-24.

Ben-Rafael, E., Sharot, S. (1991) *Ethnicity, Religion and Class in Israeli Society,* Cambridge: Cambridge University Press.
Blau, P.M. (1964) *Exchange and Power in Social Life,* NY: John Wiley and Sons.
Bourdieu, P. (1982) *Ce que parler veut dire,* Paris: Fayard.
Bourdieu, P. (1987) *Choses Dites,* Paris: Minuit.
Bourdieu, P., Passeron, J.-C. (1970) *La Reproduction—Elements d'une Theorie du Système d'Enseignement,* Paris: Minuit.
Brewer, M.B., Kramer, R.M. (1985) "The Psychology of Intergroup Attitudes and Behavior" *Annual Review of Psychology,* 36: 219-243.
Brewer, M.B., Miller, N. (1984) "Beyond the Contact Hypothesis: Theoretical Perspectives on Desegregation." Miller, N., Brewer, M. (eds.) *Groups in Contact: The Psychology of Desegregation,* New York: Academic Press.
Brosh, H. (1988) *The Effect of Learning Arabic in Elementary and School on Achievement in Literary Arabic in the Seventh Grade,* Tel Aviv: The School of Education, Tel Aviv University.
Chomsky, W. (1957) *Hebrew: The Eternal Language,* Philadelphia: Jewish Publication Society of America.
Cooper, R.L. (1989) *Language Planning and Social Change,* Cambridge: Cambridge University Press.
Cooper, R.L., Fishman, J. A. (1977) "A study of language attitudes" in Fishman, J.A., Cooper, R.L., Conrad, A. W. (eds.) *The Spread of English—The Sociology of English as an Additional Language,* Rowley (Mass.): Newbury, 239-276.
Dorian, N. (ed.) (1989) *Investigating Obsolescence: Studies in Language Contraction and Death,* Cambridge: Cambridge University Press.
Dorian, N. (1982) "Language loss and maintenance in language contact situations" in Lambert, R. D., Freed, B.F. (eds.) *The Loss of Language Skills,* NY: Rowley.
Edwards, J. (1988) *Language, Society and Identity,* Oxford: Basil Blackwell.
Fasold, R. (1987) *The Sociolinguistics of Society,* Oxford: Basil Blackwell.
Fishman, Cooper, Conrad (eds.) *The Spread of English—The Sociology of English as an Additional Language,* Rowley (Mass.): Newbury, 239-276.
Fishman, J. (1989) *Language and Ethnicity in Minority Sociolinguistic Perspective,* Clevedon, Philadelphia: Multilingual Matters.
Fishman, J. A. (1987) "English: Neutral tool or ideological protagonist? A 19th-Century East-Central European Jewish intellectual views English from afar," *English World Wide* 8, 1: 1-10.
Giddens, A. (1987) "Structuralism, post-structuralism and the production of culture" in Giddens, A., Turner, J. (eds.) *Social Theory Today,* Oxford: Basil Blackwell, 195-223.
Giglioli, P.P. (ed.) (1987) *Language and Social Context,* Harmondsworth (UK): Penguin Books.
Gordon, M.M. (1964) *Assimilation in American Life,* NY: Oxford University Press.
Gorny, Y. (1986) *The Arab Question and the Jewish Problem,* Tel-Aviv: Am Oved (Heb).
Grillo, R.D. (1989) *Dominant Languages: Language and Hierarchy in Britain and in France,* Cambridge, U.K.: Cambridge University Press.
Gumperz, J.J. (1982) *Discourse Strategies,* London: Cambridge University Press.
Gumperz, J.J. (1987) "The speech community" in Giglioli, P.P. (ed.) *op. cit.,* 219-231.
Habermas, J. (1988) *Le Discours Philosophique de la Modernit?,* Paris: Gallimard.
Hechter, M. (1975) *Internal Colonialism,* Berkeley: University of California Press
Hechter, M. (1978) "Group formation and the cultural division of labor," *American Journal of Sociology* 84: 293-318.
Hewstone, M., Brown, R. (1986) "Contact is not enough: An intergroup perspective on the contact hypothesis" in Hewstone, M., Brown, R. (eds.), *Contact and Conflict in Intergroup Encounters,* Oxford: Basil Blackwell.

Homans, G.C. (1974) *Social Behavior: Its Elementary Forms,* NY: Harcourt, Brace and World.

Horowitz, D., Lissak, M. (1989) *Trouble in Utopia: The Overburdened Polity of Israel,* Albany: State University of New York Press.

Horowitz, D.L. (1975) "Ethnic identity" in Glazer, N., Moynihan, D.P. (eds.), *Ethnicity: Theory and Experience,* Cambridge, Mass: Harvard University Press, 111-140.

ICBS (1989) *Statistical Abstract of Israel,* 1989, No. 40, Jerusalem.

Isaacs, H. (1967) *American Jews in Israel,* NY: J Day.

Kraemer, R. (1978) *Intergroup Contact Between Jews and Arabs in an Israeli High School,* Tel-Aviv: School of Education, Tel-Aviv University.

Kraemer, R. (1990) *Social Psychological Factors Related to the Study of Arabic among Israeli Jewish High School Students,* Tel-Aviv: Tel-Aviv University, School of Education.

Lal, B.B. (1983) "Perspectives on ethnicity: Old wine in new bottles," *Ethnic and Racial Studies* 6: 15-173.

Landau, J.M. (1987) "Hebrew and Arabic in the State of Israel: Political aspects of the language issue," *IJSL* 67.

Levy, S., Guttman, L. (1976) *Values and Attitudes of Israeli Youth,* vols. 1&2, Jerusalem: Institute of Applied Social Research (Heb).

Lustick, I. (198) *Arabs in the Jewish State: Israel's Control of a National Minority,* Austin: Texas University Press.

Mar'i, M.K. (1989) "Arab education in Israel" in Krausz, E. (ed.) *Education in Comparative Context—Studies of Israeli Society,* New Brunswick: Transaction, 91-118.

McKay, J., Lewine, F. (1978) "Ethnicity and the ethnic group: A conceptual analysis and reformulation," *Ethnic and Racial Studies* 1: 412-427.

Myrdal, G. (1962) *An American Dilemma,* NY: McGraw-Hill.

Nakleh, K. (1975) "Cultural determinants of collective identity: The case of the Arabs in Israel," *New Outlook* 18/7, 31-40.

Peres, Y. (1976) *Ethnic Relations in Israel,* Tel-Aviv: Sifryat Hapoalim (Heb).

Ronen, M., Seckbach, F., Cooper R.L. (1977) "Foreign loanwords in Hebrew newspapers" in Fishman, Cooper, Conrad (eds.) *op. cit.,* 229-235.

Rosenbaum, Y., Nadel, E., Cooper, R.L., Fishman, J.A. (1977) "English in Keren Kayemet street" in Fishman, Cooper, Conrad (eds.) *op. cit.,* 239-276.

Rosenfeld, H. (1978) "The class situation of the Arab national minority in Israel," *Comparative Studies in Society and History* 20: 374-407.

Rubinstein, A. (1980) *The Constitutional Law in Israel,* Tel-Aviv: Shocken.

Seckbach, F., Cooper, R.L. (1977) "The maintenance of English in Ramat Eshkol" in Fishman, Cooper and Conrad, *op. cit.,* 168-178.

Semyonov, M., Lewin-Epstein, N. (1987) *Hewers of Wood and Drawers of Water,* Ithaca, NJ: Cornell Institute of Labor Studies.

Smooha, S. (1976) "Arabs and Jews in Israel: Minority-majority relations," *Megamot* 22/4: 397-424 (Heb).

Spolsky, B. (1989) "Bilingualism" in Newmeyer (ed.), *The Cambridge Survey IV/ Language: The Socio-Cultural Context,* Cambridge: Cambridge University Press, 100-118.

Wardhaugh, R. (1987) *Languages in Competition,* Oxford: Basil Blackwell.

Woolard, K. (1989) "Language convergence and language death as social processes," in Dorian, N. (ed.), *op. cit.* 355-368.

Part 4

Electronic Media and Social Diversity

13

Twenty Years of Television in Israel: Are There Long-Run Effects on Values and Cultural Practices?

Elihu Katz and Hadassah Haas

Television broadcasting was introduced in Israel late, after years of debate over its likely effects. Opponents of the medium, led by David Ben-Gurion, thought that renascent Hebrew culture would be undermined by the introduction of foreign values, that the People of the Book would turn into the people of television, that ascetic and pioneering values would be uprooted by consumerism, that ideological politics would be displaced by personality politics. Those in favor of the introduction of television argued that the medium carried no intrinsic message, that it would do whatever it was told: inform, educate, teach Hebrew, absorb immigrants, foster creativity, enfranchise marginal groups, show Israel's achievements to itself and to the world.

The absence of television seemed more acute on the eve of the Six Day War of 1967 inasmuch as TV broadcasts were being received from the surrounding Arab states. Indeed, television was introduced in Israel shortly after this war—not only to right the ostensible propaganda disadvantage, but because it was thought, wishfully, that the new medium would make for effective communication between Israelis and people in the newly occupied territories. Some of those who opposed television thought that this was simply a handy rationalization, but in the post-war euphoria, not many opponents were left.

In 1970—but without any specific reference to the fact that television broadcasting had just begun—the Ministry of Education and Culture commissioned a major study of the uses of leisure, culture and communication in Israel (Katz and Gurevitch, 1974). Twenty years later, in 1990, a repeat study was commissioned by the Ministry and the US-Israel Bi-National Science Foundation. Based on face-to-face interviews with national samples of 3000 Israelis (the 1990 study includes the Arab sector as well), the two studies are comparable in almost every respect. By good fortune, therefore, we are in a position to assess the long-run effects of introducing television on a whole society. This is much easier said than done, however, because so many other things have happened during the 20 years between the studies. It is only at great risk, therefore, that one can attribute causality to television in accounting for the changes in Israeli culture and society during this period. It is especially ironic, because not a few of the changes that emerge from comparing the two studies coincide with the predictions of its effect—more often with those of its opponents than with its proponents.

Thus, the trouble with trying to analyze the effects of 20 years of television is that this same 20-year period also includes two wars, a doubling of the population, and an increase in the level of general education such that the society, on average, is three years more educated than in 1970. Moreover, 1977 saw the first overturn of Israeli politics from left to right and the coming to political maturity of the second generation of immigrants from Asian and African countries. The new parity between citizens of Eastern and Western background challenged not only the long-standing political consensus, but also the (predominantly Western) cultural order. During the 20-year period, an additional hour of leisure was added to the day, a second day off from work was given (Friday) and a rise in the standard of living achieved. To study the long-run effects of television, therefore, one has to know how to sort out the effects of television from those of war, affluence, education, political change, cultural pluralism and so on!

Having sounded the warning, let us proceed nevertheless to examine changing trends in the values and cultural practices of Jewish Israelis over these twenty years, and to speculate about the extent to which they may be attributable to television.[1] To accomplish this, the paper will proceed as follows: (1) it will present an overview of the ways in which television broadcasting was institutionalized in Israel; (2) it will consider the patterns of television viewing; (3) it will report on major changes in the patterns of consuming culture and the arts, including reading; (4) it will review the study's findings concerning value changes in Israeli society during this period; (5) it will report on the changes in the functions and gratifications provided by the media, old and new, with respect to these values. Having done so, we shall return to weigh the possible long-run effects of television.

Television: The Israeli Version

From its inception, broadcasting in Israel was a monopoly service provided at first by the Government, and, from 1965, by a BBC-like authority financed by a license fee and directed by a Board of Governors representing the political spectrum but independent of Government. When television was established in 1968, joining radio as one of the services of the monopolistic Israel Broadcasting Authority (IB), Israel Television operated only one channel—which it yielded during the daytime hours to the Educational Broadcasting service of the Ministry of Education. Cable television by subscription was introduced in the early 90s, and a second over-the-air channel (like the British ITV) was introduced in 1993, financed by advertising but overseen by a public Board, different from that of the IBA.

Before the very recent introduction of multiple channels, Israel TV had excelled in coverage of news and public affairs, although this achievement was sometimes impeded by the overly politicized appointments of the Governing Board and of the Director General. As good as it was at public affairs, it was poor, at best, in original drama and light entertainment. Jokers used to say that Israel television could well do without drama and entertainment, since there is plenty of that in the news.

In its best days, the main 9 pm news attracted 70% of the population on an average evening. Critics and advocates of multiple channels objected that a society cannot claim to be democratic if it has only one television channel and one major news bulletin. Yet, the evidence shows that this highly politicized society collected itself for the nightly news magazine and willingly accepted its agenda for political discussion. There was no evidence of brainwashing: hawks and doves, Jews and Arabs viewed the monopolistic news magazine, believed it on the whole, and used it to talk politics not only in like-thinking groups but across political divisions.[2] Indeed, the 9 pm news magazine became a sort of civic ritual during which the society communed with itself. There was an informal norm that attendance was "required," and that there were to be no intrusions during the news—no telephone calls, for example. American politicians now are talking wishfully about how to organize "electronic town meetings"—having blithely exchanged their three channels for hundreds. Rather than undemocratic, the lesson of 15 years of Israel TV is that participatory democracy may be enhanced, rather than impeded, by gathering its citizens in a single public space set aside for receiving and discussing reliable reports on the issues of the day.

The introduction of multiple channels has changed the picture. The heavy emphasis on news and public affairs has given way to much lighter entertainment on the new channels. Even the many cheap-to-produce political talkshows are sprinkled with very high doses of sensation, scandal, personalities, provocations, and pop. And advertising interrupts everything. Ironically, the introduction of a competing news magazine (at the same hour as the original) has lowered the total number of viewers of both programs—as if the very offer of choice abolished the norm of collective viewing of the television news.

Like in other countries—not only the smaller ones—a high percentage of television programming is imported from abroad, especially from the United States. The new second channel promised to commission many more programs from local producers, but with double the hours of broadcasting, the overall ratio of domestic to imported programming has declined, if anything, to well below 50%. If one also takes account of the dozen or more cable channels—now reaching some 60% of the population—the proportion of homemade programming is tiny.

The idea that *fewer* hours of broadcasting might result in better programs does not occur to anybody. Since its inception in 1968, Israel TV has gone from three nights per week of experimental broadcasting, to six nights per week, and, after a religious/political/ cultural battle over Sabbath-eve broadcasting, to seven nights. The next frontier was breakfast television. And with the inauguration of cable channels and the second over-the-air channel, television in Israel has become the non-stop public utility so familiar in the rest of the world.

The Viewers

Apart from a few religious and secular ascetics, every home (94%) has a television set, and the modal viewing time is 2-3 hours. More telling, perhaps, is that one third of the leisure time of adult Israelis is spent viewing television. There are five hours unspoken for on working days, of which an average of 1.7 hours go to viewing TV, and of the combined 14.1 hours of leisure on the two days of the weekend, 4.3 hours go to TV.[3] Compared to 1970, the added hours of leisure come from a shorter workday and a longer weekend, in addition to the reduced time spent on housework, averaging over an hour a day. In a large sense, television may be said to be consuming all of the extra leisure time made available since 1970 without major harm to other activities. Surprisingly, it has not even reduced time spent outside the home. Nevertheless, in close-up, one should note the decline in time spent sleeping, eating, reading newspapers and books, and listening to the radio. Time spent on each of these activities has been reduced since 1970, although only by minutes, not hours, per day.

Men watch more hours of TV than women. Older people and the less educated are heavier viewers.

When the first channel was just being launched in 1970, Israelis ranked their preferences among television offerings as information first, entertainment second, and culture third. Fifty five per cent put information in first place. In 1990, information and entertainment were ranked first by a smaller proportion of viewers (43%), tied for first place with entertainment (43%). That does not mean that they wish the quality of programming to be lower: other data suggest, rather, that they are asking for more variety. They also want more "familiar" programs—those that are home-produced—even while criticizing the news for being too domestic and not worldly enough.

It is very difficult to answer the question whether television has increased or decreased attention to civic affairs. Israel is considered to be a country of avid news consumers, and during the years of monopolistic national broadcasting the most highly rated program on television by far was the evening news. Radio news bulletins and magazines were, and still are, highly attended. Yet, comparing 1990 with 1970, we note some decline in viewer preference for news over other genres, and a substantial decline in the total audience for TV news (especially since the introduction of competing channels). The level of newspaper reading remains very high (some 90% read a daily newspaper), but the habit of reading two newspapers has given way to reading only one—especially since the major evening tabloids are distributed, in effect, at the same hour as the morning papers. Also the number of newspapers has declined.

Is television responsible for any of this? Perhaps so. It may be argued that in its first years, television presented itself as the national showcase for news, reduced attention somewhat to the other news media, and gradually redirected audience attention elsewhere, to what Postman (1986) would call amusement. But, like others of the ostensible long-run effects of television, this is no more than an interpretation, a surmise; it may well be that the sources of change originate elsewhere and that changes in television viewing habits is more an effect than a cause.

Cultural Practices, 1970–1990

Has television affected other forms of consuming culture? What about the arts?

It is important to recall at this point that the amount of time spent outside the home—except for the aged—remains virtually unchanged between 1970 and 1990, and therefore unaffected by television. Enough extra leisure is available for people to include 2-3 hours per day of TV viewing in their time budgets[4] without sacrificing some 2½ hours "outside"—visiting, meandering, going to meetings, and consuming culture.

What has changed during these 20 years is what people do when they go out. Compared to 1970, there has been a major decline in the consumption of the arts. There is a per capita drop in the scope and/or frequency of attendance at cinema, theatre, concerts, museums, and lectures. This is very surprising since we had reason to expect an *increase* in participation in the arts inasmuch as the society is three years more educated since 1970, and education is positively correlated with consumption of the arts.

Ironically, the box-offices are unaware that there has been a decline in per capita consumption of the arts. The reason they don't notice is because the population has doubled, so that in 1990 the theater and concert halls are as full as they were in 1970! Only we, the researchers, know that a sea-change is in progress! Employing a variety of measures it can be shown that the scope of the audience, or frequency of attendance, or both, have lowered the extent of involvement in the institutions of "high" culture. Nobody is surprised that cinema attendance is down—casually putting the blame on television—but the same drop applies to theater, concerts, museums, etc.

Before making the wrong interpretation, however, it should be added that attendance at sporting events is also down. In 1990, per capita attendance at such events is lower than it was in 1970—both in scope and in frequency.

By contrast, there has been a rise, between 1970 and 1990, in the rate of going to pubs, eating out in restaurants, domestic and foreign travel, and participatory sports.

Our reading of these findings suggests that there is a decline in what may be called *spectacle* and a rise in those activities that are active, interactive, intimate, where participants bring their own programs along. In other words, there is a decline in those things which require one to sit in a particular place at a particular time, to watch a curtain go up and listen to some professional performer deliver a message from the stage. Correspondingly, leisure pursuits that have to do with activity, interactivity, flexible time, one's own small group and one's own agenda are on the rise.

Let us consider whether television may be to "blame." Television might explain these changes in the sense that it has given us an overdose of spectacle. People are fed up with staring; there's enough spectacle in the living-room, and when one goes outside the home one looks for something different. When people do go out they want to do more than stare. They want to be active, interactive, intimate, creative, and so on.

Any explanation, of course, would have to account for the decline in reading as well. Clearly, reading is not a spectacle. Nor does television displace the functions of reading, as we shall see. But reading does involve a lot of looking, and so perhaps the explanation does apply—at least until we find a better one.

Another possibility is that television satiates the appetite for the arts and the other media. We would all intuitively agree that cinema attendance has been hurt by television. The fact is, however, that people are seeing *more*, not fewer, films than they did in 1970, but they are seeing them on TV. This may be equally true for theater, concerts, sports, even museums, as well as reading fiction and reading news. The arts, especially cinema, are the content of television. According to McLuhan's (1964) rule, each new medium incorporates its predecessor as content. Perhaps television gratifies these needs for experience of the arts.

One must also take account of the alleged decline of the performing arts in other countries, too.[5] Of course, television may be the cause here as well, but a competing explanation would suggest that the culture of pluralism and postmodernism has challenged the Western canon and shaken up the entrenched hierarchy of "high" and "popular" art. It may be that people—even the upwardly mobile—don't "have to" prefer Beethoven to rock any more. We have already noted the coming of age of the second generation of Israelis whose parents originate from Africa and Asia, and the highest drop in arts participation is among the Israeli-born of 20-30 years, not only among those of Eastern origin but among those of Western parentage as well. The fact that the decline is no less strong among the Western groups born to television rekindles the possibility that television may be a cause.

What we are suggesting is that television may have preempted the other performing arts by doing what they do, as well as fostering an awareness that the rest of society is doing the same thing at the same time. In this sense, television offered the "togetherness" of a spectacle, superceding the spectacle of going to the theater, a concert, or to a political rally to share an experience with others who are present. Is it possible, we are asking, that the collective experience of viewing television—of viewing one-channel, public television—has satiated not only the desire for spectacle but the further need for widely shared experience and deliberation? Rather than contributing to the atomization of society and undermining its culture, as the opponents feared, Israel Television may have moved the collectivity from outside to inside, but served the collectivity very well, nevertheless. Stated otherwise, we are speculating on the possibility that 20 years of monopolistic public television offered Israelis a strong new taste of collectivity—in the double sense of simultaneous communion with very large numbers of one's compatriots, and shared content of collective import. Cardiff and Scannell (1987) make much the same case for the early days of both BBC radio and BBC television. Dialectically, we further propose that this "togetherness" and its implicit obligations became tiresome and oppressive after a while (as did other aspects of collective culture) and pushed people to find groups of intimates with whom to do "other" kinds of things.

Value Changes, 1970–1990

Another area in which we have observed change between 1970 and 1990 is the area of values, and these changes also reverberate with some of the concerns of the opponents of television. But almost nobody would venture that television is powerful enough, in itself, to have induced change in such deep-seated values. It is more reasonable that the impetus for change comes from elsewhere, and that the institutionalization of television and the viewing habits that it cultivates are only part of a larger picture. Let us now examine these changes, paying particular attention to values such as individualism versus collectivism and hedonism versus asceticism, that have entered our discussion so far.

At the outset, it should be emphasized that the society is very traditional on the whole. Compared to other western-oriented societies, family, nation and collectivity are very important, as is connection with the religious tradition. National and traditional holidays involve almost everyone, whether in religious or secular guise. Escapism is very low. But changes are taking place, slowly but surely.

We asked a series of value questions in this national survey about the "importance" Israelis attribute (1) to self, (2) to family, (3) to friends, (4) to state and (5) to peoplehood. Questions touched on affective and cognitive aspects in each of these realms. We asked, for example: How important is it for you to know yourself, to want to study, to make your day an orderly one, to feel that you are using your time well, to strive for a higher living standard, to escape from everyday reality, to overcome loneliness, and so on. This is the domain of self-concern. For the primary group area, we asked about the importance, cognitively and emotionally, of spending time with family and friends. With respect to state and people, we asked how important is it to you to understand what's going on in the world? How important is it to you to understand the true character of our political leaders? How important is it to you to believe in our leaders, feel pride in our state, and so on.

Many of the changes are small but consistent and significant; a few are very sharp. Table 1 displays these changes over time. Overall, there is an increase in concern for self and a decreased concern for society and state. There is more egoism than there was 20 years ago. Although concern for the future is still predominant, concern for the present has risen sharply. Pleasure is more highly valued, and there is an increase in the valuation of leisure as compared with work. Indeed, the importance of leisure is now more or less equivalent to the importance of work, whereas in 1970 work was more important than leisure, future was far more important than present. In sum, there is a rise in what might be called hedonism and individualism, and in the legitimacy of concern with self. These are big words for small changes, but they are very clear in the data.

Table 1
The Importance of Needs—1990 and 1970 (Percent citing the need as "very important")

	1990 (N=1450)	1970 (N=1960)
Self identity		
1. Cognitive needs (A1, B1)		
1. To develop good taste	66	61
* 2. To know myself	74	66
* 3. To want to study	65	56
4. To organize my day	69	63
5. To feel I am making good use of my time	76	72
6. To strive for a higher standard of living	57	54
* 7. To obtain practical information for daily life	70	47
2. Affective needs (A2, B1)		
* 8. To be entertained	68	54
9. To experience beauty	64	64
10. To re-experience past events	35	32
11. To raise my morale	83	77
3. Affective-escapist needs		
* 12 To overcome loneliness when I am alone at home	56	37
* 13. To release tension	74	61
14. To escape from the reality of everyday life	22	16
15. To relive the experiences of other people	17	20
Family		
4. Affective needs (A2, B2)		
16. To spend time with family	89	85
Friends		
5. Cognitive needs (A1, B3)		
17. To learn how to behave among others	54	52
18. To participate in discussions with my friends	66	63
19. To feel that others think as I do	34	36
20. To feel that I am influential	48	47
6. Affective needs (A2, B3)		
* 21. To spend time with friends	68	55
State		
7. Cognitive needs (A1, B4)		
22. To understand what goes on in Israel and in the world	82	87
23. To get to know the true qualities of our leaders	47	50
24. To follow the way government performs its functions	58	60
25. To know what the world thinks about us	67	70
26. To understand those who disagree with government's policy	46	41
27. To understand how the Arabs feel	31	33
8. Affective needs (A2, B4)		
* 28. To have confidence in our leaders	63	77
§ 29. To feel part of the Israeli society	73	—
30. To feel pride in our State	84	90
§ 31. To feel close to the Israel Defense Forces (Zahal)	80	—

*	32. To feel that I am participating in current events	39	46
	People		
9.	**Affective needs (A2, B5)**		
*	33. To feel in a festive mood	60	70
	34. To get closer to the Jewish tradition	47	51
§	35. To feel part of the Jewish people	83	—

§ Question not asked in 1970.
* Values that have changed significantly (7% or more) between 1970 and 1990

Their counterpart—the decline in collectivity-oriented values—may be observed in the lesser importance attributed to feelings of belonging to the larger society in matters such as the values of "having confidence in our leaders," "feeling that I am participating in current affairs," and "having pride in our state," although the latter is still at the top of the list. Organizational and political membership has experienced a decline. While the family retains its high place at both time periods, and is highly correlated with orientation to the collectivity, the value of spending time with friends has taken a major leap, and we know, from our study, that friends pull towards pleasure and pluralism and away from the burdens of the collectivity (Katz, Trope, and Haas, 1984). There is also a large increase in concern with "overcoming loneliness when I am alone at home."

Just as we asked in the case of changing cultural practices, we asked again in the case of changing values: does television have any share in these changes? Is television to "blame" in any way for the slow invasion of individualism and hedonism? It seems a fair guess that the answer is no. No one can deny that in its twenty years of existence as the sole national channel, Israel TV has demonstrated an incredible ability to seat the society together every night, to celebrate national achievements and religious occasions, indeed, to symbolize "togetherness."

In fact, if television has had any influence on values, we propose that it may have slowed these new trends. Rather than promoting individualism, pluralism or hedonism, it is more likely to have held them back, while reinforcing the sense of belonging to the civic sphere and the nostalgia for collectivity that permeates movements of national liberation such as Zionism. It is true that the opponents of television forecast a rise in self-oriented concerns and a decline in collectivistic ones: that the personal will supplant the collective, that egoism will displace altruism, that pleasure will uproot dedication. The only trouble with the prediction is that it does not at all correspond to the message of the first twenty years of Israel television, or to the shared experience it offered.

Function of Television and the Other Media

To this point, we have acted as observers comparing changes in culture and values with what we know about the institutionalization of Israel TV, its organizational form, content and function. We wish to turn now to ask the viewers what *they* think are the functions of television and the other media. Do they see things as the researchers do?

To do so, we asked respondents to assess the helpfulness of each of five media—radio, television, book, newspaper, cinema—for satisfying each of the "values" outlined in the previous section (and in Table 1). For example, following the value question, "How important is it for you to understand what's going on in the world?" we asked further, "How useful are newspapers for this purpose? How useful are books for this purpose?" and so on for the five media. We are really asking which media best satisfy each of the respondents' needs or values.[6]

In 1970, the newspaper was the predominant medium. Of the 35 concerns or values about which we inquired, the newspaper fulfilled more different functions than the other four. In 1990, television had displaced the newspaper very clearly as the medium which best fulfills more different kinds of concerns.[7]

That television has displaced the newspaper as the most diversified medium is not so surprising. The important point is that it ranks ahead of the other media in the area of the collectivity, especially in the emotional aspect of attachment to nation and people. More surprising, perhaps, is that television is rated the medium most helpful in satisfying national values that are not only affective but cognitive, i.e. not only "to feel pride in our state" but "to understand the true character of our leaders".

After its widespread diffusion in the early '70s, television also became important in satisfying many other functions as well, such as overcoming loneliness and spending time with family. But in the minds of most Israelis, television takes only second place to books or cinema or both with respect to personal values such as knowing oneself, cultivating good taste, being entertained, aesthetic experience, spending time with friends, improving morale. In short, Israelis appear to be saying that television has outdistanced the other media—especially newspapers—in cognitive and affective aspects of relating to the collectivity even more than to the self or to interpersonal relations.

Table 2
Grading of Media for Satisfying Needs of Population (1990)

Type of Needs					
Self identity					
1. Cognitive needs	Television	Newspaper	Book	Radio	Cinema
2. Affective needs	Cinema*	Television*	Book	Radio	Newspaper
3. Escapist needs	Book	Television	Radio	Cinema	Newspaper
Family					
4. Affective needs	Television	Cinema	Radio	Newspaper	Book
Friends					
5. Cognitive needs	Television	Newspaper	Book	Radio	Cinema
6. Affective needs	Cinema	Television	Radio	Newspaper	Book
State					
7. Cognitive needs	Newspaper*	Television*	Radio	Book	Cinema
8. Affective needs	Television	Newspaper	Radio	Book	Cinema
People					
9. Affective needs	Television	Radio	Book	Newspaper	Cinema

* Tied for first place.

The book, for its part, has retained all of its functions and even increased slightly in the number of important concerns it is thought to serve. Although the frequency of reading (not the overall percentage of readers) has declined somewhat, the book is holding its own from a functional point of view. Substantively, we can say that the book best fulfills functions related to self, especially affective ones. It is supreme among the five media in these functions. In Victor Nell's terms, "it is the affective part of self which the book best serves."

Along with books, cinema continues to share the self-oriented and affective realm, that is, the emotional aspects of self-fulfillment. Cinema has become altogether different from television, functionally speaking, over the period of 20 years. If in 1970 cinema was considered the universal medium of entertainment, by 1990 it has become an art and behaves like the other arts, in the sense of being correlated with education: the higher the education the higher the consumption of cinema, and of theater, concerts, museums and galleries. This was not true for cinema prior to the inception of television.

The cinema and television do not fulfill each other's functions any more. What we now have is a cinema that is allied with books on the one hand, and television which is allied with radio. This may be truer in Israel than elsewhere, since news and public affairs dominate the broadcasting media, and the populace is highly politicized. It also explains the displacement by television of the functions of the newspaper. In 1970, people apparently thought that TV would join film as a medium of fiction and pleasure, but this expectation has not so far been fulfilled. Instead, TV joined newspapers and radio as a medium of current affairs. Yet the picture may reverse again as television channels multiply, and TV may yet rejoin cinema as a medium of pleasure.

In a word, after 20 years of Israel television, Israelis see it as it saw itself, namely, as a medium of the collectivity. More important than self-gratification, Israelis experienced their one-channel television as a way to connect with the larger society and its civic concerns. Escapism and entertainment are thought to have been better served by other media.

Conclusion

In comparing Israel of 1970 with Israel of 1990—prior to the diversification of channels now replacing the 20-year old monopoly—we have documented three areas of change: (1) The content of values has moved, however slowly, in an individualistic direction, in the direction of pleasure at the expense of civic obligation. (2) There is a decline in participation in the performative arts, and in events that transpire at fixed times and places, with large numbers of participants. By contrast, there is a rise in activities that involve small groups of people doing their own things, at times and places of their own choosing. (3) The perceived division of labor among the media suggests that Israeli Jews identify their public television (prior to the new competition) as having served collective functions rather better (although not more frequently) than individualistic or hedonistic functions.

Simply stated, the data suggest that Israeli society—its values, its cultural practices—is moving slowly away from the collectivism that characterized it (and still does, relative to other societies) and towards greater self-indulgence. But Israel television cultivates collectivism—as its viewers and observers both think. If so, and if television can affect basic values at all, we must infer that the process of value change has been *slowed* by television. As critical school theorists used to say, non-change or slowed change may be the major effect of the media of mass communication (Katz, 1980).

Nor can television be held directly responsible for the decline in the patterns of collective consumption of culture and the arts. The most compelling argument we can find to connect the two is that individualistic and interactive patterns of "going out" are, ironically, a reaction against the collectivism of staying home with television.[8] In the simplest sense, if Israel television has successfully transformed the home into a theater or forum, then people want to do something else when they go out. In a larger sense, however, it suggests a saturation not only with the togetherness of Israel television but with togetherness and sacrifice made by the state and society during the first four decades of its embattled history. As in the case of values, Israel television is pulling *against* the stress of change, rather than with it.

Yet there is a nagging sense in which this may not be true. The message of television may be collectivistic, and its symbolic function likewise, as rightly perceived by its viewers. But there is also the reality of the *medium* as technology, and the way in which it situates its audience. While it may not keep them from going out, the fact is that its offerings can only be consumed at home. People may talk about the programs the next morning (30% do), but is this the equivalent of going out to a meeting of one's trade union, or political party, or going out to the theater? Whether television has made home-and-family into a locus of political action and cultural experience is still an open question. It is equally possible that it has done no more than give people the illusion of being "engaged," in line with what Lazarsfeld and Merton (1948) call the "narcotizing dysfunction" of broadcast news, or what Gerbner et al. (1979) think of as pulling people out of society and into the isolation of their living rooms.

And one wonders, similarly, whether television as a medium has not had a major share in the personalization of politics that is now sweeping the country. Primary elections have displaced the power of the party chiefs in selecting candidates for the parliament, and a populist law has been passed calling for the direct election of the prime minister, to the consternation of most social scientists. There is good reason to believe that television has weakened the party system by moving it indoors and, willy nilly, making it intimate.

Thus, early opposition to the introduction of television in Israel may have (1) been right, but for the wrong reasons, and (2) been right, but prematurely. Being right for the wrong reasons, the opponents suspected that television harbored a subversive message, not so much realizing that it was the medium itself rather than the message that may be problematic. Being right but prematurely, they could not have anticipated that the function of national integration would be so well served by Israel Television during its first two decades. But they may be right from now on. In the era of commercial, multi-channel narrowcasting, Israel may now have to make way for the escapist self-indulgence prematurely anticipated by the early opponents and latter-day critics like Houston and Postman.

Perhaps even more important than the message or the medium, the influence of television may be related to the form of its institutionalization in a particular society. The manifest and latent effects of a monopoly channel, operated by an independent Authority, in a newly democratic society, with a strong collective will, may be altogether different from the competitive, mixed commercial/public, multi-channel system now beginning to broadcast to a much more individualistic society of Israelis.

To summarize: (1) In spite of a persistent collectivism, we perceive a slow but sure trend towards self-gratification among Israelis at the expense of some decline in the pioneering values that characterized the society twenty and more years ago. (2) We perceive a decline in collective forms of out-of-home leisure in favor of more differentiated and pleasure-oriented pursuits typically enjoyed with small groups of friends. (3) Since its establishment 20 years ago, over one-third of leisure time in Israel is spent viewing television and some (but by no means all) of the functions of other media have been subsumed by television. (4) The safest thing to say about the long-run effects of television on the changes in Israel culture and society is that it is an impossible question to answer. (5) If one has to choose—on the basis of these comparative data—whether Israel television gave more support to the individualizing trend or to the norm of collectivism, there is a much stronger case to be made for the latter. The collectivism we have in mind has to do with shared and simultaneous pursuits, governed by norms of self-sacrifice and mutual obligation, performed in the knowledge that everybody else is similarly occupied; the Jewish Sabbath would be a classic example. (6) If Israel television did indeed serve as a bulwark against individualistic and hedonistic trends, it did so because of its message (offering a shared agenda to the society), because of the technology of electronic simultaneity and because of its independent-but-monopolistic form of organization. (7) At a deeper level, however, some of the latent aspects of the message (patriotism, perpetual tension, etc.) and of the medium (the atomistic way in which it situates viewers, its mode of personalization of issues) may also have pulled in the other direction. (8) There is good reason to expect that the new multi-channel television with its emphasis on choice and consumerism will give much stronger support to individuating trends.

To repeat, the closest parallel to the argument of this paper about the first 20 years of television in Israel is Cardiff and Scannell's (1987) analysis of the national integration which was fostered during the early days of BBC radio and then BBC television.*

Notes

1. While the 1990 study included both Jews and Arabs, the 1970 study interviewed only Israeli Jews and therefore this comparison is limited to the Jewish population.
2. To repeat, Israeli Arabs are not included in this comparative study because the 1970 study did not encompass the Arab sector. It is noteworthy, however, that Israel Television is the primary and most reliable television news source mentioned by Israeli Arabs in 1990. We make no attempt here, however, to analyze the functions of television for the Arab sector.
3. These data are from "time budget" analysis where the interviewee is aided in reconstructing how he/she spent the past 24 hours. Averaging an activity such as TV viewing in this way includes the 0 hours of those who did not view at all "yesterday." Hence the discrepancy between the 2-3 hours of the modal viewer and the slightly lower figures (1.7 on weekdays, 2.3 on Fridays, 2.0 on Saturdays) noted here. Each fraction of an hour equals 6 minutes; thus 1.7 equals 102 minutes.
4. TV viewing averaged one hour in 1970 when many people were still without sets of their own, and the number of broadcast hours was small.
5. We have roughly comparable data from several European countries and the U.S. However, no systematic analysis has yet been undertaken across cultures.
6. Questions about the utility of the media were asked only with respect to those values considered at least "somewhat important" by the respondent, and with respect to those media to which the respondent was exposed at least to some extent. Thus, a respondent who attributed "no importance at all" to the need "to experience beauty" was not asked which media helped gratify this need. If he/she never goes out to see a film, questions about the helpfulness of cinema were not asked.
7. The discussion that follows is based on changes in the roles of the five media with respect to each of the 35 different needs or values. Table 2 groups these needs into 9 categories, and averages them.
8. That does not mean that the higher standard of living and self-indulgence is not to be found in Israeli homes. Our argument, rather, is that the home is home to television, and that television is experienced as "we."

* Some of Meyrowitz (1985) also has bearing.

References

Cardiff, David and Paddy Scannell (1987). "Broadcasting and National Unity." In James Curran, Anthony Smith and Pauline Wingate, eds., *Impacts and influences.* London: Methuen.

Gerbner, George, Larry Gross, et al. (1979). "The demonstration of power." *Journal of Communication* 29: 177-196.

Houston, Beverle (1994). "Viewing television: The metapsychology of endless consumption." In Nick Browne, ed., *American Television: New directions in history and theory.* Chur, Switzerland: Harwood.

Katz, Elihu (1980). "On conceptualizing media effects." In Thelma MacCormack, ed., *Studies in Communication,* Vol. I. Greenwich, CT: JAI Press.

Katz, Elihu and Michael Gurevitch (1974). *The Secularization of Leisure.* London: Faber and Faber

Katz, Elihu and Michael Gurevitch (1976). *The Secularization of Leisure: Culture and communication in Israel.* London: Faber and Faber; Cambridge, MA: Harvard University Press.

Katz, Elihu, Ya'acov Trope and Hadassah Haas (1984). "Primary groups, mass communication and integration in armed forces and nation." In Erik Cohen, Moshe Lissak and Uri Almagor, eds., *Tradition and Modernity: Essays in honor of S. N. Eisenstadt.* Boulder, CO: Westview Press.

Lazarsfeld, Paul F. and Robert K. Merton (1948). "Mass communication, popular taste and organized social action." In Lyman Bryson, ed., *The Communication of Ideas.* New York: Harper.

McLuhan, Marshall (1964). *Understanding Media: Extensions of man.* New York: McGraw-Hill.

Meyrowitz, Joshua (1985). *No Sense of Place.* New York: Oxford University Press.

Postman, Neil (1986). *Amusing Ourselves to Death: Public discourse in the age of television.* New York: Viking.

14

Video Watching and Its Societal Functions for Small-Town Adolescents in Israel*

Rafael Schneller

Leisure and Television

Free time has rapidly increased as a function of shorter working hours and the speed of modern transportation. However, this "freed" time has been increasingly absorbed by new entertainment technologies and "colonized" by Western media imperialism (Sahin and Robinson, 1982). The most powerful colonizer by far is off-the-air network television and its cable and videocassette extensions. TV, in all of its forms, has expanded to such an extent that it now consumes most of the time not otherwise committed at home. Furthermore, it has taken time away, not only from traditional mass media, but also from Compulsory activities (Adler, 1981).

The presence of free time among adults is also reflected in the younger population. The regular school program leaves plenty of free time in the afternoons, evenings and weekends. Although some have labeled these non-school hours "leisure" (Ibrahim, 1981), others note that at least a portion of them are filled by daily necessities and obligations (Dumazedier, 1967; Peterson, 1982). According to Sahin and Robinson (1982), leisure should include only the activities that are "beyond necessity." Pure leisure activity exists when a person perceives his freedom to act or socialize as important and participates in an activity just for intrinsic reasons (Neulinger, 1974, 1976).

In Israel, TV has assumed the primary role in pure leisure since its introduction in 1968. Even in the pre-video era (prior to 1981), TV accounted for 20% of all "free-time" activities in the daily schedule of Israeli youth and up to 40% of all "pure" leisure (Schneller, 1984a).

TV and Adolescence

Adolescence is viewed as a critical period for the development of self-concept, in the search for identity, and for integration into society (Erikson, 1968; Rapoport and Rapoport, 1975; Sebald, 1977; Kelly, 1982). Since these processes are based heavily on social interaction, leisure and youth activities constitute a central context for testing, accepting and forming new identities (Kelly, 1982). These activities help the adolescent find his/her unique place in society through free role experimentation and broad experiences of identification (Erikson, 1968). With the introduction of video to Israel, screen watching forms the bulk of leisure activity even more than before. Thus, it is reasonable to ask about the contribution of media involving screen watching in adolescent socialization and personal growth. In addition, some maintain that mass media are crucial to the development of the adolescent's personality (Sebald, 1977). There are others, however, who argue that the impact may be limited, since TV presents only "parasocial" interaction without identification with the person on the screen (Rosengren et al., 1976).

Concern has also been expressed about what the young are *not doing* while occupied by TV or video. Hayakawa (1969) states that the average 18-year-old American has lost 22,000 hours of potential interaction with other human beings due to television watching. In his words, "There is simply no substitution for human interaction, which includes misunderstandings, expressing and solving problems and getting to know real people." The various lists of leisure activities (see Bule, 1971; Ibrahim, 1981; Sahin and Robinson, 1982) reveal many areas of "lost opportunities" for socialization. A recent study by Schneller (1984a) based on written diaries logged every half hour from the close of school until bedtime, showed a negative correlation ($r = 0.30$, $p < .05$) between TV viewing and public and outdoor activities. These activities included participation in social and cultural events, youth movement activities, excursions, and outdoor games. Thus, TV watching itself and outdoor social activities may be viewed as "rival activities" (Himmelweit, 1958; Brown et al., 1974).

A marked decline in TV viewing from childhood to adolescence has been reported in many studies (Himmelweit, 1958; Katz, 1970; Feilitzen, 1979; Adler, 1981). Schneller (1984a), in a sample of Israeli youth, found a decrease in daily TV viewing from 1.88 hours for seventh graders to 1.58 hours for tenth graders. A contrasting increase was found in many out-of-home activities for the same population (from .64 hours for seventh graders to 1.06 hours for tenth graders). This shift can be seen as a function of changing developmental needs, and leisure selection can be viewed as a reflection of these needs (Tinsley et al., 1977). Himmelweit (1958) characterizes changes in leisure selection as a "displacement" of needs satisfaction: "When existing facilities, including mass media, do not satisfy newly aroused needs, they are, at least partly, displaced by other activities that can provide the wanted satisfaction."[1] The question arises, then, to what extent mass media can serve as displacement for real social activity if that activity is located out of reach of other environmental factors.

Leisure in Small Towns

Data relating to TV activity and its impact have been reported mainly in studies conducted in metropolitan environments. Questions arise, then, about the applicability of these studies to other settings, for example, the small town (S-T).

A city is a mosaic of social worlds, reflecting diverse populations, subcultures, ways of life and social organizations (Bell, 1965). It offers a variety of cultural institutions and activities and numerous opportunities for leisure activities. A different situation exists in the S-T. Demographic and geographic factors influence the demand for and the availability of leisure facilities in any one community. The amount and kind of facilities also depend on local or societal attitudes toward leisure and recreation (Parker, 1976). As a result, many alternatives for leisure are unavailable to S-T youth. This is what Neulinger (1982) has labeled "leisure lack." Moreover, in spite of limited leisure activities, it is not unreasonable to assume that the social and psychological needs of S-T adolescents may be the same as those of their urban peers. The satisfaction of these needs in a context of limited cultural resources results, then, in heavy use of TV, peer association, or school activities and events (Allen, 1968; Katz, 1970; Kuvlevksi, 1973).

Israel's off-the-air television selection is rather limited. It has operated only since 1969 in a single-channel, government-controlled, non-commercial format (which is similar to what has been reported in some Nordic countries; Roe, 1985). Israeli telecasting in Hebrew for the general public is limited to six hours daily, including entertainment, children's and youth programs and the news. This is substantially less than the fare offered in most other countries.

Screen watching has changed drastically since 1981 with the start of the video revolution in Israel. First of all, video expanded availability of programs to people and places that had been restricted formerly. Second, video offered programs of unlimited content, in any quantity, independent of broadcasting schedules. The past dearth may help explain the unusual boom in VCR sales. Israel is now one of the relatively heaviest consumers of VCR sets, with an average ownership rate of one VCR for every three households (Schneller, 1984b). This rate is surpassed only by Saudi Arabia (Boyd and Najai, 1984). Thus, limited TV offerings have given way to very high video consumption.

Video and the Small Town in Israel

Small towns in Israel differ from the central cities (C-C) not only in size and the lifestyles and occupations of their inhabitants, but also because they are populated primarily by newcomers who immigrated during the last 30 years. The small towns of Israel are located mainly in rural areas, psychologically quite distant from metropolitan centers. Most of them were established to aid the settlement of large immigration waves in the 1950s, shortly after the establishment of the state. Their populations originated generally from Afro-Asian communities with very little tradition of leisure. In the multicultural immigrant society that makes up modern Israel, the socialization process is often more complicated than in long established and relatively stable settings. The adolescent not only must become acculturated to social patterns of home and family, but also must accommodate the values and norms of a society that is strange even to his or her parents' generation. In such a context, actual relations and activities with adolescent and adult representatives of other cultures (both newcomers and long-standing immigrants) are crucial to social integration and identity. While urban populations have plenty of opportunities to engage in these activities, those in small towns, cut off from the multicultural environment, do not.

The innovation of video is far more than a quantitative extension of existing media. It allows the individual to control choice of content, viewing time and place, and recording and replaying, all independent of outside factors. Since the needs for control and choice are characteristic of adolescence (Brown, 1974; Roe, 1981, 1983a, 1983b), it is likely that S-T adolescents will strive for the same freedom of choice as their urban counterparts. Moreover, since the level of gratification or "need equivalence" (Himmelweit, 1958) of video is much higher than that of TV, the S-T adolescent is expected to show preference for this new medium. One would then expect a process of "functional reorganization" in the move from TV to video (Brown et al., 1974). In this process, many of the functions of TV are taken over by extended video watching. In particular, the escapism needs of S-T adolescents can be more efficiently satisfied by this medium. In this reorganization, TV and radio are not dropped totally. Rather, they become complements to video because of their similarity in content and because their programs can be easily recorded on videocassette for replay at a later time (Johnson-Smaragdi and Roe, 1986). On the other hand, TV is transformed to satisfy those needs not met by video.

If the social situation fails to satisfy personal and social needs by offering only impoverished real-life opportunities for relationships, there is a great likelihood, according to Rosengren and Windhall (1972), that mass media will serve as a substitute, or, at least, as a supplement/complement to this type of interaction. In addition to the descriptive aim of this study, it will also investigate the relevance of Rosengren and Windhall's assumption for S-T adolescents in Israel. Taking into account the high "need equivalence" of video in the Israeli media situation, it is expected that this medium will complement TV as the main leisure activity of this population. Ownership, audience, viewing, and a variety of other aspects of media use in this population will be compared to a similar group from Israeli C-C. The data will be treated both quantitatively and qualitatively.

Data collection for this study was designed to examine the following predictions:

(1) More owners of videocassettes will be found in S-Ts than in cities.

(2) The relative number of adolescent video watchers in S-Ts will be higher than in cities.

(3) Among the active video watchers, the amount of viewing time will be greater in S-Ts than in cities.

(4) TV viewing will decline in S-Ts more than in cities.

(5) Recording of TV programs will occur more in S-Ts than in cities.

Method

Subjects

The subject population consisted of two subgroups. A nonrandom sample (Group A) was drawn from among high school students in C-Cs and S-Ts.

The C-C portion of the sample included 56 classes of seventh through twelfth graders from the chief metropolitan area of Israel. They were selected according to the following demographic characteristics: a total of 16 classes consisted of longtime residents in Israel, by and large, of "Western" origin; 19 classes consisted of immigrants, largely from Afro-Asian countries; 21 classes were mixed, in terms of both origin and length of residence in Israel. The total number of subjects in sample A was 1,730, 888 boys and 842 girls.

The balance of the subjects in this group came from S-Ts in seven locations throughout the country (27 classes, N = 748, 394 boys and 354 girls). The small towns included in the study were nonagricultural settlements with 5,000-15,000 residents.

Group B consisted of a different population of active video watchers only. It included those who watched both TV and video as well as those who recorded TV programs for playback. A total of nine classes of twelfth graders from cities were chosen from among the various types of high schools, and five classes were drawn from four similar S-Ts. A total of 165 students came from these urban classes and 101 from classes in S-Ts. The students' ages ranged from 14 to 18 years. The sample was divided approximately equally between boys (N = 127) and girls (N = 138).

Procedure

For Group A, a survey was conducted orally by the classroom teacher. Inquiries (yes/no) were made about regular video watching and about ownership. The form completed by the teacher included the location and type of school, number of students in the class, their gender and the responses to the two questions.

Students in Group B provided written responses to questions about age, sex, amount of TV watching and amount of video watching. TV and video items included questions about viewing in general and about specific programs, the amount of time spent viewing for the last three days, changes in TV viewing with the appearance of video, and video recording of TV programs.

Data Analysis

The data were analyzed by t-tests and chi-square statistics for differences between C-C and S-T populations. In addition, the differences between the two age groups and the two locations were tested.

Results

Video Owners

Prediction A. The percentage of video owners in C-Cs versus S-Ts is presented in Table 1 for sample A as a whole (grades 7-12) and is broken down for upper and lower high school classes.

It was predicted that video equipment would be relatively more widespread in S-Ts than in C-Cs, given a large number of viewers and a high degree of viewing. The results of the survey only partially confirm this prediction. The total population of the two locations differ significantly, but only because of the upper classes. No such difference was obtained for the younger group.

Table 1
Video Owners in C-Cs and S-Ts

Locations:	C-C (N=1730)		S-T (N=748)		df	X^2	p <
Classes	N	%	N	%			
7th – 9th N = 1351	277	30.88	153	33.70	1	10.25	0.01
10th – 12th N=1127	285	34.21	132	44.90	1	15.3	0.0001
Total N = 2478	562	32.43	285	38.10	1	7.31	0.0069

The marked increases from 33.7% to 44.9% across the two age groups in S-Ts, compared with a modest (nonsignificant) difference of only 3.3% in C-Cs, demonstrates the important role of video in the lives of S-T youth in later adolescence. This role may be related to the lack of other need-satisfying leisure opportunities in S-Ts, which contrasts with what is available and accessible to their age peers in the central cities.

Video Watchers

Prediction B. The central interest of this study was the comparison of TV and video watching among S-T adolescents and those in C-Cs. The percentage of video watchers in C-Cs versus S-Ts is presented in Table 2 for Group A as a whole and is broken down for upper and lower high school classes.

As expected, a much higher number of video watchers was identified in the S-T population for both subgroups. In contrast to ownership, this holds true for video watchers of the lower age group as well; that is to say, this younger group, too, must seek substitutes for existing media.

Table 2
Video Watchers in C-Cs and S-Ts

Locations:	C-C (N=1730)		S-T (N=748)		df	X^2	p<
Classes	N	%	N	%			
7th – 9th N = 1351	379	42.25	236	51.98	1	9.98	0.02
10th – 12th N=1127	341	40.94	160	54.42	1	15.18	0.0001
Total N = 2478	720	41.60	396	53.20	1	27.30	0.0001

The inconsistency between ownership and video watching demands an explanation. Culture may be one of the factors contributing to relatively limited S-T ownership. As noted earlier, S-Ts in Israel are populated mainly by Afro-Asian immigrants, who maintain a high level of cohesion among extended family members. Thus, screen viewing in a wider family gathering and joint ownership were both documented in probes following the initial survey. Further support for this factor can be found in the main reason reported for group viewing, that is, that "it is boring to sit alone and to watch with nobody to talk to." This social pattern of "togetherness" is quite typical of S-Ts and characteristic of their ethnic makeup. In contrast, in the upper classes, the need for autonomy in choosing contents, timing, and peers for viewing seems to clash with the traditional framework of the extended family and may lead to an increase in video ownership.

Amount of Screen Viewing

Prediction C. A further dimension of video watching is the amount and distribution of average viewing hours. Table 3 presents the average amount of TV and video viewing in both populations of high school students in Group B.

Table 3
Video and TV Viewing in C-Cs and S-Ts (average daily hours)

Locations:	C-C (N=165)		S-T (N=101)		p<
Media	h[1]	SD	h[1]	SD	
Video	2.87	1.784	4.24	2.022	0.007
TV	3.16	1.209	2.83	1.917	n.s.

note: N = 264.

The data reveal much higher video consumption by S-T adolescents compared with those in C-Cs. As a matter of fact, the gap between the adolescent populations in these different areas may be even greater than what is shown in the table. Underestimation of differences may be a result of examining data for this sample only among active video users and not from the general population. However, even in the population surveyed, the difference in viewing time for video was almost 50%.

Of interest is the fact that no significant differences between the locations were documented for TV viewing. However, the results show that in C-Cs video viewing is less than that of TV viewing, but in S-Ts it is remarkably high. It can be suggested, then, that video seems to be only a supplement (or, perhaps, a complement) for C-C adolescents, but, for S-T adolescents, it is more of a substitute (or at least a need satisfier). Taking into account that the percentage of actual viewing in the total adolescent population is considerably higher in S-Ts than in

C-Cs (see Table 2), nonviewing leisure time of urban youth by far outweighs that of S-Ts.

The comparison of mean viewing times provides only a general picture of the differences. More meaningful perhaps is a breakdown into levels of low, medium and high amounts of viewing for each population. These differences are presented in Table 4.

Table 4
Distribution of Daily Video and TV Viewing in C-Cs and S-Ts

Locations:		C-C (N=165)	S-T (N=101)	p<
Media	*Viewers*			
	Light 1-2 hours	58.0	9.6	df = 2
Video	Medium	29.4	52.4	$X^2 = 18.75$
	3-4 hours			
	Heavy > 5 hours	12.4	38.0	p < 0.0001
	Light	37.0	49.8	df = 2
TV	Medium	51.8	38.9	$X^2 = 1.12$
	Heavy	11.1	11.1	n.s.

This table shows that the relative allocation of time to video and TV differs in the two locations. Differences in the distribution of viewing time between S-T and C-C populations are highly significant for video watching ($p < .0001$) and nonsignificant for TV viewing. Moreover, in contrast to video watching, where S-T adolescents logged more hours of watching than their urban counterparts, for TV viewing, the urban population reveals more medium and heavy users, while the S-T population shows more light users.

Comparison of combined TV and video viewing shows that, overall, 50% of S-T adolescents spend a total of five hours or more in front of the screen, compared with only 24% in C-Cs. For video alone, more than 90% of S-T adolescent users watch daily for three hours or more. Both figures are more than twice as great as that in C-Cs. A breakdown for males and females did not show any significant difference.

These data support the prediction that video is a larger consumer of leisure time among S-T adolescents than among urban Israelis in the same age group. Taking into account obligatory activities such as homework, domestic duties and grooming as well as TV viewing, S-T youth have very little time for other leisure activities.

TV Use Among Video Owners

Prediction D. The high needs equivalence of video for S-T adolescents led to a prediction that TV viewing in this population would be less than that in a comparable urban group. The statements of both S-T and C-C adolescents about their TV viewing after the introduction of video show a very high degree of similarity for the two populations. Only about one-third of either group reported less TV viewing, and only a small percentage (5.6%) reported not watching TV at all after the introduction of video.

Thus, both populations basically added video watching to previous TV consumption, and the prediction was not borne out. This finding supports our interpretation for Table 3 that video is mainly complementary for C-C adolescents, while it is the main substitute for the denied needs of real face-to-face interaction in S-Ts.

Recording

Prediction E. Recording of TV programs or "duplication" of existing videocassettes for limited replay is one of the most characteristic features of video. The unique functions of this activity and its particular importance in the S-T situation led to the prediction of a higher rate of recording in this population. But this prediction, too, was not borne out.

Only 13% of the S-T video owners reported recording, versus 63% in the cities. The recorded programs were mainly of the escapist type. A possible explanation for this finding could be the general passivity of the S-T population, which is shown by their consumption of ready-made and ready-to-use products. Such an explanation may also account for a general lack of cultural alternatives in S-T other than those supplied by public agencies.

Discussion

The aim of this study was to explore the role of TV and video in the leisure of S-T adolescents compared to those in C-Cs. The findings show a much higher degree of screen watching among S-T youth than among their urban peers. This difference is accentuated when the data are broken down for heavy, medium and light users. Although screen watching in both S-Ts and C-Cs occupies most of the adolescent's pure leisure, in C-Cs it does leave a certain amount of time to other activities, mainly those involving outdoor socialization. Heavy screen watching is assumed to be the result of a lack of other need-satisfying leisure opportunities (Rosengren and Windhall, 1972; Kuvlevski, 1973; Katz, 1974). The findings of this study for S-T adolescents are consistent with this assumption and with the view of Rosengren and Windhall (1972) that mass media will serve as a leisure substitute in a situation of impoverished real-life activity.

All of these findings have implications for the socio-psychological development of the S-T adolescent as well as for the S-T community. Adolescence has been characterized by the search for personal and social identity. Direct personal contact with real persons, situations, problems and events have been recognized as indispensable for shaping adolescents' identities and assisting them to make a place in society. These contacts are generally available for urban youth through a wide range of interpersonal and cultural encounters and a great variety of outdoor leisure activities. A very different situation exists in the small town. Adolescents there can usually find only limited outdoor and social leisure facilities and cultural events. The social needs of adolescents as they mature remain largely unsatisfied, and the opportunities for identity-forming experiences in real life are unfulfilled.

Screen watching has thus taken the place of real socialization as almost the sole leisure activity of S-T adolescents. Video watching has displaced TV as the primary form of entertainment, particularly for "escapist" gratification (Maccoby, 1954, cited in Brown et al., 1974). This medium accounts for most available, pure leisure time, and, for heavy users, it even cuts into obligatory activities.

It has already been mentioned that a high degree of screen consumption affects the viewer in at least two ways. Indirectly, it prevents the viewer from doing, that is, participating actively in the socialization process. The quantitative data seem to indicate that there is hardly any time left for other leisure activities, particularly those leading to real social interpersonal interaction.

On the other hand, heavy screen consumption may also have positive effects on socialization. In pointing out the benefits TV experience may have on social development, Sebald (1977) emphasizes that human beings are symbolic creatures and need not rely on only the actual presence of persons or objects to form views of themselves and the world. Mass media provide a constant barrage of stimuli, which, according to Sebald, bear significantly on the development of the human personality.

However, others claim that this mediated meeting with people on the screen cannot be a substitute for real interaction. According to Kelly (1982), it is critical that leisure, in providing opportunities to explore, build, and express community, be real. Thus the easy interaction with TV may come at the cost of community.

The direct social effects of a high degree of consumption of and dependence on mass media are attributed mainly to the presentation of a highly distorted view of man and the world in the telecasting of "pseudo-real" environments such as styles of living, behavior, status and social activities (Sebald, 1977). This distortion holds even in the case of purportedly informative programs like the news (Celsing, 1984). These pseudo-realities may seriously tempt the young to identify and select models for emulation, leading to an unrealistic pseudo-identity and to unrealistic aspirations and expectations (Mills, 1969). Instead of gaining their own identity, mass media turns the viewer into a mass man with a mass identity (Van der Haag, 1969). According to Mills (1969), "Mass media tells him who he is, what he wants to be, how to get that way and how to feel that he is that, even when he is not." By reducing human contact, escapist media block real-life experiences and bring about the loss of a picture of the real world. The lack of realistic social experience during adolescence extends beyond the individual, creating a generation of pseudo-realistic adults. Mass media alienate people from personal experience and intensify their moral isolation from each other, from reality and from themselves.

Even though ssome opportunities for direct experience do exist in S-Ts, they are blocked by mass media consumption. Once TV viewing becomes a habit, it impairs the capacity for meaningful experience. There are even those who have described this habit as having the same effects as an addiction (Van der Haag, 1969).

It has been argued that the starting point of the media consumption habit is the unavailability of other leisure alternatives in the S-T environment. One could suggest an alternative conception. According to Check and Burch (1976), the most frequent S-T leisure activities are of a passive indoor type, for example, reading and screen watching. S-T societies put their energies into home and family life, both of which are characteristic of Israeli S-Ts. Residents of these settlements primarily emigrated from cultures with patriarchal family structures and were quite unaware of the necessity for outdoor experience to assimilate into the new life. Living in a modern Western-oriented society has not changed these basic patterns. Thus, one can assume that in the S-T situation, the point of departure for explaining media consumption is passivity and intrafamily orientation. Since no serious demands for outdoor leisure facilities have been made by local residents, these resources remain relatively limited. Home activities, in particular media use, satisfy some of the adolescent's personal needs. However, without traditional ties, strong role models and ready opportunities to satisfy interpersonal needs, the S-T adolescent retreats almost totally to screen watching and especially to video and its relatively high level of need satisfaction. In this way, the adolescent seeks to build an identity in the pseudo-reality of a pseudo-world.

Thus, the selection of content for screen viewing ought to focus on fiction, especially of an escapist variety. Rosengren and Windhall (1972) support this view, stating that a high degree of dependence on and involvement with screen media goes together with a preference for and consumption of content that reflects a low degree of reality.

Moreover, according to Kelly (1982), "if a major portion available for leisure is diverted from social interaction to screen watching, the loss may be more than the physical activity of the medium would suggest; TV's—and video's—easiness may enjoy the cost of community." This implies that the deleterious effects of heavy video consumption go beyond the adolescent's individual identity, affecting his/her relationship to the community, and perhaps even represent a loss for the community and society in general. In conclusion, Roe's (1983a, 1983b) statement that, while video use is functional for the individual, it may be dysfunctional for society, seems to be an apt description of the S-T situation.

Further research, focused on extra-screen leisure activities in these two populations, could supply more insight into the competition between video watching and real socializing.

* AUTHOR'S NOTE: This study was supported by the Research Authority of Bar-Ilan University and the Schnitzer Foundation for Social Research on the Israeli Economy and Society. I am also indebted to Dr. A. Leslow for his valuable cooperation.

Note

1. Himmelweit used the concept of *displacement* mainly for analyzing the move from other mass media or nonmedia leisure activities toward the newly introduced TV in England. Here, this term is used for just the opposite purpose: displacement of needs satisfaction from TV by outdoor interpersonal activities.

References

Adler, R.P. (ed.) (1981). *Understanding Television.* New York: Praeger.

Allen, I.L. (1968). "Community size, population, composition and cultural activity in smaller communities." *Rural Sociology* 33, 3: 328-338.

Bell, W. (1965). "Urban neighborhoods and individual behavior," in M. Sherif and C.W. Sherif (eds.) *Problems of Youth.* Chicago: Aldine.

Boyd, D.A. and A.M. Najai (1984). "Adolescent TV viewing in Saudi Arabia." *Journalism Q.* 61: 295-301.

Brown, J.R., J.K. Cramond, and R.J. Wilde (1974). "Displacement effects of television and the child's functional orientation to media," pp. 113-136 in J.G. Blumler and E. Katz (eds.) *The Uses of Mass Communications: Current Perspectives on Gratifications Research.* Beverly Hills, CA: Sage.

Bule, C.N. (1971). "One measure for defining leisure activity." *Journal of Leisure Research* 3, 2: 120-126.

Celsing, A. (1984). *Seeing Is Believing.* Stockholm: Journalist Hogskolan Shrifserie.

Check, N.H. and W.R. Burch (1976). *The Social Order of Leisure in Human Society.* New York: Harper and Row.

Dumazedier, J. (1967). *Towards a Sociology of Leisure.* New York: Free Press.

Erikson, E.H. (1968). *Identity: Youth and Crisis.* New York: Norton.

Feilitzen, C.V. et al. (1979). "Open your eyes to child's viewing." Stockholm: Swedish Broadcasting Co.

Hayakawa, S.I. (1969). "Image and reality." *Bulletin of the National Association of Secondary School Principals* 53, 5: 35-48.

Himmelweit, H.T. et al. (1958). *TV and the Child.* London: Oxford University Press.

Ibrahim, H. (1981). "Leisure behavior among contemporary Egyptians." *Journal of Leisure Research* 13, 2: 89-104.

Johnson-Smaragdi, V. and K. Roe (1986). *Teenagers in the New Media World* (Lund Research Papers in the Sociology of Communication, No. 2). Lund, Sweden: University of Lund, Department of Sociology.

Johnson-Smaragdi, V. and K. Roe (1983a). *The Influence of Video Technology in Adolescence* (Media Panel Report No. 27). Lund, Sweden: University of Lund, Department of Sociology.

Katz, E. (1970). *Culture in Israel.* Jerusalem: Institute for Communication.

Katz, E., J.G. Blumler, and M. Gurevitch (1974). "Utilization of mass communication by the individual," pp. 19-32 in J.G. Blumler and E. Katz (eds.) *The Uses of Mass Communications: Current Perspectives on Gratifications Research.* Beverly Hills, CA: Sage.

Kelly, J.R. (1982). *Leisure.* Englewood Cliffs, NJ: Prentice-Hall.

Kuvlevski, W.P. (1973). "Rural youth — current status and prognosis," in D. Gottlieb (ed.), *Youth in Contemporary Societies.* Beverly Hills, CA: Sage.

Mills, C.W. (1969). "Some effects of mass media," in A. Casty, *Mass Media and Man.* New York: Holt, Rinehart and Winston.

Neulinger, J. (1974). *The Psychology of Leisure.* Springfield, IL: Charles C. Thomas.

Neulinger, J. (1976). "The need for and the implication of psychological concepts of leisure." *Ontario Psychologist* 8: 13-20.

Neulinger, J. (1982). "Leisure lack and quality of life." *Leisure Studies* 1, 1: 53-64.

Parker, S. (1976). *The Sociology of Leisure.* London: George Allen and Unwin.

Peterson, R.A. (1982). "Measuring culture, leisure and time use," in D.C. Whitney and E. Wartella (eds.), *Mass Communication Review Yearbook,* Vol. 3, Beverly Hills, CA: Sage.

Rapoport, R. and R.N. Rapoport (1975). *Leisure and the Family Life Circle.* London: Routledge and Kegan Paul.

Roe, K. (1981). *Video and Youth: New Patterns of Video Use* (Media Panel Report No. 18). Lund, Sweden: University of Lund, Department of Sociology.

Roe, K. (1983a). *The Influence of Video Technology in Adolescence* (Media Panel Report No. 27). Lund, Sweden: University of Lund, Department of Sociology.

Roe, K. (1983b). *The Uses and Effects of Videoviewing Among Swedish Adolescents* (Media Panel Report No. 31). Lund, Sweden: University of Lund, Department of Sociology.

Roe, K. (1985). "The Swedish moral panic over video 1980-1984." *Nordicom Rev.* 1: 20-25.

Rosengren, K.E. and S. Windhall (1972). "Mass media consumption as a functional alternative," in D. McQuail (ed.) *Sociology of Mass Communication.* Harmondsworth: Penguin.

Rosengren, K.E. et al. (1976). "Adolescent-TV relations: three scales." *Communication Research* 3, 4: 347-366.

Sahin, H. and J.P. Robinson (1982). "Beyond the realm of necessity," in D.C. Whitney and E. Wartella (eds.) *Mass Communication Review Yearbook,* Vol. 3. Beverly Hills, CA: Sage.

Schneller, R. (1984a). "TV and other leisure activities in Israel." *Studies in Education* 39: 137-158. Haifa: University of Haifa.

Schneller, R. (1984b). "The video invasion into Israel: Findings and challenges." Presented at the 14th International Conference of IAMCR, Prague.

Sebald, H. (1977). *Adolescence: A Socialpsychological Analysis,* second edition. Englewood Cliffs, NJ: Prentice-Hall.

Tinsley, H.E.A. et al. (1977). "Leisure activity and needs satisfaction." *Journal of Leisure Research* 9, 2: 110-120.

Van der Haag, E. (1969). "Of happiness and of despair we have no measure," in A. Casty (ed.) *Mass Media and Man.* New York: Holt, Rinehart and Winston.

15

VCR Narrowcasting in the Kibbutz*

Dov Shinar

Technology has played an increasingly significant role in the dialectics of developing and questioning communication philosophies, structures and functions. Viewed in this perspective, the race for technological innovation in television, particularly in the last two decades, has been the focal point of the struggle for self-preservation on the part of profitable corporations and the pressures for devising alternative models.[1] Large screens, high definition images, improved color, and alphanumeric methods illustrate efforts to improve, rather than change, the product and service of big, centralized systems (Hurwitz, 1978). VCR, videocassette, low-powered broadcasting, and other "small" technologies have been associated with change in communication models. Premeditated or coincidental, their development has triggered expectations and initiatives to use narrowcasting as a means to reinvent television (Kalba, 1979; Willener, 1976).

In philosophical and ideological terms, small media technologies promised to counterweight the inadequacies of the established models. Liberals and Marxists alike have admitted that wherever it has been used, television has divided communities between givers and receivers, programmers and watchers, distributors and consumers (Walsh, 1980).

Some have seen these qualities as inherent to the medium (Groombridge, 1972; Mander, 1978), while others have been battling for the democratization and the demystification of television. In the framework of more comprehensive demands to democratize democracy, claims were made in the liberal camp for a broadcasting reform, intended to achieve a more equitable distribution of communication resources, curb manipulative control, and encourage citizens' participation and initiative (Henderson, 1974; Rogers, 1976; Branscomb & Savage, 1978; White, 1984). Others demanded to radically change the vertical, centralized, alienating nature of capitalist-controlled media-structures into an emancipatory model, designed to enhance genuine relevance, popular involvement, and affirmative action (Enzensberger, 1972; Freire, 1974; Pasteka, 1979; Beltran, 1980). Accountability and public involvement were advocated as ways to demystify television. Their common philosophy has been "the right to communicate," which, based on Article 19 of the Universal Declaration of Human Rights, states that "everyone has the right of opinion and expression," including *association, information, and development* (MacBride, 1980: 173).

The concepts of *access, participation* and *self-management* gradually emerged as practical expressions of the right to communicate. Access refers to the opportunities available to the public to choose programs and to have a means of effective feedback to transmit its reactions and demands to communication organizations. Participation implies a higher level of involvement in the production process and in management and planning of communication services. Self-management is the most advanced form of participation, in which the public exercises the power of decision-making, and is fully involved in the formulation of policies and plans.

In the areas of policy and practice, this conceptual development resulted in a variety of alternative communication movements and experiments, in which advocates of radical change, proponents of moderate social decentralization and social institutions—such as trade unions and religious organizations—were united in their opposition to the hegemony of the established media and in their support of various combinations of access, participation and self-management. Small, portable, easy-to-operate, inexpensive technologies seemed to be the perfect means for implementing their objectives.

In media research, too, established models have been challenged by newly proposed relationships between product and process, source and recipient. Concepts such as channel combinations, functional interchangeability, and division-of-labor among different media emerged from findings on the limitations of individual media in satisfying communication needs (Katz & Gurevitch, 1976). Effect-oriented, product-based research (which accepted media premises that the program is the ultimate goal and viewed planning/production/distribution processes as geared to their attainment), had to face the proposition implied in the right to communicate—that *participation* in all communication processes may be as important as the final product. Likewise, an alternative pattern was proposed to the traditional tight separation between production/transmission and consumption roles, in terms of less rigid boundaries between individual and community as recipient and as source (Willener, 1976).

Research problems typical of the established mass media—referring to control, structure, and resources; organization; operation and management; content and penetration; ethics and privacy; transfer/adoption of models; and legislation—appeared in different fashion, posed new theoretical and methodological challenges, and caused some researchers to ask whether the hitherto almost exclusive concern with the mass media had become obsolete.

VCR and Broadcasting Reform: Revived Promise and Disenchanting Performance

The advent of the VCR in the 1970s originally implied the possibility of genuine change. The flexibility of the new technology in terms of playback and off-air recording increased freedom in the choice of contents, distribution, and timing of use and reduced dependence on monopolistic broadcasting sources. In contrast with earlier versions of access, promoted earnestly or as lip-service by the established media, which did not imply relinquishing control (such as phone-in and audience-participation shows), the VCR triggered a true decentralization of control over television consumption. Advocates of television reform wanted more, however. Their search for grassroots models was geared to all television processes—planning, production, distribution and consumption. They wanted to use video to enable individuals and groups to exercise greater control over the environment, to develop critical awareness and political organization, to create channels for local expression and interaction, and to foster cultural identity and artistic relevance.

For some ten years before the introduction of the VCR, activists had been experimenting with earlier generations of audio-visual technology—8 mm and 16mm film and open-reel, low-gauge video—in order to attain these objectives. Following the Canadian "Challenge for Change" prototype, dozens of projects mushroomed around the globe. These were well-intentioned, idealistic, but sometimes naive endeavors to establish nonprofessional *community* television.[2] The fact that none of them succeeded has been attributed, in part, to the cumbersome and unreliable pre-VCR equipment (Worth & Adair, 1972; O'Sullivan-Ryan & Kaplun, 1980; Nigg & Wade, 1980; Walsh, 1980). Thus, it did not take long for grassroots communicators to perceive the promising prospects of VCR technology. VCRs were easier to move and operate, cheaper, compatible with ENG and cable, offered a better storage capability than open-reel tapes, and easier to edit. A new technological promise thus served to revive the ideology of community television.

Unfortunately, the VCR experience has been as unrewarding as that of previous technologies. Few experiments to stimulate dormant civic feelings through community television have survived their euphoric infancy to become full-fledged communication systems. True, some evaluations pointed to successful cases in North America and Europe (Berrigan, 1977, 1979; Brownstein, 1978; Burns & Elton, 1978; Moss, 1978; Lewis, 1984). These examples are, however, a marked minority among hundreds of experiments conducted in all parts of the world. In addition, success has usually referred to continued activity and growth, whereas "little research which could substantiate the claims of video in the area of social animation has been carried out..." (Berrigan, 1977: 211), leaving open the question of the net value of access and participation.

Explaining the Failure

The very promise of community television has thus remained ambiguous. As the improved technology did not provide satisfactory blueprints for a broadcast reform, new ideas were sought to replace the notion that appropriate technology would suffice to trigger a communications revolution. The resulting conceptual effort produced three variables, based on sociocultural rather than technological factors: the *compatibility* of the medium with the social context in which it is being applied; the *demand* for participatory communications; and the availability of adequate *resources* (Berrigan, 1977; Postgate, Lewis, & Southwood, 1979; Lewis, 1984).

The first variable (considered by diffusion researchers to be essential for effective adoption (Katz, 1973)), is the level of compatibility between an innovation and an adopting unit. Many experiments to establish small-scale participatory television revealed unsatisfactory compatibility levels: some researchers claimed that media participation cannot be achieved without the parallel institution of participation in other spheres (Gonzaga-Motta, 1984), while others argued that community television was introduced in the industrialized world in neighborhoods whose populations shared geographic proximity, but which did not satisfy basic sociological requirements of community (Mattelart & Piemme, 1980). The transplantation of models has triggered another compatibility problem: notwithstanding differences in structural, cultural, and technological contexts, in political tensions and in financial capabilities, many community television ventures in Europe, Oceania, and the Third World borrowed their conceptual premises from the United States and Canada, resulting in faulty adaptation (Berrigan, 1977; O'Sullivan-Ryan & Kaplun, 1980). The transplantation of the once fashionable Canadian "Challenge for Change" model to the Australian "Video-Access" project, for example, revealed incompatibilities between the imported emphasis on "process"—community members' involvement in planning, production, distribution and utilization—and the final product, the program. Australian analysts found the Canadian emphasis on process incompatible with the Australian reality: "Process," they reported, "is only the philosophy of access providers. Access users must feel they are capable of making a 'good' product or their interest wanes" (Lewis, 1984: 76).

In the Third World, the open-society and equal rights premises underlying the imported models often proved incompatible with typical restrictions on decentralized public opinion mechanisms, with the low valuation placed on citizens, and with a frequently poor self-image (O'Sullivan-Ryan & Kaplun, 1980; Lewis, 1984).

The second variable—need and demand—highlights additional difficulties. A sociocultural resistance to participation was observed in most urban and rural experiments in North America and Latin America, as well as in Western Europe (Berrigan, 1977; Lewis, 1984; Atwood & Mattos, 1984), suggesting that either there was no need for community television at all, or that the application of the medium could not overcome local barriers, or worse, that the experimenters were not aware of the problem. Thus, the assumptions about communities' readiness to accept participatory television and about their automatic adoption of simultaneous source/recipient roles revealed wishful thinking rather than proven fact.

Finally, the promise of community television has been found to be intimately related to the financial, technological and human resources available for the development of both process and product. The lack of funds has been a universal constraint. In the Third World, community media have seldom been included in major financial priorities. Elsewhere, the costs of decentralization have always been a deterring factor, especially where they involved competition with commercial enterprise. Thus, experiments in Asian, African, and Latin American countries went through financial ordeals, along with Western European efforts, with Australian and even Japanese ventures and with many cases in the United States and Canada (Berrigan, 1977; Nigg & Wade, 1980; Fauconnier, 1983; Lewis, 1984; Prehn, 1985). Technology has been another source of constraint. Indeed, the advent of the VCR, computerized editing systems, and time-base correctors has eased production difficulties considerably, but these items have remained relatively expensive, have demanded moderately high skill levels, and have not been available to most community groups. Manpower and training constraints have included everywhere difficulties in recruiting and training community groups in technical, artistic, journalistic, and human relations skills; in developing adequate leadership; and in mobilizing back-up support (Berrigan, 1977; Nigg & Wade, 1980; Lewis, 1984).

VCR Narrowcasting in the Kibbutz: The Promise

The introduction in the late 1970s of narrowcast television in the Israeli *kibbutz* (collective rural community) provided an opportunity to clarify the conditions necessary for achieving the objectives of community television. Unlike the small-scale, on-again off-again nature of most previous experiments, the sizable acquisition and application of narrowcasting equipment, and the expected presence of compatibility, demand, and resources promised to satisfy substantive and methodological requirements. Thus, out of a sample of 71 kibbutzim (the plural of kibbutz in Hebrew) with cable facilities, five systems were introduced in 1978-1980, 45 in 1981-1984, and 21 in 1985 (Shinar & Shur, 1986).

This chapter reports a study undertaken between 1985 and 1986, under the auspices of the Yad Tabenkin Institute for Kibbutz Studies, aimed at exploring the promise and performance of kibbutz cable television as a community medium and at making policy recommendations. At the same time, the study—including a "Kibbutz Video Survey," content analysis of programs, and three in-depth case-studies—was considered useful in learning about the more general conditions necessary for the viability and effectiveness of community television.

The Kibbutz Video Survey (Shinar & Shur, 1986) included a detailed questionnaire on the introduction, operation and resources of local cable stations, sent to informants in all 263 kibbutzim in Israel. 182 informants, featuring a fair representation of the total distribution of kibbutzim by size, age and ideological orientation, returned completed questionnaires. Content analysis was used to investigate 33 local programs produced in nine kibbutzim and all items of the first seven editions of "Arutz Lakibbutz" (Kibbutz Channel), an overall kibbutz movement newscast screened in 98% of the kibbutzim surveyed, through local cable systems or direct closed-circuit. The in-depth case studies included interviews with kibbutz members and with key figures in kibbutz television, as well as an analysis of relevant documents. In 1985, at least 121 (40%) of the 263 kibbutzim owned one VCR or more. At least 52 kibbutzim owned cameras and 22 owned electronic editing equipment. VCRs were being used for overall community purposes in 71 kibbutzim, while local cable stations enabled members of at least 52 communities to view rented and self-produced programs in their homes. Direct closed-circuit screenings were being conducted in an additional 14 communities, with local schools and special interest groups using video in another 50 kibbutzim. In addition, two fully-equipped and staffed central units were operated by the nationwide kibbutz organizations for the production and distribution of programs to their affiliates, and four regional centers were active in training and production (Shinar & Shur, 1986).

Compared to other cases, kibbutzim were found to satisfy most requirements identified for community television. Unlike many other earlier sites for community television projects, kibbutzim are full-fledged communities, not only in terms of geographic proximity, but also in shared values, symbols and lifestyles. Kibbutz life is based on voluntary, selectively accepted membership, pragmatically engineered according to a combination of socialist and Zionist ideologies. Notwithstanding differences between individual communities (Krausz, 1983), the kibbutz has been found to provide the motivation, participation and mutual responsibility necessary for the formation and persistence of community. Production and consumption, for example, are collective. Most members work together in agriculture, industry and services. All members receive goods and services from the kibbutz via collective institutions such as a communal dining hall, laundry and clothing store. The socioeconomic status of kibbutz members is not directly related to the goods and services they receive or produce. Unlike other systems, the farm manager, the head of the industrial plant, or the highest officials receive no more than other members; status is achieved not through seniority, wealth, or family rights, but through the contribution to the community. Finally, in addition to internal kibbutz relations, the concept of community also applies to inter-kibbutz dimensions, whereby the affiliation of individual kibbutzim to the central organizations that form the Kibbutz Movement Federation provides ideological, cultural and practical cooperation.

The introduction of community television in the kibbutz displayed a significant awareness of model-transplantation problems. The point of departure for recommending the adoption of the medium was a search for the solution of well-defined kibbutz problems. The first policy paper issued in 1981 by the Kibbutz Movement's Communications Committee suggested that the very existence of the kibbutz as such depends on the active involvement of its members in all spheres of life. Efforts to maintain and promote active involvement were guided by the premise that, as a unique way of life, the kibbutz has been compelled since its early days to look for compatible answers to its problems, through local experimentation rather than through the adoption of models developed elsewhere. Thus, community television was considered a possible means to promote involvement by stimulating public dialogue and reaction to local, regional and national issues, by encouraging members to express their views and concerns, and by bringing up matters to public knowledge and public discussion (Kibbutz Communications Committee, 1981).

The position taken by kibbutz media activists in the "process versus product" and "providers versus users" dilemmas was that while the model being locally devised could not function without a strong process component, attention should be given to producing a viewable and meaningful product, together with an awareness of the fallacy involved in trying to imitate broadcast television (Tamir, 1985).

The second variable identified in community television research—demand—is present in the kibbutz reality almost by definition. The equality of rights and duties, the mutual dependence among members, and the principles of direct democracy are but a few sources of this need for participation and communication in kibbutz life. They are complemented by the fact that kibbutzim are not isolated communities.

Although making up no more than 3% of Israel's population, active involvement in national affairs has been a major tradition of the movement, as expressed by the role of kibbutz members in the struggle for the establishment of the state and of the country's public life, security affairs, economy and culture. A steady flow of communications is necessary for personal and institutional functioning as well as for maintaining morale, motivation, involvement and solidarity. In addition, the demand for information has been strongly emphasized by the economic and occupational changes that have affected the kibbutz in recent years. Technological development, professional advancement and economic growth have increased the need for internal and external communications. This has been a complex task for kibbutz members and institutions, with implications for the comprehension of a changing environment, accessibility to events, and exertion of the right to participate in decision making (Katz & Golomb, 1983).

Changes in the collective ideology have been an additional source of demand for participatory communications. Kibbutzim have developed from isolated groups of young, pioneering idealists to communities of several hundreds of members and a wide range of personalities, interests and skills. During almost one century of existence, natural erosion affected ideological zeal and collective orientations, coupled with the impact of a rising standard of living and a diminishing isolation from the urban middle class. Personal property has been increasingly tolerated, revealing a more liberal attitude toward the formerly rigid concept of equality. The family unit has been competing with the hitherto predominant community orientation, as illustrated by the decision adopted by most kibbutzim to have the children spend the night at home instead of at the communal house and by families taking some of their meals at home instead of at the communal dining hall. These trends of affluence have exposed the kibbutz collective ideology to threatening influences. One generally approved conclusion called for strengthening community ties through the activation of communication channels tailored to local needs (Magen, 1985).

Field data from the Kibbutz Video Survey support this conclusion: about 2/3 of the informants in 171 kibbutzim (63%) reported the awareness of the need for improved communications in their communities—40% among a majority of members and 23% among part of the membership. Economic and financial information were the leading topics in demand. A greater demand was found for internal rather than external communications. Most communities reported being well-provided by the mass media with information on the world, the region, and the country, while the demand for communications with non-kibbutz communities was found to be lower than the need for communications on kibbutz cultural continuity, local artistic expression, and links between kibbutz members and the movement. The majority of respondents proposed to introduce local television (79.6%), to improve the local newsletter (81.7%), and to intensify interpersonal relations (79.2%) as ways to meet the demand.

Kibbutz television has been fortunate in the third potential problem-area: resources. In the late 1970s, when cable television was first introduced in the movement, there were no real problems of technology, funding and manpower. At that time, major technological difficulties had already been solved and became a problem of funding and skill. Also during those years, kibbutzim were experiencing unprecedented financial growth. No difficulties were found in installing transmission cable systems (usually a by-product of the installation of telephone lines) or in purchasing production and playback equipment, sometimes of a quality far exceeding the needs of community television. During the first five years of kibbutz television, the overall sum invested by kibbutzim in the purchase of VCRs and other production/playback equipment was estimated at three million US dollars. This sum is about three times higher than the budget allocated by all kibbutzim to their members for the purchase of books.[3] In the area of manpower, the kibbutz has earned a reputation for problem-solving inventiveness and for the ability to perform cooperative assignments. Thus, the demands posed by community television for positive attitudes to innovation and participation as well as for autonomous initiative and decentralized structure were met by a favorable predisposition.

Compared with findings on the destructive influence of external initiative, excessively centralized authority, and governmental control (Berrigan, 1977; Lewis, 1984), the promise of community television in the kibbutz was brighter than elsewhere.

Compared with the controversial introduction of television sets in the kibbutz movement in the late 1960s, the diffusion of VCR narrowcasting equipment in the late 1970s indicates a stronger acceptance of video, notwithstanding obvious differences in pace and proportion.[4] Two different patterns emerge from the comparison of data gathered for the diffusion of television sets (Gurevitch & Loevy, 1972) and of VCR equipment (Shinar & Shur, 1986) in the kibbutz, in terms of the percentages of kibbutzim

Table 1
Diffusion of Television and Community VCR in the Kibbutz Movement (percentages of kibbutzim)

	Television (N = 231 kibbutzim)	VCR *(N = 263 kibbutzim)*
First measuring Early introduction	(April 1968) 19.5% (45)	(mid-1980) 1.9% (5)
Second measuring 12 months preceding study	(June 1968) 25.1% (58)	(mid-1984) 19.0% (50)
Third measuring At time of study	(June 1969) 61.0% (141)	(mid-1985) 27.0% (71)
Percentage of growth between first and second measuring	5.6%	17.1%
Percentage of growth between second and third measuring	35.9%	8.0%

where both types of items were available at the time of each study (third measuring), twelve months earlier (second measuring), and at the time of their introduction (first measuring). The diffusion pattern of television sets displays an initially modest rate of growth (5.6%), from 19.5% in the first measuring to 25.1% in the second. This was followed by a dramatic increase (35.9%) to 61% twelve months later, suggesting that an uphill path led to opening the way for large-scale adoption. Indeed, the introduction of television in the kibbutz was met by strong resistance, on the grounds of its alleged destructive influence on the collective, participatory, and local creativity ethos (Gurevitch & Loevy, 1972). The diffusion of VCR and other narrowcasting equipment indicates, in contrast, an initially high rate of adoption (17.1%), from 1.9% in the first measuring to 19% in the second. A modest increase (8%) to 27% took place in the following twelve months, suggesting that the VCR had to overcome fewer early obstacles, but that some difficulties did emerge to slow the pace of diffusion.

The Performance: Process

Trial and error experiments, coupled with uncoordinated efforts were typical of the performance of kibbutz television in its first formative years. Sixty-nine percent of the local stations (47 out of 69 cases) were introduced as a result of individual or group initiative rather than of collective resolutions taken by kibbutz communal institutions. Public discussion on the introduction of cable television took place in the general assemblies of no more than 23 kibbutzim, one-third of the cases studied. The guidelines formulated by kibbutz communication activists did not reach the local level or were rejected altogether.

About half of the 241 television crew members for whom data were available in the Kibbutz Video Survey, had no training at all; about one quarter were given only basic training in kibbutz movement crash courses, while another quarter had longer training. Local operations were run by staffs with an average size of five members, with a range from three to eight. About half of the staffs (23 out of 53 for whom data were available) had been working without any systematic procedures and 19 crews formulated general guidelines, while only seven crews had overall policies. Preproduction meetings were never conducted in more than half of the kibbutzim and only 20% had regular staff meetings. Decisions on production and distribution are made by the station staff alone in 21 sites, by the staff jointly with kibbutz committee members in 22, and by the staff jointly with a specially-elected committee in 10 kibbutzim. Work on video productions usually is conducted at the expense of staff members' free time. Only 20% of the crews said they had adequate time for planning, production and distribution assignments. Likewise, most stations lacked autonomous budgets and depended on the kibbutz's cultural committee or secretariat for funds. Nevertheless, few complaints were reported on the application of censorship through this dependence. In fact, almost half of the stations reported on their satisfaction with current budgetary arrangements. The major basis of control has been public opinion, usually through informal criticism.

Planning and coordination of production and transmission have been as casual as station operation. The objectives for the introduction of community television, formulated in 69 kibbutzim with local stations, do not display a high degree for compatibility with the areas rated in 171 kibbutzim as highest in perceived need of communication improvements (see Table 2). Economic and financial information were rated as priority areas for the improvement of local communications, but were assigned much lower priority among kibbutz television objectives. Entertainment was not mentioned at all as a priority area for communications improvement, but more than 40% of the local stations have had it as a major programming item. Education and culture were given low priorities among the areas of need, but were considered the most important objectives for the introduction of television.

In addition, the strong community orientation of kibbutz video activists in the initial days does not appear to have reached either the field or the leadership. The failure of kibbutz television founders to persuade the movement's central bodies even to discuss the official adoption and recommendation of the community television model obviously reduced the model's legitimacy and acceptance at the local level.[5] Local crews have been only sparsely guided by central units. The available guidance, given mainly in crash courses, included orientation on the purchase and operation of equipment and production work, with little concern about the basics of journalism, station development and community activation. Ideological, operational and professional guidelines have not been provided, given that blueprints on these matters were never developed at the central level. This is hardly surprising, since production has become the major objective at a relatively early stage. Central units have become staffed with trained crews, their programs have been recorded on ¾ inch high-band tape (in order to achieve broadcast quality, which could enable them to market their product to professional television), and assistance of outside contractors has been sought in editing the final product. Following broadcast television standard practices, productions of local crews have seldom been considered qualified to be included in the "Arutz Lakibbutz" (Kibbutz Channel) movement-wide periodical news magazine, and decision making has been highly centralized.

The Product

Although there is some locally produced video, loaned, rented and purchased materials make up the major part of kibbutz TV programming, a pattern not unlike the use of home-VCR. Programs produced by the kibbutz movement's central units—particularly Arutz Lakibbutz—have been transmitted in all 69 community stations studied. In addition, programming in 59 stations has included off-air recordings from Israel Television, mainly to compensate for the overlap

Table 2
Kibbutz Communications Demand and Kibbutz Television Supply

Demand				*Supply*					
Areas in which the need for communication improvements has been most acutely felt (% kibbutzim) N = 171		*Objective for introduction of cable television (% kibbutzim)* N = 69		*Major emphases in kibbutz television local transmissions (% kibbutzim)* N = 69		*Major topics in kibbutz television local productions (% kibbutzim)* N = 175		*Major topics in "Arutz Lakibbutz" (Kibbutz Channel) (% kibbutzim)* N = 51	
Economics	73%	Social, educational, cultural improvement	72%	Entertainment	42%	Current events	32%	Culture, society, education, heritage	45%
Finance	70%	Documentation	60%	Involvement	30%	Economic reports	30%	Kibbutz external relations	29%
Society	62%	Communications improvement	57%	Information	14%	Daily problems	18%	Economics, finance	18%
Education	55%	Economic improvement	57%	Documentation	14%	Trivia	15%	Welfare	8%
Culture	55%	Democratization	55%			Welfare	5%		
Welfare	48%								
Entertainment	75%								

in scheduling between kibbutz communal functions and popular television programs. The most outstanding example has been occurring on Saturday nights, when kibbutz general assemblies coincide with the broadcast of the major weekly sports program. Rented feature films have been another popular item in 54 stations, followed in 32 kibbutzim by off-air recordings from Israel Instructional Television.

Local productions, recorded, edited, and transmitted on ½ inch VCR (except for 9 stations with ¾ inch U-matic equipment) were less widespread. Features on local topics have been transmitted on irregular schedules in 32 kibbutzim and periodical local news magazines in 18. Less common local programs include items to be discussed in coming general assemblies, electronic bulletin boards, games and contests, productions for kibbutz festivities and live coverage of kibbutz committee meetings.

Table 3
Programs Transmitted on Kibbutz Television (n = 69 kibbutzim)

	% Kibbutzim
Import from kibbutz movement: Arutz Lakibbutz (kibbutz channel)	98.5
Recordings from Israel TV	85.5
Rented feature films	78.2
Recordings from Israel instructional television	46.3
Locally produced features	46.3
Locally produced newscasts	26.0
Preparation for coming general assemblies	18.8
Games and specials	14.4
Electronic bulletin board	8.6

Kibbutz productions, central and local alike, have made up only a small part of the transmission schedules. With an average duration of 20 to 30 minutes, local programs have been transmitted once in three to four weeks, and kibbutz movement programs once in four to six weeks. Local stations have emphasized current events and information, with particular reference to social issues. A typical local news magazine may include a discussion on a topical issue such as the composition of nursery school age-groups; whether or not to conduct Bar Mizvah celebrations; items from the field, such as dog life on the kibbutz, fire prevention, etc.; items on kibbutz local artists; items on the local industrial plant, agricultural farm, etc.; financial reports; and variety items such as celebrations and humorous events. Special programs have dealt with recognized problems, such as the adherence to cults, kibbutz members returning from army service, and documentation of festive, political and other events. Arutz Lakibbutz has dealt with kibbutz identity (such as the role of the kibbutz in Israeli society, moral/ideological stocktaking); internal mechanics (such as innovations in education, the introduction of an automatic banking machine and budgetary cuts); current information and arts/entertainment topics. Along with this service, the public relations function of the program has been clearly shown in the preference for safe topics, such as cultural and social reports (45% of the items) rather than economic and financial controversy (18% of the items, notwithstanding a much higher audience demand) and in the preference for covering kibbutz official institutions (46% of the items) rather than events (26%) and individuals (19%).

Productions of kibbutz movement central units have generally received greater human, financial, organizational and technical resources than local productions. However, their tendency to imitate broadcast television in contents and formats, and the attempts to assume critical positions toward the kibbutz establishment have been incompatible with their didactic, mobilized tone. Formality and pompousness were identified in more than 80% of the items analyzed. Messages have been usually positive, expressing praise, pride, and confidence in more than 50% of the items; consensus and some criticism in 45% to 50% of the items; and negative feelings, including frustration, doubt, and mistrust in 10% to 30% of the messages transmitted. A typical Arutz Lakibbutz program may include: items on the contribution of the movement to Israeli society, items on current information (such as the agricultural season, the situation of kibbutz industrial plants), items of general interest (i.e., educational innovations, construction, movement's staff returning home), and entertainment items.

The influence of broadcast television has been apparent in Arutz Lakibbutz and local productions alike. In the former, it has been expressed in visual treatment (sets, background, performing and announcing style) and in verbal and symbolic language, including artwork. In the latter, this influence can be recognized in the imitation of program structures and formats. Local programs, however, have been typified also by some conscious or accidental attempts to develop a specific style, illustrated by the lack of manipulation of reality and by the development of a rhetoric of intimacy, expressed in an informal familiar tone, and in the fact that characters do not have to be identified to the viewer.

Efficiency and Effectiveness

The performance of kibbutz television as a community medium has not yet measured up to its bright promise. In terms of efficiency, most local stations have displayed a casual approach to planning, production, distribution and feedback. The central units have become increasingly centralized and alienated from the field. A tendency toward professional broadcasting rather than community narrowcasting is apparent in both cases.

In terms of effectiveness in goal achievement, access has been selective, having provided little opportunity for kibbutz members to come closer to the system. Although kibbutz members were consulted on transmission schedules, they have had little influence over the selection of imported and locally produced programs. Access has been even more limited at the central unit level, expressed by a minimal share of local crews (and none on the part of individual members) in the selection of materials and feedback.

Participation has been as limited as access, with little involvement by the public in planning processes and decision making. Such participation has included, at best, voting in the general assembly for or against the allocation of funds to the local crew. There has been no public participation in central units' decision making. Moreover, few conscious efforts were reported for the recruitment and encouragement of large numbers of kibbutz members to participate in program production. Out of 48 kibbutzim for which data were available on this matter in the Kibbutz Video Survey, 26 reported strong interest and 17 reported some interest by members in being involved in the work of the local station. Explicit interest in participating in production was expressed by 28 of the 66 respondents in one of the in-depth case studies; by 24 out of 110 respondents in the second case study; and by 28 out of 200 respondents in the third case. This amount of demand is certainly not matched by the 5-member average size of crews in the 69 stations studied nor by the average number of participants in the production of the 33 local programs analyzed (3.5 participants per kibbutz in 9 communities with an average population of 200 adults each).

One consequence of these shortcomings has been the virtual absence of self-management. Kibbutz television has come to be considered as a hobby of a few video activists in local stations and as the privilege of professionals in the central units.

Conclusions: The Missing Variable

The faulty performance of kibbutz cable television cannot be ascribed to the absence of basic prerequisites, compatibility, demand and resources, since kibbutzim have been generously equipped with them. The findings of the present study point to other explanations. First, the formative phase of kibbutz television was not guided by a clear conceptual framework. The efforts invested since the late 1970s by the movement's community television founding fathers in devising applicable blueprints did not find significant expression in the field. The ineffective diffusion of community television principles among crews and audiences reflects the lack of policy and the weakness of dissemination channels. These have been powerful obstacles to the attitudinal and behavioral charge required by the adoption of participatory media. The adherence to the professional model—in which only one component of the community media model, namely production, is the major objective—was not free from the commitment to use television for sociocultural improvement. Thus neither access and participation nor centralized specialization and professionalism became full and legitimate objectives. The confusion between elements from both models has prevented the achievement of most of their goals.

Problems of systemic balance provide a second explanation. A stronger emphasis has been given to certain components of television systems (such as transmission and production equipment and imported programming) than to other components, including planning, training in journalism practices and community activation, and developing operational blueprints.

Finally, the lack of recognition of community television as a specific medium provides an additional explanation. The view of local community stations as miniature broadcasting organizations, implied in the overemphasis given to production, has meant giving up the particular qualities of community television. In this sense, the difference between the professional and community models is that the former promotes essential norms (such as planning and creativity, correct camera work, and high-quality editing) as ultimate goals, while the latter prescribes the use of these norms for the achievement of social and cultural objectives, including the promotion of community self-expression and authenticity, the opening of channels for public involvement, and multidirectional communication avenues.

Since the completion of the study in 1986, no significant changes have been reported in the situation depicted by the study. A recession in kibbutz economy has caused the discontinuation of subsidized productions. Arutz Lakibbutz has further emphasized its professional aspirations, mainly through offering advertising services to kibbutz-based industrial plants, in order to compensate for the loss of income. At the local level, less than a dozen new stations became operative. The movement's leadership has not acknowledged the participatory model nor has it encouraged its development.

Thus, notwithstanding the presence of most prerequisites identified in previous research, kibbutz television has displayed acute performance problems, notably a low level of institutionalization, consistent lack of planning and a confusion of models. Consequently, compatibility, demand and resources can be considered *necessary* conditions, without which community television is doomed from the outset. The variables emerging from the analysis of kibbutz television—conceptual framework, systematic balance, and recognition of the medium's specific qualities—may be considered at least as some of the *sufficient* conditions for the effective application of community television.

Notes

1. Research data indicate, for example, that Third World governments that embarked on "big technology" investments abandoned regional provision in broadcasting and the press, and that almost everywhere local and regional media operators have been pressured to upgrade their equipment in order to compete with big media organizations (Lewis, 1984: 7).
2. "Community television" is used here to mean "a station characterized by the local nature of its ownership, programming, and the market it is designed to serve...that provides for management, operation, and programming primarily by and for the members of the local community...[and that] should allow for community access and reflect the interests and special needs of the audience..." See Canadian Radio-Television and Telecommunications Commission (1986). Public Notice CRTC 1986-176 proposed Regulations Respecting Television Broadcasting, pp. 18-19.
3. The average annual budget for the purchase of books allocated to each kibbutz member is 10 shekels (Israel) or U.S. $6.60. Multiplied by 30,000 members, it amounts to some U.S. $200,000 annually and U.S. $1 million over five years. In addition to this earmarked allocation, members use funds from their general personal budgets for purchasing books.
4. Differences in absolute pace and magnitude of adoption and diffusion can be accounted for by the easier installation and use of television sets and the more complex nature of narrowcasting systems (infrastructure, cost, training and organization).
5. This unfavorable background for participatory media suffered a further setback when, following the rotation principle in the staffing of central positions in the

movement, time came for the group of community television initiators to go back home. They were relieved in late 1982 by a team of more professionally inclined communicators who concentrated on the promotion of centralized production. Although this team was relieved by another in 1986, the professional inclination is still predominant in 1988.

References

Atwood, R. & Mattos S. (1984). Mass media reform and social change: The Peruvian experience. In G. Gerbner and M. Siefert (Eds.), *World Communication: A handbook.* New York: Longman.

Beltran, L. R. (1980). Farewell to Aristotle: Horizontal communication. *Communication* 5(1).

Berrigan F. (Ed.). (1977). *Access: Some western models of community media.* Paris: Unesco.

Branscomb, A., & Savage, M. (1978). The broadcasting reform movement: At the crossroads. *Journal of Communication* 28(2).

Brownstein, C.N. (1978). Interactive TV and social services. *Journal of Communication* 28(2).

Burns, R., & Elton, L. (1978). Programming for the future. *Journal of Communication* 28(2).

Enzensberger, H. M. (1972). Constituents of a theory of the media. In D. McQuail (Ed.), *Sociology of Mass Communications.* Middlesex, England: Penguin.

Fauconnier, G. (1983). Serving two cultures: Local media in Belgium. In G. Gerbner & M. Siefert (Eds.), *World Communication: A handbook.* New York: Longman.

Freire P. (1974). *Pedagogy of the Oppressed.* New York: Seabury.

Gonzaga-Motta, L. (1984). National communications policies: Grass roots alternatives, in G. Gerbner & M. Siefert (Eds.), *World Communication: A handbook.* New York: Longman.

Groombridge, B. (1972). *Television and the People.* London: Penguin.

Gurevitch, M., & Loevy, Z. (1972). The diffusion of television as an innovation: The case of the kibbutz. *Human Relations* 25(3).

Henderson, H. (1974, March). Information and the new movements for citizenship participation. *Annals of the American Academy of Political and Social Science.*

Hurwitz,S. (1978). The corporate role. *Journal of Communication,* 28(2).

Kalba, C. (1979). The video implosion: Models for re-inventing television. In R. Adler & W. Baer (Eds.), *The Electronic Box Office.* New York: Praeger.

Katz, D., & Golomb, N. (1983). Integration, effectiveness and adaptation in social systems. In E. Krausz (Eds.), *The Sociology of the Kibbutz.* New Brunswick, NJ: Transaction.

Katz, E. (1973). *On the Use of the Concept of Compatibility in Research on the Diffusion of Innovation.* Jerusalem: The Israel Academy of Sciences and Humanities Proceedings V(5).

Katz, E., & Gurevitch, M. (1976). *The Secularization of Leisure.* London: Faber and Faber.

Kibbutz Communications Committee (1981). *Kibbutz Communications in the Age of Electronic Media.* Working paper. Tel Aviv: Kibbutz Movement Federation. (Hebrew).

Krausz E. (Ed. (1983). *The Sociology of the Kibbutz.* New Brunswick, NJ: Transaction.

Lewis P.M. (1984). *Media for People in the Cities: A study of community media in the urban context*. Paris: UNESCO.

MacBride, S. (1980). *Many Voices, One World*. Paris: UNESCO.

Magen, A. (Ed.). (1985). *Communications Technology in the Kibbutz*. Tel Aviv, Israel: Yad Tabenkin Institute for Kibbutz Studies. (Hebrew).

Mander, J. (1978). *Four Arguments for the Elimination of Television*. New York: Morrow.

Mattelart, A., & Piemme, J.M. (1980). New means of communication: New questions for the left. *Media Culture and Society*, 2.

Moss, M.L. (1978). Research on community uses. *Journal of Communication*, 28(2).

Nigg, H., & Wade, J. (1980). *Community Media*. Zurich, Switzerland: Regenbogen-Verlag.

O'Sullivan-Ryan, J., & Kaplun, M. (1980). *Communication Methods to Promote Grass-roots Participation. Paris: UNESCO.*

Pasteka, J. (1979). *Right to communicate: A socialist approach*. Paris: UNESCO.

Postgate, R., Lewis, P.M., & Southwood, W.A. (1979). *Low Cost Communication Systems for Educational and Development Purposes in Third World Countries*. Paris: UNESCO.

Prehn, O. (1985). *Community Television in Denmark*. Aalborg: University of Aalborg.

Rogers, E. (1976). Communications and development: The passing of the dominant paradigm. *Communication Research* 3(2).

Shinar, D., & Shur, S. (1986). *Kibbutz Video Survey*. Tel Aviv, Israel: Kibbutz Movement Federation. (Hebrew).

Tamir, A. (1985). *Closed Circuit: Video in the Service of the Kibbutz*. Tel Aviv, Israel: Sifriat Poalim. (Hebrew).

Walsh, B. (1979-80, December-January). Community television. *Cinema Papers*.

White, R.A. (1984). Communication strategies for social change: National TV versus local public radio. In G. Gerbner & M. Siefert (Eds.), *World Communications: A Handbook*. New York: Longman.

Willener, A. (1976). *Videology and Utopia: Explorations in a new medium*. London: Routledge and Kegan Paul.

Worth, S., & Adair J. (1972). *Through Navajo Eyes: An exploration in film communication and anthropology*. Bloomington: Indiana University Press.

Part 5

In Times of Elections

16

Voters as Consumers: Audience Perspectives on the Election Broadcasts

Gadi Wolfsfeld

Televised advertisements have become a central component of the Israeli election campaign in recent years. Millions of shekels are poured into the production of these commercials, and their content and tone have an important impact on the pace and agenda of the election campaign. The newspapers carry daily reviews of the previous evening's broadcasts as various pundits attempt to rate the effectiveness of the ads in the perennial attempt to determine who is "winning" the campaign. The underlying question appears to be: who is doing the best job at manipulating the public?

The controversy over whether or not these ads should be broadcast takes place during every election campaign. In addition to making the usual complaints about the dominance of "style" over "substance," many commentators are alienated by the often vicious attacks of the two major parties on one another. Questions are also raised about whether or not the ads really have any effect on anyone. This controversy continued during the 1992 election campaign, and concerns over the waste of public monies were fueled by press reports that the number of people who were viewing the election broadcasts had declined.

In order to evaluate the utility of the election broadcasts, or whether or not there is a need to change the existing format, we need to be more specific about their purpose. The approach that will be adopted in this article is best described by Joslyn (1990), in which he calls on researchers to look at election campaigns as "occasions for civic education." While the intended goal of the election broadcasts is persuasion, they also provide an important channel for the dissemination of political information about the candidates and positions of the various political parties. This type of information can be valuable for many citizens, including those who have already decided on how they will vote. The broadcasts can also serve other positive functions, such as stimulating a greater level of political interest, discussion, and participation in the election campaign.

We see voters as intelligent *consumers* of political information (Himmelweit, Humphreys, and Jaeger 1985; Popkin 1991) who are perfectly capable of evaluating whether or not the election broadcasts are meeting their needs. This perspective differs from a good deal of the previous research in political communication, which looks almost exclusively at the "effects" of such commercials on candidate images and voting behavior (see, e.g., Biocca 1991; Kaid, Nimmo, and Sanders 1986; Kaid and Boydston 1987). The ideas which are presented in this article do, however, dovetail rather well with the "uses and gratifications" school of thought, which also looks at these issues by looking at the needs of the audience (Blumer 1985; Blumer, Gurevitch, and Katz 1985; Caspi 1984; Caspi and Levinsohn 1993; Donohew, Palmgreen, and Rayburn 1987).

The starting point for any evaluation of these broadcasts should begin by comparing what the public expects from these broadcasts with what they are getting. Accordingly, we shall examine the 1992 election broadcasts by asking voters about the utility of the election broadcasts. The discussion will be divided into two sections. The discussion in the first section will look at the attitudes and behavior of the general public. It is important to look at such issues as the size of the audience for such ads, reasons for watching and not watching the ads, and the general level of satisfaction with what is being broadcast.

The second part of the study will focus on a more specific group of consumers: the undecided voters. Many voters in this group should be actively searching for political information in order to make their decision about their final "purchase." It will be useful to find out about the size and nature of this group and who among them finds the broadcasts helpful as a voting guide. We shall also present some results that indicate the amount of help voters say they received from the one political debate that was televised as compared to the other political ads that were broadcast. All of these factors will allow us to better evaluate the overall utility of the broadcasts for the electorate.

In this paper we shall attempt to answer these questions based on a national survey that was carried out a few days after the election in 1992. The survey was carried out by the Guttmann Institute of Applied Social Science Research in Jerusalem.[1] The survey was conducted by telephone among five hundred and four Jewish adults above the age of 19.[2]

Table 1
Television Viewing for Three Elections

Amount of Viewing	1981* (*N*=1,111) (%)	1988 (*N*=508) (%)	1992 (*N*=504) (%)
All or almost all	61	33	25
3-4 times each week		23	12
1-2 times each week	15	12	23
Infrequent		7	21
None	23	26	19

Note: the survey in 1981 was carried out using personal interviews while the surveys in 1988 and 1992 were carried out by telephone. No survey data were available for the 1984 election.

*In 1981 the response categories were all, some, and none. The 15 percent figure refers to all of those who answered some.

I. The General Public: A Shrinking and Skeptical Audience

The first question that should concern consumer advocates is whether or not people are using the product. There's not much point in investing so much money in public education if a good deal of the population is cutting class. Survey data published during the election campaign suggested that the television ads were attracting a smaller audience than in previous elections. It is possible to examine this question directly by utilizing data collected during two previous election campaigns: 1981 and 1988.[3]

As can be seen in table 1, people were indeed watching fewer ads in the election campaign of 1992. While 61 percent of the population reported watching all (or almost all) of the ads in 1981, that figure decreased to 33 percent in 1988 and to 25 percent in 1992. There was also a dramatic drop since the previous election in the percentage who were watching the ads several times a week.

It is important to emphasize, however, that these findings suggest not that *fewer people were watching the ads* but rather that *people were watching the ads less*. The percentage of citizens who watched at least one set of broadcasts remained fairly stable over the years, and may have even increased slightly in 1992. Most voters apparently decided that there was no need to watch the broadcasts every night and preferred to tune in from time to time. Although presumably one could argue for the convenience of being able to choose which night to watch, the fact that 63 percent of the population watched two or fewer ads a week should cast certain doubts about the wisdom of broadcasting the commercials six nights a week, at least under the present format.

Table 2
Campaign Interest for Three Elections

Frequency of interest	1981 (*N*=1,111) (%)	1988 (*N*=508) (%)	1992 (*N*=504) (%)
All the time	31	23	21
Most of the time	29	26	24
Occasionally	27	26	34
Never	13	25	21

Why did the voters watch fewer ads in 1992? The primary reason offered by pundits was that the decline in viewing was indicative of a more general indifference to the 1992 campaign. Dozens of news articles, radio broadcasts, and several television features were devoted to a discussion about the lack of popular interest in the campaign. The political parties were reported to be having much more trouble mobilizing volunteers to work in the campaigns, and the numbers who were attending rallies appeared to be much smaller than in previous elections.

The notion of political indifference, in a sense, places the "blame" for a lack of viewing on the voters. If the Israeli public is simply not interested in the political campaign, then there is really not much the political leadership can do to better inform them. Yet, it has been documented that Israelis have one of the highest levels of political interest in the Western world (Wolfsfeld 1988), and thus the potential for viewing should be very high.

The evidence collected for the present survey does not support the notion that the decrease in viewing in 1992 was related to a drop in interest in the campaign. In addition to the previously discussed questions about viewing habits, respondents in the 1981, 1988, and 1992 elections were also asked: "How much do you take an interest in and follow the election campaign: in newspapers, the radio, and television?" The results of this comparison are presented in table 2. While there does seem to have been a decrease in voter interest when one compares the extremely heated campaign of 1981 to that of 1988, there was no further drop in interest between 1998 and 1992. Although one would hesitate to reject the many claims of party activists on the basis of one survey question, these findings do cast some serious doubts as to whether or not the extent of voter indifference was as widespread as was claimed.

Another explanation that was offered for the decline in viewing had to do with changes in the mass media system in Israel. The introduction of cable television to Israel, while not yet complete, offered many Israelis the option of watching something possibly more attractive than election propaganda. The survey sample was divided into two groups according to whether or not the respondents had access to cable televi-

Table 3
Reasons for Not Watching Election Broadcasts

Reason	Percentage of Respondents
Preferred to do other things	36
Already decided on vote	12
They had nothing new to say	12
Don't like when people try to "trick" me	9
Don't want to watch political propaganda	8
Don't believe the claims and promises of political parties	8
Not interested in politics	8
The politicians don't relate to me seriously	5
Watched cable television	1
Watched something on another channel	1
I didn't understand what they were talking about	1

Notes: Total N=508; total exceeds 100 percent due to rounding.

sion in their homes. Although in some geographic areas this might be related to other demographic variables, the fact that many major cities still had not yet installed cable offered a reasonable test of the "cable hypothesis." When we compared those with cable to those without, *no significant differences* were found in the extent to which either group watched the political commercials. It would seem then that people's decisions about how many broadcast ads to watch are unrelated to the number of program alternatives they face.

An additional way to approach this problem is simply to ask those voters who watched the smaller number of broadcasts about their reasons for not viewing. We asked those who watched less than once a week why they didn't watch. As can be seen in table 3, the most popular reasons were that they preferred to do other things, that they had already decided how to vote, and that the ads had nothing new to say. A further refutation of the cable hypothesis comes from the fact that only 2 percent of those who didn't watch said that it was because they were watching something else on television.

It is also noteworthy that so few Israelis suggested that they weren't watching due to a lack of interest in politics. Most Israelis are interested in politics and, as shown, do follow the campaign in the news media. The most reasonable conclusion is that the election broadcasts are simply not providing the type of information and format that would attract a wider audience.[4] This point becomes even clearer when we look at the public's attitudes towards the ads.

Figure 1
Public Attitudes toward Frequency of Ads
Total does not equal 100 percent due to rounding.

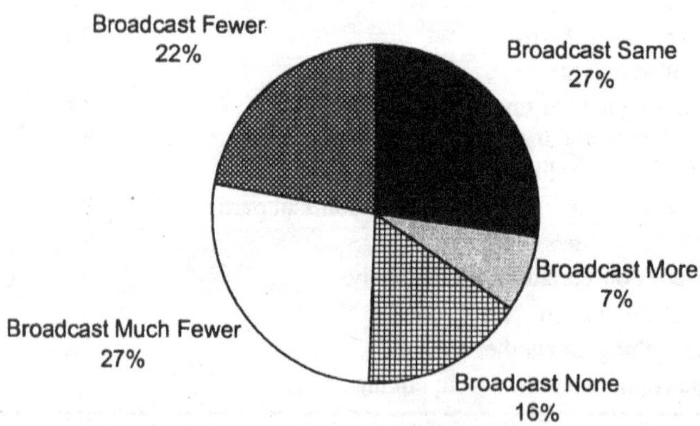

Attitudes Towards the Ads

In general it can be said that most Israelis have a negative attitude toward the election broadcasts. This is perhaps best illustrated by their responses to questions about whether they would like to see more or fewer ads broadcast during election time. As can be seen in figure 11.1, the majority of Israelis would prefer to see fewer political ads on television, and a meager 7 percent would like to see more.[5] It is perhaps meaningful to point out that the 16 percent of those sampled who suggested that the ads be completely discontinued did so without that possibility having even been mentioned by the interviewers.

People are also very unlikely to find the ads very helpful in deciding for whom to vote. Although we shall deal with this issue more directly in the second section of this piece, it is important to note that only 2 percent of the sample reported that the ads offered them a good deal of help in this direction, and another 7 percent reported that it offered them some help.[6] If this is considered one of the primary functions of these broadcasts, they are clearly missing the mark.

Another way to gauge how seriously voters are taking the ads is to look at some of the reasons they give for watching them. Previous work on this topic (Caspi 1984; Caspi and Levinsohn 1993) has concluded that voters are much more likely to watch for reasons of entertainment than for voting guidance. The gap is especially dramatic when one asks respondents to list the "most important reasons" for watching. When this question format is used, the proportion listing voting guidance as their principal reason for voting ranges between 2 percent and 11 percent of the public (Caspi 1984).

In the present study we used a more conservative measure that attempts to gauge whether or not voting guidance was *one* of the reasons for viewing the election ads. The respondents were presented with five different motivations that had been found important in previous studies and asked whether each of them was one of the reasons they watched the programs. The results are presented in figure 2, and it is useful to bear in mind that the proportions refer only to those who actually watched a number of broadcasts, rather than to the whole electorate.

It is important to recall that this survey was conducted after the conclusion of the election campaign. Therefore these replies tell us something about how people came to think of these broadcasts as well as why they initially chose to watch. As in the past we find that the most frequently cited reason for watching the election broadcasts in 1992 was entertainment. This was the only motivation cited by a majority of the audience, and this suggests that most viewers do not take these broadcasts very seriously.

The other motivations, on the other hand, fall much closer to the notion of civic education. The fact that a significant minority of viewers did turn to the ads in order to get information for the purposes of political discussion and debate, to keep up with the electoral race, and to obtain help in their voting decisions, is one of the few findings that suggests something positive about these ads. It could be argued that the use of entertainment is a perfectly legitimate means of achieving some more significant educational goals.

In general, however, the evidence presented here suggests that the Israeli election broadcasts are not meeting the needs of the general public. People are watching fewer broadcasts than in the past, and a large majority would like to see fewer political ads put on the air. The major reason for watching is entertainment, and considering the public cost of these ads, the broadcasts are not realizing their potential.

We turn then to the second part of the discussion, which focuses more specifically on the utility of the ads for undecided voters.

II. Undecided Voters

Undecided voters should provide the most motivated audience for the election broadcasts. Certainly they are the primary target for the political ads, and at least some of these citizens should be expected to use these broadcasts as a source of information in making their final decision. In this essay, "undecided voters" refers to those respondents who reported (after the election) that they had debated between two parties before making their final choice.[7] A surprisingly high 49 percent of the voters fall into this category. We also made a further distinction between "internal floaters" (34 percent of the sample), who debated between two parties within the same political camp, and "external floaters" (15 percent) who weighed the options of voting for parties from two different camps.[8]

It is helpful to begin by telling something about the social background and interests of these three groups before turning to an account of their attitudes and behavior with regard to the election broadcasts. We shall, throughout these analyses, attempt to better understand the undecided voters by comparing them in background, attitudes, and

Figure 2
Viewing Motivations

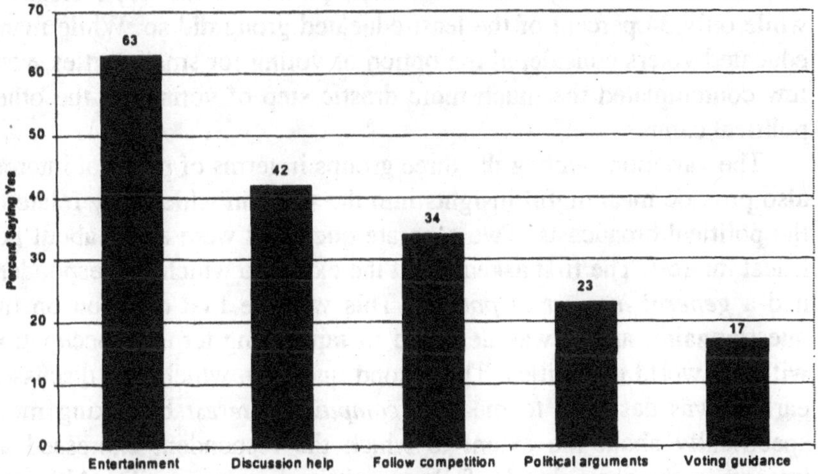

Note: Figures indicate the percentage of respondents who said yes to each category. Respondents were allowed to say yes to more.

behavior to committed voters. In terms of age, undecided voters tended to be younger than committed voters. Thus, while only 23 percent of those who were over the age fifty-six reported being undecided, 64 percent of those between the ages of twenty and twenty-five fell into this category. As we might expect, then, political commitment is something that grows with time.

In detailing the differences in education, it is important to distinguish between internal floaters and the external floaters. Those voters with higher levels of education were the least likely to be external floaters. Thus, only 9 percent of those who finished a university degree were external floaters, while 17 percent of those with less education fell into this category. There were no significant educational differences, on the other hand, between committed voters and internal floaters; those with a university education were just as likely to fall into one of these categories as the other.

These results have a certain internal logic about them. Studies have shown that greater education leads to more political interest and a greater tendency to think about politics in an ideological manner (Barnes and Kaase 1979; Converse 1964; Neuman 1986; Wolfsfeld 1988). As the platforms of the small parties tend to be more ideologically focused, they are more likely to appear to the better-educated voters. In the present sample, for example, 50 percent of the college-educated respondents said they voted for small parties in the 1992 election, while only 34 percent of the least-educated group did so. While many educated voters considered the option of voting for small parties, very few contemplated the much more drastic step of voting for the other political camp.

The variations among the three groups in terms of political interest also provide meaningful insights into the ways in which they relate to the political broadcasts. Two separate questions were asked about political interest. The first asked about the extent to which the respondent had a *general interest in politics*. This was the first question on the questionnaire, and it was designed to tap a long-term preoccupation with the world of politics. The second question, which was discussed earlier, was designed to measure *campaign interest* by asking more specifically about the extent to which the respondent expressed an interest in the campaign by following it in the mass media. Although the two variables are correlated with one another ($r = .31$), the distinction between the two types of political interest proved to be a useful one.

The results shown in figure 3 show that while there are significant differences among the groups in terms of general political interest ($X^2 = 19.24$, $p < .001$), there are no such differences when it comes to following the campaign.[9] The fact that undecided voters have less long-term political interest than committed voters do makes perfect sense. The fact that such differences disappear at election time, however, is a far more intriguing finding. It suggests that many citizens normally uninvolved in politics suddenly develop an interest during the election campaign. Lacking previous interest, they remain unencumbered by many political commitments, a seductive prize for all of the political parties.

This state of affairs offers an important opportunity for those who hope to use the election broadcasts as an opportunity for civic education. Television has become a truly mass medium whose visual format can attract an extremely large audience. The fact that so many Israelis tend to watch television news on a regular basis (Cohen, Adoni, and Bantz 1990) demonstrates the potential for these broadcasts. Only television can provide political information in a format that can appeal to almost everyone, even those who do not normally read about politics in the newspapers.

This line of argument is given support by the fact that we found no significant differences in the amount of broadcast viewing by the three groups. This is consistent with the earlier finding about a lack of difference in campaign interest, which, it turns out, is the best predictor of broadcast viewing ($r = .53$). This reinforces the notion that election campaigns can serve an important equalizing function by closing the gap between those who are more or less involved in politics.

Despite the similarity in viewing patterns, however, there are critical differences in the ways in which each voting type relates to the political ads that reflect each group's needs. There is a good deal of evidence pointing to the fact that *the weaker the level of political commitment the more seriously the viewers relate to the broadcasts.* The first piece of evidence is presented in figure 4 which, shows that it is the external floaters who are most likely to watch the ads either to gain voting guidance or to follow the competition, and that they are the least likely to view the ads as a form of entertainment. The differences with regard to voting guidance are especially significant and offer an important clue to what follows.[10]

The most important question from a consumer's viewpoint is whether voters are in fact getting help from the election broadcasts in making their voting decision. There were two questions in the survey

Figure 3
Political Interests and Voter Profiles

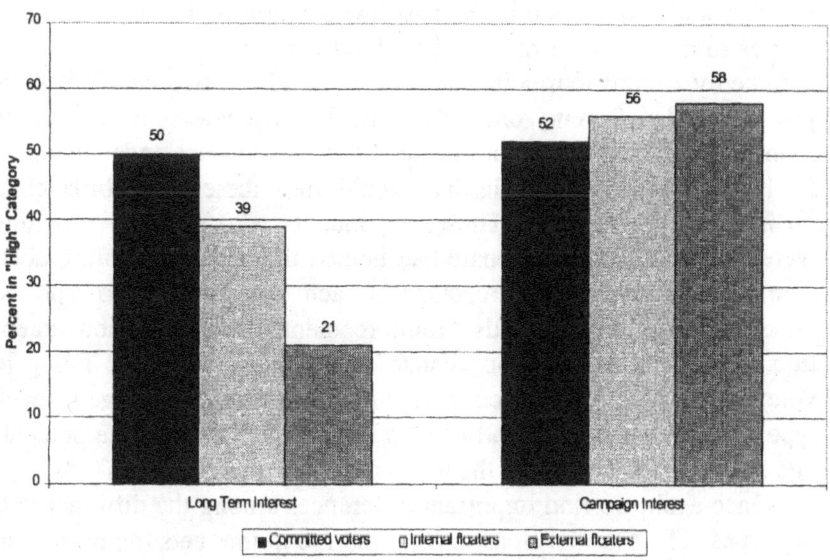

Figure 4
Voter Profiles and Viewing Motivations

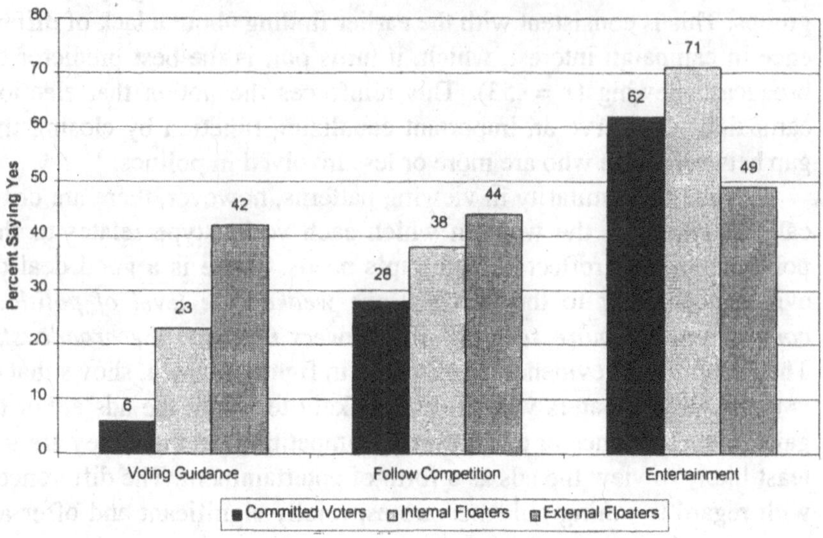

that related to how much help the viewers felt they were getting from the broadcasts. The first was a general question about how much the broadcasts helped them make their voting decision.[11] The second question focused more specifically on one particular broadcast: the debate between the two candidates for prime minister that has become a standard part of the election campaign.

The standard method in the past few elections is for the two major parties to devote some of their broadcast time to debates in which an assumedly neutral journalist asks questions of the two candidates for prime minister. Seventy-one percent of the respondents in our survey reported watching the debate in the 1992 election, an understandably far higher number of people than would view the election broadcasts on a more typical night. Those respondents who reported watching were asked whether the debate had helped them in their voting decision. We calculated the percentage in each voting type who reported either "no help" from the ads, "reinforcement" of their previous intention, or help in a "decision change" about how they were going to vote.[12] The results presented in figure 5 show the percentage of each type that received some kind of help from the debate and the percentage that received help from the much more numerous political ads.

Once again we find important differences among the different voting types. The external floaters form the group that gets the most help in their voting decision from both the political ads and the debate. The differences between the committed voters and the internal floaters are less consistent, but it is the external floaters who feel the most positive about the information they are getting from these broadcasts during the election campaign.

Yet another confirmation of this pattern of results can be found by examining the differences in attitudes about how many ads should be broadcast. Although, as was shown, most Israelis would like to see fewer ads broadcast, there are once again significant differences among the three groups. While 71 percent of the committed voters wanted fewer broadcasts, 65 percent of the internal floaters felt that way, and only 51 percent of the external floaters wanted fewer ($X2 = 12.12, p < .01$). The external voters clearly got more out of these ads than did the other two groups.

Let us try to put all of this into some type of perspective. Those citizens who find themselves debating between the two major political camps during the election campaign turn out to be the least educated members of the population, the youngest, and the ones who have the least long-term interest in politics. Many of these voters do become interested at the time of the election and then depend on the television broadcasts for information that apparently helps them in their voting decision.

It is important, however, not to exaggerate the size of this group. Only fifteen percent of all those who were surveyed fell into the category of external floaters, while 40 percent of these voters hoped to receive voting guidance from the broadcasts, only 22 percent actually did. To put it differently, if we remove all of the people who did not watch the broadcasts as well as those who denied getting any help from the ads, we are left with about 3 percent of the public who claim to have used the ads to make an internal camp decision and about 2.5 percent who used the ads to decide between the two camps.

It is true that the last few elections in Israel have been very close and that even a small percentage in either direction could have determined the shape of the government. However, when one looks at those few external voters who had the potential of changing the election outcome, one finds that they split fairly evenly between the two camps.[13] Even the most mediacentric of observers would have a hard time using these data to make a case that the election broadcasts had a major impact on the final election results.

Figure 5
Help from Ads and Debate

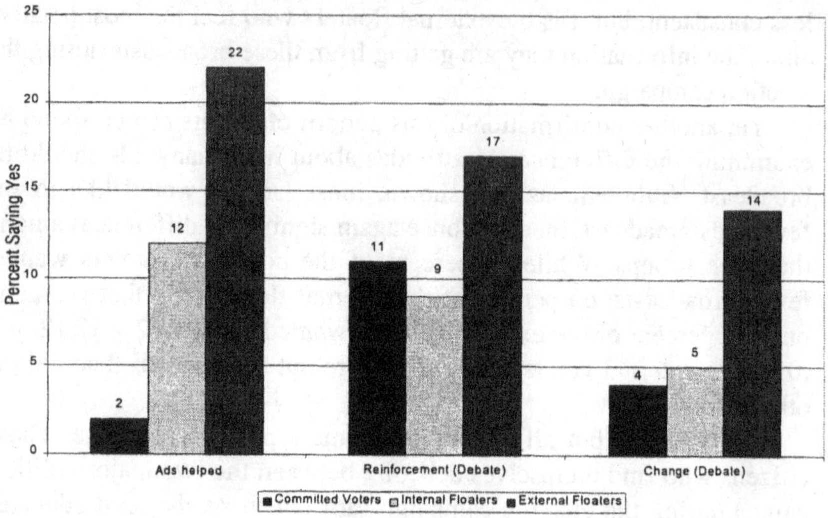

III. Conclusion

The overall conclusion of this article is that the election broadcasts in Israel are not meeting the needs of the voters. The election campaign offers an important opportunity to get citizens involved in the political process. The vast majority of Israelis are watching fewer ads than they did in the past, and it is clear that they are not satisfied with what they are seeing. Most voters do not take these ads very seriously, and most would prefer to have fewer ads broadcast.

At the same time, one cannot ignore the half-full side of the glass. This was one of the first studies in Israel to show that the televised ads and the debate do have an impact on an important segment of the voting public. While further research is needed to better specify this process, it is clear that many less committed voters do exploit these broadcasts as a source of information for voting guidance.

The fact that many of these voters appear to be less-educated and less-interested in politics in between the elections can be thought of in either a positive or a negative light. On the one hand, it could be argued that television serves as a great equalizer, in that it not only creates a general excitement about the election campaign, but also offers useful information for those who might otherwise be left out of the democratic process. The fact that no correlation was found between education and either campaign interest or viewing can be cited in support of this position. A more cynical perspective, however, would point to the generally low level of the ads and raise questions about the manipulation of the uninformed through style rather than substance. This becomes an especially important issue, because it is those who float between the two camps who ultimately determine the election.

In any case, it is clear that some type of reform is warranted. There are many alternatives that can be considered, but one possibility that seems especially appealing is to decrease the number of ads while increasing the number and scope of the political debates. Some might argue that this type of format would attract even a smaller, more elite audience than those who now watch the broadcasts. Yet, the admittedly small amount of evidence that was presented in this paper showed that it was the less-sophisticated external floaters who reported receiving the most amount of help from the one debate that was held. We also found no differences in the educational level on long term political interest between those who watched and did not watch the debate.[14]

The key to planning and evaluating such changes, we would argue, is to look at these broadcasts as an incomparable opportunity to inform the public. Policy makers would be well advised to consult the voters about what they would like to get out of such broadcasts rather than depend exclusively on the advice of professional politicians. This would surely offer one way to narrow the rather large gap that now exists between public expectations and government performance in this field.

Notes

1. I want to thank Chana Levinsohn, of the Institute, who provided a great deal of help in both designing the questionnaire and carrying out the survey.
2. It should be noted that over the years the institute has found very few differences when comparing this sample size to the more conventional sample size of more than one thousand.
3. Data for 1981 and 1988 were graciously supplied by Dan Caspi and Chana Levinsohn (see Caspi 1984 and Caspi and Levinsohn 1993). All three surveys were carried out by the Guttmann Institute for Social Science Research. In 1988 there were two surveys that dealt with this topic. We chose to present the one that took place between October 19 and 23 because it was the closest in size, method, and timing of interviews to the one carried out in 1992. A comparison with the other survey results leads to exactly the same conclusions about the decrease in viewing in 1992.

4. There are, of course, other possible explanations for the decrease. An important factor that was not mentioned in the public discourse was the change in the broadcast time of the election ads. In all previous elections the ads had been given the slot immediately after the evening news, which is by far the most popular program in Israel. In 1992 the ads were shown *before* the news, and this may very well have had a detrimental effect on the size of the viewing audience.
5. Four percent would like to see many more, and three percent would just like to see more.
6. Respondents were also asked whether they thought the ads were helpful to "others." In keeping with what is known as the "third person effect" (Davidson, 1983) in communication, 23 percent, that is, a somewhat larger group, believed that the ads probably helped other voters to decide. This suggests that many are overestimating the utility of the ads in this regard, and this may offer one reason why so many ads are being broadcast.
7. The question asked was "Between which parties did you deliberate *(Mitlabet)* in your decision who to vote for?" A total of eighteen response categories were included, one of which was "I did not debate, it was clear to me who I was going to vote for in the elections."
8. Religious parties were considered to be part of the right-wing camp, as all of them had expressed a preference to continue their coalition with the Likud.
9. Note that the results are summarized by looking at the percentage who fall into the "high" category among each group; this is an arbitrary dividing point. The "high" category in long-term political interest was composed of those respondents who answered that they followed politics "a very great deal" or "a great deal" on a six-point scale. The "high" category in the campaign-interest scale was composed of those saying they followed the campaign "all the time" or "most of the time." We also looked at the alternative definition for high campaign interest that excluded the "most of the time" respondents. The results were essentially the same: although the external floaters exhibited somewhat *less* campaign interest than the other two types, the differences were still not statistically significant.
10. The statistical differences for these groups are as follows: Voting guidance ($X2 = 52.39, p < .001$), follow competition ($X2 = 5.98, p < .05$), and entertainment ($X2 = 7.06, p < .05$). No significant differences were found with regard to two of the motivational variables: for use in political arguments and for use in political discussions.
11. The question was: To what extent did the election broadcasts help or hinder you in your decision about who to vote for? The response categories were: (1) the broadcasts helped me very much, (2) helped, (3) didn't help and didn't hinder, (4) hindered, and (5) hindered very much.
12. The initial response categories were: (1) reinforced my previous decision who to vote for, (2) changed my previous decision who to vote for, (3) helped me decide because before that I didn't have any decision, (4) the debate did not help me to decide, and (5) the debate didn't change anything for me. Those who gave responses four and five were placed in the no-help category, those who gave response one were put in the reinforcement category, and those who gave responses two and three were placed in the decision-change category.
13. When one looks at all of the external floaters one finds that 51 percent reported voting for a right-wing or religious party, and 48 percent for a left-wing party. Looking at the even smaller number who say that the ads helped them in their decision, it turns out that 58 percent voted for the left, and 41.7 percent voted for the right.
14. The format of the debates could also be varied, as was graphically illustrated in the presidential debates held during the American election in 1992.

References

Barnes, Samuel M., and Max Kaase, eds. 1979. *Political Action: Mass Participation in Five Western Democracies.* Beverly Hills: Sage.

Biocca, Frank (ed.). 1991. *Television and Political Advertising, Volume 1: Psychological Processes.* Hillsdale, N.J.: Lawrence Erlbaum Associates.

Blumer, Jay G. 1985. "The Social Character of Media Gratifications." In *Media Gratifications Research: Current Perspectives.* ed. Karl E. Rosengren, Lawrence A. Wenner, and Philip Palmgreen. Beverly Hills: Sage.

Blumer, Jay G., Michael Gurevitch, and Elihu Katz. 1985. "Reaching Out: A Future for Gratifications Research: Current Perspectives." In *Media Gratifications Research: Current Perspectives,* ed. Karl E. Rosengren, Lawrence A.Wenner, and Philip Palmgreen. Beverly Hills: Sage.

Caspi, Dan. 1984. "Following the Race: Propaganda and Electoral Decision." In *The Roots of Begin's Success,* ed. Dan Caspi, Avram Diskin, and Emanuel Gutmann. Kent, England: Croom Helm.

Caspi, Dan, and Chana Levinsohn. 1993. "To Influence and to be Influenced: The Election Campaign to the 12th Knesset." In *Who's the Boss in Israel,* ed. Daniel J. Elazar and Shmuel Sandler. Detroit: Wayne State University Press.

Cohen, Akiva A., Hanna Adoni, and Charles R. Bantz. 1990. *Social Conflict and Television News.* Sage Library of Social Research 183. Newbury Park, Calif.: Sage.

Converse, Phillip. 1964. "The Nature of Belief Systems in Mass Publics." In *Ideology and Discontent,* ed. David E. Apter. New York: Free Press.

Davidson, W. Phillips. 1983. "The Third Person Effect in Communication." *Public Opinion Quarterly* 47:1-15.

Donohew, Lewis, Phillip Palmgreen, and J. D. Rayburn, II. 1987. "Social and Psychological Origins of Media Use: A Lifestyle Analysis." *Journal of Broadcasting & Electronic Media* 31:255-78.

Himmelweit, Hilde, Patrick Humphreys, Marrianne Jaeger, and Michael Katz, 1981. *How Voters Decide.* London: Academic Press.

Josylyn, Richard A. 1990. "Election Campaigns as Occasions for Civic Education." In *New Dimensions in Political Communication,* ed. David L. Swanson and Dan Nimmo. Newbury Park, Calif.: Sage.

Kaid, Lynda Lee, and John Boydston. 1987. "An Experimental Study of the Effectiveness of Negative Political Advertisements." *Communication Quarterly* 35:193-201.

Kaid, Lynda Lee, Dan Nimmo, and Keith Sanders, eds. 1986. *New Perspectives on Political Advertising.* Carbondale: Southern Illinois University Press.

Newman, W. Russell. 1986. *The Paradox of Mass Politics.* Cambridge: Harvard University Press.

Popkin, Samuel L. 1991. *The Reasoning Voter: Communication and Persuasion in Presidential Campaigns.* Chicago: University of Chicago Press.

Wolfsfeld, Gadi. 1988. *The Politics of Provocation: Participation and Protest in Israel.* Albany: SUNY Press.

17

Was It on the Agenda? The Hidden Agenda of the 1988 Campaign

Hanna Herzog

Elections as Symbolic Contests

The cost of Israel's election campaign reached a new high in 1988, even though repeated findings have proved that the time and money invested in electioneering do not significantly change voting positions. The effectiveness of election campaigns has been questioned since the first investigations into political communication.[1] Contemporary studies confirm the earlier findings that electioneering does not directly change people's political opinions.[2] On the contrary, political attitudes are developed and crystallized through long-term social and political processes.

Nevertheless, researchers agree that election propaganda does have a function in strengthening existing attitudes. It provides information and rationalizations for those who seek to confirm their positions. It encourages those who hesitate, and activates their predisposition. In order to make his views clear, each candidate contrasts his positions with those of his opponents; as a result, electioneering sharpens the differences among the contenders. In Israel, the propaganda focuses on making a clear distinction between the left and the right.

Although election campaigns do not change voters' attitudes, they do play a role in the long-term process of developing political cognition. Campaign communications, like other forms of political communication, frame and interpret information.[3] Reality has no objective meaning; it is interpreted and constructed by the public and by political sponsors such as politicians, parties, social movements and journalists. The same reality is experienced in different ways by different people because of their different interpretations. These constructions are powerful because they suggest answers to troubling and threatening conditions; they give explanations for success and failure; they define problems, determine enemies and give rise to fears and hopes. At the same time, they foster political disputes and tensions.[4]

The construction and interpretation of reality involves the use of political language that includes symbols, slogans, metaphors, name-calling, classification and catch-phrases. Symbols, like other social constructing devices, endow social experiences with meanings; they are laden with values and emotions. Political symbols convey rational and emotional attitudes, values and legitimization. Since they are part of the familiar, day-to-day realities, we are not conscious of their demands. At the same time, these social constructs are subject to constant pressures and changes. This is a continuing process in society, and is not specific to time; however, an election campaign has special social qualities that make it an active arena for producing and reproducing a political symbolic world.[5]

The literature ascribes ritualistic and dramatic metaphors to campaigns. An understanding of these metaphors in Turner's concept of liminality will illuminate the social quality of election time. The liminal stage in a ritual or a drama is an intermediate, transitional phase. The subjects pass through a period of ambiguity, a marginal stage between the known previous structure and the unknown but structured future. They become more attentive and sensitive to visual and verbal symbols, especially collective symbols.[6] As a liminal period, campaign time is a competitive symbolic environment for the voters and the politicians.

The Hidden Agenda

Traditional analyses have dealt with the issues on the campaign agenda, and with the disputes over those issues. If there are no conflicts over meaning, says Edelman, an issue is not political.[7] But even though consensual elements are not perceived as political issues, they are powerful means to political ends and thus constitute a hidden agenda that should not be ignored. I suggest that we examine the factors that mold social meanings, the ways in which challenging alternatives are presented, and the ways in which events and symbols become meaningful. This will enable us to discern not only what was contested on the open agenda, but also what went unquestioned on the hidden agenda and was thereby reinforced. Indeed, symbols are most effective when their symbolic function is unnoticed. Such an analysis can reveal the limits of the political discourse.[8]

This chapter takes that approach, and explores the hidden agenda by posing several questions. What visual and verbal symbols were negotiated in 1988, compared with previous campaigns? Which meanings competed, and which were taken for granted? The analysis is based on historical collections of Israeli political advertising,[9] and 1988 newspaper ads and television commercials. Because of limited space, only a few illustrative posters are presented; others are described. The analysis is qualitative, but nevertheless deals with the more salient and repeated poster themes.

The symbols used to contest the two most controversial issues on the open agenda implicitly reinforced two subjects on the hidden agenda; both of the latter are unquestioned foundations of Israeli society. First, the open dispute over the location of the territorial boundaries of Israel affirmed the national consensus over the nation's right to land. Second, the open dispute over which party was most capable of leading the state affirmed the national consensus on the Jewishness of the state.

Intense Dispute Creates Consensus: The Territorial Issue

Both traditional Jewish nationalism and the modern national movement, Zionism, are territory-oriented; the Land of Israel (Eretz Israel or Zion) is a central pillar of both. For many centuries, the Land of Israel was primarily a metaphysical and abstract concept with no clear boundaries; only its center, Jerusalem, was defined and real. Abstract as it was, the Land of Israel became the mobilizing symbol of the modern Jewish movement. Zionism could not exist without Palestine. But since Zionism did not specify the exact area of its territorial aspiration,[10] there were political struggles within the Jewish community over where the borders should be.

This dispute over the location of the boundaries goes back to the Yishuv (the Jewish community in Palestine prior to the establishment of the State of Israel in 1948). A common symbol for territory is a map. The map of the Land of Israel has had a prolonged resonance in the nation's political culture. During the Yishuv, the map stood for the

Figure 1

idea of nation building; then, as now, it encompassed Zionist ideas such as returning to the Land of Israel, building the country and developing a new society. Figure 1 shows the cover of a 1930 bulletin issued by Tnuva, a marketing cooperative; it refers to the dairy products of the Land of Israel. The map has no real boundaries, since it simply symbolizes the idea of cultivating the land. The rising sun and the soil are symbols of the future. The concept of "return to the land" is visualized not by just any land, but by the Land of Israel. On the other hand, Figure 2 shows a 1930 poster for the right-wing Herut Movement (predecessor of the Likud); the map encompasses all of Palestine on both sides of the Jordan River, with the legend: "All of it is mine!"

The State of Israel was born against a background of territorial conflict. The conflict between Jews and Arabs was over the right to the land; the conflict between Jews and Jews was, as before, over the limits of the land. With the cease-fire lines drawn up by the 1949 armistice agreement, the green line became a fact and the issue became temporarily less salient.

The map has been an important vehicle for conveying the major ideas of the political parties. During the 1950s, Mapai (predecessor of the Labor Party) showed Israel within the green line on its posters promoting its achievements in immigration, employment and defense

Figure 2

Figure 3

(Figures 3, 4 and 5); Herut expressed its philosophy (both banks of the Jordan) with the headline "Never!" over a map of Israel within the green line being split off from Jordanian territory (Figure 6). During

Figure 4

Figure 5

the early 1960s, the boundary was virtually a non-issue, the Six Day War put it back on the agenda and the Yom Kippur War intensified the dispute.

Figure 6

Figure 7

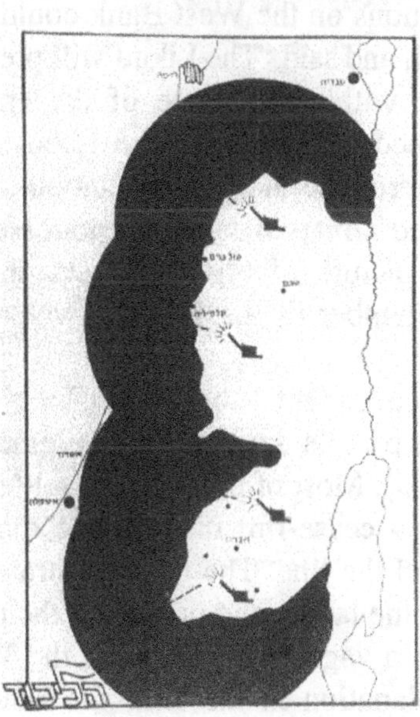

On election posters dealing with the territorial issue, the parties use maps to illustrate both Israel's right to the land and their concept of the most desirable borders. In 1977, the Likud used security as the

Figure 8

rationalization for extended boundaries. Its brochure featured a map showing how Arab cannons on the West Bank could reach most of the populated areas of Israel, and said "The Likud will prevent this! 2,500,00 Israeli citizens will be within the range of the enemy's guns if an Arafat state is established." (Figure 7). The Labor Alignment, which favored territorial compromise and good relations with a Jordanian-Palestinian state, showed a map of Israel without clear border lines as the background for a picture of Shimon Peres shaking hands with Yossi Sarid, a leftist member of the Knesset who was then with the Alignment (Figure 8).

The map on an Independent Liberals leaflet showed settlements built or planned by the party's agricultural settlement movement, the Zionist Worker (Figure 9). Most of the existing settlements were inside the green line (the 1949 cease-fire line), while most of the planned settlements were beyond the line. The map illustrated a major Zionist concept—settlement of the land—and presented the party's position on the territorial dispute in a vague way, showing the West Bank and the Sinai. There is no explanation in the text; the headline simply says "The settlement map of the Zionist Worker."

A poster announcing a speech by ultra-right-wing Rabbi Meir Kahane, head of the Kach party, depicted a Torah-shaped boundary encompassing a large area of the Middle East, including Israel and

Figure 9

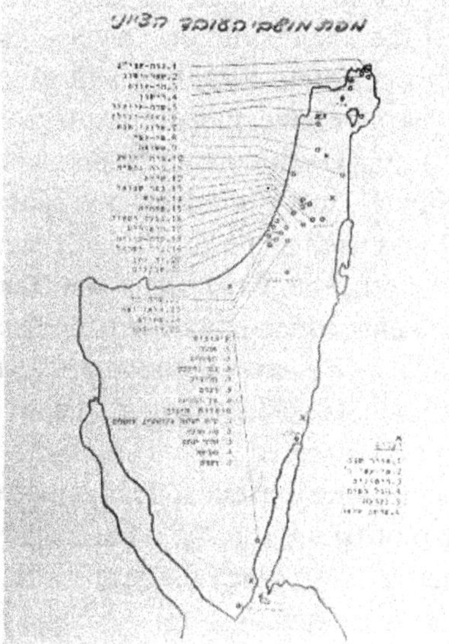

Figure 10

parts of neighboring Arab countries; this was the border of the Promised Land mentioned in the Bible. The headline read, "Those who are with the Lord are with Kahane" (Figure 10).

As these posters and brochures from 1977 show, there were clear differences among the parties in regard to the most desirable boundaries. Each party used the same symbol - a map. Each party tried to associate its map with a different meaning, and to identify this meaning with the party. The symbolic meanings projected by the propaganda were security (Likud), settlements (Independent Liberals), true and confident leadership (Labor Alignment) and faith in God (Kahane).

The same symbol was used again in the 1981 campaign. On a map of Greater Israel (including the West Bank and the Gaza Strip), the Likud listed 144 settlements which had been established since the party came to power in 1977. "We are on the map," said the ad, which declared that the settlements had "changed the map of the land of Israel. This map cannot be reversed."

In response, the right-wing extremist Tehiya party asked: "Are you on the map?" On a map of Israel, it listed what it said were the faults of the other parties - such as voting against application of Israeli law to the Golan Heights, and withdrawing from the Sinai and destroying the houses that Jewish settlers had built there.[11]

In 1984, all the parties displayed maps and repeatedly used the terms "the country" (ha'aretz) and " Land of Israel" (Eretz-Israel).

Again, in 1988, the map was a key symbol in the election propaganda. Referring to oft-declared intent of the Arabs to throw the Jews

Figure 11

into the sea (an expression used by President Nasser of Egypt), the Likud superimposed a "no left turn" sign over a map of Israel with the warning: " Left is only to the sea. Danger! The Labor Party turned left." (Figure 11).

Moledet, the extremist right-wing party that advocated "transfer" of the Arabs from the West Bank, used a map with two arrows. A white arrow with a star of David at its head pointed to the sea; a black arrow with a crescent moon at its head pointed to the east bank of the Jordan River. The poster read: "Who will go, we or they? The choice is in your hands." (Figure 12).

Attacking the proposed international conference to negotiate a peace agreement, the Likud used the image of a vise squeezing the map of Israel (Figure 13). Tehiya used its traditional symbol: a young Israeli holding the flag of Israel, with the map behind him. The text says "only a government with a strong Tehiya will keep the Likud from giving up and compromising on parts of the Land of Israel...only a government with a strong Tehiya will break the intifada." (Figures 13 and 14).

Symbols and slogans using the same ideas dominated Labor's 1988 campaign. Criticizing the Likud's handling of Taba affair, in which all of the disputed territory was awarded to Egypt, Labor declared: "Whoever shouts 'not a single inch' remains without a single inch." Another

Figure 12

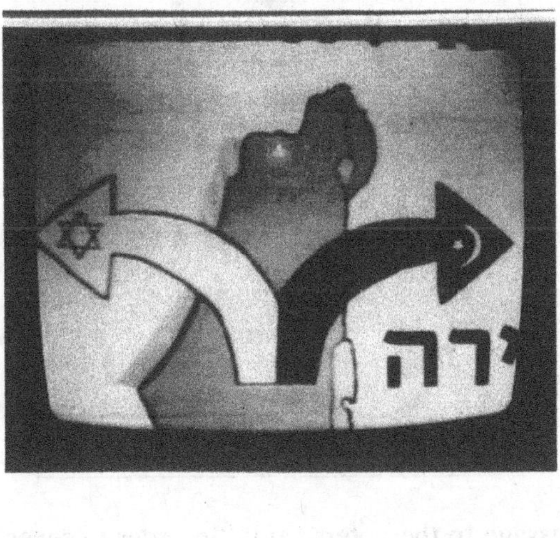

Figure 13

Figure 14

campaign message to the voters said: "In order to sever yourself from Gaza and put a boundary to the intifada, vote for Labor." The double meaning of the word "boundary" (limit, end) expressed Labor's posi-

Figure 15

tion that Gaza should be excluded from the Jewish state, and also its promise to end the intifada.

On a map that gave the Jordan River as the eastern boundary, Labor ran a newspaper ad showing the 176 kibbutzim of the United Kibbutz Movement (Figure 15). The ad made a play on the Hebrew word emet, which means "truth" and also identifies the Labor Party on the ballots. The headline read: "On borders, on security, on settlement—the true/Labor map." The ad declared that "the map indicates dedication to the vision. It is a map without which the State of Israel is exposed. It is a map against which the Likud is plotting." "Exposed" has the double meaning of "exposed to enemy attack" and "unsettled and uncultivated." The manifest message was a call to empower the kibbutz movement and to enhance its Zionist role. Indirectly, the ad noted the importance of the land and expressed a commitment to it.

In an ad for the National Religious Party, a scenic photograph showed religious youngsters standing in a forest and praying. The headline reads: "Religious Zionism - eighty years on the map. Generation after generation." Another NRP ad depicts a map of Israel covered with a skullcap; the eastern border is the Jordan River. The headline says, "Without faith, it will not work" (Figure 16).

By using the same symbol—a map of Israel—to express different attitudes toward the territorial issue, the parties sharpen their disagree-

Figure 16

ment over the boundaries but at the same time enhance the national consensus over Israel's right to the land.

The non-Zionist parties are also involved in this symbolic discourse. In 1984, the Progressive List for Peace referred to its support for the green line as the permanent border of Israel, calling it "the green line against the next war. The Likud's line is a black line, Labor's line is a gray line, our line is a green line. A line of partnership, a line of hope, a line of life." The platform of the Communist-oriented Hadash party referred to the "new line to peace" Using the same symbols and terminology as the other parties to take part in the boundary issue, these parties, too, legitimized the nation's right to the land - a right that is one of the foundations of Israeli society.

The intense, emotional debate over the territorial boundaries was a key issue on the open agenda. The symbols used by the parties in this debate reinforced the national consensus on the right to the land, putting this right on the hidden agenda. The unspoken consensus was self-evident - and this is precisely what made it such a powerful political tool.

Defining the Social Boundaries

From the time the state was established in 1948, Israel has faced several questions about its social boundaries. Since it is a democratic state, all Israeli citizens—Jew and non-Jew alike—are included within its formally defined collective boundary. However, various social definitions of the state draw different social boundaries. Some of these are described below:

1. If the criterion of a Jewish state is accepted, non-Jews are excluded by definition from the collective.
2. If statehood itself is a criterion, another social border is drawn. The state is a realization of the Zionist aspiration—but its existence is opposed by non-Zionist ultra-Orthodox Jews, who therefore exclude themselves from the collective.
3. The above criteria also exclude Israelis who live abroad. Some people believe that living is Israel is a requirement for an Israeli citizen to be included in the collective. Thus, those who leave the country are excluded and stigmatized.
4. The "Who's a Jew" controversy pits Orthodox and ultra-Orthodox Jews against Conservative, Reform and secular Jews. The first group is trying to narrow the definition, while the others want to preserve or broaden the definition.

Conflicts over social boundaries are attempts to define the identity, qualities and character of a society. The boundaries are mainly symbolic, but they can be as impassable as real walls. While these conflicts are a continuing social process, they become especially salient during election time—which, with its special quality as a liminal period, serves as an appropriate setting for negotiations aimed at confirming or changing social borders.

However, there is no open conflict over the definition of Israel as a Jewish state. By consensus, Jews are included in the collective; by implication, non-Jews are excluded. The debates over other issues affirmed the consensus, thereby placing it on the hidden agenda.

The National Camp Controversy

In the 1984 campaign, the Likud placed a new issue on the symbolic agenda: the question of which party was most representative of the nation. The Likud's banner proclaimed, "We are the national camp." This verbal symbolism was aimed at pushing the left wing to the periphery of Israeli society by implying that they were non-nationalists. Such a move is possible only when nationalism is a taken-for-granted value.

Labor reacted with rage. For years, it had been identified as the representative of the national spirit; it was generally perceived as the nation builder. Labor's political dominance had been accompanied by cultural and spiritual hegemony as well.[12] Now the Likud, after only two terms in power, was trying to usurp this domination.

The image of national identity was especially appealing to Jews of Asian-African origin (often referred to as Orientals or Sephardim), who provided two-thirds of the Likud's support.[13] Several related factors explain their switch from Labor to the Likud. The major reason was the decline in Labor's ability to govern.[14] Furthermore, when Labor began agreeing that the territorial boundaries should be changed, it not only moved closer to the Likud's position, it also legitimized the other party as an alternative to Labor. Labor's loss of political power and the Likud's legitimization paved the way for Asian/African Jews to change their vote.[15] Many of them were lower-class and underprivileged, so all of them were labeled as such. There was no legitimization for cultural ethnic pluralism or political ethnicity. To solve the problem of social marginality, and to eliminate the stigma attached to being "Oriental," they voted against the Labor regime which they held responsible for their social situation. The Likud mobilized their feelings of deprivation by offering them a shared base for identification that returned their pride and made them part of the nation.[16]

By including Jews of Asian-African extraction in the "national camp," the Likud not only affirmed their nationalism; it also provided them with legitimization to criticize the political elite and to claim acceptance (if not leadership) by virtue of greater loyalty to the society's nominal values.[17] It was no accident that the first time "I am in the national camp" appeared in the Likud's newspaper ads during the 1984 campaign, it was pictured as coming from the mouth of an Eastern-looking man. This verbal symbol not only tied the Sephardim more closely to the Likud, but also stung Labor and other parties that considered themselves as patriotic as the Likud. Labor's angry response was: "Division of the people is a national catastrophe. We are all one people," or, "We are all in the Zionist camp." The Likud's effort to stigmatize Labor as non-nationalist, and Labor's strong reaction, reflected the taken-for-granted definition of the collective in national terms.

The 1984 election campaign was very nationalist. The dominant colors were blue and white (the colors of the Israeli flags). The most conspicuous symbol was the six-pointed Star of David, which was used by most of the parties. Other frequently used symbols were the Israeli flag, the Israeli identity card, and the menorah (seven-branch candelabrum). All of the parties participated in the discourse over the national definition, and each tried to endow the national symbols with its own flavors.

By using symbols that emphasized the national identity, the parties affirmed the social boundary between Jewish and Arab citizens—thereby placing the unchallenged cutoff line on the hidden agenda. While the dispute over which party best represented the national identity flared on the open agenda, the location of the nation's social border was unquestioned. Thus the dispute remained within the accepted social boundaries.[18] By not questioning the nationalist borderline, the parties strengthened Jewish identity as the criterion for inclusion in the collective; without saying so, they excluded the Arabs.

The nationalist symbols, including the Israeli flag, were conspicuously absent in the parties' campaign propaganda in the Arab sector. The absence of these symbols indirectly helped establish the social boundaries of the collective.

Elections are virtually the only Israeli institution in which the Arab citizens participate on an equal footing with Jews. Moreover, their voting power makes them a very sought-after group during election campaigns. The right to vote is a symbolic confirmation of their belonging to a democratic regime and to Israeli society. But Israeli Arabs are exposed to contradictory symbolic messages: on one hand, they are included in the democratic process; on the other, they are excluded from the collective. The contrast became even greater during the 1988 campaign.

The Likud's 1984 "national camp" slogan drew protests from the party itself, as well as from rival parties; these led the Likud to drop the slogan at the end of the campaign.[19] However, the slogan was stronger than the protesters; when it reappeared in the 1988 campaign, no one in the Likud questioned its use. The Likud's ads proclaimed that "Victory of the national camp over the left camp is a historical necessity." Tehiya agreed, and added that the victory of the national camp was possible only with a strong Tehiya.

As in 1984, the 1988 campaign was dominated by the blue and white colors, the star of David, and other unquestioned national symbols. The waving flag of Israel was the opening scene in most of the television commercials. The contest was over who best represented these symbols; Tehiya declared that "We should add blue to our faded flag."

The Enemy Threat and the National Collective

Political parties commonly evoke the threat of an enemy in order to win electoral support; this helps them renew their own commitment and mobilize allies.[20] In 1988, both Labor and the Likud exploited the population's fear of the Arabs; each party offered its solutions for the Arab-Israel conflict.

Labor frightened the public with demographic data while trying to rationalize the need for territorial compromise. It used the social boundaries on the collective as its logic: annexation of the West Bank (as the right-wing parties wanted) would mean the loss of a Jewish majority in Israel and the end of the democratic nature of the state. Labor declared that "there are no easy solutions, but Labor has a plan for a democratic, Jewish Israel."

Similarly, the Likud used the Arabs to frighten Labor supporters. Citing various news sources, the Likud equated the enemy's plans with Labor's interests: "The PLO will suspend the combat in order to help Labor;" "The PLO will ask the Israeli Arabs to strengthen Peres's chances of establishing a dovish government." By identifying Labor with the enemy, the Likud defined themselves as the patriots - the most legitimate representative of the national collection.

The issue of how to solve the Arab-Israeli conflict topped the open agenda. In representing their competing solutions, the Likud and Labor confirmed that the Arabs were the unquestioned threat to the nation - thereby adding this consensus to the hidden agenda.

Inclusion of the Ultra-Orthodox: Change in the Political Discourse

Judaism is a pluralistic religion, in which the various streams are differentiated by their degree of religiosity. At one extreme are the secular Jews; at the other, the ultra-Orthodox. Cutting across these differences in religiosity are differences in ethnicity between Ashkenazim (western Jews from Europe and North America) and Sephardim (eastern Jews from Asia and Africa). Ethnic differences in the religious sector were institutionalized during the Mandate period, when two chief rabbinical positions were established - one Ashkenazi and one Sephardic.

The ultra-Orthodox stream of Judaism began in Europe as a reaction to the modernization and secularization of Jews, on one hand, and the uprooting of Eastern European Jewry and its migration to the west, on the other.[21] Thus, the ultra-Orthodox were originally (and for many years) entirely Ashkenazim. They opposed Zionist ideas, and denied its semi-Messianic aspirations and its attempts to create a collective Jewish life not based on halacha (traditional Jewish law). In principle (although not always in practice), the ultra-Orthodox excluded themselves from the Zionist collective. After the state was established, the ultra-Orthodox Agudat Israel party served in the Knesset and in even in Government coalitions. But it did not recognize the legal existence of the state; symbolically, the party refused to fly the national flag or to celebrate Independence Day; thus, it remained on the margins or even out of the social collective boundary that emerged in Israel.

Two major changes in the political discourse of the Zionist parties enabled the ultra-Orthodox non-Zionist parties to enter the debate on Zionist issues, and thus to include themselves symbolically in the emerging new social order. One was the shift from the term "the State of Israel" to "the Land of Israel"; the second, from "Israelis" to "Jewish people." Agudat Israel's commitment has been to the Jewish people; for years, it rejected the idea of Jewish statehood, and excluded itself from the discussions of related issues. As Friedman explains, the ultra-Orthodox community does not create new terms; to deal with modern life, it reinterprets the traditional terms found in the Torah and in the literature on halacha (traditional Jewish law). The ultra-Orthodox could not discuss ways of realizing a Jewish state without negating their traditional belief in the Messianic revival.

But in 1967, the Six Day War enabled a transition from the "non-legitimate" (in ultra-Orthodox eyes) term "State of Israel" to a "legitimate" one, "Land of Israel." And in the 1980s, the dispute over who best represented the nation led to the replacement of the word "Israelis" by the phrase "Jewish nation." Since the discourse focused on the Jewish nation rather than on an Israeli state, it opened the door to ultra-Orthodox participation. The public discussion used more terms relating to a Jewish nation and the Land of Israel than to citizens and an Israeli state; thus, the ultra-Orthodox had more opportunities to use their own legitimate terms.

By the same process—but coming from the opposite direction—the secular sector found itself closer to the ultra-Orthodox. The more Jewish terms the secular people could use to define and perceive themselves, the less alienated they felt from the Orthodox. Jewish tradition became a source of legitimization for the political claims of all the parties—each of which endowed it with its own meaning. In addition, other factors such as organizational activity and material achievements were no less important in increasing the involvement of the ultra-Orthodox parties. The most notable result of these changes was the increased Asian-African vote for the ultra-Orthodox parties, mainly Shas (Sephardic Torah Guardians).

Sephardic ultra-Orthodoxy emerged in Israel in the 1950s as the immigrants from Asian and African countries were absorbed. These Oriental Jews did not have the freedom or the resources to develop in their own way; they were forced to develop their religious life within existing channels—mainly the national-religious or the ultra-Orthodox. The attitudes and practices of ultra-Orthodoxy are alien to Asian-African Jews, who are basically more tolerant, more involved in everyday life, less oriented toward halacha. They appreciate scholarship, but do not shut themselves away in yeshivot. Since the pre-state period, most Sephardim have been a hardworking, productive community—unlike the Ashkenazi ultra-Orthodox, whose males are yeshiva students and live off philanthropic donations. For the Sephardim, the establishment of the State of Israel was a realization of the return to Zion; therefore, they did not criticize the Zionist viewpoint as did their Ashkenazi counterparts.

But reality forced those Sephardim who chose an ultra-Orthodox way of life in Israel to accept the Ashkenazi standards. The symbolic expression of this process was their giving up of traditional Sephardic dress in favor of the black garments brought to Israel by the East European Jews. The Ashkenazi ultra-Orthodox controlled the centers of power, and dominated the halachic sphere; they are perceived as adhering to the highest standards of religiosity.

However, even though the ultra-Orthodox parties had a relatively long history of legitimization, Oriental Jews did not tend to vote for ultra-Orthodox parties; they preferred to support the National Religious Party. The reason: for many years, the ultra-Orthodox were on the fringe of the political arena - and thus excluded from the social boundaries of Israeli society. Sephardic voters, who were already marginal because of their origin and social-economic status, were reluctant to further weaken their position by supporting marginal parties.

In Israel, it has been the norm for ethnic parties to be stigmatized and negated; this has prevented the Asian-Africans from channeling their feelings of ethnic deprivation into ethnic political organizations. But in 1984 a split in Agudat Israel resulted in the formation of Shas, an ethnic ultra-Orthodox party which also received support from voters who were not ultra-Orthodox. This changed Israel's ethnic political landscape. Traditionally, the ultra-Orthodox parties had been supported by Ashkenazi voters; since the establishment of Shas, however, there have been growing numbers of Sephardim among the voters for ultra-Orthodox parties.

When the political discourse shifted to the issue of which party best represented the national collective, the ultra-Orthodox parties plunged into the discussion. This helped to legitimize them, so that they became less stigmatizing and marginalizing to their supporters.[22] One reason why deprived Sephardim in underdeveloped towns and poor neighborhoods voted for Shas in 1988 was to express their resentment in being pushed to the fringes of Israeli society. The effectiveness of the party's mobilization effort, based mainly on patronage, was supported by the change in the subject of the political discourse.

Shas campaigned under such slogans as "The Land of Israel to the people of Israel according to the Torah of Israel," "Care for the poor families" and "Return to the beauty of the Sephardic tradition." In 1988, Shas used the legitimization of ethnic division within the religious sector, and the inclusion of the ultra-Orthodoxy in the political discourse, to enhance its political power.

The Hidden Symbolic Agenda: Conclusion

The question of "What was on the Agenda?" is usually studied through content analysis of the issues; this approach would reveal that the issues on the 1988 agenda were security, the economy and internal social issues. Such an approach claims that electioneering and other political communications do not influence voters' attitudes; rather, they set out the issues on which voters' choices are made. Political advertising does not tell the public what to think, but what issues to think about. The analysis focuses on the divergent positions taken by the parties.

This chapter suggests an additional dimension of analysis: the visual and verbal symbols used in the election campaign, which is an active arena for a symbolic contest. The parties endow the symbols with meanings. While the symbolic contest over issues on the open agenda emphasizes the disputes between the parties and the uniqueness of each party, it also reaffirms a hidden agenda of taken-for-granted elements. Thus, the hidden agenda tells the public what issues *not* to think about. Our theoretical argument is demonstrated through the analysis of two issues: the location of the territorial boundaries, and the collective borderline.

In 1988, every party used a map as a symbol in contesting the issue of where Israel's territorial boundaries should be. Each party endowed this symbol with its political attitudes, as shown by the boundaries on its map. By focusing on the land rather than on the state, the ultra-Orthodox parties were able to enter the political discourse.

In contesting the issue of which party represented the national collective, the parties used visual national symbols such as the Star of David and the Israeli flag, and verbal symbols such as "We are the national camp." By locating itself in the center of the collective, a party pushes the others toward the periphery. By emphasizing Jewish nationality rather than Israeli citizenship, the ultra-Orthodox non-Zionist communities included themselves in the social collective.

On both issues, an unquestioned national consensus was used to support the parties' positions. On the first issue, the Jews' right to the land was unquestioned; the question was *where* the territorial boundaries should be drawn. On the second issue, the definition of the collective as Jewish was unquestioned, since it was agreed that the collective boundaries included Jews and excluded Arabs; the question was *who* best represented the Jewish nationalism. Paradoxically, an intense dispute is a powerful mechanism for producing a consensus on commonly shared values.

Notes

1. B.F. Berelson, P. F. Lazarsfeld, and W. N. McPhee, *Voting* (Chicago: University of Chicago Press, 1954).
2. Cf. Israeli studies: D. Caspi, "Following the Race: Propaganda and Electoral Decision" in D. Caspi, A. Diskin, and E. Gutmann (eds.), *The Roots of Begin's Success: The 1981 Israeli Elections* (London: Croom, and Helm, 1984) pp. 245-272; J. Elizur and E. Katz, "The Media in the Israel Election of 1977," in A. Arian (ed.), *The Elections in Israel—1977* (Jerusalem: Academic Press, 1980) pp. 253-276.
3. D. A. Graber, *Processing the News* (New York: Longmans, 1984).
4. M. Edelman, *Constructing the Political Spectacle* (Chicago: The University of Chicago Press, 1988).
5. H. Herzog, "The Election Campaign as a Liminal Stage: Negotiations Over Meaning," *The Sociological Review* 35(3)1987: 559-574.
6. V. Turner, *The Forest of Symbols* (Ithaca: Cornell University Press, 1967); Turner, *Drama, Fields and Metaphors: Symbolic Action in Human Society* (Ithaca: Cornell University Press, 1974).
7. Edelman, *Constructing the Political Spectacle*, p. 104.
8. Herzog, "The Election Campaign as a Liminal Stage," p. 571.
9. C. Berlin, *Knesset 9: An Exhibition of Ephemera from the 1977 Israeli Elections for the Ninth Knesset* (Cambridge: Harvard University Library, 1978); Herzog,

Contest of Symbols: The Sociology of Election Campaigns Through Israeli Ephemera (Cambridge: Harvard University Library, 1987); B. Donner, *To Live with the Dream* (Tel Aviv Museum of Art: Dvir Publishers, 1989); private collection of the author.

10. B. Kimmerling, *Zionism and Territory* (Berkeley: University of California Press, 1983) pp. 8-0, 16.
11. Herzog, "The Election Campaign as a Liminal Stage," p. 145-146.
12. Y. Shapiro, *Democracy in Israel* (Tel Aviv: Massada, 1977) (Hebrew); C. S. Liebman and E. Don-Yehiya, *Civil Religion in Israel* (Berkeley: University of California Press, 1983).
13. M. Shamir and A. Arian, "The Ethnic Vote in Israel's 1981 Elections," in A. Arian (ed.), *The Elections in Israel, 1981* (Tel Aviv: Ramot, 1983).
14. Y. Shapiro, *Democracy in Israel* (Tel Aviv: Sifriyat Poalim, 1984) (Hebrew); Shapiro, *Elite without Successors* (Tel Aviv: Sifriyat Poalim, 1984) (Hebrew).
15. Shapiro, *Chosen to Command: The Road to Power of the Herut Party* (Tel Aviv: Am Oved, 1989), pp. 162-180 (Hebrew).
16. Herzog, "Between Political and Cultural Ethnicity: The Ethnic Lists," *Medina Mimshal Vihasim Benleumiyyum* 25(1986):91-114 (Hebrew).
17. C. S. Liebman, "The Religious Component in Israeli Ultranationalism," *The Jerusalem Quarterly* 41 (Winter 1987), pp. 127-144.
18. Cf. Liebman and Don-Yehiya, *Civil Religion*; B. Kimmerling (ed.), *The Israeli State and Society* (New York: State University of New York, 1989).
19. *Jerusalem Post*, 12 June 1984.
20. Edelman, *Constructing the Political Spectacle*, p. 66.
21. M. Friedman, "Life Tradition and Book Tradition in the Development of Ultra-Orthodox Judaism," in H. Goldberg (ed.) *Judaism Viewed from Within and from Without: Anthropological Studies* (Albany, N.Y.: State University of New York Press, 1987), pp. 235-255; S. Deshen, "Israeli Judaism: Introduction to Major Patterns," *International Journal of Middle Eastern Studies* 9:1978, pp. 141-169.
22. Herzog, "Between Political and Cultural Ethnicity," pp. 91-114.

18

The Silenced Majority: Women in Israel's 1988 Television Election Campaign

Dafna Lemish and Chava E. Tidhar

Introduction

The important role of television in political campaigns has been demonstrated and analyzed in the political communication literature. Juxtaposed to other forms of television coverage such as newscasts, debates, or interviews on talk shows, political broadcasts are a unique phenomenon: here political parties and the candidates determine the form and content of the campaign through paid advertising (Conti, 1987). They control the tone of their campaign and the image that they wish to project. Television commercials are a primary mechanism used by parties to project their political goals and views of economic, political and social realities.

The presence/absence of women, as well as the way they are portrayed in such campaigns, project the party's ideological stance towards women: its view of women as potential voters, the degree and nature of the party's commitment to special issues, and needs of women as well as their roles in society.

Analyses of such representations should be understood in the broader perspective of the discussion of women's imagery in popular culture. In reviewing this work, Rakow (1986a) suggests that attention be focused on the kind of images presented, whose images they are, and their meaning and consequences.

With the above issues in mind, the purpose of the present study is to reveal the ideological-value system transmitted through portrayals of women in the 1988 election campaign in Israel.

Portrayals of Women in the Media

Descriptive and content analysis studies concerned with women's media image in the U.S.A., Europe, Japan and Canada have focused on questions dealing with comparative gender representations in terms of frequency of appearance, occupational roles, behavioral patterns, personality characteristics, age, physical appearance and products advertised by women—in a comparative framework of females and males (Janus, 1977). These studies reveal distinct patterns in the portrayal of women on television.

- Women appear on the screen less than men, they are frequently younger, and are often shown in traditional feminine occupations (Tedsco, 1974; Muramatsu, 1977; Weibel, 1977; Tuchman et al., 1978; Henderson et al., 1980; Downs, 1981; Kuplowka, 1985; Thoveron, 1986; Steeves and Smith, 1987).
- When compared on the basis of male-engendered characteristics and the criteria for social success, women are presented as less logical, less active, less independent, and less dominant. On the other hand, they are portrayed to be more emotional, more dependent, and more vulnerable (Busby, 1975). In general, then, women are presented as subordinate to men (Lemon, 1978; Turow, 1974; Greenberg, 1980).

A recent study carried out by Tidhar (1988) analyzed 134 Israeli produced non-fiction programs broadcast between January and April 1988. This study found that Israeli programs portrayed women in the same patterns as in the above mentioned countries. Gender bias was found to be particularly salient in news programs where men were older than women. Women appeared more often than men in affiliated and traditional roles (e.g. wife of/mother of; participating in social and voluntary tasks).

A review of the literature on the images of women used in Israeli advertising reveals basic exploitation of female stereotypes as sex objects (Lemish, 1989). They are portrayed as helpless, dependent, ineffectual, emotional, vulnerable, subordinate, childish and plain stupid. These findings are consistent with gender stereotypes on television commercials studied in other countries, such as the U.S.A. (Vestergaard and Schorder, 1983); England (Livingston and Green, 1986); and Italy (Furnham and Voli, 1989).

Overall, images on Israeli television and advertising demonstrate the concept of "symbolic annihilation" described by Tuchman et al. (1978)—a treatment of condemnation, trivialization and absence of women in the media.

In some countries a gradual transition was observed in recent years from traditional gender differences to a more "liberal" model where women are presented in the visual media to be more like men. However, such a portrayal ignores the uniqueness of feminine work style, values and experience (Cantor, 1989; Foss and Foss, 1989). Authentic portrayals may constitute further development of women's presence on television (Dervin, 1987). Such a development is only possible through ideological changes which recognize the role media play in the reconstruction and legitimization of the overriding patriarchal structure (Seiter, 1986).

Women in Israeli Politics

Studying portrayals of women in political campaigns can be understood by comparing their symbolic representation (e.g. in political television commercials) and their actual presence in political life. In this way, one seeks to understand the important relationship of "self" and "image" (Kaplan, 1987). Contrary to the image that Israeli women attained equality (the "pioneer woman," "female soldier," the late political leader and prime-minister Golda Meir), as a whole there is almost total male domination of the political, economic and judicial systems in Israeli society. For example, only 5.8% of the current Israel Parliament are women (7 women out of 120 members). There are no women cabinet members in the government.

Overall, Israeli political life is still perceived as a manly arena dominated by power relationships, toughness and aggression. Therefore it is not a place for women (Weiss and Yishai, 1980; Izraeli et al., 1982). The uniqueness of the Israeli reality, where issues of security and war receive national attention and resources, is one potential explanation for prevailing male domination.

Since the party system in Israel is controlled by men in strategic positions in party committees who determine the list of representatives, power management and favoritism effectively block women's ability to penetrate the system or to attain leadership positions. Though women have organized themselves in caucuses within central parties, these caucuses have been manipulated to isolate women from the center of power by assigning them to handle "feminine-marginal" issues—education, social welfare and health.

Two well-known politicians, commonly perceived as exceptions, actually prove the above point. Shulamit Aloni is the leader of The Citizen Rights Party (Ratz), a left wing liberal party known for its concern for human rights and separation of religion and state, and Geula Cohen the leader of The Revival Party (Hatchiya), a right wing ultra-nationalistic party which focuses its efforts on the right of Jews to settle in an extended Israel and demands a strong hand in the treatment of the uprising in the Occupied Territories. Each of these parties is represented by four parliament members. As leaders of dramatically opposed parties, these two women received special attention in this study.

Another interesting political phenomenon is the Israeli Women's Movement, developed in the 1970's. Presently the movement has directed most of its efforts to the struggle for peace and co-existence with the Palestinians and, therefore, is identified with protest movements (Tidhar and Lemish, 1990).

It is of special importance to note that the 1988 election campaign in Israel was conducted almost exclusively through political television broadcasts on the sole channel of Israeli television. The 40 to 50 minutes of prime-time evening viewing were devoted to such broadcasts, six days a week during the four-week election period established by law.

Bearing in mind the biased portrayal of women on television in general, it seems that images of women and their representation in such a campaign should be of particular interest to the understanding of the current status of women in Israeli politics.

Research Questions

Based on the above discussion, the general research question posed was as follows: "How were women presented in television coverage in the 1988 Israeli election campaign?"

Secondary questions and domains of study were as follows:

1. What proportion of women to men was presented in the television campaign?
2. How were women presented in comparison to men? (How often did they speak to the camera; How often and in which manner were they introduced; How were they visually portrayed—camera distance, background, etc.—and in what modes of expression?)
3. In what functions were women presented—their status in life and their role in the story?

4. To what degree, and how, were changes in women's roles in society and gender equality issues expressed in the campaign?

Method

1. *Quantitative content analysis:* A content analysis was carried out on 171 television election broadcasts based upon the conceptualization presented earlier. The sample included 90%[2] of the broadcasts of four parties: two major parties—the "Likud" (nationalistic party) and the "Ma'arach" (labor party); and the two parties led by women—"Ratz" and "Hatchiya." In addition, analysis was carried out on one out of every five broadcasts of each of the other parties, regardless of whether or not they succeeded in entering the Israeli parliament. This sampling limitation should be kept in mind. Broadcast time allocated to each party varied according to the relative representation in Parliament. Therefore the unit of analysis was persons and not broadcasts.
2. *Qualitative analysis:* Qualitative analyses of selected broadcasts provided in-depth case studies. Those included every broadcast devoted to women and/or women's issues, all the presentations of party-leaders Aloni and Cohen and the special role of the two permanent presenters of the Likud and Ma'arach parties.

Procedure

All broadcasts of the 1988 election campaign were recorded on videocassettes. A structured coding form was developed according to the above conceptualization. The form included the following categories:

- the number of men and women appearing on each broadcast by age, role and political status;
- presentational characteristics such as camera distance and background;
- the manner in which each person was introduced;
- treatment of women and men via introductory patterns;
- appearance in a central or marginal role in the broadcast;
- the person's dominant mode of expression (rational, emotional or comic).

The coding was carried out by two trained female coders from the Institute for Study of Media and Family. In order to ensure reliability two procedures were employed: (a) the consensus model, in which the two coders checked against each other a sample of the broadcasts, and (b) an external checking of a small sample (12%) against a third independent male coder from the Graduate School of Education at Bar Ilan University.

Results

Quantitative Content Analysis

The results of this study indicate some biases typical to the representation of women in the media, such as frequency of appearance, age, centrality and mode of expression. However, in several aspects, the progressive-democratic parties[3] and the two parties which were led by women (Ratz and Hatchiya) deviated from conventional biases. These parties showed more progressive representations of women in leadership roles, introductory patterns and salience of appearance.

Frequency of Appearance

The presentation of Israeli women on the 1988 election campaign is consistent with their frequency of appearance on Israeli news programs in general.

Table 1
Women and Men Presented on the 1988 TV Election Campaign in Israel by Political Party

Political Party	*All*	*Men*	*Women*
	#	%	%
All Parties*	2883	87%	13%
Likud	858	88%	12%
Ma'arach	838	87%	13%
Ratz	104	88%	12%
Hatchiya	119	88%	13%
Progressive Democratic Parties	135	84%	16%
Religious Parties	655	85%	15%
Other Small Parties	63	73%	27%
Parties without Women	111	100%	-
*With female presenters of the two major parties	2987	84%	16%

As indicated in Table 1, 87% of all the persons appearing on the 1988 campaign were men and 13% were women. Even when the female presenters on the Likud and the Ma'arach broadcasts were added, the bias still prevailed with 84% men and only 16% women. These proportions remained across the different political parties with two exceptions: (a) In the five broadcasts which represent the very small parties that never got to Parliament, the presentation of women reached 27%; (b) On the other hand, nine parties in our sample did not show even a single female on their election broadcasts. It was surprising to discover that included in this group was the "She'nui" party ("change"), which emphasizes in its ideological platform civil rights in general and gender equality in particular (She'nui, 1988).

The overall gender bias in frequency of appearance is so strong that it overrules all the other differences, which may be found when comparing the relative proportions of men and women presented in various capacities. Consequently, even when some differences were in favor of women, the end result was a male dominated campaign on the television screen.

Type of Visual Exposure

Camera distance. Camera distance affects proximity, salience and intimacy. Close-up shots create greater familiarity and involvement whereas long shot create more distant and alienated attitudes.

Table 2 indicates a higher proportion of women than men taken in a medium shot and a relatively lower proportion taken in a long shot. This difference was particularly marked in broadcasts of the progressive democratic parties. The small parties and Ratz tended to present a relatively higher proportion of women in close-up shots.

Appearing alone or in a group. Singling out appearances in election campaigns may emphasize the importance attributed to the person shown as a political figure or representing an issue. There were no overall distinct differences in the proportions of women and men seen alone. However, some marked differences were found between parties; the proportion of those seen alone were higher among women in the two parties whose leaders are women and in the progressive democratic parties. In the two major parties (Likud and Ma'arach), the reverse was true.

Table 2
Women and Men Appearing on the 1988 Election campaign in Israel by Type of Visual Presentation—Camera Distance (close, medium shot, or a long shot), and by Political Party

	CAMERA DISTANCE		
Political Party	*Close Up*	*Medium Shot*	*Long Shot*
All Parties			
Total	5%	66%	29%
Men	5%	65%	30%
Women	5%	74%	21%
Likud			
All	6%	84%	9%
Men	6%	85%	9%
Women	4%	82%	14%
Ma'arach			
All	7%	61%	32%
Men	7%	60%	32%
Women	6%	64%	30%
Ratz			
All	5%	77%	18%
Men	3%	78%	19%
Women	13%	69%	15%
Hatchiya			
All	-	67%	33%
Men	-	67%	33%
Women	-	71%	29%
Progressive Democratic Parties			
All	9%	50%	41%
Men	8%	47%	45%
Women	14%	62%	24%
Religious Parties			
All	1%	53%	46%
Men	1%	48%	51%
Women	1%	81%	18%
Other Small Parties			
All	5%	78%	17%
Men	-	80%	20%
Women	18%	70%	12%
Parties with no Women			
All (Men)	11%	34%	55%

Table 3
Treatment of Women and Men Appearing on the 1988 TV Election Campaign by Political Party

	INTRODUCTORY PATTERNS		
Political Party	*Speaking to the Camera*	*Title + Profession*	*Treated with Disrespect*
All Parties			
Total	19%	13%	7%
Men	18%	13%	7%
Women	20%	8%	2%
Likud			
All	19%	11%	6%
Men	20%	13%	6%
Women	17%	1%	4%
Ma'arach			
All	21%	13%	10%
Men	21%	13%	11%
Women	21%	10%	1%
Ratz			
All	41%	45%	21%
Men	38%	42%	24%
Women	62%	61%	-
Hatchiya			
All	25%	21%	27%
Men	21%	19%	30%
Women	57%	36%	-
Progressive Democratic Parties			
All	33%	17%	1%
Men	33%	17%	1%
Women	33%	19%	5%
Religious Parties			
All	5%	5%	-
Men	5%	5%	-
Women	4%	1%	-
Other Small Parties			
All	40%	7%	-
Men	41%	7%	-
Women	35%	6%	-
Parties with no Women			
All (Men)	15%	11%	-

Note that the columns in this table are independent and derived from different sets of analyses.

Age. As in traditional media representation of women, women were younger than men. In all the political parties except Hatchiya, the proportion of women under 30 years was higher than the proportion of men in this age bracket.

Treatment of Characters

Speaking to camera. Table 3 indicates overall small gender differences in people speaking to the camera on the 1988 Israeli television election campaign (20% and 18% respectively). However, due to the built-in bias mentioned earlier, only 14% of all those who appeared speaking to the camera were women and 86% were men. Two distinct variations were found between parties: (1) As could have been expected, in the two parties whose leaders are women, the relative proportions of women speaking to the camera was higher (62% and 57% among women as opposed to 38% and 21% among men); (2) In all the other parties, the majority of characters appeared without speaking to the camera with no gender differences.

Introductory patterns. In the two parties whose leaders are women, as well as in the progressive democratic parties, relatively higher proportions of women than men were introduced with reference to their title and profession and relatively lower proportions of women appeared on the broadcasts without any introduction. In all other parties, the reverse was true, and traditional media representation was preserved.

Respectfulness

A slightly higher proportion of men were treated with disrespect (7% versus 2%). The differences were particularly marked in the two political parties led by women (Ratz and Hatchiya), where none of the women appearing on the broadcasts were treated with disrespect as opposed to approximately one in four of the men. A less marked difference of the same nature was also found in the Ma'arach, where only 1% of the women were treated with disrespect as compared to 11% of the men. A possible explanation is the tendency to treat political opponents with disrespect (N.B. the opponents are usually men in the Israeli political arena).

Forms of Expression. Table 4 shows the percentage of women and men appearing on the television election campaign by their dominant modes of expression. As in traditional portrayals of women in the media, higher proportions of emotional expressions were found among women compared to men in all of the parties. The differences were particularly marked in the two parties whose leaders are women. However, in the other modes of expression, some deviations from traditional representations were found:

(a) Except for the two parties (Ma'arach and Hatchiya) about equal proportions of men and women were presented expressing themselves rationally. Only in those two parties were the portion of rational expressions lower among women;

(b) The small percentages of comic expressions were most common to male figures, especially in Ratz;

(c) Except for the Ma'arach and the religious parties, a slightly higher proportion of men than women were seen on the broadcasts without expressing themselves.

Table 4
Women and Men Appearing on the 1988 TV Election Campaign in Israel by Political Party and the Character's Dominant Mode of expression (rational, emotional, comic)

Political Party	*Rational*	*Emotional*	*Comic*	*None*
All Parties				
Total	12%	9%	1%	78%
Men	13%	8%	1%	79%
Women	9%	15%	*	76%
Likud				
All	17%	7%	*	76%
Men	16%	7%	*	76%
Women	17%	10%	-	73%
Ma'arach				
All	16%	9%	*	74%
Men	17%	8%	*	74%
Women	8%	17%	1%	74%
Ratz				
All	36%	12%	10%	42%
Men	36%	9%	11%	44%
Women	38%	31%	-	31%
Hatchiya				
All	15%	20%	-	65%
Men	17%	13%	-	70%
Women	-	71%	-	29%

Table 4 (cont.)

Progressive Democratic Parties				
All	10%	11%	-	79%
Men	10%	11%	-	80%
Women	10%	14%	-	76%
Religious Parties				
All	*	4%	*	95%
Men	1%	4%	*	95%
Women	-	5%	-	95%
Other Parties				
All	3%	22%	-	75%
Men	2%	20%	-	78%
Women	6%	29%	-	65%
Parties with no Women				
All (Men)	7%	16%	-	77%

*Less than 1%

The Relative Importance Attributed to Men and Women in the Broadcasts

Status. Table 5 presents the proportion of women and men appearing in the election campaign according to their political status and their position within the broadcast.

As may have been expected, in the two parties led by women, women leaders appeared more often than men leaders. In the progressive democratic parties about equal proportions were presented as leaders, whereas in all of the other parties the proportion of men leaders was higher. In the two major parties as well as in the small parties, a higher percentage of women than men appeared as members of the public whereas in the rest of the parties the reverse was true. On the whole, as in the political reality, of the 623 leaders who appeared on the broadcasts only 36 were women.

Women as central figures in the broadcast consisted of only 11%, whereas men consisted of 89%. Of all women appearing in the broadcasts, 13% appeared as central figures as compared to 16% of the men. The right wing party Hatchiya, led by a women, seems an exception where the proportion of central figures among women was by far higher than among men (71% and 23% respectively). However, the appearance of "women" in this case is misleading, since it consisted of repetitive appearances of the leader herself.

Table 5
Women and Men Appearing on the 1988 TV Election Campaign in Israel by Political Party, Position Within the Party, and Status in the Broadcast

	POLITICAL STATUS			
Political Party	*Leader Member*	*Party Public*	*Member of*	*Central Figure*
All Parties				
Total	22%	10%	68%	16%
Men	23%	9%	67%	16%
Women	10%	17%	73%	13%
Likud				
All	28%	6%	65%	15%
Men	32%	5%	63%	16%
Women	3%	12%	85%	8%
Ma'arach				
All	28%	13%	60%	18%
Men	29%	13%	57%	19%
Women	11%	7%	81%	14%
Ratz				
All	36%	19%	45%	30%
Men	33%	20%	47%	30%
Women	54%	15%	31%	31%
Hatchiya				
All	30%	13%	56%	29%
Men	28%	14%	58%	23%
Women	50%	7%	43%	71%
Progressive Democratic Parties				
All	20%	10%	70%	16%
Men	20%	6%	74%	17%
Women	19%	29%	52%	14%
Religious Parties				
All	4%	10%	86%	5%
Men	5%	5%	90%	5%
Women	1%	35%	64%	4%
Other Parties				
All	17%	10%	71%	52%
Men	20%	11%	69%	61%
Women	12%	6%	82%	29%
Parties with no Women				
All (Men)	14%	14%	72%	21%

Note that the last column is independent of the others and derived from a different set of analysis.

Roles. Table 6 indicates a relatively higher proportion of street testimony and of unidentified characters among women as compared to men, and as in reality, a higher proportion of politicians among men. No marked differences were found between parties in this respect.

Table 6
Roles in Which Women and Men Appeared on the 1988 TV Election Campaign in Israel

Role	*Men* 2505=100%	*Women* 378-100%	*All* 2883-100%
Politician	26%	10%	24%
Street Testimony	6%	13%	7%
Authority	2%	1%	1%
Military Official	1%	-	1%
Blue Collar Worker	1%	1%	1%
Social Service	*	1%	1%
Dependency Role	*	3%	1%
Symbol	1%	-	1%
Others	2%	1%	1%
Unidentified	62%	70%	64%

*Less than 1%

No marked differences were found between political parties in regards to role differentiation.

Qualtitative Anaylsis

The qualitative analyses focused on those broadcasts that featured women as main characters, and/or issues of primary concern to women. In these political broadcasts women served the following roles:

Women as Persuaders

The two major parties—Likud and Ma'arach— featured female presenters in their broadcasts. Both women were in their 20s, pleasant looking and fashionably dressed. Similarly to news presenters, they opened and closed the broadcasts, connected different segments with "sense-making" comments and "helped" the audience to arrive at the "appropriate" conclusions. Clearly, they were not expressing their own opinion, but represented the party's line; what the leaders themselves would not say directly, the women presenters said on their behalf, in a seemingly "objective" interpretation of the political reality.

Women as Party Leaders

The two parties led by women—Ratz and Hatchiya—differed in their presentation of the leaders. Aloni (Ratz) was portrayed in a factual, formal and serious manner. While occasionally she talked directly to the audience, she was usually presented through detached profile close-ups and involved in various activities. She presented her arguments in a rational manner with very little emotional expression.

Cohen (Hatchiya), on the other hand, was presented in a down to earth, warm and folksy manner. In most of her appearances she talked directly to the viewers in the same medium-shot position, wearing the same white blouse and decorative pin. Her speeches—mostly of the conversational type—were very judgmental of others and full of practical advice. She used many hand motions and facial expressions.

Women as Politicians

It is interesting to note that of all the broadcasts sampled, three chose women politicians to present party issues: two from the progressive-democratic parties (Hadash—on the Arab-Israeli conflict; Mapam—on special education) and one from Hatchiya (other than the leader—on security in the occupied territories).

None of the two major parties enabled women to present any of the party's stands on issues. The Ma'arach, however, devoted an entire broadcast to its women-politicians, presenting five different women in their political activities, four of which were in feminine areas—care of elderly and young children, health reform and contact with Arab women. Clearly, the broadcasts talked *about* women party members rather than women talking on behalf of the party. Cynically, this particular broadcast ended with the two leading males (Peres and Rabin) presenting the party's program for peace, security and foreign affairs.

The Nurturing Women

In four broadcasts, laywomen—rather than politicians—were drafted to talk abut the Israeli-Arab conflict. They were all presented in their dependency roles; their argument and its justification stemmed from a role as a girlfriend, a mother, a grandmother—of males. In this function, the women represented the home front, voicing the concerns of men in war or reflecting on the implication of their men's possible or actual death.

(a) *The Ma'arach's "widow"* was widowed as a pregnant young wife who at present faces the upcoming mandatory military service of her son. In an edited emotional monologue, she portrays the anti-war protective mother who wants peace "for my son and his friends." She makes no rational arguments and provides no claims beyond her motherly need to protect her flock.

(b) *The Likud's mother* is officially presented as a "mother's voice" (contrary to the politicians' voice). As the mother of four grown sons, she argues against concession and doesn't believe in "peace at any cost." "This is too dangerous" she claims. Even though she defines herself as a "rational women," her edited monologue consists of emotional statements, often personal in nature.

Hadash, the communist Arab-Jewish party, presented two women in the nurturant role.

(c) "*The girlfriend*" read a letter from her soldier boyfriend serving in the Occupied Territories. Though reading his letter loudly, she was clearly voicing *his* inner-struggle. It expresses sensitivity pain and confusion, none of which was directly expressed by any man during the campaign. It seems that only the female voice can serve as a legitimate channel of expressing such deep emotional distress.

(d) The *"Arab peasant grandmother"* provides a detailed factual and quite restrained testimony of the circumstances through which her son was accidentally killed in the Intifada, and left her with 10 souls for which to provide. Towards the end, her eyes fill and her voice cracks with emotion, yet she remains very dignified and self-controlled. "The grandmother" seems to represent women as the traditional victims of war—they are left behind to care for the orphans.

The Equal-Rights Women

Three of the parties devoted a full broadcast to the issue of gender equality. To our surprise, two parties were religious. Hamafdal, the National Religious Party, presented their women's caucus efforts in the area of education from daycare to adult.

Meimad, the central religious camp, devoted its broadcast to a plea to women, "You are equal, your vote is equal." A woman-politician promised a solution to women's inequality within the religious perspective and committed herself to work towards that goal.

The most elaborate gender broadcast was presented by Ratz. It started with a clever graphic comparison between two unidentified figures who were not enjoying equal rights (later we learn that they differ only in their organs). Then Aloni, speaking directly to the camera, claims—"I am a second-rate citizen, and so are you." She continues by describing her party's efforts in this area and the continuation of this struggle. It is important to note that of all parties in political life in Israel, Ratz indeed is the one which most often raises issues relating to women and their struggle for social change.

The Exceptional Woman

Only one broadcast presented a woman expressing an opinion on general political issues. A high-school student from a development town provided clear cut opinions and advice and presented judgmental arguments against the Ma'arach. It is interesting to note that this performance elicited reaction in the other media and became one of the most debated "milestones" of the entire campaign.

Discussion

As in other studies concerning the representation of women in the news and current affairs programs, in our study we found some traditional male biases in frequency of appearance, in age representation, in centrality and in roles. The low frequency in which women appear in the 1988 election campaign reflect their overall misrepresentation in the real political arena.

These findings are particularly interesting in light of the fact that most parties included in their political platform issues of gender equality with varying degrees of emphasis and detail. However, this aspect of the parties' platform is not reflected in the television campaign. While we have no data on whether and to what degree Israeli citizens read those platforms (N.B. the Ma'arach platform was published but one week before the election), we do know the intensity to which most people were exposed to the television campaign. Close to 60% reported viewing the campaign three or more times a week. At least 50% reported viewing all of the broadcasts (Caspi and Levinson, in print).

In the progressive-democratic parties—those generally more concerned with equality issues—women's representation on the television campaign was indeed more equal to that of men. In the two parties led by females, a relatively higher proportion of women were represented speaking to the camera, appeared without other people around them, were introduced by title and profession and were shown in leadership roles. It is worth noting, however, that whereas Ratz allocated time in their broadcasts to women's issues, in Hatchiya it was mainly the female leader's appearance which inflated the results in these directions. In this respect, the television political campaign reflected political reality rather than a mechanism for social change.

Over the last decade, a number of research studies based upon assumptions derived from social learning theory, analyzed the attitudes and behaviors that are learned and applied by television viewers (for example, research on the learning of family roles [Buerkel et al., 1982]; learning of sex role expectations [McGhee and Frueh, 1989; Miller and Reeves, 1976]; and the learning of altruistic behaviors [Collins and Getz, 1976]). Television figures offer a significant source of vicarious role taking. In addition, by providing access to situations and social realities, which are remote from viewers' daily life experiences, television influences the shape of general viewpoints and viewers' conceptions of social reality.

This perspective seems particularly relevant to political life, with which most of our acquaintance is through the media. The naive viewer of the 1988 television election campaign in Israel would still see women as marginal to the political arena and as relating mainly to the traditional nurturing roles. However, this viewer will find the signs of change where reality actually backs it—among parties concerned with human rights.

Notes

1. This study was supported by a grant from the New Israel Fund to the Institute for the Study of Media and Family. The authors wish to thank Ornat Torin for coordinating the data analysis and to her and Tchiya Dov for hours of patient content analyzing. Finally, our thanks to Dr. Peter Lemish for his editorial contribution.
2. 10% of the broadcasts were unavailable for analysis due to technical difficulties.
3. Progressive-democratic parties include the socialist parties and the Arab-Jewish parties, commonly defined in Israel as "the left." Due to the various connotations that "left" has in the western world, we preferred the above term.

References

Baehr A. (1980). The 'liberated women' in television drama. *Women's Studies International Quarterly*, 3 29-39.

Buerkel-Rothfuss, N. L., Greenberg, B.S., Atkin, C. K. and Neuendorf, K. (1982). Learning about the family from television. *Journal of Communication*, 191-201.

Busby, J. L. (1975). Sex role research in the mass media. *Journal of Communication*, 107-130.

Cantor, M. (1989). The politics of culture: Feminism and the media. In A. A. Berger (ed.) *Political culture and public opinion* (pp. 149-163). New Brunswick: Transaction Publishers.

Caspi, D. and Levinson, H. (in print). To influence and to be influenced. In D. Elazer and S. Sandler (eds.), *Israel in the polls 1988-1989.*

Chazan, N. (1989). Speech before a group of New Israel Fund donors. Jerusalem.

Collins, W. A. and Getz, S. K. (1976). Children's social responses following modeled reactions to provocations: Prosocial effects of television drama. *Journal of Personality*, 44, 488-500.

Conti, D. B. (1987). *Non-verbal messages in televised presidential political advertising—pragmatic politics with electoral benefits.* Paper presented at the Annual Meeting of the Eastern Communication Association, Syracuse, N.Y.

Dervin, B. (1987). The potential contributions of feminist scholarship to the field of communication. *Journal of Communication*, 107-120.

Downs, A. C. (1981). Sex role stereotyping on prime-time television. *Journal of Generic Psychology*, 128, 253-258.

Foss, K. A. and Foss S. K. (1989). Incorporating the feminist perspective in communication scholarship: A research commentary. In K. Carter and C. Spitzack (eds.), *Doing research on women's communication: Perspectives on theory and method* (pp. 65-91), Norwood, N.J.: Ablex.

Furnham, A. and Voli, V. (1989). Gender stereotypes in Italian television advertisements. *Journal of Broadcasting and Electronic Media*, 33, 175-185.

Greenberg, B.S. (ed.) (1980). *Life on television: Content analysis of U.S. TV drama.* Norwood, N.J.: Ablex.

Henderson, L., Greenberg, B. S. and Atkin, C. K. (1980). Sex differences in giving orders, making plans and needing support on television. In B. S. Greenberg (ed.), *Life on television: Content analysis of US. TV drama* (pp. 49-63). Norwood, N.J.: Ablex.

Izraeli, D., Friedman, A., Schrift, R., Raday, F., and Buber-Agassi, J. (1982). *The Double Bind: Women in Israel.* Tel Aviv: Kibbutz Meuchad Press. (Hebrew).

Janus, N. Z. (1977). Research on sex roles in the mass media: Toward a critical approach. *The Insurgent Sociologist*, 7, 19-31.

Kaplan, A. (1987). Feminist criticism and television. *Channels of Discourse*, 211-253.

Kuplowska, O. (1985). *Images of Women in Television: A Survey of selected findings.* Paper presented at a workshop on Media and Ethnic Women, Edmonton Alberta.

Lemish, D. (1989). *Pretty women—ugly stereotypes: Images of women in Israeli advertising.* Unpublished paper.

Lemon, J. (1978). Dominant or dominated? Women on prime-time television. In G. Tuchman, A. Kaplan-Daniels, and J. Banet (eds.), *Hearth and Home: Images of women in the mass media* (51-68). New York: Oxford University Press.

Livingston, S. and Green G. (1986). Television advertisements and the portrayal of gender. *British Journal of Social Psychology*, 25, 149-154.

McGhee, P.E. and Frueh, T. (1989). Television viewing and learning of sex role stereotypes. *Sex Roles*, 6, 179-188.

Miller, M. and Reeves, B. (1976). Dramatic TV content and children's sex role stereotypes. *Journal of Broadcasting*, 20, 35-50.

Muramatsu, Y. (1977). The image of women in Japanese television dramas. Tokyo: N.H.K.

Rakow, L.E. (1986a). Feminist approaches to popular culture: giving patriarchy its due. *Communication*, 9, 19-41.

Rakow, L.E. (1986b). Rethinking gender research in communication. *Journal of Communication*, 11-26.
Seiter, E. (1986). Stereotypes and the media: A re-evaluation. *Journal of Communication*, 14-26.
Sharfman, D. (1988). *Women and Politics*. Haifa: Tamar. (Hebrew).
She'nui (1988). Abbreviated platform to the 11th Knesset.
Steeves, H.L. and Smith, M.C. (1987). Class and gender in prime-time television entertainment: Observations from a socialist feminist perspective. *Journal of Communication Inquiry*, 7, 44-63.
Tedesco, N.S. (1974). Patterns in prime-time. *Journal of Communication*, 24, 119-124.
Thoveron, G. (1986). European televised women. *European Journal of Communications*, 263-288.
Tidhar, C.E. (1988). *Women in Israel's broadcasting media and on Israeli television*. Paper presented at the symposium on women and communication in an age of science and technology. Tokyo
Tidhar, C.E. and Lemish, D. (1990). *Women in the Intifada: The view of television news coverage*. Paper presented at the annual meeting of the International Communication Association, Dublin, Ireland.
Tuchman, G., Kaplan-Daniels, A. and Banet, J. (eds.) (1978). *Hearth and Home: Images of women in the mass media*. New York: Oxford University Press.
Turow, J. (1974). Advertising and ordering: Daytime, primetime. *Journal of Communication*, 24, 138-141.
Vestergaard, T. and Schroder K. (1983). *The Language of Advertising*. Pp. 71-100) Oxford: Blackwell.
Weibel, K. (1977). *Mirror, Mirror. Images of women reflected in popular culture*. New York: Anchor.
Weiss, S. and Yishai I. (1980). Women's representation in Israeli political elites. *Jewish Social Studies*, 17, 165-176.

Part 6

In the Shadow of the Israeli-Arab Conflict

19

Decoding Television News: The Political Discourse of Israeli Hawks and Doves

Tamar Liebes

The Hebrew University of Jerusalem

Present-day Israel is a one-issue country. In regard to the Israeli-Arab conflict, its population is divided between hard-liners on the right—those who will not yield occupied territories in exchange for peace—and those more inclined to compromise. Members of the young generation are politically more hawkish than their parents.[1] This move to the right can be seen in voting behavior, but even more significantly it is evident in the rise of hatred of Arabs and the recent emergence of population "transfer" as an acceptable solution. In a study analyzing this trend from the perspective of political socialization that takes place *within* families, we find that whereas all parents have a better than random chance to reproduce their political outlook in their adolescent children, hawks are more successful than doves.[2]

Our study indicates that the difficulty dovish parents have in socializing their children to their ideological outlooks can be explained by (1) the influence of the dominantly hawkish peer group (which leaves open the question of what influences these peers), (2) the continual conflict into which this young generation is born, not least as it implies giving up a lot of years to army service, (3) the longing for an unambiguous and clear-cut solution to the conflict, expressed also in the impatience of the young with parental views that they regard as ambivalent and inconsistent, or even dangerous,[3] and (4) the nationalist surge following the '67 war, which, tinged with fundamentalist sentiments, became the dominant political discourse of Prime Minister Begin and the Likud Party.

Our study set out to explore the possibility that television news also has a role in the process of socialization. Our conclusion is that television seems to favor the hawks, and the object of this article will be to show how this happens in a democratic country where the public television system is not manifestly biased.[4] If there is an allegation of bias, it comes from the hawks who claim that television's representation of the conflict distorts reality. Yet, we propose that it is the hawks, not the doves who find the portrayal more compatible. The doves, on the other hand, have to make an effort to construct a reality that is more complex, less "closed," less predictable, less black and white. These attempts can be seen as ways of excusing, completing, and balancing the picture of reality on the television screen and in the minds of others although the doves are not necessarily aware that television is inadvertently not on their side. That routine television news tends to this kind of hawkish bias can be discerned with respect to the representation of other social problems as well.

In what follows, we show how these conclusions emerge from a study of the *Intifada*, i.e. the uprising of the Palestinians in the territories occupied by Israel in the 1967 war. Our starting point is based on the observations of (1) the centrality of the evening newscast on Israel's only, public channel, viewed nightly by almost the entire population (70 percent on an average night),[5] (2) the salience of viewing in the context of family (as most households still own only one television set), (3) the frequency of discussing the news and the general belief in its credibility. In this context—ostensibly homogenizing, even hegemonic—one can also observe, paradoxically, that there is (4) an increasing dichotomization of Israeli society into "hawks" and "doves." We set out to analyze the types of "negotiation" carried out by hawks and doves, both in interaction with the television text and in conversations with other family members focused around the nightly evening newscast.

The data come from two sources: replies to a questionnaire of a representative sample of 400 parent/adolescent pairs in Jerusalem, which inquired into political ideologies, patterns of media exposure, attitudes toward media, political involvement and knowledge, mutual perceptions of parent and child, and the perceptions of both of the distribution of political attitudes in the general public. From the questionnaire data family profiles are constructed in terms of the degree of ideological similarity between parent and son or daughter, with respect to their preferred solution to the Arab-Israeli conflict and their attitudes toward Arabs, the centrality of the news and the bias of journalists, and their attitudes toward censorship.

We returned to the homes of the 55 families who agreed to receive us for a second visit, in time for *Mabat*, the nightly news program.[6] During the viewing, the interaction with the screen and among family members was documented[7] and, following the broadcast, we initiated a family discussion about the news, by asking either parent or child to tell what he or she had seen, as if the others were not present. The other family members were told to feel free to interrupt in order to ask, correct, or comment.[8] In most cases this was enough to trigger a lively discussion, moving from the events of the day to general political discourse. The conversations were recorded and transcribed by the interviewers, and not surprisingly, they tended to concentrate on the Arab-Israeli conflict, as the political identity of Israelis is defined in terms of attitudes toward this issue.

To demonstrate that the everyday routines of Western journalism favor hawkish readings of Israel television news, we (1) examine these conventions of television news, (2) pointing out their likely bearing on viewer decodings of the *Intifada*, and then turn (3) to an examination of actual decodings by viewers whom we are able to identify as hawks and doves, and their interactions with their children with respect to the news. In conclusion, (4) these findings are discussed in the context of television coverage of protest movements and other types of social and political disruption, in an effort to generalize as well as to identify the conditions under which the generalization is most likely to apply.

The Framing of Reality by Television News

Let us consider the characteristics of television news—and Israeli television news in particular—bearing in mind that we are interested in the different ways in which such news enters family debate on all sides. On the whole, there is considerable agreement among media researchers—sociologists, political scientists, and communication scholars—about the attributes of television news, even if there is disagreement over the relative weight to assign to commercial, organizational, and professional routines and whether to define them as "hegemonic."

Researchers agree, first of all, that Western journalism is a social warning system, exposing the exception rather than the rule, the *deviant* rather than the norm, disorder rather than order, dissonance rather than harmony. Functionalists argue that publicizing deviance works to reaffirm the norm; calling attention to a breach demands the attention of those in charge of the norm.[10] Publicizing the deviant, however, may raise the issue of the validity of the norm that has been violated, sometimes conferring status on the violation itself.[11]

Deviance is one of the forms of conflict, and *conflict*, often violent, is the major preoccupation of television news. Gans's study, for example, shows that news consists mainly of (1) crimes, scandals, and investigations, (2) conflicts within government, and (3) violent protest—in that order.

The presentation of conflict, most media scholars agree, tends to *simplify* real-life issues and to stereotype participants. Thus, a complex, tortuous process of conflict, including a number of different actors is framed, typically, as a disconnected series of discreet and violent eruptions, preferably between two opponents. Critical theorists argue that conflicts are often shown as more soluble than they are to demonstrate the need for strong government to handle threats to the social order. In this view, the inflation of acute crises diverts attention from the chronic maladies that underlie them.[12] But this is probably less true the longer a conflict persists. In the case of a chronic conflict such as that in Northern Ireland, for example, television may downplay each incident in the series and thus risk a loss of credibility among viewers, or it may inflate their seriousness in order to justify punitive retaliation, or it may vacillate between the two.

Thus, a third characteristic of television news is its focus on *events* rather than on processes of the contexts of these events. This is the result of the institutional structure that determines the "rhythm" of television news. The nightly show consists of events that take place between one newscast and the next,[13] and that lend themselves to individual packaging as "items." This parade of problems may well conceal the likelihood that some underlying cause may connect them. Hallin would explain this tendency in terms of the bias of news to strategic, rather than value, issues.[14] Decontextualization, then, is another explanation for the bias of the news toward the unexpected and deviant. Interpretation of the unexpected would make it more expected, and thereby reduce its psychological appeal. Explanation, says Edelman, is scholarship, not news.[15]

A bias for events means a bias for *action*, especially on television. Thus, a fourth characteristic of news is the preference for action. Television favors action, but not necessarily the people who act. The journalists' rule is that weaker groups have to act in order to gain access, while for establishments, talk counts as action. This inequality means that in clashes between "in" and "out" groups, the less-favored side may be shown acting, voiced-over by the reporter, while the stronger side is invited to argue its own case.[16] By the same logic, the more violent the action, the greater chance of a deviant group to make it past the television gatekeeper. Gitlin goes so far as to claim that journalists acquire an insensitivity to the voice and life-worlds of working-class and minority people.[17]

Constructing social reality as a series of simple, dramatic episodes is also the reason for the *personification* of the social and political institutions and trends that are involved. Personalities, rather than social forces, are responsible for conflict. In conflicts that are not associated with known public figures, such as in the coverage of protest, the journalists themselves have the power to create leaders that personify one or both sides and to introduce them to the public. Once chosen, such characters—say, a demonstrator or police officer—may be personalized to various degrees: by showing the character in action, by giving him or her a voice, or by closing up on his face, or by showing him in roles other than those the character plays in the news story. Personalization, it is thought, gives support to the side that is personalized, and may de-intensify the conflict if both sides are personalized. In international confrontations, television personalizes "us" rather than "them."[18] This is true also of confrontations between establishment and deviant groups and follows from the asymmetry of presenting elites as talking vs. dissidents as rioting.

Finally, the *rhetoric* of news programs—like that of other television drama—also provides entertainment. In retelling facts, journalists are telling stories.[19] This implies that the more dramatic the plot-line—the more intense the conflict, and the more visual—the better its chance of making the news. Thus, the rhetorical constraints of having to tell a good story reinforces the normative definition of the news. More than that, they bring the personae in the news who are familiar with journalistic practices to act in accordance with journalists' exceptions. The greater the dependence on the journalist, the more likely the actor is to conform to his or her role in the journalist's script, as has often been noted in the case of extremist behavior of deviant groups wishing to call attention to themselves.[20] Thus, real life sometimes expresses the self-fulfilling practices of journalists.

The Framing of Protest by Television News

Israel Television treated the *Intifada* as a form of violent protest, rather than as an all-out rebellion or civil war. Coverage followed the form of, say, the urban riots in the U.S. in the sixties, even if American blacks can be said to have employed illegitimate means in the name of legitimate ends such as equality within the society, while the Palestinian rioters may be said to be employing illegitimate means and, by Israeli criteria, in the name of illegitimate ends.[21]

As in the U.S. riots or the Catholic protest in Northern Ireland, cameras focus on the violence of the demonstrators from over the shoulders of the security forces. The "news" is the violence of the demonstrators while the soldiers—though highly visible—are shown to be carrying out their jobs. Gans adds, concerning the U.S. riots, that police violence was largely ignored, and that the routine police brutality in the ghetto—a major clue to the eruptions—did not qualify for inclusion in the news. Schiff and Ya'ari make much the same point about the daily humiliations suffered by the Palestinians under the Israeli occupation.[22] There was little room for the long-term effect of government policy in the territories on Israel Television news (although much attention was given to the subject in other political programs). Policy takes a long time to be formulated and evaluated and defies the simplifications of television news. Talk defers to action, and process defers to specific incidents.

As noted above, however, the inequality of the two sides leads to a disparity between the display of violent action on the two sides. When the cameras arrive, they exacerbate—sometimes even provoke—the violence of the protesters whose aim is to call Israeli and world attention to their plight. The cameras—and all kinds of journalists—have the opposite effect on the soldiers who are aware that the filming of over-reaction on their part may lead to military and public censure and even court-martial.[23] Beyond the site of confrontation, the event continues in the statements of police and army commanders and politicians, thus tipping the balance even more in favor of demonstrators' *action*—rocks, Molotov cocktails, and road blocks—versus reason and restraint on "our" side.

Nevertheless, within the context of clashes, the demonstrators are presented as stronger than they are, reflecting the army's having granted them, willy nilly, the role of adversary. The face of the enemy, however, is hidden symbolically, due to the bias of television news (as we will demonstrate in detail), and, of course, because the Palestinians themselves cover their faces in self-protection. This adds to the image of the "other" as threatening, even demonic. We know them only as the masked enemy, and see them not as people, but as role players in the conflict. Only occasionally, when we are shown the mother of the stone-throwers or a Palestinian intellectual, do we get a glimpse of them as people.

On "our" side, however, the violence results in human suffering. Ordinary people are seen to be victimized: babies in hospitals, grieving families, funerals are extensively shown. The human tragedy of the other side does not exist on screen, not only because it is "our" public network, but because Israel television reporters would not be welcomed by families of Palestinian victims. Thus, all the constraints of television's presentation of the conflict combine with the cognitive processes through which viewers understand other people, to humanize "our" side and to dehumanize the other side.

How the News Reinforces the Attribution Error of Viewers

The rhetoric of television news on social conflict—framed as a confrontation between an "other" and "us"—makes it easy for viewers to commit the fundamental attribution error. The main claim of attribution theory in its classic version is that people tend to attribute their own failures to external (situational) causes, and the failures of others to internal (dispositional) causes.[24]

In his critique of attribution theory, Richard Eiser suggests that it should incorporate Schank and Abelson's "schemata" model, according to which we explain other people's behavior in the same way in which we understand the plot of a dramatic play.[25] In both, our knowledge of the rules and roles we associate with a certain social context applies to understanding and predicting behavior. If this idea is valid for perception of others in real life, it should be all the more valid in the understanding of real characters who are "mediated."[26] In the drama of the news on screen, we meet characters *only* in those roles that are relevant for the genre.

In the case of the *Intifada*, television's presentation constrains viewers to attribute situational reasons to soldiers' behavior, and dispositional reasons to protestors' behavior.[27] Soldiers perform their role in an institutional context; Palestinians are individually responsible.[28] The process whereby television reinforces the fundamental attribution error works in the following way: Compared to "our" side (1) Arabs are shown almost only in their role within the "script" of the conflict, the most news-worthy context from the point of view of journalistic function and dramatic attributes. (2) In this script, well recognized by viewers, Arabs appear as "terrorists," which in the two-year-old *Intifada* version is the stone-throwing youth, his face covered with a *kafia*, so as not be identifiable. Choosing to be "faceless" to protect himself also makes him threatening, inhuman, almost a demonic figure for viewers who do not see him as the young person he is. (3) For most Israelis, and even more so for children, television is the only source of acquaintance with Arabs, who become identical to "terrorists" on television. (4) The "terrorist" script shows the different incidents as arbitrarily violent, causing suffering to innocent victims. Hardly shown is the human suffering on the Arab side and the situational or ideological context within which rioting might make sense.[29] Thus, in terms of the attribution error, television contributes to the perception of terrorism as intrinsic to Arabs and helps viewers to think of Arabs as "bad".

Of course, in the context of clashes between stone throwers and the army, Israeli soldiers are shown as no less violent, but "we" are much less likely to be perceived as inherently bad because (1) "we" know ourselves not only through television—virtually every Israeli man is a soldier himself or the parent or son of one—and we know the external context that "justifies" our behavior, (2) television helps by showing "us" not only in the role or "soldiers" but also in the private role of family members, who suffer the consequences of violence, and (3) the ceremonies that accompany personal tragedies are used to lend meaning to the fate of individuals in terms of the national ideology.

Table 1
"Us" and "them" on TV and in viewers' experience

	The conflict					
	In television's presentation			In viewers' experience		
	Intifada combatants	Intifada victims	Other TV roles	Off-screen reality	Collective symbolic reality	Viewers' attributive frame
"us"	"good"/"bad" soldiers	"good" family member, citizen	political and professional elites	familiar	"good"	external
"them"	"bad" terrorists	not shown	not shown	unfamiliar	"bad"	internal

Table 1 summarizes this argument. On television, both "us" and "them" are cast as "bad"—the soldiers are "bad," especially when they deviate from prescribed behavior, and the violent Palestinian youth are "bad." These roles constitute the conflict as seen "on stage."[30] When Israel television shows "off stage" roles of the *Intifada* it does so only of "us," focusing on our side, showing the "good" side of those who might have created a "bad" impression on the stage of the conflict. Other items show "us" either as victims of the *Intifada* or as actors in a variety of social and political roles (as do other programs). Israelis are thereby personalized and humanized by television, whereas Palestinians—not often shown "off stage"—are seen only in their roles in the "on stage" conflict, and consequently are depersonalized and cast simply as "bad."

This asymmetrical picture is reinforced by viewers' own perceptions independent of but reinforced by what is shown on television. Israelis are familiar with their own side, of course, and are fully aware, from personal experience, of the moral dissonance experienced by Israeli soldiers and the human tragedies that result from the conflict. But they are unfamiliar, in their personal experience, with the parallel context on the other side. The resulting construction of reality by viewers is therefore dichotomized into the "we" who are pressured into being "bad" for external reasons, and the "they" who are "bad" for internal reasons, because that's the way "they" are.

How the Rhetoric of Television News Is Decoded by Hawks and Doves: Evidence from Family Discussions

The second part of this article shows how the rhetoric of a monopolistic news program on Israel's one TV channel is differently decoded by Israeli hawks and doves. The hawks, we argue, are better "served" by television rhetoric in the sense that no harm is done if it is mistaken by them to be veritable reality. The doves, for their part, find television news disturbing in its black and white biases, unless they know the code by which "their" reality can be inferred from the journalistic presentation.

Television Frames Play into the Hands of Hawks

Israeli hawks see the conflict as insoluble, "apocalyptic" rather than "serial,"[31] in short as a no-compromise, zero-sum game reflected in the relentlessness of the nightly news. Images making "us" good and "them" bad provide an acceptable script for these Israelis and help to formulate the script for news initiates.

The family discussions provide rich evidence that hawks describe reality in television terms: television incidents showing "bad" Arabs are used as proof for reminding us what the Arabs are "really" like. Television is attacked for not tilting the balance even *more* in this direction in providing the situational justification for our looking bad.

Paradoxically, in spite of "proving" them right, hawks complain that television distorts reality, that journalists are doves, sometimes traitors, who support the Arab side. This paradox is expressed in an exchange between father and daughter in the Ben Ya'akov family.[32] Aharon Ben Ya'akov and his wife, in their forties, are moderate hawks of Eastern-European origin. Ruth, his 15-year-old, Israeli born, daughter[33] is an extreme hawk. The family's older son, who studies medicine, was not home. Like other adolescents in the study, the daughter Ruth associates herself "officially" with the *Techia* party, which regards the occupied territories as an integral part of Israel and calls for massive settlement in the West Bank, but supports a much more extreme position in terms of believing in "transfer" as a desirable solution to the conflict. Whereas both father and daughter believe that television is not "objective," Ruth claims that her understanding of the conflict is based on what she sees on television. "If this is the case," argues her father sarcastically, "you should be an extreme dove!" The hawks' hostility against television news can be understood in terms of an expectation of what the news *should* show, which is different from the journalists' definition. Television, they believe, should show the "normal" aspect of reality and not give undue attention to deviance and conflict.[34]

In addition to belief in "good" news per se, concern is expressed over the show of violence to the world. It is an instrumental view of television expressing anxiety about the effect of television on others, i.e., a "third person effect."[35] This is ironic in view of the hawks' own reaction to "bad" Arabs on television. They seem to lack awareness that violence on television affects public opinion in the direction of imposing tougher control.[36] Thus, there is a paradox in the hawks' hostility to television. In spite of the fact that it plays into their hands, Mr. Ben Ya'akov's belief that television is "leftist" is typical, although he can get evidence to the contrary from his own daughter! The daughter is an extreme hawk, worrying even the moderately hawkish father, and she professes to receive her knowledge from television. The discussion between father and daughter in the Ben Ya'akov family indicates some of the processes that contribute to the move right and to the role of television in this move:

Television is the source

Father (explaining to interviewer): We try not to enter into family confrontations.

Daughter: One doesn't come out alive.

Father: Because Ruth is very extreme in her opinions and I am rather unsuccessful imposing upon her my more balanced type of thinking. (To daughter) Where do you think that (your opinion) came from? What does it grow out of?

Daughter: From television, from media, and from everything that is happening.

Indeed, Ruth's refusal to acknowledge the relevance of anything that interferes with her most simplistic black and white picture of reality seems to reflect the imprinting of television. Whereas the father is careful to affirm the justice inherent in our "case" in terms of the historical rights of the Jews to the land of Israel and the contemporary suffering of the Jews, the daughter docs not need any "proof."

The generational gap is well illustrated when father and daughter discuss what is for her "the murder" of PLO operations commander Abu Jihad, referred to in the news, which took place in Tunis a month or so prior to the discussion. "I would call it the 'execution,'" corrects the father, intent on making sure that nobody confuses the image of "our" justice with that of terrorists. Ruth does not see why bother. She takes it for granted that we are good and does not think it needs proving. Her favorite way to solve, or rather, to dismiss the Palestinian problem is "let them get lost" ("*sheya'uffu*"). Her wish for the Arabs to "vanish" which she expresses time and again during the conversation, is brutal but vague. It is vague because she prefers not to know *how* this vanishing will occur; it is brutal because it expresses an attitude of dehumanization of Arabs, entrenched deeply enough to make such a wish legitimate in thought and in conversation.

Resolving the conflict by the disappearance of the rival can be understood as part of Ruth's impatience with the ambivalence and ambiguity she senses in her father: "You are contradicting yourself. Either they are poor or they are terrorists who should be squashed," she scolds him. But this weariness with the complexity of the situation is reinforced by television's simplistic view of reality, which shows that "they" are, indeed, brutal and inhuman enough to justify "vanishing."

The daughter of the Ben Ya'akov family is a faithful representative of the majority of adolescents in other families who (1) regard the Arabs as inhuman, (2) admit that they receive their information from television, (3) claim that television shows "90%" or "almost all" of what Arabs are like, and (4) declare they do not want to know any data from other sources that may confuse this picture.

The Doves' Attempt to Amend Television's Black and White Picture of Reality

If hawks complain that television's picture is not sufficiently black and white but admit to depending on television for their perception of the conflict, doves express unease with this dichotomized representation and try to transform it into a more balanced picture. In discussions with children and others, dovish parents fail to make their point, however. They are stymied by the consensus against anchoring "evil" terrorist acts in any ideological context that would shift the argument away from disconnected acts of brutality in the direction of a dispute between two political claims. Moreover, although they know intuitively that there is something wrong with the reality on television, they are not aware of the journalistic criteria and generic constraints that make up television's code. Not having critical tools at their disposal, their objections to the simplistic framing seem subjective and unfounded. The only chance doves have to persuade their children—sometimes their siblings or parents—to their position is when they can point to the fundamental attribution error and show how television reinforces the viewers' distorted perception.

However doomed to failure, doves sometimes try to balance the picture by drawing on their own experience, giving personal evidence to show that "they" are not only "bad" and that we are not only "good."[37] In terms of the prevalent image of the Arabs their effort is to change the equation of Arabs and terrorists, to expand the image of Arabs as human beings, to counteract the tendency to depersonalize them.

The following exchange is taken from the discussion of the Horwitch family. Sally Horwitch, in her late thirties, an immigrant from the United States, is the mother of two teenage daughters and a younger son. In discussion with her oldest daughter Sharon, the mother tries to change her daughter's image of Arabs as terrorists by calling on her personal experience:

"Arabs have children and worry about them."

Mother: We know Arabs who are married and have children and they worry a lot about their children, and love them.

Daughter: I did not say "all the Arabs," I said "some of them."

Mother: What happens is that the young ones are making a lot of noise, the ones who throw stones, and suddenly they [soldiers] come and blow up everybody's houses. It's terrible.

Although she seems to be successful here, later in the discussion it becomes evident that her two daughters reject the idea of Arabs as parents who love their children: "In that case why are they ready to kill their daughters?" they ask, referring to widespread ideas about moral fundamentalism.

Mrs. Dekel, another dovish mother, tries similar tactics. Na'ama Dekel and her husband Haim are both in their forties and are originally from Syria. They have two children: a nineteen-year-old boy, now doing his army service, and a fourteen-year-old daughter, Yaffa, who is at home. When discussing the news with her daughter, Na'ama Dekel contrasts "bad" Arabs on television with "real" Arabs who are "normal."[38] They are ordinary people, she says, with family and work worries, who are struggling to survive under Israeli rule, in the threatening shadow of their own evil image on television.

"They have families."

Mother: And I think that not all of them are terrorists or stone-throwers, and not all of them burn tires, and altogether that they are human beings, people who want to live.

Daughter: But why...

Mother: And they feel very uncomfortable. They work, these people, this family; and there are other families I know who work. They feel very uncomfortable in this situation. They have to get up and go to work, despite all of the threats, and their children haven't been going to school, and they want to live. And I believe them. I believe all those who say that they would like to live with us. If there are some hotheads it doesn't mean that they are all like that. And I don't hate them and I would be ready to live with them as well as with any other person.

Trying to be more specific, Mrs. Dekel draws on her personal acquaintance with Arabs whom she has met in her profession as a teacher, but the more personal she gets the more she defeats her own purpose. The few people one knows can always be discarded as exceptions to the rule, whereas the rule—in her daughter's eyes—is on the screen for all to see:

"I've had Arab students...they're human beings like everyone else."

Mother: I've had Arab students, so I know; nice people. People. They're human beings like everyone else. They want to live. They should let them live. I know they always choose Jewish schools and not Arab schools. They're so grateful for whatever you do for them.

Daughter: OK, but that's Arabs? 10 percent are like that.

Int.: And the rest?

Daughter: The rest, let them leave.

Mother (to interviewer): Meanwhile every place I took her to, I took her once to a friend, an Arab as well, in Jaffa, who studied with me.

Daughter: OK, I said 10 percent.

Na'ama Dekel does not give up. Toward the end of the discussion she reminds her daughter of a friendly encounter with an Arab family when the daughter herself admitted that "they are terribly nice; they don't look like Arabs at all." Mother is trying to show daughter that when faced with "real" Arabs she herself was surprised to see that they are different from Arabs on television. Where she fails is in not being able to show *why* television should not be considered more representative than her personal experience:

"What about Hani?"

Mother: And Hani's parents?

Daughter: Hani is something else.

Mother: Because you know them; you've got to know them, you've got to live with them.

Int.: Hani?

Mother: The student whom we visited on the holidays they came to see us here. And suddenly she (indicating daughter) said, "Oh mother they're terribly nice, they don't seem like Arabs, they don't look like Arabs at all."

Father: But they are *Israeli* Arabs.

Daughter: OK, OK, because they live in Israel. But the ones in the territories, what about them?

Mother: What about them? Do you know them?

Daughter: No, it's enough to hear about them on television, that's bad enough.

Mother: It's not enough.

Like other daughters and sons, Yaffa prefers not to be confused with contradictory images. Television's message is clear-cut, making it easy for us not to have to worry whether some of them may be "good" and some of us not so good. Mother ends up losing the battle to the hawkish father and daughter who believe that television is the source for learning about social reality.

A similar argument about the representativeness of the image of "bad" Arabs takes place in the Levy family. This is a politically atypical family. Both parents, in their forties, are hawks, their son Ron (15) following suit, but the older daughter Maya (17) is an intelligent combative dove who feels the responsibility for the soul of her little four-year old sister. Drawing on the family's acquaintances with Ahmad who had worked for them, Maya tries to fight the "terrorist" image and receives the same response Na'ama Dekel got from her daughter: 99% of "them" want to kill "us." It is clear that television's picture wins over personal experience.

What about Ahmad?"

Daughter: Why do you admit Ahmad into the house then?

Mother: Who?

Daughter: You.

Mother: He doesn't come in order to...he doesn't want to kill.

Daughter: Ah, so *he* doesn't want to kill....

Mother: What, him??

Son: Ninety percent of them...

Mother: Ninety-nine percent of the Arabs hate the Jews.

In addition to balancing the image of faceless "bad" Arabs with personalized, "good," known ones, doves use the tactics of balancing the image of "good" Jews with "bad" violent ones. Thus, in the Dekel's living room, mother Na'ama claims that she was never hurt by Arab terrorists, but her car was damaged by fanatic ultra-orthodox Jews:

Jews can be violent as well.

Mother: And I was saying, no Arab ever threw a stone at me, but some Jew did. On a *Shabbat* I got hit by a stone, on my car, and they threw a garbage bin at me, and they almost jumped on us; she's (daughter) my witness here, just next to the house. I believe more in the Arabs than the religious Jews. I'm more afraid of them. I don't know, this is my opinion. In the morning I sit in the kitchen and I hear under this window, "*shabbes* (the Sabbath) and *prizes* (whoring)," here under this window is the problematic street *Yam Suf,* it's famous and they want to close it. (Religious groups want to close it to traffic on *Shabbat.*) If I got into my car I don't know what they would do to me. They would come in the tens and hundreds, and would anybody pay attention? So they arrest them. And in the evening they release them.

In a similar manner, Maya, the older daughter in the Levy home—the only dove in her family—tries to show that among "us" there are terrorists as well:

Terrorists should be punished

Daughter: Specifically and it doesn't matter if it is a Jew or an Arab. When he (a Jewish extremist who shot a hand missile into an Arab bus in Jerusalem) is throwing explosives on a bus—then he is wrong. He is wrong because he kills someone who is innocent. If a person comes and shoots a missile on a bus he *can't* be right.

Another tactic doves use to rearrange the distribution between "good" and "bad" is to raise the possibility of an exchange of roles, asking family members—what would you feel and do if you were in their place? Thus, in discussing the blowing up of houses of Palestinian terrorists, Sally Horwitch, swept into a heated argument with her daughter, demands to know:

"What would a Jew do in his place?"

Mother: It always makes me terribly angry because they say that for an Arab his house is more important than anything else. I would like to see them coming up to a Jew and blowing up his house. What would he do? Would he not scream? What is this?

Maya, the Levy's daughter, also senses that by changing places in fantasy, the motivations ascribed to the other side may turn less deterministic and more situational. Thus, when—as in all families—the discussion inevitably turns to possible solutions to the conflict, she demands of her younger brother Ron to imagine how he would have felt if he were a Palestinian terrorist whose friend was killed by the Israelis:

Changing roles.

Daughter: What if you were in their place and they would kill your friend? Would you be afraid or would you hate them more and say, I will not give them anything. I will revenge myself.

Son: I don't know, I haven't experienced it.

Daughter: Think! Think!

In this exchange, Maya, in her relentless attempts to win her brother over to her views, is trying to create understanding, maybe empathy, by changing places psychologically, thereby creating a subjunctive mood. She then tries an even more daring tactic by anchoring terrorist acts in their ideological context. What television news shows, she says, are arbitrary acts of violence that sound dangerously similar to the activities the pre-independence Zionist terrorist movements were practicing against the British. This kind of analogy between "our" freedom fight and "their" terrorism is rare in these discussions. And indeed the daughter creates an outrage in the family; her alternative framing of television is considered a threat as it contradicts the interest of Israeli viewers in suppressing the sacrilege of the analogy in order to reduce the dissonance it arouses:

"What about the Jewish underground?"

Daughter: If you would want to found a (new) state, you would do exactly the same thing.

Mother: How can you compare (us) to them?

Father: You must understand one thing. The *Etsel* and the *Lechi* (the Jewish extremist undergrounds) who were attempting to speed up the end of the British mandate over Palestine did not go to murder; not women or children. They fought an empire. They didn't throw stones on children or on...women and children.

(Uproar. Everybody speaks at the same time and the tape is impossible to transcribe).

It is noteworthy that although Maya talks only subjectively and does not refer explicitly to historical analogies ("If you wanted to found a state...") the father reacts defensively as if she had explicitly attacked the Jewish underground. It is crucial for him to keep Arab terrorism "pure," i.e., uncontaminated by an ideological context that may endow it with some legitimacy. This discussion illustrates that the hawkish position depends on maintaining the fundamental difference between "us" as "good" and "just" and them as "bad" and "inhuman." And any challenge to this division of the world is very threatening.

In the course of the discussion in the Levy family, while accusing her mother of socializing her children to a black-and-white view of the conflict, the daughter Maya refuses to frame the problem in terms of "good" versus "bad." In fact, she puts her finger on the attributional error that is inherent in this formulation:

Pointing to the attribution error.

Daughter (to her Mother). You are saying to Chen (the young sister): "bad Arabs." Where else would she know it from? She will grow up, see the situation, and decide for herself.

Mother: It's not my fault that she sees the situation.

Daughter: But that's what you tell her.

Mother: That's what I say because that's what I think.

Daughter: But here you are wrong! That how's you educate your children! I too, when I was in sixth or seventh grade, I used to say "Kill the Arabs" because that's how I was educated at home; that's what you said to me: "Bad Arabs." That's what I knew.

Mother: And now you think they are good?

Daughter: I don't think they are good but I understand the problem, and think that it should be solved.

In the last statement, fifteen-year-old Maya redefines the conflict in terms of a *situational frame*, making it solvable on principle, thus displacing the frame according to which the differences are intrinsic and therefore unchangeable.

Television's representation of the conflict is framed by most viewers simplistically, as a dichotomized perception of the conflict. It "proves" to the hawks that their apocalyptic view of conflict as a zero-sum game is correct. Doves have a much harder time in mediating television's message and are more concerned about the possibility that television contributes to the move to the right. They are ambivalent about viewing and look for ways to amend this image. But without the ability to understand and articulate journalistic practices and the ensuing generic constraints on the text, they remain at the level of arguing against the unrepresentativeness of television without being able to give good reasons for their intuition. Developing an awareness of journalistic practices and generic constraints—i.e. learning and teaching their families critical viewing—may help doves to "keep" their children, ideologically speaking. The fact that media literacy depends on higher education may explain why the only chance doves have to reproduce ideologically similar children is when they are highly educated.[39]

Conclusion

This article—based on observations of interaction within Israeli families—has shown that the coverage of the Palestinian uprising on Israel Television news constrains viewers to perceive the violent actions of the protestors as an expression of their predispositions, while the violent actions of the soldiers confronting them are considered to be situationally motivated. As television is the main source for understanding political reality, this framing better serves the politically uncompromising. It facilitates the socialization of their children, while making the task more difficult for parents with more dovish views. The latter must teach their children to read the news in a more sophisticated way, through an understanding of the biases implicit in journalistic practices, all the more so in the case of broadcast journalism.

Similar conclusions may be inferred from the work of others who have studied conflict on television. The present study, however, makes it possible to be more specific (1) about the types of links between the bias of television and the perceptual apparatus of viewers, and (2) about the type of conflict on television that might be expected to generate what psychologists call the fundamental attribution error, as well as (3) the kind of viewers and readers who might be expected to be more or less affected by this error.

It is evident—but worth reiterating, nonetheless—that the case we have examined generalizes best to the kind of conflict that constitutes a direct challenge to the established means or ends of a society. Thus, it does not apply to legitimate contests such as election campaigns—where adversaries are equally matched within the norms. Nor does it apply where the adversaries are unequal in reality but made equal by television—as was the case with fluoridation contests, where the small minority of opponents was raised to equal status by the media.[40] Here, too, the routines of journalism overrule the personal predilections of journalists.

Labor disputes and licensed demonstrations of all kinds come a step closer in that they typically involve unequal contests. Even if the confrontation begins within the rules and for legitimate ends, the weaker side is often tempted to trespass the normative boundaries in order to attract media attention. The staging of a strike is a publicity-seeking ceremony and rules of coverage may incite strikers to excessive action. Media attention may then result, showing the bosses as rational and responsible, speaking from behind their desks, while the striking workers are shown n action, giving the impression of trouble making and lesser reasonableness.[41]

Such displays of disorder approximate those of social an political protest, especially when they escalate into violent confrontation, partly in response to the requirements of the rules of access to the media. It is to such situations—where violent protest engenders violent response on the part of agencies of the law—that the generalizations of the present study apply. Industrial protest like militant protest—against unpopular wars, or against nuclear proliferation, against military or colonial "occupation"—evoke differential attributions both on the part of television and on the part of viewers. In such cases, the conventions of the medium compound the attribution error of viewers. Together they distance "us" from "them" and then assign inherent or dispositional blame to "them" while excusing "us" situationally.

This process of distancing and stigmatization also may apply to certain forms of television treatments of marginal groups whose very existence is sometimes portrayed as threatening core values. This is all the more likely when such groups—the poor, the homeless, the sexual minority—attract the media by provoking an event, or more typically, by being associated with threat, whereby homosexuals are carriers of AIDS, or the homeless are trespassers and squatters. In effect, this is to frame a chronic problem in terms of an acute confrontation between a healthy peaceful "us" and an unwelcome and threatening "them." Unlike protestors, these groups do not often seek exposure; their representation may be the result of our own "moral panic."[42] The main point is that they are seen to threaten society—not necessarily by protest, but by existing on its margins—and thus invite viewers to activate the attribution error.

While a number of studies have touched on these themes, as we have shown, most of them are based on content analysis or on interviews with journalists and producers. The present study, however, benefits from the presence of *real* readers and viewers who come to the media not as *tablulae rasae* but with their own social psychologies and ideologies. The media commit the attribution error not only because journalists are also viewers but because the conventions of news facilitate such perceptions, for professional or hegemonic reasons or both. Viewers take it from there, having to assimilate what they see and read through the prisms of attribution and of attitudes. From the readers in this study, we conclude that differential attributions characterize different kinds of readers. Thus, we find that Israeli hawks accept the constraints of the television text, and employ it to reinforce their political discourse. Israeli doves, on the other hand, experienced unease with the *Intifada* coverage. Few knew how to decode it by taking account of the journalistic rules of the selection and treatment of violent protest on television. Others, with similar leanings but without a sufficient degree of media literacy, find themselves unaided by television in presenting their case to family and others. It is a fair guess that such people—at least in the present circumstances—"lose their children," ideologically speaking. In this restricted sense it may be said that the hawkish reading is "hegemonic"—not because television news is the official spokesman of the rightist government and not because its journalists lean toward the right, but because its professional code inadvertently contains an ideological bias in favor of establishments, majorities, and popular norms. The dovish reading, therefore, may be considered "oppositional" in that it is predicated on an awareness of, and correction to, this bias.

Acknowledgments

I wish to thank the Spencer Foundation for its support in the various phases of the project of which this article is a part. I am also grateful to Professor Elihu Katz for his advice throughout, to Professor Nancy Griswold for her useful comments, and to Rivka Ribak for her help.

Notes

1. Data presented in E. Katz and H. Levinsohn, "Too good to be true: notes on the Israel elections of 1988," *International Journal of Public Opinion Research* 1 (1989): 111-123, and T. Liebes, R. Ribak, and E. Katz, "Ideological Reproduction," *Political Behavior* 13 (1991) show that doves are typically older and of European origin. They have higher education and income, and tend to be less religious. The hawks are younger, of Eastern origin, less educated and more religious. The overlap between these demographic variables makes for further polarization of the two groups. On the decline of Left Wing Zionism and the role of the young in the shift to the Right, see also L. Weissbrod, "From Labour Zionism to New Zionism," *Theory and Society* 10 (1981): 777-803.
2. Liebes et al., "Reproduction."
3. Theoretically the perception of inconsistency can lead to extremism in one of two directions, i.e., to a move either to a totally dovish position or to an extremely hawkish one; but, taking into account that the educational system is based on the Zionist ideology, anything that is perceived as giving up any territory of the Jewish state is not an acceptable alternative for most young people.
4. To this day, Israel has a single, publicly-owned television channel, modeled on the BBC, with a central daily news program broadcast during primetime. Although political pressures and security considerations do exist, Israeli television conforms to the norms of Western journalism.
5. Other sources of information do not carry such impact. Although two-thirds of the families in our survey read a newspaper, generally an evening one, they admit to being dependent on television news for political information—the children even more so than the parents. One might expect the image of Palestinians in the eyes of Israeli Jews to be influenced by personal contact with Israeli Arabs, but because Arab citizens—who constitute 17 percent of all Israeli citizens—live mainly in all-Arab towns and villages, with an Arabic-language school system (see the annual report of Israel's Central Bureau of Statistics), contact is in fact rare.
6. Three of the groups were discarded for technical reasons. The distribution of the profiles of the remaining 52 was similar to that of the 400 families. No obvious bias distinguished those who agreed to be interviewed. Planned before the start of the Palestinian uprising, the study was in fact carried out during the *Intifada*. A sample of 200 families of Israeli Arabs from Nazareth also participated in the project. These are analyzed in T. Liebes, "Socialization to conflict: Identity formation among Jewish and Arab adolescents in Israel," paper given at the 12th World Congress of Sociology of the ISA, Madrid, 1990.
7. As the television sound made it impossible to record the interaction.
8. In half of the discussions, we asked the adolescent (who was interviewed in the questionnaire) to retell and the parent to interact, and in the other half we switched the roles.

9. See, for example, H.J. Gans, *Deciding What's News* (New York: Vintage Books, 1979); M. Edelman, *Constructing the Political Spectacle* (Chicago: University of Chicago Press, 1988); T. Gitlin, *The Whole World is Watching* (Berkeley and Los Angeles: University of California Press, 1980); S. Hall, "Encoding and decoding," in S. Hall et al., editors, *Culture, Media, Language* (London: Hutchingson, 1985): 128-138; W. L. Bennett, *News: The Politics of Illusion* (New Hyork: Longman, 1983); D. L. Paletz and R. M. Entman, *Media, Power, Politics* (New York: The Free Press, 1981); G. Guchman, *Making News* (New York: Free Press, 1978); G. Murdock "Political deviance: The press presentation of a militant mass demonstration" in S. Cohen and J. Hyoung, editors, *The Manufacture of News* (London: Constable, 1973); and J. Fiske and J. Hartley, *Reading Television* (London: Methuen, 1978).
10. P. F. Lazarsfeld and R. K. Merton, "Mass communication, popular taste and organized social action," in L. Bryson, editor, *The Communication of Ideas* (New York: Harper and Brothers, 1948).
11. J. C. Alexander, "The mass media in systemic historical and comparative perspective," in E. Katz and T. Szeesko, editors, *Mass Media and Social Change* (London: Sage, 1981). See also, E. Katz, "Publicity and pluralistic ignorance: Notes on the spiral of silence," in Baier, Kepplinger, and Reuman, editors, *Public Opinion and Social Change* (Opladen: Westdeutscher Verlag, 1981). See also Gouldner's discussion of news and deviance in A. Gouldner, *The Dialectics of Ideology and Technology* (New York: Oxford University Press, 1975): 107-108, which draws on H. Molotch and M. Lester, "Accidents, Scandals and Routines," *Insurgent Sociologist* vol. 2 (1973): 2-11. Gouldner suggests in addition that journalists lose control of their readers, because even if they intend to hold up deviance as violation of norm, some readers may adopt the deviance as counter-cultural.
12. A. A. Cohen, H. Adoni, and G. Drori, "Adolescents' perceptions of social conflicts in television news and social reality," *Human Communication Research* 10 (1983): 203-225 and A. A Cohen, H. Adoni, and C.R. Bantz, *Social Conflict and TV News* (Newbury Park: Sage, 1991) offer an extensive literature survey relating to the presentation of social conflict on television in their study of viewers' perceptions of television news.
13. J. Galtung and M. Ruge "The structure of foreign news," *Journal of Peace Research* 2 (1961): 64-91. See also, M. Schudson "When? Deadlines, dateline and history," in R. K. Manoff and M. Schudson, editors, *Reading the News* (New York: Pantheon Books, 1986).
14. D. Hallin, "The American news media: A critical theory perspective," in J. Forester, editor, *Critical Theory and Public Life* (Cambridge: MIT Press, 1985).
15. M. Edelman, *Constructing the Political Spectacle.*
16. Glasgow University Media Group, *Bad News* (London: Routledge and Kegan Paul, 1976).
17. T. Gitlin, *The Whole World*, 268-269.
18. In a recent article in the *New York Times* (17 Sept. 1990) Walter Goodman argues that television acts as a deterrent of war in the Gulf Crisis by showing victims, actual and potential, on both sides.
19. E. Epstein, *News from Nowhere* (New York: Random House, 1973); I. Roeli, "Don't confuse me with facts: Storytelling in the news," *American Behavioral Scientist* (1989); and R.K. Manoff, "Writing the news (by telling the story)," in Manoff and Schudson, editors, *Reading the News.*
20. G. Wolfsfeld, *The Politics of Provocation: Participation and Protest in Israel* (Albany: State University of New York Press, 1988).
21. The means consist of various forms of disruption and violence as elaborated below.

22. Z. Schiff and E. Ya'ari, *The Intifada* (Tel-Aviv, Schoken, 1990).
23. Many of the items do present clashes where soldiers confronted with violent rioters, respond by firing rubber or plastic bullets, and sometimes live ammunition.
24. R. E. Nisbett and L Ross, *Human Inference Strategies and Shortcomings of Social Judgement* (Engelwood Cliffs, N.J.: Prentice Hall, 1980); S. Moscovici, "The phenomenon of social representation," in R. M. Farr and S. Moscovici, editors, *Social Representations* (Cambridge University Press, 1984); and T. F. Pettigrew, "The ultimate attribution error: Extending Allport's cognitive analysis of prejudice," *Personality and Social Psychology Bulletin* 5 (1979): 461-476.
25. J. R. Eiser, "Attribution theory and social cognition," in J. Jaspers, F. D. Fincham, and M. Hewstone, editors, *Attribution Theory and Research: Conceptual Development and Social Dimensions* (London: Academic Press, 1983); R. C. Schenk and R. P. Abelson, *Scripts, Plans, Goals and Understanding* (Cambridge: Cambridge University Press, 1977).
26. S. Livingstone, *Making Sense of Television* (Oxford: Pergamon Press, 1990).
27. S. Iyengar, *Framing Effects in Politics: Television and Political Responsibility* (Los Angeles: University of California Los Angeles, forthcoming). In a series of experiments, Iyengar shows that viewers' framing of social problems depends on the ways these problems are presented on the screen—i.e., as due to either social or individual responsibility. Although this approach is somewhat similar to ours, we have three reservations. Firstly, as social psychologists have shown, the psychological statuses of the two kinds of explanations are not equal: people tend to explain the problems of the other dispositionally; secondly, television's representations, we suggest, display this attribution bias; and lastly, not all viewers are affected in the same way—people differ in ideological outlook, which equips them with different degrees of critical distance. In an application of Iyengar's design to the case of the homeless, J. G. Powers *Mass Communication of Otherness and Identification* (unpublished dissertation, University of Southern California, 1990) adds the notion of stigmatized presentation to the individual-structural dimension. We argue that restricting presentation of the socially deviant to their deviant role is stigmatizing in itself.
28. M.S. Wetherell and J. Potter, "Narrative characters and accounting for violence," in J. Shotter and K. E. Gergen, editors, *Texts of Identity* (Greenwich, Conn.: JAI Press, 1988).
29. Schiff and Ya'ari, *Intifada*, offer a detailed account of the reasons leading to the uprising.
30. E. Goffman, *Frame Analysis* (Cambridge, Mass.: Harvard University Press, 1974).
31. K. W. Back and K. J. Gergen, "Apocalyptic and serial time orientations and the structure of opinions," *Pubic Opinion Quarterly* 27 (1963): 427-442.
32. All family names were changed.
33. All the adolescents cited in this article, and most of the adolescents in the study, were born in Israel.
34. T. Liebe and R. Ribak, "A mother's battle against the news: A case study of political socialization," *Discourse and Society* (2) (1991): 203-222.
35. W.P Davison "The third person effect in communication," *Public Opinion Quarterly* 47 (1983): 1-15.
36. G. Murdock, "Talking about terrorism: Television and the context for political discourse," in P.A. Bruck, editor, *The News Media and Television* (Carleton University: The Center for Communication, Culture and Society, 1988).
37 In this context it should be noted that parents and adolescents rarely refer to conversations they have had with soldiers who are directly involved in the conflict. This can be understood when taking into account (1) the relatively small number

of soldiers who are repeatedly assigned to handle the uprising, and (2) the fact that soldiers who are serving in the territories are often reluctant to talk about it. For further discussion see T. Liebes and S. Blum-Kulka, "Managing moral conflict: The discourse of Israeli soldiers in the *Intifada*," paper presented at the annual meeting of the International Communication Association, Dublin 1990.

38. Public opinion surveys have not shown gender differences in political attitudes.
39. The "Reproduction" paper, in analyzing the 400 families' questionnaire data, shows that although hawkish parents have about an 80 percent chance that their children will be like them ideologically regardless of the parents' education, doves have a chance of reproducing only when the parents are highly educated.
40. See R. Crain, E. Katz, and D. Rosenthal, *The Politics of Community Conflict: The Fluoridation Decision* (Indianapolis: Bobbs-Merrill, 1969).
41. Glasgow University Media Group, *Bad News* (London: Routledge and Kegan Paul, 1976).
42. Cohen and Young, *The Manufacture of News.*

20

The Intifada as a Meta-Televisual Dialogue

Yosefa Loshitzky

The notions of meta-fiction, self-reflexivity and intertextuality have been exhaustively studied and used in the disciplines of literature, theatre and film studies (see e.g. Alter, 1975a, b; Feuer, 1977, 1982; Polan, 1978; Hutcheon, 1980; Stam, 1985; Siegle, 1986). Although self-reflexivity is an old practice in cinema and the other arts, its contemporary importance lies primarily in the significant role it plays in what came to be known as the modernist critique of representation. Within this conceptual framework, self-reflexivity refers to the anti-illusionist, anti-realist stance of the project of modernity, whose primary goal was to shift the focus of artistic activity from what has been considered a naive attempt to 'mirror' the world to an exploration of the artistic medium itself.

The mimetic referentiality of nineteenth-century aesthetics, with its traditional realism locked into the dogma of representation, was substituted by self-reflexive art modes marked off by drawing attention to themselves as 'man-made' constructions. The whole validity of 'representational seeing' has been continually raised and attacked by modernism, suggesting an unavoidable disparity between reality and artistic illusion. The complexity of modern art as such has led to a devaluation of the imitation of nature a the basic premise of art. The whole process of representation or depiction has been called into question. It should be mentioned, however, that the development of photography has accounted, in part, for the crisis of representation by eliminating the need of the work of art to create likenesses.

The critique of representation, characterized by anti-realist manifestations in art practice and theory, is essential to current Marxist theories of aesthetics and culture, which consider attitudes and policy towards the notion of realism and reflection as central to their conception and definition of art and its relation to society. While orthodox Marxism (Lukacs, 1971) advocated the practice of realism in art (both critical realism and socialist realism) neo-Marxist theories of culture (Althusser, 1969, 1971) criticized the use of realism in art and the privileged status it has enjoyed in classical Marxism. Modernist self-reflexivity was viewed by the Althusserian school a producing knowledge about the working and formation of cultural and ideological codes.

Only recently, however, have media scholars (Eco, 1984; Feuer, 1984; White, 1986; Olson, 1987; Silberman, 1987) introduced the concepts of meta-television and intertextuality into the arena of television criticism and research. These critics and analysts—being directly or indirectly influenced by Baudrillard's notion of the simulacrum (Baudrillard, 1988)—emphasize that by employing the strategies and mechanisms of self-referentiality, medium reflexivity, metagenericism and autodeconstruction, television creates in its viewers' minds 'an increasingly hermetic, self-encompassing world" (White, 1986; 52) based on an imaginary dialectic continuity which constructs homology between the world *on* TV and the world *of* TV. Umber Eco (1984) goes even further, coining the term 'Neo-TV' for this meta-television, which he opposes to 'Place-TV'. According to him, while Place-TV at least pretended to talk about the external world, Neo-TV talks less and less about the external world and more about itself and the contact that it establishes with its own public.

These critics attribute the spread of the phenomenon of meta-television to various motives. According to White (1986) the rationale behind the use of these strategies in American commercial TV is economic. They are a promotional practice which both 'supports viewership of the individual programs by cross-fertilizing audiences' (1986:53) and reinforces network audience flow. Eco's explanation seems to rest with the same framework. Neo-TV's self-reflexivity is essential for its economical survival, maintained through continuous control over the viewer. In contrast to the economic or ideologically based rationale, Olson's view of the same phenomenon is more culturally and aesthetically inclined. Relying on Feuer's (1984) thesis that self-reflexivity is a sign of artistic maturity, Olson proceeds in the claim that the operations of self-conscious television or meta-television are indications of its maturity, evidence that television has reached the stage of popular postmodernism which is inherently self-reflexive and anti-realist.

Although these critics, and in particular White, claim that the all-encompassing world constructed by television does not distinguish between fact and fiction, between information and entertainment, their analysis is confined to popular television shows—*Moonlighting, Saturday Night Live, Simon and Simon* and so on—which belong to the world of fiction and entertainment and not to the world of fact and information epitomized by television news, the medium's high-status genre. The purpose of this essay is to remedy this noticeable lacuna in the critical use of the concept of self-reflexivity by expanding it to the domain of TV news. I propose to consider the construction of self-reflexivity in the news genre as a reinforcement of journalistic authority. This is accomplished by establishing and validating television itself (both as an institution/industry and as a narrative form) as a legitimate source of knowledge rather than as ideology. My analysis as well as my conclusions are based on and confined to the sub-genre of in-depth news, which differs from the network daily news genre.

I shall illustrate my arguments through the classification and investigation of levels of self-reflexivity in the 'Town Meeting' centrepiece of ABC's *Nighttime in the Holy Land*, a week-long series of live broadcasts from Jerusalem transmitted during 1988. I chose this program for several reasons. Ted Koppel's *Nightline in the Holy Land,* especially the Town Meeting segment, garnered enthusiastic responses from the American press. It received special praise for 'proving that TV news, can, when moved to take the time, reach beyond its obsession with bang- visuals' (*Newsweek*, 1988: 48). Against the backdrop of criticism commonly levelled at TV news' crisis reporting, this reception from rival print journalism is exceptional.

Criticism of media crisis coverage in general (Roch, 1986) and of TV news in particular usually focuses on four issues: (1) lack of historical context; (2) oversimplication of complex situations; (3) factual inaccuracy; and (4) lack of balance (Elizur, 1988). Yet, according to the American press, Koppel's programme avoided all these flaws and 'demonstrated how extraordinary television can be' (*Newsweek*, 1988:48). Against the backdrop of criticism commonly levelled at TV news' crisis reporting, this reception from rival print journalism is exceptional.

Criticism of media crisis coverage in general (Roch, 1986) and of TV news in particular usually focuses on four issues: (1) lack of historical context; (2) oversimplication of complex situations; (3) factual inaccuracy; and (4) lack of balance (Elizur, 1988). Yet, according to the American press, Koppel's programme avoided all these flaws and 'demonstrated how extraordinary television can be' (*Newsweek*, 1988:48). Koppel's success in 'transcending' the four most common shortcomings of TV news crisis coverage makes his programme an exemplary text which serves to highlight the critical value of using the interdisciplinary theoretical concept of self-reflexivity challenges not only the TV news claim to truthful representation of reality but also the philosophical and ideological assumptions underpinning criticism of crisis coverage by TV news.

TV news' claim that it truthfully represents reality has been under attack from a number of anti-empiricist theoretical positions. A critical review of the intellectual history of the anti-empiricist theoretical positions. A critical review of the intellectual history of the anti-empiricist position is beyond the scope of this article. Nevertheless, we can trace the origins of the anti-empiricist position in media studies—the 'critical paradigm' to use Katz's words (Katz, 1987)—to the Frankfurt school's critique of positivism and their elaboration of a critical social theory. French semiology (Barthes 1957 1964, 1977), British cultural studies (Hall, 1977, 180), discourse analysis (Van Dijk, 1988), and especially the news research undertaken by the Glasgow University Media Group (1976, 1980, 1982) and various American researchers (Gans, 1979; Gitlin, 1980), have contributed, each in its own way, to the development of the critical paradigm. Although the theories and the tools of these schools are significantly different both from the Frankfurt School's critical theory a well as for each other, they all share the assumption that the mediations of television news represent an ideology-laden version of the world.

The use of the critical category of self-reflexivity constitutes an important contribution to the critical paradigm, supporting the idea propagated by the anti-empiricist schools of thought of replacing the notion of transparency with the concept of the construction of reality, a construction which is essentially ideological.

My classification of levels of self-reflexivity in the 'Town Meeting' in *Nightline in the Holy Land* relies on the published discussions of critics and scholars in film, television and literature studies and on an original model which I developed in a previous study of self-reflexive cinema (Loshitzky, 1987).

The 'Town Meeting'

The ABC television network organized a 'Town Meeting' as the centerpiece of a week-long series of live *Nightline* broadcasts from Jerusalem. The event, which Koppel introduced as an unprecedented live televised forum took place at the Jerusalem Theatre in West Jerusalem and lasted three hours and ten minutes. Four Israeli officials and three Palestinian community leaders sat on opposite sides of the Jerusalem Theatre stage and responded to questions posed by Koppel and by members of the mixed audience. The panelists also gave their verbal reactions to some televised reports on the Intifada and other contextual issues prepared by ABC correspondents in Israel and the Occupied Territories. These reports were seen simultaneously by the audience and panelists in the theatre and by the American television audience at home. The live televised event ended with a special report on a human-interest story.

Journalist-Superstar a Self-Conscious Performer

John Fiske (1982, 1987) emphasizes that, contrary to the common view of news as a form of realism that works through metonymy, news makes sense of politics through metaphor. 'Using the metaphor of drama makes sense of it as a "stage" upon which talented individuals "perform" as stars' (Fiske, 19878:291). Although in the context of his analysis Fiske uses the term stars to refer to individual politicians or members of the ruling elite, the description fits the television news personality as well. As Margaret Morse (1986:57) puts it, 'among all the news personalities, the three network anchors are the super-subjects of the news as a totality and possess a national role and identity.'

In his opening remarks from the Jerusalem Theatre, Koppel confides to the camera: "It has been suggested to me that if we truly understood what we are trying here today, we would never have done it.' Despite his acknowledged ignorance, he came to Jerusalem to cover the Intifada and to conduct a public/televisual dialogue between the parties to the conflict. My argument is that within the context of American TV, Koppel's stardom is a legitimate source of knowledge. From his TV news persona, Koppel derives the authority to conduct an Israeli-Palestinian dialogue although, as he implied in the quoted opening remark he is far from being a Middle East expert.

This mode of inverting ideology into knowledge invokes a recent American TV commercial promoting Vicks cough medicine as an 'adult formula'. In this commercial a male actor confides to the camera: 'I am not a real doctor but I play one on TV.' White (1986) views the association of actor and character in the commercial as evidence of 'how the world of television fiction is drawn into relation with the equally constructed world of television people' (1986:58). This, of course, does not apply in Koppel's case, but it can be used as a fruitful point of departure to understand the relationship between the conscious performance of the TV news personality and journalistic authority. It can also provide some clues to questions regarding how journalists establish reliability and 'what is their psychology of evidence and of witnessing' (Katz, 1988).

To return to my comparison of Koppel's confession with the actor's confession in the cough-medicine commercial, we see that the commercial's association between actor and character is the source of authority (the authority of non-professionals, of non-doctors to recommend medicines) within the world of television. Similarly, the association between journalist and superstar anchor is the source of authority for non-expert journalists not only to report and cover international crises but also to conduct political dialogues. It is not accidental that the title of *Newsweek's* enthusiastic review of Koppel's show as 'ABC's Mideast Peace Talks'. This title, of course, not only attributes political power to ABC but implicitly suggests that, to use White's (1986) formulation, the world on TV is the same as the world of TV and therefore a televisual dialogue may, ontologically, enjoy the same status as a 'real' one.

Furthermore, because of his stardom the credibility of Koppel's witnessing is established *a priori* as more authoritative than any other's. This explains in part why ABC was willing to support Koppel's journey to Jerusalem, an undertaking which entailed enormous logistics. Although ABC has a staff of correspondents in Israel, the ultimate report on the Intifada as well as the ritualized performance of the 'Town Meeting' necessitated an authority figure. As Leach puts it in his discussion of ritual, 'There is usually a "conductor", a master of ceremonies, a chief priest, a central protagonist, whose actions provide the temporal marker for everyone else' (Leach, 1976:45)

Fiske (1987) distinguishes three stages of "clawback' (Fiske and Hartley 1978) in television news 'that correspond with spaces that are both material and symbolic' (1987-288). The central space is that of the studio news anchor, the 'subject of the news' (Morse, 1986:58) who speaks the discourse of 'the truth'. The second stage is that of the reporter whose function is 'to mediate between "raw reality" and the final truth spoken by the news reader' (Fiske, 1987: 288). And the third stage is that of the eyewitness, the one who appears to speak the real truth. Fiske observes a vital contradiction in this state of affairs because the truth that exists only in the studio depends for its validation upon the eyewitness. Koppel, who in regular *Nightline* broadcasts functions as the program's anchor and interviewer, performs in this special edition of *Nightline* the role of the reporter as well as that of the eyewitness. His performance in *Nightline in the Holy Land* encompasses the three stages of clawback and resolves the contradiction Fiske discusses. Koppel's stardom is first translated into authority and then into an authenticating function. Through the complex nexus of all three the stages of the structure of crisis reporting are brought under discursive control.

Audience Awareness

The 'Town Meeting' dialogue (which, ironically, Koppel described as a dialogue of the deaf in the broadcast following it) operates on several levels: (a) between the Palestinian and Israeli panelists; (b) between the panelists and the mixed studio audience (Palestinians and Israelis); (c) between the panelists and the American television audience (more important than the live audience from the point of view of public relations and industry promotional practice); (d) between Koppel and the panelists; and (e) between Koppel and both audiences. Thus, the complexity of the dialogue is based on the multiplicity of audiences. Thus, the complexity of the dialogue is based on the multiplicity of audiences, the actual in-theatre audience, as well as the implied television one.

Jane Feuer (1977) argues that the self-reflective musical film mediates a contradiction between live performance in the theatre and 'the frozen form of cinema' by implying that the musical is really a folk art and that the audience participates in the creation of musical entertainment' (1977:171). One of the mechanisms used in the musical to mask its being a form of mass-production is to suggest that the audience participate spontaneously in the making of the show. It does so by using theatrical audiences in the film itself in order to provide a point of identification for cinema audiences. Hence, 'the audience in the film is there to express the adulation the number itself sought to arouse from the film's audience' (Feuer, 1977: 170). The incorporation of the immediate performer-audience relationship into the film enables the musical to enjoy the advantages of both media.

Feuer's arguments apply to television as well, and to the dialectics of audience-performer in Koppel's show in particular. From a metagenericist perspective, the 'Town Meeting' audience is a studio audience which belongs to the world of the talk show (like Johnny Carson's *Tonight Show* and the David Letterman show on NBC) and the game shows which, as Robert C. Allen (1987) proposes, 'represent their addressees as a group', and not to that of the commercial and the news program which 'tend to characterize their addressees individually' (1987-94). However, Koppel emphasizes repeatedly that his audience is completely different from the audiences in entertainment shows. It did not come for sheer 'fun' but to engage in an important political dialogue. In reality, his audience was composed of highly involved individuals of two nations engaged in a bitter political conflict. Consequently, Koppel's show manipulates the expectation that the built-in audience in this live event will be not only a passive observer but also at times an active performer.

Indeed, Koppel's description of the live audience creates the illusion of the audience being a performer as well. The voice-over narration which accompanies shots of people coming to the Jerusalem Theatre emphasizes the uniqueness of his audience. It stresses that these people came of their own accord and were willing to suffer considerable inconvenience and hardship in order to participate in the event:

> These people have driven through much of the night by bus, from the Occupied Territories of Gaza. They have come to the Jerusalem Theatre to be with other Palestinians from the West Bank and Israeli Jews for an unprecedented live televised forum. [Caption: Killed: 174 Palestinians: 2 Israelis]. This tragically is what we've come to expect when we talk about Israeli-Palestian confrontation—a dialogue of violence.

Throughout the broadcast Koppel recognizes the presence of the Jerusalem Theatre audience as well as the active absence of his audience in America and gives them both a sense of participation in the performance. 'It's going to be difficult and I appreciate the fact that you liked the comment', he tells the Palestinian section of the theatre audience which had cheered Koppel's response to a statement by Likud Knesset Member Dr. Eliyahu Ben-Elissar. 'Later on', he continues, 'you're going to hate some of them. I promise you that before this evening is over, all of you will feel frustrated by me...'. Yet, in the talk show, 'although the studio audience is addressed and individual members are allowed to speak, the roles of host, guests, and characterized audience are demarcated' (Allen, 1987:95).

Koppel's introductory, transitional and concluding remarks, all indicate double audience awareness. His concluding remarks express gratitude to the live audience but at the same time recognize his American audience. "The fact that these people were willing to come here this evening and talk—if not directly to each other at all times at least through me to each other—is perhaps a more unprecedented event than those of you back in the United States can appreciate."

The Stage Metaphor: Story as Allegory and Utopianism

From the cultural-anthropological and socio-psychological perspective, the Intifada represents a case of social drama (Turner, 1974). This perspective was fully adopted by *Nightline*, which translated it into reflexive televisual terms. Koppel presented the broadcast to the American audience as an 'unprecedented live televised forum', thus indicating not only genre awareness but also the wish to transcend traditional generic distinctions by inventing a new and unprecedented genre. Unlike media events (Katz and Dean, 1985), the 'Town Meeting' broadcast (as the name itself, and not accidentally so, makes clear) emphasizes the dialogic nature of the elaborately planned event. On many occasions, during the 'Town Meeting' broadcast as well as throughout the series of broadcasts of *Nightline in the Holy Land*, Koppel stresses that his main goal in coming to the Holy Land was to replace 'a dialogue of violence' with a 'more productive kind of dialogue'.

The repetition of the dialogic motifs and structures in *Nightline*, a device which is also evident in the logic of Koppel's monitor interviews during the broadcasts before and after the 'Town Meeting', serves as an implicit, yet reflexive comment about the presumably superior skills of television over reality to solve conflicts and to engage adversaries in a productive process of negotiation. Indeed, here we have not only an example of homology between the world on TV and the world of TV—the political dialogue transformed into a televisual dialogue—but also a suggestion that the world of TV is superior to the world on 'Town Meeting' in terms of mitigating crises. Indeed the whole construction of the 'Town Meeting', as the name itself suggests, attempts to both imitate and recall the Athenian, and later New England model of direct democracy based on close dialogue between the town public and its representatives. In Koppel's program, however, the town square is replaced by a real theatre stage whose background decoration is a large painting depicting the city of Jerusalem. The primary theatre stage (itself a symbolic stage) is echoed and mirrored by the reflective stage of the TV screen.

As a type of entertainment performed before a double audience the 'Town Meeting' renders a utopian sensibility which, as Richard Dyer in his study of entertainment and utopia (1977) observes draws attention 'to the gap between what is and what could be' (1977:185). Although Dyer's analysis centers on film musicals, he claims that the categories of entertainment's utopian sensibility which he outlines (energy, abundance, intensity, transparency and community) may have wider applications to other cultural performances including television news. From this vantage point, the 'Town Meeting' provides a utopian televisual vision of a better social order based on a dialogic rather than a principle of conflict.

This utopian sensibility, the desire to present the world of TV as a possible alternative to the real world, is assimilated into the setting itself. The real Jerusalem Theatre stage becomes a symbolic stage on which the adversary parties negotiate under the skillful conducting of Koppel, the master of ceremonies. To intensify the sense of drama and draw attention to the constructed theatricality of the performed event, Koppel partitioned the stage with a fence that he crossed in a symbolic manner. This symbolic performance was followed by self-reflexive commentary on its motives and meaning.

> It has been suggested to me...*[by whom...?]* that we need a symbolic divider between our Israeli guests on the one hand and our Palestinian guests on the other. I must tell you that it has been so difficult to arrange this broadcast that that was one small price that we were prepared to pay... Let me, in fact, as I move across our fence right now, let me go immediately to one of our panelists ....

This performance, naturally, elicited laughter from the audience. The fence served as a prop to induce discussion and provide an entertaining exposition of the Israeli-Palestinian conflict for the American audience. Yet, the entertaining performance only emphasized the event's utopianism, the symbolic wish to cross borders and to represent a televisual image of something better than the Mideast reality does not provide.

The 'Town Meeting' ended with a story that consciously imposed a symbolic closure on the openness and lack of resolution of the ongoing events in the Israeli-Palestinian conflict. Koppel described it as a 'note of some slight optimism'. It was, in fact, a soft, human-interest story. Because of the importance of this story to my analysis, I will briefly summarize it.

The story is about a house in Ramleh, a town in the center of Israel (not in the Occupied Territories). The house was built by Akmed Khairy, who planted a lemon tree in its garden. In 1948, the Khairy family was forced to leave Ramleh because of the advancing Israeli forces. They settled in the West Bank. A family of immigrant Jews moved into the house. After the 1967 war, Bashir, the oldest son of the Khairy family, returned to visit the house he had left when he was a young child. Bashir became friends with Dalia Landau, the oldest daughter of the Jewish family which had moved into his house. She offered to give the house back to him.

A few years later Bashir was sent to prison for a terrorist bombing in which two people died. Early in 1988, Israel deported Bashir and three other Palestinians to Lebanon, where they were given a hero's welcome. The following day an open letter from Dalia to Bashir was published in an Israeli newspaper. In this letter, she appealed 'to both Palestinians and Israelis to understand that the use of force will not resolve this conflict on its fundamental level'. Against a background of shots of the lemon tree, the reporter's voice-over narration ending the story tells that

> the house in Ramleh is being rented now. Neither Bashir's family nor Dalia's lives there anymore. The lemon tree that brought such pleasure to both families bears little fruit these days. Its branches have been cut back. But the tree itself is not dead.

Hayden White (1981), who studies the relationship between narrative and history, observes that 'narrativity, certainly in factual storytelling...is intimately related to, if not a function of, the impulse to moralize reality'. Hence, every story is a kind of allegory which 'points to a moral, or endows events, whether real or imaginary, with a significance that they do not possess as a mere sequence' (1981:13-14). In the case of the story of the house in Ramleh, this impulse follows the tradition of the classic Hollywood narrative (Bordwell et al., 1985) where social and political conflicts are personalized into conflict between individuals. The story of the house, in a self-reflexive manner, surpasses the boundaries of realism and becomes an allegory for the Israeli-Palestinian dilemma.

The story of the house is used as a deliberate closure of the 'Town Meeting'. The broadcast does not simply end; it concludes, and in a conscious manner. In introducing the story, Koppel exposes the program's desire to create a *moral* drama (White, 1981:20) as he confides to the multiple audience that 'we *wanted* to *end* on a note of some slight *optimism*'. The moralizing impulse of the closure contains both an image of utopian vision—the temporary sharing of the same house by an Israeli, Dalia and a Palestinian, Bashir—and the disruption of that same image—the terrorist activity.

Conclusion

In this essay I trace three self-reflexive devices utilized by the 'Town Meeting' broadcast: the television news personality's conscious performance/acting, audience awareness and the stage/metaphor—story/allegory. All three strategies are used so as to construct a television world which offer a utopian vision of a better and more perfect world than the 'real' one. This utopia-invested 'picture of the world' is legitimized through the authority and the credibility of the journalist superstar, and is reinforced by what seems to be the active and spontaneous participation of the audience which stands in metonymic relationship to the community at large—a community in the sense of McLuhan's (1964) global village. The studio audience and the home audience become television's fictive 'we' (Stam, 1983) and a false sense of almost universal community is established.

This analysis, which lies within the tradition of the anti-empiricist critiques of the news, is in line with the critical paradigm which tends to see the news (as well as other cultural artifacts) within the terms of ideological construction. Yet, despite the infusion of the critical paradigm and a set of other interdisciplinary methods and focal issues—generally put together under the rubric of cultural or critical studies—into communication research, the tension between the two competing traditions of the field is still in effect. A recent example of this rivalry is found in Greg Philo's book *Seeing and Believing: The Influence of Television* (Philo, 1990) which contains sharp criticism of some of the ideas propagated by the ideological approach in the news.

An in-depth critique of this book is, obviously, beyond the scope and intentions of this article. However, I chose to refer in my conclusion to some of the arguments found in this book for several reasons. First some of the claims presented in Philo's study are relevant to the theoretical and conceptual framework of my analysis, if not in detail then at least in spirit. Second, the book presents the findings of a recent study and as such its theoretical conclusions are one of the latest contributions to the empiricist/anti-empiricist debate. Third, despite the fact that Philo is joint author of all the books published by the Glasgow University Media Group, some of his conclusions, as well as his rehabilitation of 'outmoded' concepts such as 'bias', 'objectivity' and 'effects' seem to be somehow alien, if not heretical, with regard to the spirit of the previous books.

The study discussed in this book investigates the reception, by different groups, of news on the British miners' strike of 1984/85. Its findings show that the different groups had a relatively monolithic understanding of the message rendered by television concerning violence during the miners' strike and concerning who was responsible for it. These findings as well as the nature of the debate within the groups which, according to Philo, demonstrates the ability of people from different groups to reject news which contradicts their experience or logic, are used by the author as a springboard to attack the theoretical position which sees the news entirely within the terms of ideological construction.

Philo's main conclusion is that television has a powerful impact on people's beliefs regardless of their different social situations. This conclusion is joined by a rejection of (1) the social importance of the notion of different decodings being generated by differently situated audiences; (20 the notion that the empirical content of the pictures is subject to relativism and cannot be used as an objective criterion to evaluate the bias, accuracy and fairness of the news.

Since this article is not a study of audience decoding, I would not argue with Philo's conclusions regarding this issue. I would mention, however, that his main conclusion served to bring communication research back to the paradigm of omnipotent media. Nevertheless, Philo's conclusion is different from the original paradigm advocated by mass society theorists, who tended to conceptualize the audience as a defenseless, atomized and lonely crowd. By contrast, Philo bases his rehabilitation of the notions of bias and effects on the evidence of the ability of the audiences he researched to reject inaccurate and 'biased' news

For me, however, it is more important to argue with Philo's according of privilege to *seeing* (in the form of visual images or pictures) as a mode of truthful representation of reality and the standard for truth in the news. As the title of his book indicates, for Philo, seeing is believing and the image is a marker of the real. Philo's conclusion regarding the power of the empirical content of the television picture (the image) is neither new nor popularly unaccepted. His rejection of what he calls the relativism of cultural studies (epitomized according to him by Fiske's work) undermines that kind of ideological analysis which suggests that every image embodies a way of *seeing* (Berger, 1972) or that seeing is believing but not all sights are equal in the eye of the camera, or of television news (Nichols, 1981).

To contest Philo's re-worked empiricism is to engage in an old controversy, since seeing has always been privileged in Western epistemology, and reality, as Sontag suggests, 'has always been interpreted through the reports given by images' (Sontag, 1978: 153) despite the fact that philosophers since Plato have critiqued traditional Western dependence on images as truthful representations of reality and the standard for truth.

I do not argue with Philo's contention concerning the power of the image and especially of the moving image. The concentration of images in our society, which exceeds the density of visual messages in any other era, only reinforces their power and provides them with an authority to define, if not—as Baudrillard argues—to replace the real. Yet power should not be confused with truth which is what Philo does when he argues that people's ability to define their understanding of the situation in a uniform way on the basis of news pictures, is evidence that such things as bias and accuracy exist. Furthermore, for him this is evidence that the relativism of a cultural studies which does not distinguish between fact and fiction is wrong, and that the former demarcation line between the two should be re-established by both newsmakers and media researchers.

My own analysis of *Nightline in the Holy Land* demonstrates both the power of the televisual image but also, and primarily its highly constructed nature. If seeing is indeed believing, then Ted Koppel's image of passionate but rather civilized television dialogue should have been a reflection of a real Israeli-Palestian dialogue. Unfortunately, it was not.

More important from the ideological point of view, however, is that Koppel neither masks his impulse to moralize and conclude in a fictional manner not apologizes for it, but consciously, not to say eagerly exposes it. And here we come back to the issue of the TV superstar and journalistic authority and to my analogy between Koppel and the actor in the cough-medicine commercial. The legitimacy of moralizing, of filling in gaps (Iser 1978) and discontinuities between the events in the chaotic and undisciplined real world, derives from the very same authority I discussed previously. This is the authority of the television news personality, as such, to cover events all over the globe, regardless of his or her expertise on these subjects, and to enjoy the same credibility and enlightenment that entitles a television actor in American commercial television to recommend medicines.

Furthermore, just as the actor may only recommend medicines, not prescribe them, so may the television superstar only recommend political medicines such as negotiations and dialogues, since he lacks the legal means formally to effect them. And yet, like the actor, he does not completely lack the practical means. The advertisers of the cough-medicine commercial used the actor not because of his actual medical authority but in spite of it. They assumed (and rightly so) that a popular television actor's power of persuasion is sufficient to advance and promote their sales. The test of the pudding, as Brecht observed, is in its eating. The commercial's success is measured by increase in product consumption rates, not by adherence to medical criteria r even to medical ethics. It would be presumptuous of me to claim that Koppel has the practical means, not only to recommend, but also to promote his solutions; this touches upon another issue which is beyond the scope of this essay and belongs to the field of mass-media effects. Nevertheless, whether or not the TV news personality has the power to change the world, he certainly has the power to construct it. The television image Koppel projects in the Town Meeting is only a picture of the world. As Gombrich (1960) teaches us, the world can never quite look like a picture, but a picture can look like a world (1960: 395). Koppel's Town Meeting is a picture of the world as American television would like it to be. It belongs to the discourse of desire.

References

Allen, R.C. (1987) 'Reader-Oriented Criticism and Television', pp. 74-112 in R.C. Allen (ed.), *Channels of Discourse: Television and Contemporary Criticism.* Chapel Hill: University of North Carolina Press.

Alter, R. (1975a) 'The Self-Conscious Moment: Reflections on the Aftermath of Modernism', *Tri-Quarterly* 33, 209-30.

Althusser, I. (1969) For *Marx*, trans. Ben Brewster New York: Pantheon Books.

Althusser, L. (1971) *Lenin and Philosophy and Other Essays*, trans. Ben Brewster. New York and London: Monthly Review Press.

Barthes, R. (1957) *Mythologies*. London: Paladin.

Barthes, R (1964) *Elements of Semiology* New York: Hill and Wang.
Barthes, R. (1977) *Image/Music/Text*, trans Stephen Heath. New York: Hill and Wang.
Baudrillard, J. (1988) *Selected Writing*. Cambridge: Polity Press.
Berger John (1972) *Ways of Seeing*. London: BBC and Penguin.
Bordwell, D., J. Staiger and K. Thompson (1985) *The Classical Hollywood Cinema: Film Style and Mode of Production to 1960*. New York: Columbia University Press.
Dyer, R. (1977) 'Entertainment and Utopia', *Movie*, 24: 2-13.
Eco, U. (1984) 'A Guide to the Neo-Television of the 1980s', *Framework*, 25: 18-25.
Elizur, J. (1988) Working papers for an international symposium on 'Future Directions in Television News Research: Content, Cognition and Control', Jerusalem: Communication Institute, The Hebrew University.

Feuer, J. (1977) 'The Self-Reflective Musical and the Myth of Entertainment', *Quarterly Review of Film Studies*, 27): 313-26.
Feuer, J. (1982) *The Hollywood Musical* Bloomington: Indiana University Press.
Feuer, J. (1984) *MTM: Quality Television*. London: British Film Institute.
Fiske, J. (1982) *Introduction to Communication Studies*. London: Methuen.
Fiske, J. (1987) *Television Culture*. London: Methuen.
——— and J. Hartley (1978) *Reading Television*. London:" Methuen.
Gans, H.J. (1979) *Deciding What's News*. New York: Vintage Books.
Gitlin, T. (1980) *The Whole World is Watching*. Berkeley: University of California Press.
Glasgow University Media Group (1976) *Bad News*. London: Routledge andand Kegan Paul.
Glasgow University Media Group (1982) *Really Bad News*. Writers and Readers.
Gombrich E.H. (1960) *Art and Illusion: A Study in the Psychology of Pictorial Representation*. London: Phaidon.
Hall, S. (1977) 'Culture, the Media and the "Ideological Effect"', pp. 315-48 in J. Curran et al (eds.), *Mass Communication and Society*. London: Edward Arnold.
Hall, S. (1980) *Culture, Media, Language*. London: Hutchinson.
Hutcheon, L. (1980) *Narcissistic Narrative: The Metafictional Paradox*. Waterloo: Wilfrid Laurier University Press.
Iser, W. (1978) *The Act of Reading: A Theory of Aesthetic Response*. Baltimore: Johns Hopkins University Press.
Katz, E (1987) 'Communication Research Since Lazarsfeld', *Public Opinion Quarterly*, 51; -45, 25-45.
Katz, E (1988) Working papers for an international symposium on 'Future Directions in Television News Research: Content, Cognition and Control'. Jerusalem: Communication Institute, The Hebrew University.
———and D. Dayan (1985) 'Media Events: On the Experience of Not Being There', *Religion* 15: 305-14.
Leach, E. (1976) *Culture and Communication*. Cambridge: Cambridge University Press.
Loshitzky, Y. (1987) 'The Radical Aspect of Self-reflexive Cinema', Ph.D. dissertation, Bloomington: Indiana University.
Lukacs, G. (1971) Critical Realism and Socialist Realism', pp. 93-135 in *Realism in Our Tie* New York: Harper Torchbooks.
McLuhan, M. (1964) *Understanding Media*. London: Routledge andand Kegan Paul.
Morse, M. (1986) 'The Television News Personality and Credibility: Reflections on the News in Transition', pp. 55-79 I T Modleski (ed.) *Critical Studies in Entertainment*. Bloomington: Indiana University Press.

Nichols, B. (1981) *Ideology and the Image: Social Representation in the Cinema and Other Media*. Bloomington: Indiana University Press.

Olson, R.S. (1987) 'Meta-Television: Popular Postmodernism', *Critical Studies in Mass Communication*, 4: 284-300.

Polan, DB. (1978) 'Brecht and the Politics of Self-Reflexive Film', *Jump Cut*, 17 (April: 29-32.

Philo, G. 1990) *Seeing and Believing: The Influence of Television*. London: Routledge.

Roch, I. (1986) 'Criticizing the Press Coverage of the War in Lebanon: Toward a Paradigm of News as Storytelling', *Communication Yearbook, 9,* Beverley Hills: Sage.

Siegle, R. (1986) *The Politics of Reflexivity: Narrative and the Constitutive Poetics of Culture,* Baltimore: Johns Hopkins University Press.

Silberman, M. (1987) 'The Politics of Representation: Brecht and the Media', *Theatre Journal*, 39(4): 448-60.

Sontag S (1978) *On Photography*, New York: Farrar, Straus, andand Giroux.

Stam, R. (1983) 'Television News and Its Spectator', in A. E. Kaplan (ed.) *Regarding Television—Critical Approaches: An Anthology.* American Film Institute Monograph Series, vol. 2, Frederick, MD: University Publications f America.

Stam R. (1985) *Reflexivity in Film and Literature: From Don Quixote to Jean-Luc Godard* Ann Arbor: UMI Research Press.

Turner, V.W. (1974) *The Ritual Process*. Harmondsworth: Penguin.

Van Dijk, T. (1988) *News Analysis: Case Studies of International and National News in the Press.* Hillsdale, NJ: Lawrence Erlbaum.

White, H. (1981) 'On the Value of Narrativity in the Representation of Reality', in W.J.T. Mitchell (ed.), *On Narrative.* Chicago: University of Chicago Press.

White M. (1986) 'Crossing Wavelengths The Diegetic and Referential Imaginary of American Commercial Television', *Cinema Journal* 25(2): 51-64.

21

One of the Bloodiest Days: A Comparative Analysis of Open and Closed Television News

Itzhak Roeh and Akiba A. Cohen

This chapter analyzes television news reports, from five countries, dealing with an incident that took place in the West Bank village of Nahalin in April 1989 during the Palestinian uprising. The analysis of both the verbal and visual texts attempts to explicate "open" and "closed" presentations of the incident by referring to three dimensions: the rhetoric of balance, the rhetoric of facticity, and the rhetoric of neutrality. The analysis suggests that the stories by both Israel Television and CBS are relatively "closed," with the Israeli case being "defensive" while that of CBS being "offensive." The other versions are appraised as lying somewhere between poetic closure and journalistic openness.

On December 9, 1987, the intifada began. As with many other historical events, nobody really knew on that day that it was the beginning. Several days earlier, an Israeli truck hit and killed several pedestrians on a road in the Gaza Strip. Rumors quickly spread among the Arab inhabitants that it was not an accident. They promptly took to the streets in a series of violent demonstrations. (Many riots and demonstrations had taken place before, but the duration and intensity of the present ones had increased dramatically.) Israeli army reinforcements were called in to quell the riots and arrest some of the demonstrators. They used live ammunition, and more Palestinians were wounded and killed (Schiff and Yaari, 1990). The situation in the area continued to escalate and casualties mounted.[1] At the time of writing, the intifada is in its 43rd month with no real end in sight. The media around the world have been covering it since it began. After the first few months of heavy and saturated coverage, there were ups and downs, with subsequent high moments when major events took place (see, for example, Lederman, 1992). This was the case on April 13, 1989, 17 months into the intifada, when in the early morning hours a unit of the Israel Border Police, a military-like branch of the police, which had only recently been deployed in the territories, entered the village of Nahalin, near Bethlehem, on a mission of arresting village residents suspected of being active in the intifada. There ensued between the military and the villagers a violent clash in which four Palestinians were killed, and a fifth died later in a related riot. Many people were wounded.

This paper analyzes comparatively the way the event was reported on television news in the 10 major stations of five countries: the British Broadcasting Corporation (BBC) and Independent Television News (ITN) in the United Kingdom; the first and second French channels (TF1 and A2F); the first and second West German channels (ARD and ZDF); the three major American commercial networks (ABC, CBS, and NBC); and the only news-producing Israeli channel (ITV). All the stories analyzed below were aired on April 13, 1989, the day the incident occurred.

The 10 news items varied significantly in terms of formal television characteristics, such as length and use of visual materials. The longest news item was that produced by Israeli Television (5:20 minutes), followed by CBS (2:34 minutes). The other items were shorter: ABC, 1:48 minutes; NBC, 1:43 minutes; BBC, 1:31 minutes; TF1, 1:55 minutes; A2F, 1:22 minutes; ITN, 34 seconds; ARD, 32 seconds; and ZDF, 20 seconds.

All the stations, except ARD in Germany, included a visual report. It is widely accepted that field coverage fulfills in television news the function of authentication: the pictures provide the reliability of an "unwritten" discourse of truth, the "raw reality" (Fiske, 1987). Yet, none of the footage was shot during the confrontation in Nahalin (see, for example, Cohen and Roeh, 1990), but rather in its aftermath, once the reporters got word of it and obtained permission to arrive on the scene.

Between Open and Closed Readings

The 10 versions of the story of Nahalin vary on at least three rhetorical dimensions which represent a tension between "closed" and "open" presentations of the incident. Davis and Walton (1983) use similar terms for news analysis, although in a slightly different way. They suggest that the reporting of the Aldo Moro story on several European stations took the form of "moral closure," at the stage when Moro was shot by his captors and his body was found in a parked car in the center of Rome. They argue that "'*The need for closure*' which overrides the '*need for balance*' in the case of reporting the Red Brigades [at this stage] means that reports will be structured and presented to demonstrate their divergence from the core values of society and the exclusion of terrorist groups from normal life" (p. 15). Davis and Walton conclude that "Consensus and closure...are merged. The visual and verbal content of the Moro story tells more about the maintenance of an ideologically safe version of consensus by media demarcation than it does about the 'events' which constitute the news" (p. 48). News stories cannot escape the above dilemma, we suggest, and the tension between poetic/ideological closure versus openness is what we seek to exemplify in the following analysis.

Among the tenets of ideal "objective" journalism are what can be classified as (a) the rhetoric of balance, (b) the rhetoric of facticity, and (c) the rhetoric of neutrality. Each of these tenets can be viewed as a continuous dimension. Balance is taken to be the journalistic practice by which opposing parties or competing points of view are given more or less "equal" presentation (both verbally and visually, both explicitly and implicitly). The facticity dimension refers to elements such as novelty, concreteness, and timeliness, on the one hand, and timelessness, poeticization, and mythologization on the other.[2] The dimension of linguistic neutrality consists of a continuum ranging from the conventional standardized and impersonal language to the loaded, personalized, and stylized.

Accordingly, the more rhetorically balanced, current/factual, and neutral/standardized the story, the more open it seems to be. Conversely, the less it is presented on a whole range of textual levels as balanced and the more poetic/mythological and loaded/stylized, the more closed it appears to be. The degree of closure or openness of a news story is a function of a weighted combination of these three dimensions.[3] Journalistic coverage, we argue and attempt to demonstrate, cannot escape the tension between professionals' claim for "open" presentation and the constraints of closure in all writing—social scientists and historians included (Geertz, 1988; White, 1981).

The ITV and CBS versions of the Nahalin incident offer disparate ideological readings of the same event, while at the same time they share certain similar rhetorical patterns. Both ITV and CBS tend to construct a "closed" pattern. Both seek to minimize potential variabilities of interpretation. It can be argued that rhetorical closure eliminates alternative readings and suggests a constrained reading in the sense that Rubin-Suleiman (1976, 1980) describes the ideological novel, *roman a these*, as a literary genre that seeks to limit the reader's freedom. It does so by using various rhetorical means that mutually reinforce each other and impose a single "correct" reading.

ITV and CBS, then, extensively use rhetorical devices to construct a rich and dense network of verbal and visual means to create their respective ideological closure. While the American network fiercely blames and condemns Israel, the Israeli broadcast makes a strenuous effort to defend its case. While ITV suggests that the violent incident is over, CBS suggests that it is only one episode in an endless chain of events. At the same time, however, as far as journalese is concerned, both versions significantly diverge from the ideal of a "balanced" coverage that tends to represent side by side the adversaries' points of view, to minimize the rhetorical presence of the reporter, and to let the reader read the story his or her way.

The CBS depiction represents a cruel, even brutal reality, for which Israel and its armed forces are held largely responsible. Moreover, the Nahalin incident is presented as an example of a particularly desperate phase of the enduring Israeli-Palestinian conflict as a whole. It is not only "one of the worst bloodlettings of the 16-month rebellion"—as the narrator puts it—but also part of a "murderous cycle" where "the vision of settlement seems to be disappearing behind a thickening cloud."

The thickening cloud of despair and insolvability is an antithesis to what Israel TV says about the Nahalin episode. The latter story is "epic" rather than dramatic, and the voice of the reporter is moderate and restrained, as opposed to the emotionally involved tone in the CBS presentation. The story does not begin *in medias res* as it does on CBS, but rather from the end, after the action is over. From the very beginning it suggests resolution or denouement: "The army is investigating the event."

The stories broadcast by the other eight stations can be described in varying degrees as more ideologically "open." None takes sides so emphatically as ITV and CBS. An important criterion for the analysis of the continuum is the degree to which some of the stories maintain the journalistic dictum of balance and neutrality. Some try, more than others, to avoid by all means an unequivocal judgment. Others at least go through the motions of presenting the contending points of view. Thus, for example, the British ITN reports that on the one hand, "Eyewitnesses say the Israelis fired indiscriminately into the crowd." but on the other, "Israel said its troops had to fire after tear gas failed to break up a riot." Also, ABC quotes Israeli officials as saying: "The police had gone in to arrest Palestinians suspected of attacking Jewish settlers" while Palestinians were saying: "The Border Police provoked the violence by abusing village women."

Following is a more detailed analysis of the 10 items.

Defensive Closure: The ITV Story

For ITV the Nahalin affair is domestic news and it is rather naive to expect Israel Television to provide a balanced view, a neutral story "from nowhere" (Epstein, 1973). And indeed, even though its rendition does not ignore the basic facts ("four Arab residents killed, 12 wounded," etc.), the opening words of the anchor refer not to the casualty count but to a quote from the Israeli authorities: "The Commander—General Amram Mitzna—appointed a special investigative team to examine this morning's bloody events in the Arab village of Nahalin in the Bethlehem district." These same lines symmetrically close the story, as told by the reporter: "An investigating team, appointed by the commanding general, will examine what happened in Nahalin today." This symmetry contributes to the closure of the story, and suggests again that things are under control.

The atmosphere of "things being under control" is given visual support in the establishing shot of a panoramic view, lasting nearly 20 seconds, in which a military helicopter flies over the hilly village terrain. It flies so high that everything below appears peaceful and serene.

It is also noteworthy that the most dominant participant on ITV is General Mitzna, who provides the "good arguments" that Israel uses to justify the action carried out by its forces. He is brought into a "dialogue" with two Palestinians from Nahalin, who are interviewed in Arabic (with Hebrew subtitles). One of them emotionally expresses his anger at being beaten by the soldiers and keeps asking: "For what reason? Nobody knows why! I asked him: Why, why?" Cut. In a close-up, General Mitzna now "replies": "It is clear that Nahalin is a special case. We entered the village because groups came from there to the main road ... and recently stones and Molotov cocktails were thrown on Israeli vehicles. And that's why we had to enter!" The interview with Mitzna, who is calm and authoritative, was shot later at a nearby army base. It is juxtaposed and in strong contrast to the two highly excited Arabs interviewed in the village shortly after the event took place.

Israeli Television, while presenting an Israeli point of view, does not ignore the norms of Western journalism. It does provide some of the rage and fury of the day, albeit mainly through verbal expression, as above, rather than visual footage, and through what can be described as "rhetorical control": Mitzna's repeated appearances contribute to the moderation which the Israeli position favors; what's more, the authoritative general clearly places the blame on the villagers when he says: "Among the casualties there are some on whom we have evidence ... not that we meant to kill them, but we know that they were active and violent participants with the Border Police." Finally, the tone of the reporter is in keeping with standardized news discourse—his lexicon is unloaded and matter-of-fact: it lacks emotion, imagery, and metaphors, as well as any other stylistic idiosyncrasies. In short, it contributes to an aura of restrained moderation. And this is precisely the way in which Israel would prefer to present itself in such hard times.

Offensive Closure: The CBS Story

The anchor begins not with the moderate, self-assured, after-the-action report, as in ITV, but rather dramatically by introducing the viewer to the statistics of how many were killed and wounded at Nahalin. To intensify the impact of the statistics, he then adds a combined-speech quote:[4] "Palestinians said the toll was much higher" followed by " ... They [Palestinians] called it a massacre by the Israeli occupiers."

The video report then begins with a highly dramatic scene followed by a concrete, close-up style statement: "The body of one of the victims was torn from a car and carried to an Arab ambulance." What the viewer sees is a body wrapped in white linen with bloodstains being held up by a crowd near an ambulance. This would become a repeated—in fact, a dominant—leitmotif: participants are readily identified as either victims or aggressors—there are no neutral bystanders—and the report is soaked with brutal images that go beyond the current political conflict between Israelis and Palestinians. It goes "deeper" than the here and now: even the corpses are still in danger, the reporter narrates, and families "defend" them from the Israeli soldiers. Also, he adds, "The wounded are hidden and carried to the hills to escape arrest."

These points are expressed later by the repeated and dominant use of mythological elements which seem, again, to take the concrete story far beyond the "here and now." For example, the same helicopter that in the Israeli version served as a tranquilizing agent, is seen here flying just above the roof tops of Bethlehem, in what might appear to be a frightening situation, which reporter Bob Simon uses as a vehicle to shift into mythological spheres: "The boy was laid to rest as an Israeli helicopter crossed the skyline where three wise men once saw a star in the East." Juxtaposing the town of Bethlehem, which implicitly suggests a mythological timeless (and spaceless) context, with the low flying military plane, creates explicit irony as Simon says: "Bethlehem today was the wrong place and the wrong time."

Two additional mythological motifs referring to Israel and its people appear in the CBS item. In the first, Simon invokes an American image for his home audience by describing the place as "the increasingly *Wild West Bank* [italics added] of the Jordan—" the place clearly being the West Bank, and the image being that of the American "Wild West." Simon goes on to say: "It seems as if anarchy had been loosed upon the territory." The word "territory" refers both to today's West Bank territories occupied by Israel and to the historic pre-statehood status of the American West. This latter reference is linked to the biblical context when he says: "the People of the Book writing their own laws ... [are] ... involved in what appears to be recreational shooting."

The mythological timelessness and spacelessness—that is, stripping the story of its concrete historical moment—is also reinforced by the assessment of the situation as being "a murderous cycle." The severity of the no-win/no-way-out situation progressively increases, with the story nearing its end, by the saliently repetitive use of the word "more" as many as eight times in the closing sentences, in a crescendo-like pattern: "more and more weapons are being fired these days by more and more Israeli solders, settlers, and policemen .... Soldiers seem to fire more quickly these days; there are more bullets, there's more hate, and more desperation." What the archive footage shows when this verbal despair is expressed are Israelis in uniform and in civilian clothing, aiming and firing their weapons in various directions—in short, the "recreational shooting" the narrator refers to.

And finally, just as the closure in the Israeli story is heightened by the symmetry of things being under control in the beginning and the end, so there is a symmetry—albeit of a different mood—in the CBS story. The report that opens with corpses being torn away, ends with a gloomy view of a settlement "disappearing behind a thickening cloud." The realization of this metaphoric expression is provided by a shot of an Israeli soldier running out of a cloud (probably tear gas) which fills the screen. This is the last picture, and, as if to add disaster to the already tragic ending of the drama, a musical marker is emphatically played.

From Poetic Closure to Journalistic Openness

The analysis of the ITV and CBS stories reveals their respective closures. Both stories are characterized by a clear deviation from the ideals of Western journalese, as if rhetoric and storytelling do not comply with professional tenets. Following is an analysis of the other eight stories, which presents them as more open, in various degrees. All serve to illustrate a built-in tension between the poles of open and closed.

The ABC Story

The ABC story is almost devoid of metaphors and mythological elements. It provides the Shamir visit to Washington (which ended on that same day) as the context for the story, thus foregrounding timely current news, avoiding the timeless poetic and mythological elements (as in the CBS story).

As far as balance is concerned, ABC generally follows the rules of journalistic practice. The reporter, Dean Reynolds, presents the two points of view following each other: "Israeli officials said the police had gone in to arrest Palestinians suspected of attacking Jewish settlers. They were forced to open fire, officials said, when they were ambushed by rock throwers ... Palestinians said the Border police provoked the violence by abusing village women." And once more: "While the [Israeli] army said it will hold an investigation, the Palestine Liberation Organization said what's really needed is international protection for Palestinians under occupation."

Current political context is suggested both at the outset and as a conclusion: "The Israeli prime minister, Itzhak Shamir, wound up his trip to the U.S. today by defending the use of force against Palestinians in the occupied territories." And then: "It's been one week since Prime Minister Shamir proposed elections for Palestinian peace negotiators." Current context is highlighted, as opposed to CBS's poetic timelessness.

The role of the Border Police is given prominence in the ABC story, and this, once more, can be seen as foregrounding of the "current" and timely constituent in conventional news coverage: "It was the first time that this unit was deployed."

Also, there is a rhetoric of journalistic caution for neutrality: "At least four and perhaps as many as six Palestinians were killed ... in an Israeli raid on West Bank village. And that raid appears to have triggered the events of today."

Moreover, the standardized journalistic avoidance of explicit statements of judgment is salient. It is not the reporter who evaluates and tells the viewers about how extreme the situation is; he only confirms this evaluation by using an official source description of the situation: "Officials called it a day of exceptional violence." Only now, supported by officials, the reporter takes the license to evaluate the situation his own words, and thus abides by the rhetorical rules of objectivity. Openness, then, is presented through balance, current information, and standardized/neutral journalistic discourse.

The NBC Story

The NBC story is characterized by a narrative line that attempts to determine the yet unclear facts—going from the known to the unknown. The dominant tone is that of detachment and of a matter-of-fact rendering of new information, avoiding drama and involvement, and getting at the true facts.

The anchor lead ends by introducing the reporter who will tell "what's known and what's not." This is followed by the reporter's opening to the story: "The details aren't clear, and the army says it's investigating. The Palestinians say Israeli border police drove into their village in the middle of the night ... They called it a massacre." And when explaining the replacement of the army by the Border Police, correspondent Martin Fletcher says: "The idea is to reduce casualties." This is mentioned despite the unexpected outcome: "Replacing soldiers with Border Police didn't make things better, but worse." This evaluation, it is worth noting, follows abundant visual and verbal indications of the worsening situation, but it is by no means a personal judgment.

There is a clear effort by NBC to provide details and contextualization for the events at Nahalin: "It was the third time in a week their village was raided ... a day before the shooting, village leaders complained ..." In describing the wounded, the reporter says: "Most ... were shot in the upper body, not in the legs, which regulations require." Despite the harshness of the situation, the reporter lets it be known that there are regulations that seek to avoid it, and thus one can almost hear in this report the voice of Israeli sources. About one third of the text deals with the nature of the Border Police unit. In describing who they are and their "known brutality," archive material is used to show their ruthless behavior. And yet, the text, as described above, attempts to mitigate the message sent by the footage, and to link the rough images to the events of the day, to produce a more balanced news account.

Significant loaded terms are avoided, and the story is not stylized in any kind of a dense pattern, thus contributing to a neutral/standardized rhetoric of news.

The BBC Story

The BBC item is in fact the most "closed" among the eight relatively open stories. This can best be exemplified by means of quasi-quotes or combined discourse. Contrary to the studio lead, which claims that "at least six people were killed and 20 wounded," the reporter, Keith Graves, quotes/mentions an Israeli version according to which "there was only one dead and four wounded." The reporter questions the credibility of the Israeli version by saying it was "trying to play the whole thing down" and "to seal the village off from the outside world." The BBC report of "at least six dead" is presented authoritatively and as factual, in contrast to the Israeli version, which is perceived here as manipulative disinformation. It is, however, noteworthy that the BBC numbers outscore all other reports, and that the true number after all was four dead and not "at least six."

Another example in the BBC story appears towards the end when the reporter again refers to the Israeli position by saying: "The Israeli military commander ... has ordered an inquiry into one of the bloodiest incidents since the uprising started." Needless to say, the military commander never said that the incident was the "bloodiest." And yet he is quoted in a combined speech as if he did. And when reporting that "many of the dead were hit in the head or the back" no mention is made, as in the NBC story, of an implicit Israeli position, namely, that army regulations limit firing to legs only.

While several phrases in the text provide what might on the surface be considered elements of current information, they are presented, however, in a manner conducive to the elicitation of drama and emotion, which are more pertinent to poetic and loaded rhetoric. For example, the reporter then "invites" the viewer to the scene by saying: "Outsiders arriving at the village ... found dead and wounded scattered around the streets." The "outsiders" in this context are actually the reporters themselves, as no other outsiders were allowed in, and the reporter rhetorically creates a sort of solidarity between himself and the viewer—both sharing, as it were, the same privileged point of view. The camera heightens the dramatic effect of the text, showing the same "wounded scattered around" and invites the audience to share the experience of the "villagers hysterical with grief and anger." Thus in the BBC news item, drama seems to override journalistic information, although the story does not resort to mythological elements.

In this reading of the story, then, there is a high degree of closure. The item also contains several instances of loaded terminology. This occurs—mitigated, however—when sources are quoted: "The Mayor of Bethlehem called it a massacre," and also, this time rather emphatically, "moderate Arab leaders described [it] as a massacre." It also occurs in the reporter's own descriptions: "villagers hysterical with grief and anger" or the "Arab Druze members of the Border Police noted for their brutality." Finally, the reporter resorts to a melodramatic contrast, juxtaposing praying and shooting, "they ... returned around dawn as villagers were leading prayers, opening fire on anyone they saw."

Curiously, the reporter in this case was not actually reporting from the scene, but rather from BBC's Cyprus bureau. His voice-over was mixed in London with the footage from the Nahalin and Bethlehem locations. This is only implicitly suggested to the viewer by his sign-off: "Keith Graves, BBC News in the Middle East" (and not from a specific location normally referred to).

The ITN Story

The ITN item is relatively brief and more "distant." The only voice heard is that of the anchor in the London studio who provides commentary on what is shown in the footage. There is no reporter on the scene. The item is relatively balanced even though the initial reference to the Arab side ("Villagers ... say") is not followed by the Israeli position. There are nevertheless two cases of balanced presentation. First, the statement "Eyewitnesses say the Israelis fired indiscriminately into the crowd" is countered by a "balanced" reference to the reason for that: "... after youths threw stones." And the second version, that of the PLO, who called the raid "a preplanned massacre" is followed by the Israeli point of view: "Israel said its troops had to fire after tear gas failed to break up a riot. The military commander is investigating."

Stylistically, the item does not contain any poetic or mythological elements. It is written in a matter-of-fact style—standardized, brief, and concise. It appears as timely, current, and almost "headlinese." Opinion or commentary is duly acknowledged as a quote, and not as a view promoted by the broadcaster.

The two instances of loaded expressions: "The Israelis fired indiscriminately into the crowd" and "preplanned massacre," as noted above, are not the reporter's own phrases; he explicitly attributes them to sources. Neutrality prevails, as it were, through a standardized rhetoric of objectivity.

The TF1 Story

The TF1 report is characterized by the classic format of a distinct beginning, middle, and end. While the first and last segments provide geopolitical and cultural context—referring to Lebanon, to Shamir's politics, and to tomorrow's (Friday's) prayers of the Muslims in Jerusalem—the middle section focuses on correspondent Patricia Alemoniere's highly personalized and emotionally charged account of the events of the day at Nahalin.

In the lead, the reporter provides bare statistical facts about the incident, that is, the number of killed and wounded, immediately juxtaposed with the clause: " ... in spite of the new proposals of Itzhak Shamir." This suggests that the nature of the political proposals is positive. It is an instance of implicit balance: people are killed *despite* Prime Minister Shamir's proposals. The bulk of the report on Nahalin, however, can hardly be described this way. If balance is achieved, it is not by the conventional point-counterpoint of quotations or attributions, but rather through the structure of the entire item, as a whole, with its different parts that counterbalance each other.

As far as current information is concerned, it can be found mainly in the lead and closing segments. The main (middle) part of the story has poetic qualities somewhat like a lyrical elegy and contains repetitions and anaphoras in a continuous mode: "the women *expressing* their anger ... the young boys *seeing* the bodies ... *weeping* because everybody was weeping" [italics added]. These emotional expressions are clear digressions from current descriptive news parlance; note the rhythmic parallelism and triplets: (a) "Nobody could go to Nahalin"; (b) "the army blocked the access roads"; (c) "the place was under curfew"; (d) "the inhabitants would have been revolting"; and (e) "the soldiers would have fired." And yet, despite the abundant use of poetic patterns, there is no instance of mythology in this account. To add to the dramatic and emotionally loaded discourse, the reporter presents in her own voice-over the text of an injured boy seen in his hospital bed. She does this in first person, in a tone that overexcitedly attempts to imitate a child's voice, clearly identifying with him and his suffering in what appears to be symbiosis between the reporter and the victim. This is an uncommon rhetorical device indeed.

Just as is the case with balance and current/factuality, so with the linguistic/rhetorical dimension, the third segment of the story returns to the standardized/neutral news discourse that characterized the introductory segment. While the middle section with its poetic devices suggests timelessness, the final segment is squarely within a well-defined time fame: "This evening the Palestinians and the Israeli men in charge were asking themselves what would happen tomorrow?" This reference to "tomorrow" is not abstract but rather concrete: it refers to the following day, Friday, April 14th, "the day of the great prayer" for the Muslims on the Temple Mount. And this time timeliness brings to a complete circle the opening statement: "This morning, in fact, four Palestinians have been killed ...."

The A2F Story

There are both similarities and differences between the second French channel and the first French channel news items in terms of their general structure. While both stations deal with what is coming up in the following day in Jerusalem, the A2F report is less dramatic and more balanced. Balance is suggested in this item by the use of visual material. The report begins with the tranquil view from the air, using the same helicopter shown in the ITV version, albeit very briefly. On the other hand, the report ends with a scene of two soldiers firing tear gas, pushing and dragging a Palestinian onto an army jeep, while brutally beating him (identical footage, except for the beating of the Arab man, is shown on the other French station). Verbally, some balance is obtained by bringing up the two positions next to each other: "The villagers affirm that there were seven dead ... The Israeli army, which opened an inquiry, speaks of four dead." And yet the balance is slightly skewed in favor of the Israeli position since the anchor in Paris already has stated the fact that four were killed. There is also some indication of the story giving preference to the Israeli version: "According to the official version, feeling threatened, they opened fire on the stone throwers." In fact, one of the visual scenes focuses on an Arab woman carrying a large stone in her hand as she walks down the street.

Current/factuality is stressed by an emphasis on concrete details, such as: "Nahalin, a village of 2,000 inhabitants, near Bethlehem" (nobody else took the trouble to be as specific). The reporter, Charles Enderlain, also refers to the Border Police as "a paramilitary unit," and is very specific about the expected event: "*tomorrow*, during the prayers of the *second Friday of Ramadan* in the mosques" [italics added]. Finally, by way of summary, he states: "The uprising has just entered its 17th month."

The language of the item is generally standardized. Only one clear example of loaded rhetoric appears in the opening line of the anchor: "The Middle East, once more with deaths in the territories ... The West Bank has in fact experienced the bloodiest day since the beginning of the year."

The Two West German (ARD and ZDF) Stories

The Nahalin incident does not attain the status of a distinct story in either of the two German stations. In both cases the very brief reports, with anchor voice-over but no lead, are presented as part of a "package" of foreign news. The ARD story consists of footage while the ZDF story presents only a full-screen geographical map of Israel with Nahalin marked on it through the duration of the item.

In the ZDF story, the rhetorical pattern of balance is maintained minimally by mentioning the Palestinian report, on the one hand, and Jerusalem Radio, on the other. In the ARD item, it is even difficult to determine balance or imbalance.

In the ARD story there is a series of current/factual elements: four Palestinians died in the incident; 30 were injured; and by way of summary it is mentioned that exactly 399 Palestinians had been killed by Israelis since December 1987. In the ZDF story, however, there is no coherent and consistent report of facts: initially "several people were killed" and in the next sentence "at least three Arabs were killed." Poetic, mythological, and loaded rhetorical terms are completely absent in both versions. In sum, both items lie closest to the "open" end of the continuum and are presented in a detached and standardized way.

Tentative Closure

The authors are clearly aware of the dangers of overgeneralization. As far as studying the coverage of the intifada is concerned, there is no doubt that one incident in an ongoing chain of events cannot do justice to the overall picture. This has been but a case study of one story, which illustrates rather than represents the diversity of television coverage. And yet, the criteria offered here seem to be useful in analyzing television news in general.

We have suggested that the open-closed distinction can usefully be borrowed from literary criticism and from historiography (Grossman, 1978) and applied to the study of news. In fact, a reconceptualization of the borrowed continuum has been worked out. Through the three-dimension rhetorical analysis of the news, the open and the closed are redescribed in terms basic to journalistic writing. In other words, basic tenets of Western journalism—objectivity, timeliness, only-the-facts—are examined as rhetorical practice. News can be better understood as a professional praxis, we believe, once we see it as ever oscillating or torn between the constraints of the closed and the open.

By implication, this article suggests that news stories should be read as vehicles of meaning production rather than (as the old legend would have it) "transmitters" of crude information. (A *rhetoric* of "only-the-facts" might well be employed, though.) The above comparative reading of 10 stories exemplifies how the same "data" are used to create diverse stories, each constituting a meaningful event. TV news stories, it is suggested, can be viewed as frames that make sense or produce meaning conceivably only within particular cultural boundaries/settings (and/or ideological environments). In other words, stories that television tells to given audiences must be in some way domesticated and, hence, diversified.

A concluding remark about the norms and conventions of the journalistic profession. The reader is certainly aware by now that professional ideologies of scientific journalism are challenged here. What is proposed above is a critical view of journalistic praxis in as much as it perceives itself as a missionary of fact-finding universalistic science. A tension (if not a self-defeating contradiction) is enclosed between, on the one hand, a professional urge to stick to "what-is," "the-way-it-is," and avoid conventional narrativity and, on the other hand, journalistic writing, which is saturated by conventional framing and by culturally bound meaning production. Again, we know that journalists believe in an "open," unstructured, unrhetorical presentation of reality-as-it-is; yet we find their text often structured, poetic, and rhetorically closed. News should be read as a battleground for the open and the closed, the professional and the poetic.

Notes

1. This paper analyzes how one intifada event was presented on 10 different stations on the same night. Its title is derived from the texts of more than one report. While it was definitely a serious event, in retrospect it was not the bloodiest of them all. Other studies of the intifada, including another one based on the same event, are to appear in Cohen and Wolfsfeld (in press).
2. The poetic and the mythological are traditionally defined as antithetical to the historical (see Grossman, 1978). In the context of news—the historiography of the present—it is suggested that the poetic and mythological tend to ignore the historicity of the narrated events and to locate them outside concrete frames of space and time. Also, to poeticize seems to suggest that the conventions of documentation and realism are violated. A different perspective for the discussion of realistic of factual journalism as opposed to poeticized journalism is Rorty's radical view on "poeticized liberal polity" (Rorty, 1989); according to him, "we need a redescription of liberalism as the hope that culture as a whole can be 'poeticized' rather than as the Enlightenment hope that it can be 'rationalized' or 'scientized' ... In my view an ideally liberal polity would be one whose culture hero is Bloom's 'strong poet' rather than the truth-seeking logical, objective, scientist" (p. 53).
3. Entman's (1989) book, in particular his discussion of "Objectivity, Bias and Slant in the News" (pp. 30-38), makes a similar point: "Journalists follow the work rules that objectivity lays down, but they cannot realize the aims of objectivity. The objectivity creed contains yet simultaneously camouflaged codes and conventions that journalists use in making their news choices" (p. 31). These choices, we propose, can well be located along a continuum between closed and open presentations.
4. "Combined speech" is a well known literary device which links direct and indirect peresentation of speech to create ambivalence. The voice of the narrator (and of the TV reporter for that matter) is mixed, as it were, with that of the quoted source of speech. It is in combined speech that bivocality occurs: there is no way to tell clearly whose voice is heard, since the boundaries between direct speech (the speaker's voice) and indirect speech (the narrator's voice) are blurred. This category of combined speech is widely analysis (see, for example, Bakhtin, in Todorov, 1984) and in literary studies (see, for example, Roeh and Nir, 1990).

References

Cohen, A. A., and Roeh, I. (1990). A five-version tale of one jeep, one Palestinian, and two Israelis: Some secrets of TV news editing that only comparative viewing might reveal. *Feedback*, 31(4), 6-12.

Cohen, A. A., and Wolfsfeld, G. (Eds.). (in press). *Framing the intifada: People and media*. Norwood, N.J.: Ablex.

Davis, H., and Walton, P. (1983). Death of a premier: consensus and closure in international news. In H. Davis and P. Walton (Eds.), *Language, image, media* (pp. 8-49). New York: St. Martin's Press.

Entman, R.M. (1989). *Democracy without citizens*. New York: Oxford University Press.

Epstein, J. (1973). *News from nowhere*. New York: Vintage Press.

Fiske, J. (1987). *TV culture*. London: Methuen.

Geertz, C. (1988). *Works and lives—The anthropologist as an author*. Palo Alto: Stanford University Press.

Grossman, L. (1978). History and literature. In R. H.Canary and H. Kozicki (Eds.), *The writing of history* (pp. 3-39). Madison: University of Wisconsin Press.

Lederman, J. (1992). *Battle-lines: The American media and the intifada*. New York: Henry Holt and Company.

Richman, A. (1989). American attitudes toward Israeli-Palestinian Relations in the wake of the uprising. *Public Opinion Quqarterly*, 53, 415-430.

Roeh, I., and Nir, R. (1990). Speech presentation in the Israeli radio news: Ideological constraints and rhetorical strategies. *Text*, 10, 225-244.

Rorty, R. (1989). *Contingency, irony and solidarity*. Cambridge, England: Cambridge University Press.

Rubin-Suleiman, S. (1976). Ideological dissent from works of fiction: Toward a rhetoric of the Roman a These. *Neophilogus*, 60, 162-177.

Rubin-Suleiman, S. (1980). Redundancy and the readable text. *Poetics Today*, 1, 119-142.

Schiff, Z., and Yaari, E. (1990). *Intifada: The Palestinian uprising—Israel's third front*. New York: Simon and Schuster.

Todorov, T. (1984). *Mikhail Bakhtin, the dialogical principle*. Minneapolis: University of Minnesota Press.

White, H. (1981). The value of narrativity in the representation of reality. In W.J.T. Mitchell (Ed.), *On narrative* (pp. 1-25). Chicago: University of Chicago Press.

22

Terrorism as Theater: Mass Media and Redefinition of Image

Gabriel Weimann

> Let me put forward the proposition that the media, particularly television, and terrorists need one another, that they have what is fundamentally a symbiotic relationship. Without television, terrorism becomes rather like the philosopher's hypothetical tree falling in the forest: no one hears it fall and therefore it has no reason for being. And television without terrorism, while not deprived of all interesting things in the world, is nonetheless deprived of one of the most interesting.
>
> —Ted Koppel, ABC anchor
> Cited in *Harper's*, October 1984, p. 47.

The "Theater of Terror"

During the early 1970s, academics and journalists noticed the emergence of media-oriented terrorism. Terror had entailed a mass psychological aspect historically. But contemporary terrorists became exposed to new opportunities for exerting mass psychological impacts as a result of technological advances in communications and transportation. The most significant change was the emergence and widespread diffusion of television broadcasting. Paralleling the growth in technology-driven opportunities for terrorist action were efforts by terrorists themselves to hone their communications skills. As one of the terrorists who orchestrated the attack on the Israeli athletes during the 1972 Munich Olympic Games testified:

> We recognized that sport is the modern religion of the Western world. We knew that the people in England and America would switch their television sets from any program about the plight of the Palestinians if there was a sporting event on another channel. So we decided to use their Olympics, the most sacred ceremony of this religion, to make the world pay attention to us. We offered up human sacrifices to your gods of sport and television. And they answered our prayers. From Munich onwards, nobody could ignore the Palestinians or their cause (cited by C. Dobson and R. Paine, 1977: 15).

During the 1970s, academic observers remarked increasingly on the theatrical proficiency with which terrorists conducted their operations. As Jenkins concluded his analysis of international terrorism:

> Terrorist attacks are often carefully choreographed to attract the attention of the electronic media and the international press. Taking and holding hostages increases the drama. The hostages themselves often mean nothing to the terrorists. Terrorism is aimed at the people watching, not at the actual victims. Terrorism is a theater (Jenkins 1975, 4).

Modern terrorism can be understood in terms of the production requirements of theatrical engagements. Terrorists pay attention to script preparation, cast selection, sets, props, role playing, and minute-by-minute stage management. Just like compelling stage plays or ballet performances, the media orientation in terrorism requires a fastidious attention to detail in order to be effective. As Laqueur put it: "The media are the terrorist's best friend. The terrorist's act by itself is nothing, publicity is all" (1976, 104). Menahem Begin, leader of the Irgun Zvai Leumi (National Military Organization) during the British Palestine Mandate (1920-1948), wrote about the media strategy of his organization. The Irgun used newspapers, posters, and radio broadcasts to gain world attention to its messages. The target audience for Irgun's propaganda extended beyond the community in Palestine. At home, Irgun sought to employ word and deed to demoralize the British military forces. Abroad, Irgun sought to enhance support among both Jews and non-Jews. "We translated our broadcasts," noted Begin, "into foreign languages and distributed them among the foreign newspaper correspondents and foreign diplomatic representatives. Our broadcasts generally contained factual news and poetical analysis. As we learnt, they received very wide publicity in the world's press, from Sydney to San Francisco. This was important in keeping the Eretz Israel problem in the focus of international attention. The voice of revolt and of freedom was carried far and wide" (Begin, 1974, 84). A special wing of Irgun, the Revolutionary Propaganda Force, "was given the task of disseminating the message of revolt. Our people expected explanations of our actions and we had to give explanations in order to secure what we wished to secure: their understanding and sympathy." Irgun learned self-consciously from the experience of underground movements in Europe about the importance of communicating its point of view and about different ways of doing so: "One of the most important means was our radio station. At first we broadcast for only five minutes a day.... Thereafter we broadcast for ten, fifteen or twenty minutes. We were never silenced" (Begin, 1974, 82-83).

Several terrorist organizations realized the potentials of media-oriented terror, in terms of effectively reaching huge audiences. A study of all incidents of international terrorism during 1968-1980 revealed a significant increase in terrorist acts that victimize Western nations (though most perpetrators are non-Western) and are directed to attract the attention of the Western media (Weimann, 1986; Weimann and Winn, 1994). No wonder that Bell argued: "It has become more alluring for the frantic few to appear on the world stage of television than remain obscure guerrillas of the bush" (1976, 89). Terrorist theory was gradually realizing the potency of the mass media. Acts of terrorism were more and more perceived as means of persuasion, when the victim is "the skin on a drum beaten to achieve a calculated impact on a wider audience" (Schmid and DeGraaf, 1982, 14).

One of the most influential theorists of modern terrorism was the Brazilian Carlos Marighela, whose "Minimanual of the Urban Guerrilla" became a sourcebook for many terrorist movements all over the world. In his publications, Marighela outlined the various uses that can be made of the media:

> To kidnap figures known for their artistic, sporting, or other activities who have not expressed any political views may possibly provide a form of propaganda favorable to the revolutionaries... Modern mass media, simply by announcing what the revolutionaries are doing, are important instruments of the propaganda. The war of nerves, or the psychological war, is a fighting technique based on the direct or indirect use of the mass media... (1971a, 87-90). The coordination of urban guerrilla action, including each armed action, is the principal way of making propaganda. These actions, carried out with specific and determined objectives, inevitably become propaganda material for the mass communication system. Bank assaults, ambushes, desertion and diverting of arms, the rescue of prisoners, executions, kidnapping, sabotage, terrorism, and the war of nerves, are all cases in point. Airplanes diverted in flight, ships and trains assaulted and seized by guerrillas, can also be solely for propaganda effects (1971b, 103).

The emergence of media-oriented terrorism led several communication and terrorism scholars to reconceptualize modern terrorism within the framework of symbolic communication theory. Thus, Karber suggested a new model of analysis: "As a symbolic act, terrorism can be analyzed much like other media of communication, consisting of four basic components: transmitter (the terrorist), intended recipient (target), message (bombing, ambush) and feed back (reaction of target audience). The terrorist's message of violence necessitates a victim, whether personal or institutional, but the target or intended recipient of the communication may not be the victim" (Karber, 1971, 529). Dowling suggested applying the concept of "rhetoric genre" to modern terrorism, arguing that "terrorists engage in recurrent rhetorical forms that force the media to provide the access without which terrorism could not fulfill its objectives" (1986, 14). Some terrorist events become what Bell has called "terrorist spectaculars" (1978, 50) that can be best analyzed by the "media event" conceptualization (for a comparative analysis of media events and terrorist spectaculars, see Weimann, 1987).

Despite the growing interest in media-terrorism relationships and the convincing evidence of the diffusion of media-oriented terrorism (Weimann and Winn, 1994; Brosius and Weimann, 1991; Weimann and Brosius, 1989, 1991), most studies monitored the coverage given but not the effects of this coverage on public opinion.

Terrorism and Media Effects

The lack of studies on the effects of mass-mediated terrorism may be partly explained by the theoretical and methodological complexity of conceptualizing and measuring media effects. Traditional scholarship on this subject has been divided between the "powerful media" paradigm, arguing major media effects, and the "weak media" paradigm which holds that media effects are minimal. Early empirical research on the effectiveness of the media was dominated by the image of an omnipotent media and a mass society. However, subsequent empirical evidence suggests that the media are less effective than was previously assumed. The flow of communication is less direct than was once thought: mass media ordinarily do not serve as a sufficient and necessary cause of opinion change but rather function among and through a nexus of mediating factors. As Berelson put it, "Some kinds of communication on some kinds of issues, brought to the attention of some kinds of people under some kinds of conditions, have some kinds of effects" (1949, 500). Two factors were found to limit media influence: audience selectivity (in exposure, perception and retention) and interpersonal influence. No longer viewed as strictly atomistic and passive, audiences of the mass media were increasingly understood to have the autonomy to avoid, resist and reject messages that challenge their preconceptions and attitudes. This selectivity and interpersonal processing of media messages have been found to act as filters of mass mediated influence, contributing to reinforcement rather than change of audience opinions.

As a result, a more complex perception of media effects has evolved, leading scholars of media effects to focus on more specific effects, and especially on those which do not trigger defense mechanisms, such as selectivity. Concepts such as climate of opinion, status conferral, cultivation and reconstruction of reality, knowledge gap, or agenda-setting may serve as examples of these specific effects that caused, to some extent, a return to the concept of powerful mass media. It appears that when the media are the sole source of information, and when no predispositions exist (or, at least, when they are not antagonized), the media increases effectiveness in shaping images, attitudes and perceptions. In the case of terrorism, the public is often informed solely by the media and does not have any established attitudes toward the conflict involved. Under these conditions, the Dependency Model (DeFleur and Ball-Rokeach, 1975; Ball-Rokeach and DeFleur, 1976) suggests that the media may have a strong impact on the public agenda, images and attitudes. The present study set out to examine this hypothesis, when related to mass-mediated terrorism.

Measuring the Impact on Public Opinion

In order to establish the causal relationship between media coverage of terrorist events and its impact on public opinion, one has to control other factors and to maintain the sequence of coverage-exposure-change. Experimental research designs are often the preferred solution for the identification and measurement of causality since they provide the ability to control or eliminate the influence of external factors and to activate the desired sequence of stimuli. An experimental design was used in the first study of the effects of press coverage of terrorist events (Weimann, 1983). In this experiment, the attitudes of subjects exposed to press reports of two separate terrorist incidents were assessed before and after exposure. The experimental group was compared to a matched control group that was not exposed to the press reports. This experiment was limited to press coverage only and the dependent variables were only evaluative attitudes.

The present study employs the same experimental design but media coverage was enriched to include both press and television coverage (separately, to enable inter-media comparison), and the impact was measured on more dimensions than merely evaluative attitudes. Specifically, the dependent variables related to specific effects, such as status conferral, agenda setting, level of information, and affective attitudes.

A random sample of two hundred Israelis, all adult Jews living in urban areas, completed seven Likert-scaled items constituting a general scale of attitudes toward terrorism. The questions explored the conditions under which terrorism might be regarded as justifiable. Scale scores, along with socio-demographic characteristics (age, education), were used to pair subjects so that they could be randomly assigned to one of the experimental or the control groups. This matching procedure was repeated four times in order to yield four experimental groups, each with 25 subjects, and four matched control groups, each also with 25 subjects. Every experimental group was then exposed to one medium (press reports or television news) with its coverage of one or two specific terrorist events. These terrorist incidents were:

The South Mollucan Train Seizure

On December 2, 1975, a group of South Mollucans seized a train near Beilen, the Netherlands, in pursuance of its goal of wresting an independent republic from Indonesia. The event involved the killing of three people and the subsequent triggering of an attack by sympathizers who stormed the Indonesian Consulate in Amsterdam. The terrorists were captured and given heavy prison sentences.

The Croatian Hijacking

On September 10, 1976, a group of Croatians seized control of a TWA jet en route from New York to Canada, redirecting it to Europe. The aircraft made "bombing runs" over London and Paris, dropping leaflets that called for the establishment of an independent Croatian state. Prior to departure, they had placed a bomb in New York, which later exploded, killing a police officer. The media event came to an end in Paris, where the terrorists surrendered to the authorities.

These particular events were selected so that they would be remote in the time, location, and experience from the subjects in question. The two events were not selected in order to be in any way representative of the full range and character of international terrorist events. They were selected because of their suitability for testing the impact of the media on the general public in situations where the public has little prior knowledge or sentiment. Following the design for the experiment, each of the four experimental groups was exposed to coverage of one of the two incidents by one of the three media. Thus, one experimental group was asked to read a full set of clippings on the South Moluccan case as drawn from Israel's leading daily newspaper, Yediot, while another experimental group was exposed to a comparable full set of clippings relating to the Croatian case. The sets of clippings were neither censored nor deliberately constructed in any particular fashion; they were a full set representing everyday coverage of the sequence of events in each instance. The two corresponding control groups were presented with randomly selected press clippings from the same newspaper but concerning events unrelated to terrorism.

Following the same procedure, the research team invited two experimental groups to view the actual televised coverage of the two events (recorded from "Mabat," the Israeli television news program) while their corresponding control groups were exposed to videotaped television news programs containing no reference to terrorism in any form. Osgood's semantic differential scales were utilized to measure attitudes and attitude changes (see Osgood and Suci, 1955; Osgood, Suci and Tannenbaum, 1957). Particular use was made of Osgood's evaluative dimension, notably scales that possessed high loadings and were vital to his first rotated factor. Subjects were provided with a list of evaluative adjectives on a 7-point scale, including such pairs as kind-cruel, just-unjust, and brave-cowardly. The post-exposure questionnaire was designed to measure a relatively full range of media effects, including agenda setting, change of awareness, change of information, and priming.

Thus, the questionnaire contained questions about the importance of the problem at issue, the need to solve it, the need to report it in the media, self-reported changes in interest and knowledge, and other indices of awareness and information. The before and after scores on the various evaluative scales were compared. If hypothetically the control groups and their corresponding experimental groups experienced the same changes in attitudes from the first measurement to the second, then the changes could not be attributed to media exposure. On the other hand, in the simplest of situations, if the experimental groups underwent attitudinal change but their corresponding control group did not, the changes among the experimental groups could properly be attributed to the exposure. A t-test for matched pairs was used to assess the significance of the difference between the "before" and "after" differences, calculated for each pair and for each scale. The average scores were computed from seven-point scales, where 1 represents the negative extreme of the semantic differential (e.g., bad, cruel, unfair, etc.), and 7 is the positive extreme (e.g., fair, brave, honest, etc.). Table 1 presents groups' means before and after exposure to press reports.

Table 1
Changes in evaluative attitudes after exposure to press coverage

	South Mollucan case			Croatian case		
	Averages	Averages		Averages	Averages	
Scale	*before*	*after*	*t test*	*before*	*after*	*t test*
Good-Bad						
Experimental	2.03	3.14	2.21*	2.17	3.09	2.09*
Control	2.12	2.21		2.23	2.19	
Just-Unjust						
Experimental	2.19	3.32	2.99**	2.74	3.48	2.78**
Control	2.22	2.17		2.76	2.80	
Kind-Cruel						
Experimental	1.85	1.87	n.s.	1.78	1.83	n.s.
Control	1.87	1.79		1.82	1.85	
Fair-Unfair						
Experimental	1.87	2.88	2.83**	1.96	2.73	2.16*
Control	1.83	1.94		2.02	1.98	
Honest-Dishonest						
Experimental	1.57	2.07	2.08*	1.76	2.32	2.10*
Control	1.65	1.70		1.72	1.59	
Valuable-Worthless						
Experimental	1.53	1.77	n.s.	1.87	1.66	n.s.
Control	1.65	1.70		1.72	1.59	
Brave-Cowardly						
Experimental	2.02	4.43	3.76**	2.43	3.97	3.51**
Control	2.16	2.28		2.35	2.24	

Note: Scales range from 1 (negative adjective) to 7 (positive adjective).
* p<.05 (two tailed)
** p<.01 (two tailed)
*** p<.001 (two tailed)
n.s. - not significant

The comparison of the scores before and after press exposure reveals that exposure does tend to affect certain aspects of the terrorists' image. While the evaluations made by the control groups changed little, most of the experimental groups' scores changed significantly, and in some instances substantially. The experimental groups' evaluations remained largely negative, but they moved in the direction of an improvement of the terrorists' image on most evaluative scales. The predominant image remained one of disapproval, but this disapproval decreased after exposure. This image-improving effect is more salient for certain evaluative dimensions, namely: brave-cowardly, just-unjust, good-bad, fair-unfair, and honest-dishonest, but not on the other scales (i.e., kind-cruel, brave-cowardly). This impact of press coverage was similar for both events even if the two events involved rather different actions, motives, and outcome. The magnitude of image improvement was almost identical for the two cases.

The next step was to study the impact of press exposure in terms of agenda-setting, status conferral and self-reported level of information and interest. Table 2 presents the responses of both experimental and control groups to a series of questions related to these aspects.

Table 2
The impact of press coverage on the public's perceptions

	Percent "agreeing" with statement			
	South Mollucan case		Croatian case	
	experimental	*control*	*experimental*	*control*
"the problem which caused the event is important"	48	16***	44	21 ***
"the problem should have been reported by the media"	53	21***	47	26***
"the problem should be solved by international institutions"	43	26***	46	24**
"people should know about this event and its causes"	47	25**	48	23**
"I know and understand the background of this event"	52	16*	47	29*
"I would like to know more about this subject"	51	32**	53	28***
"this is a topic I might discuss with my friends"	38	29 n.s.	34	32 n.s.

Note: the statistical significance of the difference between the groups' proportions is tested under the null hypothesis of no difference.
* p<.05 (two tailed)
** p<.01 (two tailed)
*** p<.001 (two tailed)
n.s.- not significant

Since each of the experimental groups was matched with a control group, the differences in response patterns presented in Table 2 should be related to press exposure. The observed differences between the groups provide abundant evidence to both agenda-setting and status conferral functions of media coverage. Thus, subjects who were exposed to press reports of terrorist incidents tended to see the issue as more important, to believe that an international solution is desirable, and to hold that media coverage and public attention were merited. Press exposure created both awareness and interest: the experimental subjects were more likely to report an interest in and knowledge of the issue in question. However, exposure did not encourage interpersonal communication. It appears that press coverage of these specific cases would not yield public discussion or debate but rather inform and shape images on the individual's level. In the next step, the impact of television coverage was measured. Table 3 presents the comparison of experimental and control groups exposed to television coverage of the two terrorist incidents.

Table 3
Changes in evaluative attitudes after exposure to television coverage

	South Mollucan case			Croatian case		
Scale	Averages *before*	Averages *after*	*t test*	Averages *before*	Averages *after*	*t test*
Good-Bad						
Experimental	2.11	2.98	n.s.	2.21	2.45	n.s.
Control	2.07	2.17		2.24	2.43	
Just-Unjust						
Experimental	2.09	3.12	2.56*	2.54	3.46	2.98**
Control	2.12	2.27		2.43	2.65	
Kind-Cruel						
Experimental	1.79	1.92	n.s.	1.75	2.87	2.27*
Control	1.96	1.87		1.97	1.80	
Fair-Unfair						
Experimental	1.87	2.01	n.s.	1.96	2.78	2.26*
Control	1.83	1.94		2.02	1.98	
Honest-Dishonest						
Experimental	1.62	2.11	2.09*	1.70	2.43	2.21*
Control	1.65	1.68		1.98	2.09	
Valuable-Worthless						
Experimental	1.64	1.87	n.s.	1.73	1.78	n.s.
Control	1.65	1.70		1.72	1.59	
Brave-Cowardly						
Experimental	2.18	4.19	3.32**	2.23	3.99	3.65**
Control	2.18	2.32		2.27	2.20	

Note: See note to Table 1.

Compared to press coverage, television coverage yielded a somewhat different impact. Again, the impact was mainly in the direction of improving the evaluations on certain dimensions (just-unjust, honest-dishonest, and brave-cowardly) for both events. The terrorists continued on balance to be regarded as unfavorable, but these disapproving images became less disapproving after exposure. However, unlike the results of the press exposure, television coverage produced different impacts for the two events. Television coverage of the Croatian incident produced more change on more scales than did coverage of the South Mollucan event. There is a good reason to believe that this difference is explained by the nature of the specific television reports on the two events. TV coverage of the South Mollucan case focused on the hijacked train and included dramatic footage of murdered hostages, masked gunmen, tense negotiations, and the terrorists' eventual arrest. Given the macabre character of some of the footage, it is perhaps not surprising that the experimental group did not change its views of the terrorists' cruelty and unfairness. By contrast, coverage of the Croatian hijackers was essentially nonviolent in theme. It focused mainly on the hijacked TWA aircraft, the leaflet drop, and the eventual landing and surrender in Paris. The Croatians' only victim, a New York police officer, was only briefly mentioned. The centrality of violence in television coverage of the South Mollucan case may be the reason for the different impact of the two incidents. Press reports on the two events were more similar and lacked the dramatic visual presentation of the victims, thus yielding similar effects in terms of image change.

While television coverage produced somewhat different patterns of attitudinal change for each incident, the broadcasts did not produce substantially differing results in terms of agenda-setting or status conferral. Table 4 presents the comparison of the perceptions held before and after exposure to television reports.

As in the case of press coverage, discussed above, television coverage conferred status on the problem and the participants, encouraging viewers to believe that the problem should be solved and that the public had a genuine interest in its resolution. The control groups generally rated the problems in question as relatively unimportant and expressed little or no interest in each case and its causes. In sharp contrast, the experimental groups were convinced that the problem is indeed important, that it should be reported by the media, and that it should be solved by international institutions. TV reports heightened subject interest in the event and its causes, increased the likelihood of

Table 4
The impact of television coverage on the public's perceptions

	Percent "agreeing" with statement			
	South Mollucan case		Croatian case	
	experimental	*contro*	*experimental*	*control*
"the problem which caused the event is important"	52	17***	49	22 ***
"the problem should have been reported by the media"	57	24***	56	27***
"the problem should be solved by international institutions"	51	23***	48	27**
"people should know about this event and its causes"	44	21**	50	24**
"I know and understand the background of this event"	27	18*	31	24 n.s.
"I would like to know more about this subject"	46	30**	42	24***
"this is a topic I might discuss with my friends"	42	26**	38	27*

Note: See note to Table 2.

personal discussion of the issue, and strengthened the subjects' assessment of the need to inform the public about the case. All of these effects are statistically significant when compared to the matched control groups

Powerful Media or Not?

The experiments revealed the impact of mass-mediated terrorism on the public, mainly in terms of image formation or redefinition. At first glance these findings may seem surprising: after all, Israelis were often targeted by terrorism and yet the results show that Israelis may be affected by media coverage to improve their images of terrorists. However, one should be cautious about the nature of the impact and the methodological limitations. Boulding (1961) has suggested three ways in which messages might engender redefinition of an image: through "addition" (when receivers interpret information about a subject they have not previously organized), through "reorganization" (when a part of the image is changed by creating new meanings or new relationships in the image), and through "clarification" (when receivers reduce their uncertainty by giving some aspects of the image higher definition). The findings of the present study regarding the media's impact on the terrorists' image may be related to all three types of image redefinition. In the specific cases involved, the media served as the sole source of information and interpretation. Thus, under such conditions, the media can form or redefine images. In many terrorist events reported from abroad, the public is dependent on the media for information and interpretation, and is relatively free from any established attitudes or perceptions. These conditions are considered by the "dependency model" as optimal for the media to achieve significant effects:

> The potential for mass media messages to achieve a broad range of cognitive, effective and behavioral effects will be increased when media systems serve many unique and central information functions... When people become heavily dependent upon the mass media for the information they need to resolve ambiguity, the defining or structuring effect of mass-mediated information is considerable (Ball-Rokeach and DeFleur, 1976, 232, 234).

The dependence on the media for clarifying terrorist events and the lack of preexisting attitudes or other sources of information can account for the relatively strong impact of mass-mediated terrorism. However, one should qualify the effects by the special circumstances and conditions activated in this study: in many other media contents the public is not that dependent on media presentations, has pre-existing opinions and perceptions and is, consequently, less affected by the media. The surprising finding in this study is the image-improving effect. Before turning to various explanations of this specific "redefinition of image" caused by the media, it must be reiterated that the findings are delimited by the measure of short-term effects, the use of particular terrorist events that may misrepresent the full domain of such events, and the choice of politically "remote" incidents. However, within these limits, the impact of the "theater of terror" can be emphasized as long as the "show" does not trigger defense mechanisms by creating cognitive dissonance.

Another interesting finding relates to different impacts of the media studied. The comparison of impact across media reveals interesting similarities and differences: both press and television led to image changes and heightened the importance attributed to the issue. Press reports were found to be somewhat more effective in forming attitudes and perceptions than television, while exposure to television coverage was more effective in encouraging interpersonal communication. These differences may be explained by the different functions of each medium, the audience's needs directed to each medium, and the different format and content of presentation in each medium. When considering these attributes, the effectiveness of the press is highlighted. Press reports are more detailed, provide more information and analysis, and appeal better to the public's cognitive needs (see, for example, Katz et al. 1973). Television presentation is more condensed and focuses on the visual, and often dramatic, features of the event. Thus, television is more effective on the emotional rather than the cognitive dimension. Television indeed might be more inherently effective at encouraging interpersonal communication than the press. Exposure to television is more of a group experience while the consumption of newspaper reports tends to be a more isolated experience (a finding revealed by many "uses and gratifications" studies, highlighting the integrative function of television).

Why Is the Impact Positive?

What is it about media coverage of terrorism that may contribute to its image-improving effect? Several aspects related to contents, the style and form of reporting terrorist events are suggestive. Let us examine some of these potential explanations.

The Rationalization of Terrorism

Media coverage of terrorist events must explain the motive for the cruel and brutal aggression, directed mainly against innocent victims. Weimann and Winn (1994) studied media coverage given to over 6,700 terrorist events. They analyzed the reports in leading newspapers in 12 countries and the American television networks (ABC, CBS, NBC). Their analysis revealed that among the sample of media as a whole, terrorists achieve an approximately 50% success rate in securing media recognition for their purported motives. The motives of terrorists were found to have a good chance of being mentioned on the first page of a daily newspaper or among the first three stories in a nightly television newscast. Among terrorist stories broadcast by the U.S. networks, approximately two-thirds discuss the terrorists' motives and do so among the first three stories in the program (Weimann and Winn, 1994, Figures 7.2 and 7.3). Paradoxically, according to the data, the more terrorists victimize innocent people, the more the media grant attention to the motives of terrorists. For each medium studied, the probability of reporting the terrorists' apparent or purported motives increases as the number of fatalities increases.

By looking for a motive, and by presenting the political or social background, media reports often rationalize terrorism. Keeping in mind that terrorists are often motivated by a true political, social, or cultural grievance, this reasoning done by reporters, media analysts and, as it often happens, the terrorists themselves when being interviewed, may lead to sympathy and identification.

The "Pornography of Death"

Very often journalists are accused as "traitors" or "terrorists' collaborators" simply because their reports appear to spread panic. In the 1995-6 bombings of busses in Tel Aviv and Jerusalem, Israel, the media were blamed for their close-up photographs and footage of dead victims and torn bodies, live interviews with hysterical witnesses, and emotional headlines (using words like "fear", "death", and "panic"). Prof. Avineri, an Israeli political scientist, even called Haim Yavin, the leading television news anchorman, a "collaborator with Hammas". According to Avineri, the newsman served the Hammas by "spreading panic" and voicing fear and anxiety. The media respond to these accusations by presenting professional news-making as guiding their selection of stories, pictures and words. And yet, one cannot avoid the ratings-oriented, competitive and emotionally charged format of mediating a terrorist event.

This format, often labeled as the "pornography of death", involves the elements of unedited coverage, live broadcasting from terrorist scenes, interviews with hostages, victims and relatives, emotional writing and shocking pictures (Weimann, 1988). While the debate on the media's responsibility and ability to control the sensationalization of the coverage is still lingering, there is a common understanding that such coverage is rewarding the terrorists. There is no doubt that terrorism aims at fear, doubts, and even panic. The media amplify the scary scenes and pictures, the agony and pain, and bring them into our living rooms. Thus, even without reference to motives, rational, background or consequences of the event, the unavoidable terrorizing effect of mass-mediated terror is in accordance with terrorism's *raison d'être.*

The Labeling of Terrorism

The motives attributed by journalists to terrorists are not the public's only source of information about the terrorists' ultimate purposes. Media audiences can also draw inferences from the terms associated with a terrorist group, including both the group's formal name and the various synonyms that the media might use interchangeably with its formal name. To use some obvious examples, a group might be labeled murderers, gunmen, or saboteurs or alternately a national liberation movement, nationalists, or patriots.

The affective or propaganda significance of the terrorists' formal names or informal labels derives from how these terms are perceived. Weimann (1985) undertook public opinion research to measure the affective valence of a wide range of labels using semantic differential scales. His analysis yielded a relatively simple threefold division into negative, neutral, and positive categories. Negative labels, according to their decoding by the public, included labels as murderers, gunmen, saboteurs, terrorists, criminals, kidnappers, and hijackers. Neutral labels were guerrilla, army, front, movement, and organization. Positive labels were freedom fighters, liberation organization, nationalists, patriots, and independence organization.

Terrorists are aware of the ramifications of language and often select favorable labels. A simple word count (Weimann and Winn, 1994, 193) shows the terms most frequently used in the titles of the world's hundreds of international terrorist groups are liberation, national, people, popular, unity, front, democratic, freedom, and independence. Other frequently used terms are justice, oppressed, peasants, workers, homeland, fatherland, patriots, victims, and sovereignty.

The "Stockholm Syndrome" of the Media

The concept of a "Stockholm syndrome" entered the popular lexicon in the wake of a protracted bank robbery in Sweden's capital in August 1973. The event gained world attention because of the psychological transformation of the hostages held captive over a five-day period. Perhaps the best-known case of the Stockholm syndrome involved the case of Petty Hearst. The California newspaper heiress, Patricia Hearst learned to identify with her Symbionese Liberation Army (SLA) kidnappers, embracing the group's "revolutionary goals," and actively participating in the group's schedule of armed robberies. The

Stockholm syndrome has been manifested in many cases of international terrorism as well, including the hijacking of an Air France flight by German and Palestinian terrorists to Entebbe airport in Uganda in July 1976 (for a collection of studies on this syndrome see Ochenberg and Soskis, 1982).

The phenomenon of the Stockholm syndrome would have little bearing on the relationship of terror and the media if it were not for the vulnerability of the media to the terrorist orchestration of events in kidnap settings. The mass media, which tend to focus on these unexpected terrorist behaviors (human gestures like the release of a pregnant woman, stroking the head of a crying child, or giving a helping hand to a frightened elderly hostage), may be themselves subjects of this Stockholm Syndrome, carrying it to their huge audiences. First, journalists can succumb to the Stockholm syndrome when they are themselves in captivity. Second, they can also report the Stockholm-like experiences of others. Both cases were manifested in the case of the South Mollucan event: Gerard Vaders was a Dutch newspaper editor aboard a train bound for Amsterdam in December 1975, when it was captured by masked gunmen, calling themselves the Free South Mollucan Youth Movement. In his extensive reporting on the 12-day episode, the Dutch journalist wrote about the growing compassion that he felt for the Mollucan terrorists (see Ochberg, 1982). After liberation, Vaders and his fellow captives became vigorous critics of the Dutch government's handling of the South Mollucans.

The case of Dutch editor, Gerard Vaders, illustrates the vulnerability to the Stockholm syndrome of newsmen. But journalists often echo the sympathies of the victims of terrorism towards their victimizers: in the case of threatening kidnappings or hijackings, the hostages often develop enormous empathy with their captors. An illustrative case is the media treatment of the TWA hijacking to Beirut in the summer of 1985. Upon his release, TWA pilot Testrake described his feelings towards the terrorists:

> We were involved on a daily intimate basis with these people. We got to observe them on a human basis as differently from a political basis. It was a sort of a split personality thing. On the one hand they had us prisoner... But they were continually exhibiting small kindnesses to us which, of course, is, I grant you, an exact opposite of their cruelty, their murderous intentions and so on. But yet they were thoughtful toward us, they did bring us little special things. Any time there was a picture of one of us in the paper, boy, we got it quicker than you folks did almost. So this exhibits their interest in us, their concern for us. And this was on a human basis so when they would bring us things like this, we appreciated it. We could see then that

> these people have just the same hopes and aspirations that we all do. They hurt for their country, they see that their country is prostrate and bleeding, that they're really in almost a hopeless situation. And yet they're people just like we are... We empathized with that aspect of it, it's a purely human thing.[1]

The presentation of the terrorists' motives and the rationalization of their actions, the use of positive labels, and the evidence of the Stockholm Syndrome in media reports of terrorism, are all speculative explanations which may serve as hypotheses for systematic analysis of media coverage of terrorism. The present study's findings on the impact of mass-mediated terrorism should encourage future research to relate the form and contents of media reports on terrorism to their various cognitive and emotional effects.

Notes

1. Citations from the TWA episode are drawn from "Excerpts from News Conference of TWA Crew", *New York Times* (July 4, 1985), 7; and from "Transcript of News Conference Held by Freed Hostages in Syrian Capital", *New York Times* (July 1, 1985), 7.

References

Ball-Rokeach, S., and M. DeFleur. (1976). "A Dependency Model of Mass Media Effects." *Communication Research* 3: 1, 3-21.

Begin, M. (1974). *The Revolt: Story of the Irgun*. Tel Aviv: Hadar.

Bell, J.B. (1975). *Transnational Terror*. Washington D.C.: American Enterprise Institute for Public Policy Research.

Bell, J.B. (1978). "Terrorist Script and Live-Action Spectaculars." *Columbia Journalism Review*, (May-June), 47-50.

Berelson, B. (1949). "Communications and Public Opinion", in W. Schramm, (ed.), *Mass Communication*, Urabana: University of Illinois Press, 527-543.

Boulding K. (1961). *The Images*. Ann Arbor, Michigan: University of Michigan Press.

Brosius, H.-B. and G. Weimann. (1991). "The Contagiousness of Mass-Mediated Terrorism", *European Journal of Communication* 6, 63-75.

DeFleur, M., and S. Ball-Rokeach. (1975). *Theories of Mass Communication*, 3rd edition. New York: McKay.

Dobson, C. and R. Paine. (1977). *The Carlos Complex: A Pattern of Violence*. London: Hodder and Stoughton.

Dowling, R.E. (1986). "Terrorism and the Media: A Rhetorical Genre." *Journal of Communication* 56:1, 12-24.

Jenkins, B. (1975). *International Terrorism*. Los Angeles: Crescent Publication.

Karber, P. (1971), "Urban Terrorism: Baseline Data and a Conceptual Framework." *Social Science Quarterly* 52, 527-33.

Katz, E. (1980). "On conceptualizing Media Effects." *Studies in Communication* 1, 119-141

Katz, E., M. Gurevitch, and H. Haas. (1973). "The Use of the Mass Media for Important Things." *American Sociological Review* 38, 164-181.

Laqueur, W. (1976). The Futility of Terrorism. *Harper's*, March 1976.
Livingston, N. (1982). *The War Against Terrorism*. Lexington: Lexington Books.
Marighela, C. (1971a). *For the Liberation of Brazil*. Harmondsworth: Pelican.
Marighela, C. (1971b). "Minimanual of the Urban Guerrilla." In J. Mallin, (ed.), *Terror and the Urban Guerrilla*. Coral Gables: University of Miami Press.
Ochberg, F. (1982). "A Case Study: Gerard Vaders," in Ochenberg and Soskis (eds.), *Victims of Terrorism*, Boulder, Colorado: Westview Press
Ochenberg, F. and D. Soskis, (eds.). (1982). *Victims of Terrorism*, Boulder, Colorado: Westview Press.
Osgood, C.E. and G. Suci. (1955). "Factor Analysis of Meaning." *Journal of Experimental Psychology* 50, 325-38.
Osgood, C.E. and P.H. Tannenbaum. (1957). *The Measurement of Meaning*. Urbana: University of Illinois Press.
Schmid, A. and J. de Graaf. (1982). *Violence as Communication*. Beverly Hills: Sage.
Weimann, G. (1983). "The Theater of Terror: Effects of Press Coverage." *Journal of Communication* 33, 38-45.
Weimann, G. (1985). "Terrorists or Freedom Fighters?" *Political Communication and Persuasion* 2:4, 433-45.
Weimann, G. (1986). "Mass Mediated Theater of Terror: Must the Show Go On?" P. Bruck (ed.), *The News Media and Terrorism* Ottawa: Carleton University Press. 1-22.
Weimann, G. (1987). "Media Events: The Case of International Terrorism." *Journal of Broadcasting and Electronic Media* 31:1, 21-39.
Weimann, G. (1998). "The Theater of Terror: Democracy's Tough Challenge". In Cohen-Almagor, R. (Ed.), *Basic Issues in Israeli Democracy* Tel Aviv: Sifriat Hapoalim.
Weimann, G. and H.-B. Brosius. (1989). "The Predictability of International Terrorism: A Time-Series Analysis", *Terrorism*, 11(6), 491-502.
Weimann, G. and H.-B. Brosius. (1991). "The Newsworthiness of International Terrorism", *Communication Research* 18(3), 333-354.
Weimann, G. and Winn, C. (1994). *The Theater of Terror: Mass Media and International Terrorism*, New York: Longman Publication.

Part 7

Society, State, and Mass Media

23

Protest, Television, Newspapers, and the Public: Who Influences Whom?

Sam Lehman-Wilzig

This study analyzes three related questions: To what extent does TV influence its audience, the newspapers, and the tactics of public pressure groups based on the existence and availability of TV in general? The study is based on a 52-day national TV strike in Israel in late 1987, with the following aspects investigated: the change in traffic accident and public protest frequency during the strike period; the change in number of articles and photos found in the newspapers; the coverage of all Israeli media regarding public protests over an extended period of time; and less quantitatively, the effect of public service announcements (PSAs) on traffic accident rates over the years. The findings indicate the following: PSAs seem to have an impact on traffic accidents; newspapers do change their product to a limited extent when TV is not available to the public; and most interestingly, despite the fact that TV does a far worse job of covering protest events, the public's erroneous perception of TV's importance has a significant impact on public pressure group behavior.

Introduction

To what extent does television influence its viewing audience? The debate rages on.[1] Does the existence of television as a competing medium to newspapers change the latter's approach to the news? The jury is still out.[2] Do public interest groups take into consideration the availability of specific media when they plan their public activity? No one seems to have even asked this question in the scholarly literature.[3]

The latter question is of particular interest, for when the whole topic of "political communication and persuasion" is brought up, almost inevitably it is addressed from the standpoint of "how the media and/or political elite persuade the public." That political communication is a two-way street may be grudgingly acknowledged, but the vast amount of scholarly energy expended in the field is almost wholly directed at the one-way avenue of top to bottom. The present study, then, is also designed to advance the cause of "bottom-to-top" political communication.

On the face of it, the three questions posed above are seemingly unrelated. As is shown here, however, they are interconnected. The opportunity for addressing all three issues simultaneously presented itself during October-November 1987 in Israel when the nation's only television station went on strike for a 52-day period. This afforded the opportunity for a rather unique "laboratory" test case, as there has been in the recent past no similar situation[4] in the democratic world where domestically transmitted television ceased entirely for so extended a period of time.[5]

In order to test the effects of such an electronic communications vacuum,[6] it was decided to focus on two readily quantifiable—but quite dissimilar—variables: traffic accidents and public protest events. Israeli television periodically mounts public service announcement campaigns (PSAs) for the prevention of traffic accidents; Israel leads the democratic world in per capita protest participation,[7] and its media do not hide the dimensions of such extraparliamentary activity.

Both phenomena, then, are widespread enough to exhibit possible sensitivity to media availability. However, the two are unalike: while traffic accidents are "accidental," their frequency may be directly influenced by the media; public protests are almost all "purposeful" (nonaccidental), albeit being influenced by the media in a much more indirect manner, as we shall see. In short, by looking at both, one may be able to see how television influences (or doesn't influence) the public in different ways: through direct, "stage-managed," and clear messages (PSAs); and/or through indirect, "reported," and ambiguous news items (protest).[8] Specific initial hypotheses were not generated; although this study's opening question has ample support in the literature for opposing conclusions, the second has hardly been addressed adequately, and the third question (especially regarding the influence on purposeful political behavior[9]) has not been addressed at all in the past. As the methodology makes clear, however, the study proceeded in a quite purposeful manner.

Methodology[10]

Regarding this study's first question, in order to uncover the number of protest events which occurred in Israel during the entire period under discussion, two daily newspapers—*Ha'aretz* (morning) and *Ma'ariv* (afternoon)—were surveyed over three 52-day periods: pre-TV strike (November 19, 1987-January 20, 1988). Data from another study (using *The Jerusalem Post* as primary source) were brought to bear for the same dates in the previous two years (1986-1987 and 1985-1986) for the purpose of comparison and control. The results are found in Table 1.

Table 1
Number of Protest Events and Traffic Accidents:[a]
Pre-, During, and Post-TV Strike[b]

Year	Pre-Strike	During Strike	Post-Strike
	......Protest Events		
1987[c]	40	11	24
1986[d]	26	35	26
1985[d]	30	41	16
	...... Traffic Accidents		
1987	2967	2172	2096
1986	2110	2114	2006
1985	1894	1900	1760

[a] As reported by the Israeli police.
[b] During each year, for the periods August 15-October 6, October 7-November 28, and November 29-January 20 of the following year.
[c] As reported by Ha'aretz and Ma'ariv together.
[d] As reported by The Jerusalem Post.

In order to ensure that the protest results were not an artifact of "extraordinary" events in Israel during the periods in any of these three years, the general Israeli news environment was looked at closely as well. Of the nine specific periods under review here, only one was marked by such an unusual news repertoire: the 1987-1988 post-TV strike period saw the commencement of the West Bank intifada (uprising). Whether this had any significant impact on the overall total of protests during this period is questionable. On the one hand, the intifada did generate six demonstrations (pro and con) during that period. On the other hand, during times of crisis the Israeli (as any other) population tends to become defensive and put off criticism of the government to another time, so that the intifada probably artificially lowered protest (on other issues) which would have occurred had the situation been "normal." In any case, even if the intifada did cause an additional six events overall to show up, this still does not change the basic thrust of the post-TV strike protest increase during the last period of 1987.

Table 1 also displays the number of traffic accidents occurring during these periods (for the TV strike year 1987-1988, and again the two preceding ones 1986-1987 and 1985-1986).[11] It affords some comparative perspective between a political consequence of the strike (protest events) and a possible social consequence (traffic accidents).[12]

Table 2
Number of Articles and Pictures in Five Dailies: Pre-, During, and Post-TV Strike

Newspaper[a]	Pre-Strike	During Strike	Post-Strike
Ha'aretz	75.0[b]	81.3	81.7
	15.6[c]	13.0	17.8
Davar	75.8	78.5	74.3
	17.8	12.6	19.6
Ma'ariv	55.8	62.0	63.6
	16.3	16.1	17.1
Yediot Ahronot	63.0	62.8	64.3
	19.8	15.5	17.0
Hadashot	110.0	114.0	110.1
	64.0	58.0	65.1

[a] For the first four newspapers listed here, only the news pages were counted, and not the editorial pages. Due to the nature of the fifth paper, all of its articles were counted, which accounts for its higher totals.
[b] Daily average number of articles during the week surveyed.
[c] Daily average number of pictures during the week surveyed.

Regarding question number two, during the same three periods one week each respectively was chosen,[13] and five daily newspapers were researched to reveal whether any change took place as a result of the TV strike in the number of articles and/or pictures which these papers presented.[14] This also served the purpose of indicating whether any increase or decline in newspaper protest coverage during the TV strike period was an artifact of a change in the overall number of items covered. The results are displayed in Table 2.

Table 3
Number of Reported Protest Events Per Medium[a]

Source	Number of Events
1. *Jerusalem Post*[b]	118
2. *Ma'ariv*[b]	91
3. *Al Ha'mishmar*[b]	59
4. *Davar*[b]	56
5. *Ha'tzofe*[b]	51
6. *Ha'aretz*[b]	41
7. *Yediot Ahronot*[b]	35
8. *Mabat La'hadashot*[c]	31
9. *Ha'modiah*[b]	30
10. *Hadashot*[b]	21
11. *Erev Tov Yisrael*[d]	17
Overall Total Reported: 420	
Overall Total Events:[e] 211	

[a] For period November 1, 1987-April 30, 1988.
[b] Newspaper.
[c] Television nightly news program.
[d] Israel Army Radio late afternoon hour-long news program.
[e] Discounting duplication of reported events by all the sources.

As to the study's third question, in addition to the three-period protest analysis mentioned above, a comprehensive six-month survey (November 1987 through April 1988) was undertaken comparing the results of protest coverage by all of Israel's media (see Table 3).[15] These included nine daily newspapers, the major news program, *Erev Tov Yisrael* (5-6 p.m.), on Israel's most popular radio channel, *Galei Zahal* (the army station), and the nightly *Mabat* news program on Israel's single television channel (state-supervised). The purpose here was to ascertain whether the electronic or print media did a better job of covering protest, compared to the perception on the part of the protest groups (as derived from Table 1) regarding which medium was more important and effective in getting their message across.

Findings and Discussion

Regarding the question of television's influence on the public, Table 1 presents some interesting—and in one respect, relatively unambiguous—evidence. First, whereas in 1986 and 1985 the level of traffic accidents held fairly consistent over the three periods (7% maximum change within each year), the television strike year exhibits a marked 27% decline between the pre-strike and strike periods (the previous two years showed almost no change whatsoever between these two periods). Were it not for a continued small decline in the 1987 post-strike period, one would have been able to state quite unequivocally that the elimination of television had a very significant impact on traffic accidents. As it is, the evidence of some relationship is strong although not absolute.

But what could explain such a connection? Two different possibilities present themselves: the influence of televised PSAs regarding how to prevent accidents, and the lessening of societal tensions as a result of elimination of television news.

The first explanation is the more readily provable. For starters, Israel's worst year for traffic accidents was 1978 (with 16,695). As a result, the government decided to spend money on regularly televised traffic PSAs, and the frequency of accidents began to decline over the ensuing decade on a steady basis.[16] When, in 1986, an increase in accidents became apparent, the authorities once again decided (in March 1987) on a higher frequency of PSAs, focusing primarily on the major problem of pedestrian accidents (which immediately began to decline in April-May of that year). From June to early October 1987 the redoubled PSAs returned to their traditional emphasis on proper driving behavior. The result? Whereas in each of the previous eleven years the July summer vacation accident rate was higher than in June, in 1987 the July totals were lower than the previous month! Yet the numbers here remained relatively high throughout the summer of 1987, with the PSA effect apparently only making itself sharply felt after the summer and Jewish holiday season ended—precisely when the TV strike began.

How convincing is this explanation? Both the long-term and short-term statistics seem to support the theory of television (PSA) influence quite strongly. However, paradoxically the very strength of the data raises a problematic question: if indeed PSAs do influence driving behavior, and the impact seems to be quite immediate, why wouldn't there be a regression in traffic accidents (to higher levels) once those PSAs went off the air (during the strike)? A possible answer, of course, is that a long-term PSA campaign may have a lasting cognitive effect for some time after the televised messages cease (the PSAs started up immediately after the strike's cessation, perhaps explaining the continued decline in 1987-1988 accidents). Such a theory (and the extent of such a lasting effect) must await further, more refined, research.

An alternative theory involves the issue of environmental stress. It is well known that increases in traffic accidents occur when the weather gets very hot. Might it not also be possible for a decrease in traffic accidents to occur as a result of less sociopolitical heat and stress?

Such a hypothesis is not at all far-fetched. At least one study in Israel,[17] and another comparing fourteen different countries (including Israel),[18] have shown a consistent relationship between "social stressors" and various forms of aggression. Concerning Israel specifically: "what is interesting to the observer are the fluctuations and historical changes in levels of aggression, and the correlations between aggression and social conditions."[19] Traffic accidents can certainly be viewed as a stress-related social phenomenon, along with homicide, rape, suicide, etc.

What, however, does the TV strike have to do with a reduction in social tension? The Israeli press was replete with articles (during the TV strike) reporting on a citizenry (and politicians) thrilled to be given a break from the steady drumbeat of televised "bad news."[20] Notwithstanding the general animosity felt by large parts of the Israeli public (and press!) toward Israeli TV, the possibility exists that indeed a respite from nightly politically charged pictures and reports had some influence in ameliorating the (usually high) general tension level of Israeli society, with a subsidiary positive impact on traffic accidents (among other social phenomena).

It must be noted, of course, that the blacking out of the TV screen was not in and of itself the cause for any objective reduction in real sociopolitical stressful factors. Rather, television acts as an important facilitator of social stress by transmitting the stressfulness of sociopolitical reality. If the above hypothesis is correct, though, the implications are quite important, not only for society, but also for researchers who wish to understand such stress-aggression correlations. It is not enough to look only at the "stressor" independent variables (e.g., national unemployment) and their impact on the dependent "social stress indicators" (e.g., civil aggression), but also at the intervening variable in this relationship—the media! It is not only the objective reality which counts; sometimes the subjective perception of that reality on the part of the public, as a result of the way that reality is presented or not presented, is the determining factor in the level of social aggression and behavior.

From the standpoint of this study's findings, the major problem with this theory is that (as noted above) the Palestinian Arab intifada commenced almost immediately after the Israeli TV strike ended. The intifada undoubtedly raised the political temperature during this post-TV strike period, but the traffic accident rate continued to decline! Thus, despite the inherent logic of the social stress theory, some proof of its effect in areas other than traffic accidents, and the fact that the Israeli public itself seemed to support the theory during the TV strike, the evidence is not conclusive. Once again, further research is necessary before any definitive statement may be made along these lines.

When we turn to the protest event data in Table 1, the evidence becomes far more substantial. Whereas in 1985 and 1986 the protest frequency numbers were initially positively curvilinear over these three periods (with a moderate average slope), in 1987 the three strike-related periods exhibited a sharply sloped, initially negative curvilinear evolution. Simply put, the number of protest events plummeted dramatically during the TV strike period (to by far its lowest level among all the nine periods surveyed here), and then rose almost equally as sharply in the post-strike period—a very strong indication that the TV strike affected Israeli protest negatively, and that the existence of television in Israel is a strong catalyst of public protest.

This conclusion is given added support when one looks at the historical evolution of Israeli protest frequency relative to the introduction of television into Israeli society.[21] Before television began in Israel in 1968, public protest events averaged about 45 annually in the preceding two decades; after 1968 the annual average skyrocketed to about 150![22] This relationship is not unique to Israel. As Etzioni noted regarding the American case: "The number of demonstrations in the pre-mass television decade (1948-1958) was much smaller than the first television decade (1958-1968).... [T]elevision has played a key role in the evolution of this particular form of political expression and in the increasing frequency with which this form is applied."[23]

Before we discuss the possible reasons for the influence or connection between television and protest, let us turn to Table 2, which has some bearing on that issue as well as on question number two: does the existence of television have a bearing on the way newspapers present the news? Here too the evidence is quite clear, albeit not totally unambiguous.

In four of the five newspapers surveyed, an increase in the number of articles was registered during the TV strike period compared to its predecessor (in the fifth, virtually no change occurred)—suggesting that the newspapers attempted to make up for the television news void. This trend is somewhat blurred, however, by the fact that in only two newspapers do we find a post-TV strike reduction in the number of articles printed (*Davar* and *Hadashot*). The evidence is almost completely unidirectional regarding newspaper pictures: in four of the five papers the number of photos declined for the strike period (in one it stayed the same), while in all five papers the number of photos increased after the TV strike ended. A reduction in the number of newspaper photos during a television strike may seem illogical at first, but given a situation in which the newspaper will not, or cannot, increase its overall size, the number of photos and articles become involved in a zero sum game. In this case, it is obvious that the written word won out over the visual presentation.[24]

In short, based on these data one can say with some assurance that newspapers are somewhat sensitive to changes in inter-media competition, and will adjust their product accordingly to a certain limited extent.[25]

Might not this be the case regarding other social actors on the national scene? Is it not possible that protest groups, for example, might also adapt their activity to the exigencies of the communications environment? Here we return to the possible explanations behind the results shown in Table 1.

Why does public protest dramatically decline during the TV strike period? The first possible answer is the one broached earlier: social stress. If television news (Israeli, at least) gets people angry, frustrated, etc., they might be less likely to take to the streets when that specific negative stimulus is eliminated. The problem with such a theory is that in the Israeli context at least, there are very few "spontaneous" demonstrations or riots (5-10% at most). Most of the public extraparliamentary activity is preplanned, group-initiated (although not necessarily by a fully institutionalized interest group), and these are far less likely to be spontaneously and psychologically affected by television-induced angst (unlike, perhaps, car drivers).

Second, public protest could also possibly be a function of the amount of political information received by the public: the more information, the greater the likelihood that "negative" stimuli (i.e., against one's specific interests) will be received by sundry public groups, which in turn might move them to demonstrate. But this theory has even greater problems with which to contend.

To begin with, as shown in Table 2, the nation's press attempted to make up for the informational shortfall during the TV strike period. From a pure (and overly simplistic) quantitative standpoint, all the five papers together managed to add on average a total of nineteen items of their pre-strike totals—far more than the number of television news items appearing on any single half-hour news program. More germane is the fact that virtually all the television news reports are on important news events which are normally covered by all the newspapers, so that qualitatively it would be very difficult to argue that television news adds much to the general informational fare. This is especially so when one considers that it is the protest group which initiates almost all the protest, and one would have to assume that the collective leadership hardly loses any important information when the TV set is black, given the multiplicity of newspaper (and other) sources from which such an elite can draw its information.

The above two theories are characterized by an assumption that the social group is acted upon by the media. This, of course, may be far from the case, or certainly not the entire picture. Equally as plausible a theory is that such groups are sensitive to and are able to exploit and adapt to the availability of different media.

The extremely marked reduction in the number of protest events that took place during the TV strike (a 73% decline), and subsequent sharp increase (118%), indicate that a conscious process of media selection was at work here. The tendency of protest groups to seek television exposure especially is a natural one. As Wolfsfeld found in his field research of Israeli protest groups: "Television, and by association, its reporters were seen by all of the [protest] participants as the most powerful of all the media."[26]

Why is there such a perception? Demonstrations are action-packed, emotion-laden events, and the visual dimension of television most completely reflects and carries that component to the audience. Newspapers are a "cold" medium designed to address the rational and cognitive needs of their audience, and as such, the nonspecificity of the protest message is not ideally suited for print transmittal, which emphasizes the details and reasoned rationale behind the events reported upon by the newspapers.

The Israeli historical relationship between television and protest, as outlined above, lends further credence to this theory of social group adaptation to media availability. It would be stretching the imagination quite a bit to argue that television news per se caused Israeli social tension to skyrocket to the extent that public protest more than trebled as a result. It would be even more outlandish to argue that television news added so much information to the general news pool as to cause such a huge rise in protest due to increased "negative" news stimuli. But it is not difficult at all to accept the possibility that many citizens who heretofore were inactive (or who felt that getting their message across through the newspapers was not very effective) might have begun to get involved in extraparliamentary activity due to the advent of this new and potent visual medium.

The remaining question, however, is how correct this perception of television influence may in fact be. The results shown in Table 3 suggest that such groups may be making quite a big mistake.

Israeli TV's coverage of protest events was quite poor compared with its print counterparts (it was somewhat better than the Israel Army Radio).[27] It covered more protest events than just two newspapers,[28] and less than the reportage of seven others—falling significantly short of three papers, seriously short of another (*Ma'ariv*), and extremely short of one more (*The Jerusalem Post*). Thus, even from the perspective of television's strength, agenda-setting, i.e., getting the specific issue to be aired in front of the public, albeit not necessarily the details of that protest message, Israeli TV fails the test. To be sure, it may very well be that those protest events which are covered by television do succeed in getting their (gross) message across in a "stronger" fashion than if merely the papers had covered them. On the one hand, from the pre-protest tactical decision standpoint (to protest or not to protest based on the availability of only the newspapers), a decision to wait until the TV strike was over was probably not a correct one. As Table 3 indicates, only 31 of the 211 actual protest events were covered by Israeli TV in the six-month period surveyed, a very low 1:7 ratio![29]

Nor does the erroneousness of the protest groups' seeming decision not to protest during the TV strike period end with the problem of limited television coverage. Another consideration is the audience being addressed by the protest. Two major audience possibilities present themselves here: either those with political influence, or potential future protesters who might be convinced to join the extraparliamentary battle. In both cases, the relevant audience is comprised mainly of the sociopolitical elite in Israeli society,[30] those who are most prone to receive the brunt of their political information from newspapers.[31] Thus, when one takes into account the kind of audience which the protesters are trying to reach, reliance on television is precisely the wrong approach to take.

Conclusions

At least two ironic conclusions emerge from the findings. First, television probably does a much worse job of reporting on protest events than the printed press.[32] Nevertheless, this fact has seemingly not permeated the social consciousness of the nation, and thus the protest groups' perception of television superiority leads them to give TV a backhanded "influence" on the existence of protest events. Put another way, television news does influence protest, but indirectly—it is the protest initiative of the groups based on the existence of television (and incorrect notion of its greater coverage) which lends a sort of pseudo-influence to television on public protest. This does not mean that the influence is any less "real;" it does suggest that it is far from direct, i.e., not based on unconscious effects emanating from television on the audience groups, but rather the latter's belief that such an effect exists. In a sense, one can say that at least here (from the perspective of the social groups), it is the medium which is more important than the message.

A second, and related, ironic conclusion has to do with those social groups themselves. As we say, they definitely seem to be rationally deciding on the timing of their political pressure relative to the availability of the television medium. However, that decision may not in fact be a rationally correct one, as the chances of their appearing on the nightly news is quite low (while the television audience may not be the one which they are most interested in addressing). In short, it is not that such pressure groups are not smart; rather, they may be too smart for their own good (or at least not as smart as they think).

In the final analysis, then, can it be said from the data here that television has a significant impact on public political behavior? Robinson and Levy are correct when they ask and reply: "how do people learn about the world 'out there'? The mythic answer—from television news."[33] However, their conclusion that it is really the newspapers which provide most of the news (at higher levels of comprehension) to the public, misses part of the point. For it is precisely the myth of television impact and power which may indirectly give television its greater influence on the public which continues to believe in that myth. The bottom line, therefore, is that while the press indeed does a better job of reporting on events (Table 3), it is still television which not only significantly influences public behavior (Table 1), but to a limited extent even influences the press itself (Table 2).

Notes

1. The literature on this topic is vast. Regarding television news specifically, see, for example, John P. Robinson and Mark R. Levy, *The Main Source: Learning From Television News* (Beverly Hills: Sage Publications, 1986), which concludes that: "Television news should not be considered the public's main source of news" (p. 232). An even more radical conclusion is reached by Peter Clarke and Eric Fredin, "Newspapers, Television and Political Reasoning," *Public Opinion Quarterly* 42(2) (Summer 1978): 148: "Television may actually exert an inhibiting effect on knowing about politics." A contrary assessment is offered by Shanto Iyengar, Mark D. Peters, and Donald R. Kinder, in their "Experimental Demonstrations of the 'Not-So-Minimal' Consequences of Television News Programs," *American Political Science Review* 76(4) (December 1982): 855: "We have shown that by ignoring some problems and attending to others, television news programs profoundly affect which problems viewers take seriously." One must note that not all the scholarly disagreements on this issue are in fact "contradictory," as some researchers are looking for influence on the public's opinions, while others (as Iyengar et al.) study television's agenda-setting role.
2. See Stephen Lacy, "Effect of Intermedia Competition on Daily Newspaper Content," *Journalism Quarterly* 65(1) (Spring 1988): 95-99. His conclusion (p. 99): The presence of television, radio and cable in a market appears to have little, if any, impact on the allocation of resources by newspaper management." However, this begs some of the more important questions; e.g., has television influenced the press from the standpoint of the way the latter's product is presented? Are there more pictures in the papers in the television age? Shorter articles? Greater use of color graphics? In short, do newspapers attempt to at least package their product differently? Impressionistically, such successfully upstart papers as *USA Today* strongly suggest that this might indeed be the case. This element is studied below in this article.
3. This is not to say that no one has looked into the interrelationship between public pressure groups and the various media. On the operational level of give-and-take in the field, a worthwhile contribution is Gadi Wolfsfeld, "Symbiosis of Press and Protest: An Exchange Analysis", *Journalism Quarterly* 61(3) (Autumn 1984): 550-55; 742. However, his research does not touch upon the strategic question of whether to demonstrate at all, given the media coverage available. Indeed, an indication of how little the whole question of mass media/political conflict has been researched is the fact that from its inception, *Journalism Quarterly,* the most senior communications journal in the field, has published a mere seven articles and/or research notes, over a period of 65 years, on the connection between the mass media and demonstrations, riots, etc., in all of the subject's manifestations.
4. A mirror-image analysis of the one presented here is K.E. Meyer, "Hut of Darkness: Television Viewing During the New York Newspaper Strike," *Saturday Review* Nov. 11, 1978, p. 56.
5. What makes the choice of Israel all the more serendipitous is the fact that polls conducted over the years show that from 75 to 90% of Israeli adults watch the nightly news broadcast at least several times a week—a very high level of news viewership. See, for example, Wolfsfeld, "Symbiosis of Press and Protest," p. 553, where he reports that "77% of the population report watching the news 'almost every night'." By way of comparison, the American totals are much lower. See Lawrence W. Lichty, "Video Versus Print," *The Wilson Quarterly* 6 (1982): 49-57; he found that less than a third of all adult Americans watch television news daily. In a more refined but geographically limited study, John P. Robinson con-

cluded that in three Ohio towns surveyed in depth, approximately 50% watch television news daily: "Daily News Habits of the American Public," *ANPA News Research Report,* No. 15 (1978).

6. All of Israel's radio stations were struck as well, except for the army radio station (*Galei Zahal*). Israelis continued to receive foreign TV, such as from Jordan and the Middle East (American Christian) channels, but, as explained below, for our purposes these were irrelevant.
7. See my "The Israeli Protester," *The Jerusalem Quarterly* No. 26 (Winter 1983): 127-38 for substantiation of Israel's leading place regarding extraparliamentary behavior.
8. Harvey Molotch and Marilyn Lester, "News as Purposive Behavior: On the Strategic Use of Routine Events, Accidents, and Scandals", *American Sociological Review* 39(1) (Feb. 1974): 101-12. Among other things, the authors differentiate between the media function of "promoting" news and "assembling" news (pp. 104-5).
9. The effects of PSAs on social behavior has at least been touched upon: Jerry R. Lynn, "Effects of Persuasive Appeals in Public Service Advertising," *Journalism Quarterly* 51(4) (Winter 1974): 622-30.
10. For an extended elaboration of the methodology regarding the scoring of protest events and a discussion of the problems inherent in such an approach, see my *Stiff-Necked People, Bottle-Necked System: The Evolution and Roots of Israeli Public Protest, 1949-1986* (Bloomington: Indiana University Press, 1990), chaps. 2 and 4. Briefly, all protest events in which ten or more adult Israeli (not Palestinian) citizens participated, were scored, including political and hunger strikes (but not purely economic strike action).
11. All the data regarding traffic accidents were graciously given to me by central headquarters of the Israeli police. My thanks for their help.
12. My thanks to Gavriel Yehuda for researching and providing both the protest and traffic accident data. This was accomplished under my supervision in a Master's eminar.
13. The weeks were: Sept. 1-7, Nov. 3-9, and Dec. 15-21.
14. This too was done by Gavriel Yehuda.
15. This survey was conducted under my supervision by a special undergraduate seminar class of students from Israel's Ministry of Defense. My thanks to them for the difficult assignment carried out quite punctiliously, and especially to Zvi Granot for the difficult task of organizing and assessing the data. It should be noted that these six months covered most of the strike period and all of the post-strike period. There was little advance warning of the TV strike, so that no such survey was conducted in the pre-strike period; as the survey included television and radio, it was impossible to score these media retroactively for that earlier period. Nevertheless, there is little doubt that the results here are representative of Israeli media coverage in general (although see note c in Table 3).
16. To be sure, the government also began to increase its capital investment in transportation infrastructure, so that the PSAs were not the sole factor here.
17. Simha F. Landau and Benjamin Beit-Hallahmi, "Aggression in Israel: A Psycho-Historical Perspective," in *Aggression in Global Perspective,* ed. A. Goldstein and M. Segall (New York: Pergamon Press, 1983), pp. 261-86.
18. Simha F. Landau, "Trends in Violence and Aggression: A Cross-Cultural Analysis," *International Journal of Comparative Sociology* 25(3-4) (1984): 133-58.
19. Landau and Beit-Hallahmi, "Aggression in Israel," p. 284.
20. See, for example, Menachem Shalev, "Politicians unruffled by quiet on airwaves," *The Jerusalem Post,* Friday, October 30, 1987, p. 7: "'The whole pace of life in the

country has slowed because of the strike,' Pazner [PM Shamir's media adviser] says, 'and it might not be such a bad thing. I think the public is generally far less nervous and agitated because it is not attached 24 hours a day to the newscasts'." To be sure, Pazner was not a disinterested party here, but his comment did reflect a widespread feeling at the time.

21. For a more elaborate analysis of this general point, see Lehman-Wilzig, *Stiff-Necked People,* chaps. 3 and 8. Many of the same points are made in my "Conflict as Communication: Public Protest in Israel, 1950-1982," in *Comparative Jewish Politics: Conflict and Consensus in Jewish Political Life,* vol. 2, ed. S.A. Cohen and E. Don-Yehiya (Ramat Gan: Bar-Ilan University Press, 1986), pp. 139-40.
22. The turning point actually occurred in 1971, suggesting some lag between television's introduction and its impact on the extra-parliamentary arena. See *Stiff-Necked People,* p. 107, for the possible reasons behind this time lag.
23. Amitai Etzioni, *Demonstration Democracy* (New York: Gordon & Breach, 1979), pp. 12-13.
24. The clearest indication that this is indeed what occurred can be derived from the *Hadashot* numbers. Not only are the article/photo results here a mirror image of each other, but this is the "television newspaper" par excellence on the Israeli scene—a newspaper (à la *USA Today*) which was established in the early 1980s for the television generation. Consequently, its editorial staff would be most sensitive to any change in the television environment.
25. This is not to say that the press can't influence television to a certain extent. See James D. Halloran, Philip Elliot, and Graham Murdoch, *Demonstrations and Communication: A Case Study* (Harmondsworth, England: Penguin Books Ltd., 1970), in which they note: "in one sense television appears to be dependent on the press.... The morning newspapers are an important source of information about the likely stories of the day" (p. 305). This is true to some extent in Israel as well. Israel Peleg noted through personal observation of the work within Israel TV's newsroom: "The suggestions for that day's line-up...are based on the reporters' sources, their [the reporters'] following national events, and also from reading the morning papers and listening to the morning news broadcasts on radio." The author, however, did not try to find out the relative quantitative proportion of each of these sources. *Objectivity in Television News* (Doctoral diss., Department of Political Science, Hebrew University, Jerusalem, November 1981), p. 116 (my translation from the Hebrew). Here is virtually virgin research territory for future quantitative work.
26. Wolfsfeld, "Symbiosis of Press and Protest," p. 553.
27. While not strictly comparable, Peleg's work, *Objectivity in Television News,* pp. 258 and 271 had a different finding. Surveying the coverage of Israeli "labor relations strife" over a 36-day period, he found that television had an item 75% of the time, as did 75% of all the four newspapers he surveyed taken together (unfortunately, he covered only the front page of the papers). Radio scored less well—in only 53% of the surveyed news programs was there such a report.
28. Perhaps three, if note c of Table 3 is taken into account.
29. Their decision was certainly not based on any thought that more Israelis watch the nightly news than read a daily paper. Israeli polls rather consistently show that about 85% read a newspaper "regularly," about two-thirds read them every day, with about half of the latter reading two papers or more daily! See Elihu Katz and Michael Gurevitch, *The Secularization of Leisure: Culture and Communication in Israel* (Cambridge, Mass.: Harvard University Press, 1976), p. 183. These numbers have hardly changed since Israeli television's inception, lending support to the findings of William A. Belson, "The Effects of Television on the Reading and the

Buying of Newspapers and Magazines," *Journalism Quarterly* 25(3) (Fall 1961): 366-81.

30. For a discussion of this seemingly "anomalous" fact regarding Israeli protest participants, see my "The Israeli Protester," *The Jerusalem Quarterly* No. 26 (Winter 1983): 127-38.
31. Of course, this is the standard phenomenon elsewhere as well. See, for example, M. Mark Miller, Michael W. Singletary, and Shu-Ling Chen, "The Roper Question and Television vs. Newspapers as Sources of News," *Journalism Quarterly* 65(1) (Spring 1988): 12-19. Among other things, they show how "preference for television is associated with lower levels of local/state public affairs knowledge" (p. 19). Somewhat the same conclusion was reached twenty years ago by Serena Wade and Wilbur Schramm, "The Mass Media As Sources of Public Affairs, Science, and Health Knowledge," *Public Opinion Quarterly* 33(2) (Summer 1969): 197-209. They found that the lower classes were more likely to use television as their primary source of political (campaign) information.
32. A discussion of why this is so would lead us too far afield, but at least one possibility can be advanced. In a half-hour televised news show, a maximum of 15 news items can be broadcast (assuming about 120 seconds per item). The average newspaper (at least in Israel) carries about five times that many items. Protests, then, have much greater difficulty in getting a spot on the TV news, even taking into account their "natural" advantages as mentioned above (e.g., action-packed, etc.).
33. Robinson and Levy, *The Main Source,* p. 7.

24

Inherent Contradictions of Democracy: Illustrations from National Broadcasting Corporations

Eva Etzioni-Halevy

The purpose of this paper is to map out and illustrate some of the major contradictions inherent in the manner in which power is exercised (and conceived of) in a democracy. The main argument is that the confrontation of the democratically elected elite's power by the power of other elites is both a danger and a necessity for democracy and that this internal contradiction finds expression in ambivalent, self-contradictory, and controversial "rules of the game" of the democratic process. This argument is supported by illustrations from the area of bureaucracy and in particular from one type of semigovernmental bureaucracy, national broadcasting corporations and their elites, in four western-style democracies.

Framework for the Analysis

The argument is presented in the framework of a democratic-elitist (or demo-elitist) perspective, a well-established but recently neglected perspective in political science and political sociology. Since theories of participatory democracy are recognized as basically normative or prescriptive,[1] and since pluralist theories of democracy which are both prescriptive and descriptive have been severely criticized on both counts[2] and have fallen out of grace,[3] three paradigms on the exercise of power in modern society have recently been competing for center-stage: Marxist theories,[4] elite theories,[5] combinations thereof,[6] and corporatist theories.[7]

These theories have much to recommend them in that they all penetrate behind the scenes and demonstrate that even in a democracy the facade of pluralism really conceals a much more concerted power structure, that on matters that really count power is concentrated in the hands of small, interlocking groups of power holders. But they have a common deficiency: mostly they have little to say on what is *distinctive* in the manner in which power is exercised in a democracy.

The Marxist view of democracy suffers from excessive vacillation. On the one hand, power is shown to be concentrated in the hands of the "ruling class," which always shapes policy to serve its own interests, and democracy is conclusively shown to afford little (if any) choice, discretion or power to the public. On the other hand, democracy is praised as being preferable to practically all other past or present political structures and as being capable of preventing the atrocities of fascism, Stalinism and similar regimes.[8] One may well ask, if democracy is so innocuous, why is it so desirable? If democracy affords no real power to the public in curbing the power of rulers, how is it so effective in preventing atrocities common in many nondemocratic regimes?

Marxist theory supplies no answer to these questions, for, while it concedes that democracy is preferable to all other regimes, it does not explain why.

Elite theory and corporatism, too, have little to contribute to the analysis of democracy. Elitists correctly point out that power holders, political elites, are universal in complex societies and that democracy is not exempt from their rule any more than other regimes are. They also offer sophisticated analyses of power elite structures. Corporatists, for their part, point to the close interaction between governmental elites and corporate and trade union elites in the making of economic policy. They correctly emphasize that such corporatist arrangements frequently short-circuit or bypass democratic institutions and procedures (although they do not supplant them). But they, too, fail to bring into relief the distinctive features of the exercise of power in a democracy.

This is precisely the topic on which the demo-elitist perspective is focused. This paradigm, as presented here, is closer to elite theory than it is to Marxist class theory, not because it holds that classes or economic inequalities are unimportant, but rather because it holds that in the *political* arena (with which this perspective is concerned) elites (including economic elites) are the main power holders. Hence, class influence on politics can best be conceptualized in terms of elite rather than class theory. Nonetheless, it is not a pure elite theory in that it attempts to integrate elements of elite theory with elements of democratic theory. In this, it follows in the footsteps of Weber,[9] Mosca,[10] Schumpeter,[11] and Aron.[12]

The democratic-elitist perspective in some of its earlier versions has been dismissed by critics as elitist in the prescriptive sense, that is, as favoring the rule of elites, hence as conservative.[13] It has also been accused of denigrating popular participation in politics as dysfunctional for democracy.

And, in fact, some scholars who in previous decades have been classified as democratic-elitists (such as Berelson, Kornhauser, and Milbrath), have argued that successful democracy depends on widespread public apathy, that if the "masses" were to participate in politics in large numbers, peaceful competition among elites—and thus democracy—would be apt to break down.[14]

But the demo-elitist perspective in its present version makes no such claims. It does not denigrate popular participation in the political arena but merely claims that any form of popular political participation—and any form of organization—is apt to generate people who are especially active and influential, that is, it is apt to germinate its own elites. And even the centerpiece of modern western democracy, the electoral principle, implies elites that can be elected or, conversely, voted out of office.

In view of this, the basic contentions of the demo-elitist perspective in its present version are as follows. There is no inconsistency between democracy and elitism: elites are as necessary for democracy as they are for all political regimes. But while elites are to be found in all political regimes, the manner in which elites vie for and acquire power and the manner in which they exercise their power over the public, as well as the extent of that power, are of the first order of importance.

It is in this that democracy is distinct from other regimes.

The distinctiveness of democracy lies in the fact that in it the exercise of power is beset by major contradictions. These contradictions, in turn, grow out of the limitations on elite power, which are also peculiar to democracy. Following Schumpeter, Lipset, and Dahl, the argument here defines democracy as an institutional arrangement whereby two or more persons or groups participate in the contest for power (or for elite positions) on the strength of their past and/or their advocated policies and/or their projected images, and whereby they acquire and exercise such power on the basis of free, regular elections by all adults, whose votes have equal value, and where there is freedom of information, of speech, of organization and of participation in the contest for power.[15]

Several observers of the Marxist and elitist persuasions have argued that elections have mainly symbolic value, affording the public no real choice of policies and conferring no real power on it.[16] In contrast, I side with the theorists of democracy who argue that elections do offer the public a choice—albeit frequently a limited choice—of elites and policies and that this is, to say the least, much more than no choice at all. In addition, I side with those who argue that, while democracy ensures neither economic nor political equality for all, its procedures open avenues for political participation and the widening of policy choices and institutionalize the struggle for economic equality more than other known political regimes. Finally, I would side with those who argue that democracy is distinctive because its procedures are more effective than those of other known political regimes in limiting the ruling political elite's power.

Democratic procedures restrain this elite's power by confronting it with an institutionalized, constantly recurring threat of replacement, which forces it to take account of anticipated public reaction to its actions. Democratic procedures also restrain the incumbent elite's power by confronting it with public scrutiny of its actions, with constant exposure and demystification of its attempts to manipulate the public, which, in turn, has a direct impact on the threat of replacement with which the elite is periodically faced. Finally, the value of the democratic procedures (as per the above definition) lies in limiting the political elite's power by confronting it in an institutionalized manner with the power of other elites such as the opposition, elites of major interest groups, and bureaucratic and judicial elites.

There is a constant temptation for elite groups or persons to enhance their power by countervening or circumventing these procedures. But it is also in the interest of elite groups or persons to enforce the procedures on each other or to serve as mutual watchdogs, and thereby to limit each other's, but ultimately also their own, power. All this cannot bring about an elite-less society. But it can do much to make life in an elite-ruled society more tolerable.

The Inherent Contradictions of Democracy

These procedures, however, have an additional result. Because of them democracy is beset by a dilemma, a paradox or an internal contradiction, which renders it a rather precarious and fragile type of institutional structure. This inherent contradiction or dilemma stems from the relationship between the principle of the acquisition of power on the basis of free elections by the entire population and the principle of freedom of organization, both of which are part of the above definition of democracy. Without freedom of organization, free elections and civil liberties would not be possible. Where there is freedom of organization, and where various sectors of the public have different interests, actual interest groups, associations, and organizations are apt to arise. As Dahl put it, "Because organizations are possible and advantageous, they are also inevitable."[17] But as Dahl has also emphasized, such organizations may be used to promote economic and political inequality or even to destroy democracy.

From a demo-elitist perspective it may be added that independent organizations are bound to give rise to their own independent elites, and the most powerful among these then counterbalance the power of the ruling political elite. As noted, this is one of the most basic devices whereby democracy curbs the power of the ruling elite. The absence or weakness of such countervailing elites would thus obviate the very essence of democracy.

However, the principle of freedom of organization—and the power of countervailing elites it generates—also contradicts the principle of the acquisition of power on the basis of election by the entire population.

For while the incumbent political elite acquires its power on the basis of such elections, the elites that countervail its power usually do not. They usually acquire their power in a non- or ademocratic manner (for example by appointment) or are elected by only a part of the population. Therefore, this power, by definition, obviates the essence of democracy. The power of countervailing elites is thus part of the very essence of democracy.

But, by the same token, it is also one of the major threats to democracy. It is one of democracy's major assets, but also one of its major defects.

This inherent contradiction is manifested in several areas of sociopolitical life. One such manifestation stems from the power of capitalist corporations and their conglomerations and elites and, to a somewhat lesser extent, from the power of trade unions and their elites in western-style democracies.

It has frequently been asked how the power of capitalists squares with the principles of democracy. The plain answer, of course, is that it does not, as Marxists have so convincingly pointed out. Other observers, however, have made the equally valid point that the most likely alternative to private enterprise capitalism, a state-controlled economy (sometimes called state capitalism), creates a more concerted, more powerful ruling class, that where the state (or the ruling elite) is the sole employer of all, only the most daring would object to its policies.[18] Effective political opposition would thus be obviated by the system, and an independent elite, countervailing the power of the ruling elite, would be unlikely to arise. A state-controlled economy thus certainly does not square with democracy.

The other alternative to capitalism, that of worker-owned enterprises (or cooperatives), is apt to give rise to organizations which (as elite theorists have pointed out) must necessarily give rise to their own elites. In fact, wherever cooperatives have been formed, this has occurred already.[19] Such elites, though not elected by the entire population, would countervail the power of the democratically elected political elite. They would thereby pose the same dilemma for democracy that capitalist elites do today: they would be both a necessity for and a threat to democracy. Democracy is thus beset by the contradiction of depending for its existence on nonstate economic enterprise whose elites also jeopardize its existence.

The power of trade union leadership, occasionally (though not always) elected by its own membership but never by the public at large, poses a similar problem for democracy. By entering into tripartite agreements with the leadership of capitalist and trade union conglomerations, the political elite can obviate at least the spirit (if not the letter) of democracy, and this problem has been well analyzed by corporatist theorists.

But, by the same token, independent trade unions are also necessary for democracy, for the denial of trade unions' (as of other organizations') independence and power and their subjugation by the state and its ruling elite are one of the hallmarks of authoritarian and totalitarian regimes, which is another way of saying that independent, powerful trade unions are an important element of democracy.

Here too, then, democracy is faced with the internal contradiction of requiring for its very existence the types of organizations and leaders whose power then threatens its proper procedures.

Contradictions of Democracy and the Rules of Bureaucracy

The same dilemma is also exemplified by the role of government bureaucracy in a democratic regime. Bureaucracy has been widely (and justly) accused of jeopardizing democracy because its nonelected elite frequently amasses great independent power as against that of elected politicians. Such accusations have been made by adherents of the "technocratic" school of thought,[20] by several Marxist scholars[21] and by others.[22] However, as Mosca and Schumpeter—but few others—have correctly perceived, a powerful, independent bureaucracy is also necessary for the safeguarding of proper democratic procedures, for the top of an independent, powerful bureaucracy is another elite which countervails and thus curbs the power of the ruling political elite.

In previous analyses I have shown that wherever the bureaucratic elite has lacked such independent power and has buckled down to the political elite—wherever bureaucracy has thus become party-politicized—it has been used by the political elite as an instrument of (political) manipulation and corruption.[23] In these cases, it has been utilized for the handing out of material benefits in return for political support, a type of manipulation which at times has greatly biased or obviated the democratic process.

Only where bureaucracy has gained independent power as against that of politicians and has thus resisted the encroachment of party politics, has this electoral manipulation been eliminated and proper democratic procedures come into force. I have, therefore, presented the thesis that bureaucracy poses a practically insoluble dilemma for democracy. A powerful, independent bureaucracy poses a threat to democracy and yet is also a necessity for its proper functioning.

Since Tocqueville, it has been taken for granted by scholars of a variety of schools of thought that, while democracy is based on controversy and conflict, it is based on an *institutionalization* of such conflict, which, in turn, presupposes widespread consensus over the "rules of the game" whereby the conflict is waged.

Further, it has been widely argued that such consensus over the rules of democracy is well entrenched especially among elites. Occasionally, empirical research has shown that in several areas this is not the case, that while consensus over rules is more widespread among elites than it is among the public, nevertheless there are several areas where such consensus is absent even among elites.[24] Nonetheless, the idea that consensus over the rules of democracy prevails among elites is still one of the stocks-in-trade of a variety of sociopolitical analyses. Moreover, in the wake of Weber's model of bureaucracy, it has long been taken for granted that bureaucratic behavior, too, is governed by clear and generally accepted rules.[25]

But if, as has been argued before, democracy is faced with basic inherent contradictions and dilemma, then this must necessarily find expression in contradictions, dilemmas, and controversies with respect to the rules of democracy. Specifically, if the role of bureaucracy in a democracy is beset by inherent contradictions and dilemmas, then the rules governing bureaucratic behavior, especially rules governing the relations between bureaucrats and politicians, must be controversial, ambivalent and even self-contradictory. And, indeed, democratic "rules of the game" put bureaucracy in a double bind: it is expected to be under the control of elected politicians and yet exempt from such control, politically responsive and politically independent at one and the same time, which is another way of saying that bureaucracy is expected to be simultaneously politicized and nonpoliticized (or politically neutral).

While this self-contradiction, lack of clarity and controversy in the role of definition of bureaucracy have not been greatly emphasized in the work of theorists and researchers, they emerge quite clearly in reports of official inquiries into bureaucracy. For instance, in the Report of the Fulton Committee of Inquiry into the British Civil Service, the following statements can be found.

> Because the solutions to complex problems need long preparation, the service must be far-sighted; from its accumulated knowledge and experience it must show initiative in working out what are the needs of the future and how they might be met. A special responsibility now rests upon the Civil Service because one Parliament or even one Government often cannot see the process through. At the same time, the Civil Service works under political direction....[It] has also to be flexible enough to serve governments of any political complexion.[26]

In other words, the public service must itself work out what the needs of the future are and yet must serve different governments which may have totally opposing conceptions of what such needs might be.

A similar dilemma regarding the role definition of bureaucracy emerges from the Coombs Royal Commission of Enquiry on the Australian Government Administration, in whose report the following pronouncement appears.

> There remains the vexed question of whether there is or should be an "ethos"...among officials...This issue arose in the Commission's work most frequently in relation to the claim that officials should be "neutral" on political issues. On the one hand, such neutrality was seen as basic to the capacity of the administration to serve equally well governments of different political persuasion. On the other hand, it was argued that a claim to be neutral frequently was either false or reflected merely a singular lack of self-awareness.[27]

Ostensibly, countries such as the United States and France have solved the problem by differentiating between political executives (in the U.S., political appointees; in France, members of ministerial cabinets) and career bureaucrats. Thus, in the United States, the Report of the Hoover Commission on the Organization of the Civil Service states:

> In the National Government, it is the function of political executives to represent within the administration the policy purposes of the President...to provide leadership in developing national policy...in short to take responsibility for governing....It is the function of the complementary group of career administrators in the National Government, who must serve whatever responsible officials are in office...to keep the government operating as effectively as possible at all times.

Apparently, things do not work out quite as smoothly in practice, for the commission then goes on to state:

Despite the need for clarity, the functions of political executives and career administrators have become excessively confused in practice. The confusion is not deliberate, but is rather the inadvertent consequence of a combination of circumstances ... [among other things] the difficulty of finding satisfactory criteria for distinguishing the role of political executives and career administrators.[28]

Controversy, Contradictions and Ambiguities in the Rules of National Broadcasting

The Thesis

In what follows, this argument is applied to and supported with illustrations from a semigovernmental bureaucracy, national public broadcasting corporations of the type found in most western-style democracies. Such broadcasting corporations are instruments of mass communication, but they are also bureaucratic-style organizations under a certain degree of government control. Thus, they are beset by the same problems that beset other parts of the bureaucracy in democratic regimes.

Unlike some other parts of the bureaucracy, broadcasting corporations are not in control of large-scale material resources and cannot allocate material benefits on any significant scale. Hence, they cannot be utilized by the political elite for electoral manipulation in the same manner as other parts of the bureaucracy. But, since they are also instruments of mass media, they can be utilized for *symbolic* manipulation or propaganda both before and between elections.[29]

Public broadcasting corporations are surrounded by rules and norms obliging them to maintain political objectivity, neutrality, and balance and prohibiting them from injecting value judgments into their programs. But, at the same time, their working rules and regulations also require them to select, interpret and comment on political topics. This is virtually a contradiction in terms. For, as the study reported below has clearly shown, it is practically impossible in the interpretation of political reality to determine objectively what objectivity actually is. Frequently one person's (or group's) objectivity is another person's (or group's) bias.

It follows that, if a national broadcasting corporation is under the control of elected, incumbent politicians, it can be pressured by these politicians to interpret objectivity in a manner that will favor the ruling party or the government with the aim of keeping it in power indefinitely. Hence, the crucial importance of the broadcasting corporation's independence from the government.

On the other hand, those at the top of broadcasting corporations (like other top bureaucrats) form a nonelected elite. Hence, it would certainly be contrary to democratic principles if they obtained and retained significant power over and exempt from the control of elected politicians and if they were allowed to impose their own (frequently controversial) conception of objectivity on the interpretation of political reality.

Thus, I argue that the dilemma which pervades the general relationship between bureaucracy and democracy reappears in the case of the relationship between broadcasting corporations and democracy: the political independence of a national broadcasting corporation is both a necessity for and threat to democracy. Hence, I argue, a national broadcasting corporation will be expected to be both politically independent and politically accountable, simultaneously controlled and uncontrolled by the government. This controversial, ambivalent, and self-contradictory character of rules is important because it results in role conflicts for politicians, top bureaucrats and top broadcasting people, and is also instrumental in fostering actual struggles among them as they interpret the rules to suit the promotion of their own interests.

The Study

Material in support of this thesis comes from a comparative study of national broadcasting corporations in western-style democracies. The first problem to be faced was the selection of countries for study. By the definition of democracy presented above, only a small number of countries can be viewed as democracies today. Since the study was to deal with national public (rather than commercial) broadcasting, one major western democracy whose most prominent broadcasting systems are commercial, the United States, had to be excluded.[30]

Budgetary and time constraints made it necessary to limit the study to four countries only, and of those, it was thought best to choose two relatively large and two relatively small countries in terms of population. Also, because the topic was the relationship between the broadcasting corporation (as a type of bureaucracy) and politics, it was thought best to select two countries with party-politicized bureaucracies and two countries with non-party-politicized bureaucracies. Language and personal constraints narrowed the choice even further. The final selection is spelled out in Figure 1.

The study itself was a qualitative one, based on a combination of two methods: (1) analysis of documents and other written material; (2) interviews with key informants. Eighty interviews, at least seventeen in and about each broadcasting system, have been conducted.

Since in West Germany public broadcasting is decentralized into a relatively large number of broadcasting stations, interviews have been conducted with media experts on broadcasting in general and with informants at West Germany's only nationwide television broadcasting station, the second television channel, ZDF.

Results: Ambiguities and Contradictions in Legal Rules and Norms

In all four countries studied, there were ambiguities, contradictions and controversies with respect to the laws and rules or norms surrounding public national broadcasting, particularly those concerning the relationship between the broadcasting corporation and the government (or the political elite).

Figure 1
The Countries and Broadcasting Systems Selected for Study

Type of Bureaucracy

		Non Party-Politicized	Party-Politicized
Size of Population	Relatively Large	Britain British Broadcasting Corporation (BBC)	Federal Republic of Germany Zweites Deutsche Fernsehen (ZDF)
	Relatively Small	Australia Australian Broadcasting	Israel Israel Broadcasting Authority (IBA) Corporation (ABC)

In Britain, this was evident from the fact that the BBC was constituted on a legal basis that would distance it to some extent from the government but would still grant the government some powers over the corporation. The legal pattern, designed to incorporate this circumscribed independence, was that of the royal charter, which defines the institution as a body corporate and requires it to acquire a license from the secretary of state of the home department. The charter and the license make no explicit provisions for BBC independence and, indeed, contain provisions that contradict it. The license (clauses 3, 4, and 13) awards the home secretary the power to instruct the corporation to broadcast the government's official announcements and to refrain from broadcasting any matters as he sees fit.

But the BBC's own official handbook states that in practice these have always been treated as reserve powers. Indeed, the handbook states: "Subject to the law of the land and the obligation under the Charter and the License Agreement, the BBC is fully independent...;" and "the corporation has enjoyed, and enjoys, complete freedom."[31] Thus, there are distinct differences between the manner in which the charter and the license, on the one hand, and the BBC, on the other hand, define the degree of the corporation's independence.

According to Briggs, BBC independence is really based on conventions rather than on laws and regulations.[32] But conventions are usually anchored in norms, and these, too, were found to be contradictory. Norms affirming BBC independence have been long-standing but not necessarily clear-cut.

According to the BBC's official handbook, the norms on which BBC independence is based date back to the time before the royal charter was granted (in 1927). But the lack of clarity of these norms also harks back to that time and is evident, for instance, in the Crawford Report, which states that the BBC should not be subject to "continuing ministerial guidance" but that the state through parliament must "retain the right of ultimate control."[33] This, of course, raises the question where "continuing guidance" ends and "ultimate control" begins.

Since then, politicians have frequently reaffirmed the principle of BBC independence as illustrated by the following statement by erstwhile Prime Minister James Callaghan in 1976: "you and we sometimes have differences but...none of these differences has ever disturbed the fundamental principle that the influential medium of broadcasting is free from political control and will so remain."[34] Respondents in this study similarly affirmed the principle of BBC independence. But one respondent expressed a widespread view when he said that the BBC should be independent from government but accountable to parliament, independent in its program making but accountable financially.[35] This raises the question whether accountability to government and to parliament (where the government necessarily has a majority) can, in fact, be kept separate in practice.

The Australian Broadcasting Corporation has been constituted as a statutory authority, a legal form which emulated the British pattern of allowing the organization "to be distanced from the government of the day, while remaining subject to a measure of governmental and parliamentary control."[36]

According to some observers, however, the ABC's status as a statutory authority does not clearly define the degree of its independence. The following statement in the report of the Coombs Royal Commission of Inquiry into Australian Government Administration gives direct evidence of the ambiguity surrounding the issue.

> The fact that a statutory body has been brought into being frequently signifies that a decision has been taken to place the performance of a particular function outside the political sphere of influence and to relieve a minister and his department of immediate responsibility for it. But the fact that certain powers are reserved to the minister means that it is the Parliament's intention that the abdication of ministerial authority should not be complete. It has not been easy to devise statutory formulae which adequately express the desired balance of ministerial and agency power and responsibilities, and there have, no doubt, been occasions when this difficulty has been compounded by the absence of any clear conception of what the minister's role should be.[37]

Unlike the royal charter in Britain, the Australian 1983 Broadcasting Act (on which the legal status of the ABC is presently based) states explicitly that it is the duty of the ABC's board of directors to safeguard the corporation's independence. However, the act also obliges the board to consider (but not necessarily to accept) ministerial policy statements. And under Section 78 of the act, the minister may direct the corporation to broadcast or to refrain from broadcasting any matter in line with national interest. Thus, the act combines the obligation to maintain independence with the obligation (under certain conditions) to accept ministerial directives.

The Dix Report states that for the ABC (as for the BBC) independence is supported by conventions irrespective of the law. But observers have argued that in Australian politics conventions are not as firmly based as they are in British politics. Indeed, the normative ambiguities surrounding such conventions have found expression even in the Dix Report itself. Thus, the report states that the accepted convention is that the ABC "not share responsibility with any other body for the content and composition of its programmes. ..."[38] The same report, however, also contains the following statement: "From the beginning of our review, many people and organizations put the view to us that the publicly-owned ABC not be a power unto itself. We share that opinion..." And, further, on the same page: "while the public interest requires accountability of its instrumentalities, it also requires independence for a body such as the ABC."[39] This raises the question whether the requirements of independence and accountability are not contradictory with each other.

This dilemma also finds expression in contradictory statements by politicians. According to the Dix Report, an affirmation of ABC independence was made as early as 1945 when Prime Minister John Curtin stated: "the Government recognizes that the intent of the Australian Broadcasting Act is to create a position of special independence of judgment and action for the broadcasting instrumentality."[40] Equivalent statements were made periodically in later years. For instance, the leader of the (Labor) government in the Senate, Senator John Button, said in the Senate in May 1983: "I stress that the Government is committed to the independence of the ABC."[41] But the Dix Report also cites a different view among politicians.

> There is another body of opinion with a different view...according to this view, the ABC is a creation of the Commonwealth Parliament and owes its existence to it....A Standing Committee of the Senate...has been studying the questions of public control and accountability of Statutory Authorities [and has expressed]...a concern to reassert an appropriate measure of Parliamentary Authority over statutory organiza-

> tions, an authority felt to have been eroded over the decades...[otherwise] they would or may well, in effect, be accountable to no one...[42]

The same ambiguity is evident in respondents' statements. Several respondents were adamant that the ABC must be independent. One respondent expressed this opinion as follows. "It should stay [independent]... there is a big danger in having an organization whose main aim is the dissemination of information...directly under a government. ..." A like-minded respondent, a representative of the Australian Journalists' Association, said:

> I believe it should be independent. I think the ABC is a major information resource in Australia...to us it is the only really independent source and we have in the past and will in the future continue to defend it from attacks by politicians. I think it should be right outside their fingers.

Other respondents, however, expressed the view that the ABC must be accountable even if this encroaches on its independence. One respondent expressed this view as follows.

> It has to be accountable to the people...and I think the only practical way it can be is through the parliament. Not to the government in power, but to the parliament. And one hopes that if democracy is in a healthy state then the checks and counter checks of parliamentary procedures will safeguard [its political independence]...I mean [the threat to the ABC's independence] is always a danger, but I don't see any way around the proposition that ... the ABC is publicly funded and therefore can't be a law unto itself.

Other respondents voiced the opinion that the ABC should be both accountable and independent: accountable financially, but independent in programming. One respondent formulated this opinion as follows:

> I don't believe that accountability necessarily precludes independence. Certainly I believe that the ABC should be independent, but I also believe that it has to be accountable...but I don't think that accountability should be able to be used by politicians...I do also think that the public interest demands that the ABC be accountable for how it spends its funds...but [it should be able to] decide independently how [those funds are] utilized.

But is this, in fact, possible? In the opinion of some other respondents, it is not: "There is no doubt...that the general pressure thing does, of course, get manifested through the financial provisions." The dilemma this creates was best expressed in the words of yet another respondent: "The ABC should be independent. But it uses taxpayers' money...I really don't know."

The same ambiguities and controversies are evident in Israel. The Broadcasting Authority Act of 1965 (as amended in 1966, 1968 and 1973) provides for a broadcasting authority that will furnish broadcasts as a national service, will see to it that such broadcasts give suitable expression to views and attitudes prevalent among the public, and will furnish reliable information. The act further provides for a minister to be in charge of executing the law and for a plenary, a board of directors (including a chairman) and a director general—all appointed by the government—for fixed, renewable terms. The act further states (Section 46) that the government shall have the right to have its announcements and the announcements of the general staff of the military and of civil defense broadcast by the authority.

In a state of national emergency, the government shall be entitled to revoke the authority's powers as per this act for no longer than thirty days (a time span that the foreign affairs and security committee of parliament may extend indefinitely).

Significantly, the act lends the government no further prerogatives of interference. But, by the same token, (like the British royal charter but unlike the Australian act) it makes no explicit provisions for the authority's independence from the government. Since the act does not grant the authority any independence from government to begin with, it is not clear what there is to revoke in case of emergency.

How much independence for the broadcasting authority is implied by the act? On this a respondent commented:

> The legal independence of the broadcasting authority is expressed in the fact that the law provides for a minister in charge of implementing the broadcasting act, but does not provide him with the authority to interfere in broadcasting....The act is not declarative but practical. Barring a state of emergency—in which the government can seize the authority—the government has no control over it. The plenary and the board of directors have a three-year term during which they cannot be dismissed. This gives them three years of relative freedom.

Another respondent, however, commented in this context that since the board of directors are government appointees, the government's control over them, even if not enshrined in law, is ensured in practice. Perhaps, the experts' diverging opinions on the Israel Broadcasting Authority Act can best be explained by the illuminating comment of one respondent: "The act is generally unclear. It is a masterpiece of hazy formulations."

Similar ambiguities and controversies are evident in Israel in the norms of the major participants. In a newspaper interview after his appointment in 1968, the first director general of the newly created Israel Broadcasting Authority, Shmuel Almog, stated that the authority must be free of government or partisan interference, although it must preserve close coordination with the foreign and defense offices on matters of foreign policy and security. The former director general of the Israel Broadcasting Corporation, Yosef Lapid (whose term ran from 1979 to April 1984), made a similar, though more detailed, statement in an interview.

> The essence of my role is to be independent from the government....To understand that the broadcasting authority needs to be truly independent and that this is not merely some lip service to democracy, you need a thorough political education. When you are appointed to a position like mine you say: I am the director general on the basis of the law and my own conscience and my understanding of Israeli democracy...and you know that for five years you must act, so that later on you will not spit into your own face.[43]

But a former member of the board of directors of the Israel Broadcasting Authority, Aharon Papo, himself a representative of the then ruling Likud on the authority, wrote the following in a newspaper article.

> The astounding fact in the ministers' response is that they treat the broadcasting authority as if it were a natural disaster that must be put up with....In their imagination—and only in their imagination—is the broadcasting authority conceived of as a fourth arm of government besides the legislature, the executive and the judiciary. The fact that the reporters and broadcasters have not been elected by the public and are only its servants has escaped their notice....Broadcasting services are not the private mouthpieces of their staff, but belong to the public that funds them...and since the public in a democracy elects a parliament which designates a government from its ranks, the government is the representative of the public through which it exerts its authority over the medium.[44]

A staff member of the IBA similarly said:

> Usually interference [by politicians in broadcasting] has a negative connotation. [But] it may be looked upon positively as well...we have the duty to give expression to the variety of attitudes in the community. Hence, interference is legitimate and we must respond...it is legitimate...even from party elements. We are asked to give coverage say, to a party convention. Why not? The question is: how much?

With some variations, the story repeats itself with regard to West German public broadcasting. The basic legal framework for West German broadcasting was created at the end of the 1940s under the influence of the western allies, whose overriding aim was to preclude a repetition of the Nazi experience and, thus, to make sure that broadcasting enjoyed freedom from state interference. But the strongest legal basis for broadcasting independence comes from the post-occupation era and is to be found in the pronouncement of the Federal Constitutional Court of 1961 to the effect that "broadcasting is the concern of the general public. It must be pursued in complete independence, in a non-partisan manner, and must be safeguarded against all forms of interference." Here, then, broadcasting independence is clearly spelled out by law. However, in West Germany broadcasting is under the authority of the states, and, as I show in greater detail elsewhere, state laws and interstate agreements on broadcasting also provide for broadcasting corporations to have governing bodies that represent the divergent political views existing in the community, that are to convey these views (including the views of political parties) to the broadcasting corporations, and that are to see to it that these views are reflected in broadcasting policies. The West German legislator has thus provided for an inherent contradiction: independence, coupled with political supervision.[45]

This contradiction is also evident in pronouncements by members of the state elites. Thus, W. Geiger, an erstwhile judge of the Federal Constitutional Court, wrote: "The requirement for citizens' freedom of information basically dictates that the State refrain from exerting an influence on broadcasting."[46] On the other hand, according to Williams, in the 1970s, several public figures expressed themselves in favor of political influence on broadcasting, most notably the chairman of the CDU/CSU working party on broadcasting who described broadcasting as an inherently political activity which, therefore, could not be further politicized by the intervention of politicians.[47] This raises the questions where state influence ends and political influence begins and whether the affirmed right of incumbent politicians to interfere is to be seen as part of their role as representatives of the state or as part of their role as representatives of the ruling party.

These ambiguities and differences of opinion come through in respondents' statements. Some respondents expressed unwavering support for broadcasting independence, for instance thus:

> We put great value on this [ZDF independence].

> I find that for journalism [political interference] is deadly.

More common, however, were less adamant or two-sided views.

> In a system of publicly funded broadcasting, the interest of the public must be conveyed in some way. The next question is whether at present the public interest is

conveyed in an acceptable manner. I think not. It is clear that there must be some supervision. The question is: how.

According to the constitution broadcasting must be independent. But you cannot divorce yourself from the political reality of a country.

Conclusion

The main thesis of this paper was that, because of the features and procedures that render democracy distinctive and limit the ruling elite's power, the exercise of this power is beset by inherent contradictions. The major contradiction is that the confrontation of the democratically elected political elite's power by the power of other elites is part of the very essence of democracy, yet is also a major threat to democracy. This inherent contradiction results in self-contradictory and controversial rules of the democratic process. This argument was illustrated in the area of bureaucracy and supported by data from a comparative study of a type of semigovernmental bureaucratic organization, national public broadcasting corporations in four countries: Britain, Australia, Israel and West Germany.

In all four countries studied, there were found to be marked inconsistencies in the legal frameworks and norms that govern broadcasting. Some legal frameworks were designed so as to distance broadcasting from direct government control, while maintaining "ultimate" government control over it, but without clear indication of where direct control ends and ultimate control begins. And precisely where the legal framework made the clearest provisions for broadcasting independence, it also made the clearest provisions for political intervention in broadcasting.

There was a widespread normative conception among political elites and among broadcasting elites that broadcasting ought to be independent. There was also the conception that broadcasting ought to be accountable. And, frequently, these two conceptions were held by the same people.

Since similar inconsistencies were found in the legal frameworks and norms surrounding broadcasting in all countries studied, the conclusion must be reached that they were not the result of oversight on the part of the drafters of legal provisions and guidelines or the result of capriciousness on the part of politicians and broadcasters. Rather, they may be seen as the result of a deep-seated ambiguity ingrained in the role definition of broadcasting corporations and their elites in a democracy and the expression of a dilemma which generally besets the role definition of elites and the exercise of power in a democracy. Such contradictions, in turn, give rise to tension and struggles between (in this case) broadcasting elites and politicians. These, however, are beyond the scope of this paper.[48]

Notes

I am grateful to Mangula Waniganayake for her most skillful interviewing at the Australian Broadcasting Corporation.

1. E.g., Benjamin R. Barber, *Strong Democracy* (Berkeley: University of California Press, 1984); H.T. Wilson, *Political Management* (Berlin: Walter de Gruyter, 1984).
2. Robert A. Dahl, *A Preface to Democratic Theory* (Chicago: University of Chicago Press, 1956); Robert A. Dahl, *Pluralist Democracy in the United States* (Chicago: Rand McNally, 1967); Robert A. Dahl, "Stability, Change and the Democratic Creed," in Charles F. Cnudde and Deane E. Neubauer, eds., *Empirical Democratic Theory* (Chicago: Markham Publishing Co., 1969), pp. 253-67; Robert A. Dahl, *Modern Political Analysis*, 2nd ed. (Englewood Cliffs: Prentice Hall, 1970); Robert A. Dahl and Charles E. Lindblom, *Politics, Economics and Welfare* (New York: Harper, 1953); David Riesman, *The Lonely Crowd* (New Haven: Yale University Press, 1961); Giovanni Sartori, *Democratic Theory* (Detroit: Wayne State University Press, 1962); David B. Truman, *The Government Process*, 2nd ed. (New York: Knopf, 1971).
3. See, for example, Michael Margolis, "Democracy: American Style," in Graeme Campbell Duncan, ed., *Democratic Theory and Practice* (Cambridge: Cambridge University Press, 1983), pp. 115-32.
4. E.g., Ernest Mandel, *Late Capitalism*, rev. ed. (London: New Left Books, 1975); Nicos Poulantzas, *State, Power, Socialism* (London: New Left Books, 1978); Ralph Miliband, *The State in Capitalist Society* (London: Quartet Books, 1973); Ralph Miliband, *Marxism and Politics* (Oxford: Oxford University Press, 1977); Ralph Miliband, *Capitalist Democracy in Britain* (Oxford: Oxford University Press, 1982); Michael Parenti, *Democracy for the Few* (New York: St. Martin's Press, 1980); Maurice Zeitlin, "On Classes, Class Conflict and the State: An Introductory Note," in Maurice Zeitlin, ed., *Class Conflict, and the State* (Cambridge, Mass.: Winthrop Publishers, 1980).
5. E.g., Thomas R. Dye, *Who's Running America?* (Englewood Cliffs: Prentice Hall, 1976); Thomas R. Dye and Luther Harmon Zeigler, *The Irony of Democracy*, 3rd ed. (North Scituate: Duxbury Press, 1975); George Lowell Field and John Higley, *Elitism* (London: Routledge and Kegan Paul, 1980).
6. For Example G. William Domhoff, *Who Rules America?* (Englewood Cliffs: Prentice Hall, 1967); G. William Domhoff, *The Higher Circles* (New York: Random House, 1970); G. William Domhoff, *The Powers That Be* (New York: Random House, 1978); G. William Domhoff, *Who Rules America Now?* (Englewood Cliffs: Prentice Hall, 1983); Michael Useem, *The Inner Circle* (New York: Oxford University Press, 1984).
7. For instance Philippe C. Schmitter and Gerhard Lehmbruch, eds., *Trends toward Corporatist Intermediation* (Beverly Hills: Sage Publications, 1979); Bob Jessop, "Capitalism and Democracy," in Gary Littlejohn, Barry Smart, John Wakeford,

and Nira Yuval-Davis, eds., *Power and the State* (London: Croom Helm, 1978); pp. 10-51; Bob Jessop, "Corporatism, Parliamentarism and Social Democracy," in Schmitter and Lehmbruch, eds., *Trends toward Corporatist Intermediation*, pp. 185-212; Alan Cawson, "Pluralism, Corporatism and the Role of the State," *Government and Opposition*, 13 (1978), 178-98; Alan Cawson, "Functional Representation and Democratic Politics: Towards a Corporatist Democracy," in Duncan, ed., *Democratic Theory and Practice*, pp. 173-84; Colin Crouch, "The State, Capital and Liberal Democracy," in Colin Crouch, ed., *State and Economy in Contemporary Capitalism* (London: Croom Helm, 1979), pp. 13-54.

8. See for example Miliband, *The State in Capitalist Society and Capitalist Democracy in Britain;* Goran Therborn, "The Rule of Capital and the Rise of Democracy," *New Left Review*, 103 (1977), 3-41; Goran Therborn, *What Does the Ruling Class Do When it Rules?* (London: New Left Books, 1978).
9. Max Weber, *The Theory of Social and Economic Organization* (New York: Free Press, 1947); Max Weber, *Economy and Society* (New York: Bedminister, Press, 1968).
10. Gaetano Mosca, *The Ruling Class* (New York: McGraw Hill, 1939). Mosca is commonly classified as an elitist, and in many respects he is one. But in the later development of his theory he also made a considerable contribution to our understanding of democracy.
11. Joseph A. Schumpeter, *Capitalism, Socialism, and Democracy*, 3rd ed. (New York: Harper and Row, 1962).
12. Raymond Aron, *Progress and Disillusion* (London: Pall Mall Press, 1968); Raymond Aron, *Politics and History* (New York: Free Press, 1978).
13. E.g., Jack L. Walker, "A Critique of the Elitist Theory of Democracy," *American Political Science Review*, 60 (June 1966), 285-95; Peter Bachrach, *The Theory of Democratic Elitism: A Critique* (Boston: Little Brown, 1967); Carole Pateman, *Participation and Democratic Theory* (Cambridge: Cambridge University Press, 1970).
14. E.g., Bernard R. Berelson, Paul F. Lazarsfeld, and William N. McPhee, *Voting* (Chicago: University of Chicago Press, 1954); William Kornhauser, *The Politics of Mass Society* (Glencoe: The Free Press, 1959); Lester W. Milbrath, *Political Participation* (Chicago: Rand McNally, 1965).
15. Schumpeter, *Capitalism, Socialism and Democracy*; Seymour Martin Lipset, *Sociology of Democracy* (Neuwied: H. Luchterhand, 1965); Dahl, *A Preface to Democratic Theory.*
16. For instance Miliband, *The State in Capitalist Society*, and Dye and Zeigler, *The Irony of Democracy.*
17. Robert A. Dahl, *Dilemmas of Pluralist Democracy* (New Haven: Yale University Press, 1982), p. 37.
18. For instance, Mosca, *The Ruling Class*; Robert Moss, *The Collapse of Democracy* (London: ABACUS, Sphere Books, 1977); Milovan Djilas, *The Story from Inside* (London: Weidenfeld and Nicolson, 1981).
19. See for example David French and Elena French, *Working Communally* (New York: Russell Sage Foundation, 1975); Ewell Paul Roy, *Cooperatives*, 3rd ed. (Danville: Interstate Printers and Publishers, 1976).
20. Examples include Mattei Dogan, *The Mandarins of Western Europe* (New York: John Wiley, 1979); Jacques Ellul, *The Technological Society* (London: Jonathan Cape, 1965); B. Guy Peters, *The Politics of Bureaucracy(New York: Longman, 1978).*
21. See for instance Mandel, *Late Capitalism*; Poulantzas, State, Power, Socialism.
22. E.g., Edward Page, *Political Authority and Bureaucratic Power* (Knoxville: University of Tennessee Press, 1985).
23. Eva Etzioni-Halevy, *Political Manipulation and Administrative Power* (London:

Routledge and Kegan Paul, 1979); Eva Etzioni-Halevy, *Bureaucracy and Democracy: A Political Dilemma*, rev. ed. (London: Routledge and Kegan Paul, 1985).

24. See for example Dahl, "Stability, Change and the Democratic Creed"; and H. McClosky, "Consensus and Ideology in American Politics," in Cnudde and Neubauer, eds., *Empirical Democratic Theory.*
25. Weber, *The Theory of Social and Economic Organization*; H.H. Gerth and C. Wright Mills, eds., *From Max Weber: Essays in Sociology* (New York: Oxford University Press, 1958).
26. Lord Fulton et al., *The Civil Service: Report of the Committee*, vol. 1 (London: Her Majesty's Stationery Office, 1968), p. 11.
27. Herbert Cole Coombs et al., *Report of the Royal Commission on Australian Government Administration* (Canberra: The Commonwealth Government Printer, 1977, hereafter cited as the Coombs Report).
28. Herbert Hoover et al., *Commission on Organization of the Executive Branch of the Government: Task Force Report on Personnel and Civil Service* (Washington, D.C.: 1955), pp. 1-2, 4.
29. On the basis of research carried out in the 1950s and 1960s, social scientists had long argued that the effect of the media on public opinion is rather limited and serves mainly to reinforce existing attitudes. More recently, however, the consensus among social scientists has been that the media, including the electronic media, have a more substantial effect on public opinion than was previously believed, especially in making the public aware of and focusing its interest on certain issues which, for their part, may work in favor of or against certain parties, politicians, or the government of the day.
30. It was thought best not be include the public television and national public radio systems in the United States in this study because they are not equal in prominence to the broadcasting systems in the countries eventually selected for this comparison.
31. *BBC Annual Report and Handbook 1985* (London: BBC, 1985), pp. 169, 170.
32. Asa Briggs, *Governing the BBC* (London: BBC, 1979).
33. Lord Crawford, *Report of the Broadcasting Committee* (Cmnd 2599, 1926), Appendix II, p. 16.
34. *BBC Annual Report and Handbook 1985*, p. 170.
35. See for example *The Sunday Times*, Aug. 25, 1985.
36. Alexander Thomas Dix, *The ABC in Review*, vol. 2 (Canberra: Australian Government Publishing Service, 1981), p. 85 (hereafter cited as the Dix Report).
37. Coombs Report, p. 86.
38. Dix Report, vol. 2, p. 76.
39. Ibid., p. 71.
40. Ibid., p. 72.
41. Cited in *The Canberra Times*, May 15, 1983.
42. Dix Report, vol. 2, pp. 72-3.
43. Name cited by permission of the respondent.
44. Aharon Papo, "The Government and Television," *Ha-aretz*, june 24, 1980, p. 13.
45. Eva Etzioni-Halevy, *National Broadcasting under Siege* (London: Macmillan, forthcoming).
46. W. Geiger, "Sicherung der Informationsfreiheit des Bürgers als Verfassungsproblem," in W. Geiger et al., *Der öffentlich-rechtliche Rundfunk* (Zurich: Edition Interform, 1978), pp. 11-43.
47. Arthur Williams, *Broadcasting and Democracy in West Germany* (Bradford: Bradford University Press, 1976).
48. On this see Etzioni-Halevy, *National Broadcasting under Siege.*

25

The In/Outsiders—Political Control on Media in Israel: A Theoretical Framework

Dan Caspi and Yehiel Limor

Since its inception, Israeli society has adopted principles of Western democracy. The Declaration of Independence of the fledgling state, born in 1948, is replete with human and democratic values, even though the term "democracy" is not stipulated explicitly therein.[1] Adoption of the rules of the democratic game was not merely incidental, as these rules enabled preservation of the pluralism that prevailed in the small pre-State Jewish society in Palestine (the *Yishuv*), with its variety of ideological and religious schools of thought (Horowitz and Lissak, 1978 and 1989). Subsequently, the democratic ethos accentuated differences between the Western, democratic, modern State of Israel and its non-democratic Arab neighbors.

The founding of the new state and the espousal of democratic principles demanded immediate introduction of governing and social institutions and the formulation of the relevant rules of the game. It became essential to define the status of the existing media institution[2], as well as its reciprocal relations with other institutions, especially the political one. The initial constellation of the new and developing society engendered expectations of obedient, disciplined media that could be recruited for collective missions formulated by the ruling political elite and which posed as national challenges.

Although the present paper alludes to mass media in Israel, it effectively paints a much broader picture, whose implications are relevant to other young democratic states as well. After presenting the mass media as performing a vital mediation function in any democracy, we shall introduce the notion of *In/Outsider*. As any mediator, the mass media consolidate themselves as a power focus. Since no power could remain uncontrolled in any democracy, a range of mechanisms is developed to ensure "checks and balances" between the *In/Outsiders* and other social institutions. The paper identifies four major patterns of media-politics relationship and numerous ways of political control over the mass media.

Mediation and Mediators

One may relate to the mass media as *mediators,* considering their position at information hubs and their transmission of a variety of messages—information, demands, claims, consensus, and support—among the various sectors and strata of society (Caspi and Limor, 1992). Mediators are essential to the realization of democratic principles that emphasize the importance of constant dialogue between the representatives and the represented, as well as the latter's monitoring and supervision of the former, thereby ensuring attentiveness to public demands and recruitment of public support for policy, whether in advance or in retrospect.

A neutral mediator is an asset, possibly a rare asset. Those who accumulate power find it difficult to maintain neutrality and complete impartiality. Even without relinquishing their pivotal status, in which most of their power lies, the media and media professionals play a significant role in the political process.

One may distinguish between two principal types of mediation: *vertical* and *horizontal*, distinguished according to their respective clientele (Caspi, 1997). In vertical mediation, the more familiar of the two, the communications media constitute two-way message channels between the political elite to the general population or elected officials and the electorate. In horizontal mediation, in contrast, the media transmit messages among various sectors of the population, the political elite and even other elites in society.

Unlike traditional mediators, political parties or trade unions, the media are not explicitly institutionalized in the political system and participate in the political process without any official status. While other mediators operate within specified limits, their aims generally well-defined within the political structure, the role of the mass media, especially insofar as political mediation is concerned, is primarily a by-product of their presence in the political arena and does not necessarily reflect any preparation whatsoever for fulfillment of such functions.

The vagueness of the media's political status renders it difficult to characterize the relevant patterns of reference to them. Furthermore, the systems of checks and balances that both typify and regulate reciprocal relations between various factors and the political system are not necessarily valid regarding the media.

In many respects, one could describe the media's special status in the political arena as "the best of both worlds": the mass media are simultaneously within and without the political establishment, wearing two pair of glasses—one of an insider and one of an outsider. Thus, we suggest to regard them as *In/Outsiders*. That particular position implies at least two main dimensions - structural and functional.

From the *structural* point of view, an outsider is one who pretends that he/she is out of the system and out of the regular control system. Usually, mass media claim for unique and special privileges. They reject any exterior control and wish to remain out of any control. But one cannot be beyond any control while operating in a social system.

From the *functional* point of view, the mass media look at the political process and cover it. But on the same very time being covered by the media, the political process is been changed. By covering the politics, the media intrude and exercise a considerable impact on it. They are perceived as observers on the sidelines, whose function is to serve as public advocates or watchdogs vis-à-vis the government, but on the other, they are involved in political processes as the *fourth estate* of the government and in certain cases may even exert influence (Cater, 1957), and even are "part of government" as well as journalists are "political actors" (Cook, 1998).

Communicators themselves repeatedly claim that their special status is partly due to their constant subjection to public scrutiny. Unlike the governing authorities, that stand for election once every four years, the media face a daily contest, with fateful decisions left to their voters/consumers. Readers, listeners or viewers decide whether to buy a daily paper and which one to buy, whether to turn on the TV and which channel to watch or whether to opt for the radio and which station to select. The indeterminate nature of the media's status in mass society is partly responsible for the tensions surrounding their activity. The double identity of *In/outsiders* originates tensions because the entire social system couldn't handle efficiently the double-identity media.

The less well defined their position in the social structure, the greater the tension anticipated between the mass media and the political system, as well as the general public. Furthermore, traditional, established mediation systems—parties and interest groups—perceive the media as powerful competition, compounding the difficulties entailed in institutionalization of the latter's political role. However, these entities, too, require the mediation services of the mass media to transmit their messages to target audiences. The two-valued reciprocal relations of competition and dependence are perhaps the basis of the internal tension characterizing relations with the mass media in every country, including Israel, as well as the reason for opposition to their full institutionalization (Lambeth, 1995).

The media-politics conflict is a self-evident situation that entails constant negotiation in determining the rules of the game. From this point of view, bargaining between the media and the political establishment in Israeli society takes place not only because of the young age of this democracy but primarily because such negotiations are among the universal hallmarks of democracy: the mass media are undergoing a still unfinished process of institutionalization and negotiation with the other institutions.

The Need to Control the In/Outsiders

The media consolidation as a power focus in democracy, *Insiders,* naturally arouses certain questions on checks and balances: If the media indeed fulfill vital mediation functions, how can the power of the mediators be restrained? How are the media to be controlled and by whom?

No simple answers may be found to these questions. Any attempt to control the media is perceived, at least *prima facie*, as a violation of the sacrosanct principles in the liberal democracy, as "freedom of the press," "freedom of expression" or "the public's right to know." Each of the involved parties had an interpretation of its own for these terms that stand at the foundation of every democratic regime.

The dual status of the mass media, *In/Outsiders,* sparks predictable tension in every democratic society, especially a society in formation such as Israel's. The media aspire towards a virtually unattainable status entailing recognition as an institution with the same rights as other inside institutions, but exemption from regulation and control by them. Consequently, the more the other institutions relate to the media as a conventional and supervisable institution, the greater the media's demand for extra privileges, such as freedom from criticism by other institutions. However, some regulation is essential because the media constitute a power base in society. Any entity that accumulates power and assumes the role of a power base cannot be exempt from the basic democratic principle of checks and balances. Hence, it is hardly surprising that other social institutions seek to regulate the media institution and balance the power it has amassed.

The various control mechanisms adhere to a set of the operative arrangements that translate the principles of social responsibility (Siebert *et al.*, 1963) into practical terms. These arrangements effectively regulate the relationship between the media and the various institutions in the society in which they operate and also determine the intensity and nature of their control. Generally speaking, such arrangements obtain control in two spheres—formal and informal—and at two levels—institution-wide (macro) and interpersonal (micro)—yielding four basic relations (see Table 1).

Table 1
Media-Politics Interaction By Level and Sphere of Relations

	Level	
Sphere	**Macro**	**Micro**
Formal	1. Laws, regulations, censorship, Editors' Committee, Press Council, journalistic ethics, spokesmanship	2. Press releases, press conferences, restrictions, spokesmanship, ethics committee intra-organizational courts
Informal	3. Briefings, manipulation, selective release of information, sanctions and prizes	4. Leaks, social ties, sanctions and prizes

Formal relations are defined in terms of legal or agreed institutionalized arrangements, including laws, regulations, ordinances and even written agreements, while *informal relations*, as their name implies, are determined outside and in addition to official ones and include manipulation of information, exchange of information and covert reward systems. Both formal and informal relations may be forged at the *macro* (institutional) level (e.g. relations between the government and the press, or a particular newspaper) or the *micro* (personal) level (such as those between a Cabinet Minister and a reporter or newspaper editor).

The greater the tension between the media and other institutions, the closer these relations will conform with Patterns 1 and 2. At times, application of legal arrangements—at the macro or micro level—suffice to attest to the existence of tension. Imposition of general restrictions on the press or individual constraints on journalists is a tangible reflection of tension and the unfeasibility of problem-solving through understanding and compromise. Reliance on the force of law shows that a mutual understanding was either undesirable or unacceptable. Conversely, greater cooperation between the parties and less tension in interaction points to a greater prevalence of Patterns 3 and 4 that are characteristic of the social responsibility model.

Media control, always and inevitably, means interference, or even actual involvement, in its activities. Exercising pressure is one of the most common control methods. For the purposes of the present discussion, we shall define pressure as "specific interference", ad hoc, meaning temporary interference. This can be distinguished from the permanent interference, which is a control pattern in its own right (Caspi and Limor, 1996a). Usually, the pressure is accompanied by use of (or the power to use) various rewards, either positive rewards (prizes) or negative rewards (sanctions).

It appears, therefore, that the communication institution—and/or certain parts of it—may be controlled in one of two main patterns: intervention and/or pressure. Each of these patterns may be implemented by using rewards and sanctions. Figure 1 outlines the conceptual framework of this discussion, showing that control via prizes and sanctions can be done in two different ways:

One way is permanent, continual intervention or interference, which uses prizes without pressure (dotted line 1) or combined with pressure (dotted line 1a). The other involves ad hoc interference only, which inevitably means exerting pressure (dotted line 2). Either way, the pressures, prizes and sanctions express the degree of control.

Using prizes and sanctions to exercise control over the media is definitely not a new idea. In the 17th and 18th centuries, European regimes were already in the habit of wooing journalists and newspaper editors, in the hope of getting favorable publicity. They did not hesitate to bribe journalists, buying off their hearts and pens alike. One major example of this is a special fund established by the British court, through which writers were paid for publishing articles in support of the crown. Democratic governments still want to control the media, but they cannot simply bribe journalists to get favorable coverage. However, as the media expands and diversifies, the attempts to influence it grow more frequent, and the methods, both direct and indirect, of using rewards and sanctions, become more sophisticated.

Figure 1
Control of the Mass Media: A Conceptual Framework

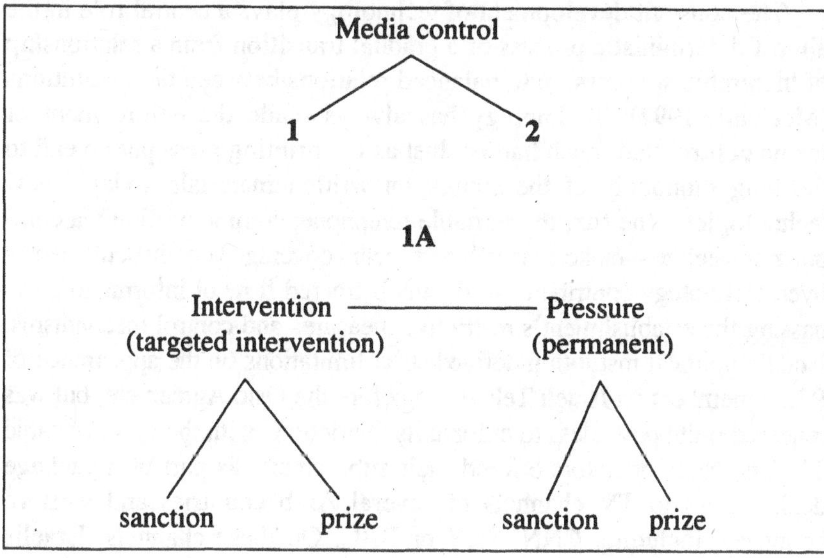

The various means of government involvement in the media's economy and finances (Picard, 1985), can naturally help the government when it wishes to influence the contents of media coverage. But attempts to influence the media, or interfere with its activities, take other forms as well. Offering exclusive information, or withholding it, also helps the government keep an eye on media organizations. In other words, any method, financial or otherwise, can serve to either reward the media, or implement sanctions against it.

Sometimes democratic governments seem to prefer sanctions, thus expressing their displeasure with the media organization's position, or with certain information it had published or aired. Such sanctions may be aimed, for instance, at the media organization's financial resources or vital cash flow. But the government does not always use overt means of pressure. While sanctions are usually out in the open and easily traceable, rewards are often well concealed and hard to discover.

Choices of Media Control

Every pattern of interaction, in every sphere and at every level, micro or macro, formal or informal, effectively entails a measure of mutual consensual control, ostensibly contradicting the Western perception of media as watchdogs. A watchdog, by definition, guards and supervises others. Hence, supervision *by* the media is far more self-evident than supervision *of* the media.

The constant development of technology plays a central role in the almost deterministic process of a gradual transition from a relationship of hierarchic suppression to balanced relations between the institutions (McQuail, 1992). Technology has always made the enforcement of media control that much harder. Just as the printing press put an end to the long monopoly of the church on written materials, today's new technologies—the fax, the portable telephone, communication via computer or satellite—make censorship of media coverage very difficult. Moreover, technology contributes to the unobstructed flow of information, bypassing the establishment's restrictive measures and control mechanisms. Israel's political institution defined strict limitations on the appearance of P.L.O members on Israeli Television before the Oslo Agreement, but was rendered quite powerless to enforce its restrictions with the onset of cable TV. The cable operators offered their subscribers, as part of a package deal, access to TV channels of several Arab countries and western countries, including CNN, SKY or BBC. On these channels, Israelis could watch Palestinian spokesmen expressing opinions, which the Israeli authorities considered as undesired political propaganda.

As effective control becomes increasingly impossible, the need for alternatives grows. It is quite unthinkable that a focus of power which grows constantly stronger, such as the mass media, should remain completely unsupervised. The need for alternatives is felt particularly by social systems, which abide by the social responsibility model. When the establishment relinquished the right for direct and open control, the mass media committed itself to some degree of self restraint (e.g. by establishing news/press councils, adopting codes of conduct etc.)—but what can the political establishment do when reporters and editors fail to conceal information, and harm essential public interests? How can such damage, caused by mistakes or bad judgment on the part of the media, be prevented or repaired?

Steering mechanisms are necessary, and not only for the benefit of society or the political establishment. The people and organizations of the media may need them as well. Because, just like any other liberty, freedom of the press is quite a heavy burden. Reporters face all kinds of unexpected situations, and are forced to deal with numerous circumstantial issues. Editors and reporters cannot be expected to know everything there is to know about every issue that happens to come up on the public agenda. Therefore, the decision on whether to publish or not to publish, cannot remain in their hands alone. The task is almost impossible, and the responsibility is too great for any person to bear. How can reporters correctly evaluate the information they have obtained? Who will editors consult when they feel uncertain about sensitive information?

True, the government has relinquished open and direct interference in journalistic considerations in return for the media's commitment to social responsibility and the public interest—but that should not hinder the continued dialogue between them, which is a natural and essential aspect of any dynamic relationship (Turow, 1992). Thus, despite the independence given to the media, the political establishment still holds on to certain tools for interfering with and influencing journalistic judgment. In other words: the diminished open and direct control compels politicians to invent alternative patterns, more sophisticated perhaps, of indirect and covert supervision. Such control patterns, which are revised every now and then, are no impediment to the media. They even help it do its job, without creating an oppressive feeling of interference or lack of freedom.

Any attempt at exerting control on the media requires the agent to consider at least the following seven basic questions, each of which entails a choice (Caspi and Limor, 1996b). The combined answers to these questions determine the manner in which pressure is exerted. These are the seven basic choices:

Choice 1: Which kind of rewards to use, whether to apply prizes or sanctions?

Choice 2: Whether to implement rewards or not to implement them?

Choice 3: Whether to exert pressure before or after the publication?

Choice 4: Whether to exert pressure on input or output of the media organization?

Choice 5: Whether to exert pressure at the macro or micro levels?

Choice 6: Whether to exert formal or non-formal pressure?

Choice 7: Whether to exert pressure ad-hoc or continuously.

The main question is, of course, the first one: Is the agent attempting to influence the media organization through pleasant means, by promising prizes, or is it threatening to use sanctions? Once this issue has been determined, responses to the succeeding questions will determine the pressure pattern. Various examples of both sanctions and prizes are listed below:

- **Implementation:** Not all factors capable of exerting pressure actually carry out their threats or promises, especially where sanctions are concerned. Agents often only threaten to apply sanctions without actually doing so. In some cases, the threat alone suffices to achieve the desired goals.
- **Timing:** The agent may choose to exert pressure either before or after actual publication. In many cases, such timing is not determined by agent alone, especially when the agent discovers that certain information has already been publicized by the media.
- **Target:** Relations between the media institution and other institutions are based on exchange of input and output. As raw information is a major input to the media, blocking the flow of such information is clearly an instrument of pressure. Similar pressure maybe applied to other vital inputs, chiefly financial. On the other hand, pressure may also be applied to outputs, e.g. refusal to purchase newspapers or cancellation of advertising will adversely affect the media organization's resources, especially its revenues.
- **Level of Pressure:** Pressure may be exerted at two different levels: macro and micro. At the macro level, prizes or sanctions are applied to the media institution as a whole, or the media organization (newspaper, radio station, television network), whereas the micro level applies to individuals, i.e. a particular reporter or editor.
- **Sphere of Pressure:** Pressure may be applied in the formal or informal sphere of interaction between the agent and the media organization or between the agent and the communicators. In the first case, prizes and sanctions are effected overtly and formally, whereas in the second, they are concealed and at times merely implied.
- **Frequency:** Pressure may be applied only once, continuously or even permanently.

The above seven choices are of a dichotomous nature and the combinations among them yield no fewer than 128 basic pressure patterns (see Table 2), half of them involving prizes and the other half sanctions.

As indicated, the dichotomous choices yield 128 basic patterns of pressure exerted on the media. These are not the only patterns, however, as each question actually has more than two responses. For example, there are numerous intermediate possibilities between full imple-

Table 2
Patterns of Pressure Exerted on the Communications Institution

Pressure Pattern	Reward: (a) Prize (b) Sanction	Application: (a) Reward realized (b) Not realized	Timing: (a) Before publication (b) After publication	Pressure on: (a) Input (b) Output	Level: (a) Macro (b) Micro	Sphere: (a) Formal (b) Informal	Frequency: (a) One-time (b) Extended
1	a	a	a	a	a	a	a
2	a	a	a	a	a	a	b
3	a	a	a	a	a	b	b
4	a	a	a	a	b	b	b
5	a	a	a	b	b	b	b
6	a	a	b	b	b	b	b
7	a	b	b	b	b	b	b
8	a	b	a	a	a	a	a
9	b	a	b	b	a	a	b
10	b	a	b	a	a	a	b
11	b	a	b	b	a	b	a
127	--	--	--	--	--	--	--
128	b	b	b	b	b	b	b

mentation and none at all, including various combinations of prizes and sanctions. The same is true regarding timing: The basic before/after distinction may be supplemented by other possibilities, most significantly that of combined application both before and after publication. Similarly, additional possibilities exist for other issues as well: Level (e.g. simultaneous application at the macro and micro levels), sphere (simultaneously formally and informal), frequency (pressure need not be one-time or continuous, but may be applied intermittently, at irregular intervals) and input/output (pressure may be applied to both at the same time).

Furthermore, two complex questions are not included among the seven choices: (1) Volume of prizes or sanction; (2) Extent of implementation. The volume of control or sanction may vary with any number of factors, such as the relationship between media professionals and those who control them, the identity of the element interacting with the media organization and the extent of its motivation to exercise control, the history of the relationship between the agent and the media organization or the manner in which control is exercised. As the number of questions is increased and the choices are defined more precisely, the number of possibilities rises accordingly, yielding thousands or even tens of thousands of pressure patterns available to would-be agents. Many such pressures are actually applied and affect routine functioning of the media organization.

Implementing Control

Identifying control patterns in this manner helps us analyze every individual case of media control. Censorship, one of the oldest and best known tools of political control, is applied continuously to the output of the organization, on the macro level and in the formal plane, before publication, and with no need for implementing the sanctions—which can either take an administrative form (closing down the paper), or follow the legal path (punishment for the editor and reporters.) An advertising boycott, on the other hand, is a sanction which necessitates implementation, only once, after publication, and is applied to the organization's input, at the macro level, in the non-formal plane. Leaks of information usually represent a one-time control pattern, applied to the media organization's output, through the implementation of a reward at the micro level, in the non-formal plane, before publication. A libel suit, on the other hand, is the implementation of a one-time sanction in the formal plane, at either the macro or micro levels, or both, and nearly always after publication.

In order to demonstrate the actual implementation of pressure, we shall bring here several examples, taken from the Israeli scene, although similar examples can be found in just about any other country.

Damaging Newspapers' Income from Circulation

One of the most common sanctions is damaging the organization's input, namely its financial resources—by either reducing its circulation or cutting its income from advertisement. In other words, a pressure pattern of sanction implementation at the macro level.

At the beginning of January 1994, Israel's Ministry of Foreign Affairs informed the management of "The Jerusalem Post", a daily newspaper, that it was cutting the number of its subscriptions from 1,100 down to 87. This paper, published in English, serves as a major source of information about Israel for the community, both in the country and abroad, and the Ministry of Foreign Affairs used to distribute it among its embassies and consulates, for promotional purposes. The decision to reduce the number of subscriptions was explained by two considerations: financial (cutting expenses) and relevant to the matter at hand (Due to Israel's improved international standing there is no longer need for so many copies at its embassies). The paper's management claimed that the cancellation was political, and the financial considerations were a mere disguise. It should be noted that in the late 1980's, the Jerusalem Post was acquired by the Hollinger Group of Canada for the sum of $16.4 million and as a result, changed its editorial line, often expressing right wing opinions, and criticizing the government.

Whatever the real reason for the massive cut in subscriptions, it reflects the political agent's potential punitive power over the press. In this case, cutting down the number of subscriptions directly affects the paper's circulation, and indirectly it also affects its income from circulation as well as advertisement.

The action taken in this case may be defined as follows: a negative reward, implemented in the formal plane, at the macro level (against the paper), after publication, applied continuously to the media organization's output. Thus, we may identify this profile of media control as b-a-b-b-a-a-b (see profile 9 on Table 2).

This was not the only case of a controlling agent deciding to implement financial sanctions against a newspaper, as retribution for its publications. The following cases provide documented proof of this:

- In the early 1950's, the IDF stopped purchasing the "Ha'Olam Ha'Ze" ("This World"), a weekly magazine, for reading rooms in military camps. This was done after the magazine, known for its criticism of government policies, published an article questioning the need for women's military service. (see profile 11 in table 2, b-a-b-b-a-b-a,).
- In the 1970's, the Aviation Industry's employees' union decided to cancel dozens of subscriptions for the daily newspaper "Davar", the organ of the Federation of Labor in Israel, following the publication of a series of articles on one of the Aviation Industry's plants.
- In the 1980's, the national bus company, "Eged", decided to "improve" its services on several long routes, and began to hand out copies of the daily paper

"Ma'ariv" to its passengers. This was done after a rival paper, "Yediot Aharonot", published a series of articles on the bus company (Caspi and Limor, 1992).

These three examples demonstrate the implementation of post publication sanctions. Sanctions were implemented at the macro level (against the newspaper), with pressure focused on the media organization's output, namely avoiding purchase of the printed paper.

Damaging Income from Advertisements

It is well known that advertisements are the largest and most significant component of a newspaper's income. In many papers, ads account for about two thirds or more of the total income (the rest comes from selling the paper itself). Therefore, when income from ads is reduced, a vital lifeline is damaged.

The two following documented examples demonstrate the use of the "ad weapon" against newspapers:

- On the eve of the Labor Federation elections in 1969, the general secretary of the Labor Party gave instructions to stop publishing his party's campaign ads in the prestigious daily paper, "Ha'Aretz". This was a punitive step against the paper, which was considered hostile to the party. A meeting brought about reconciliation, and the Labor Party renewed the ads, which brought the paper quite a substantial income. This is an example of a pressure pattern composed of the following elements: negative reward, realized, post-publication, applied to input (income from advertisements), macro, formal and continuous—b-a-b-a-a-a-b. (see profile 10 on Table 2)
- In the early 1990's, certain elements in the Knesset (the Israeli Parliament) accused the Ministry of Construction and Housing of punishing the daily newspaper "Hadashot" with an advertisement boycott, for an article criticizing the minister. This was a sanction, which may be described as a macro, non-formal pressure pattern, applied continuously, after publication.

It should be noted that just as stopping advertisement can serve as a sanction, an increased flow of ads to a particular paper may be regarded as a reward. The following example demonstrates this:

- In the early 1970's, a dominant figure in one of Israel's opposition parties (Rafi) claimed that companies owned by the Labor Federation (ruled at the time by the governing party), were supporting the "Ha'Olam Ha'Ze" weekly magazine, which had published many articles against Rafi's leader—through frequent advertising. After the affair was exposed, the leader of the Labor Party gave the word, and the advertising was stopped. In this case, the increased flow of advertisements to a particular magazine was a macro, non-formal pressure pattern, applied for the most part before publication.

Legal Action

Many examples show that controlling agents prefer legal action as a means of coercing the media organization, and forcing it to either publish or refrain from publishing certain information. Usually, such legal action is a sanction implementation pattern applied before publication, in the formal plane and at the macro level. The following two examples demonstrate this:

- In 1984 the leader of the "Kach" Movement, Meir Kahana, petitioned the Supreme Court, claiming that the Israeli Broadcasting Authority had ostracized him, refusing to air his interviews or report his activities, thus violating both his freedom of speech and the Broadcasting Authority Law. Kahana petitioned the Supreme Court after the board of governors of the broadcasting authority decided to strictly limit the coverage of the Kach movement and its leader. The Supreme Court overruled the board of governors' decision, thus helping a political group implement a pre-publication macro control pattern.
- Just before Israeli Television began to broadcast its historical documentary series, "The Pillar of Fire", which deals with the Holocaust and the national struggle that preceded the establishment of the state of Israel, a group of educators and public figures petitioned the Supreme Court, asking it to prevent or delay the broadcast. The group argued that the Jews of Asia, Africa, and the Balkans were not fairly represented in the series, and that the producers had ignored historical facts regarding the contribution of eastern Jews to the Zionist movement and the establishment of the state of Israel. The Supreme Court turned down the petition, on the grounds that (among other things), the court's interference would constitute "under these circumstances, an inappropriate censorship of the (broadcasting) authority's activities." This case is an example of the implementation of pre-publication macro-formal pressure, exerted by a common interest group.

Pressure in the Field of Information

The following two examples demonstrate two opposite situations: The first is a (partially successful) attempt to prevent publication, and the second—a (successful) attempt to ensure publication.

- In January 1994, the five companies operating Israel's cable TV were planning to broadcast a documentary on the investigation of a young boy's murder—a case which shocked the entire Israeli public some years ago. The film reconstructed the investigation of the suspects and their conviction, based on their own confessions. The boy's parents wished to prevent the broadcast, claiming it might offend them, because the script questioned the identity of the killers, largely adopting the defense counsel's position, that his clients were innocent. Three of the five companies agreed to cancel the broadcast. The other two disregarded the pressure and aired the film as planned. The pressure exerted by the family, with the help of certain public officials, wasmacro-formal and, of course, applied before publication.

- At the beginning of 1994, the Society for the Deaf petitioned the Court against the Israeli Broadcasting Authority. The society's representatives argued that according to a law approved two years earlier, one quarter of all pre-taped programs must have subtitles. The law also requires at least one weekly news program to include sign language translation. Even before the law was passed, the society negotiated this issue with the broadcasting authority, which occasionally complied with its requests. When the Supreme Court ruled in favor of the petition, the broadcasting authority was forced to add subtitles to the morning and afternoon news, and sign language translation to one news edition every day. In this case, the Society for the Deaf chose to apply a macro-formal control pattern, implementing post-broadcast pressure—which was in effect pre-broadcast, since its purpose was changing future broadcasts.

Discussion

It would be erroneous to express the interaction solely in terms of pressure applied to media organizations. This approach presents an unbalanced picture of such relations, perceiving the media as hapless victims requiring protection from the pressures of malicious agents seeking to limit journalists and constrain freedom of information. This view, conforming with the traditional conception of the media as the underdog, ignores several key aspects of the prevailing situation (Paletz and Entman, 1981). First, pressure is often applied in reaction to what the media have done or are likely to do, either before or after publication, as noted above. In such cases, interference and/or pressure is a response to a stimulus. It is difficult to imagine a situation in which an injured party would not attempt to defend itself or limit the scope of damage accruing from undesirable publicity. Second, even if pressure is applied without prior stimulus, editors and journalists still have various means of repelling it. The very arrangements that enable control of the media, such as formal agreements, laws and regulations, also have the power to relieve editors and journalists from a wide range of pressures. Third, in many cases, media organizations are subjected to cross-pressures applied by various interest groups that essentially cancel one another out. For example, an interest group's opposition to the airing of a television commercial encouraging the consumption of alcohol is likely to be countered by the advertiser's interest in promoting sales.

The media, which handle information, and especially the news media, participate in the process of power distribution. Doing this, it both acquires power for itself, and poses a threat to those who hold the information, and their monopoly. Therefore, the desire (and perhaps also the stimulus) to control the media, stems from the urge to control the information and its flow processes.

When the media participate in the process of power distribution, the political institution and its components see no reason to give up their part in controlling the flow of information. In this state of affairs, the political institution and the communication institution may come to blows, but when the atmosphere is one of social responsibility, both sides prefer dialogue to conflict. Being in a unique position, of *In/outsiders*, the arrangements for controlling the media institution, are constantly being negotiated and renegotiated.

The Israeli case seems to illustrate the continuos and Sisyphus process of media institutionalization in a new democracy. Dialogue with the *In/Outsiders* began during the British Mandate. The British authorities required official arrangements—laws, ordinances and regulations—to establish and regulate the activity of the mass media, Jewish and Arab alike. The Mandatory Press Ordinance (1933), like the Defense (Emergency) Regulations (1945), institutionalized one aspect of the relations obtaining between the press and the ruling authorities.[3]

Although many of these arrangements are still valid in the State of Israel, the overall picture of interaction between the communications institution and other social institutions does not resemble the one that prevailed in the Mandatory period. The rules of the game change constantly, as is demanded by changes in both institutions. Consequently, comprehension of the interaction between the two institutions demands not only examination of the background to the rules of the game but also examination of the changes within each institution and their implications.

Until the establishment of the State, the Hebrew press was, as indicated, largely a mobilized press that manifested Zionist zeal—and not only because of the party ownership of many newspapers and clandestine radio stations. The political and media institutions were also similar in terms of ideology, interests and a common goal, namely liberation from the yoke of foreign rule. The establishment of the State of Israel naturally required reassessment of media-politics relations. Moreover, the various partners in the game were no longer necessarily on the same side of the playing field facing a common rival.

During the first few years after the establishment of the State, the political institution continued to perceive the printed and broadcast press as a branch of the establishment that has to be controlled and regulated. This conception was anchored not only in the outlook that supported use of media tools for promotion of ideological and national aims but also in past experience, wherein the communications and political institutions cooperated with one another in virtually every respect. The direct party ownership and control of many newspapers only reinforced this conception and enabled its unchallenged application.

Moreover, in the transition from the Mandate to an independent state, the new ruling authorities upheld the principle of nationalization, entailing the dismantling of power bases among parties and the transfer of their functions to the new government. The young state appropriated vital services—defense, education, housing and employment—for which political movements were responsible in the Mandatory Period. The Prime Minister's Office's assumption of responsibility for radio broadcasting was yet another inevitable reflection of the overall trend towards appropriation of services for the good of the state. Control of the airwaves, like the disbanding of underground organizations, was intended to neutralize private, uncontrolled power bases.

When no explicit laws have been enacted—and at times even when they have—the legal system, i.e. the courts, arbitrate and settle disputes between the media institution and other social institutions, especially the political one. The U.S. Supreme Court, for example, is often asked to interpret the First Amendment. Its rulings guide all partners in the democratic game and effectively shape the practical patterns of relations among them.

Social responsibility principles were accepted in Israel as part of democratic norms, with the changes demanded by the special circumstances of a young democracy. Generally speaking, a *mixed model* appears to apply regarding regulation of the media-politics relationship. The mixed model combines principles of social responsibility, especially in the normative sphere, with remnants of the authoritarian conception, particularly insofar as practical manifestations are concerned.

There are some similarities between the Israeli mixed model and the *development media* model (McQuail, 1994), common in Third World societies and countries, that sanctifies various objectives and values the media's role in their achievement, such as national development in the political, economic, social and cultural spheres, as well as promotion of democracy and reinforcement of solidarity with other developing countries. The media institution and its journalists are expected to join in realizing the national goals of the new state, demanded to stay more *Insiders* than *Outsiders*. However, the Israeli *mixed* model may reaffirm the *In/Outsiders* status of the mass media as well as their vital role for a young democracy.

Notes

1. The Declaration of Independence is a declarative document rather than a legal one. Nevertheless, five years after the establishment of the State, the Israel Supreme Court determined that "the legal system on which the political institutions in Israel were established and according to which they operate attests that this is indeed a state whose foundations are democratic." Accordingly, the Court stipulated that if the Declaration of Independence "expresses the nation's vision and credo, we are obliged to accord all due attention to its provisions" (High Court of Justice 87/53).
2. The common sociological approach suggests to regard any communication system, including various media and organization, as a social institution. That sociological term "refers to arrangements involving large numbers of people whose behavior is guided by *norms* and *roles*". (Jary and Jary, 1995, p. 324.)
3. Additional Mandatory regulations determined or somehow limited the activity of other media (e.g. the Criminal Law Ordinance (1936) and the Cinema Ordinance (1927)).

References

Caspi, D. (1997). "Introduction: The Pillars of the Israeli Democracy". in: D. Caspi. ed. *Communications and Democracy in Israel*. Jerusalem. Van Leer and Hakibutz Hameuhad. (in Hebrew).

Caspi, D. and Y. Limor (1992). *The Mediators: The Mass Media in Israel 1948-1990*. Tel-Aviv: Am Oved / The Hebrew University. (in Hebrew).

— (1996a). *The Media Institution*. (Vol. III of *Mass Communication*). Tel-Aviv: The Open University. (In Hebrew).

— (1996b): "One Thousand Ways to Control the Media". Paper presented at ICA annual convention, Chicago, IL (May 1996).

— (1998). *The In/Outsiders: The Media in Israel*. Cresskill, NJ: Hampton Press.

Cater, D. (1957). *The Fourth Branch of Government*. Boston: Houghton Mifflin.

Cook, T. (1998). *Governing the News: The News Media as a Political Institution*. Chicago: The University of Chicago Press.

Giffard, C.A. (1975). Ancient Rome's Daily Gazette. *Journalism History*, 2(4), 106-9.

High Court of Justice (1953). *73/53, 87/53 - Kol Ha'am vs. Minister of Interior*. 7(2) P.D, pp. 871-899. (in Hebrew). (The official translation appears in *Selected Judgments of the Supreme Court of Israel (1948-1953)*, 1990).

Horowitz, D. and M. Lissak (1978). *The Origins of the Israeli Polity*. Chicago: Chicago University Press.

— (1989). *Trouble in Utopia: The Overburdened Polity of Israel*. Albany: State University of New York Press.

Jary, D. and J. Jary. (1995), *Dictionary of Sociology*. Collins.

Jervis, R., R.N. Lebow and J.G. Stein (1985). *Psychology and Deterrence*. Baltimore: John Hopkins University Press.

Lambeth, E. (1995). Global Media Philosophies. In: J.C. Merrill, ed., *Global Journalism: Survey of International Communication* (pp. 3-19). New York: Longman. (3rd ed.).

McQuail, D. (1992). *Media Performance*. London: Sage.

— (1994). *Mass Communication Theory*. London: Sage.

Paletz, D. L. and R.N. Entman (1981). *Media, Power, Politics*. New York: Free Press.

Picard, R. (1985). *The Press and the Decline of Democracy*. Westport, CT: Greenwood.

Siebert F., T. Peterson and W. Schramm (1963). *Four Theories ot the Press*. Urbana: University of Illinois Press.

Turow, J. (1992) *Media Systems in Society*. New York: Longman.

[illegible] (1993). The [illegible] Boulder, [illegible] Westview Press.
[illegible] (1990). [illegible] Albany: State University of New York Press.

26

Speech Presentation in the Israeli News: Ideological Constraints and Rhetorical Strategies[1]

Itzhak Roeh and Raphael Nir

It is widely accepted that news discourse is "free" from both rhetoric and ideology Western journalists would all too eagerly support such a claim, and add to it the myth of objective-mirroring of reality. It is, therefore, of particular interest for the student of news to uncover rhetorical devices related, as they are, to specific ideological "environments."

It is found (in the Israeli case) that the various ways of speech presentation contribute to the dominant "rhetoric of objectivity" in the news. First, it is the preferred indirect-speech technique that contributes to the standardized, no-digression, impersonal type of discourse. And secondly, for direct and combined speech to occur—ideology seems repeatedly to be consulted. Such digressions tend to be colored by the speaker's judgements, and, indeed, only in some situations, are quotations permitted to be presented with their original flavor.

The news tries hard to avoid an overt expression of such flavors. Direct speech is, therefore, very rare, and mimetic elements of combined speech are somewhat controlled—or, perhaps concealed—in the preferred grammatical indirect speech. Moreover, as a rule, it is the speech of non-elite, enemy, and other non-very-important speakers which is presented in combined speech. Ideological permission to deviate from indirect speech is also given to less important, less respected issues.

Patterns of speech presentations become, thus, clues for a system of values, for cultural hierarchies.

Beyond Direct and Indirect Speech

The various techniques of speech presentation in narrative fiction have been widely researched and described by scholars of both literature and linguistics (for example, McHale, 1978; Rimmon-Kenan, 1983). Speech and conversation are of primary importance in all stories, as a large portion of the activities of the actors is expressed as "speech-acts" (Austin, 1962). The problems of speech presentation are inherent in the complex communication-setting of reporting and the reported communication acts which characterize it: the utterance of the quoted speaker is interwoven with that of the narrator. The narrator can rhetorically "control" the presentation by the way in which s/he reports the actor's speech.[2] The more indirect the speech presentation, the greater the narrator's involvement as well as his/her degree of control over what is being reported. Strategies of presentation may be ordered along a continuum, with original utterances presented on the one end, and on the other end utterances which have been filtered by the narrator. Between these two poles, different degrees of directness and indirectness in the manner of reporting the utterance can be located.

A number of models have been developed to describe these strategies (for example, McHale, 1978; Rimmon-Kenan, 1983; Leech and Short, 1981). Most of these efforts have dealt with written discourse and, more specifically, with narrative fiction. There has been considerable discussion among students of literature and the media concerning whether there are any significant stylistic and linguistic differences between speech presentation in poetics and in the press (Fiske and Hartley, 1978; Roeh, 1982; Short, in a lecture, Brussels, 1984). In this article, we will attempt to apply tools developed in literary criticism to analyze the forms of speech presentation found in news broadcasting on Israel Radio.

Radio news is a special genre of discourse. From a functional-communicative perspective, it can be categorized as "informative" discourse (Kinneavy, 1980), and, in this respect, it does not differ from the printed press. The clear rhetorical differences seem to stem from the nature of the medium—vocal versus graphic or typographical—but it is not quite that simple. Radio news is not typical oral discourse in which the criterion of spontaneity applies (Tannen, 1982), i.e., it is a written text transmitted by vocal means. This implies a combination of planned discourse and paralinguistic devices typical of oral communication: the announcer's intonation and vocal variations. These characteristics have significant implications for differences in strategies for speech presentation in radio news and the printed press.

The presentation of reported utterances plays an important role in both radio and newspaper news. In a random sample of 300 news bulletins broadcast on Israel Radio from 1980 to 1982, we find that no less than 80% of the items contain different modes of speech presentation. This study is an attempt to examine these modes of speech presentation and to account for the relationships between them and the underlying ideology. Our assumption is that rhetorical regularities constitute—or, if you will, express—ideological stance, and that this study will help explain some aspects of the "world picture" created in radio news (Roeh, 1982).

Every presentation of speech in the news contains some degree of "intervention" (or rather, mediation). In the extreme case of airing an original recording of the quoted speech in the speaker's voice, the intervention consists of the editor's selection of passages for broadcast. The announcer leaves the stage, as it were, and refrains from intervening. Mediation/intervention increases as the form of speech presentation becomes progressively more indirect. One may argue that there is a correlation between ideological factors influencing the narrator's position and the manner in which he/she chooses to formulate his/her words. As we will show, in certain cases of direct and combined speech, an ironic attitude toward the quotation might be suggested; in others, the delivery can express a position of identification or support.

Leech and Short's model of speech presentation in fiction (1981: 318-336) serves as a point of departure for our analysis, providing a basis for understanding and organizing the unique characteristics of speech presentation on the radio. Their model posits five types of speech presentation:

1. Narrative report of speech-act (NRSA)
2. Indirect speech (IS)
3. Free indirect speech (FIS)
4. Direct speech (DS)
5. Free direct speech (FDS)

These categories are ordered along a continuum "from pure narrative words to pure character words" (Toolan, 1988: 128). At one pole the narrator is in full control of the manner in which the speech act is presented: the original utterance is not transmitted at all, and there is virtually no difference between a report of a verbal communicative act and a report of any other type of action or event. On the other end of the continuum is the category of free direct speech (FDS), a presentation of the utterance as originally expressed. FDS excludes even formal markers such as a colon or quotation marks, and usually any speech-act verb as well. This is the most direct technique in written speech, involving minimal intervention on the part of the narrator who ostensibly relinquishes control over the words of the speakers and lets them speak for themselves as in a drama. In fiction, this reluctance to intervene is particularly striking in the technique of stream of consciousness. As we will see, free direct speech is problematic on the radio news because the announcer cannot entirely avoid mediation: his voice must be heard!

Between the poles of the spectrum are three categories in which, with regard to the written text, the narrator has partial control over the reported speech. In the indirect speech form, the utterance is reported from the point of view of the narrator; the presentation here entails changes in deictics (words specifying person, place and time), syntax (sentence structure), punctuation (a colon and quotation marks are not used) and register (if the original utterance is formulated colloquially, the tendency is to relay it in print in a more formal register).

Free indirect speech (FID), also known as "combined speech," has drawn considerable attention in studies on literary style (for example, Golomb, 1968; Even, 1968; Banfield, 1973, 1982; Steinberg, 1982; Stanzel 1984). By FID an attempt is made to partly imitate the speaker's style and, in this way, to convey an impression of the original utterance while maintaining the grammatical pattern of indirect speech. In addition to its mimetic character, free indirect speech can include some of the formal principles of direct speech, particularly deistic markers of time, place, and person (Borer 1981).

As mentioned above, the various forms of combined speech can reflect different attitudes of the narrator. They can point to distance between the narrator and the quoted speaker or, alternatively, to the narrator's greater identification with the speaker. The narrator can also use combined speech to camouflage a particular position or to create ambiguity as to his attitude vis-a-vis the quotation.

Speech Presentation on Israel Radio News

The style of news on Israel Radio's hourly reports is highly uniform (Roeh, 1982). It is a serious style, "reverent" and highly standardized. A certain characteristic register for radio news reports, which can be labeled "Radio News Reporting Style" (RNRS), has crystallized in the 19 daily news bulletins broadcast hourly from 6 a.m. to 1 a.m. This register, modeled very much after the classic style of the BBC news, is distinguished by lexical, morphological and syntactic traits as well as by an authoritative, "holier-than-thou" intonation. In the typical RNRS sentence, as in modern Hebrew in general, a nominal phrase is followed by a predicate. As a rule, neither colloquialisms nor highly stylized literary expressions are used. First- and second-person pronouns are never permitted, and one finds no trace of idiosyncrasy. RNRS, in other words, is an "unmarked" variety of news discourses. Moreover, the Israel Broadcasting authority employs a language supervisor to guard against digression from the grammatical norms of classical Hebrew, which adds to the standardized reverence of RNRS. Although no comprehensive and detailed description of this style has yet been developed, Israeli Hebrew-speakers, who are avid listeners of radio news, most certainly have internalized RNRS, and thus can easily sense stylistic deviations.

The salience of RNRS increases when it is compared with the language of the radio's current affairs news magazines (broadcast three times daily—morning, noon and evening). There is a clear distinction on Israel Radio between the two genres of news programs. The bulletins mediate—or "tell"—and they rely primarily on indirect speech. The current affairs broadcasts, on the other hand, "show" and so lend themselves to more varied presentation techniques, such as the use of first-person and direct speech.[3]

The prevalence of indirect speech can be further explained by the distinctive nature of the news bulletin: it is presented in its entirety by one announcer. This generic constraint implies that the narrator must present direct speech by taking upon him/herself the role of an actor expressing/transmitting the words others have spoken But the medium of speech permits only limited markings of direct speech, unlike the colon and quotation marks of printed discourse which clearly define the boundaries between the narrator and the cited speaker. The presenter is, therefore, compelled to modify his/her intonation in order to assume the position of the quoted source. Doing so necessarily suggests interpretation—something the news generally seeks to avoid, and it will, therefore, prefer indirect over direct speech. Indeed, a shift out of Radio News Reporting Style, out of indirect speech, is one of the few means available to the presenter to convey to the audience a hint of an ideological message. Combined speech can provide the vehicle for that.

The question of when a digression from RNRS is permissible is our overriding question, since it may point to connections between rhetoric and ideology in the news.[4] In the following sections, we will discuss how different techniques of speech presentation color the news ideologically.

To analyze the techniques of speech presentation on the radio news, we found it necessary to modify the model constructed for poets. We suggest the following categories:

1. Recorded speech (RS)
2. Direct speech (DS)
3. Free indirect speech (FIS)
4. Indirect speech with signaled citation (ISC)
5. Free direct speech (FDS)*
6. Indirect speech (IS)
7. Reported speech-act (RSA)

* The reasons for the location of FDS here are specified on p. 21.

Arranging the categories along a continuum yields:

1, 2	3,4,5	6,7
direct	combined	indirect

In our corpus of 300 items, speech presentation was found in 242 items, with the following distribution:

	Category	%
1.	(RS)	0.6
2.	(DS)	1.9
3.	(FIS)	33.1
4.	(ISC)	2.5
5	(FDS)	6.0
6	(IS)	44.6
7	(RSA)	10.3

The table illustrates that the proportional representation of categories 1 and 2 (direct presentation of speech) is quite low (3.7%), and that indirect speech (categories 6 and 7) is the most common (54.9%). Combined speech (categories 3, 4 and 5) is found in 41.6% of the items that include speech presentation. To understand the significance of these findings, we will now review the characteristics of each of the categories.

Analysis of the Findings

Recorded Speech

Recorded speech (RS) is an extreme case of direct speech (DS) and is used very rarely in Radio News Report Style (RNRS). Only two out of the 300 news items in our corpus employ this technique. RS is indeed a distinct stylistic choice and, hence, has high rhetorical value. It should also be stressed that although RS is the least mediated presentation of speech in RNRS, it is a highly controlled discourse by virtue of its scarcity. The very decision to use it implies a strong statement. What does recorded speech connote and what accounts for its relative absence?

As our corpus illustrates, it takes a traumatic event for a news item to present related speech "as-it-is," with minimal mediation. One of the two items using RS tells the story of a kidnapped boy whose life is seriously threatened; the other is about a well-known personality who committed suicide. These are two clearly emotionally charged stories, and the language is accordingly loaded and empathic.

In the first story, the mother urges the kidnappers to let her son go; in the second, the lawyer of the deceased reads the letter found with the body. It is the mother speaking herself, not the usual "translation" into detached indirect speech; it is the lawyer reading the letter from beginning to end, not the more usual edited paraphrase. Both are in the first person; both express a strong, emotional point of view, which RNRS typically avoids.

What explains these exceptions? A strong sense of high drama seems to be the compelling factor. Surprise and shock, grief and compassion can easily be communicated. A deep sense of identification with the victims can easily be shared by broadcasters and listeners alike. A wide consensus underlies the situation, where no partisan views, let alone dissenting responses, can be expected. Also, it can be argued that referential information is scarce at such moments, and is replaced by emotional appeals, by expressions of shock, wonder or dismay which constitute the information of the moment. These are clear instances of "showing": the extreme and rare events "speak for themselves."

Direct Speech

Direct speech (DS) is a clear exception to the rule of RNRS. It occurs in our data in 2.9% of presented speech units. Once again, the question is when this digression is "permitted." Not surprisingly, some of the conditions that account for the freedom to digress in recorded speech resurface here, where some of the same rhetorical characteristics are involved.

Two of the seven stories that include a DS unit are those already mentioned, the kidnapped child and the suicide, which were subsequently repeated in the news. The first opens with the statement that there is no new information to add to that already reported. The mother then pleads again withe kidnappers. But it seems that high drama cannot repeat itself without variation, and the newscaster now takes the mother's role, reading the text in her name. Direct speech is mediated not only in terms of the newscaster's intonation and cadence, but also through the limited editing involved: the original recorded speech is now divided into two parts, with the newscaster's opening and linking clauses:

1. The mother addressed the kidnappers, saying "Please, keep your promise: let our son come back home. I appeal to your conscience, and for heaven's sake, let him go." And to her son the mother said, "We are doing everything we can so that you can come back home." (Literally translated from the Hebrew text).

Not only is such an explicit piece of DS unusual for the news, so, too, is its dominant "conative function" (in Jakobson's terms [1960]). It seems, again, that only the exceptional situation—where universal compassion is presumed—allows for such an exceptional deviation. Indeed, when such an "emotional consensus" is assumed, a newscaster is expected to take sides and to relinquish the normal modus operandi of detached presentation. It is inconceivable, after all, to suggest a neutral, indifferent point of view when the story refers to innocent victims; the rhetorical rules of "objective" presentation will not do.

In the story of the suicide, the deceased had been a controversial political figure. The adversarial attitudes of public figures eventually will be expressed and broadcast.

But this can wait. The morning the news breaks is a time for emotions to be aired and disputes controlled. Thus, the trade union secretary is quoted in DS at the very outset of the 12.00 p.m. news bulletin:

2. "The Union is deeply shocked," said the secretary-general.

Other illustrations of DS are the Israeli defense minister's criticism of the PLO, and an Israeli political personality's call on the nation to actively defend democracy against fanatics who threaten it. Common to them is the use of emphatic expressions, which may be seen as serving Israel's mainstream ideology: Arens harshly derides the PLO, and Mr. Pa'il provocatively calls on us to save democracy from its enemies.

3. Minister of Defense Arens says: "We in Israel have known this for many years. This is not a national liberation movement but a conglomerate of terror gangs fanatically engaged in terrorist operations."

4. Mr. Pa'il states: "Since the police are inactive, we have no other alternative but to create an organization for self-defense to stop future pogroms."

These two illustrations exemplify different rhetorical strategies, clearly suggesting a committed point of view. These are constructed through parallelism, repetition and contrast (example 3), or through loaded lexicon ("terror gangs," "fanatically," "pogroms") embedded in an adversative syntactic pattern ("this is not but...," "we have no...but..."), as in examples (3) and (4).

Direct speech, then, is problematic for RNRS because it exerts pressure on the single narrator to interpret. He must either assume an involved, committed point of view, or a detached, ironic stance.[5] When the ideological and/or emotional climate is one of acceptance, compassion or consensus, a committed position seems permissible. Alternatively, when the story under consideration implies ideological indifference, neutrality or lack of emotional involvement, the approach will be ironic. Although both empathy and irony are hypothetically possible when DS is used, in our corpus we find only the former, the committed. We do find the detached, ironic attitude—though mitigated—in combined speech presentations. This largest sub-category here is free indirect speech.

Free Indirect Speech

Progressing along the continuum from direct to indirect speech, the first free indirect speech illustrations represent a subcategory: They are characterized by pronouns that help represent the point of view of the quoted speaker, and are closest in style—and committed attitude—to direct speech. As can be seen, they imply a clearly, "unproblematic" ideological standpoint and so they are particularly emphatic.

5. The Minister of Defense said that the Lebanese experience, indeed, supports *our* stance...and it is clear to *us* that to give up the territories... is to jeopardize *our* security.

6. The Minister of Defense said that there is no limit to that which *we* owe *our* widows, but there is a limit to *our* resources.

These are the only two illustrations in our corpus using the first person in an indirect speech pattern, and they are thus hardly distinguishable from the preceding DS units. To be sure, indirect speech subordination, as in (5) and (6), creates some distance between the presenter and the quoted speaker, but this distance is highly modified (perhaps "compensated" for) by the explicitly suggested committed point of view: the digressive first person that recurs three times in both (5) and (6) by no means conveys the "objective" position usually suggested by the typical RNRS indirect speech pattern. On the contrary, the presenter quotes the Minister using his own expression: "We are talking about our security, our widows." The implied point of view is, obviously, loaded and committed.

Moreover, in example (6), the Hebrew formulation provides not only syntactic and lexical parallelism and contrast ("there is no limit to"/"there is a limit to") but also a rich network of consonance where l's and s's repeatedly counter-echo to reinforce the opposition between an unlimited moral pledge and rather limited material support.

Ein gvul laxov she'anu xavim la'almanot/ax yesh gvul la'masha'bim shelanu.

Most examples of FIS, which oscillate between direct and indirect speech, can be described as those where mimetic elements (representing the original style of the speaker) are identifiable. These elements contribute to a rhetoric of authenticity, even though the news register typically tends toward a high degree of narrator mediation and control. The question raised then, is which mimetic elements "penetrate" indirect speech—turning it into free indirect speech—and where?

Approximately 80 instances in our sample contain mimetic elements. As a rule, these are marked deviations from RNRS and can be grouped as follows:

(a) Parallelisms and repetitions
These can be further divided into syntactic (additive or adversative), lexical (equivalent and oppositional) and phonological patterning (assonance, consonance, alliteration, rhyme).

(b) Literary, figurative and idiomatic expressions
(These can be described as mainly "upward" digressions from RNRS.)

(c) Colloquialisms
("downward" digressions).

(d) Intensifiers
Typical here are adjectives like "only" and "indeed," but some collocations also occur.

(a) *Parallelisms, repetitions.* In most cases where mimetic penetration into indirect speech creates FIS, more than one linguistic level is activated. Some of the different levels interact and reinforce each other. The more interactions, the more difficult it is to "translate" FIS into standard RNRS.

The most recurrent pattern is parallelism and repetition on the syntactic level (which, again, involves in most cases some of the other deviations which produce rhetorical density). Examples abound, and the following represent just a few:

7. Mr. Peres said to Mr. Shultz that Washington should understand [a] that Arafat is not moderate and [b] that he has not changed his policy.

[Hebrew: *Mar Peres amar lemar Shultz she'Washington tzrixa lehavin [a] she'eyn Arafat matun [b] vexi lo shina klal et mediniyuto.]*

8. The lawyers concluded that Mr. L. [a] did not commit any crime, [b] was innocent, and [c] all his efforts were [i] on behalf of the bank, [ii] on behalf of the working people, and [iii] on behalf of the state of Israel.
[Hebrew: *Orxey hadin hisiku ki [a] mar L. lo bitze'a kol avera, [b] haya xaf mipesha, [c] ve kol ma'amatzav hayu [i] lema'an habank, [ii] lema'an hapoalim, [iii] ulema'an medinat yisrael.]*

The highly elaborate rhetorical patterning heightens the emphatic expression—one can feel a touch of crescendo: Mr. L. is described in favorable terms that become more and more powerful, or "seductive," as we proceed from one additive clause to another. Repetition of the syntactic structure itself creates a sense of seduction, as descriptions become increasingly approving, from "did not commit any crime" to the more positive "innocent," to the complimentary "on behalf of the bank," to the laudatory "on behalf of the state of Israel."

9. An official in Bonn says that [a] in Germany it is well known that there is terror in Syria and [b] that Syria is involved in acts of terror in Germany.

This is parallelism of a particular nature: a mirror repetition, or symmetry, is created by "in Germany, terror, Syria: Syria, terror, in Germany."

As we have noted, an emphatic expression built on a multilevel, repetitive, additive pattern is hard to translate into the conventional third-person indirect speech of RNRS. It can be argued that rhetorical value—its highly marked stylistic character—helps such an utterance to be included in the news:

10. Member of Parliament Zaiger says that [a] the public owns most of the banks' capital, but [b] the rights to vote and decide are in the hands of the few.
[Hebrew: *Haver hakneset Ziger omer ki [a] hatzibur maxzik berov menayot habankim, aval [b] zexuyot hahatzba'a netunot bidey me'atim].*

This is an adversative parallelism pattern, where the emphasis is based on the rhetorical power of contrast. In our corpus, however, most parallelisms (40 out of 50) are additive.

In the following (Hebrew) example of additive syntactic parallelism, we see a highly patterned network of consonance, rhyme and meter:

11. The deputy Prime Minister has said that

[a] there is no absolute solution//to the problem of emigration, and

[b] there is not way//to fight it.

Hebrew: [a] *ein pitron muxlat//leva'ayat ha'aliya.*

[b] *ve'ein derex axat//lehilaxem ba.*

Parallelisms as in the above, where syntax, lexicon, meter, and vocal properties all interact and reinforce each other, produce a particularly powerful, rhetorically seductive expression. If rhetoric is to be measured in terms of its power to minimize choices of interpretation and response (Paine, 1984; Suleiman, 1983), then such a multilevel rhetorical strategy can be said to be "successful" in that it might eliminate or weaken alternative readings.

Most syntactic parallelisms include lexical repetition. In some cases, such repetitions are particularly salient and contribute to the rhetoric of authenticity and emphasis, as in the following:

12. The king of Morocco says that [a] Israel from its viewpoint... [b] Morocco from its viewpoint...and [c] Arab countries from their viewpoint...will contribute to the process of negotiation.

Finally, the category of repetition may also include phonological patterning. Consonance, for example, although not always easily spotted, should be looked for within patterns of heightened rhetoric, to which it contributes its share. Where vocal properties are thus patterned, the poetic function of speech is further reinforced—attention is focused on the patterns of speech rather than on meaning, and the processing of information is slowed down, as Jakobson and the Russian Formalists strongly insist.

The combination of consonance, meter and rhyme noted above is worth repeating here:

Hebrew: 11a. *Ein pitron muxlat//lega'aya ha'aliya, ve'ein derex axat/lehilaxem ba.*

(b) *Literary, figurative, idiomatic expressions*. This category of digression more often than not suggests a detached and, at times, ironic point of view and, only in a few cases, a committed one. Clearly, this group of illustrations would be more illuminating in Hebrew—how does one convey upward deviations when it is "literariness," archaisms or idiomatic expressions that makes the difference? We will try by relying on English paraphrase.

What, then, are the reality materials involved? What are the ideological conditions that permit one point of view rather than another? The actors involved in some of these examples, for instance, are the

Iranian minister for foreign affairs, the Libyan ambassador to the U.N., Jordan's King Hussein, the leader of a coup in Nigeria, and a criminal. common to them all is the fact that ideologically they are seen to be deserving of derision. Interestingly, the literary expressions used contribute to a characterization of these actors as unreliable, as the following examples might show:

1. The Iranian minister, while criticizing the U.S. for its threat to leave UNESCO, uses an archaic, Mishnaic idiom. UNESCO will profit from such a decision, he argues, using "high" Hebrew—and the intonation for the newscaster is necessarily ironic. Neither the argument nor the person who utters it can be taken too seriously.

2. The Libyan ambassador surprisingly alludes to the same Jewish linguistic tradition His is a tail-piece, where it is reported that the ambassador refuses to pay the rent for the (huge) house where he resides. The rent is too high, he complains, and he is being harassed by the municipality for some evil reason. The lexicon to describe this harassment is again Mishnaic, high Hebrew; and the position of the narrator—as revealed through the newscaster's unavoidable intonation—is detached and ironic, and suggests that the speaker is unreliable.

3. The story of a burglar caught red-handed is another example of the characterization of an actor as untrustworthy. Here the narrator is permitted to take sides. The court is quoted reverently, and he suspect presented unfavorably. The news is surely not expected to treat criminals with respect. The suspect is reported a saying that he was "just walking innocently in the bosom of Nature when, by sheer chance, he found the key that happened to fit ..."

(c) *Colloquialisms*. The digression downward—to spoken rather than to literary language—contributes to the rhetoric of reliable authenticity. If the use of archaic Hebrew by an Iranian minister raises suspicion as to its authenticity, the use of colloquial Hebrew by an Israeli minister raises suspicion as to its authenticity, the use of colloquial Hebrew by an Israeli minister appears reliable enough.

On a continuum from the committed point of view to the detached, ironic position, colloquialisms can represent varying degrees of both. When the expression verges on slang—when digression or incongruity is particularly strong—irony appears to be more dominant than the sense of reliability. Since it is almost impossible to demonstrate these ambiguities through translation, we reluctantly suggest the above generalizations as findings. In only 9 of the 80 FIS cases are colloquial elements identifiable, and all of them are minimal—one or two words in length. Colloquialism is, therefore, a rhetorical device which the news tries to minimize. The explanation again may well be the norm of a high language standard, reverent and serious, and strongly supported by organizational control.

(d) *Intensifiers*. There are approximately 20 units free indirect speech using intensifiers:

13. The prime minister says that *all* the steps taken by the [Lebanese] president are insufficient.

"All" (Hebrew: *kol*) recurs in 9 units, and it contributes to an emphatic reading that captures the flavor of the original utterance. Other intensifiers function similarly with varying degrees of rhetorical power:

14. [McFarlane] said that [this] can, *indeed*, open a new page.

15. [The police] say that it is *absolutely* unjustified.

16. [A Syrian spokesman] says that the Americans *themselves* are to blame.

17. [The Histadrut secretary] said that with such inflation...these demands are the *only* way out.

Some common, though not idiomatic, collocations also function as intensifiers:

18. Participants...asked the president to secure *full and absolute* sovereignty over all Lebanon's lands.

19. He believes that it depends on what will be said and written, *here and elsewhere.*

To conclude, free indirect speech is generated by an ideological base that constrains the limits of linguistic variation. It is characterized by loaded, evaluative and emphatic expressions, by different linguistic digressions, by marked rhetorical devices and highly patterned forms of presentation. All of them embody a permission to deviate from RNRS's dominant rhetoric of "no opinion," "only the facts."

Indirect Speech with Signaled Citations [ISC]

Ambiguities of mediated speech mixed with a free flow of original, authentic speech are explicitly controlled in this small category of five cases in our corpus. Here the narrator specifically signals that he/she is letting another participant speak. The parenthetical expressions "as he calls it," "as he puts it," "according to her definition," make it clear that the narrator is maintaining distance, that what he/she is about to say is the language of the source, not of "the news."

This category is noteworthy as an illustration of a rhetorical strategy closest to marked direct speech in print. The explicit signal "as he puts it" before a quote is somewhat analogous to the use of quotation makers in print. An attempt is made to clearly distinguish the source's words from the narrator's paraphrase, so as to avoid ambiguities.

However, the category is so small that generalizations regarding ideological constraints are difficult to draw. One item refers to an utterance by PLO leader Arafat, a case in which distance is expected on Israel Radio:

20. The massacre of his people, *as he calls it.*

Another refers to the KGB, which the news is supposed to treat with suspicion.

21. The head of the KGB says that the Soviet authorities will act firmly against—*as he puts it*—subversive elements in his country.

In these cases an ideological stand is obvious: "We" Israelis shouldn't believe them.

Free Direct Speech (FDS)

To the extent that free direct speech refers to the literary technique "stream of consciousness,"[6] it is foreign to our corpus. The narrator of the news can by no means let the characters speak or reflect freely in a way analogous to the free flow of consciousness in twentieth-century fiction. Moreover, as a rule, there are no stylistic markers (either mimetic or deictic) in FDS that may create an impression of an authentic, original utterance. What we suggest calling FDS can be so denominated for two main reasons: grammatically the quoted speech is not subordinate to the main clause, and no formal markets tell us exactly where the boundaries of the citation are. The pattern is identical in all fourteen cases of FDS:

- FDS opens the news item;
- the citation is presented in the opening clause;
- it is followed by the main clause, always assuming the same form:

  "so" + declarative verb + source.

For example:

22. France will not sell any more ammunition and weapons to Libya, *so said* the French ambassador to Beirut.

As for the news value of the stories in this group, most of them are considered as of high news value: they refer to issues of political existence and survival, national security and elite personalities. Generally, reference is to "very important," well-placed and prestigious sources, and they talk about Israel's relationships with the big power, its military and economic predicament and related matters. These make up the "right stuff" of most news stories, and of most, if not all, of the stories that constitute the indirect speech category.

In both IS and FDS, language is characteristically unmarked (i.e., no lexical or grammatical digressions from RNRS are present). It is hard to find among the FDS stories any of the rhetorical elements described above which are typical either of direct of combined speech. Likewise, the correlating reality-materials and ideological conditions of those strategies are rare in this group. The narrator does not suggest less control, and no mimesis, no authenticity, is offered. Moreover, the pattern of unmarked presented speech opening the sentence helps blur the speech presentation of the citation. "France will not sell any more ammunition and weapons," can easily be taken as either reported political action or the thoughts and intentions of politicians. One cannot necessarily assume that this is a quotation unless the clause which follows—"so said the French ambassador," for example—so suggests. (The newspaper, of course, provides the reader with quotation marks so as to avoid ambiguity.)

To sum up, then, free direct speech is a category used for reports of high news value. Therefore, ideology is not likely to permit linguistic deviation, which might imply distance or any recognizable detached point of view. Judged as serious news, it is rhetorically characterized by a high degree of control—by standardized presentation. The pattern of "so said" or "so announced" is required to reinforce the authority and truthfulness of the presented statement, as is the rule with most other serious news. We find, therefore, that FDS is the closest to indirect speech in the news.

Indirect Speech and Reported Speech Acts [IS and RSA]

As already noted, indirect speech, including the reporting of speech acts, is the most typical presentation strategy of radio news bulletins:

over half of the cases of speech presentation are reported in IS or RSA. Moreover, indirect speech is actually much more frequent than the numbers indicate, as it is in essence the dominant grammatical framework of "combined speech." As this paper has tried to show, these "combined" strategies are, in fact, indirect presentations, which include mimetic or direct speech elements.

The typical structure for indirect speech without mimetic elements is:

> "*quoted source—declarative verb—subordinate conjunction—clause*" with the source and the verb differing according to the circumstances. The deictics of person, place and time change with the point of view of the narrator. On the radio news, however, only the pronouns change—third person replaces first person. As for location, the quoted source usually relates to a place by specifically naming it—Beirut, Haifa, Washington and so on—rather than by using demonstrative pronouns such as "here" and "there." Thus, a variation in the narrator's position does not require a change in the signaling of the location. As to time, there is generally no difference in position. By their very definition, the events reported in the news are "new;" that is, they are near the time of the broadcast, and so the perspective of the narrator and the source are both in the present. We therefore do not find transitional changes such as from "now" to "then." Also, there are almost no changes in tense with the shift from narrator to source, since Hebrew syntax does not require agreement of tense among the various verbs in the quote.

When the presented speech consists of more than one sentence, the reporter tends to repeat the declarative clause. This is due to the linear nature of vocal presentation. The listener cannot be helped along by graphic markings such as quotation marks, and he/she must be reminded that what is being said is not the direct report of the narrator but the relayed words of someone else. Given this, declarative clauses abound in indirect speech: he-said..., he-continued..., he-added...., etc.

Indirect speech presentation is typical of RNRS, the unmarked style of radio news, where, for example, first- or second-person is not used and the tendency is to refrain from using loaded lexical expressions (Roeh, 1982). The reporter plays the role of the "outside observer" without assuming ideological responsibility toward the events or the citations—with an uncommitted point of view. Therefore, indirect speech does not use rhetorical devices such as parallelism, repetition or figurative language, which might disclose the narrator's position toward the text.

A mere report of a speech act (RSA) can be situated at the extreme pole of the speech presentation continuum, a clear case of "telling." This strategy is far more frequent in journalism, print and electronic, than in fiction. The reason for this, apparently, is that in a news report, the reporter is usually not interested in rendering the item in its original version, and often actually is unable to do so. This category also includes items reporting about future plans, in which the newscaster relates a speech act that will take place. Because the words have not yet been spoken, they clearly cannot be quoted, even through indirect speech:

23. Foreign Minister Shamir will ask the Market leaders to improve trade conditions between Israel and the Market countries.

Indeed, in half the cases of RSA (8 out of 17), the declarative verb is in the present or future tense. The former is used to signal a speech act that has already occurred as well as one which will take place on the day the item is reported. From the narrator's point of view, then, the present tense refers to either the past or the present.

This presentation strategy transfers the emphasis from the rhetorical to the illocutionary aspect of the utterance—it focuses on the essence of the speech act. In other words, RSA emphasizes the speaker's intention and does not reflect how the words were originally uttered. The content clause common to indirect speech is replaced by a noun phrase, which may be viewed as the nominalization of the underlying sentence. The declarative verb is more often modal in RSA than it is in IS, where the modality can be gleaned from the paraphrased quotation itself.

In a sizable number of cases it is difficult to determine whether the report is of a speech act or of a regular action. This intermediate group includes, for example, items where the declarative verb is "to decide." The "decision" may not necessarily be performed as a speech act; it may be the conclusion of the narrator. For example,

24. In Kiryat Netaphin, the residents and those of nearby Bidiya decided to establish in Shomron a "house of peace," which will reflect the culture and folklore of Jews and Arabs.

In RSA, then, the narrator's rhetorical control over the report of the events is the greatest, but it is expressed through the declarative verb, not through mimetic reported speech.

In our examination of the categories along the reported speech continuum, we began with recorded speech, where mimetic elements are most dominant, and concluded at the diegetic pole with a report of a speech act, where mimesis is not found at all. As noted, the instances of speech presentation in the news are far from evenly distributed among the seven categories. The standard practice is to relay citations in an indirect manner and, thus, to create an impression of the absence of a particular, let alone committed, point of view—of a rhetoric of objectivity (Roeh et al., 1980). The few instances of direct and recorded speech, as well as most cases of combined speech, help us realize how strongly bound by ideological constraints the rhetoric is. So the point of view of the dominant ideology is disclosed. This is illustrated in the link between rhetorical strategies and reality materials, or the kinds of individuals whose speech is presented.

The initially autonomous, non-ideological aesthetic pressure to use a variety of different, often contrasting, strategies of presentation is, ultimately, ideologically constrained. Elements of this variety, such as "showing" or "telling," mimesis or diegesis, serve the ideological mainstream. For direct, and otherwise mimetic, speech to be permitted into a dominantly indirect speech territory, specific aspects of reality must be addressed. And, as direct speech or mimetic elements in indirect speech—generally loaded and emphatic in our corpus—can disclose a narrator's attitude, the overall trend in the news will be to avoid them, unless wide consensus is presupposed. Rhetoric can draw upon consensus which is either "positive" or "negative;" it can be loaded and committed in support of a mother's appeal for her kidnapped child (example 1), or it can be loaded and ironically detached, as in the case of the Iranian minister's criticism of the U.S., or of the Libyan ambassador's complaint to the U. N. Enemies are easy to be manipulated.

Ideology is probably not as hegemonic as some critics would have it, but "resonant"—as Geertz (1973) would put it—it seems to be. It apparently does not fully determine the rules of presentation, but it does seem to largely delineate the limits of linguistic variation. Or so appears to be the case in Radio News Report Style on Israel Radio.

Notes

1. This study was supported by a grant from the Israel Academy of Sciences.
2. By "narrator," we refer to Booth's concept of "implied narrator" (cf. Booth, 1961).
3. This follows the well established distinction between "telling" and "showing" in literary theory, for example, Booth (1961), Rimmon-Kenan (1983), Stanzel (1981).
4. Our conception of ideology is grounded in the culturalist-pluralist approach more than it follows the Marxist view (see, for example, Geertz's "Ideology as a Cultural System" [1973]). We assume that mainstream ideology does express itself in the news and, presumably, is particularly influential (although not unequivocally

dominant) where a monopolistic radio and television system operates, as is the case in Israel. For the purpose of this study, however, the question is not whether ideology stems from a materialistic base "to distort reality" but, rather, how, as a constraining power, it competes and interacts in the cultural market with technological and symbolic determinants—such as in the medium of radio, and patterns provided by the Hebrew language—to ultimately produce an output that is ideologically colored.

5. This has been discussed by literary critics such as Rimmon-Kenan 1983) and Golomb (1968).
6. (Cf. Toolan, 1988: 128).

References

Auerbach, Eric (1953) (1958). *Mimesis: The Representation of Reality in Western Literature.* Princeton: Princeton University Press.

Austin, John (1962). *How to Do Things with Words.* Cambridge, MA: Harvard University Press.

Banfield, Ann (1973). Narrative Style and the Grammar of Direct and Indirect Speech. *Foundations of Language* 10: 1-39.

——— (1982) *Unspeakable Sentences.* New York: Routledge and Kegan Paul.

Booth, Wayne C. (1961). *The Rhetoric of Fiction.* Chicago: Chicago University Press.

Borer, Hagit (1981). Linguistic Aspects of the Combined Discourse. *Hasifrut* 30-31, 35-57 (Hebrew).

Even, Joseph (1968). Represented Speech: A Concept in the Theory of Prose and Its Use in Hebrew Fiction. *Hasifrut* 1, 1: 140-152 (Hebrew).

Fiske, John and Hartley, J. (1978). *Reading Television.* London: Methuen.

Frye, Northrop (1957). *Anatomy of Criticism.* Princeton: Princeton University Press.

Geertz, Clifford (1973). *Ideology as a Cultural System.* In *The Interpretation of Cultures.* New York: Basic Books.

Golomb, Harai (1968). Combined Speech: A Major Technique in the Prose of Agnon. *Hasifrut* 1, 2: 251-62 (Hebrew).

Jakobson, Roman (1960). Linguistics and Poetics. In *Style in Language*, T. Sebeok (ed.). Cambridge, MA: M.I.T. Press.

Kinneavy, James L. (1980). *A Theory of Discourse.* New York: Norton.

Leech, Geoffrey N. (1983). *Principles of Pragmatics.* London and New York: Longman.

Leech, Geoffrey N. and Short, M.H. (1981). *Style in Fiction.* London: Longman.

McHale, Brian (1978). FID: A Survey of Recent Accounts. *Poetics and Theory of Literature* 3: 249-87.

Paine, Robert (1984). Politically Speaking: Cross-Cultural Studies of Rhetoric. Memorial University, Newfoundland, ISER.

Rimmon-Kenan, Shlomit (1983). *Narrative Fiction.* London and New York: Methuen.

Roeh, Itzhak (1982). *The Rhetoric of News in the Israel Radio.* Bochum: Studienerag N. Brockmeyer.

Roeh, Itzhak; Katz, Elihu; Cohen, Akiva; and Zelizer, Barbara (1980). *Almost Midnight: Reforming the Late Night News.* Beverly Hills: Sage.

Ron, Moshe (1981). FID: Mimetic Language Games and the Subject of Fiction. *Poetics Today*, 1/2: 17-39.

Stanzel, Franz (1981) Teller-Characters and Reflector-Characters in Narrative Theory. *Poetics Today* 2/2: 5-15.

Stanzel, Franz (1984). *Theory of Narrative.* Cambridge: Cambridge University Press.

Steinberg, Meir (1982). Point of View and the Indirections of Direct Speech. *Language and Style*. 15/2: 67-117.
Suleiman, Susan (1983). *Authoritarian Fictions: The IdeologicNovel as a Literary Genre*. New York: Columbia University Press.
Tannen, Deborah (1982). The Oral/Literate Continuum in Discourse. In *Spoken and Written Language* D. Tannen (ed.) Norwood, N.J.: Ablex.
Toolan, Michael J. (1988). *Narrative—A Critical Linguistic Introduction*. London and New York: Routledge and Kegan Paul.
Weizman, Eldaah (1984). Some Register Characteristics of Journalistic Language: Are They Universals? *Applied Linguistics* 5/1: 39/50.

27

The Rabin Myth and the Press: Reconstruction of the Israeli Collective Identity

Yoram Peri

The assassination of Prime Minister Yitzhak Rabin on Saturday night, November 4, 1995, was one of the most dramatic events that had ever occurred in Israeli history. A few days earlier, during the Israeli Oscar award ceremony, Rabin had said, "For us in Israel, life is bigger than the movies". He had no idea how portentous his words had been. Rabin's assassination occurred in the backdrop of a severe crisis of national identity. The media is a major factor in the process of shaping the new Israeli identity, and therefore it held a crucial role in the aftermath of the assassination.

But what was this role? Was the media the public sphere, "an instrument for enlightenment" (Scannell, 1992:339) where free and unrestricted discourse took place? Or perhaps the national press and broadcasting were agencies contributing to the reproduction of existing political and economic orders by underpinning their legitimacy through their complex practices of representation (Hall et al. 1980; Hall, 1977, 1982)?

I will argue the latter: that in spite of the fact that the media was seen as the central arena for deliberation about the national identity, such a discourse did not take place. Dominant groups in society have used that critical event in order not only to reintegrate society but to reinvent it (Anderson, 1983). They did so by broadening the hegemonic coalition and by distancing and discrediting the others. Their tool was the media, which deconstructed Rabin's biography and used the martyrdom to reconstitute the mainstream secular Zionist story.[1]

The unit of time under study was the week starting with the day of the killing. Could a shorter period of time have been chosen—from the assassination to the end of the funeral, sundown on Tuesday, November 7th—the most relevant analytical tool could be the concept of "media event", such as a coronation, or the assassinations of Kennedy (Dayan and Katz, 1992) or Indira Gandhi (Minwalla, 1990 quoted in Dayan and Katz). A week was chosen however, not just because of its association with the Jewish custom of *shiva*—the seven-day period of mourning—but primarily because this was the duration of the national period of mourning, the period of time in which—to use Schramm's analysis of the Kennedy assassination—the crisis ended and the social system returned to equilibrium (Schramm, 1965:7).

The *shiva* was, first of all, the unit of time set by the media programming for the national ritual of mourning. This was the liminal period in which, the event—the assassination and what it evokes—"occupies society's center" (Dayan and Katz, 1992:89). Indeed, the week culminated in a mass rally that paralleled the one that had served as the setting for the assassination, in the very same town square, with the name now changed from Kings of Israel Plaza to Rabin Plaza. It was at this rally that the widow of the assassinated Prime Minister also crowned the successor, Shimon Peres. But, above all, what marked the end of the week-long ritual of national mourning was the fact that this was when the media returned to their routine schedule of programs.

The Political Ritual that Followed Rabin's Assassination

The assassination of Rabin plunged Israelis into bewilderment, shock, and deep anxiety. For many, the anger and bereavement were intense and felt personally; even for those outside the political center, the mourning was not an expression of tertiary loss (of someone remote), but of primary loss (of a member of one's family or someone in a primary relationship). On the collective level, the assassination created a liminal moment, as defined by Victor Turner (1969, 1974), a situation of intense communal emotion, heightened social relations, communitas, a reflexive condition in which society "looks at itself and asks not just what it is, but what it should be".

Indeed, from the moment that word of the assassination became public, Israeli society opened the parentheses of a liminal moment: Although there were no acts of sedition, incitement or outbursts of aggression, behavior was characterized primarily by an interruption in the daily routine and high emotional intensity. The public drew together for a secular ritual of national mourning in which the media played a key role. In modern society in which the media perform an important function in the bestowal of meaning and as a primary source of social cohesion (Jensen, 1991:2), the ritual itself dons the garb of a media event. It becomes a secular ritual that television does not just cover, but shapes and creates; a political ritual fraught with secular symbolism that casts light on the core values of society and the components of the collective memory (Lukes, 1975:12).

In fact, in the spirit of Rabin's remark about the movies and "real life" in Israel, it is not hard to create this symbolism. Instead of the invisible hand of a highly imaginative director, reality itself provided an ample supply of details: the site of the murder—a dim area at the foot of the stairs to the stage; the context—a mass rally intended to condemn political violence; the "Song of Peace" at the end, its printed words stuffed deep inside the jacket pocket of the murder victim and stained with his blood during the assault; the fact that the Bible reading of the week was the Sacrifice of Yitzhak [Isaac]; the day on which tradition holds that Rachel the Biblical matriarch died; and, finally, the funeral in Jerusalem with Senator Ted Kennedy casting earth from the Arlington grave of his assassinated brother, John Kennedy, upon the fresh tomb.

The media, especially the two television channels, were the main factors shaping and constructing the political ritual (Gusfield and Michalowicz, 1984), and they did so according to the acknowledged model of a media event. Entry into the liminal period was marked, first and foremost, by upsetting the regular schedule of programs and creating an intense level of media transmission. The new programming was characterized by live or "direct" broadcasts and round-the-clock coverage. Even channels were unified—nine radio stations consolidated into one—and an attempt was made to consolidate the two television channels, which succeeded only for coverage of the funeral. Commercials were, of course, suspended on both radio and television.

Not only was the schedule of programs disrupted, distinctions between various types of television genres became vague, narrative forms intermingling. Instead of the standard division into drama, news, documentation, fiction, and entertainment, the ongoing broadcast on each channel was blended into one program that combined these genres. "The conferral of media event status," in the words of Dayan and Katz, "consists in pulling it away from the news and translating it into a fictional register" (1992:114). The text that was created thus blurred the distinction between news and fiction.

Even the traditional role of the newscasters was altered. From an ostensibly neutral and objective stance, reporting events "from a distance", newscasters became identified with, involved in, and expressive of the political center (Levi, 1981). These were no longer skeptical, critical, ironical, and occasionally cynical independent journalists, but rather partners to the cultural and political elite in playing the game, spelling out its views, and serving as a kind of preacher or town-crier for the government. This was reflected in the style of Haim Yavin—Mr. Israel Television—on Channel One. Yavin, who had once been reprimanded for daring to express a political view by raising his eyebrow to an interviewee, now spoke in the tones of a preacher suffused with deep faith. The delivery changed, assuming a dimension of holiness, of deep drama, while underscoring symbols and their ongoing interpretation.

Similar phenomena were evident in the newspapers during this period. The routine newspaper style was supplanted by a poetic, lofty rhetoric. Journalists lost their standing as observers, disinterested parties. They knowingly and openly assumed an active role in distributing and replicating values. This was reflected not just in the writing, but also in the decisions of the editors. Stickers were enclosed in the weekend editions of Israel's two tabloid newspapers, Yediot Aharonot and Ma'ariv, one saying "No more violence", accompanied by a photograph of Rabin and the Ma'ariv logo, and the other with the words "Shalom Haver". The Yediot Aharonot sticker had a distribution of almost one million copies.

Another disruption was in the direction of the flow of messages in both the electronic and printed media. Most messages flow from the media to the audience, but here the flow increased in the opposite direction, from the audience to the media. The number of listeners who called into the television stations increased several-fold, with a similar rise in calls and letters from readers to the newspapers. The media themselves allowed the general public—as opposed to those in positions of authority—to appear much more than usual.

Messages during this period also changed their character from the routine monologue to the more dialogic, to use Bakhtin's term (1981). However, audience involvement was not just to express an opinion about the situation, but also to influence the program content itself. For example, members of the Broadcasting Authority decided, upon directives from the Ministerial Committee for Ceremonies and Symbols, to continue its mourning programming for 48 hours from the end of the funeral. When regular programming was partially resumed on the third evening, however, the media were deluged by viewer response demanding that the special programs be continued. Channel Two had a similar reaction from its viewers. Listeners also largely dictated the character of the programs on the Radio. "We operated according to the 'publicometer'—telephone calls from listeners," said Moshe Shlonsky, director of the popular IDF Radio station. [2]

But the entire week of mourning was more than just a media event, even though it occurred in the context of a crisis similar to the assassination of Kennedy or Indira Gandhi. Media events revolve primarily around one location where the event takes place, with most participants in the political ritual sitting at home and watching it with their families and friends, like the audience for a theatrical ritual. "Media events have shifted the locus of ceremoniality from the piazza and the stadium to the living room" (Dayan and Katz, 1992:211). Even if viewers dress up for the event and insist that they are taking part in a celebration (Minwalla, 1990), it is still basically passive participation.

What took place in the second week of November 1995 was quite different. First of all, it took place not only on the air but simultaneously in the presence of a large public. About a quarter of a million people participated in the mass rally in Kings of Israel Plaza on the night of the assassination, and some 35% of all television owners in Israel watched it from their homes. On the very night of the assassination, no fewer than 93% of the population had already heard about it—about 60% from the television and some 20% from the radio (*Teleseker* Survey, December 1995). Approximately half (42%) immediately called their friends and relatives to tell them what happened (*Yediot Aharonot* Survey, November 9, 1995). From that moment, pilgrimages began to the Rabin home in Jerusalem and later to their private home in Tel-Aviv, to the plaza where Rabin was shot, a day later to the expanse in front of the Knesset where his body lay in state, and finally to Mt. Herzl where he was buried. From the time of the assassination until the end of the burial, approximately 80% of the

1.5 million households in Israel viewed at least part of the special broadcast on television.

During the course of the week, between a quarter and a third of all Israelis took part in outdoor events at the three pilgrimage sites. [3] Several hundred thousand congregated at the family site, the home of the victim, and the political-civic site of the plaza. According to estimates, close to one million people passed by the coffin lying in state at the Knesset, and about half a million took part in the funeral cortege or visited the graveside on Mt. Herzl. More than a hundred thousand letters poured into the Office of the Prime Minister or his home, and these included texts, poems, pictures, drawings, or gifts. Hundreds of condolence albums were also sent with expressions of sympathy from thousands of people. This does not fit easily into a description of a media event that moves from the piazza or stadium to the living room. It was more like an "epidemic of communitas", the need of people to be together, to talk to each other, to feel close with each other.

Moreover, behavior in a media event is determined in advance; it is known and expected. The assassination of Rabin, however, evoked a wave of spontaneous and unplanned public behavior. The most dramatic expression of this was the congregating of tens of thousands of youth in the Kings of Israel Plaza at all hours of the day and night throughout the week. The sitting in small circles in the light of the memorial candles, the melancholy songs they sang, and the atmosphere suffused with religiosity surprised and greatly moved the Israeli public. This spontaneous behavior in the plaza, and to a lesser extent at other pilgrimage sites, brought out the television cameras, although this was not planned. In fact, the boundaries were blurred here too, as reality on the streets and television reality intermingled. The congregating of people in the plaza or in the expanse in front of the Knesset drew the cameras, which caused even more people to congregate there. Reality influenced television behavior, which in turn shaped reality, in a cycle. Thus the border dissipated between symbolic behavior on the street and television ritual at home, and the thin tissue dissolved that had separated "true" and "apparent" reality.

The literature that deals with political ritual notes several roles that the media perform in dramatic events such as the assassination of a head of state or a president. Together with the politicians, the media participate in shaping the pattern of national mourning, are a key to constructing the event, and bestow upon it symbolic meaning, i.e., what might be termed an engineering of symbols. The media enable the participation of everybody in the ritual, create social networks, and contribute to shaping the social structure. They facilitate the expression of grief and enable catharsis over the experience of loss (Schlesinger, 1987).

Political ritual has important functions in re-asserting the political order that was damaged by the assassination. The murder of the supreme political authority generates a series of onerous political problems that impinge upon the very roots of government, the democratic political culture, and the normative system (Elderman and Simon, 1971; Marvick and Marvick, 1971). It is necessary to re-establish command quickly by selecting the heir and conferring legitimacy immediately upon his or her rule. There is a need by the audience to repledge allegiance, to reformulate its contract with the successor, and to undertake to do battle with the forces that caused the assassination and shook up the political system. On the other hand, the heir uses the ritual to consolidate power by pledging to continue along the path of the predecessor and to restore life to its normal course. Legitimacy is premised upon social re-integration and it is the media that build the social networks and re-shape the social order, just as they reinforce the core values set by the political center.

But in the situation in which Israeli society found itself at the time of the assassination, the media performed not just these roles—which media have performed in similar circumstances, such as the Kennedy assassination—but an additional function: articulation of the collective identity (Barbero, 1993). As will be shown, the assassination took place in the context of identity crisis and could therefore have developed into a "critical discourse event" (Herzog and Shamir, 1994), a significant social event in which a public debate ensues about issues fundamental to society, with various interpretive groups competing to bestow symbolic meaning on them. The national media, press and electronic alike, gave the impression that such deliberation did take place, and ample articles were devoted to analysis of the causes and consequences of the murder. However, although the media could have been the major arena for such negotiations, this process did not take place at all. On the contrary, the dominant elite groups seized control over the media, and sounded their voice whereas all other voices were ignored, silenced, or excluded. The exclusion of these interpretations of the collective identity made the one presented by the elite unacceptable to the rest of society, thus deepening the social division and segmentation, rather than integrating the mourning.

The Struggle for Collective Identity in Deeply Divided Society

The significant feature of Israeli society at the time of the assassination was that it was a society deeply divided. The debate over the peace agreements with the Palestinians and the Arab states was not just waged over the future of the territories that were occupied in 1967. A much deeper struggle has preoccupied Israeli society for over twenty years concerning the definition of its collective identity. Thus, the question of peace borders involves more than just geographical, strategic, or political issues, but entails a re-definition of the social borders with the "other" (LaPierre, 1984)—the relationship between the Jewish people and the nations of the region and the world, and the particularistic character of its national culture (Schlesinger, 1987:285). Efforts to define the collective have evoked a bitter struggle in Israel, and this struggle is what fuels and exacerbates the political debate over the peace process.

Trying to define the collective identity is an almost obsessive preoccupation in Israeli society, with no agreement among the various camps to accept the status quo, i.e., the coexistence of a plurality of definitions. On the contrary, each tries to shape the entire collective according to its definition of the civic religion. Even those who had once chosen a strategy of withdrawal and isolation (the anti-Zionist Orthodox groups) seek now to force their definition on the entire society.

It was in this context that Rabin was assassinated, as testified by the assassin himself. Yigal Amir could not bear to have Rabin, representative of one school of thought about collective identity, be in a position of such great influence, and because Amir had no way to curb this influence, he sought to exclude Rabin from the social negotiation. "I wanted to get rid of him," he said, "it didn't have to be murder. I wanted to neutralize him. Had he been injured and left the game, that would have been good enough. He didn't necessarily have to die". [4]

Israeli and international media structured the assassination as a clash between the victim and his murderer, Rabin versus Yigal Amir, leader of the peace camp versus the representative of the fundamentalist, nationalist-religious, peace-rejecting camp. However, the arena of struggle over the definition of the collective identity in Israel is much more complex and inhabited by at least four main streams of thought:

The central, hegemonic stream is the Zionist camp, which includes the traditional groups in the labor movement and also large segments of the nationalist camp. Despite differences among various factions in this stream, a broad common denominator enables their consolidation under the rubric of Zionism, neo-Zionism, or post-state Zionism. This stream stands on an ideological platform of Zionism and democracy, grasped as a democratic, Jewish nation-state.

The second, small but important as it is composed of the intellectual and cultural elites that dominate the symbol-making of Israeli society, is the post-Zionist stream. This group calls for basing the collective identity of Israel on the civic definition of all citizens of the state, without regard for their Jewish-Arab ethnic origin. It seeks to sever the link of Israeli citizens from the Jews in the diaspora, to eliminate the religious roots of Israeli identity, and to base Israeli society first and foremost on universalistic values.

The third is the non-Zionist ultra-Orthodox stream, which views Israeli society as one grouping of Jews, just as there continue to be groupings of Jews in various countries in the world. For this stream, the basis for defining the collective identity is particularistic and exclusively religious.

And the fourth stream has been called fundamentalist. These are the religious-Zionists, who advocate an ideology that integrates nationalism and religious faith, in the spirit of the teachings of Rabbi Kook and his disciples, Gush Emunim. This group seeks to base collective identity on particularistic Jewish values, but, in contrast with the third stream, the territorial component of the sacred homeland assumes much greater importance. [5]

Hence, this is not merely a debate about political orientation—foreign relations and security. Nor is it only a dispute over the nature of the constitutional arrangements, the basis for political authority, and the legitimacy of the state institutions. Rather, this is a much deeper rift concerning the relevance of various components in the repertoire of the civic religion, the nature of the collective identity. It includes complex questions such as: What are the bounds of civic space; and even, what is the meaning of time—is it sacred or empty in the sense of Walter Benjamin; and, having returned to the homeland, are the Jewish people now living in a sacred era, with all that implies, or an era bereft of religious meaning? [6]

Thus, the assassin sought not just to halt the peace process, not just to prevent the withdrawal of Israeli governing institutions from Palestinian cities in the West Bank, but also to arrest the process of "Hellenization" of Israeli society. As he awaited his victim at the edge of the mass rally, Amir chatted with the policemen there, castigating the singer Aviv Gefen, pop-culture hero of Israeli youth, who symbolized for him a foreign culture, and claimed that "most of the participants in the rally are Arabs". In other words, those who came to the rally and who claim for themselves the right to shape the identity of Israeli society in their own image are fundamentally illegitimate because they are the "other".

This analysis enables us to understand the connection between Yitzhak Rabin, 73 years old and the last of the Palmachniks (the elite units during the War of Independence), and the young Aviv Gefen, grasped simplistically by the other streams as the symbol of self-indulgence, foreign culture, nihilism, and a lack of national roots. The bond forged between the two a moment before the rally began and which was expressed there reflects the closeness between the representative of the generation of "candle children" and the representative of the generation of 1948, both members of the first stream in our categorization, the neo-Zionists.

As the peace process gained momentum and the IDF expedited its evacuation from the territories, tension rose between the various streams, especially between the first and the third. Those in the nationalist religious-Zionist camp were under particular strain, as their fear grew that the political process would also resolve the debate about collective identity. The peace process threatened to shatter their dream, destroy their spiritual world, and they found themselves in an untenable existential terror. Voices were raised during this period in their ideological journal Nekuda that called for far-reaching measures, even severing ties with Israeli society and the state.

In the final analysis, on Saturday night November 4th, the three shots of Yigal Amir brought about a crisis of anomie, in Durkheim's terms. [7] The assassination of Rabin—the Prime Minister who represents political stability and the Minister of Defense who is the symbol of security more than anyone else in Israel—produced a palpable sense of insecurity, a fear of social disintegration, and apprehension of what the future holds in store: subversion of the public order, the crumbling of the normative system, civil war, even war with foreign powers. If Mr. Security was murdered, anything can happen. "A danger of clashes and loss of control threatens to split Israel from within," wrote a level-headed political analyst the day after the assassination (Dan Margalit, *Ha'aretz*, November 5, 1995). It's no wonder that a poet used even more dramatic language: The assassination, she wrote, was "something supernatural that toppled everything we believed in. Our entire world has been transfigured" (Dalia Rabikovitch, *Yediot Aharonot*, November 6, 1995).

The media, which during times of crisis usually serve to restore social integration, reshape the social structure, and recreate the national consensus—the renewed social contract—performed a much more special function in Israel because of the deep cleavage in society. The media responded to the assassination in ways that had significance for the definition of the collective identity, taking advantage of the event to crystallize that identity. This was done by promoting the political ritual surrounding Rabin, building the myth of the man who became a symbol in his death. This the media accomplished by addressing a critical point in the collective identity—construction of the collective memory. "Collective identity relates to a collective memory through which the contemporary group recognizes itself through a common past, remembrance, commemoration, interpretation and reinterpretation" (LaPierre, 1984:196). In modern society, the media join the intellectuals in their traditional role of "the selective interpretation of history" (203-204).

Indeed, in the course of the week, the media were intensely preoccupied with the personality of Rabin, deconstructing his biography and constructing it anew, with the finished product elevated from a personal to a collective biography. In fact, the media used elements of Rabin's biography to shape a collective memory in order to construct a collective identity for Israeli society. The man Yitzhak Rabin metamorphoses into a symbolic representation of all Israeli society. "He was us," wrote Yonatan Gefen (*Ma'ariv*, November 6, 1995). "We wept for our father figure, and more so for ourselves. For Yitzhak Rabin, and more so for our own image..." in the words of Ofer Shelach (*Ma'ariv*, November 11, 1995).

This is the significance of constructing the Rabin myth in the week following his assassination. It was not the cultural tradition of "Speak of the righteous only after their death", but well beyond. This was a case of constructing a collective memory, "a reshaping of practices through which people construct themselves as cultural authorities" (Zelizer, 1995:4) [8]. What then was the identity assumed by Rabin, which indeed became the identity of Israeli society as a whole? What are its characteristics? Its components? What are the events that shaped it and how was it structured?

Personal Biography and the Reconstruction of the Collective Memory

In an effort to answer these questions, I reviewed all articles written about Yitzhak Rabin in the five national daily Hebrew newspapers during the period of the event. This included all biographical items that mentioned Rabin in two "quality" papers—*Ha'aretz* and *Davar_Rishon*, the two popular newspapers—*Yediot Aharonot* and *Ma'ariv*, and the business daily *Globes*, which also carries general news.

The corpus studied included all sections of the newspapers, all pages, and all types of writing—news, features, and commentary. In the first few days, there were more news stories, but the proportion of features increased during the period of mourning. The length of the articles varied widely, from short items to detailed profiles of 3,500 words. Altogether, 348 articles of various length were examined. They represented the main forum for public discourse—the daily newspapers, whose combined circulation soared during the week of the assassination to almost one million copies in print, which means that they reached almost 80% of Israeli households.[9]

A content analysis was performed on the texts. Items were graded on three variables: (1) mention of traits characteristic of Rabin or events of his life used to reflect traits characteristic of him (e.g. "He was a hero and loved Israel"—Shalom Rosenfeld, *Ma'ariv*, November 10, 1995); (2) the comparative importance of various traits: importance was determined both by the number of appearances of each trait and the weight ascribed to it by the writer (e.g., "Rabin was the most outstanding example of..." Editorial, *Ha'aretz*, November 5, 1995); and (3) any explicit or implicit statement that this trait relates not just to Rabin the individual, but that it reflects the collective personality of Israeli society. (Example of an explicit statement: Yitzhak Rabin "symbolized the new Israeli", Orit Harel, Ma'ariv, November 10, 1995; or "the Palmachnik who is my private father, who is Rabin, who is the collective [father], my protector," Talma Admon, *Ma'ariv*, November 10, 1995).

Also analyzed were the linguistic techniques and methods used by the writers in reconstructing the collective biography. It was not always easy to establish causal connections between the traits/events related to Rabin the man and those related to the Israeli collective as a whole. Techniques commonly used to draw this connection were, for example, metaphor, metonymy, or analogies. ("Yitzhak Rabin was the first Jewish flower to bloom in the earth of the homeland from out of the ashes of exile and the Holocaust," Gabriel Ben-Simchon, *Davar Rishon*, November 19, 1995). The solidarity theme also appeared frequently through use of the "royal we"—not in the sense of 'I the king', but meaning 'You + I', to create a sense of involvement, a merging of the writer and the audience of readers into one cultural community, as in Meir Shalev's words: "And the pining...for a generation of young people that is disappearing before our very eyes" or "We'll continue along his restrained but determined path" (*Yediot Aharonot*, November 6, 1995).

What then is the reconstructed image of Rabin as it emerges from the contents of the media? The list below shows the six traits most often used to depict Rabin, both in terms of the number of times they were cited and the importance attributed to them by the writers. Additional traits appeared in the texts, but much less frequently than these (from several to 20 mentions). The first two traits appeared approximately 140 times, the third and fourth appeared up to 100 times each, while the last two traits appeared several dozen times.

The traits in order of relative importance were:

- Israeli sabra
- peacemaker
- Zionist
- Americophile
- Anti-politician
- Empathetic figure

In order to have a perspective for the content analysis of the tests published during the week of the assassination, a group of articles published in the previous three years, since Rabin became Prime Minister in 1992, was also examined. News, features, and commentary were sampled from the same periodicals used in the post-assassination research, i.e., the five Hebrew dailies. These articles were deliberately chosen for their resemblance to those published after the assassination, i.e., they were longer; more comprehensive, descriptive, or critical; and focused on Rabin's character, personality, methods of work, or behavior. However consisting of 16 items only and due to the fact that they have been published during a long period of three years, they could not have been compared with the same content analysis to the corpus of the 348 articles, and their reading was rather interpretative.

The term "sabra", like "the Palmach generation" or "the generation of 1948", is a broad, inclusive concept. In the newspapers, it appeared in its generalized "sabra" form or as one or more components of the sabra archetype—warrior, unpolished but authentic, straight-talking, a do-er, devoted to his comrades and willing to sacrifice himself for the good of the whole, and so forth. The components of this image are discussed at length in research about the myth of the sabra. "The symbol of the new Jew, comely, with cowlick" (David Grossman, *Ma'ariv*, November 6, 1995). "His image epitomizes the sabra spirit of the pre- and early-state period—straight-talking and to the point" (Hila Komem, *Davar*, November 6, 1995).

In describing the sabra, much use is made of the symbols of the period, images and metaphors taken from songs of the War of Independence and especially the world of the Palmach. This was "a generation different and more wonderful than all the others—the Palmach generation. A generation that was the antithesis to the freeloader spirit, the antithesis to shirking one's duty, the antithesis to messianism, the antithesis to pomp and ceremony, the antithesis to extremism, the antithesis to demagoguery. It was a generation that spurned praise, but yes, a silver platter and yes, what comradeship" (Meir Shalev, *Yediot Aharonot*, December 6, 1995). Naturally, nothing negative or critical was linked to the concept of sabra or Palmachnik. In the past, the "redheadedness" of the sabra or Palmachnik was a hook on which writers could hang negative qualities—over-simplification, hot-headedness, aggressiveness, or lack of sophistication. Yoel Marcus (Ha'aretz) juxtaposed the negative red-headedness with the positive "analytical mind" of Rabin. Following the assassination, however, the concept "red-head" had only one meaning—all positive. "A proud, sweet sabra with blonde curls and freckles on his nose...We wanted to be like him..." (Gabriel Ben-Simchon, *Davar Rishon*, November 12, 1995). The lack of polish of the sabra also undergoes a face lift that transforms it into a commendable quality: "Rabin had an unpolished style, but there are two kinds of lack of polish: that of Weizmann, who stands beside Rabin's grave and says, 'We drank, we ate...' Rabin's lack of polish was a kind of honesty...never crude..." (Sami Michael, *Davar Rishon*, December 5, 1995).

The death of Rabin turned him into a "peacemaker", the symbol of the longing and desire of Israeli society for peace. This element in his personality emerged prior to the assassination, of course, and winning the Nobel Peace Prize in 1995 reinforced it. However, prior to the assassination, Rabin was still being criticized for his hesitancy about the peace process, for the halting pace of progress (e.g., not evacuating Hebron, or the tough policies toward Palestinians in the territories). The assassination at the conclusion of a peace rally and in the context of opposition to his peace policies bolstered the transformation of his image vis-a-vis the Arab world. During the week of mourning, no texts appeared like those that had been frequent in the past describing the warrior, violent, and tough side of Rabin ("break their bones", "tighten the siege of Beirut", etc.). Indeed, even the military component of his personality, an aspect impossible to ignore, was used to emphasize his character as a man of peace. "Soldier for peace", "warrior for peace", and similar expressions appeared frequently. In a typical profile: "The old soldier who led the state of Israel to victory in the Six Day War will now fight for peace" (Yael Gvirtz and Anat Meidan, *Yediot Aharonot*, November 5, 1995).

The longing for peace of the neo-Zionist stream is regarded among the other camps, especially among the fundamentalists, not as a noble expression of lofty goals, but as a product of weakness, short-sightedness, a reflection of materialistic, hedonistic, American values, a lack of national pride and historical consciousness, and even—among the extremists—as treason. Peace, formerly perceived by the neo-Zionists as instrumental, a deal, the product of weariness and an unwillingness to carry on the fight, was elevated through the restructured image of Rabin to the level of a value that holds its own against the values represented by the other streams.

The third concept frequently used by writers in describing Rabin is that of Zionism. In an editorial in Ha'aretz the day after the assassination, Rabin is described as "a man who more than any other reflected the rebirth of Israel". Zionism, as manifested in the descriptions of Rabin is elevated to supreme heights. In the words of Yaron London (*Yediot Aharonot*, November 6, 1995), Zionism is no less than "the most daring and most successful social and national revolution in modern times". The concept "Zionism" embodies not just the simple, limited meaning—advocating the right of the Jewish people to gather in its historic homeland and enjoy national independence—but also its broader meaning—love of homeland, statehood, nation-building and state-building, the public over the private weal, and collective values over individual rights. This was Rabin according to the new portrait, and this was and should be Israeli society. "The only value remaining [in our era] is that of personal fulfillment, financial success. Rabin represents the complete opposite of this. He, who could have done things on his own behalf, never gave it a moment's thought" (Gabi Bashan, *Ma'ariv*, November 9, 1995).

The diplomatic chapter in the life of Rabin—serving as ambassador to Washington, followed by his special tie to the American nation and country—is a critical element in his personal biography and its collective meaning. The term "diplomat" does not refer to the values, content, or status of this profession. On the contrary, Rabin was described as an undiplomatic diplomat. The heart of the matter was the partner, the United States. "Rabin conducted an ongoing love affair with America...which returned the compliment" (Akiva Eldar, *Ha'aretz*, November 8, 1995). The emphasis was on the fact that Rabin was Israel's most prominent ambassador to the United States "and focused on fostering the strategic alliance between the two countries..." (Moshe Zack, *Ma'ariv*, November 6, 1995).

Although Rabin based the foreign and defense policies of Israel on its links to the U.S. as an ultimate national resource, the description of his attitude to the United States goes beyond international relations and strategic considerations. Rabin is described as an authority on American society and politics, an unabashed advocate of American values and the American way of life, and the importer of the American dream to Israel. Prior to the elections, Rabin was criticized more than once for his quasi-American, presidential style of governing (Yoel Marcus, *Ha'aretz*, February 19, 1993), for his exaggerated American orientation in both foreign affairs and defense (Uzi Benziman, *Ha'aretz*, March 12, 1993), and primarily for his republican values that replaced the social-democratic underpinning of the labor movement. After his death, Rabin is portrayed as having imported to Israel an uncommonly positive product: "American culture that won his heart...the Protestant ethos, values, and beliefs...etc." (Gabi Bashan, *Davar Rishon*, November 9, 1995).

The deconstructed description of Rabin's personality is particularly dramatic in representing him as something other than a politician. Though Rabin was involved in political affairs while still in uniform during the War of Independence and held political jobs for 26 years after ending his army career, he was perceived as the antithesis of a politician. "Rabin has never been a politician...not a functionary, he was an outsider to the party ambiance," according to Yael Gvirtz and Anat Meidan (*Yediot Aharonot*, November 5, 1995). In an era in which public criticism of politics is harsh and being a politician implies something negative, those who can avoid this label enjoy a marked advantage. In the United States, the outsider—one who does not come up through the Washington corridors of power, but emerges from "authentic" society—has an edge in running for president. But it's a little hard to define a politician who spent a quarter century in Washington as an outsider. Perhaps this was an image that the politician Rabin created for himself? Rubik Rozental in *Davar Rishon* (November 6, 1995) suggests that in contrast with other politicians, "Rabin never created for himself an image, but always remained himself."

Of particular irony was the reconstructed image of Rabin as an empathetic figure—a devoted family man, someone who likes people, is surrounded by friends, amiable, sociable, sensitive to and concerned about others. This assortment of qualities was emphasized in particular throughout the event and yet it is in absolute contradiction to how Rabin was described throughout his public career—closed, introverted, lacking close friends, one whose body language and handshake expressed a painful shyness and discomfort with others, accused of never greeting the woman who served him tea every morning in Labor Party headquarters, as someone surrounded and influenced by a closed circle of patricians and the wealthy. But the portrait drawn of him after his death was diametrically opposed to this: "[He was] the opposite of a snob, never arrogant, he treated with equal respect and seriousness simple people and those with power and position" (Hila Komem, *Davar Rishon*, November 6, 1995). He who was described by the newspapers as "autistic", whose hand gesture of impatience for and dismissal of others, even ministers in the government, was remarked about (Daniel Ben-Simon, *Davar*, October 17, 1994), now appears as "sensitive and attentive, one who loved to converse and listened without interrupting" (ibid).

Keep in mind that the issue is not which of these portrayals is "accurate", but the very fact that a change did take place in describing Rabin during these two periods, and why. The conclusion appears obvious. The picture drawn of Rabin in the newspapers prior to the assassination was much more complex than that drawn afterwards. In almost all the articles prior to his death, negative expressions appear beside the positive expressions, and sometimes often. The change has less to do with a difference of opinion over his policies, which is less relevant for our discussion, but with the image, character, and components of his personality, and their symbolic significance. In fact, some of the positive expressions mentioned frequently the week after the assassination had never appeared at all in the past, though their opposite had been. It's not so surprising, then, that after the assassination, Rabin was transformed into the collective figure desired by the writers, since after all, in the words of Yonatan Gefen, "He was us" (*Ma'ariv*, November 6, 1995).

Conclusion: How Hegemony Won and Lost

Who participated in the building of this version of the biography, a version that sought to give a particular character to the collective identity by linking it to the collective memory? Scrutiny of the writers whose articles, statements, and quotes crammed the Hebrew press during this period reveals that these were representatives of three elite groups: the political, the media, and the cultural. No real difference was found between direct statements—opinion pieces written by authors or politicians—and reportage written by professional journalists. No significant difference was found either in the ranking of traits/events among these three groups—cultural, media, or political. The similarity among the three was so striking because all were members of one interpretive community.

Zelizer notes that the concept "interpretive community" was taken up in fields beyond media research, and notes that it is not precisely a socio-economic group, but distinguished by how it structures cultural forms and social reality (1994). Thus, interpretive communities are culture-groups in a sense broader than just media audiences.

Examination of the national media in the week of Rabin's assassination reveals the absence, disappearance, of major social and cultural groups from the public discourse. Most noticeably missing were the Arab community, the Russian immigrants, the "other Israel"— referring to the residents of development towns of primarily Mizrahi origin—and, of course, the ultra-Orthodox and nationalist Zionists. All are interpretive communities with a different perception of reality, who are engaged in a struggle with each other, and particularly with the hegemonic group, over defining the collective identity of Israeli society. Their under-representation on television caused the leaders of the Arab population to protest to the Broadcasting Authority during the week of mourning that they were being excluded from the programs.

The dominance, of the neo-Zionist discourse group over the editing tables in the newspapers and electronic media, the proximity of this group to the cultural-entertainment elite in Tel-Aviv, and the ideological-political affinity of this stream to the political elite were clearly reflected in the reaction to the assassination. Hence, it was not surprising to find a link between those who participated in shaping the collective profile, i.e., shaping the collective identity of Israel, and the specific characteristics of this identity. In fact, the image created during the reconstruction of the collective identity was that of the hegemonic interpretive community. In a liminal moment, Turner notes, a society looks upon itself and asks not just who it is, but primarily who it wants to, feels it should, become (Turner, 1977). The reflection of the restructured image of Rabin is what this community wanted to become.

When Shils and Young studied the significance of the coronation ceremony in Britain, they regarded it as a symbol of the values that unify British society, the suppliers of consensus despite political differences (Shils and Young, 1953). Birnbaum took issue with this claim, well before Gramsci's concept of hegemony became popular. In "Monarchs and Sociologists"', Birnbaum argues that he is not at all sure that the interpretation of the ceremony by the various classes was identical. On the contrary, the ceremony expresses the values of the upper and middle classes, glossing over the social gap and conflict (Birnbaum, 1955). In this spirit, Lukes also analyzed political rituals in Britain, noting that these rituals "help to define as authoritative certain ways of seeing society" (Lukes, 1975:306). It is an authoritative interpretation intended to serve the needs and interests of the ruling groups and to maintain their dominance.

In the Israeli context, the hegemonic interpretation of the collective identity by the neo-Zionist-Ashekenazi-Labor elite, which had been unchallenged since the formative years of the Israeli society, faced a serious challenge in the last decade. The assassination was an extreme symbolic act of someone who wanted to undermine the authoritative position of that elite as the sole legitimate interpreter of the collective identity.

The ascension of what was perceived to be a real threat, and the crisis brought on by the assassination, caused the hegemonic elite to respond with all its power. A situation in which everything is fluid and in flux, which can be shaped and kneaded before it hardens, is a situation that must not be missed. Gramsci (1971) refers to a crisis as the moment of the blink in which frameworks are re-organized; what gels at this moment is solidified in the collective memory. Into these circumstances in which most members of the collective yearn for a different life, for a more desirable situation, the hegemony comes and offers its own model.

The Rabin myth constituted and disseminated by the media, in addition to the political ritual celebrated that week, was the most significant practice used by the hegemonic neo-Zionist groups to consolidate their position and world-view. To broaden their base of support, they initiated ties with the younger generation. The identification of the "candle children" with the late Prime Minister caused an overnight change in the old-timers' attitudes towards the individualistic, pleasure-oriented culture of the younger generation. They were praised by spokespeople of the elite for their dedication to the peace process, the ultimate goal of the Zionist movement. When the television management was asked why the live broadcasting from Rabin Square did not attract more youngsters to the spot, thus distorting reality rather than reporting it, the answer was "this is where the important story takes place".[10]

The feeling that the entire people in Israel reacted in a similar way to the political murder and shared the martyr's values and attributes was created because of the shutting out of all the other voices, and the denial of the national media access to the other interpretive communities. When, during the week's mourning, reporters presented some views of Israelis who thought differently about the assassination and its causes, these were censored by the editors. They felt "the lesson of the tragic event was that we were too lenient about incitement. After the horrific event we had to be more strict about it".

The official state institutions reacted similarly. The Attorney General issued new directives about freedom of expression, arguing that verbal incitement could harm the public order. The police hauled in some individuals who were disrespectful of Rabin's memory and several offenders who had been accused of incitement in the past two years but never tried suddenly received a trial date.

These actions aroused the ire of some civil rights organizations, and indeed the new policy was lifted after several weeks. The Attorney General, for example, restated his position as "an ethical directive, not a binding legal order". But that was too late. At 'the moment of the blink'—the significant moment in history in which a public debate ensues about issues fundamental to society, with various interpretive groups competing to bestow symbolic meaning on them the critical discourse did not take place.

It took no less than five weeks for the first reservations to be heard publicly. Yoel Marcus, though a member of the hegemonic group and a senior journalist at *Ha'aretz*, expressed his reservations about the new, rose-colored image of Yitzhak Rabin. The article was met with a harsh reaction from Rabin's widow, who announced that she would immediately cancel her subscription to the newspaper. Another month was needed before representatives of the other interpretive communities were able to protest in the general press what had happened. The first, Yitzhak Laor, made his statement in reference to the memorial album for Rabin. Entitled "Group Picture with Mirror", Laor's article criticized the literary wheeler-dealers, always close to the ruling powers, who demean themselves by exalting Rabin and serve the goal of national unity by "a Rabin festival... as if there is no other way for culture other than togetherness and kitsch, identity and unity, as if plurality that does not merge cannot exist" (*Ha'aretz*, January 26, 1996). The other writer, a prominent member of the fundamentalist stream and editor for many years of their journal *Nekuda*, forcefully attacked the Israeli media for "taking sides in the debate", for presenting the views of only one political camp and not allowing other views to reach the public.[11]

Beyond this, no national media efforts were made by other groups to challenge the collective portrait of Israeli society as shaped by the cultural-political-media elite, or the monopoly it claimed in fashioning this portrait. They expressed their wrath at the media and the hegemonic group only in their internal media: Russian-language weeklies, synagogue newsletters, notices pasted up in their neighborhoods, and other community media. There the postZionist Russian immigrants could criticize the political ritual as "a personality cult like the one we knew in the USSR", and the ultra-nationalists argued that "Rabin has brought it [its death] upon himself because he betrayed the Jewish people".[12]

Many more months had to pass before Israelis realized, after the Ministry of Education published the report of an investigative committee, that the teens who sat in Rabin Square singing and crying were only one fraction of their age-group, while others, and not insignificant numbers, were critical of his policy, indifferent to the event, or even supportive of the killing.[13]

The suppression of the public discourse during the period following the assassination did not result in the molding of the Israeli collective memory or the reinvention of the entire Israeli collectivity. The other narratives, stories, and aspirations, images and social forces were simply concealed, but they broke through and burst forth six months later in the May general elections, unveiling the tormented and shattered Israeli identity. In the Knesset, a "coalition of minorities"—parties that represent the Russian, the nationalist, the religious and the ultra-Orthodox communities—have made unprecedented achievements. Prime Minister Shimon Peres, Rabin's partner and heir, had to hand his seat over to Binyamin Netanyahu, the leader of the Likud party and the nationalist camp. No wonder the election results were described by the defeated camp as "the second assassination of Rabin".

Notes

1. I deeply thank Elihu Katz for his valuable comments of an early version of the manuscript.
2. Interview with Moshe Shlonsky, Director of IDF Radio, December 17, 1995. Information about Channel One was obtained in an interview with the Director-General Ya'ir Stern on the same date. Interviews were also held with producers and program writers for radio and television and with editors of the daily newspapers.
3. This is an estimate of the Police, but various figures appeared in the newspapers. Although only an estimate, the magnitude speaks for itself.
4. Interview by the Police investigators 25.12.1995, The Police Archive.
5. The foremost intellectual forum of the post-Zionist stream is the periodical Teoriya U-Vikoret and, of the fundamentalist stream, the monthly Nekuda.
6. A taste of this fascinating debate appeared in the daily Ha'aretz shortly before the assassination and immediately following, with contributions (between September 12 and October 7) by Shlomo Avineri, Zeev Sternhell, Baruch Kimmerling, and others. Also see the article by Mordechai Rotenberg in *Davar Rishon* from January 5, 1996 and Oz Almog in *Ha'aretz* from December 19, 1995.
7. Yigal Amir claimed that his mission was to redeem the nation from Yitzhak Rabin. In Hebrew, "Yigal" derives from the root "ga'al", which means "redeem" and "Amir" contains the word "ami", which means "my nation". The leftover "Yi" and "R" in his name are a reference to Yitzhak Rabin.
8. For the distinctions between "speech community", "discourse community", or "community of memory", see Zelizer (1992:89).
9. Other Hebrew periodicals were also examined, such as the weeklies *BaMahane* (published by the IDF), *LaIsha* (a women's magazine), and less regular periodicals that appear after the assassination. However, as these magazines are directed to specific readers and not to the general public they results are not included in the report above.
10. See note no. 2.
11. Yisrael Harel in an interview on the television program "Shetah Hefker", December 27, 1995.
12. In November 1996, the first commemoration of the assassination, such expressions were very common in the alternative, community, media.
13. A letter of the director general of the ministry of education, 8 October 1996. See also Rapoport, 1997.

References

Anderson, Benedict (1983) *Imagined Communities*, London: and New York: Verso.
Bakhtin, Michail (1981) *The Dialogic Imagination: Four Essays*, Austin: University of Texas Press.

Barbero, J. Martin (1993) *Communication, Culture and Hegemony: From the Media to the Mediation*, Trans: Elizabeth Fox and Ronald White, Sage, London: Sage.

Birnbaum, N. (1955) "Monarchs and Sociologists: A Reply to Professor Shils and Mr. Young", *Sociological Review* 3: 5-23.

Chaney, David (1983) "A Symbolic Mirror of Ourselves: Civic Ritual in Mass Society", *Media, Culture and Society* 5:119-135.

Crotty, William J. (ed.) (1971) *Assassinations and the Political Order*, New York: Harper and Row.

Dayan, Daniel and Elihu Katz (1992) *Media Event*, Cambridge, Mass. and London, England: Harvard University Press.

Durkheim, Emil (1915) *The Elementary Forms of the Religious Life*, Glencoe, Ill.: Free Press.

Elderman, Murray and Rita J. Simon (1971) Presidential Assassinations: Their Meaning and Impact on American Society, in W. J. Crotty, (ed.) *Assassinations and the Political Order*, New York: Harper and Row, 455-488.

Gramsci, Antonio (1971) *Selection From the Prison Book*, New York: International publishers.

Gusfield, Joseph R. and Jerzy Michalowicz: (1984) "Secular Symbolism: Studies of Ritual, Ceremony, and the Symbolic Order in Modern Life", *Annual Review of Sociology* (10): 417-435.

Hall, Stuart (1977) "Culture, the Media and the 'Ideological effect'", in J. Curran et al. (Eds.) *Mass Communication and Society*. London: Edward Arnold.

Hall, Stuart (1982) "The Rediscovery of "Ideology": Return of the repressed in Media studies"' in M. Gureveitch et al. (Eds.) *Culture, Society and the Media*. London: Methuen.

Hall, Stuart et al. (1980) *Culture, Media, Language*. London: Hutchinson.

Herzog, Hanna and Ronen Shamir (1994) "Media Discourse on Jewish/Arab Relations", *Israel Social Science Research* (9) 1and2: 55-88.

Jensen, Klaus Bruhn (1991) "The Qualitative Turn", in Klaus L. Jensen and Nicholas W. Janowski, *A Handbok of Qualitative Methodology for Mass Communication* Research, London and New York: Routledge.

Johansson, Olof (1995) "Swedish Reaction to the Assassination of the Swedish Prime Minister Olof Palme", *Scandinavian Political Studies*, 18 (4): 265-283.

Lapierre, G. (1984) "L'identite Collective, Object Paradoxal: D'ou Nous Vient-il?", *Recherches Sociologiques*, 15 (2/3): 155-164.

Levi, Mark R. (1981) "Disdaining the News", *Journal of Communication*, 31(3): 24-31.

Lukas, Steven (1975) "Political Ritual and Social Integration", *Sociology*, 9(2): 289-308.

Marvick, Dwaine and Elizabeth. W. Marvick (1971) "The Political Consequences of Assassination", in W. J. Crotty, 489-544.

Minwalla, S. (1990) *The Assassination of Indira Gandhi*, Unpublished .Annenberg School of Communication, University of Southern California, Los Angeles. Quoted by Dayan and Katz (1992).

Rapoport, Tamar (1997) *The Many Voices of Israeli Youth*, The Hebrew University of Jerusalem. (in Hebrew).

Schlesinger, Philip (1987) "On National Identity: Some Conceptions and Misconceptions Criticized", *Social Science Information*, 26 (2) 219-264.

Schramm, Wilbur (1965) "Communication in Crisis", in Bradley S. Greenberg and Edwin B. Parker (ed.) *The Kennedy Assassination and the American Public*, Stanford, California: Stanford University Press, 1-25.

Shils, Edward and Michael Young (1953) "The Meaning of Coronation", *Sociological Review,* 1: 63-81.
Turner, Victor W. (1969) *The Ritual Process*, Chicago: Aldine.
Turner, Victor W.(1974) *Dramas, Fields and Metaphors: Symbolic Action in Human Society*, Ithaca, NY: Cornell University Press.
Turner, Victor W. (1977) "Process, System, and Symbol", *Daedalus*, 106:61-80.
Verba, Sidney (1965) "The Kennedy Assassination and the Nature of the Political Commitment", in Greenberg and Park, 348-360.
Wolfsfeld, Gadi (in press) "Framing political events", in Tamar Liebes and James Curran (eds.) *Media, Culture and Identity*. London: Routledge.
Zelizer, Barbie (1994) *Covering the Body, The Kennedy Assassination, the* Media, *and the Shaping of Collective Memory*, Chicago and London: Chicago University Press.

Part 8

Thinking about the Future

28

Greetings from a Viewer from Afar: The Objectives of Israel's Sociology of Language

Joshua A. Fishman

There are several reasons why I have accepted the invitation of the Editors to greet those who are most directly involved in and concerned with Israeli research on sociolinguistic topics. I have done so, most of all, because I am always eager to show my solidarity with the people and the academics of Israel and I try to do so, even from afar, whenever an appropriate opportunity presents itself. Secondly, I knew that my nearby neighbor in this prefatory position would be Elihu Katz, whose unfailing encouragement and kindness throughout my prolonged 1970-1973 sabbatical at the Hebrew University in Jerusalem I will never forget. However, neither of these reasons implies any great familiarity with either recent or current sociolinguistic efforts in Israel and, therefore, I am well aware that the substance of my remarks may lag significantly behind the intensity of their emotional foundations. Even as late as the late-70s, I was able to competently review and comment upon the state of Israeli sociolinguistics, but now, some 25 years since my departure, I am much less able to do so. I apologize in advance for any errors in fact that may creep into the following remarks, which of necessity, must be more broadly opinionated than precisely informed.

Why Be Interested in the Sociology of Language

The small economy of Israeli academic life has, nevertheless, produced an admirably large handful of sociologists that are clearly of international repute and of intergenerational importance. I do not have the impression that this is as yet the case in connection with the sociology of language. There are few full-time sociolinguists in Israel and, necessarily, fewer still are the doctoral training programs and the research centers that focus squarely on developing sociolinguistic expertise and that can do so in a reliable, long-term fashion (if, indeed, there are any at all). Sociolinguistics is largely a "sometimes thing" in Israel, something that many people undertake every once in a while (most of them not really being trained in this area of specialization and treating it as if it were something that any reasonably alert person could do). Not surprisingly, therefore, it has not yet developed into something that has contributed noteworthy theories, topics or methods of its own to the worldwide sociolinguistic enterprise, or even to local Israeli theory or policy. I think there are several probable reasons for this state of affairs and that these reasons relate to Israeli sociology, on the one hand, and to Israeli linguistics, on the other.

What Could the Sociology of Language Contribute to General Sociology in Israel?

Why hasn't the sociology of language found a secure home within sociology per se in Israel? This question cannot be satisfactorily answered by turning it around and asking, "Why hasn't the sociology of language found a secure home within sociology per se in the USA?" The reasons are profoundly different in the two contexts. The reality of popular sociological thinking is very thin in the USA, where psychological answers, on the one hand, and economic answers, on the other hand, constantly have more appeal than do sociological ones. Individual initiative rules supreme, and the sociology of language has aroused little interest among American sociologists because they are still struggling with the realization that sociology per se has generally aroused little attention or interest. In Israel, however, social groups and societal influences are more palpably real and central to the everyday convictions and concerns of laymen and academics alike. Sociology has come to the fore as a central national pastime and academic pursuit, and the reasons for the failure to include the sociology of language in that pursuit must be looked for in Israeli reality, rather than in American or international terms.

The sociology of language provides access to additional variance in the study of situational factors governing social group-membership, sub-ethnic group-membership religious group-membership, kinship group-membership, political group-membership, occupational group-membership, age-group-membership, etc. All modern societies, and those based on massive and highly varied immigration even more than most, reveal complex and recurring multiple group memberships. The fluctuating boundaries, the saliencies, the conflicts and congruencies between these memberships are what sociology has to offer the social sciences and the public at large. However, it is language (usage, users, uses, language attitudes and overt behaviors toward languages and language groups) that is, for sociolinguistics, the key and accompaniment to all of these multiple-group-memberships. The socially patterned repertoires of varieties of talking/writing, as they exist in different networks faced by repertoires of expected and unexpected rounds of interaction (both *within* themselves as well as *between themselves and other networks* that are substantially non-overlapping membership with them), is what sociolinguistics is "into" and what it has to offer sociology as a whole. It is a potentially very refined perspective that is capable of yielding very refined (not to say complex) results, but, of course, it requires linguistic sophistication at the points of problem definition, theory-based hypothecation, data collection, data analysis and theoretical revision. Some of this sophistication must come initially from linguistics (more about that later), but sociology itself must decide whether it is really interested in finding all of the additional societal variation and cleavages that sociolinguistic research would quickly reveal. Thus far, Israeli sociology has had more than enough societal variation to cope with and is basically uniformist in outlook and in assumption. It is a science that monitors, broadcasts and dearly prefers the consolidation of that fractured "new Jewish people," the Israelis, that contentious "goy ekhad be-arets," and for this ideologically suffused purpose it is in no need of, is not ready for and is even opposed to any tools that will reveal how extremely unconsolidated and increasingly unconsolidating modern social reality really is.

What Can the Sociology of Language Contribute to Israeli Linguistics?

Israeli linguistics is, if anything, even less hospitable to sociolinguistic emphases (and to working along with sociologists) that are sociology/

sociologists vis-a-vis matters and expertise sociolinguistic. As the inheritors of millennia of linguistic sophistication by grammarians on various continents, Israeli linguists who keep an eye on Israeli linguistic reality are still the bearers of the burden of the revival of Hebrew. Although increasingly realistic descriptions of "Hebrew as she is spoken" are beginning to come to the fore, the recognition of the true variance in vernacular Hebrew, of the degree of patterned avoidance of Hebrew that exists in some circles and of the abandonment of "authentic" models and normative agencies in the course of the language's growth and change, has been and still is an uphill struggle. Even if the Hebrew language's normative and prescriptive passions do not burn as brightly or as hotly as they used to, the wholesale abandonment of these views and even of the language as a whole for particular functions and by particularly prestigious social networks brings "no cheer to Mudville" where "mighty Casey has struck out."

Thus, the low saliency of Israeli sociolinguistics has a deeper grounding than merely the usual reluctance of linguists to learn sociology and social research methods (rather than sloppily re-inventing them as they go along), or the total ignorance that exists among sociologists with respect to linguistics and linguistic field methods. Many smaller countries and smallish academic economics have managed, nevertheless, to produce several eminent, somewhat younger, sociolinguists, as the generation of the founding fathers "moves on," who are strongly involved not only in research but also in training even younger specialists in this field via interdisciplinary programs of specialization that are fully stabilized and connected with supportive training departments and research centers. I look forward eagerly to such developments in Israel as well.

Breaking through the Triumphalist and Consolidationist Myth

I do not presume to have a substantive agenda for Israeli sociolinguistics, although I do tend to think that individual researchers, research institutes and even academic departments should have such agendas and differ, one from the other, in connection with their priorities and preferences. Fractured Israeli societal reality must have a sociolinguistic counterpart and I am eager to find it. I am tired of reading that Hebrew has now finally been fully revernacularized, when the processes of revernacularization have still not been unveiled in all of their historical variation and when so many Israelis at home and abroad so commonly prefer to speak English with each other (not to mention publishing in English for each other—as with the vast majority of the papers in this volume—while pretending that this is being done only "in order to reach the rest of the world). I am tired of reading about the growing proportion of Israelis who are Hebrew speaking (even when Hebrew may be the fifth or sixth language in which they function), while the situational, demographic and pragmatic bases of their multilingualism is roundly overlooked. The grass-roots spread of English and other LWC's (languages of wider communication) in Israel remains generally undocumented, both within the realm of informal individual as well as formal (individual and institutional) life. The Yiddishization of Jerusalem is a reality which an iconoclastic American researcher disclosed a decade ago because an Israeli conspiracy of silence surrounded it then and still surrounds it now. The gloating about "the death of Yiddish" becomes evermore shocking when one realizes that it has gone on for a hundred years now and that it masks an unwillingness to face an ideologically undesired reality to the contrary. Will Russian be similarly derided and laughed under the rug, or is a realization of its long-term internal and external utility bubbling below the surface? How much Hebrew do different kinds of Israeli Arabs know and use and how much do they want to know and use? Are Jewish Israelis counting on English to make it unnecessary for them to learn Arabic in order to get along with Arab Israelis and with the Arab world in general? Is Ashkenazi Hebrew still alive and well in Ashkenazi Ultra-orthodox yeshivas and does it, too, have vernacular (i.e., non-text-related and non-translational) functions? What is the role of other-than-Hebrew-and-other-than-English in political campaigning? In advertising more generally? Do Jewish Israelis really need/read the Hebrew subtitles to English movies, and how is the role of English (and of other-than-Hebrew as well as other-than-English) in television changing with the introduction and rapid rise of cable TV? And above and beyond all other topics, what are the intra-linguistic variables that show age/social class/sub-ethnic topical and situational variation in Hebrew today? "New ways of analyzing variation" in Hebrew should, by right, be a fully owned Israeli intellectual property, but it is not even significantly so. Nor is the study of "foreigner talk." Nor is the study of child language acquisition (or of child bilingual or bi-dialectal acquisition) sufficiently infused with Israeli contributions. And whatever has become of the "Academy of the Hebrew Language" as a factor influencing spoken and written Hebrew and what does that teach us about the inter-generational role of language academies? Perhaps the "Ulpan industry" and/or the "ESL industry," which, between them, have sometimes seemed to employ the bulk of Israeli linguists and their graduate students, have "brainwashed the teachers" even more than they have influenced the students. Perhaps the Emperor is more scantily clad than anyone has bothered to say or even see?

Follow-up Research

In the 70s, there were several pioneering studies of the Hebrew Academy's impact on attitudes toward and usage of its neologisms, of the spread of English in Israel at the level of the "man in the street," of the ability of the police to use the languages of the populace, of Hebrew baby-talk, and of Yiddish and of Judesmo at the neighborhood-life level. These all need to be followed up. Intellectual fields can only prosper when they have historical depth, when they are aware of their own histories and when newer studies can build on earlier ones. It is high time that sociolinguistic efforts in Israel were revived from their recent doldrums, so that scholars throughout the world can become aware of and interested in pioneering Israeli data and theory in areas such as these. Instead, Israeli teachers and researchers are constantly replaying the records that were initially "cut" (prepared) elsewhere. Israel is a periphery, rather than a center, in the sociolinguistic world today. This should not be the case, given its dynamics, intellectually, societally and linguistically.

Where Can Good Sociolinguistic Research Come from?

One of the best early sources of good sociolinguistic research, before self-propelling theoretically issues begin to flow spontaneously, as they so frequently do when research traditions become established and differentiated one from the other, is a keen insight and curiosity with respect to the major social problems of the time. Contra-cyclical and non-conformist views are often particularly provocative. In the world of stylish post-modernism, who more than Israelis should realize that the pre-modern world is also still very much with us? Can secularism and religion co-exist, not only in the same country but in the same social networks? If mixed economies can prosper, can mixed ethnicities also prosper? Does conflict resolution at the micro-level have anything to teach us at the macro-level? If the ravages of deprivation and brutality can be overcome at the individual level, can societal scars and trauma also be overcome? If messianic dreams can persist notwithstanding centuries of messianic tarrying, can post-modernism also persist notwithstanding the massive return of unreconstructed fundamentalism, terror and tribalism? Can sub-national, national and international allegiances and values co-exist? If the components of complex sociolinguistic repertoires can be situationally linked, is this also the case for the components of ideological, identificational and cognitive repertoires? Sociolinguists are formed by good hypotheses, good research design skills and by "a-ha" recognitions vis-a-vis the nature of linguistic co-contributions to the solutions to and the theoretical elaboration of all of the above questions as well as many more.

My Personal Path and Preferences in the Sociology of Language

Is there a danger of parochialization as a result of the pursuit of topics such as the above? Not really. If the problems are theoretically anchored, they will lead outward into the world of general theory, as well as inward into the world of complex Israeli reality. In all of my own work, I have tried to derive insight into Jewish topics from the vantage point of general theory, just as I have tried to derive general theory from empirical research on Jewish concerns. I have always found Jewish sociolinguistic concerns to be very richly provocative for the further growth of general theory, every bit as much as I believe that these concerns have benefited from being tackled from a general theoretical point of view. General sociolinguistics has prospered from stimulating research on Norway and India, on Ethiopian markets and Puerto Rican neighborhoods in the Greater New York Metropolitan Area, on Frisian towns and on Maori villages, on Catalan policies and on Quebecois anxieties, on Aboriginal "outback stations" in Northern Australia and on Hasidic shtiblekh in Brooklyn. I refuse to believe that a strong injection of Israeli reality into the sociolinguistic literature would have anything but positive results, provided that this injection were theoretically well anchored, on the one hand, and clearly aimed at theory testing and revision, on the other hand. I am also a strong believer in mutual enrichment between applied and theoretical concerns. A national sociolinguistic survey, such as those recently concluded in the Basque Country, Ireland, Friesland, Belgium and Wales (not to mention the earlier surveys undertaken in Ireland, East Africa and New Zealand) might be a boon to the piecemeal efforts at educational, intergroup and linguistic inquiry now struggling separately to get off the ground.

* * * *

I have no doubt that the inclusion of Israeli sociolinguistic efforts within the annual volumes in this series will have highly beneficial results. Such inclusion will not only record the existence, but will also stimulate the growth in numbers, quality and provocativeness of Israeli sociolinguisitics/sociology of language over the years to come..

The current selection of papers is extremely impressive, both in depth and in breadth, and, indeed, several of them tackle many of the most fundamental problems of Israeli society and, indeed, of the discipline worldwide, involving as they do many of the most creative members of this field of study. The great linguistic laboratory which Israel constitutes cannot help but stimulate the level of awareness of and involvement in "language in society" that such a laboratory so richly deserves and so desperately needs. Of course, it is easy for me, as an outsider living in a relatively peaceful and affluent setting, to give gratuitous and critical advice to colleagues working under very difficult and often beleaguered conditions. How wonderful it would be if peace and calm could quickly come to Israel and its neighbors. However, setting aside the wisdom of waiting until that state of affairs materializes, it is often also desirable to have an outsider look in and make suggestions even when the circumstances for their implementation are less than optimal and may long continue to be such. Countries all over the globe are struggling with less than optimal circumstances. Those may, indeed, be the only circumstances around. These comments of mine come with good wishes and with fond hopes that they may stimulate thought, discussion and decisions on behalf of a more vibrant sociolinguistic future in Israel, "af al pi khen," notwithstanding the difficulties that may exist.

29

An Agenda for the Sociology of Communication in Israel

Elihu Katz

Scorekeepers of the miracles of Israel, ancient and modern, sometimes need to be reminded to include two communications miracles on their lists. One of these is the revival of the ancient Hebrew language as the taken-for-granted medium of daily life. This miracle owes a debt to that other miracle of communication: the survival of the Jewish people by virtue of the preservation of their Book, and, of course, vice versa. What better starting point for a sociology of language an communication? Given the ready access to the scriptures, the rabbinic literature and to historical accounts, how can one resist reexamining the Tower of Babel or the leadership of Moses. The same holds for contemporary affairs: how can one resist studying the resurrection and diffusion of a language, the evolution of the Hebrew-language press as a medium of national liberation, or the process of producing and celebrating newly invented holidays? How can one resist studying the irony of the search for television programming appropriate to the Jewish Sabbath, or the dilemma of how to represent both the unity of the nation and its multi-cultural heritage, including that of its Palestinian citizens?

Proposing an agenda for a sociology of communication in Israel seems all too easy. The trouble is that sociologists—not only in Israel—do not show much interest in communication, certainly not in the mass media. The reason for this is not clear since the fathers of sociology showed much interest, but the fact is that the mass media were relegated, together with public opinion, to that residual of social psychology called "collective behavior". The irony is that the institutions of public opinion and communication are central not only to any notion of social control, or nation-building participatory democracy, but also to the contradictory tendencies towards segmentation and globalization which are undermining the nation state everywhere.

The gap left by sociology has now been preempted by a new multidisciplinary enterprise called communication or media studies which is in vogue almost everywhere. Most sociologists of communication, like myself, have relocated in these departments, and have joined forces with political scientists, social psychologists, sociolinguists, legal scholars and humanists (cinema studies, rhetorical studies, language and literature). In Israel, the Hebrew University was the first to found such a department in 1963, abetted by the sociological leadership at the time, and by now, most of the other universities have followed suit. Many of the contributors to this volume are members of these departments, which are—among other things—generating sociologies of communication (but not so different from the sociologies of politics being generated by the equally interdisciplinary Political Science). Of course, research on communications and the media occupies scholars elsewhere in the University a well, including departments of sociology. (My secret ambition, I confess, is to make a tour of the academic community, with the aim of letting certain colleagues know that—wittingly or not—they are doing communications).

The agenda I wish to propose relates to the interdisciplinary, but heavily sociological, research on communications that deserves to be done in Israel Some of it is being done. Obviously, an agenda of this sort is personal—bounded by what the writer considers interesting and by his necessarily limited knowledge. Wherever possible, I shall illustrate by reference to work that has been done, or is being done.

The People of the Book

Some years ago, Hanna Adoni and I attempted to review some of the functions of the Book for the survival of the Jews. In the absence of a territorial domain, the Book served as a kind of "portable homeland," we thought, a perpetual reminder of a shared past and a promised future. It was the repository of the foundational myths of peoplehood and of the collective memory of national experience. Of course, to accomplish these tasks, the Book had to be read. And so, indeed, literacy was a near-universal requirement (at least for men), and scholarship in the Book was a major source of communal status and authority. Reading of the Book, as well as study and worship were communal matters, carried out by organized groups, in public. An obvious by-product was the obstinate preservation of the Hebrew language for these purposes. The Book generated prescribe codes for living and legislating.

However well known, these propositions deserve the attention of communications scholars, especially those interested in sociologically-tempered technological theories. How can a literary canon, and its exegesis, keep a dispersed people alive, and together, over so long a period and so many places? Generalizations about writing and printing surely apply, *a fortiori,* to this People of the Linear Medium. Or would graven images have accomplished the same tasks? What characterizes peoples with written constitutions? Answers to questions like these may be known to others, perhaps, but they are not known to us—professionally, that is.

Communication history is not a popular specialty, and almost seems at odds with the jet-setting and internetting that stereotype media scholars. But that's a shame, given the natural resources so readily available. To my knowledge only one or two Israeli scholars are studying media histories, although it is almost a national pastime to study the Semitic alphabet, Assyrian tablets, the process of canonization, not to speak of Biblical genres, midrashic hermeneutics, and the like. All kinds of academics—not just Jews—are busy studying Genesis, but it hardly occurs to Israeli social scientists.

The Institutional Structure of Communication in Israel

The same holds true for the history of communication in Israel, beginning with the period prior to the establishment of the state. Again, there are innumerable studies and writings on how Hebrew took root and warded off competing languages including the other Jewish vernaculars. *We,* as professional students of language and communication, should also know the answers, instead of simply joining the chorus who compare the success of Hebrew in Israel with the apparent failure of the Gaelic in Ireland.

No less interesting is the history of communication media in Israel. The indigenous Hebrew press, and organs of the political groupings that formed before or during the early migrations are the obvious starting points. In spite of their different voices these journals formed a loyal vanguard of national liberation—in which politicians doubled as journalists, as they did in many other national movements. The party press, around which politics was organized, then gradually, and reluctantly, gave way to a few privately owned newspapers, of whom the two most successful, circulation-wise, have moved in a strongly populist direction. What little we know of this process is thanks to political scientists, sociologists, and historians with no special interest or competence in the comparative sociology of communication.

The social history of broadcasting is equally interesting from a comparative point of view. Why, for example, did it take so long (from 1948 to 1965) to realize that democracy implies an independent broadcasting service, not one directly administered by the Prime Minister's office? Why was television so late in coming? Who has the good sense to institute a BBC-like monopoly service—financed by a license fee and officially independent of Government—when the broadcasting law was reformed in 1965? And why are ostensibly patriotic conservative governments so anxious to rid themselves of public broadcasting—a they have tried to do elsewhere in Europe—and to abandon the airwaves to the advertising-driven second service and the dozens of cable channels?

Division of Labor Among the Media

Which media serve which functions is one of the questions that have been regularly researched. But even this research ha been largely individualistic rather than macro-sociological. The role for Israeli media in national integration, for example, has not been studied frontally—except perhaps in wars. Did television make a difference, for politics, for culture? Why did the party press disappear? Has the segmentation of television lessened the sense of shared experience, shared fate, and shared agenda that characterized the once-monopoly channel that was Israeli television? Does the Russian-language press promote the integration of immigrants?

And what is the meaning of the Israeli rush to adopt new media technologies—such as the internet or the cellular telephone? Do these media function primarily as economic tools, or are they extensions of the concern for security or other more personal domains? How to explain that such a tiny society—where opening a window allows you to talk to half the population—is so addicted to mediated communication?

> And what of newspaper reading? Slowly, but surely, people are reading only one newspaper, rather than a morning and evening paper. There is the irony that even while the number of television channels is multiplying the number of newspapers is dwindling. At the moment, Yedior Aharonot probably reaches more people daily than does any one of the television channels! The meaning of this success needs to be written—and rewritten.

Israeli society—still one of the most politicized—has been slow in producing television-cloning tabloids offering easy-to-read versions of scandals and soundbites. But there is more than a hint that the serious press is in trouble, with only one remaining Hebrew-language daily, however distinguished, and the public satisfied that television news is doing a more credible job, instead.

Media and Politics

During the long period of debate over whether/when to introduce television broadcasting in Israel, a concern was voiced—a political echo of the fear that TV would undermine renascent Hebraic culture—lest television personalize politics; Israelis were great ideologues at the time. Now that ideology has declined and personality politics have arisen—primaries, personalized campaigning, direct election of prime minister decline in political party activity—it is certainly time to ask whether television has anything to do with this. In asking, one must be careful to sort out the verbal from the visual as well as the transplanting of politics from "outside" to the living room.

There has also been a marked decline in collectivity-orientation in the society, and a corresponding rise in the legitimacy of self-interest and materialism. Israel television oozed collectivism and carried no commercial advertising during its 20 years of one-channel monopoly. Is it possible that 'Dallas' has some share in the (slow but steady) rise of egoism and materialism? Is there some basis for the hypothesis of American cultural imperialism?

Research on these broader questions of political culture deserve to be joined to the much more developed—but narrowly-defined—research on strictly political communication. For example, what effect has live broadcasting of Knesset debates had on the MKs and on the public image of the legislature? This kind of question links the specifically political to the broader concerns of the culture. So do the ceremonial broadcast of events such as the various peace ceremonies on the one hand, and the gruesome aftermath of terrorist events, on the other.

Election campaigns bring out the entire communications research fraternity. There is interest in the role of the press in agenda setting, the character of political advertising, the rhetoric of appeals ("fear" appeals for example, which are thought to have been effective in 1996), the segmented party-political broadcasts aimed at their particularistic constituencies. Interesting as they are, these concerns—well represented in this volume—deserve to be set in the larger concern of redesigning the election campaign, and putting the media to better use within it.

During elections, but not only during elections, the media take the role of representing the society to itself, and this is a heavy responsibility when such representation is translated into voting intentions. Voters (not just Israelis) make decisions based on their assessment of how others are going to vote. Moreover, this aspect of journalism has taken a new turn in recent years as the press takes the lead in sponsoring and publicizing opinion polls. Parenthetically, it may be noted that opinion polling is but one aspect of the "precision journalism" that tracks the stock market, the weather, the changing number of students in religious schools, etc., on which interpretive journalism increasingly rests.

It is noteworthy, I believe, that Israeli citizens do not understand the normative role of journalism as a "watchdog." Apart from "media watch" groups that champion balance (and purport to he able to demonstrate leftist bias in the media), there is a recurrent antipathy toward the legitimacy of criticizing government (when government is on "our" side). This is more complex than it sound because the norm of social responsibility is not at all alien to Israeli newsmakers who sometimes impose self-censorship in the name of security matters or in the name of denying voice to racists such as the Kahane movement. Serious work must be done on who/what is to say/said! There is much to be done altogether at the nexus of communication and law.

Newer (cognitive) theories of media effect further accent this question of media responsibility. According to this argument, change is accomplished by the media not by changing individual minds but by changing norms, whereby people come to believe that valued other people believe that it is socially acceptable or unacceptable to smoke or to hate. And thus the power of the media lies in their ability—intended or not—top represent the norm of non-smoking (or smoking), or by the norm of ethnic tolerance (or intolerance), or by the norm of respect for government (or disrespect). This is by no means a new idea—it underlies the lobbying by many groups for a better image throughout the history of cinema and broadcasting. But it makes the job of journalism all the more difficult, and all the more vulnerable.

Media and Conflict

The question of image directs attention to the larger question of intergroup relations and conflict. This is another of the areas that has been much—but still not enough—stuied by Israeli sociologists of communication and others. Of the three longstanding intergroup conflicts—Arab/Jewish, religious/secular, and Ashkenazi/Sephardi—most attention has been given, in cinema and broadcasting research, to the conflict between Arabs and Jews, domestic and international. The one-dimensional image of the Arab as enemy may have given way, after the *intifada* and, certainly since Oslo, to multidimensionality. The larger problem, however, is how little they are seen, and this holds especially true for Israeli Arabs, given their struggle for equality and resources.

Religious Jews, on the other hand are ubiquitous on television, variously as ultra-orthodox, ultra-nationalists, or intellectuals of religious persuasion. It would be of considerable interest to understand these images are juggled by television viewers most of whom are quite sympathetic to religious tradition, even if they declare themselves ideologically secular. Even mainstream religious Zionists are now perceived as "threatening" to more secular Jews and their neighborhoods, and the media appear to be exacerbating the gap, or so it seems to me. It is also true that the observability of these groups has been lessened in recent years, as particularistic tendencies and group media displace the push towards shared public space that characterized the earlier years of the state. The separatism is so marked in certain extreme groups that the mainstream media lost track of them; so did the security services, it appears.

The representation of Israelis of Eastern origin has been enhanced manifold, quantitatively and qualitatively, dating perhaps to the central role which the Begin government assigned to development towns and to its recognition that a second and third generation of immigrants from Asia and Africa had come to political maturity. Willy-nilly, all of the media reflect and promote this change, I believe, and it is a subject worthy of tracking over time.

Media and Culture

Apart from representing society to itself, the media also have an important role in culture. This has two different aspects: first media *are* culture, in the sense that, functionally, 'our' *Dallas* is mutatis mutandis like our grandparents' *Genesis* (or at least the Book of Esther); and, second, the media intervene in our ability to participate in non-media culture.

The idea that the media are the content of culture has been much emphasized by James Carey to counterbalance the other sense whereby the media only 'deliver' culture. Thus, media are able (or used to be able) to assemble society to commune together, to share an experience, to imagine the whole. The media offer role models and reference groups and moral themes to emulate or reject.

Research in Israel should try to untangle, even now, the extent to which the media do or don't deserve credit for having taught Hebrew, the extent to which the collectivity-orientation of these media fore-stalled individualism, preserved the sabbath, helped in immigrant absorption, mobilized the society for war. It is still worth trying to determine the effect of introducing graven images, as the people of the Book became the people of television. By now, we also ought to know something of the effect of channel multiplication on the quality of broadcasting.

Anything but boring, such audience research can be very intriguing. For example, consider the simple hypothesis that television is responsible for the decline in per capita attendance at the performing arts, museums, and sporting spectacles because it keeps people home. But research shows that this hypothesis is wrong. While it consumes almost 40% of leisure time, television in Israel has *not* kept people from going out as often as they did prior to TV. Why, then, when Israelis do go out, are they less likely, since TV, to go to the theater or to a concert or a football game? To answer this question one must move to other levels of analysis, and then to compare research to see whether the same phenomenon is evident in other countries following the introduction of television. At the same time, it may also be said that people are now seeing *more* movies, and *more* symphonic concerts than they did before—thanks to the delivery function of television.

The trouble is that we always seem to be taken by surprise. If systematic hypotheses about the likely effects of books on society and culture had been formulated in the 16th century, and if there were departments of sociology and communications to do the work, we might not have had to wait until the 20th century to ask the question, and try to answer it only in retrospect.

But what excuse have we for hardly knowing what to ask, and what to look for, as television implanted itself in the 20th century household? We hardly know anything about the role of television in the lives and minds of children, for example. Perhaps we will do better with the internet. Whether the internet will further erode the nation/state by creating affinity networks that trespass national boundaries illustrates the scope of the agenda relating to the new media of telecommunication. Think Big, is the message.

Selected Bibliography in English

Books

Arian, A. (1995). *Security Threatened: Surveying Israeli Opinion on Peace and War*. New York: Cambridge University Press.

Barness, A. (1961). *The Israel Press—A History*. Jerusalem: The Israeli Publishing Institute.

Ben Rafael, E. (1994). *Language, Identity and Social Division: The Case of Israel*. Oxford: Oxford University Press.

Ben Rafael, E. and Elite, O. (1994). *Language and Society in Israel*. Beer Sheva: Ben Gurion University Press.

Bentolila, Y. (1984). *The Sociophonology of Hebrew as Spoken in a Rural Settlement of Moroccan Jews in Israel*. Jerusalem: The Hebrew University.

Birnbaum, S.A. (1967). *Yiddish: A Survey and Grammar*. Manchester: Manchester University Press.

Benbau, I. and Sermoneta, J. (eds.) (1985). *Judeo-Romance Languages*. Jerusalem: The Hebrew University and Misgav Yerushalaim.

Blank, M. (1989). *The Human Language*. Jerusalem: Bialik Institute.

Blau, J. (1988). *Studies in Middle Arabic and its Judeo-Arabic Variety*. Jerusalem: Magnes Press.

Blum-Kulka, S. (1997). *Dinner-Talk: Cultural Patterns of Sociability and Socialization in Family Discourse*. Mahwah, New Jersey, London: Lawrence Erlbaum.

Blum-Kulka, S. and Kasper, G. (1993). *Interlanguage Pragmatics*. Oxford: Oxford University Press.

Bruck, P. (ed.) (1988). *The News, Media and Terrorism*. Ottawa: Carleton University Press.

Caspi, D. and Katz, E. (1986). *Media Decentralization—The Case of Israel's Local Newspapers*. New Brunswick: Transaction Books.

Chomsky, W. (1957). *Hebrew: The Eternal Language*. Philadelphia: Jewish Publication Society of America.

Cohen, A.A. and Adoni, H. (1990). *Social Conflict and Television News*. Newbury Park: Sage Publications.

Cohen, A.A. and Wolfsfeld, G. (eds.) (1992). *Framing the Intifada: People and Media*. Norwood, New Jersey: Ablex Publishing Corporation.

Dayan, D. and Katz, E. (1992). *Media Events*. Cambridge: Harvard University Press.

Dromi, E. (1993). *Language and Cognition*. Norwood, N.J.: Alex Publication Corporation.

Etzioni-Halevi, E. (1987). *National Broadcasting under Siege—A Comparative Study of Australia, Britain, Israel and West Germany*: New: St. Martin's.

Fishman, A. (1972). (ed.) *Advances in the Sociology of Language*. The Hague: Mouton.

Fishman, J., Cooper, R.L. and Conard, A.W. (1977). *The Spread of English—The Sociology of English as an Additional Language*. Newbury: Rowley.

Frenkel, E. (1994). *The Press and Politics in Israel: The Jerusalem Post from 1932 to Present*. Connecticut: Greenwood Press.

Gordon, A. 1993. *Content Analysis of International News in Selected Israeli Newspapers and American Newspapers*. L.A.: Louisiana State University Press.

Katriel, T. 1986. *Talking Straight in Dugri Speech in Israeli Sabra Culture*. Cambridge: Cambridge University Press.

Katriel, T. 1997. *Performing the Past: A Study of Israeli Settlement Museums*. Hillsdale, NJ: Laurence Erlbaum.

Katz, E. and Gurevitch, M. 1976. *The Secularization of Leisure: Culture and Communication in Israel*. London: Feber and Faber.

Katz, E. and Szescko, T. 1981. *Mass Media and Social Change*. Beverly Hills: Sage Publications.

Katz, E. and Wedell, G. 1977. *Broadcasting in the Third World*. Cambridge: Harvard University Press.

Lederman, J. 1992. *Battle lines: The American Media and the Intifada*. New York: Henry Holt and Company.

Liebes, T. and Katz, E. 1990. *The Export of Meaning—Cross Cultural Reading of Dallas*. New York: Oxford University Press.

Loshitzki, Y. 1997. *Spielberg's Holocaust: Critical Perspectives on Schindler's List*: Indiana University Press.

Marcus, S. 1965. *The Judeo-Spanish Language*. Jerusalem: Kiryat Sefer.

Morag, S. 1963. *The Hebrew Language Tradition of the Yemenite Jews*. Jerusalem: The Academy of the Hebrew Language.

Moshayov, D. 1977. *The Press in Israel*. Jerusalem: Government Press Office.

Neev, O. 1973. *Broadcasting in Israel*. Philadelphia.

Nimmo, D. and Mansfield, M. 1982. 'Government and the Newsmedia—Comparative Dimensions' : Baylor University Press.

Rabin, C. 1973. *A Short History of the Hebrew Language*. Jerusalem: The Jewish Agency.

Roeh, I. 1982. *The Rhetoric of News in Israel Radio*. Bochum: Dr. Drockmeyer.

Roeh, I., Katz, E., Cohen, A.A. and Zelizer, B. 1980. *Almost Midnight: Reforming the Late Night News*. Beverly Hills: Sage.

Shinar, D. 1987. *Palestinian Press in The West Bank—The Political Dimension*. Jerusalem: Jerusalem Post.

Shur, S. forthcoming. *Language and Nation Building: Political aspects of the Hebrew language revival*. Haifa: Haifa University.

Soesman, A. 1993. *Attrition of Native Language Vocabulary in Dutch Adult Immigrants to Israel*. Tel Aviv: S.N.

Spolsky, B. 1986. *Language and Education in Multilingual Settings*. Clevedon Avon: Multilingual Matters.

Spolsky, B. 1989. *Conditions for Second Language Learning*. Oxford: Oxford University Press.

Spolsky, B. and Cooper, R. 1991. *The Languages of Jerusalem*. Oxford: Calderon Press.

Watts, R.J., Ide, S. and Ehlich, K. 1992. *Politeness in Language*. Berlin—New York: Mouton de Gruyter.

Wexler, P. 1990. *The Schizoid Nature of Modern Hebrew: A Slavic Language: Search of a Semitic Past*. Weisbaden: Otto Harrassowitz.

Wolfsfeld, G. 1997. *Media and Political Conflict*. Cambridge: Cambridge University Press.

Wyant, Y. (ed.) 1989. *Canadian-Israeli Perspectives on Culture, Women and Media.* Jerusalem: Academon.

Journal Articles

Adams, W.C. 1981. 'Television Coverage of the Middle East'. Washington: George Washington University.

Adoni, H. 1978. 'Functions of Mass Media in the Political Socialization of Adolescents'. *Communication Research* 6: 84-106.

Adoni, H. 1984. 'Media and the Social Construction of Reality: Toward an Integration of Theory and Research'. *Communication and Research* 11: 323-340.

Adoni, H. 1985. 'Media Interchangeability and Co-Existence: Trends and Changes in Production, Distribution and Consumption Pattern of the Print Media in the Television Era'. *Libri* 3: 202-217.

Adoni, H. 1995. 'Literacy and Reading in a Multimedia Environment'. *Journal of Communication* 45: 152-176.

Adoni, H. and Akiba, C.A. 1978. 'Television Economic News and the Social Construction of Economic Reality'. *Journal of Communication* 28: 61-70.

Adoni, H. and Cohen, A.A. 1980. 'Children's Fear Response to Real Life Violence on Television: The Case of the 1973 Middle East War'. *International Journal of Communication Research* 6.

Adoni, H., Cohen, A.A. and Mane, S. 1984. 'Social Reality and TV News: Perceptual Dimensions of Social Conflicts in Selected Life Areas'. *Journal of Broadcasting* 28: 33-49.

Adoni, H. and Shadmi, E. 1978. 'The Portrait of the Citizen as a Young Reader—The Function of Books as a Political Socialization of Youth in Israel'. *Reading Research Quarterly* 16: 121-137.

Amara, M. 1995. 'Hebrew and English Lexical Reflections of Sociopolitical Changes in Palestinian Arabic'. *Journal of Multilingual and Multicultural Development* 16: 165-172.

Ariel, M. 1988. 'Female and Male Stereotypes in Israeli Literature and Media: Evidence from Introductory Patterns'. *Language and Communication* 8: 43-48.

Bachi, R. 1956. 'A Statistical Analysis of the Revival of Hebrew in Israel'. *Scripta Hierosolymitana* 3: 179-247.

Bahbah, B. and Kital, S. 1985. 'Perspectives in Conflict: Role of the Palestinian Media in the West Bank, the Gaza Strip, and East Jerusalem'. *Journal of Communication* 35: 16-25.

Barnett, G.A., Wigand, R.T., Harrison, R.P., Woelfel, J. and Cohen, A.A. 1981. 'Communication and Cultural Development: A Multidimensional Analysis'. *Human Organization* 40: 330-337.

Ben Rafael, E. and Brosh, H. 1991. 'A sociological Study of Second Language Diffusion The Obstacles to Arabic Teaching in the Israeli School'. *Language Problems and Language Planning* 15: 1-24.

Ben-Rafael, E. 1994. 'A Sociological Paradigm of Bilingualism: English, French, Yiddish, Arabic in Israel'. *Israel Social Science Research* 9: 181-206.

Bentolila, Y. 1994. 'Bilingualism in a Moroccan Settlement in the South of Israel'. *Israel Social Science Research* 9: 89-108.

Blum-Kulka, S. 1982. 'Learning to Say What You Mean in a Second Language: A Study of the Speech Act Performance of Learners of Hebrew as a Second Language'. *Applied Linguistic* 3: 29-59.

Blum-Kulka, S. 1983. 'The Dynamics of Political Interviews'. *Text* 3: 131-153.

Blum-Kulka, S. 1990. 'You Don't Touch Lettuce with Your Fingers: Parental Politeness in Family Discourse'. *Journal of Pragmatics* 14: 259-288.

Blum-Kulka, S. 1993. 'You Gotta Know How to Tell a Story: Telling, Tales and Tellers in America and Israeli Narrative Events at Dinner'. *Language and Society* 22: 361-402.

Blum-Kulka, S. and Olshtain, E. 1984. 'Requests and Apologies: A Cross-Cultural Study of Speech Act Realization Patterns'. *Applied Linguistics* 5: 196-213.

Blum-Kulka, S. and Snow, C. 1992. 'Developing Autonomy for Tellers, Tale and Telling in Family Narrative-Events'. *Narrative and Life History* 2: 187-217.

Broddason, T., Cohen, A.A. and Greenberg, B.S. 1987. 'News Diffusion of the Palme Assassination among Journalists in Iceland, Israel and the United States'. *Europen Journal of Communication* 2.

Cais, J. 1983. 'Socialization and Verbal Behavior: An Israeli Example'. International Journal of the Sociology of Language 41: 57-75.

Carbaugh, D. 1993. 'Communal Webs: Communication and Culture in Contemporary Israel'. *Quarterly Journal of Speech* 79: 156-163.

Caspi, D. 1981. 'The Agenda—Setting Function of the Israeli Press'. *Knowledge* 3: 401-414.

Caspi, D. 1981. 'On Politicians' Criticism of Mass Media'. *Journal of Broadcasting* 252: 181-193.

Caspi, D. 1983. 'Media Decentralization in a Centralized System: The Case of the Local Press in Israel'. *Gazette* 31: 171-184.

Caspi, D. 1983. 'On the Control of Media by Politicians: A New Perspective'. *Political Communication and Persuasion* 2: 263-277.

Caspi, D. 1984. 'On the Control of Media by Politicians'. *Political Communication and Persuasion* 2: 263-275.

Caspi, D. 1986. 'Electoral Rhetoric and Political Polarization: The Begin—Peres Debates'. *European Journal of Communication* 1: 447-462.

Caspi, D. 1989. 'In Search of a Theory of Television News and Public Relations'. *American Behavioral Scientist* 33: 216-220.

Caspi, D. and Limor, Y. 1978. 'How the Yom Kippur War Affected Israeli Legislator Media Exposure'. *Journalism Quarterly* 55.

Caspi, D. and Limor, Y. 1983. 'The Servants of Two Masters: The Evaluation by the Public and its Representatives of the Mass Media in Israel'. *Mass Communication Review* 10.

Caspi, D. and Limor, Y. 1996. 'One Thousand Ways (and more) to Control the Mass Media'. *Forthcoming*.

Cohen, A., Barnet B.G, Wig and R.T, Harrison R.P, Wolsfel J. 1981. 'Communication and Cultural Development: A Multidimensional Analysis'. *Human-Organization* 40: 330-337.

Cohen, A., Adoni, H. and Drori, G. 1983. 'Adolescents' Perceptions of Social Conflicts in Television News and social Reality'. *Human Communication Research* 10: 203-225.

Cohen, A.A. 1976. 'Radio versus Television: The Effect of the Medium'. *Journal of Communication* 26: 29-35.

Cohen, A.A. 1981. 'People without Media: Attitudes and Behavior during a General Media Strike'. *Journal of Broadcasting* 25: 171-180.

Cohen, A.A. 1985. 'Attention to the Mass Media among Straight and Split Ticket Voters'. *Human Communication Research* 2: 75-78.

Cohen, A.A. 1987. 'Decision Making in VCR Rental Libraries: Information Use and Behavior Patterns'. *American Behavioral Scientist* 30: 495-508.

Cohen, A.A. 1989. 'Answers without Questions: A Comparative Analysis of Television News Interviews'. *European Journal of Communication* 4: 435-451.

Cohen, A.A. and Adoni, H. 1980. 'Children's Fear Responses to Real-Life violence on Television: The Case of 1973 Middle East War'. *Communication* 6: 81-93.

Cohen, A.A., Levy, M.R. and Golden, K. 1988. 'Children's Uses and Gratifications of Home VCRs: Evolution or Revolution'. *Communication Research* 6.

Cohen, A.A. and Salomon, G. 1979. 'Children's Literate Television Viewing: Surprises and Possible Explanation'. *Journal of Communication* 29: 156-163.

Cohen, J. 1997. 'Relationship Between Attachment Models and Parasocial Interaction'. *Journal of Broadcasting and Electronic Media* 41: 516-529.

Cooper, R.L. 1983. 'Preface to Sociolinguistic Perspective on Israeli Hebrew'. *IJSL* 41: 5-8.

Cooper, R.L. and Danet, B. 1980. 'Language in the Melting Pot: The Sociolinguistic Context for Language Planning in Israel'. *Language Problems and Language Planning* 4: 1-28.

Cromer, G. 1987. 'The Polluted Image: The Response of Ultra-Orthodox Judaism to Israeli Television'. *SSR* 71: 198-199.

Cromer, G. 1995. 'Secularism is The Root of All Evil: the Haredi Response to Crime and Delinquency'. *International Journal of Group Tensions*: 109-121.

Dorani, E. and B., N. 1993. 'Cable Television in the Kibbutz: A Case Example'. *Israel Social Science Research* 8: 197-199.

Dotan, J. and Cohen, A.A. 1976. 'Mass Media Use in the Family During War And Peace: Israel 1973-1974'. *Communication Research* 3.

Etzioni-Halevy, E. 1988. 'Inherent Contradictions of Democracy. Illustrations from National Broadcasting Corporations'. *Comparative Politics* April: 325-340.

Eyal, C.H. 1985. 'News Paper Political Advertising and News in the 1984 Israeli Elections'. *Journalism Quarterly* Autumn: 601-608.

Fellman, J. 1974. 'The Hebrew Revival: A Myth?'. *Orbis* 23: 350-354.

Fellman, J. 1975. 'The Hebrew Language on the eve of its Revival'. *Orbis* 24: 349-353.

Fellman, J. 1978. 'A Note on the Hebrew and the Irish Revivals'. *Orbis* 27: 315-316.

Fisherman, H. 1990. 'Attitudes toward Foreign Words in Contemporary Hebrew'. *International Journal of the Sociology of Language* 86: 5-40.

Fishman, G. and Weimann, G. 1995. 'Reconstructing Suicide: Reporting Suicide in the Israeli Press'. *Journalism Quarterly* 72: 551-558.

Fishman, G. and Weinmann, G. 1997. 'Motives to Commit Suicide: Statistical vs. Mass Mediated Reality'. *Archives of Suicide Research* 3: 1-14.

Fishman, J. 1965. 'Who Speaks What Language to Whom and When'. *La Linguistique* 2: 67-88.

Fishman, J. 1967. 'Bilingualism with and without Diglossia-Digglosia with and without Bilingualism'. *Journal of Social Issues* 23: 29-38.

Fishman, J. and Weinmann, G. 1985. 'Presenting the Victim: Sex Bias in Press Reports on Crime'. *Justice Quarterly* 2.

Forgas, J. 1985. 'Language and Social Situations'. New York: Springer-Verlad.

Frenkel, E. 1977. 'The Russian Press in Israel'. *Soviet Jewish Affairs* 7: 24-36.

Galnoor, I. 1979. 'The Politics of Public Information'. *Transaction/Society* May/June: 20-30.

Galnoor, I. 1981. 'Israel's Polity: The Common Language'. *The Jerusalem Quarterly* 20: 65-82.

Glinert, L.H. 1995. 'Inside the Language Planners Head: Tactical Responses to a Mass Immigration'. *Journal of Multilingual and Multicultural Development* 16: 351-371.

Gold, D. 1989. 'A Sketch of the Linguistic Situation in Israel Today'. *Language in Society* 18: 361-388.

Goren, D. 1980. 'The News and Foreign Policy: An Examination of the Impact of the News Media on the Making of Goreign Policy'. *Research in Social Movements, Conflict and Change* 3: 119-141.

Greifat, Y. and Katriel, T. 1989. 'Life demand Musayara: Communication and Culture in Contemporary Israel'. *International and Intercultural Communication Annual* 13: 121-138.

Gurevitch, M. 1971. 'Television and the Sabbath Culture in Israel'. *The Jewish Journal of Sociology* 13: 65-71.

Guttman, N. 1997. 'Beyond Strategic Research: A Value Centered Approach to Health Communication Interventions'. *Communication Theory* 7: 95-124.

Hazani, M. 1991. 'Aligning Vocabularity, Symbols Banks, and Sociocultural Structure'. *Journal of Contemporary Ethnography* 20: 179-202.

Herzog, H. 1987. *Contest of Symbols—The Sociology of Election Campaigns Through Israel Ephemera*. Cambridge: Harvard University Library.

Herzog, H. 1987. 'The Elections Campaign as a Liminal Stage: Negotiation over Meanings'. *The Sociological Review* 35: 559-574.

Herzog, H. and Ronen., S. 1994. 'Negotiated Society? Media Discourse on Israeli Jewish/Arabs Relations'. *Israel Social Science Research* 9: 55-88.

Hicks, R.G. and Gordon, A. 1974. 'Foreign News Content in Israeli and U.S. Newspapers'. *Journalism Quarterly* 51: 639-644.

Hoffman, J.E. 1974. 'The Prediction of Success in Language Planning: The Case of the Chemists in Israel'. *International Journal of the Sociology of Language* 1: 39-65.

Hofman, J.E. 1974. 'Predicting the Use of Hebrew Terms among Israeli Psychologists'. *International Journal of the Sociology of Language* 3: 53-65.

Jaffe, M. 1997. 'Media Interactivity and Self Efficacy: An Examination of Hypermedia First Aid Instruction'. *Journal of Health Communication* 2: 235-251.

Kaplowitz, I. 1992. 'Arabic in Israel: The Sociolinguistic Situation of Israel's Arab minority'. *International Journal of the Sociology of Language* 98: 29-66.

Katriel , T. 1992. 'Lefargen: A Study in Israeli Semantics of Social Relations'. *Research on Language and Social Interactions* 26: 33-55.

Katriel, T. 1989. 'Hahlafot: Rules and Strategies in Children's Swapping Exchanges'. *Research on Language and Social Interaction* 22: 157-178.

Katriel, T. 1989. 'An Overview of Research on Language and Social Interaction in Israel'. *Research on Language and Social Interaction* 22: 347-356.

Katriel, T. 1991. 'Sodot: Secret-Sharing as a Social Form among Israeli Children'. *Research on Language and Social Interaction* 24: 141-157.

Katriel, T. and Nesher, P. 1986. 'Gibush: The Rhetoric of Cohesion in Israeli School Culture'. *Comparative Education Review* 30: 216-231.

Katz, E. 1973. 'Culture and Communication in Israel: The Transformation of Tradition'. *Jewish Journal of Sociology* 15: 5-21.

Katz, E. 1989. 'Journalists as Scientists: Notes toward Occupational Classification'. *American Behavioral Scientist* 33: 236-246.

Katz, E. 1992. 'The End of Journalism? Notes on Watching the War'. *Journal of Communication* 42: 5-13.

Katz, E., Adoni, H. and Parness, P. 1977. 'Remembering the News: What the Picture Adds to the Recall'. *Journalism Quarterly* 54: 231-239.

Katz, E., Gurevitch Michael and Hadassah., H. 1973. 'On the Use of the Mass Media for Important Things'. *American Sociological Review* 38: 164-181.

Katz, E. and Tamar, L. 1984. 'Once Upon a Time in Dallas'. *Intermedia* 12: 28-32.

Katz, E. and Tamar, L. 1990. 'Interacting with 'Dallas': Cross Cultural Readings of American TV'. *Canadian Journal of Communication* 15: 45-66.

Katz, P. 1982. 'Ethnicity Transformed: Acculturation in Language Classes in Israel'. *Anthropological Quarterly* 55: 99-111.

Koplewitz, I. 1990. 'The Use and Integration of Hebrew Lexemes in Israeli Spoken Arabic'. *Multilingual Matters* 71: 181-195.

Kraemer, R. and Birenbaum, M. 1993. 'Language Attitudes and Social Group Memberships'. *International Journal of Intercultural Relations* 17: 437-449.

Kraemer, R. and Olshtain, E. 1994. 'The Social Context of Second Language Learning in Israeli Schools'. *Israel Social Science Research* 9: 161-180.

Kraemer, R., Olshtain, E. and Badier, S. 1994. 'Ethnolinguistic Vitality, Attitudes, and Networks of Linguistic Contact: The Case of the Israeli Arab Minority'. *International Journal of the Sociology of Language* 108: 79-95.

Kraemer, R. and Olshtein, E. 1989. 'Perceived Ethnolinguistic Vitality and Language Attitudes: The Israeli Setting'. *Journal of Multilingual and Multicultural Development* 10: 197-212.

Kressel, G. 1989. 'The Power of Words'. *Israel Social Science Research* 6: 1-22.

Landau, M.J. 1987. 'Hebrew and Arabic in the State of Israel: Political Aspects of the Language Issue'. *IJSL* 67.

Lehman-Wilzig, S. 1989. 'Protest, Television, Newspapers and Public: Who Influences Whom?'. *Political Communication and Persuasion* 6: 21-32.

Lemish, D. 1997. 'The School as a Wrestling Arena: The Modeling of a Television Series'. *European Journal of Communication Research* 22: 395-418.

Lemish, D. and Tidhar, C.E. 1991. 'The Silenced Majority: Women in Israel's 1988 Television Election Campaign'. *Women and Language* 14: 13-22.

Leslau, W. 1945. 'Hebrew Elements in Judeo-Arabic Dialect of Fez'. *Jewish Quarterly Review* 36: 61-78.

Levinson, H. 1981. 'The Television Series 'Holocaust' in Israel'. *International Journal of Political Education* 4.

Levy, A. 1986. 'Mass Media as Intermediary of Conscious and Unconscious Group Fantasy: The Case of Sharon'. *Journal of Psychohistory* 14: 121-130.

Lichter, R. and Lichter, L. 1988. 'Israel in crisis: Coverage of Israel's Palestinian Problem'. *Media Monitor* 2: 1-3.

Liebes, T. 1984. 'Ethnocriticism Israelis of Moroccan Ethnicity Negotiate the Meaning of 'Dallas''. *Studies in Visual Communication* 10: 46-71.

Liebes, T. 1988. 'Cultural Differences in the Retelling of Television Fiction'. *Critical Studies in Mass Communication* 5: 277-292.

Liebes, T. 1992. 'Decoding Television News: The Political Discourse of Israeli Hawks and Doves'. *Theory and Society* 21: 357-381.

Liebes, T. 1992. 'Our war/Their War: Comparing the Intifadah and the Gulf War on U.S. and Israeli Television'. *Critical Studies in Mass Communication* 9: 44-55.

Liebes, T. 1992. 'Television, Parents, and he Political Socialization of Children'. *Teachers College Record* 94: 73-86.

Liebes, T. and Katz, E. 1986. 'Patterns of Involvement in Television Fiction: a Comparative Study'. *European Journal of Communication* 1: 151-172.

Liebes, T., Katz, E. and Ribak, R. 1991. 'Ideological Reproduction'. *Political Behavior* 13: 237-247.

Liebes, T. and Ribak, R. 1991. 'Democracy at Risk: The Reflection of Political Alienation in Attitudes toward the Media'. *Communication Theory* 1: 239-252.

Liebes, T. and Ribak, R. 1992. 'The Contribution of Family Culture to Political Participation, Political Outlook and its Reproduction'. *Communication Research* 19: 618-641.

Liebes, T. and Ribak, R. 1994. 'In Defense of Negotiated Reading: How Moderates on Each Side of the Conflict Interpret Intifada News'. *Journal of Communication* 44: 108-124.

Liebes, T. and Rivka, R. 1991. 'A Mother's Battle against TV News: A Case of Political Socialization'. *Discourse and Society* 2: 203-222.

Liebes-Plesher, T. 1984. 'Shades of Meaning in President Sadat's Knesset Speech'. *Semiotica* 48: 229-265.

Limor, Y. 1978. 'How the Yom Kippur War Affected Israeli Legislators' Media Exposure'. *Journalism Quarterly* 55: 474-481.
Loshitzki, Y. 1991. 'The Intifada as a Meta-Televisual Dialogue'. *Media, Culture and Society* 13: 557-571.
Manor, Y. 1984. 'Integration Hasbara into Policy'. *Jerusalem Quarterly* 33: 25-39.
Markowitz, F. 1993. 'Israelis with a Russian Accent'. *The Jewish Journal of Sociology* 35: 97-111.
Maschler, Y. 1994. 'Appreciation ha'araxa 'o ha'aratsa'['valuing or admiration']'. *Text* 14: 207-238.
McNamara, T.F. 1987. 'Language and Social Identity: Israelis Abroad'. *Journal of Language and Social Psychology* 6: 215-228.
Mendes, C., R. 1982. 'Language Maintenance and Shift among Jerusalem Sephardim'. *IJSL* 37: 25-39.
Morag, S. 1959. 'Planned and Unplanned Development in Modern Hebrew'. *Lingua* 8: 247-263.
Nahir, M. 1978. 'Normativism and Educated Speech in Modern Hebrew'. *ILSL* 18: 49-67.
Nasser, M. 1973. 'Freedom's Double Edge: Arab Press under Israeli Occupation'. *Journalism Quarterly* 52: 207-212.
Negbi, M. 1986. 'Paper Tiger: The Struggle for Press Freedom in Israel'. *The Jerusalem Quarterly* 39: 17-32.
Nir, R. 1984. 'Linguistic and Sociolinguistic Problems in the Translation of Imported TV Films in Israel'. *International Journal of the Sociology of Language* 48: 81-97.
Nir, R. 1986. 'Electoral Rhetoric in Israel—The Televised Debates.'. *Language Learning* 38: 187-208.
Nir, R. and Roeh, I. 1987. 'Who Says What How: Declarative Verbs on the Israeli News'. *Hebrew Studies* 28: 147-159.
Nir, R. and Roeh, I. 1992. 'Intifada Coverage in the Israeli Press: Popular and Quality Papers Assume a Rhetoric of Conformity'. *Discourse and Society* 3: 47-60.
Nossek, H. 1994. 'The Narrative Role of the Holocaust and the State of Israel in the Coverage of Salient Terrorist Events in the Israeli Press'. *Journal of Narrative and Life History* 4.
Pail, M. 1974. 'A Way toward Peace: The View of 'Moked''. *Middle East Review* 7.
Poll, S. 1980. 'The Sacred-Secular Conflict in the Use of Hebrew and Yiddish among the Ultra-Orthodox Jews of Jerusalem'. *IJSL* 24: 109-126.
Rabihiya, Y. and Wolfsfeld, G. 1988. 'Communication and Control in Times of Crisis: Israeli Censorship in Occupied Territories'. *Canadian Journal of Communication* December: 96-101.
Rabin, C. 1983. 'The Sociology of Normativism in Israeli Hebrew'. *International Journal of the Sociology of Language* 41: 41-56.
Rabin, H. 1981. 'What Constitutes a Jewish Language?'. *International Journal of the Sociology of Language* 30: 19-28.
Roeh, I. 1989. 'Journalism as Storytelling—Coverage as Narrative'. *American Behavioral Scientist* 33: 162-169.
Roeh, I. 1991. 'Monologue, Dialogue and Ideology: The Discourse of Equality on Israel Radio—1957-1987'. *The Australian Journal of Communication* Issue on the Language of Radio.
Roeh, I. and Akiba, C.A. 1993. 'Two Israelis: Some Secrets of TV News Editing That Only Viewing Reveals'. *Propaganda Review* 10: 26-31, 62-63.
Roeh, I. and Ashley, S. 1985. 'Criticizing the Press Coverage of the War in Lebanon: Toward a Paradigm of News as Storytelling'. *Communication Yearbook* 9: 1-45.
Roeh, I. and Feldman, S. 1984. 'The Rhetoric of Numbers in Front Page Journalism: How Numbers Contribute to the Melodramatic in Popular Press'. *Text* 4: 347-368.

Roeh, I. and Nir, R. 1990. 'Speech Presentation in the Israeli Radio News: Ideological Constraints and Rhetorical Strategies'. *Text* 10: 225-244.

Roeh, I. and Nir, R. 1991. 'Covering the Intifada in the Israeli Press: 'Popular' and 'Quality' Papers Assume a Rhetoric of Conformity'. *Discourse and Society* 2.

Roeh, I. and Nir, R. 1991. 'The Passing of Speech in Israel Radio News: Rhetoric Strategies and Ideological Limits'. *Hebrew Linguistics* 31.

Roeh, I.C., Akiba A. 1992. 'One of the Bloodiest Days: A Comparative Analysis of Open and Closed Television News'. *Journal of Communication* 42: 42-55.

Rosenbaum, Y. 1983. 'Hebrew Adoption among New Immigrants to Israel: The First Three Years'. *International Journal of the Sociology of Language* 41: 115-130.

Salomon, G.C., Akiba A. A. 1977. 'Television Formats, Mastery of Mental Skills and the Acquisition of Knowledge'. *Journal of Educational Psychology* 69: 612-619.

Schneller, R. 1988. 'Video Watching and its Societal Functions for small-town Adolescents in Israel'. *Youth and Society* 19: 441-459.

Schuman, H., Steeh, C. and Bobo, L. 1993. 'Pluralistic Ignorance Revisited: Perception of Opinion Distribution in Israel'. *The International Journal of Public Opinion Research* 5.

Shamir, J. 1987. 'Horse Race Journalism and Pollsters' Performance in Israel'. *Political Communication and Persuasion* 4: 371-383.

Shamir, J. 1988. 'Israeli Elite Journalists: Views on Freedom and Responsibility'. *Journalism Quarterly* 65.

Shamir, J. 1995. 'Information Cues and Indicators of the Climate of Opinion: The Spiral of Silence Theory in the Intifada'. *Communication Research* 22: 24-53.

Shapira, R. and Aviad, E.R. 1994. 'A Symbolic Interactionist User's Guide to the Answering Machine: 22 Reflections on Vocal Encounters in an Emerging Social World'. *Symbolic Interaction* 17: 411-429.

Shinar, D. 1982. 'The Portrayal of the Elderly in Four Israeli Daily Newspapers'. *Journalism Quarterly* 59: 92-96.

Shinar, D. 1993. 'VCR Narrow Casting in the Kibbutz'. *Israel Social Science Research* 8: 175-196.

Shinar, D., Tomer, D. and Biber, B. 1980. 'Images of Old Age in Television Drama Imported to Israel'. *Journal of Communication* 30: 50-55.

Shtarkshall, R. and Basker, E. 1985. 'Radio and Family Planning in Israel: Letters to Broadcasters'. *Journal of Communication* 35: 69-81.

Simon, R. 1983. 'Print Media Coverage of the War in Lebanon'. *Middle East Review* 16: 5-16.

Stock, E. 1954. 'The Press of Israel: Its Growth in Freedom'. *Journalism Quarterly* 31: 481-490.

Weil, S. 1977. 'Verbal Interaction among the Bene Israel'. *International Journal of the Sociology of Language* 13: 71-85.

Weil, S. 1983. 'Women Language in Israel'. *International Journal of the Sociology of Language* 41: 77-91.

Weimann, G. 1982. 'On the Importance of Marginality: One More Step into the Two-Step Flow of Communication'. *American Sociological Review* 47: 764-773.

Weimann, G. 1983. 'On the Strength of Weak Conversational Ties'. *Social Networks* 5: 245-267.

Weimann, G. 1983. 'Pre-Election Polls in the Israeli Press'. *Journalism Quarterly* 60: 283-300.

Weimann, G. 1983. 'The Theater of Terror: The Effects of Press Coverage'. *Journal of Communication* 33: 38-45.

Weimann, G. 1984. 'Images of America: The Impact of Americanized TV in Israel'. *International Journal of Intercultural Relations* 8: 185-197.

Weimann, G. 1984. 'Terrorists or Freedom Fighters? Labeling Terrorism in the Israeli Press'. *Political Communication and Persuasion* 2: 433-445.

Weimann, G. 1985. 'Mass-Mediated Occultism'. *Journal of Popular Culture* 19: 81-88.

Weimann, G. 1987. 'Conceptualizing the Effects of Mass-Mediated Terrorism'. *Political Communication and Persuasion* 4: 213-216.

Weimann, G. 1987. 'Media Events: The Case of International Terrorism'. *Journal of Broadcasting and Electronic Media* 31: 21-39.

Weimann, G. 1990. 'The Obsession to Forecast: Pre-Election Polls in the Israeli Press'. *Public Opinion Quarterly* 54: 396-408.

Weimann, G. 1990. 'Redefinition of Image: The Impact of Mass-Mediated Terrorism'. *International Journal of Public Opinion Research*: 16-29.

Weimann, G. 1995. 'Zapping in the Holy Land: Coping with Multi-Channel TV in Israel'. *Journal of Communication* 45: 97-103.

Weimann, G. 1996. 'Cable Comes to the Holy Land: The Impact of Cable TV on Israeli Viewers'. *Journal of Broadcasting and Electronic Media* Forthcoming.

Weimann, G. 1996. 'Can the Media Mediate? Mass Mediated Diplomacy in the Middle East'. *Journal of Conflict Processes* 2: 31-41.

Weimann, G. 1997. 'Can the Media Mediate? On Mass Mediated Diplomacy in the Middle East'. *Journal of Conflict Processes* 1: 46-59.

Weimann, G. and Fishman, G. 1988. 'Attribution of Responsibility: Sex-Based Bias in Press Reports on Crime'. *European Journal of Communication* 3: 415-430.

Weimann, G. and Hans-Bernd, B. 1991. 'The News Worthiness of International Terrorism'. *Communication Research* 18: 333-354.

Wexler, P. 1981. 'Ashkenazic German (1760-1895)'. *International Journal of the Sociology of Language* 30: 119-130.

Wexler, P. 1987. 'Interdialectical Translation as a Reflection of Lexical Obsolescennce and Dialect Distance: The West Yiddish Bible Translation of 1679 in the Biblia Pentapla'. *Journal of the Sociology of Language* 67: 7-26.

Wexler, P. 1991. 'Yiddish: The Fifteenth Slavic Language. A Study of Partial Language Shift from Judeo-Serbian to German'. *International Journal of the Sociology of Language* 67: 7-26.

Wolfsfeld, G. 1984. 'Collective Political Action and the Media Strategy: The Case of Yamit'. *Journal of Conflict Resolution* 28: 363-381.

Wolfsfeld, G. 1984. 'The Symbiosis of Press and Protest: An Exchange Analysis'. *Journalism Quarterly* 31: 128-144.

Wolfsfeld, G. 1984. 'Yamit: Protest and the Media'. *Jerusalem Quarterly* 31: 128-144.

Wolfsfeld, G. and Rabihiya, Y. 1988. 'Communication and Control in Times of Crises: Israeli Censorship in the Occupied Territories'. *Canadian Journal of Communication* Special Issue.

Yaeger-Dror, M. 1991. 'Linguistic Evidence for Social Psychology Attitudes: Hyperacommodation or (r) Singers from a Mizrahi Background'. *Language and Communication* 11: 309-331.

Zelizer, B. 1993. 'Pioneers and Plain Folks: Cultural Constructions of 'Place' in Radio News'. *Semiotica* 93: 269-285.

Zemach, T. and Cohen, A.A. 1986. 'Perception of Gender Equality on Television and in Social Reality'. *Journal of Broadcasting and electronic Media* 30: 427-444.

Zilberg, N. 1995. 'In-Group Humor of Immigrants from the Former Soviet Union to Israel'. *Israel Social Science Research* 10: 1-22.

List of Contributors

Muhammad Amara is a sociolinguist of Israeli Arabic and a lecturer in Political Science and English Studies at the Bar-Ilan University

Eliezer Ben-Rafael is a sociologist of plurilingualism in Israel, and a professor of Sociology, at the University of Tel-Aviv

Yaakov Bentolila is a sociolinguist of Moroccan Jews in Israel, and a senior lecturer in the Department of Hebrew Language and Literature, at the Ben-Gurion University of Beer Sheva.

Shoshana Blum-Kulka is a sociolinguist who has studied the development of English in Israel, and an associate professor in the Department of Communication, at the Hebrew University of Jerusalem.

Hezi Brosh is a sociolinguist who studies the role of Arabic in Israeli education, in the School of Education at the Tel-Aviv University.

Dan Caspi is a specialist of mass communication in Israel and an associate professor at the Open University, chairs the Israeli Association of Communication.

Akiba Cohen is communication scholar who investigates the mass media, and a professor of Communication, at the Tel-Aviv University.

Gerald Cromer is a social psychologist of communication, and a senior lecturer in the Department of Psychology, at Bar-Ilan University.

Eva Etzioni-Halevy is a political sociologist who is a specialist in bureaucracy and elite studies, and she is a professor of Sociology, at Bar-Ilan University.

Haya Fisherman is a sociolinguist interested in the role of English in the development of Hebrew, she works in the Department of Communication, at the Haifa University.

Josuah A Fishman is a founding father of the Sociology of Language, and a professor emeritus at the Yeshiva University.

Hadassah Haas is a researcher of communication and leisure time, and a former senior lecturer at the Gutman Institute of Applied Research in Jerusalem.

Hayim Hazan investigates aging, life cycles, symbolic activity and communication, and is a professor of Anthropology in the Department of Sociology at the Tel-Aviv University.

Hanna Herzog is a political sociologist who specialized in political communication, gender and ethnicity. An associate professor in the Department of Sociology at the Tel-Aviv University.

Tamar Katriel is a sociolinguist of Hebrew and Israeli culture, she is an associate professor in the Department of Communication and Education, at the Haifa University.

Elihu Katz is a sociologist of communication and a leading figure of communication studies; he is an emeritus professor of the Hebrew University at Jerusalem and a professor of the Anneberg School of Communication, at the University of Pennsylvania, Philadelphia.

Sam Lehman-Wilzig is a researcher of ex-parliamentary activity. He chairs the Unit of Press and Public Communication at Bar Ilan University, is an associate professor in the Department of Political Science, at Bar Ilan, Ramat Gan.

Dafna Lemish is a researcher of gender and mass media, she is a senior lecturer in the Department of Communication, at the Tel-Aviv University.

Tamar Liebes is a researcher in mass media, and an associate professor in the Department of Communication, at the Hebrew University of Jerusalem.

Yehiel Limor is a mass media researcher the New School of Media Studies, at the College of Management, in Tel-Aviv.

Yosefa Loshitzky is a senior lecturer in the Department of Communication at the Hebrew University of Jerusalem.

Raphael Nir is a sociolinguist, a professor of Communication and Education at the Hebrew University of Jerusalem, and the Open University at Tel Aviv.

Yoram Peri is a political sociologist who is interested in culture and language, and he is a lecturer in the Department of Communication, at the Hebrew University of Jerusalem.

Aviad E. Raz is an anthropologist of culture and a lecturer in the Department of Behavioral Sciences, at the Ben-Gurion University.

Itzhak Roeh, a researcher in mass media, a senior lecturer in the Department of Communication at the Hebrew University of Jerusalem.

Rafael Schneller is a researcher of mass media and verbal and non-verbal communication, he is a senior lecturer in the School of Education at Bar Ilan University.

Rina Shapira is a sociologist of education and a professor of Sociology and Education in the Department of Sociology and the School of Education, at the Tel-Aviv University.

Dov Shinar is a researcher in mass media, and a professor in Communication and the Dean of the New School of Media Studies, at the College of Management, in Tel-Aviv.

Bernard Spolsky is a sociolinguist and a specialist in plurilingualism, and a professor of Language, in the Department of English Language and Literature, at the Bar-Ilan University.

Chava Tidhar is a researcher of gender and communication, Israel Educational Television, Ramat Aviv.

Gabriel Weimann is a sociologist of networks and communication, and a professor of Sociology and Communication in the Department of Communication and Sociology, at the Haifa University.

Gadi Wolfsfeld is a researcher in political communication, and an associate professor in the Department of Communication and Political Science at the Hebrew University of Jerusalem.

Narspy Zilberg is researcher at the Social Studies Center, Jacob Blaustein Institute for Desert Research, Ben-Gurion University of the Negev, Sed Boker. She studies cultural anthropology and communities of immigrants from the former Soviet Union in Israel.